The Pursuit of Knowledge Under Difficulties

The Pursuit of Knowledge
Under Difficulties

From Self-Improvement to
Adult Education in America,
1750-1990

Joseph F. Kett

Stanford University Press
Stanford, California

Stanford University Press
Stanford, California
© 1994 by the Board of Trustees of the
Leland Stanford Junior University
Printed in the United States of America

CIP data appear at the end of the book

Original printing 1994
Last figure below indicates year of this printing:
04 03 02 01 00 99 98 97 96 95

Stanford University Press publications are distributed
exclusively by Stanford University Press within the
United States, Canada, Mexico, and Central America;
they are distributed exclusively by Cambridge
University Press throughout the rest of the world.

To Jennifer and John

Acknowledgments

I welcome this opportunity to thank several individuals for assistance on this book. Dorothy Ross and David Shi read the original draft of the manuscript and made valuable suggestions for improvements. It is a pleasure to express my gratitude to each, not only for their comments but for their intellectual companionship over the years. My colleague Elizabeth A. Meyer, a historian of ancient Rome, sprinted across two millennia to read the same draft, pausing along the way to borrow a razor from William of Occam. Her numerous and keen criticisms proved of great value to me when I revised this version. Helen Lefkowitz Horowitz critiqued a later draft, saved me from sundry gaffes, and directed my attention toward topics that I initially had slighted. My thinking about the issues raised in Chapters 6 and 7 has been sharpened by Fred H. Matthews. Coming at the subject from different directions, Joan Jacobs Brumberg and Brian Balogh each made extremely helpful suggestions for improving Chapter 9. I thank Lois Banner for assisting me with a point in Chapter 12 and Michael Kammen for bibliographical suggestions. I am also grateful, in fact very grateful, to Philip Nowlen for his criticisms of a draft of Chapter 12. He nudged me to recognize the centrality of World War II in post-1940 developments, and he led me to a better understanding of the current continuing-education scene. My wife Eleanor read none of the drafts but made all of them possible by patiently initiating me into word processing.

I would also like to thank Lottie McCauley and Ella Wood of the history department staff at the University of Virginia for their patience in putting up with my often unreasonable requests and for the innumerable forms of aid they gave me while I was working on this book.

J.F.K.

Contents

Preface

Exploring the history of continuing and adult education entails making sense of astounding statistics, frustratingly loose terminology, lofty idealism, and base huckstering. In the following pages the reader will encounter examples of all of these: a school that enrolled 100,000 new students a year, another that taught biblical prophecy by mail, and a lexicon that includes such terms as continuing, adult, further, recurrent, popular, and second-chance education, as well as educational extension and, more recently, lifelong learning. With variations, all of these terms describe education attained after the apparent conclusion of conventional schooling. In the twentieth century the clients of schools devoted to this type of education have usually been over the age of 21, hence legally adults, but adult education is best defined in terms of its function rather than by a targeted age group. The distinguishing feature of adult education has been its role in providing additional learning for those who believed that they had completed their education only to find that they desired or required more.

When I commenced this study, I did not expect to write a history of adult education. My interest lay rather in the myriad societies that arose before the Civil War to encourage self-education and mutual improvement. I was familiar with success literature, which trumpeted the possibilities of self-education, and I hoped to gauge the scope and purpose of self-education in antebellum America. It soon became clear that Americans construed self-education very broadly. They equated it with what a contemporary Briton called "the pursuit of knowledge under difficulties." A "self-taught man" acquired liberal education discontinuously, by some mixture of formal schooling and private study. Inasmuch as most Americans of the antebellum period acquired liberal education in just this way, it was plausible for contemporaries to emphasize the wide dispersal of self-education in their society. To use their language, what mattered was the availability of the "means" of culture: books, libraries, magazines, mutual improvement societies, and formal schools. These were all points on a continuum along which individuals moved, but they were not arranged in any regular order. The autodidacts whom Americans praised throughout the nineteenth century possessed some formal schooling and, not infrequently, more than the average. But they bobbed in and out of schools, improvement societies, and stints of private study in a seemingly chaotic way. Just as the prevailing antebellum conception of self-education did not exclude some formal education, it was not restricted to adults. Self-improvement manuals were widely employed by students in academies and colleges as well as by private students. As a universal duty, self-improvement was not age specific. Boys and girls as well as men and women formed mutual improvement societies throughout the nineteenth century. Not until the 1920s did the term "adult education" enter common usage. Significantly, it did so after radical changes in the preceding three decades had greatly enhanced the importance of formal and sequential schooling in American society. In other words, the prolongation of formal education and establishment of sequential (uninterrupted) schooling as an ideal made it possible by the 1920s to equate self-improvement with adult education.

Yet even in the 1920s supporters of adult education recognized their indebtedness to the tradition of self-improvement, which in the nineteenth century was embodied not only in the solitary endeavors of autodidacts but in sundry institutions of self-improvement, including literary societies, lyceums, mechanics' institutes, the Lake Chautauqua Assembly and its many offshoots in the 1870s and 1880s, and university extension. Arising at different times and reflecting a variety of impulses, these institutions nonetheless shared a number of characteristics that linked them to each other in the minds of contemporaries and that facilitated their adoption in the twentieth century as forerunners of adult education. First, they aimed primarily at working youths and adults, and, appropriately, conducted their programs and "exercises" in the evening or, in the case of the Lake Chautauqua Assembly, during summer vacation. The architects of these institutions of popular self-education routinely invoked the inspirational images of lonely autodidacts who pursued knowledge after an exhausting day at the anvil or printer's press. From the promoters of mechanics' institutes in the 1820s and 1830s to the advertisements of early twentieth-century correspondence schools, the image of the self-taught Benjamin Franklin exerted an especially powerful attraction for the designers of in-

stitutions of popular self-education, who rarely failed to point out that
Franklin himself founded an institution of self-improvement, the famed
Junto.

The campaign that led in 1862 to the passage of the Morrill, or Land-
Grant College, Act also witnessed frequent invocations of Franklin's image. While funding colleges for the children of workers rather than for
workers themselves, the Morrill Act indirectly stimulated the development of adult education. The failure of the land-grant colleges to attract
students to their residential programs in the late nineteenth century led
them to pioneer a distinctive form of university extension in the early
twentieth century. Today, advocates of community colleges, which have
absorbed many of the functions of the university extension movement and
which enroll huge numbers of working adults, often invoke the Morrill
Act as a precedent for their "outreach" programs aimed at adults.

In addition, institutions of popular self-improvement have long been
permeated by voluntarism. At some level all education can be described as
voluntary; even in an age of compulsory school laws, children can choose
to become truants or students. Yet long before compulsory school laws,
Americans commonly talked of "sending" children to school and "joining" literary societies, a verbal distinction that accurately reflected their
association of institutions of mutual improvement with choice. Throughout the nineteenth century, self-education was associated with an often
strenuous act of the will: to choose a course of mental improvement was
to embark upon an ambitious enterprise that involved self-denial, persistence, and resilience. Not infrequently, diarists recorded the day on which
they started their program of self-education.

By whatever names institutions of self-improvement have passed—lyceums, mechanics' institutes, chautauquas, "people's" institutes or colleges, or adult schools—they have made voluntary education paramount,
and for this reason they provide windows through which to examine popular motives for acquiring knowledge and for preferring one kind of
knowledge over another. Does this mean that the institutions commonly
associated with formal education, such as high schools, academies, and
colleges, have been less voluntary in the sense of being dependent on student satisfaction? On balance, the answer is yes. Although formal schools
often have instructed adults, they have primarily targeted those under the
age of 21, who are presumably less mature and hence more in need of
structure and direction. Formal educational institutions have enjoyed tax
support and/or endowments, which have afforded them a measure of insulation from those who called for allowing students to learn whatever
they desired, and they have inherited curricular traditions that have a life
of their own.

Yet it is impossible to write a history of continuing and adult education without alluding constantly to developments in formal education. For example, in the century after 1750, colleges contained little enclaves of self-education and mutual improvement called literary societies, and these resembled and at times inspired their extramural counterparts. In Chapter 3 I will describe features of the antebellum academies that made them virtual institutions of continuing education: they lacked fixed curricula; they were remarkably attuned to student interests; many of their students were in their twenties; and their structure was compatible with, indeed virtually invited, frequent interruptions of study. In this respect, the distinction between formal educational institutions and those of popular self-improvement was by no means always clear. The same was true after the Civil War, but for a different reason. In the 1870s and 1880s, nearly all institutions of popular self-improvement started to become more similar to established institutions of formal education by introducing annual curricula, textbooks, courses of study, and even quizzes, examinations, and certificates. This convergence culminated in the 1890s, when university professors started to organize "university extension" in direct competition with institutions of popular self-improvement.

None of these developments collapsed the distinction between the two types of education. For example, although the organizers of the Lake Chautauqua Assembly (the progenitor of numerous post–Civil War experiments in adult education) briefly incorporated the Assembly as a university, their rhetoric constantly invoked the image of solitary autodidacts, and they emphasized knowledge as a source of moral inspiration so much that they embarrassed their supporters in the universities. Similarly, university extension did not develop in the United States along the lines its name implied, for after a brief experiment in the 1890s with extending the university curriculum, university extension in the first two decades of the twentieth century became a largely self-contained enterprise within universities, one prone less to competition with established university departments than with the innumerable proprietary schools that offered fast, cheap adult vocational education.

A third link between nineteenth-century institutions of popular self-education and twentieth-century adult education has been their shared emphasis on rendering knowledge relevant to human affairs. As voluntary institutions dependent on the support of their participants, they have stressed the integration of learning and living. In the twentieth century this tilt toward relevance has usually taken the form of a preoccupation with job training and personal therapy. Yet for most of the nineteenth century those who joined literary societies, mechanics' institutes, and chautauquas did not equate relevance with the acquisition of job-specific skills. Rather, most participants rallied behind the flag of "culture," the ideal that Matthew Arnold in 1869 equated with "the best that has been thought and known." Those in quest of Arnoldian culture studied types of knowledge that would elevate them beyond everyday concerns. The same was true of those who pledged allegiance in the nineteenth century to the ideal of Useful Knowledge—the belief that mastery of science would make farmers and artisans more productive. Even the founders of mechanics' institutes, who resolutely preached the doctrine of Useful Knowledge, disdained teaching trades. Yet the institutions of popular self-education discovered ways to make these ideals broadly relevant to human affairs. For example, antebellum literary societies stressed the acquisition of kinds of knowledge that could be displayed in public, and in this respect their programs were especially suited to young lawyers and physicians in an age when the professions had intimate ties to public life. Similarly, the most successful antebellum lyceum lecturers were those who proved adept at tailoring higher knowledge to the moral and social concerns of their auditors.

A final thread that has connected institutions of popular self-education with each other and with twentieth-century adult education has been democratic idealism. Before the American Revolution, educators almost invariably described self-improvement through the acquisition of higher knowledge as a gentlemanly duty. In contrast, calls for widening the public's access to education beyond the rudiments mounted after the Revolution. For the most part, republican educators of the late eighteenth century looked to formal institutions of education—academies and colleges—to accommodate new popular demands for education, but by the 1820s, when it became clear that states were not prepared to fund the colleges that republican educators had envisioned, educators increasingly emphasized the effectiveness of popular self-education.

In the first half of the nineteenth century, the ideal of popular self-education became intertwined with contemporary calls for "diffusing" knowledge among the multitude beyond the perimeters of established educational institutions. This objective in turn aroused the support of an assortment of dreamers and visionaries, who expected that institutions of popular self-education would serve a range of social and moral as well as educational goals. In the 1820s the Connecticut educator Josiah Holbrook, as resolute a visionary as one could imagine, pleaded for "associations of adults for mutual improvement." He expected these "lyceums" to sprout in every state, in fact throughout the world, and he puffed them as cures for gossip, intemperance, ignorance, and sectional strife. Throughout the 1840s and 1850s, a resilient band of visionaries condemned the belletristic tilt that they detected in all existing educational institutions. They also called for new institutions to serve manual workers, the honest farmers and artisans who were being educationally disfranchised by the assortment of political demagogues and lawyers who favored classical over practical education. The passage in 1862 of the Morrill Act, with its endorsement of universities for the "industrial classes," owed a good deal to these visionaries. Established in the 1870s with the modest objective of training Sunday-school teachers, the Lake Chautauqua Assembly quickly became an extraordinarily ambitious enterprise for elevating the intellectual horizons of the evangelical middle class. Inspirational and personal ties linked Chautauqua to the early university extension movement in the 1890s, which included among its goals the reconciliation of class antagonisms by the diffusion of knowledge. When this movement declined, Progressive idealists revived university extension in the early 1900s by orienting it toward vocational education for the common people and toward democratic social service. In the 1920s disillusioned Progressives turned to adult education with the expectation that it alone could afford opportunities for spontaneous education and for the integration of learning and living that public-school and university bureaucracies long had stifled. In the 1970s and 1980s, advocates of "lifelong learning" have sounded disconcertingly like Josiah Holbrook in their precise recording of each page read and lesson taken as evidence of the irresistible momentum of education.

While their designers have perceived institutions of popular self-improvement and adult education as embodiments of democratic idealism, educational democracy can be assigned various meanings. The one most often embraced by adult educators has been the satisfaction of popular aspirations for knowledge. Whatever original purpose they have avowed, institutions of popular self-improvement and adult education have been led toward this definition of democracy by their dependence on student fees. This reliance has hindered adult educational institutions from providing a second chance for those denied formal education in their school years, because the satisfaction of "aspirations," the willingness to teach anyone anything anywhere, has prevented adult schools from providing a parallel or equivalent to traditional formal education. To lure clients, adult schools have taught all sorts of exotic subjects that cater to avocational and seemingly trivial interests, and they have displayed a kind of formlessness that has provoked controversy over whether adult education, in the absence of coherent institutional goals, can afford a second chance to the disadvantaged. At several points in this study I will contrast adult education in the United States with its counterpart in Great Britain, where the political left long has perceived adult education as a way out of the class system. For reasons that include but ultimately transcend financing, this has never been a major objective of adult education in the United States.

The history of the pursuit of knowledge under difficulties reflects only in part the successive ideologies framed by visionary enthusiasts for educating the out-of-school population. More fundamentally, it is the history of that population itself. Josiah Holbrook did not invent the popular literary society; rather, he baptized existing societies as lyceums. Literary societies and other institutions of popular self-improvement owed more to their clients than to educational philosophers like Holbrook.

The history of the relationship between the designers and clients of institutions of popular self-improvement and adult education reveals some general tendencies. The most striking has been the proclivity of architects and promoters of these institutions to scale down their expectations of their clients' intellectual abilities. Each successive generation of designers has lowered its expectations on the basis of its understanding of the experience of its predecessors. Whereas in the 1820s both Josiah Holbrook and the promoters of mechanics' institutes expected to transfer a replica of the knowledge of the learned to the uneducated, by the 1840s lyceums and mechanics' institutes were popularizing knowledge in novel ways, for example by sponsoring lectures about science rather than scientific instruction. In the 1870s and 1880s, Chautauqua devised new ways to popularize academic subjects like history, literature, and the classics. The history of university extension between 1890 and 1910 is that of ever-more-reductive approaches to popularization and the gradual downgrading of academic education. During the 1930s their experience with adult students enrolled in classes sponsored by the Works Progress Administration persuaded some adult educators of the need to overcome adult illiteracy (a minor interest of adult educators before 1930), while it convinced others that even literate adult students lacked a serious dedication to learning. In turn, assumptions derived from the 1930s shaped the thinking of educators after World War II.

Conditioned by contact between educators and ever wider segments of the public, this long-term tendency toward diluted expectations has led educators to frequently underestimate the seriousness of adult students. By targeting the base of the student pyramid, educators have often failed to understand its middle and upper levels. As the prestige of collegiate education rose in the late nineteenth and twentieth centuries, some participants in self-improvement societies used their studies as springboards for entering colleges. For example, although the founders of late-nineteenth-century chautauquas expected little more than to prick an interest in education and displayed little interest in feminism, some women used these institutions to prepare for entry into colleges, and they avowed a distinct ambition to take their places alongside men in the world of learning. After World War II, adult educators were both astounded and discomfitted by the eagerness of veterans to enroll in colleges, for such enthusiasm for college did not conform to their association of adult education with avocational fun and games.

The surge of students who reentered college in the 1970s and 1980s, which had a similarly jarring effect on professional adult educators, was foreshadowed by a variety of extramural continuing education programs in the 1960s, in which women not only raised their awareness of the value of completing college but also explored subjects like women's studies. Long before the 1960s, subjects that would make their way into the American collegiate curriculum either first appeared or first aroused widespread interest in institutions of educational extension, and the clients for these subjects followed the subjects themselves into the colleges and universities. The very fact that American adult education has not consistently aimed to transfer advanced education to the less privileged has facilitated this kind of relationship, for extension classes have not necessarily been designed as copies of campus courses. Ultimately, the history of adult education offers opportunities for examining evolving American conceptions of education itself; by virtue of its sensitivity to popular aspirations, adult education reveals a great deal about what Americans have thought constituted the process of education.

Had this study been completed thirty years ago, it would have ended on an anticlimactic note, for by 1960 adult education had attained a secure but marginal niche in American education. At that date, adult education encompassed classes for adults who were trying to acquire high-school diplomas, courses that offered instruction in job-specific skills or in vocationally useful personality skills (e.g., the Dale Carnegie courses), and an assortment of recreational/avocational classes for old dogs eager to learn new tricks. Professionals in the field of adult education assumed that older students took courses to satisfy interests that arose from their situations in life and that bore little comparison to those of youthful undergraduate or graduate students. The remarkable surge of older students into colleges and universities since the late 1960s has shattered many of these assumptions. By the end of the 1980s, nearly 40 percent of American undergraduates were aged 25 or over. To an extent that has dismayed veteran adult educators, many of these older students have sought carbon copies of the education afforded their younger counterparts; indeed older students seem to relish enrolling in the same courses as teenagers and, not infrequently, testing themselves against younger competitors. Today, no one can plausibly describe adult education as a marginal activity, but professional adult educators have become increasingly marginal to the education of adults.

The Pursuit of Knowledge
Under Difficulties

Chapter 1

Literature, Philosophy, and Self-Education in Eighteenth-Century America

B y such terms as philosophy and literature, eighteenth-century scholars and statesmen signified the content of education beyond the rudiments. These words had much broader applications than the academic specialties with which each is now associated. Inspired by Francis Bacon, especially his *The Advancement of Learning* (1605), and by Sir Isaac Newton, the learned of the Age of the Enlightenment interpreted philosophy as the investigation of the underlying rationality of the universe, the discovery of the laws of nature, ethics, and economics. While we view Adam Smith as an early economist, no such profession (or subject) existed in the eighteenth century. Rather, Smith was a philosopher, specifically a moral philosopher. Literature had the same breadth as philosophy.[1] Thus colleges were called "literary institutions" and academic endowments "literary funds" well into the nineteenth century. But literature, which included drama, verse, and history, as well as much of the subject matter of philosophy, connoted knowledge gleaned from written sources. In comparison, philosophy, while employing the written word, also emphasized outdoor investigations of nature and the conduct of experiments. The foremost colonial institution for encouraging scientific experiments was called, appropriately, the American Philosophical Society.

Because philosophy and literature possessed broad and overlapping applications, contemporaries often used these terms interchangeably, or by synecdoche made a part such as moral philosophy stand for the whole. Collectively, philosophy and literature did not exhaust the eighteenth-century's lexicon of knowledge. An older terminology, one familiar to seventeenth-century Puritans, persisted into the eighteenth and indeed into the nineteenth and twentieth centuries. Puritans had called for the advancement of the "Artes and Sciences."[2] By "artes" they meant the seven arts embodied in the trivium (grammar, rhetoric, and logic) and quadrivium (music, arithmetic, geometry, and astronomy) that boys had studied in Europe for over a millennium, while "sciences" referred to the three "philosophies" handed down from the Middle Ages (natural, moral, and mental).[3] These were the subjects suited to a *liber homo* and hence became the linguistic root of liberal education as well as of twentieth-century faculties of arts and sciences. Yet while persisting into the eighteenth century, this older terminology acquired new connotations and applications to reflect the expanding perimeters of knowledge. Francis Bacon's emphasis on the useful applications of general principles and on the possibility of discovering general ideas by investigation of manual trades led to the increasing association of the "arts" with manufactures, commerce, and agriculture in the belief that these could be improved by knowledge, and to an increasingly common distinction between these "mechanic arts" and the "fine arts" of painting, sculpture, music, engraving, and architecture. In *A Brief Retrospect of the Eighteenth Century* (1803), Rev. Samuel Miller accommodated the widening boundaries of knowledge by employing a more specialized terminology: not only the mechanic and fine arts but "mechanical philosophy" (electricity, galvanism, magnetism, motion and moving forces, hydraulics, pneumatics, optics, and astronomy) and "natural history" (zoology, botany, mineralogy, geology, meteorology, and hydrology).[4]

Depending on one's perspective, American colleges in the eighteenth century either reacted slowly to new scientific knowledge or did as well as could be expected in view of their limited resources. In no sense were they centers of scientific experiment. In contrast, the colleges quickly embraced another new term and concept, that of belles lettres. Popularized by English translations of Charles Rollin's *De la manière d'enseigner et d'étudier les belles lettres* (1728) and by Hugh Blair's *Lectures on Rhetoric and Belles Lettres* (1783), belles lettres encompassed many of the same studies as literature, including languages, poetry, rhetoric, history, and moral philosophy, but Rollin's well-deserved reputation sprang from his skill in making study relevant. He told readers how to analyze the literary qualities of a work to develop "a just and exact discernment," which would lead them through every branch of knowledge to whatever was most beautiful, curious, and useful, and how to study history to derive models of behavior.[5]

Although disagreements abounded in the eighteenth century between advocates of one or another subject, these contentions developed within a broad framework of agreement, slowly emerging in England between the sixteenth and eighteenth centuries, that learning was valuable not merely for clergymen but for the sons of gentlemen who were bound for secular pursuits. Rooted in the Italian Renaissance and disseminated in sixteenth-century England by Sir Thomas Elyot, Roger Ascham, Sir Humphrey Gilbert, and Sir Philip Sidney, this ideal was closely linked to that of the polite gentleman, who blended learning, manners, and public service.[6] Thus arose the notion of "polite learning," which was as antagonistic to dissolute and ignorant gentry as to the scholastics of the medieval universities.[7] The boundaries of polite learning were capacious. In his first collection of essays Francis Bacon wrote that "histories make men wise; poets, witty; the mathematics, subtle; natural philosophy, deep; moral, grave; logic and rhetoric, able to contend."[8] In *Queene Elizabethe's Achademy* (1570), Sir Humphrey Gilbert, himself a specimen of the new-style gentleman, urged the sons of gentlemen to study navigation, military sciences, and the arts as well as the ancient and modern languages. Even if the universities had yet to grasp the value of music and drama, they also were worthy studies in the eyes of humanists of the English Renaissance.[9] Inasmuch as all knowledge was to be reflected in a higher order of public activity, it was logical for gentlemen to investigate whatever subjects might render them publicly useful. Francis Bacon's contention that knowledge had to be dedicated to the systematic development and improvement of the arts was at once part of the fabric of Renaissance humanism and a foreshadowing of the role that Enlightenment philosophers would later assign to education.[10]

These ideals did not pass unperturbed from the Renaissance to the Enlightenment, for in America they had to pass through the medium of seventeenth-century Puritanism. For all the importance that Puritans attached to print culture, few in the seventeenth century viewed literary refinement as an end in itself. As Larzer Ziff has observed, "the principal relation of the book to [Puritan] society was that of documenting the perception of reality common to all members of all classes within it." In the thinking of Puritan clergy and laity, books were "icons of truth" rather than means by which the educated delineated a distinctive and socially exclusive sphere of literary culture.[11] On the whole, however, Puritanism complemented rather than challenged the value of secular learning, for while Puritans distanced themselves from the ideal of polite gentlemanliness, their outlook accommodated a broad view of the accomplishments of what Cotton Mather called "the Christian Philosopher." Although careful to subordinate classical and scientific knowledge to Scripture, Puritans assigned to the human understanding a substantial role in bringing men and women to God. Even as they drove music from their churches and assailed drama and erotic poetry, Puritans admired and studied the ancient classics and displayed a pronounced interest in science on grounds succinctly stated by Mather: "Philosophy is no Enemy, but a mighty and wondrous *Incentive to Religion*."[12] No American Puritan suffered at the hands of Enlightenment rationalists the insult that Renaissance humanists had hurled at the medieval schoolman Duns Scotus, whose name was corrupted in the sixteenth century to dunce. Eighteenth-century clergymen, like the Presbyterian Samuel Stanhope Smith, who investigated the cause of color pigmentation and who introduced the first professorship of chemistry at Princeton, participated actively in the American side of the Age of Reason.[13]

The Value of Learning

By 1750 literature and philosophy in the Anglo-American world rested on several clear but narrow foundations. Such knowledge was valuable to ministers, who mined it for insight into the glory of God and who, in their role as pedagogues, transmitted it to the rising generation. In addition, knowledge still led, as in the Renaissance, to the ideal of the gentleman. Americans lacked a titled nobility and a court, but, as John Adams recognized, each region had its distinguished families, which were accorded deference by their social inferiors. British magazines familiarized Americans with the image of the Restoration gentleman; in the late seventeenth century, John Winthrop's grandsons eagerly awaited the arrival of gentlemen's magazines from London, which provided them with appropriate models of dress and behavior. In the early eighteenth century, Virginia grandees constructed great houses along the James River that were modeled on English country estates.[14] The cultivation of knowledge could complement dress, manners, and furnishings; William Byrd II, who built Westover in the late 1720s, disciplined himself to read Latin and Greek authors each morning and accumulated the largest private library in the colonies.

Yet, as schoolmasters well knew, the mere possession of intellectual culture did not transform one into a gentleman, and knowledge was by no means a necessary attribute of gentlemanly status. William Byrd II's social and political position in Tidewater Virginia depended far less on his library than on his estate; Byrd did display his literary polish in his publications, but these were intended mainly for his admirers in England rather than for his peers in the Virginia gentry. In contrast, during the second half of the eighteenth century the development of the professions of law and medicine broadened the foundations of the pursuit of knowledge and made the achievement of gentlemanly status more accessible to men of the "middling sort."

Throughout the seventeenth and early eighteenth centuries, the number of full-time legal and medical practitioners in the colonies had been exceedingly small. Ministers customarily treated the medical ailments of their parishioners; merchants prescribed quinine and other remedies from their stock of imported commodities; sheriffs and bailiffs read legal digests and pleaded causes. In contrast, during the second half of the eighteenth century, elite practitioners of law and medicine, the latter often medical graduates of Scottish universities, initiated a drive for higher professional standards. Professional lawyers began to form societies like Massachusetts's Suffolk County Bar Association to wrest practice from "the hands of Deputy Sheriffs, Pettyfoggers, and even Constables."[15] Lawyers increasingly proclaimed the need for liberal learning as part of this push for standards. After 1764 New York demanded two years of college education before admission to legal practice. John Adams was among the members of a Massachusetts law club formed in 1765 to study political philosophy as well as law.[16] James Otis, Jr., in Massachusetts and George Wythe in Virginia insisted that their legal apprentices—Thomas Jefferson was among Wythe's—saturate themselves with literature as well as with the intricacies of the law.[17] Similarly, the establishment of mid-century clubs for elite full-time physicians culminated after Independence in the chartering of state medical societies that sought to control entrance into the profession by raising educational standards.[18] The rising status of each profession was also symbolized by the beginnings of professional education within institutions of higher education. The University of Pennsylvania established the colonies' first medical school in 1766; a handful of others followed by 1800, and by that year several colleges, including William and Mary, Transylvania, Columbia, and the University of Pennsylvania, offered lectures in law. But in the eighteenth century it was at least as important for ambitious professional men to cultivate literature and philosophy as to master the techniques specific to their craft.

On the surface, the ministry was an exception to this trend, for the Great Awakening spurred criticism among revivalists of the ideal of a learned ministry, which in the eyes of radical New Lights like the Presbyterian Gilbert Tennent could easily disguise an unconverted ministry. Yet the very virulence of New Light attacks testified to the value that many clergymen had come to place on reason rather than on inner religious experience. In turn, opponents of revivals responded to the onslaughts of "enthusiasts" by emphasizing reason all the more. New Lights themselves often were more ambivalent than hostile to an educated clergy. Failing to detect vital piety at Harvard or Yale, Tennent pleaded in 1741 for "seminaries of learning" restricted to those possessing "plain evidences of experimental religion."[19] Tennent himself was a graduate of the Log College, an academy founded by his father at Neshaminy, Pennsylvania, and so named in derision by its anti-revival opponents. Other alumni of the Log College, including Samuel Blair and Samuel Finley, founded New Light academies in the mid-eighteenth century. The physician Benjamin Rush, who attended his uncle Samuel Finley's academy in Maryland, recalled how its students performed farm chores to improve their health and "to implant more deeply in our mind the native passion for rural life."[20] But in other respects Finley's school was typical of eighteenth-century academies. Its curriculum stressed Latin and Greek, while Finley himself took pains to reprove the "slightest act of incivility."[21] New Light academies had no quarrel with liberal education. As Samuel Finley recalled in his sermon at Samuel Blair's funeral: "He studied several branches of mathematics, and especially geometry and astronomy; nor will these seem tasteless studies to one who had such a savour of living piety, when it is considered that he saw the glory of God in all his works, and admired and adored him in all."[22]

Unable to persuade conservative synods to license the graduates of the Log College, New Lights secured its chartering in 1746 as the College of New Jersey (Princeton). The transformation of the Log College into Princeton responded both to discrimination by Old Lights and to the value that New Lights attached to liberal learning. Although New Lights valued a converted ministry above all else, "they cherished the rhetorical skills conferred by a liberal arts education."[23] The Awakening contributed directly to the founding of more colleges in the three decades after 1740 than in the preceding century. Even those New Light preachers whose humble station denied them a liberal education saw the value of one. Isaac Backus, who was converted during the English evangelist George Whitefield's tour of New England in 1741, had only a common school education. But Backus, who became New England's leading Baptist and an implacable opponent of New England's Standing Order, made "persevering efforts" to acquire literary culture.[24]

The learned professions of the eighteenth century all led to public life, usually in the form of office holding. At least in New England the ministry itself was a kind of civil office, subject to popular election and supported by taxes.[25] Throughout the colonies physicians and especially lawyers held public offices and in sundry ways participated in public affairs, and such participation became a major rationale for acquiring refined knowledge. Thus Thomas Jefferson advised his nephew in 1785 to learn Spanish for use "when you become a public man." Similarly, Rollin contended that literature and philosophy were especially valuable for public men, a category that he applied to all those in employments "which oblige us either to speak in public or in private, to write, or to give an account of our administration, to manage others, gain them over, or persuade them."[26] Of course professional men were not the only ones to fit this description, but, especially in the urban centers where they thrived, intellectual culture could readily compensate for their lack of a landed estate or distinguished pedigree.[27]

The association between the acquisition of knowledge and participation in public life sharpened in the late eighteenth century as the writings of British "real" Whigs brought Americans into contact with the tradition of civic republicanism. With roots in antiquity, Renaissance Italy, and Commonwealth England, the idea of a republic depended less on any specific configuration of structural characteristics than on the state of mind of its citizens. Plain living, simple manners, and above all popular understanding of public affairs would preserve republican liberty as surely as luxury and self-absorption would fertilize the ground for despotism.[28] The fact is certain, proclaimed John Adams in 1765, that "wherever a general knowledge and sensibility have prevailed among the people, arbitrary government and every oppression have lessened and disappeared in proportion."[29] Republicanism not only advanced a powerful motive for the "diffusion" or popularization of knowledge but summoned the gentry to educate itself in the history of ancient and modern republics as well. This was precisely the course charted by James Madison upon his graduation from the College of New Jersey in 1771, and by the 1780s the nation's colleges were rife with plans to modernize their curricula.[30] At Yale, President Ezra Stiles proposed in 1777 to add a professorship of law, while at William and Mary a few years later Thomas Jefferson used his ex-officio position on the college's board to introduce the study of public administration and natural and international law. In 1784 the regents of the University of the State of New York proposed a drastic expansion of Columbia University's curriculum to embrace subjects like Roman and international law.[31]

The flurry of interest in modernizing the curriculum extended to vocational subjects as well as to politics and history. Indeed the practical imperative had gained ground even before the Revolution. In his *Proposals Relating to the Education of Youth in Pennsylvania* (1749), Benjamin Franklin had designed a curriculum for an academy that would teach the keeping of accounts, the history of commerce, and the principles of mechanics as well as arithmetic, English, and geography, all with the intent that boys might be fitted for "any Business, Calling or Profession."[32] In 1754 the newly founded King's College (later Columbia University) had proposed to teach navigation, surveying, husbandry, and commerce, and indeed "every thing *useful* for the Comfort, the Convenience and Elegance of Life."[33] For a brief period in the second decade of the nineteenth century, Jefferson envisioned organizing the curriculum of what would become the University of Virginia around professions and vocations, including even a school of "technical philosophy" for mariners, soap makers, tanners, carpenters, and wrights of every sort.[34]

These tilts toward practicality reflected the prevailing ideal of Useful Knowledge. Derived from Francis Bacon, elaborated by Franklin, and em-

braced by Jefferson, Useful Knowledge called for the reduction of speculative truths to practice, the grounding of theories upon experiments, and
the application of science to the improvement of agriculture, commerce,
and "the common purposes of life." Useful Knowledge competed with the
classical languages, belles lettres, and the study of law and political philosophy for the attention of the educated. Yet even as colleges accorded mor.
space in their curricula to the sciences—by 1788 all eight colleges founded
in the colonial period had established professorships of natural philosophy (physics)—they distanced themselves from anything that smacked of
vocational education. When Philadelphia's Academy was organized in
1749 (it would soon become the College of Philadelphia, and in 1779, the
University of Pennsylvania), its trustees essentially scuttled Franklin's *Proposals* by describing the college as primarily "An Academy for Teaching
the Latin and Greek languages."[35] Similarly, King's College quickly gravitated to the more familiar collegiate curriculum, and Jefferson ultimately
organized the curriculum of the University of Virginia into liberal and
professional rather than vocational "schools": ancient languages, modern
languages, natural history, mathematics, anatomy and medicine, moral
philosophy, and law.[36]

   With its increasingly large component of natural sciences and belles
lettres, the eighteenth-century collegiate curriculum was scarcely fossil-
ized, but the widespread belief that collegiate education should prepare
young men for public life worked against trade training, which most assumed could safely be left to apprenticeship. Even Jefferson, an ardent Baconian, inveterate tinkerer and practical experimenter, and self-conscious
reformer of higher education, ultimately rejected "technical philosophy"
for mariners, carpenters, and wrights at the University of Virginia. Although he did not state his reasons for this rejection, he clearly intended
that the university educate southern, Democratic-Republican political
leaders in order to counter the Federalist influence at New England universities. As members of Jefferson's aristocracy of talent and virtue, such
leaders need not have been born to gentlemanly status. It was enough that
they be educated to be gentlemen, which is to say, liberally educated. To
be sure, Jefferson provided for practical education at the University of Virginia, for a school of law, for the study of agriculture as a subdivision of
chemistry, and for teaching the science of "bombs, balls, and other projec-
tiles" in the school of mathematics. But none of this meant that Jefferson
saw the university's mission as training lawyers, farmers, or military officers. In an age when law was an avenue to public life, when experimental
agriculture was an avocation of gentleman-farmers, and when gentlemen
routinely assumed military roles in crises, instruction in these subjects harmonized with Jefferson's underlying goals for higher education and with
his desire to expand the boundaries of liberal education. In the eyes of Jef-

ferson's contemporaries, to acquire a liberal education was to answer a calling, a summons from "the multitude of mankind who are grovelling in the Earth."[37]

The Roads to Learning

The tradition that stretched from Renaissance humanism to Enlightenment rationalism did not exclusively associate liberal education with colleges or universities. None of the major English humanists of the sixteenth century who wrote specifically on education trusted England's ancient universities, which they saw as bastions of scholasticism, corrupt Latinity, and papistry. In *The Schoolmaster*, Roger Ascham urged the private education of youth in the houses of gentlemen, a path earlier delineated by Sir Thomas Elyot in *The Boke Named the Governour* (1531). Sir Humphrey Gilbert proposed "Queene Elizabethe's Achademy" as a morally safe alternative to the universities. A young gentleman of the English Renaissance could also acquire a suitable education at the inns of court in London or on his grand tour. Francis Bacon interrupted his studies at Gray's Inn to travel for two and a half years in France. Sir Philip Sidney's three-year tour, commenced when he was nineteen, combined study under Protestant masters with travel in France, Germany, Italy, Poland, and Hungary. In addition, grammar schools, of which there were several hundred in England by 1600, introduced boys to the classical languages and taught them correct English.[38] The triumph of Puritanism in mid-seventeenth century England boosted these schools, for Puritans seized them as vehicles for popularizing education, while Anglicans attacked them for "diverting those, whom Nature or Fortune had determin'd to the Plough, the Oar, or other Handicrafts, from their proper design, to the study of Liberal Arts, and even Divinity itself."[39]

Of these routes to liberal education, attendance at grammar schools was by far the most accessible in colonial America, and especially in New England. In 1647 the Massachusetts Bay Colony required every town of a hundred families to establish a grammar school; Connecticut and Plymouth adopted similar laws in 1640 and 1673, respectively. Like their English counterparts, seventeenth-century New England grammar schools were essentially Latin schools. In the eighteenth century their curriculum expanded to include the sciences and some mathematics, and the seaport towns were the site of a growing number of private grammar schools. These schools usually taught either "academical" subjects (Latin, Greek, logic, rhetoric, English grammar, mathematics, natural philosophy, astronomy, and geography) or useful ones (navigation, mensuration, bookkeeping, shorthand, and surveying).[40] In addition, some private schools taught the "female branches," a category that included a good deal of English grammar and prose styling, a little arithmetic, such genteel subjects as ornamental handwriting and painting, and useful female arts like sewing and needlework.[41]

But did grammar schools provide a liberal education, or merely a preparation for one? Contemporaries thought the latter. To the extent that they envisioned grammar schools as other than college preparatory schools, they tended to stress their offering of useful vocational subjects for young men bound for the trades. In urban areas, where demand for vocational education was keen, private schoolmasters taught a rich variety of vocational specialties. In contrast, although probably more than half of their students never attended college, the tax-supported grammar schools persisted primarily as schools for teaching Latin, which was required by the colleges. One obvious objection to this classical bias was that boys who were not bound for college spent a lot of time acquiring the rudiments of classical languages that they would never perfect. It seemed absurd to school would-be tradesmen in a dead language that they would quickly forget upon leaving school.[42] In response, pressure mounted after the Revolution to orient the public grammar schools more toward vocational goals, but it proved nearly impossible to pry the public grammar schools from their self-image as Latin preparatory schools. For example, while boys who attended the Hartford Grammar School were allowed after the Revolution to study navigation and surveying as a practical concession to calls for a more flexible curriculum, the school's regulations of 1790 prescribed that the master attend principally to instruction "in the Study of the learned Languages and of those branches of the Arts and Sciences, usually taught in Collegiate Schools."[43] Regardless of their vocational goals, boys could not even enroll in the school unless they possessed a Latin accidence and dictionary.

In the nineteenth century a growing number of young people would turn to academies, a type of educational institution that arose in late-eighteenth-century New England and then spread throughout the United States between 1800 and 1860, as a cheap and accessible substitute for colleges. But this was not a role to which eighteenth-century grammar schools were suited. The academies flourished by offering liberal, ornamental, and vocational subjects and by attracting older youth in their late teens and twenties as well as young boys and girls. In contrast, the eighteenth-century public grammar schools focused on Latin, lacked the curricular range of the academies, and mainly attracted boys under the age of fourteen. The youthfulness of their students alone restricted the ability of the grammar schools to provide a liberal education, for the latter required more than mastery of Latin or indeed any sequence of subjects. Above all, it required opportunities for training and practice in rhetoric, the art of persuasion indispensable to public men.[44] On balance, it is easy to understand why contemporaries did not view grammar schools as self-sufficient institutions of liberal education. Even Jefferson, who often proclaimed the need to diffuse knowledge and who tried unsuccessfully to legislate a system of public grammar schools into Virginia, failed to assign any role to them save as threshing machines for identifying the most talented, college-bound youth.

Barricading themselves behind intensive Latin study, the public grammar schools of New England faced financial distress during the Revolution and increasing local opposition after it. Their preoccupation with Latin ran counter to the demands for vocational education that were widely voiced in urban areas and that drew support after the war from most educational theorists. Typically, although himself a scholar and classicist, John Adams thought that a new nation needed less of the ornamental and more of the useful and mechanical arts.[45] Further, New England towns had long chafed under the requirement to maintain grammar schools, a burden that became more onerous as their population shifted toward outlying districts. In practice, grammar masters for decades had taught the rudiments of learning to small children as well as Latin to boys, but townspeople nevertheless preferred the establishment of primary schools closer to home. In 1789 a Massachusetts law authorized towns to establish school districts to serve outlying residents, released towns with fewer than two hundred families from the requirement to maintain grammar schools, and, by stipulating that grammar-school students demonstrate their ability to read English before their admission, indirectly reinforced the penchant of the remaining grammar masters to get on with the teaching of Latin. In the same year New Hampshire decreased local responsibility for Latin schools, and, in a series of complicated maneuvers in the 1790s, Connecticut achieved the same result.[46] These laws depleted the number of public Latin schools, which in Massachusetts alone fell in the 1790s to about half of the colonial number.[47]

In view of the limitations of grammar schools, it is not surprising that most eighteenth-century American scholars linked liberal education primarily to colleges. Indeed the connection had become well ingrained in seventeenth-century Massachusetts, many of whose luminaries, like John Cotton, Thomas Shepard, and Thomas Hooker, were graduates or fellows of Emmanuel College, a Puritan foundation at the University of Cambridge. By establishing a college in 1636, even before they had provided for grammar schools, the founders of the Bay Colony initiated one of the more enduring love affairs in American history.

The Advantage of a College Education

In retrospect, eighteenth-century colleges might seem remarkable mainly for their poverty. Until the latter part of the century, when professorships began to multiply, much of the burden of collegiate instruction fell on college presidents and on tutors, who were recent graduates. At one point in Harvard's history, its president taught all of its courses, and Yale did not appoint its first professor until 1755, more than half a century after its founding. At the start of the Revolutionary War, only some 2,500 college graduates resided in the North American colonies. Yet of the 55 delegates who attended the Constitutional Convention in Philadelphia in 1787, 23 were collegians.[48] Further, although it was fairly common for eighteenth-century collegians not to graduate, only one of these 23 men, Alexander Hamilton, did not hold the A.B. degree. In rough terms, the chances of a college graduate in the United States serving as a delegate to the convention were one in 100. In contrast, the chances of any white adult male serving were approximately one in 20,000 for the entire population of white adult males.[49] Individual colleges accounted for equally impressive records. Of 338 graduates of the College of New Jersey (Princeton) from 1748 through 1768, 21 participated in the Continental Congress, 4 became U.S. senators, 7 entered Congress, and 2 became justices of the Supreme Court. In addition, these 21 Princeton classes produced 44 state legislators, 12 state judges, 5 state attorneys-general, and 2 governors.[50]

Had eighteenth-century colleges served as necessary stepping-stones for the sons of elite families, the prominence of graduates in public life would have been less remarkable. In reality, however, most sons of upper-crust families did not attend college, and the colleges did not draw their students exclusively from the gentry. Rather, their students came from a variety of social ranks. In his biographical directory of students in Princeton's first 21 classes (1748-68), James McLachlan identified the occupations of the fathers of 152 alumni: 76 of the fathers were farmers; 45 practiced one or more of the learned professions. Just under 30 percent of the fathers were professionals, while three-fourths of the sons (251/338) became professionals.[51] Attendance at Princeton clearly facilitated the movement of young men from agriculture into the professions, which in turn had close ties to public life. Emphasizing rhetoric and ornamental learning, the collegiate curriculum and extracurriculum were highly useful for these young men, certainly more so than a curriculum founded on trade education. In the eighteenth century, farm youth attended colleges to learn to become gentlemen, to occupy positions of influence in the rapidly growing professions, and to prepare themselves for public life.

Some collegians came from modest families, but very rarely from impoverished ones. Joseph Tichnor of Princeton's class of 1758 was the son of a shoemaker who left him a middling estate of 56 acres. As one of the least expensive of the colonial colleges, Princeton was receptive to young men of modest means, but Tichnor was poor even by Princeton's standards. In 1757 the college's president, Aaron Burr, had to pay Tichnor's bills.[52] Most of these relatively poor collegians were bound for the ministry. Typically, they were young men who only conceived the desire for a liberal education after a religious conversion experience and who entered and graduated from college at relatively advanced ages.[53] The popular image of eighteenth-century collegians as callow boys is misleading, for while some students graduated at fifteen, many were well over twenty at graduation. The proportion of Yale graduates who were age 23 or over at graduation fluctuated from a fifth to a quarter for much of the century and then rose to nearly 30 percent toward the end of the century.[54] Daniel Farrand, who was "brought to bow at the feet of Jesus" during George Whitefield's New England tour in 1741, did not enter Yale until he was 24. Farrand later entered Princeton, from which he graduated in 1750 at the age of 28. Some students were practically graybeards. Benjamin Haitt, a farmer's son who became a Presbyterian clergyman, was 36 at his graduation from Princeton in 1754.[55] In contrast to would-be lawyers and physicians, who usually needed family connections to secure desirable professional apprenticeships, young men marked by saving grace and little else could find patrons within the ministry who would guide them toward liberal education. Because conversion experiences often occurred in the teen years or later, these pious but poor youth were likely to stumble late into college. Whereas Princetonians who went into business graduated on average at 19 and those who became lawyers or physicians at 20, on average the Princetonians who became ministers graduated at 24.[56]

While in general clergymen thus experienced later graduations than lawyers or physicians, aggregate data fails to do justice to the waywardness and unpredictability of eighteenth-century collegians' lives. Graduates not infrequently practiced more than one profession, and the personal connections and interests forged in colleges nudged individuals in unanticipated directions. Hugh Henry Brackenridge, the grandson of a Scottish tenant farmer who was killed at the Battle of Culloden, grew up in a poor family in western Pennsylvania, exhibited early piety, gained the patronage of a minister, and after teaching school between his fifteenth and twentieth years, entered Princeton. There he joined with James Madison, William Bradford, and Philip Freneau in the American Whig Society, and he and Freneau wrote a poem, *The Rising Glory of America*, which was filled with patriotic prophecies and composed to be read at the college's 1771 commencement. Brackenridge's exposure to his secular-minded superiors might have weakened his resolve to become a minister and certainly highlights the mingling of social ranks in colleges. While Brackenridge did study theology after graduation, he inclined more to law and most of all to literature. Moving to Pittsburgh in 1781 to establish a legal practice, he won fleeting fame for his authorship of *Modern Chivalry*, arguably the first American novel.[57]

Not only could young men of modest estate gain access to colleges, but eighteenth-century colleges possessed incomparable resources for imparting a liberal education as well. Poor in comparison with the lavishly endowed institutions of higher education that arose later, they nevertheless appeared formidable to contemporaries. In 1756 the largest building in Britain's American colonies was Princeton's Nassau Hall.[58] At a time when few libraries were open to the public (nearly all such libraries were located in the seaport towns), colleges afforded young men access to books in relative abundance. At the start of the eighteenth century, the Harvard College Library held the largest single collection of books in New England; Yale, founded in 1702, quickly accumulated a more modern collection of books than Harvard.[59] Colleges also served as magnets for scholars from the increasingly vigorous Scottish universities, including John Witherspoon and Samuel Stanhope Smith at the College of New Jersey and William Smith of King's College, and thus enabled Americans to stay abreast of intellectual developments in the land of Adam Smith, David Hume, and Lord Kames. Equally important, colleges brought likeminded young men together and thereby broke down the isolation that afflicted intellectually inclined youth in America's vast agricultural hinterland. Trying to decide whether to attend the College of William and Mary or continue "my Studies in the Greek and Latin" at home in Albemarle County, the seventeen-year-old Thomas Jefferson opted for the "more universal Acquaintance" offered by the college.[60]

Collegiate and Self-Education

Eighteenth-century colleges did not engage in what later generations would call university extension, adult education, or "outreach." Colleges did not establish off-campus programs; professors did not embark on lecture tours. None of this means, however, that colleges neglected their public responsibilities. In an age when charters were not conferred routinely or automatically, the eighteenth-century colleges possessed acts of incorporation that made them bodies politic, authorized to govern themselves in the interests of the common weal, and hence similar in some respects to towns.[61] Colonial and, later, state governments directly granted money to colleges that by current standards were private institutions; more than half of the money donated to Harvard in the eighteenth century came from the Massachusetts government.[62] In the context of eighteenth-century assumptions, colleges could best serve the public by turning callow youth into leaders of public life. Yet the effect of colleges on public life was by no means restricted to offices held, discoveries made, sermons preached, causes pleaded, or patients cured by their graduates, for collegians absorbed from their student years, and especially from the student literary societies, a culture of self-education and mutual improvement that they projected into their later lives and habitats. In the eighteenth century the ideal of liberal education was bound intimately to that of self-education, both in the general sense that a liberal education included the acquisition of qualities of character, for example, the habit of placing civic duty above self-interest, and also in the sense that a liberally educated person possessed a knowledge of many subjects—history, the law of nations, modern polemics, and modern poetry—that rarely formed part of the collegiate curriculum.

In the 1720s a group of Harvard students formed a club to promote "right reasoning and good manner" by monthly disputations and issued a manuscript magazine, the "Telltale," that was modeled on Joseph Addison's *The Spectator.*[63] But the main growth of literary societies came after 1750 with the Flat Hat club at William and Mary, the Critonian and Linonian societies at Yale, and the American Whig and Cliosophic societies at Princeton. By 1800 Harvard, Brown, Dartmouth, Dickinson, Williams, North Carolina, and Union colleges were home to one or more of these societies, which stimulated student interest in subjects like fiction, poetry, and public speaking and which could boast of libraries that were always more accessible and at times larger than the official college libraries.[64]

Reinforcing the quest for knowledge, literary societies were part of a culture of gentlemanly self-education that flourished in the eighteenth century. Collegiate- and self-education were complementary ideals rather than competing alternatives. The eighteenth century's two major treatises on self-education, the *Treatise on the Conduct of the Understanding* by Locke and *The Improvement of the Mind* by Isaac Watts, the English dissenting minister and popularizer of Locke, were familiar vademecums for college students and continued to be used as college textbooks into the nineteenth century. The collegiate curriculum left a great deal to self-instruction, for no college even pretended to cover the range of topics that students might seek to learn. Until late in the century, colleges neglected instruction in modern languages. No college offered French before 1779, and while courses in French rode the crest of republican enthusiasm for the French Revolution, they receded with the wave. By the early 1800s colleges were retreating from the 1790s experiment that had allowed students to substitute French for Hebrew or Greek.[65] Students had to fall back on private tutoring or self-education to learn modern languages. For example, as a student at the medical school of the University of Edinburgh, Philadelphia's Benjamin Rush taught himself Spanish and Italian.[66] Colleges also left political theory to self-instruction. After his graduation from Princeton in 1771, James Madison returned to his Virginia home and read extensively in government and public law in order to understand the momentous issues of his day.

To describe self-education as a gentlemanly culture conveys its planned, patterned quality. Eighteenth-century manuals on self-education not only exhorted young men to improve their minds but told them how to do so. One favored activity was the keeping of commonplace books. Locke thought so highly of the practice that he devised a new way to organize these journals.[67] In the eighteenth century commonplace books served some of the functions later encompassed by Bartlett's *Familiar Quotations*. Madison copied portions of the memoirs of Cardinal de Retz and extracts from Montaigne into his commonplace book.[68] Jefferson recorded quotations from Bolingbroke, Milton, Shakespeare, and Ossian into his.[69] Commonplace books were not only convenient places to record quotations that might otherwise slip from memory; they also forced young men to reflect on what they were copying and in this way helped them form resolutions to regulate their lives. In addition, they were useful places to fashion and re-fashion sentences in order to enhance their precision and concision.[70]

While the keeping of commonplace books was a solitary endeavor, nothing in the eighteenth century's conception of self-education excluded activities that involved more than one person. Of the five methods for improving the mind recommended by Isaac Watts—observation, reading, meditation, attendance at lectures, and conversation—two were group activities. Conversation, under which Watts included "disputes of various kinds," is a fair description of the activities of the collegiate literary societies.[71] Conversation also seeded the literary correspondence that collegians continued after graduation. Recent graduates reinforced each other's literary bent by letter. In 1772 William Bradford, a recent Princeton graduate, wrote to Madison: "I propose making History and Morality my Studies in the ensuing winter, as I look upon them to be very necessary in whatever employment I may hereafter engage. 'Gnothi se auton' 'Know Thyself' as the celebrated maxim of the antients; and perhaps we shall not find an easier way of doing this than by the Study of History." A year later Bradford advised Madison to take *The Monthly Review*, an influential British magazine.[72] But correspondence was more than a way to pass on advice; for some, it acquired the stature of an art form. Writing to his friend James Kent in 1782, young Simeon Baldwin of Connecticut compared the pleasures of literary communication to "Rapture itself."[73]

Such techniques of self-education as elevated conversation and literary correspondence indicate how blurred the line was between private study and mutual improvement. Most forms of gentlemanly self-education involved contact with others. Young men frequently prepared for college under the guidance of a learned person and, as Jefferson's frequent letters of counsel to his young acquaintances reveal, they continued to offer or seek intellectual guidance after graduation. Even when preparing for a profession, graduates commonly engaged in self-directed liberal education. Legal and medical apprentices commonly used interludes, or created interludes, in their formal professional preparation so that they could advance their liberal cultivation of knowledge. Just as James Otis encouraged his legal apprentices to read broadly, an activity that had occupied Otis himself for a year and a half after his graduation from Harvard in 1743, so Jefferson took leave of George Wythe's law office for months at a time in order to study at his home near Shadwell, Virginia.[74] Similarly, for many college graduates readying themselves for the pulpit, professional preparation, almost always conducted under the personal supervision of a veteran minister, involved an extension of the collegiate literary society. Nathaniel Emmons, one of the leading New Light Congregationalists in late-eighteenth-century Massachusetts, encouraged his pupils to read widely in ethics, metaphysics, and civil polity as part of his self-described "liberal" design of ministerial preparation.[75] In addition, upon graduation some young men entered the households of learned elders, not with any specific intent to prepare for a profession but to place themselves in an environment congenial to self-education. After graduating from Princeton, Aaron Burr, who was the son of a Princeton president of the same name, went to live with Joseph Bellamy, a leading Massachusetts New Light theologian and a follower of Jonathan Edwards (Burr's grandfather), in order to resolve some theological doubts that had arisen in his mind while he was a student. Then in the spring of 1774 Burr moved into the house of his brother-in-law, Tapping Reeve, a Connecticut lawyer and the founder of the first law school in America, where he passed his time "occupied in reading, principally history."[76] Whether Burr was tutoring himself or being tutored or, as seems most likely, engaging in some combination of both, he was pursuing a course of informal study that was common among eighteenth-century college graduates.

Urban Clubs

Toward the middle of the eighteenth century the seaboard cities provided the setting for literary clubs that brought together recent graduates, prominent professional men, and established merchants. Similar societies had long existed in London, where the "Society for free and candid enquiry," popularly known as the Robin Hood Society, dated to 1613. The so-called Kit-Cat Club, founded at the start of the eighteenth century, counted Sir Richard Steele and Joseph Addison among its luminaries; Addison boasted that he had "brought philosophy out of closets and libraries, schools and colleges, to dwell in clubs and assemblies, at tea-tables and in coffee-houses."[77] A mid-eighteenth-century historian of the Robin Hood Society stated that "for the diffusion of useful knowledge it was thought expedient to admit every person that chose to come and for that purpose to assemble at a Public House."[78] In 1752 the society's membership, then 300, included bakers, shoemakers, lamplighters, schoolmasters, and apothecaries. Thereafter it acquired a more gentlemanly hue and in this respect became more like the Kit-Cat Club, but it continued to admit "lower mechanics." Nicholas Hans's account of these societies discloses their ties to deism and Dissent.[79]

In comparison, American literary societies initially sprang from the desire of graduates to recreate the sense of intellectual coterie that they had known in collegiate literary societies. In literary societies, graduates formed alliances with older physicians, lawyers, and merchants who in some instances hoped to revive the club life they had known in London or Edinburgh. Inasmuch as New York City and Philadelphia had become beehives of intellectual activity by 1750, replete with self-taught printers and booksellers, it would have been possible for Americans to recruit men of middling social rank to their clubs. At times they did so, but on balance the Americans faced a different challenge than the British. Specifically, the former felt the need to create urban intellectual institutions, and they naturally gravitated toward those in authority. Thus shortly after his graduation from Yale in 1741, William Livingston cooperated with other New York lawyers to establish a "Society for Improving themselves in Useful Knowledge."[80] In the 1750s Livingston would also contribute to the founding of the New York Society Library and King's College.

The Revolution boosted the establishment of an elite urban culture by injecting new vitality into the urban colleges as well as by pricking interest in history and political theory. When King's College became Columbia College in 1784, it did more than assume a patriotic title. By the mid-1780s a politically conservative, almost hidebound, college controlled by Anglican clergymen was transformed into an interdenominational college managed by an urban, professional elite. With its reorganization, the college developed new ties to New York City's civic leaders. In 1784 students organized the college's first literary society, "for the purpose of improving themselves in Polite Literature."[81] In turn, this society foreshadowed and fed members into the Uranian Society, a gentlemen's club formed in 1788 without any formal tie to Columbia but with a membership that included Columbia students and recent alumni. The Uranian Society attracted young men of distinguished families: Colden, Livingston, Verplanck, and Clinton. To these youth it afforded opportunities for debate, primarily on political topics but also on issues of religion and ethics, and a collection of books that by 1793 was valued at £188 and that well represented the genteel literary tastes of the day: Dryden, Goldsmith, Samuel Johnson, Pope, Swift, Gibbon, the *Federalist*, and histories of the American Revolution by William Gordon and David Ramsay.[82]

The Rising Glory of America

Although the Uranians appear to have disbanded by 1794, similar clubs sprouted not only in New York City but as well in Hartford, Boston, Baltimore, Wilmington, and Charleston. They bore such names as the Debating Club and the Belles-Lettres Club or, in one New York City instance, simply the Gentlemen's Club. Indeed competition from rivals may have doomed the Uranians. William and Peter Irving, the older brothers of Washington Irving, belonged to the Calliopean in New York City, before which William declaimed "a piece from Pope." Another brother, John Irving, was active in the Belles-Lettres Club.[83] All such clubs were permeated by a belief in America's Rising Glory. Like Britons, Americans concluded that a flourishing commerce and a liberal government would nurture literary vitality, and with the achievement of independence this conception of the relationship between political, economic, and cultural health imparted an urgency to expectations of a flowering of letters. Ezra Stiles and Benjamin Franklin had amassed evidence of the relentless growth of the American population, Thomas Paine had broadcast the defects of the English constitution, and the successful conclusion of the war seemed to remove the last obstacle to the budding of republican culture. In 1783 students at Washington College in Chester, Maryland, hailed the forthcoming "Reign of LEARNING and of PEACE." The result was an unprecedented spurt of versification, essay writing, and experiments in the writing of fiction.[84] Fully half of the magazines started in America between 1741 and 1794 began publication in the brief period from 1786 to 1794, and the years 1786 and 1787 alone witnessed the launching of more new magazines than had been started from 1764 to 1783.[85]

Just as his Princeton education had exposed the provincial farm boy Hugh Henry Brackenridge to the polished James Madison, urban gentlemen's clubs brought together collegians and non-collegians. On the still small stage of American literature, authorship in the form of writing essays or verse or experimenting with fiction could bring a young man to public attention and impart gentlemanly status to aspiring middle-class youths, regardless of whether they had attended college. The rising professions, especially law, complemented the effects of the literary flowering. In what would become a common pattern, the grammarian Lindley Murray chose to study law because he wished for a profession "attached to literary pursuits."[86] The Irving brothers came from a middle-class family several notches below the Livingstons and Clintons, but Peter attended Columbia, became a physician, dabbled in letters, and introduced his younger brother Washington, who never attended college, to literary circles.[87] In his first publication, *The Letters of Jonathan Oldstyle, Gent.* (1802), the nineteen-year-old Washington posed not only as a gentleman but as an aging and crusty one. Similarly, while studying law but privately hatching literary ambitions, sixteen-year-old Charles Brockden Brown joined a Belles Lettres Society in Philadelphia. This society, which apparently lasted from 1786 to 1793, aimed exclusively at the "literary improvement" of its members.[88] Perhaps because of his Quaker family's prejudices against colleges, Brown's formal education had ceased when he left the Friends' Latin School in 1786, the same year that he joined the Belles Lettres Society. The latter became his surrogate college, or perhaps more accurately, his surrogate collegiate literary society. Its members critiqued each other's literary efforts, and Brown recorded the society's proceedings in a journal whose labored orotundity gives insight into his fledgling attempts to become a writer:

This society is in its infancy; the vital principle is scarcely roused to action. At a more advanced period, when its operations shall have gained some degree of stability, when conjecture is ripened into fact, and when the views and reasonings of mistaken foresight have yielded to the certain and more obvious conclusions of experience, this subject will find employment from abler pens, and deservedly receive a thorough investigation.[89]

Brown's Belles Lettres Society is better described as a mutual improvement society than as a gentlemen's club. Admittedly, the distinction is slippery, for gentlemen's clubs engaged in mutual improvement, but they attracted a mixture of leading professional men, public officials, recent college graduates, and well-recommended aspirants to letters like Washington Irving. In contrast, the Belles Lettres Society was a kind of literary boys' club. Such clubs proliferated in the seaboard cities toward the end of the eighteenth century and in the first few decades of the nineteenth, and they attracted store clerks as well as legal and medical apprentices, all of whom fit the loose contemporary category of "young men"—youth from their early to mid-teens to their twenties. Decidedly less elite than gentlemen's clubs, they nevertheless fed on the same literary aspirations, which included authorship and service to America's Rising Glory. At a time when literary reputations could be quickly, if not necessarily easily, acquired, such clubs served some of their members as staging grounds for gentlemen's clubs. Brown himself, who began to publish essays in the *Columbian Magazine* while still a year and a half shy of his twentieth birthday, experienced just such a graduation, for as his reputation grew, he came to be counted as a member of the elite Friendly Club whenever he visited New York City.[90]

In sum, the Rising Glory motif pried open the doors of elite literary clubs to young men of middling social rank without in any significant way challenging the idea that the pursuit of literary culture was primarily a gentlemanly activity. Much the same can be said for the growing number of formal and informal societies that inclined to philosophy rather than to literature. Before the end of the eighteenth century, two learned societies had been established in North America on the model of England's Royal Society: the American Philosophical Society (Philadelphia, 1743) and the American Academy of Arts and Sciences (Boston, 1780). In addition, in urban centers gentlemen gathered informally for clubs or "parties," where they discussed and corresponded about experiments that "let light upon nature" and thereby improved "the arts of living."

Like literary clubs, philosophical societies were urban institutions that made room for non-collegians as well as for college graduates and, again like gentlemen's clubs, philosophical societies had a mildly leveling effect, for the cultivation of science as well as literature could impart genteel status. On the surface, indeed, philosophical societies were far more open to ordinary artisans, for they fully incorporated the ideal of Useful Knowledge, which long had proclaimed that the gentry had much to learn from the "Mechanick Arts." By the late eighteenth century, the pantheon of Useful Knowledge included such inventive mechanics as Franklin and David Rittenhouse. In his *Notes on the State of Virginia* (1784), Jefferson, who in 1796 would become the American Philosophical Society's third president, hailed Rittenhouse as an example of what untutored genius might accomplish in America, while Jefferson's friend, the physician Benjamin Rush, contended that Rittenhouse was fortunate to have escaped "the pernicious influence of monkish learning upon his mind in early life." Had he secured a liberal education, "Rittenhouse the philosopher, and one of the luminaries of the eighteenth century, might have spent his hours of study in composing syllogisms, or in measuring the feet of Greek and Latin poetry."[91]

Rush's admiration for Rittenhouse exemplifies how gentlemen and artisans occasionally encountered each other on terms of equality in learned societies. As a medical-school graduate of the University of Edinburgh, Rush possessed far more education than Rittenhouse, who like Franklin had only a grade-school education. The idea of Useful Knowledge was a leveler of sorts, for just as it encouraged inventive artisans like Franklin to study the laws of physics, it prompted learned physicians like Scotland's William Cullen to investigate such mundane processes as bleaching. Additionally, since neither colleges nor medical schools, the sole institutions for the study of science, pretended to encompass the entire range of natural knowledge, even the educated engaged in extensive self-instruction. For their part, learned societies served in effect as mutual improvement clubs in which those who knew more of one or another scientific branch instructed those who knew less.

Yet this culture of self-education made learned societies appear more democratic than they were. In the eighteenth century and for much of the nineteenth, individuals who attained eminence in science often did so in branches they had never studied in school, but those lacking more than a grade-school education rarely attained eminence. Of the 81 men and one woman of science born before 1776 who are listed in Clark A. Elliott's *Biographical Dictionary of American Science*, only eight fell into the category of "private study, self-taught."[92] The great majority of members of learned societies were either college or medical-school graduates (sometimes both). For example, of the 62 incorporators of the American Academy of Arts and Sciences, 54 were Harvard graduates and another six held honorary degrees from Harvard.[93] Membership in a learned society or an invitation to one of the eighteenth century's many informal clubs where gentlemen met to investigate nature did not in itself bridge the wide chasm between artisans and their social superiors. Reflective of the gentry's prevailing view of inventive mechanics was the patronizing tone of an observer at one of the parties given by Caspar Wistar (1761-1818), a Quaker physician and professor of anatomy at the University of Pennsylvania. After meeting "several ingenious men of a class something below that of the ordinary members" of Wistar's circle, the observer related:

When an operative mechanic attracts notice by his zeal for improvement in any branch of science, he is almost uniformly invited to the Wistar meetings. The advantage of this policy is obviously very great. A modest and deserving man is brought into notice. His errors are corrected, his ardour is stimulated, his taste improved. A healthy connexion is kept up between the different classes of society and the feeling of mutual sympathy is duly cherished.[94]

Franklin and Rittenhouse managed to transcend the normal limits of their social rank, but a brief glance at their careers indicates how dependent on luck and timing as well as talent such ascents were. Born in 1732, Rittenhouse passed the first 35 years of his life in the obscurity of Norriton township, Pennsylvania, where he made halfhearted attempts at farming and far more persistent efforts to fabricate clocks and to study science. Perhaps his first piece of good fortune was to inherit a translation of the First Book of Newton's *Principia* from an uncle. His second was to meet William Barton, a graduate of the University of Dublin who would have stayed in Ireland had the estate he inherited not been so encumbered by debt. Barton moved to Norriton in 1751, married Rittenhouse's favorite sister, and kept him supplied with scientific books from Britain. It is possible that Barton brought Rittenhouse to the attention of Reverend Richard Peters, the governor's secretary who in 1763 employed Rittenhouse to assist in surveying the dividing line between Pennsylvania and the lower counties of Maryland and Delaware. In turn, Peters brought Rittenhouse to the notice of Reverend William Smith, who came to Philadelphia to preside over its Academy (founded by Franklin) and who guided the Academy's development into the College of Philadelphia. Aware that Rittenhouse was planning to construct a planetarium or orrery and eager to purchase it for the College, Smith arranged the College's conferral of an honorary M.A. degree on Rittenhouse in 1767. A year later Smith secured Rittenhouse's election to the American Philosophical Society, of which Peters was a member, and in 1769 the Society selected Rittenhouse's Norriton farm as one of the three observation sites for the impending transit of Venus. Rittenhouse's many contributions to the cause of American independence, including his assistance in the manufacture of cannon and gunpowder in Pennsylvania, did nothing to dim his reputation, and in 1779 he secured appointment as the first professor of astronomy at the University of Pennsylvania, the new name for the College of Philadelphia.[95]

Franklin's career, which differed from Rittenhouse's in many ways, illustrates how a clever man could effect the ultimate achievement of self-instruction: the transformation of an artisan into a gentleman. One of seventeen children of a Boston tallow chandler, Franklin possessed only an elementary education, but he compensated for this by private reading, correspondence with learned men, and his founding of the Junto, a "club for mutual improvement," in the fall of 1727. The forerunner of the American Philosophical Society, the Junto was composed mainly of young men like Franklin. Its membership included several printers, a copier of deeds, a glazier, a surveyor, a joiner, a clerk, and one young gentleman of means. Franklin used the Junto for various purposes. Its members conducted self-conscious investigations of virtue, which led Franklin to portray basic Christian qualities like industry, frugality, and chastity as avenues to wealth rather than as handmaidens of piety. In a manner at once ponderous and tentative, Franklin used the Junto to map out a kind of calculating behavior that in the nineteenth century would come to be recognized as appropriate to the middle class.[96] Yet Franklin himself employed the Junto and his other forays into self-improvement less to reinforce his position as an artisan than to make his way into the world of gentlemen. Even before he was twenty, Franklin's interest in books had marked him as a youth of promise and had helped him secure an interview with a colonial governor, William Burnet. The Junto brought him to the attention of Philadelphia's select society, including James Logan, a Quaker merchant and the owner of one of the largest private libraries in the colonies. Franklin and Logan cooperated in launching the Library Company of Philadelphia in 1732. It was Logan who beseeched the Royal Society in London to recognize the claims of Thomas Godfrey, a member of the original Junto, to have invented an improved quadrant.[97]

Useful Knowledge was indeed highly useful for Franklin. Benefiting from his earnest cultivation of philosophy, his studious efforts to acquire literary refinement by reading Joseph Addison's *The Spectator*, and his accumulation of a personal fortune as printer to the Pennsylvania assembly (a position he secured through the kindly intervention of his social superiors), Franklin acquired most of the marks of a gentleman. His career serves as a reminder that gentlemanly status was open to a talented, ambitious, and educated (whether self- or college-) youth.

Rather than viewing Franklin and Rittenhouse as typical of even eminent cultivators of science in the eighteenth century, it is more accurate to see them as fortunate beneficiaries of gentlemanly patronage. Such patronage was forthcoming in part because even the well educated were often self-instructed in the branches of science in which they made their mark and in part because, amid the Revolutionary era's flush of republican patriotism, Franklin and Rittenhouse nicely fit the image of the United States as a nation of opportunity for "natural aristocrats." When in his *Notes on the State of Virginia* Jefferson responded to the Abbé Raynal's deprecatory dismissal of America for failing to produce genius, he based his counterblast on Franklin and Rittenhouse, the latter "second to no living astronomer" and in genius the first, "because he is self-taught."[98] Similarly, Connecticut's Simeon Baldwin greeted independence with the hope that "many a Ritenhouse among our Mechanick genii and an American Cincinnatus on every farm" would soon appear.[99]

City and Countryside

Toward the end of the eighteenth century and throughout the nineteenth, organized intellectual life spread beyond the perimeters of the seaboard cities into interior locales. It was not just that new towns and cities sprang up or that intellectual institutions inevitably followed the flow of population. Rather, a leading feature of American cultural life between 1780 and 1900 was the proliferation of self-conscious intellectual outposts, of towns and villages whose inhabitants earnestly established academies and colleges, library societies and literary societies. In contrast, even allowing for the smaller scale of the eighteenth-century population and for the fact that nearly all Americans lived between the Atlantic coast and the Appalachians, pre-Revolutionary America contained few equivalents to the decentralized intellectual culture that would typify the nineteenth century. Culturally and intellectually speaking, the gap between the seaboard cities and the interior was profound.

To be sure, there were exceptions to this generalization, such as ministers in New England towns and intellectually inclined members of the southern gentry. Yet although the colleges, where ministers dominated the faculty, warmed to belles lettres and other species of secular learning after the mid-eighteenth century, village ministers did not necessarily evince a keen interest in learned fields other than theology. As for the South, much of Virginia was little more than a rowdy frontier in the eighteenth century. Jefferson and Madison were what one historian has called "biological sports" in the Chesapeake society, for few members of the gentry shared their taste for learning.[100] George Tucker, a Virginia intellectual of the generation after Jefferson, recalled that among members of the eighteenth-century gentry, "Literature was neglected, or cultivated, by the small number . . . rather as an accomplishment and mark of distinction than for the substantial benefits it confers."[101] Most members of the colonial Virginia gentry lived primarily in a world of oral culture, into which print culture, the disposition to acquire ideas and information from books, pamphlets, newspapers, and magazines, infrequently and inconsistently intruded.[102] Even in Virginia, towns like Petersburg and Fredericksburg were vastly more congenial environments in which to cultivate literature and philosophy than were the plantations.[103] For rural youth of modest means, in other words for most youth, the obstacles to acquiring higher or "polite" knowledge were formidable.

The career of Devereux Jarratt, who became a leading Episcopal minister in Virginia, reveals the obstacles to learning that confronted a struggling youth of poor parents in the eighteenth century.[104] Born in 1732 in New Kent county in Tidewater Virginia, Jarratt was the son of a carpenter and came of age in the colonial South's vast rural working class. His parents ate plain food and wore simple clothing that was "suitable to their humble station." Jarratt quickly discovered the chasm between Virginia's plain folk and gentry:

We were accustomed to look upon, what were called *gentle folks*, as beings of a superior order. For my part, I was quite shy of *them*, and kept off at a humble distance. A *periwig*, in those days, was a distinguishing badge of gentle *folk*—and when I saw a man riding the road, near our house, with a wig on, it would so alarm my fears, and give me such a disagreeable feeling, that, I dare say, I would run off, as for my life. Such ideas of the difference between *gentle* and *simple*, were, I believe, universal among all of my rank and age.[105]

This difference extended to education. Jarratt's parents had no ambition higher than to teach their children to read and write, to understand arithmetic, and to memorize prayers and parts of the Bible. Jarratt prided himself on being able to recite chapters of the Bible from memory after hearing them read a few times and before he had learned the alphabet. Frequently interrupted, his formal schooling ended when he was twelve or thirteen years old.[106] Jarratt then went to work as a carpenter, still never having heard of philosophy, rhetoric, or logic, "for there were no books on such subjects among us." But he managed to procure a manuscript book on arithmetic, and he became so skilled in "the *Division of Crops*, the *Rule of*

Three and *Practice*" that his fame spread to Albemarle County, a hundred miles north of New Kent, where an overseer, Jacob Moon, hired him to conduct a school.[107]

Jarratt then passed several years as an itinerant schoolmaster. No one mistook him for a gentleman, for he owned little more than the shirt on his back, lacked a liberal education, and retained his shyness in the presence of his superiors. But in the household of one of his employers he encountered an intense New Light gentlewoman, a Mrs. Cannon, who sparked his long-dormant interest in religion. Jarratt soon conceived a desire "to be better acquainted with the meaning of the scriptures," and although he did not own a single book, by some means "I got hold of a little old book, in a smoky condition, which I found to be [William] Russel's seven sermons."[108] Russel's sermons stimulated him to find an exposition of the Bible. It is revealing that Jarratt hypothesized that such a book should exist, for "I had never heard of any exposition, or did I know there was any such in the universe."[109] Soon he learned that a gentleman living five or six miles distant "owned a very large *book*" that explained all the New Testament. This turned out to be William Burkitt's *Expository Notes, with Practical Observations on the New Testament*, first published in 1724. Jarratt's reading of Burkitt accelerated his religious development. Soon he became a lay preacher and was urged by friends to become a minister.[110]

With his New Light tendencies, Jarratt distrusted the Church of England, but he also knew that the Presbyterians required their ministers to know Latin and Greek. "This obstacle appeared insuperable, as I was totally ignorant of these languages, and without the means of acquiring the knowledge of them."[111] At this juncture—Jarratt was now in his late twenties—he embarked on the study of the ancient languages under the direction of Alexander Martin, a recent Princeton graduate who had become a tutor in the house of a Virginia gentleman. By now inclining toward the doctrines of the Church of England rather than Presbyterianism, Jarratt visited London and was ordained as an Anglican minister.

By far the most detailed record of an eighteenth-century Virginian who was not born into the gentry, Jarratt's narrative of his life reveals the hurdles that stood between a carpenter's son and the acquisition of knowledge. Jarratt not only lacked the classical languages; more basically he did not possess a map of knowledge. He scarcely knew where to begin his liberal education or even what constituted liberal education. In addition, his autobiography discloses the importance of religious zeal in opening otherwise locked gates. Jarratt's occupation, schoolmaster, did not entitle him to genteel status: when he first entered the Cannon household, he was mistaken for the son of a neighborhood pauper.[112] By his own account,

Jarratt acted the part of a hypocrite, feigning piety to curry the favor of Mrs. Cannon. Later his piety became authentic, but it still continued to serve him well. It was Mrs. Cannon's spouse who paid for Jarratt's instruction in the classical languages by Alexander Martin.[113]

The conditions that Jarratt encountered were representative of those in rural Virginia during the mid-to-late eighteenth century. Even an inexpensive book might easily cost half the price of a hog, while multivolume works like Tobias Smollett's *Complete History of England* sold for £9, a colossal sum to someone like Jarratt.[114] An investigation of estate inventories in late-eighteenth- and early-nineteenth-century Virginia has revealed that fully half the free household heads did not own a single book, that most individuals who owned any books possessed only a few religious works, and that outside of a handful of river ports like Fredericksburg and Petersburg (the latter not incorporated until 1784), individuals with small-to-middling estates rarely owned more than a few books.[115] Thus while a flourishing print culture, a disposition to acquire ideas and information from books, existed in the river ports among those of middling as well as upper rank, in the vast hinterland, where most Virginians lived, it was rare to encounter individuals with large private libraries who were not members of the wealthy gentry, and even within the gentry the penetration of print culture was extremely inconsistent.

Jarratt benefited from his intellectual curiosity and a nimble mind, but without piety he would never have attained prominence. Of all professions, the ministry was by far the most receptive to poor young men. But piety did not routinely lead young men to a thirst for knowledge. The Methodists and Baptists attached little importance in the eighteenth century to educated ministers. It was Jarratt's luck (although he called it providence) to fall in with the Presbyterians, who did. Even the Presbyterians did not encourage pious but poor youth to investigate all spheres of learning. Piety gave direction to Jarratt's efforts to educate himself, but it also focused his strivings on religious rather than secular literature. Collegians at New Light Princeton pursued belles lettres, but the ideal of the man of letters was beyond Jarratt's grasp and indeed that of most eighteenth-century youth of Jarratt's class. While it was possible for Jarratt and such other poor Virginia youth as the Presbyterian Drury Lacy to acquire on their own a familiarity with subjects like geography, geometry, and English grammar and to learn enough Latin and Greek to be licensed in the ministry, "polite literature" was usually a closed book to them.[116]

The conditions that Jarratt encountered, representative of those in rural Virginia in the eighteenth century, were widespread outside Virginia. Although New England had a much higher literacy rate than Virginia and a long tradition of vernacular print, the recollections of New Englanders born into rural families resemble Jarratt's. Describing the cultural milieu in which his father—who was born in Epping, New Hampshire, in 1759—came of age, William Plumer, Jr., related:

> Newspapers were then hardly known in the circle where he moved. Pamphlets were scarce and confined mostly to religious topics, the occasional sermon, the controversial tract, or the painful experience of some Christian professor; or, what was more attractive, the narrative of some Indian captivity, or wild sea adventure, or shipwreck, the capture of a Spanish galleon, or the death of Capt. Kidd. Bound volumes were still more rare, and of those which he could obtain few were of much value.[117]

Such was the senior Plumer's craving for knowledge that "if he heard of a book, within many miles of his home, he could not rest till he had visited its privileged owner, and obtained the loan of it. He often went great distances on foot to borrow a book, of which he had heard perhaps, only the title, from a person he had never seen."[118]

Inasmuch as many parts of New Hampshire were still in the frontier stage in the 1760s and 1770s, Plumer's experience may have been unusual. Yet the kinds of books that the younger Plumer described, devotional books and chapbooks that related marvelous events, had circulated for generations in New England, where they formed the staple reading of the common people in town and country alike.[119] The polite literary culture that developed toward the middle of the eighteenth century differed from this traditional culture in many ways. Genteel culture valued style as much as substance, investigated natural laws more than revelations of wonders, and was far less embedded in oral traditions.[120] In addition, polite culture was mainly an urban phenomenon, while the vast majority of people lived outside of cities. As late as 1800, when London contained a million and Paris half a million inhabitants, the largest American city, Philadelphia, numbered fewer than 70,000 people. Furthermore, the recollections of young men whose early years were passed in settled agricultural areas of New England describe conditions more closely resembling Plumer's youth than that of Franklin. For example, while the future inventor John Fitch acquired the rudiments of education in his town school, as a farmer's son in mid-eighteenth century Windsor, Connecticut, he smacked into obstacles at every turn in his quest for education. Although Fitch's father allowed his son to attend school for extended periods until he was eight or nine years old, thereafter young Fitch had to work on the family farm:

> Altho I was exceedingly small of my age and hardly able to swingle more than two pounds of flax in a day and not able to thrash more than two bushels of grain in a day with the steadyness of a man of thirty, yet for that pityful trifeling labour I was prevented from going to school any more than one month in the dead of winter, when he [would] see that I was nearly crazey after learning.[121]

When Fitch was about eleven years old, he heard of "a book that would give me information of the whole world which was Salmon's Geography."[122] Confronted by his father's refusal to purchase the book for him, young Fitch planted a potato patch in his spare time, sold the produce, and took his ten shillings to a merchant in the neighborhood "who delt to New York who promised me to get the book who did it according to promise but the book cost twelve shillings and I was two shillings in debt."[123] Fitch managed to pay off the debt, but his memory of his father's parsimony remained with him through life.

Fitch's experience underscores the contractual relationships that bound boys to their fathers. His aspirations for knowledge beyond the rudiments had no place in the agricultural society of Windsor. Lacking piety as well as wealth and contemptuous of his father's Presbyterianism, he was hardly a likely subject for a conversion experience, had no interest in the ministry, and no prospects of acquiring a liberal education.

The experiences of Jarratt, Plumer, and Fitch not only illustrate the slow movement of books and ideas in the colonial hinterland but also testify to the importance of personal connections in obtaining a liberal education. To acquire a liberal education, a young man had to encounter someone who already possessed one. Sons of the gentry easily surmounted this obstacle, and in New England's larger towns, grammar schools afforded boys of different social ranks an opportunity to prepare for college. But throughout colonial society, personal connections were important and not readily available to young men from poor families or to the sons of artisans and farmers who lived far from towns. The latter often depended on religious conversion experiences to bring them to the attention of clergymen, who in turn undertook to prepare them for college. It was no accident that the colonial college most receptive to poor youth, Princeton, was also the most evangelical. But in the wake of the Revolution, a debate developed among educators tinged by the Enlightenment over the appropriate structure of republican education. Well-read and articulate, these theorists distanced themselves from the sectarianism spawned by religious revivals and sought to construct models that would make education more accessible to talented youth. In the process, the republican educators brought to the table a number of questions that would persist into the nineteenth century, including who should acquire a liberal education and of what sort.

Republican Education

Nearly all participants in the late-eighteenth-century debate on education agreed on a number of propositions. First, by education they meant instruction in formal schools, not the informal influences encountered in the home or on the job. Even Jefferson, who often extolled newspapers as instruments of popular education and who described education as a life-long enterprise, omitted any reference to newspapers, libraries, or other non-scholastic means of education in his Bill for the More General Diffusion of Knowledge, which he introduced in the Virginia House of Burgesses in 1779. While this omission might seem surprising, it can be explained by a second point of agreement. Education had to be "universal," which at the minimum meant that it had to affect all white male youth. Benjamin Rush, a physician, friend of Jefferson, and member of the American Philosophical Society, viewed newspapers as a promising vehicle of popular self-education, but he also recognized that newspapers did not circulate widely, and he averred that newspapers would not diffuse knowledge until towns were more widely established in the countryside.[124] In the eyes of both Rush and Jefferson, education gleaned by reading the newspapers or participating in public affairs left too much to chance in a society where random circumstances could not be presumed favorable to self-education for the many. Most republican educators continued to associate self-education and mutual improvement with the leisurely pursuit of knowledge by gentlemen. Learned philosophical societies might accommodate the occasional Rittenhouse, the "ingenious Mechanick," but such societies made no pretense to universality. In contemporary typology they engaged primarily in the "advancement" of knowledge, and the consequent diffusion of conveniences, rather than in the diffusion of knowledge itself.

In addition to favoring formal schooling, the republican educators agreed on the need for a tiered system of public, national (or regional) schools. At a time when "public" education usually meant either the education of children in groups (as opposed to private tutorial at home) or schools not restricted to members of a particular denomination, the republicans advanced the more modern equation of public with tax support. In fact, they often attacked private schools that charged tuition, partly on grounds that they excluded the poor and encouraged aristocratic pretensions ill-suited to a republic. Noah Webster condemned American colleges as "nurseries of Inequality."[125] In addition, they looked to tax-supported schools to forge what Webster called "our National Character," or what Benjamin Rush described as "republican machines."[126] In language that foreshadowed the rhetoric of public-school reformers in the 1830s, they urged that schools take dissimilar children and turn them into similar citizens.[127]

Preoccupied with developing a system of public schools that would nurture republican sentiments, educational theorists struggled and often disagreed over a key issue. Assuming universal education in the rudiments of reading, writing, and arithmetic, what proportion of the population was to receive more advanced education? Republican educators responded to this question with considerable ambivalence. For example, Jefferson proclaimed his "quixotism for the diffusion of knowledge," but the most striking feature of his Bill for the More General Diffusion of Knowledge was his preoccupation with winnowing the talented. Like most of his peers, Jefferson assumed that colleges would train an elite to conduct public affairs. What mattered was the composition of the elite, specifically its accessibility to talented but poor youth. His proposed bill divided Virginia first into wards (or "hundreds"), each with its own public elementary school, and then into twenty large districts, each with its own grammar school for instructing male youth in Latin, Greek, English grammar, and advanced arithmetic. The state would support one "public foundationer" in each grammar school—collectively, these foundationers were the "twenty geniuses" to be "raked annually from the rubbish"—and only one would ultimately proceed at public expense to the College of William and Mary.[128]

Jefferson's plans reflected his conventional division of society into the laboring and learned classes, a distinction that appeared to restrict liberal education to the few. Educated together in the elementary schools, the two classes thereafter would separate, the former to engage in agriculture or craft apprenticeships, the latter to proceed to grammar schools and colleges en route to public affairs or the professions.[129] Yet Jefferson, who crisply drew the laboring/learned distinction in a letter to his nephew Peter Carr in 1814, immediately muddied it by proposing that the curriculum of what would become the University of Virginia include an evening school of "technical philosophy" to which mariners, carpenters, shipwrights, pumpmakers, clockmakers, machinists, opticians, metallurgists, founders, cutlers, druggists, brewers, distillers, dyers, painters, bleachers, soapmakers, tanners, powdermakers, saltmakers, and glassmakers would resort "to learn as much as shall be necessary to pursue their art understandingly, of the sciences of geometry, mechanics, statics, hydrostatics, hydraulics, hydrodynamics, navigation, astronomy, geography, optics, pneumatics, physics, chemistry, natural history, botany, mineralogy and pharmacy."[130]

Inasmuch as Jefferson's final plan for the University of Virginia dropped the school of technical philosophy, it is possible to view his 1814 proposal as an eccentric fragment of almost crackpot proportions. How were artisans scattered over a vast area supposed to attend the evening school of a university whose location Jefferson had selected because of its proximity to his home, not because it bordered any population center? And what benefit exactly were they to derive from immersion in academic subjects? Before dismissing his idea, however, we should recognize that other republican educators were moving in a stumbling and ambivalent way toward the same notion: a type of liberal education that would be useful to the many rather than the few. On the one hand, all accepted Jefferson's stress on a pyramidal system of public schools to winnow talented youth.[131] On the other hand, they were heirs to the tradition of Useful Knowledge represented by Bacon and Franklin. This tradition encouraged them to equate philosophy with applied as well as speculative truths. At the very least, the mingling of theory and practice served pedagogical goals. Franklin had contended that academic pursuits could be made interesting if teachers skillfully associated the knowledge contained in books with practical activities; descriptions of the "prodigious Force and Effect of Engines and Machines used in War" would prick interest in the principles of mechanics.[132] But in the wake of the Revolution, some republican educators were willing to go further than Franklin, who had employed neither the language nor motifs of republicanism, by portraying utility as a way to diffuse liberal education. If, as Franklin had argued, drawing connections between practice and theory would rivet the attention of boys, it might also stir the intellectual curiosity of republican citizens. As long as knowledge was applied to "some necessary and useful purpose of life," Rush wrote, "the excellency of knowledge would be obvious to everybody."

Of the several republican educators, the lexicographer Noah Webster went farthest in stressing the diffusion of Useful Knowledge, and, significantly, he downgraded the importance of colleges and universities. In contrast to Jefferson, Webster saw the intermediate level of education, post-primary and precollegiate, as critical in the new republic, for few young people would persist in school long enough to benefit from a college or university. Nor, indeed, should they, for university education bred "a fondness of ease, for pleasure or for books, which no efforts can overcome."[133] Such education was useless, for "why should a merchant trouble himself with the rules of Greek and Roman syntax or a planter puzzle his head with conic sections?"[134] In fact, it was worse than useless, for it bred habits inimical to the drudgery of the countinghouse; "what is now called a *liberal education* disqualifies a man for business."[135]

Rather than turning boys loose in stores at fourteen "without an idea of their business," Webster contended, their education should be prolonged to the age of fifteen or sixteen by the addition of vocationally useful subjects: the principles of trade, insurance, and husbandry.[136] The key word here was "principles." Although he doubted the suitability of existing liberal education for those in the ordinary callings of life, neither Webster nor the other republican educators associated useful education with teaching craft techniques. Rather, popular education could be both useful and liberal if it focused on the broad principles that undergirded the common trades.

Consistent with his republican commitment to education that would simultaneously be useful, liberal, and popular, Webster also voiced advanced ideas about the education of women. In contrast to Franklin, who blithely equated "youth" with boys, Webster believed that republics had a duty to educate all of their citizens to discharge the obligations of their stations. Just as colleges unfitted young men for practical activities, parents too often pushed their daughters beyond their stations by encouraging their mastery of the harpsichord and minuet rather than the sort of "solid" education Webster advocated for them: English, history, geography, poetry, and arithmetic. Rather than educating women to amuse and beguile men, Webster wanted to teach them to discharge their duties as republican citizens. Similarly, Rush, whose widely reprinted *Thoughts Upon Female Education* was originally delivered as a lecture to the board of visitors of the newly chartered Young Ladies' Academy of Philadelphia in 1787, called for women to be taught bookkeeping on the grounds that they would act as stewards and guardians of their husbands' estates and executrices of their wills. In 1793 Priscilla Mullin used her valedictory to this academy to call for admitting women to male professions, but her proposal was highly unusual. Neither Webster, Rush, nor even the feminist Judith Sargent Murray envisioned education as a spearhead for merging gender spheres. Rather, the republican educators contended that education would enable women to exert a more intelligent moral influence on children and young men, for where the latter inclined to dissipation, women "are among the last to be corrupted."[137]

No consensus existed among republican educators that women should be educated beyond the rudiments. But the fact that post-primary education for women was becoming a controversial issue says a good deal about the value that late-eighteenth-century republican educators attached to the many rather than the few. Although Webster's insistence on educating females to be chaste intellectual companions for men and to raise children properly was nearly identical to ideas being advanced at the same time in England by Hannah More and others, he invariably returned to the unique requirements of the American republic, specifically the need to provide the great majority of citizens, including women, with useful education.

In their plans to popularize liberal education, most republican educators targeted the requirement of colleges that boys study the dead languages. Criticism of the bonding of Latin and liberal education did not originate with the republicans. In his mid-century *Proposals*, Franklin devoted a rambling, learned footnote to proving that the ancients above all valued instruction in their own tongues and that the colonists should accord similar reverence to English.[138] But in contrast to Franklin's polite and rather cautious language, Rush portrayed the subservience of educators to Latin and Greek as monarchical, unjust, even conspiratorial, as well as anti-republican. Rush once asked John Adams whether men did not employ Latin and Greek "as the scuttlefish emit their ink, on purpose to conceal themselves from an intercourse with the common people."[139] As long as "Latin and Greek are the only avenues to science, education will always be confined to a few people," he argued. Unburdening the curriculum of Latin and Greek "would greatly increase the number of our students in the colleges and thereby extend the benefits of education through every part of the country."[140] A "liberal or learned education in a republic" should include the study of eloquence, more powerful than the sword in bringing about the Revolution; the history of the ancient republics and the progress of tyranny in the states of Europe; chemistry, vital to agriculture and manufactures; and the principles of commerce and money, which if properly understood would guard against landed monopoly.[141]

In the political divisions of the 1790s, Rush became an ardent Republican, Webster an equally ardent, if fractious, Federalist. Gradually, however, political lines crystallized on the issues raised by the republican educators. As Federalists fell into opposition after 1800, most of them took the line that the ancient languages formed the necessary prop for all liberal education and the bastion against the barbarism of Jefferson's followers. Benjamin Rush's call for turning citizens into "republican machines," innocuous when first voiced in 1786, had acquired far different and decidedly partisan connotations by 1802. For their part, most Republicans assailed ancient-language requirements in grammar schools and colleges. In addition, Republicans generally were more sympathetic than Federalists to the diffusion of knowledge, which they associated with the overthrow of Latin and Greek requirements.[142]

This choice of the ancient languages as a battlefield made the issues appear more crisply defined than they were in actuality. By channeling their discontent toward a single enemy—the study of the ancient languages as a requirement for a liberal education—Republicans satisfied themselves that they were dethroning "monarchical" education without clearly delineating the contours of republican education. Many Republicans continued to cherish the classical languages even as they opposed mandating them, and none was willing to part with the study of eloquence or history. Although a useful education usually meant the opposite of an ornamental one, republican educators did not consistently attack the latter.[143] Rather, they clung to a kind of republican gentility. They assumed that society would continue to be guided by leaders whose educational attainment would be far above average, but the diffusion of Useful Knowledge would ease the process of accommodating the upwardly mobile by establishing a fundamental ground of sympathy between social ranks: leaders who respected the accomplishments of craftsmen and farmers; tradesmen and yeomen who at least glimpsed the theoretical interests of leaders.

To say this is to suggest that the preference of late-eighteenth-century republicans for Useful Knowledge was, at some level, political. Useful Knowledge was far more compatible with republican expectations of national development than any other philosophy of education. The point is not just that the mass of citizens had to receive some education to exercise the franchise. Rather, they required a type of education simultaneously liberal and useful if they were to be properly bonded to republican gentlemen. The inherited conception of liberal education, tied to Latin and eloquence, promised nothing like this. By definition, it excluded all those not bound for public life, including all women and all yeomen and artisans who aspired only to discharge the duties of their stations. In contrast, Useful Knowledge would establish the basis for mutual respect among different ranks, while maintaining the hierarchy appropriate to an orderly republic. Rather than depending on inherited wealth or on their possession of types of knowledge incomprehensible by the many, the superiority of leaders would depend on their greater advancement in kinds of knowledge possessed by all citizens.

Although preferable on political grounds, Useful Knowledge was open to sundry objections. Consistent with their objective of advancing knowledge, the eighteenth-century philosophical societies had welcomed a few inventive artisans and a larger number of gentlemanly cultivators of the soil who wished to improve agriculture. What was unclear was how Useful Knowledge could be reconciled with the goal of diffusing knowledge throughout society. Ordinary artisans and farmers lacked the "genius" and the leisure to engage in intellectual exploration. Why was it important for clerks to study the history of commerce? Were the occupations of printer, carpenter, and clockmaker sufficiently similar to justify educating boys in the principles of mechanics? While gentlemen might investigate agriculture, did it make sense for boys to study it in schools at a time when no textbooks or recognized science of agriculture existed?

Drawn on political grounds to the ideal of diffusing Useful Knowledge, the republican educators failed to answer these questions, and for the most part they failed to raise them. Jefferson stopped thinking about them after he jettisoned his plan for a school of "technical philosophy." His final plan for the University of Virginia was both original and coherent, but it derived its coherence from the ideal of gentlemanly investigator rather than from that of diffusing knowledge. Gentlemen should know something of military tactics or law or agriculture as well as the classical languages, history, and the sciences, for just as gentlemen would benefit from the ornament of literature when they sought to persuade others in public halls, they would also serve in the course of their lives as military officers and as justices of the peace, and not infrequently they would join agricultural improvement societies.

For all of the difficulties surrounding its implementation, the ideal of diffusing Useful Knowledge persisted into the nineteenth century, and it did so with distinctly political overtones. In 1862 the framers of the Morrill, or Land-Grant College, Act called for the "liberal and practical education" of the "industrial classes," and they did so in language that clearly linked "liberal" and "practical" as conjunctives rather than as alternatives. By the early 1900s, proponents of Useful Knowledge were ready to experiment with new forms of university extension that were redolent of Jefferson's plan for adult education in a school of technical philosophy.

In reality, however, the democratization of knowledge in the nineteenth century would depend less on popular interest in applied science than on a widening of the audience for polite literature, and it would take the form of a much greater reliance on self-education and mutual improvement than the republican educators had envisioned. Although the American Revolution did little to persuade mechanics to become philosophers, it encouraged commoners to avail themselves of the benefits of literature. As the editors of the *Christian's, Scholar's, and Farmer's Magazine* proclaimed in 1789, it is "of essential service to the community, that our young men, in general, who shall devote themselves to commerce, and to mechanical and agricultural employments, should possess considerable degrees of literature."[144]

Conclusion

Eighteenth-century education was democratic in neither theory nor practice, but within the context of a society divided into social ranks it afforded opportunities for upward mobility for those who could find patrons. This was true not only of the pious young men who benefited from patrons in the ministry but of noncollegians of middling social rank, who consorted with gentlemen in literary societies, and of the occasional "ingenious Mechanick" invited by his betters to participate in the meetings of philosophical societies as well.

Such instances of mobility occurred within the framework of deep cultural divisions between town and country and between social ranks. The depth of these divisions and the meager intellectual resources available outside of cities contributed to the importance of collegiate education and help to explain the preoccupation of republican educators with devising an elaborate pyramid of formal educational institutions. Republican educators did not entertain high expectations for self-education, which they understandably perceived as a privilege available to gentlemen and their clients, not as a means for opening education to a wider range of talented youth. The latter objective demanded that academies and colleges become more widely diffused by reconciling liberal and practical education in ways yet to be defined.

Chapter 2

The Uses of Knowledge in
Antebellum America

Speaking before the Harvard chapter of Phi Beta Kappa in 1826, the jurist Joseph Story proclaimed the "general diffusion of knowledge" as one of the striking features of the age.[1] In the same year the Connecticut educator Josiah Holbrook devised a grand scheme for "lyceums," local literary and scientific "associations of adults for mutual improvement" throughout the United States and, in fact, the world, for the study of "Mechanics, Hydrostatics, Pneumatics, Chemistry, Mineralogy, Botany, any branch of the Mathematics, History, Political Economy, or any political, intellectual, or moral subject."[2] Although lyceums did not develop along the lines Holbrook envisioned, in the form of organizations for sponsoring popular lectures they became a vast enterprise between 1830 and 1860 and took their place alongside sundry other agencies for popularizing knowledge: libraries in such unlikely places as steamboats and hotels, inexpensive books and periodicals, the penny press, and mass public education.[3]

Historians usually have identified the three decades before the Civil War as the period especially marked by the democratization of knowledge, a view often echoed in the writings of contemporaries. For this period the available explanations are convenient, almost too convenient: the transportation revolution, which speeded communications; Jacksonian democracy, which elevated the common man; and technological advances that brought down the price of printed material. Yet notions of democratization after 1830 can be as misleading in application to cultural as to political history, for the process of change was gradual and consisted of rivulets that, while they converged after 1830, had begun a half-century earlier with the proliferation of academies, library companies, periodicals, and mutual improvement societies. This early diffusion of knowledge did not depend on missionaries like Holbrook, who was determined to plant the seeds of knowledge everywhere; rather, it was primarily a local movement in which townspeople, women as well as men, made organized and often costly efforts to improve their access and that of their children to literature and science.[4]

In the eyes of contemporaries, academies, library companies, periodicals, and mutual improvement societies alike were "means" of spreading knowledge. Yet this phrasing is misleading to the extent that it assigns primacy to institutions. More accurately, individuals created institutions to educate themselves and others. While it is true that people read books because they became available, it is equally true that books (and periodicals and lectures) became more available because people chose to read and to listen. Even after 1835, when improvements in transportation contributed to the emergence of lyceum lecturers as a speaking aristocracy addressing a silent democracy, audiences retained the right to vote with their feet, while lecturers found that they could never stray far from the expectations of their listeners.[5]

A variety of motives spurred the popular quest for knowledge in the late eighteenth and early nineteenth centuries.[6] The upheavals of the Revolution and its aftermath stimulated wider popular engagement in public life. Those exposed to public life either as observers or as participants found new incentives to acquire knowledge, in part to comprehend the allusions of speakers and in part to form their own opinions. Increasingly, "no man's opinion was accepted solely because of his station, and more and more men with no station were expressing opinions."[7] The religious agitation that accompanied popular politicization stimulated the spread of sects and denominations hostile to hierarchy and nurtured a poor man's enlightenment in which shoemakers and carpenters debated religious and philosophical issues once reserved for the educated clergy. The occupational specialization that attended economic change led to the formation of mutual improvement societies specific to one or another occupational group, whether merchants or mechanics, while aspirants to the legal and medical professions discovered new uses for literary and philosophical cultivation.

Well established by 1800 as a suitable activity of gentlemen, the pursuit of knowledge adapted successfully if not always smoothly to nineteenth-century democracy. It did so because American democrats who talked of leveling social distinctions were inclined to level up rather than down—to make genteel culture more accessible to the multitude rather than to eradicate it. In this context, the pursuit of knowledge served both aggressive and defensive functions; it was both a way for individuals to advance within professions and intellectual occupations and a means by which occupational groups guarded their flanks by aligning themselves with genteel culture.

For the most part, these developments affected men more than women. In contrast to the late nineteenth century, when women came to dominate organizations of mutual improvement, males spearheaded the formation of knowledge societies in antebellum America. Yet women also engaged in self-improvement in the first half of the nineteenth century. The prevailing tendency to associate the quest for knowledge with disinterestedness legitimated female intellectual improvement as never before. Because intellectual improvement was acquiring abundant new practical applications in the early nineteenth century, contemporaries rarely felt compelled to argue the point. Rather, they contented themselves with general affirmations of the relationship between knowledge and both personal and social benefit, and they portrayed the pursuit of knowledge as a moral calling, an outlet for high-minded selflessness formerly channeled exclusively into religion. This rhetoric of selflessness proved inviting to women, but it should not disguise the fact that women too were finding new (if limited) vocational uses for knowledge.

Academies, Library Companies, and Periodicals

Academies, which taught Latin but which did not depend on tax support, began to emerge in New England in the 1760s, aided by the towns' evasion of the requirement to maintain Latin grammar schools. By 1800 Massachusetts and Connecticut each contained at least 21 academies, most of which had been founded in the 1780s and 1790s.[8] Perhaps because they have been interested mainly in public education, historians have been content to classify academies as transitional institutions between the decline of the Latin grammar schools and the rise of the supposedly more democratic public high schools of modern America. This neglect is strange, for academies grew swiftly not only in late-eighteenth-century New England but also in states like North Carolina that were not known for traditions of learning. Further, although not supported by taxes, academies were not quite "private" institutions, for they received considerable public support in the form of land grants, lottery proceeds, and in the case of the larger ones, charters.[9] Bernard Bailyn has aptly described academies as quasi-public institutions that developed in response to "a powerful folk movement in which large numbers of people, organizing locally, built for themselves, without prescriptive traditions, plans, or principles of education, institutions to serve vague, unformed cultural needs."[10] Some of the larger academies, like the ones established respectively by Samuel and John Phillips at Andover and Exeter, benefited from lavish individual endowments, but more commonly local patrons banded together to aid academies by providing many small benefactions rather than a few handsome ones.

Among other accomplishments, academies significantly widened the educational opportunities of women. Eighteenth-century Latin grammar schools had exclusively taught boys. The so-called English grammar schools, which the smaller towns maintained as cheap alternatives to the Latin schools legally required of the larger towns, had been open to girls only on occasion. Girls could attend private schools, that is, schools conducted by a single master for profit, but these flourished mainly in the seaports, where they served the daughters of prosperous merchants and public officials. In short, until the rise of the academies in the late eighteenth century, girls had few opportunities to obtain education beyond the rudiments. While some of the more famous academies were exclusively for boys, others were restricted to girls, and the majority were coeducational. Even in the coeducational academies, girls were instructed in separate "ladies' departments" and denied the range of subjects open to boys. But with public support and numerous benefactions, academies were able to hire several teachers, and from their inception they offered a remarkably broad range of courses, including college subjects like astronomy and natural philosophy. At least one late-eighteenth-century academy billed its curriculum as comparable "to that of any College on the continent."[11]

Leicester Academy in central Massachusetts was an average specimen of the incorporated New England academies. Chartered in 1784, on condition that its petitioners raise 1,000 pounds exclusive of real estate to support it, Leicester Academy was described by contemporary accounts as "another channel to public education."[12] Leicester was "public" according to the common understanding of that term in eighteenth-century America. Not only did it benefit the public but no legal barriers restricted entrance.[13] Although located in Leicester, it admitted tuition-paying students from anywhere. The academy also garnered a good deal of popular support. It was not tax-supported, but the subscription required by its charter was made up by several small bequests. One of the contributors, Reuben Swan, was the keeper of a public house in Leicester, a man "in no way distinguished among her citizens."[14] Swan's gift, £50, made him one of the school's larger benefactors. Timothy Bigelow, an army veteran in "somewhat straightened" circumstances, donated £30. The largest bequest was £150. Most of the contributors, Emory Washburn noted in his 1860 chronicle of the school, belonged to the class of men "whose independence of thought and opinion gave character and consistency to the public sense of the community at large," but who possessed little formal education.[15]

Leicester Academy contained few amenities and did not have a campus. Its classes met in a two-story former private dwelling, distinguished from other dwellings mainly by a cupola and bell bequeathed to it. It offered a Latin course, which included Greek and logic, and an English course, which included writing, arithmetic, and surveying. In theory, its prospective students were to be examined before admission "as to their acquaintance with the first rudiments of learning," but Washburn averred that "this preliminary examination, if ever employed, was based upon such extremely 'first rudiments' as to amount to no check to the admission of students." Although Leicester added new subjects like chemistry and French from time to time, its facilities were meager. Students learned geography by memorizing textbooks, for there were no maps. The school's "textbooks" were actually the same books used by young men and women who studied on their own: Hugh Blair's *Lectures on Rhetoric and Belles Lettres*, Isaac Watts's *The Improvement of the Mind*, and Jane Marcet's *Conversations on Chemistry*, the last a British work designed for use by young ladies studying at home. Washburn's description of the texts nicely captured the flexible quality of academy education: so far from constituting a required course of study, the texts were designed "as elementary books for the various pupils who might resort to the academy for longer or shorter periods, . . . according to their respective opportunities or purposes for an education."[16]

Modest if not humble in its origins and growth, Leicester Academy exemplified the popular pressures for advanced education in late-eighteenth- and early-nineteenth-century New England. The same pressures led to the formation of scores of social libraries in the same period. The so-called society or social library can be defined as a voluntary association of individuals who contributed money to a common fund to purchase books.[17] Some social libraries were formed as joint-stock companies; others relied on the annual fees of subscribers; a very considerable number blended features of each type by pooling capital to buy books and then opening collections to a wider public on an annual fee basis.[18] Historians of American libraries have portrayed social libraries as a kind of necessary but inferior prelude to the development of tax-supported libraries after the middle of the nineteenth century. Yet what is most striking about the social libraries is the timing of their establishment. The path from the social to the tax-supported library was twisting and replete with odd reversals. Only when the social libraries were manifestly in decline did they "lead" to the tax-supported libraries. In what amounted to an act of euthanasia, municipalities purchased their collections after mid-century. Rather than progressively gaining strength in the nineteenth century, social libraries flowered only at the end of the eighteenth and in the first few decades of the nineteenth centuries.[19]

The overall effect of social libraries was greatly to increase access to literary culture. In contrast to the library societies of the pre-Revolutionary era, which typically were composed of the leading male residents of seaports, those established between 1780 and 1820 took root mainly in farming communities of the hinterland and at times included female shareholders.[20] In addition, although the practice did not become widespread until after the Civil War, women occasionally organized their own "ladies'" libraries; one such library was funded in Dublin, New Hampshire, in 1799 and was still in operation in 1851.[21]

The involvement of women in library associations was consistent with the post-revolutionary era's stress on the importance of educating females for their role as mothers in republican families by substituting serious reading for frivolity and fashion. This doctrine, effectively voiced by Benjamin Rush and Judith Sargent Murray, complemented the widely circulated preachments of Hannah More in Britain, most notably her *Strictures on the Modern System of Female Education*, in which More made the case for female intellect on the grounds that Christian mothers had themselves to become readers and thinkers to guide their children around the shoals of infidelity.[22] Yet women who joined literary associations and cultivated the habit of reading did so out of desire and interest rather than merely to act out a prescribed duty. Women often flayed themselves for reading too much fiction, but a taste for reading implanted by novels could easily lead to a preference for works of history or narratives of adventure, which opened a world of wonders as arresting to readers of the nineteenth century as vivid depictions of martyrs or the Final Judgment had been to those of the seventeenth.[23]

The distinctive contributions of these libraries included extending literary culture into the hinterland, shrinking the cultural distance between the substantial interior towns that could sustain booksellers and less populous places, and widening the circle of access to genteel or liberal learning. A composite of social libraries would resemble one of contemporary libraries of well-read gentlemen. When in 1793 Thaddeus Mason Harris, the librarian of Harvard College, devised a model catalogue for a social library, which he defined as a "*small* and *cheap* library, intended to suit the taste and circumstances of common readers," he included theology, religious history, civil history, biography, voyages and travel, geography and topography, ethics, logic, metaphysics, law, poetry, drama, fiction, natural philosophy, natural history, chemistry, the fine arts, agriculture, and manufactures.[24] That Harris envisioned libraries as instruments of serious self-education is suggested by his tripartite division of these categories: books to improve the memory, reason, and imagination. Although Harris's treatise does not appear to have been widely used as a primer on library formation, social libraries typically included many of these categories.

Genteel taste included works on religion, but with some exceptions the holdings of social libraries were not decisively tilted either toward defenses of Christianity or toward the writings of deistical skeptics. More commonly, social libraries restricted their theological holdings by excluding all sectarian works or by stipulating in their bylaws the exact proportion of books that could be purchased in different categories.[25] Nor were social libraries formed to satisfy a taste for fiction. Someone eager to read the latest novel was likely to rent it from one of the many circulating libraries that arose in the eighteenth century as profit ventures. No shareholder of a social library could have echoed the boast of the proprietor of a circulating library in eighteenth-century Newport that 5,000 of his 8,000 volumes were "novels, tales, and romances."[26]

Overall, the holdings of social libraries were extremely eclectic, and this was true even within specific categories. One encounters histories ranging from the ancient Egyptians and Carthaginians (Charles Rollin) to Charles V (William Robertson) to the American Revolution (David Ramsay). Yet there was a common thread, for social libraries were sources of higher and more comprehensive knowledge than could be gleaned from newspapers or pamphlets, neither of which they purchased. Similarly, shareholders bought relatively few books on farming, insurance, or navigation, although these were available for purchase. Whether they selected works on history or philosophy or science, they sought works that advanced broad and general views. By the same token, shareholders usually tried to avoid polemical books on politics or theology; libraries were intended to mute rather than intensify local divisions.[27]

In some instances, voluntary library associations arose to encourage publications by their members. As late as 1900 a "book club" signified an association for reprinting scarce books or fostering the publication of original compositions by members.[28] Thus the Literary Confederacy, formed in New York City in 1817 by William Cullen Bryant and Gulian C. Verplanck among others, was classified as a book club, for its principal purpose was to foster publication in periodicals by its members. Rooted in such coteries, the typical periodical of the early 1800s had a modest circulation of a few hundred readers, most of whom lived within a 50-mile radius of its place of publication, and it survived only for a few years.[29] Not until 1811 did an American magazine celebrate its tenth birthday. Nor can it be said that the early periodicals met highly specialized interests. Before 1820 most periodicals were miscellanies with contents as eclectic as the subtitle of the *Massachusetts Magazine: Monthly Museum of Knowledge and Rational Entertainment, Poetry, Music, History, Biography, Geography, Morality, Criticism, Philosophy, Mathematics, Agriculture, Chemistry, Novels, Tales, Observations, Etc., Etc.*[30] Adhering to the literary models established earlier in the century in Britain by Joseph Addison and Richard Steele, American magazines took names like the

"Trifler," "Rambler," or "Fireside Talker" that underscored their eclectic and literary character.[31] At a time of sharpening political and religious divisions, libraries and periodicals institutionally embodied a view of secular knowledge as conducive to refined feelings and as removed from controversy and daily events alike.

Mutual Improvement Societies

Mutual improvement societies bore resemblance to eighteenth-century gentlemen's clubs and had ties to library associations. During his brief residence in Rhode Island between 1729 and 1731, the Anglican bishop and philosopher George Berkeley inspired an organization known as the Literary and Philosophical Society of Newport, which first engaged in debates and discussions and gradually turned to forming the Redwood Library and Athenaeum.[32] The link between libraries and what fairly can be characterized as mutual improvement societies ("gentlemen's clubs" becomes an inappropriate moniker for societies whose members were no longer necessarily male or genteel) continued to grow in the nineteenth century. In Lexington, Virginia, a society known first as the Belles-Lettres, later as the Republican and the Lexington Literary Society, and finally as the Franklin Society, was organized in 1800 to debate current political issues and cultural topics. In 1811 it began a library, and in time it would count Stonewall Jackson among its members.[33] Starting as a discussion club devoted to literature, the Detroit Young Men's Society organized a library after one of its members realized that it would be cheaper for members to purchase books and circulate them freely among themselves than to continue to rent them from local merchants.[34] Young men's literary associations followed a similar course from Buffalo to Cleveland, Detroit, and Sioux City.[35]

While often linked to library associations, mutual improvement societies had a life of their own, or more accurately, lives of their own. "Mutual improvement" is merely a tag for a variety of antebellum societies that bore a lexicon of titles: "literary," "Franklin," "belles-lettres," "young men's," "mechanics'," "mercantile," and the ubiquitous "lyceum," which a contemporary aptly defined as "a literary club of almost any description."[36] Eighteenth-century gentlemen's clubs and learned societies had appropriated some of the same titles, but by the 1840s the quest for knowledge through voluntary associations had a far broader base than in 1780.

The difference was partly geographical. The gentlemen's clubs of the eighteenth century had taken root in seaboard cities, not in the interior. By 1840 literary associations had become a feature of towns and cities across the northern tier of states. In the early 1840s, some 3,500 to 4,000 American communities contained societies for sponsoring lectures, and these societies frequently did double duty as mutual improvement organizations.[37] Pittsburgh had a Chemical and Physiological Society (1827), the Chatham Literary Association (1838), and a Young Men's Mercantile Library Association (1847).[38] As early as 1817 Detroit could count a City Library Association among its institutions; soon it possessed an Athenaeum (1831) and a Young Men's Society (1832). Even smaller cities contained several associations. Lynn, Massachusetts, had a Franklin Club (1837 or 1838), the Silsbee Street Debating Society (1841), the Natural History Society (1842), the Social Union for literary and scientific study (1843), the Gnomological Society (1849), the Exploring Circle (1850), and the Young Men's Debating Society (1852). A literary association was established in Cedar Falls, Iowa, in 1859, six years after the town's incorporation.[39]

The clientele of literary societies also changed. In 1805, twenty young Boston women organized the Gleaning Circle, in which they read and discussed books on history, geography, travel, astronomy, and poetry, but pointedly omitted novels and romances. This society probably took its name from *The Gleaner* (1798), the title of the collected essays of the feminist Judith Sargent Murray (1752–1820). The daughter of a wealthy Gloucester shipowner, Murray began to write for Boston magazines as "Constantia" in the mid-1780s (she moved there in 1793), and was among the first women to acquire a literary reputation in the new nation. Her contemporary, the historical compiler Hannah Adams (1755–1831), probably was the first American woman to try to support herself by authorship. As the daughter of a Medfield, Massachusetts, farmer turned bookseller, Adams belonged to a social rank several notches below Judith Sargent Murray and owed her prominence more to the increasing circulation of print in New England's agricultural towns. By the 1820s a penchant for reading characterized a growing number of young women in New England, while voluntary associations of women for moral reform proliferated. These forces coalesced in the early factory villages. The merchant capitalists who financed Lowell, Massachusetts, as a showcase of benevolent industrialism encouraged lyceums and similar institutions of improvement, and on their own the factory operatives formed mutual improvement societies in Lowell and other factory towns in the 1830s and 1840s. The *Lowell Offering*, which began publication in 1840 to print the poems, stories, and essays of the mill operatives, arose in the context of an already flourishing culture of mutual improvement among female factory workers.[40]

In contrast to eighteenth-century gentlemen's clubs, which had viewed themselves as magnets for those who already possessed literary and scientific taste and accomplishments, nineteenth-century mutual improvement clubs functioned more like schools. Often teenagers, their members composed and debated as "exercises in self-improvement," and some of the larger societies, notably the mercantile library associations and mechanics' institutes, offered evening classes. Nearly all reached out to their communities by sponsoring public lectures on general topics suited to popular tastes rather than on specialized scientific topics. Aided by newspapers and railroads, which advertised and speeded their comings and goings, individuals as diverse as the ethereal Ralph Waldo Emerson and the world traveler Bayard Taylor formed the core of a class of national lyceum lecturers in the two decades before the Civil War.

A distinctive feature of antebellum literary societies lay in their recruitment of entire segments of locales. These segments might be defined by age (all "young men"), by gender, or by race. In response to their exclusion from white literary societies and stirred by the nascent abolitionist movement, free people of color formed scores of their own literary associations in the 1830s. William Lloyd Garrison addressed some of these and gave his name to at least one, the New York Garrison Literary Association. More commonly, black literary associations omitted both racial designations and anti-slavery from their titles and instead copied the classical imagery of white societies by adopting such titles as the Phoenix Society (New York City), the Boston Philomathean Society (patterned after an organization of the same name in New York City), the female Minerva Literary Association (Philadelphia), the Demosthenean Institute (Philadelphia), the Adelphic Union for the Promotion of Literature and Science (Boston), and the Theban Literary Society (Pittsburgh). Rather than acting overtly as anti-slavery societies, these organizations aimed to prepare their members for participation in the anti-slavery cause by teaching intellectual skills and by engendering pride in racial intellectual attainments. Typically, their members organized libraries and reading rooms, encouraged provisions for schooling black children, sponsored lectures, and engaged in sundry exercises and debates "to improve their minds, strengthen their intellectual faculties, and cultivate a refined literary taste."[41]

Knowledge of Most Worth

Franklin's career had shown that the cultivation of knowledge could contribute to the fulfillment of personal ambition, and the frequency with which literary clubs borrowed his name suggests that their members grasped the relationship between knowledge and individual advancement. Yet beyond general assertions that the pursuit of knowledge would build character, contemporaries rarely described these personal benefits. With few exceptions, antebellum literary associations ignored technical instruction in occupational skills. The most celebrated antebellum lyceum lecturers did not speak on subjects that possessed any apparent relevance to the working lives of their auditors; rather, they discoursed on the Goths, life among the Turks, the scenery of Switzerland, and human qualities like beauty, character, or wit. It cannot even be said that lecturers were schoolmasters who taught subjects from the platform. Emerson, who virtually invented the profession of platform lecturing, sprinkled his lectures with allusions that must have baffled many of his listeners. Contemporaries commented on his "epigrammatic and somewhat disconnected style," his "bead string of suggestions, fancies, ideas, anecdotes, and illustrations." Neither primarily a teacher nor an entertainer—he gestured woodenly and usually read his lectures—Emerson can best be characterized as a public philosopher with a genius for making higher knowledge relevant to universal human interests rather than to vocational paths.[42]

Just as eminent lecturers usually downplayed the relationship between higher knowledge and vocational advancement, self-improvers usually emphasized their disinterestedness. As a seventeen-year-old store clerk in Orono, Maine, in the 1840s, Benjamin Browne Foster came across an advice book that ridiculed "the practice of composing and oratory by those who were not students by profession." The argument that merchants and mechanics should confine themselves to their business outraged Foster, who responded that man's "higher destiny" decreed that he "should endeavor by writing, or otherwise, to enlarge, cultivate and adorn his intellect." Representative of young men fast breaking with Calvinism, Foster saw self-culture as an end in itself. Indeed the vocational value of "composing and oratory" for Foster, who opened the Orono store each morning at five o'clock, spent his day unloading and selling supplies, and disdained collegiate education as an exercise "in committing useless absurdities in extinct tongues," was not at all apparent. Yet although Foster defended self-improvement as valuable in itself, he would find many uses for it. He had already acquired "an itch for scribbling," which he scratched by submitting weekly articles to the editor of the *Piscataquis Farmer* in Dover, Maine, in exchange for a subscription to the paper. In time, he would attend college, study for the ministry, and become a lawyer.[43]

Much like Foster, Isaac Mickle, Jr., who was born into a wealthy family in the vicinity of Camden, New Jersey, in 1822, commenced a program of self-improvement before settling on a vocation and, like Foster, he viewed self-improvement as valuable in itself. But Mickle's diary goes beyond Foster's in illustrating the practical uses of literary cultivation.

Although Mickle attended several private schools or academies in southern New Jersey, his diary recorded little about his formal schooling beyond notations of rows between classmates and an unflattering portrait of a teacher named Cox, whose insistence on suffixing his academic degree to his name yielded the curious moniker "O. Cox, A.B." The bulk of

Mickle's entries pertained to excursions and picnics with young ladies, his attendance at political rallies, and his arduous regimen of self-improvement. Mickle spent five to six hours a day in private reading and his journal, itself an instrument of self-improvement, is strewn with comments on ancient writers, American histories and biographies, and works on political philosophy. In addition, as a teenager Mickle and his friend William Jeffers converted Mickle's study "into a gymnasium for our mutual improvement in rhetoric," each taking and giving "lessons in articulation, and action, a knowledge of which comes amiss in no sphere of life."[44] But perhaps Mickle's most important instrument of self-improvement was the Washington Library Society, which he often called simply the "Washington."

Mickle described the Washington as a public library, which meant simply that the young men who joined could borrow books, many of which were lent by Mickle himself, who owned some 300 books by the time he was fourteen. In 1838 this society consisted of eighteen young men, all "highly respectable" and all between the ages of fourteen and twenty. In addition to serving as a library, the Washington acted as a debating society for members and it sponsored public lectures. The Washington brought Mickle into contact with young men outside the circle of his social class: young carpenters, coopers, clerks, and dry-goods merchants. Mickle was surprised to find one of its members, a "friendless carpenter boy" named Samuels, composing his speech for an upcoming debate in his shop, using his workbench for a desk, all in all "a surprising effort for one in his circumstances."[45] Regardless of their social class, the young men of the Washington became "highly respectable" by practicing self-improvement, a course that set them off from the town's street-corner society of young men who idled away their time "swearing, cursing each other, lying, insulting females, and using indecent and offensive expressions."[46]

Representative of swiftly growing antebellum towns, Camden contained fewer than 1,000 inhabitants at Mickle's birth in 1822 and around 10,000 at his death in 1855. Mickle identified two other debating societies in Camden during the late 1830s: the Franklin, "conducted by boys," and the Union. In 1838, when Camden's population was around 3,000, the Union invited members of the Washington, the "Juniors," to its celebration of General Washington's birthday, and thereby it underscored one of the functions of male literary societies: to bring young men of promise to the attention of those of higher rank. Just as Samuels, the "friendless carpenter boy," could consort with Mickle in the Washington, Mickle used the Washington as a base for his ever-widening range of contacts. In Mickle's day Camden was becoming large enough to arouse concern about the character of its young men, but it was still small enough for established businessmen and professionals to identify youth of promise. Select society valued literary cultivation, which it viewed as a spur to sobriety and self-discipline (on attaining his majority, Mickle was elected to the board of the Camden Temperance Society) and as potentially useful.

Although the circle of Mickle's associates in self-improvement had a short radius, the platform lectures that became popular in the 1830s and 1840s served as an important bridge between self-improvers and the larger community. Mickle used his frequent trips to Philadelphia to recruit speakers for the Washington and by the early 1840s organizing and attending lectures had become one of his principal activities. Within the span of three weeks in January 1842, Mickle attended a lecture on a Wednesday evening by the editor of a Trenton newspaper, who spoke on the Goths, Huns, and Vandals, was present at a lecture the following Tuesday on phrenology, planned to attend a lecture the next evening (it was cancelled when the speaker fell ill), accompanied a young lady to a temperance lecture two nights later (Friday), and on the following Monday went to Trenton to find material for a lecture on the history of West New Jersey by a Camden physician. On Wednesday he attended a lecture in Camden on "The Power of Knowledge" before journeying to Philadelphia, where on Thursday and Saturday evenings he heard Orestes A. Brownson speak on "Civilization." Mickle arranged to speak with Brownson privately on Monday, then returned to Camden to catch a lecture on Wednesday (again cancelled), and on Friday attended a temperance lecture.

As public figures, touring lecturers afforded Mickle opportunities to observe the style and behavior appropriate to public life; most often, his attention was riveted by a speaker's dress, appearance, or platform manner. For example, what he noticed about the Philadelphia lawyer David Paul Brown were his facility with Latin quotations, his costly finger ring, florid style, and overweening vanity.[47] Yet it would be misleading to think of Mickle's penchant for lectures as a kind of harmless interlude in his serious program of self-improvement. Although his diary abounds with references to books he read, he rarely analyzed his reading. What is most striking are the quotations in English, Latin, and French that he extracted from his reading and sprinkled throughout his diary. Just as the Washington's debates gave him opportunities to display his learning, his frequenting of lectures enabled him to witness public figures exhibit theirs. Enchanted by public life—at the age of fourteen he upheld Andrew Jackson in the Washington's debates, and he named his sailboat after Martin Van Buren—he chose the legal profession "as almost the only way to offices of government and jurisprudence."[48]

Yet Mickle kept self-improvement and politics in separate compartments. Talking politics struck him as a "very questionable employment."[49] Like the lectures he attended, most of the Washington's debates avoided

partisanship. Mickle and his friends debated "whether the Negro or Indian had suffered more from the discovery of America," whether greater
intelligence would yield greater happiness, or whether honor or wealth
was a keener stimulus to activity. Self-improvement led Mickle into a
world both more abstract and open-ended than politics, where the alternatives were always clearly defined, and it also gave him a chance to hone
and acquire potentially useful skills, facts, and ideas. Early in the century
Timothy Dwight averred that what New Englanders sought from education was the ability to adduce relationships among the sundry objects of
their thought, to comprehend generalizations, and to put them to use.[50]
Dwight's comment can fairly be applied to the kind of lectures that Mickle
frequented. In an age when employers paid for phrenological analyses of
prospective employees and when fiancées used phrenology to assess the re-
liability of prospective spouses, the phrenological lectures that Mickle often attended were likely to prove practical as well as enlightening.[51]

The relevance of literature and philosophy to vocational advancement in antebellum America depended on a configuration of social and
cultural circumstances that took shape in the late eighteenth century and
then came to have a wide impact in the first half of the nineteenth century.
We have earlier seen how law and medicine were emerging as full-time
professions in the second half of the eighteenth century. By the end of the
eighteenth century urban clerks were starting to form a distinct occupational class in insurance companies, banks, and merchants' and stock exchanges. As urban merchants and clerks distanced themselves from productive activity to concentrate on retailing and keeping accounts, the gap
between mercantile and mechanical pursuits widened.[52]

Still embryonic, antebellum occupational specialization occupied the
ground between the colonial era—when sheriffs and bailiffs pleaded legal
causes, ministers prescribed medicines for their parishioners, and artisans
sold the products they made—and the late nineteenth century, when evening schools proliferated to teach new technologies like the typewriter and
new subjects like accountancy. In this nascent (antebellum) stage of occupational specialization, formal professional schooling hovered on the periphery of legal and medical apprenticeships, and mercantile and mechanics' institutes engaged in relatively little trade training. For the most part,
aspirants to specific professions or occupations acquired relevant trade
skills by observing veteran practitioners in the workplace. At the same
time the cultivation of literature and philosophy was acquiring new relevance for the upwardly mobile. Urban growth, which saw the number of
towns containing 2,500 to 10,000 inhabitants rise from 56 in 1820 to
over 350 by 1860, encouraged occupational specialization, but without a
history of guilds that tied workers to the practice of a single trade, the
United States entered this period of relative occupational specialization

with traditions that were antithetical to permanent specialization. "He brings a field to tillage and leaves other men to gather the crops; he embraces a profession and gives it up," Alexis de Tocqueville wrote of the American. As opportunities for non-manual labor proliferated in the wake of the transportation revolution and the democratization of politics, liberal learning could become highly useful even for those with unformed goals.

Law and Learning

The legal profession that Mickle chose affords abundant illustrations of all of these tendencies. Mickle's various sallies into self-improvement hinged on coalescing circumstances that gave literary cultivation heightened relevance to the law. The link between literary polish and the practice of law as a serious, full-time profession, forged in the 1750s and 1760s by elite practitioners in seaboard cities, was strengthened as political and economic developments created new opportunities for full-time lawyers. The revival of economic activity after 1815 and the economic transformations that attended the transportation revolution increased the amount of litigation, while the gradual democratization of American politics afforded lawyers new opportunities for holding office and displaying their talents in public. The American Revolution, the writing of state constitutions, the federal constitutional convention, and the inter-party competition between Federalists and Republicans after 1790 were so many theaters in which lawyers could display their talents. The gradual democratization of politics after 1800 increased the number of public offices, especially at the state level, and provided lawyers with additional opportunities for public service.[53]

The relationship between the expanding legal profession and the cultivation of knowledge took various forms. With literary associations inherited from the eighteenth century, law was one of the more appealing callings for those whose interests were primarily literary rather than legal.[54] Born in Maine in 1793, John Neal left school at the age of twelve and moved to Baltimore with the intention of becoming a merchant, but after a series of reverses he changed his mind and took up the study of law. Like many young men of his day, Neal also evinced an interest in writing, and to develop his literary skills he joined the Delphian Club. Formed in 1816 by aspiring young men eager to publish, the Delphian gave Neal a chance to hone his style and to rub elbows with sophisticated college graduates like his close friend John Pierpont. Jehu O'Cataract and Pertinax Particular, a sample of the clubbable names with which Delphians baptized themselves, critiqued each other's compositions and published a periodical, the *Portico*. Yet although Fenimore Cooper would soon make it one, authorship was not a plausible profession in the United States of 1820, and Neal wrote his first novel merely to finance his legal studies.[55]

Neal's early career was representative of one of the trends that fed the rise of literary societies and periodicals alike: while studying for the law or some other profession (but most often the law), young men joined literary societies to gratify private authorial ambitions. Isaac Mickle, Jr., for example, shared Benjamin Browne Foster's "itch" for writing, and while studying as a legal apprentice, Mickle assumed the editorship of the Camden *Eagle*. An anthology of poets of the Old Northwest compiled in the mid-1860s by William T. Coggeshall underlines the close connection between law, literary cultivation, and writing.[56] Nearly half of the 97 poets anthologized by Coggeshall made their livings as lawyers. Yet this statement fails to do justice to the permeable nature of careers in the first half of the nineteenth century, for, like John Neal, the great majority of these lawyer-poets were lawyers only for a period. Born in 1804, Otway Curry was successively a carpenter, newspaper editor, and lawyer. Along the way, Curry, who did not undertake the study of law until his mid-thirties, anonymously contributed verse to newspapers. Similarly, Frederick W. Thomas, born in 1811, was at one time or another a lawyer, a minister, a professor of rhetoric at the University of Alabama, and a journalist.[57]

Authorship of poetry was merely one among several ways in which a lawyer could display an attachment to literature. Nearly a quarter of the lawyers who practiced in antebellum New Hampshire fit one or more of the following categories: they had established local reputations as scholars in fields outside of the law; they wrote and published books, pamphlets, or orations on non-legal topics; they held offices in cultural institutions such as athenaeums and state historical societies; or they edited or wrote regularly for newspapers.[58] Even in the West lawyers often had literary interests. Commenting on lawyers in Springfield, Illinois, during the early 1830s, James H. Matheny once wrote: "Aside from the practice of the law, the leading men of the bar cultivated in no little degree the intellectual life. Political oratory was perhaps their principal interest, but they delivered occasional addresses and lectures upon themes, literary, historical, and even scientific."[59] Thus the prairie lawyer and future congressman Edward Dickinson Baker, whose literary attainments were acquired by self-education, built a local reputation in and around Springfield with lectures on "Art," "Robert Burns," "The Sea," "The Life and Death of Socrates," and "The Influence of Commerce on Civilization." This was at a time when Springfield could be aptly characterized as "crude in appearance and fact. The streets were alternately rivers of black mud or Saharas of flying dust."[60]

The presence of such literary lawyers reflected a paradox of western life. On one hand, many westerners were ignorant and some disdained learned men. Yet westerners valued public eloquence, and political parties sought to attract the educated to their cause.[61] Frontier folk enjoyed elaborate and extravagant public addresses; the grandiloquent stump speech was a form of popular theater as well as popular education. When a state legislator in Missouri appealed for laws to provide care for the insane, he quoted *Macbeth*, recited poetry, and invoked examples from Greek and Roman history.[62]

This paradoxical attitude toward learning was exemplified in the life of John Reynolds, who was born in Pennsylvania in 1788, came to Illinois as a boy, and enjoyed a swift rise in public life: associate justice of the Illinois Supreme Court at the age of thirty, and then respectively state legislator, governor, and congressman. Reynolds traced his success to his familiarity with the common people, and a memorialist agreed that he had learned all the catchwords and figures of speech "invented by vulgar ingenuity and common among a backwoods people."[63] Yet although Reynolds sometimes "feigned to be an illiterate," he passed himself off as a graduate of an (unspecified) out-of-state college and sprinkled his public addresses with Latin quotations. Contemporaries esteemed him as a "ripe scholar" who understood "the Latin and Greek perfectly," as one who "had drunk deeply of the Pierian spring."[64] In public he always played the role of a gentleman by wearing an expensive black suit, polished shoes, and a silk hat.[65]

The reality appears to have been more subtle. It is unlikely that Reynolds had ever attended a college, and his classical learning seems to have been superficial. In his autobiography he claimed to have studied and admired Virgil, but his banal and rather pandering comments—"His pastorals are innocent, and as the ladies would say, 'sweet.' His Georgics are good. Many of the best principles of agriculture are there laid down"[66]—indicate something short of intoxication at the Pierian spring. Contemporaries thought his learning deep only because "a few Latin phrases and illustrations were quite enough to give him a reputation for learning among men who did not know a word of Latin."[67] Most of his acquaintances had no way of knowing whether he was speaking in Latin or in tongues. What they found striking was his familiarity with many subjects, including the classics.

The close ties between the legal profession and politics and the continuing value of literary attainments for public speakers contributed greatly to the spread of mutual improvement societies. According to one of its early members, the Young Men's Society of Detroit served as "a species of gymnasium for the mental exercises" of the young lawyers who dominated it.[68] Literary exercises helped present and future legal practitioners to sharpen debating skills and to amass a stock of potentially useful quotations. In addition, lawyers who associated themselves with literary cultivation boosted their reputations and that of their profession. The pursuit of knowledge was not only a way for individuals to distinguish themselves but also a means by which established professionals inculcated respectable behavior in neophytes and shielded their callings from the popular criticisms that swirled around all of the antebellum professions. Literary and philosophical cultivation had a certain defensive or didactic quality as a way for ministers and doctors as well as lawyers to blunt criticism of increasingly specialized but still fledgling vocations; at the same time, the fact that prominent leaders in professions and vocations emphasized the defensive role of knowledge imparted the sanction of elites to intellectual pursuits and made them attractive in the eyes of the upwardly mobile.

Piety and Learning

Even as professions and occupations were acquiring distinct shapes in antebellum America, many of them were coming under attack for undemocratic or anti-republican tendencies. The frontier religious revivals that opened the nineteenth century burst with criticism of overeducated clergymen whose sermons chilled the heart.[69] The Methodist circuit rider Peter Cartwright derided "pews, literary institutions and theological institutes."[70] Such itinerant preachers as Alexander Campbell and Elias Smith, who called themselves merely "Christians," urged the dissolution of all barriers between clergy and laity. Whether calling for a more accessible ministry or none at all, the early Methodists, Baptists, and "Christians" viewed literary refinement as subversive of religious ardor. This hostility to hierarchy spilled over into medical reform. The followers of the untutored herbalist Samuel Thomson, among them Elias Smith, contended that the learned "Latin and Greeklings" of the medical profession had deliberately contrived baffling medical terms to confuse plain people and that, once pruned of needless complexity, medicine could become comprehensible to anyone.[71]

Paradoxically, these attacks on the learned professions arose within the context of the ever-widening circle of print culture and expanding provisions for education during the early 1800s. The same individuals who declaimed against literary polish taught themselves grammar and composition, frequently in the wake of religious conversions, and then used their new knowledge to communicate with their followers. Elias Smith, who until he was fifteen had been unaware of the existence of dictionaries, came across Isaac Watts's writings of self-improvement after his conversion, learned from Watts to look up each new word in a dictionary, and became the editor of the radical *Herald of Gospel Liberty*. Born in 1769 (the same year as Smith) and similarly self-taught, Samuel Thomson began as a boy to experiment on friends with local herbs and soon acquired a reputation as a healer in his native New Hampshire. At this stage of his life, Thomson showed little interest in the medical profession, which scarcely existed in rural New England, where most medical practice was still conducted by part-time healers—midwives, ministers, and others judged by their neighbors as peculiarly skillful in the treatment of disease. But by the first decade of the nineteenth century Thomson found himself increasingly harried by lawsuits from the now numerous full-time physicians, and it was in this context that he constructed a medical system and launched a movement to secure repeal of recently enacted laws regulating entry into the medical profession.[72]

Thomson's writings reveal a speculative if crude mind; he had nothing against theories as long as anyone could understand them. In this respect he resembled the Methodist itinerant Peter Cartwright. Cartwright enjoyed displaying such learning as he possessed. Noting that Methodist preachers "were called by literary gentlemen illiterate, ignorant babblers," he recollected how he confounded "one of these Latin and Greek scholars, a regular graduate in theology," by replying first in German and then in Dutch when addressed by the scholar in Greek. Knowing neither German nor Dutch, the polished graduate concluded that Cartwright was speaking in Hebrew, "immediately caved in, and stated to the company that I was the first educated Methodist preacher he ever saw."[73] Cartwright tolerated educated ministers of "the right stamp, and the right spirit."[74] What rankled was the patronizing tone of "velvet-mouthed and downy D.D.'s" who attributed their failure, and Cartwright's success, to the ignorance of frontier folk.

Despite the strident attacks on learned clergymen that permeated the religious revivals of the early 1800s, between 1800 and 1840 evangelicals contributed in many ways to the widening popular quest for literary culture. Evangelicals did not value secular learning as an end in itself, but they craved converts, not only among the poor but among educated social leaders. They loathed riches but envied the literary polish of the gentry and took special delight in converting the upper crust. This motive linked eastern evangelicals like Lyman Beecher, who yearned to keep revivals respectable lest evangelicals be compelled to abandon the educated portion of the community to Unitarianism, with the brawny Cartwrights of the West.

The requirements of denominational apologetics gradually propelled evangelicals toward respect for education. An unlearned ministry might easily become a defenseless ministry, incapable of contending orally or in the religious press with rival denominations. Of course such a ministry might not need to know more than the Bible and its own theology.[75] Yet the distinction between secular and religious learning was not always crisp. Dan Young, an early "shouting" Methodist, recorded in his diary that, while working the Methodist circuit in Vermont in 1807, he studied Greek and read "Locke on the Human Understanding."[76] The Scottish commonsense philosophers like Adam Ferguson and Thomas Reid, who combatted the corrosive epistemological skepticism of David Hume, enjoyed a wide following among American Protestants in the early nineteenth century. The devout could also find well-documented warnings against the dangers of luxury in the histories of the ancient world by Gibbon, Rollin, and Oliver Goldsmith that made their way into social libraries. By familiarizing themselves with secular learning, clergymen could guide their parishioners around the shoals represented by Thomas Paine or Lord Byron. As early as 1830 Nathan Bangs transformed the *Methodist Magazine* into the more literary *Methodist Quarterly Review*. Above all, the revivalists grasped the significance of print as a medium of popular communication; it was the sea in which they swam. In 1835 a leading Baptist counted the number of reams of paper, 2,500, and pages printed, 7,000,000, by his denomination in its missionary efforts.[77]

Religious conversion experiences themselves imparted a desire, however vague, for self-betterment. In the revivals of the Second Great Awakening, a new psychology of conversion crystallized. Now conversion became less an ascertainment of one's divine election than one's conviction that the past's slate had been wiped clean. A few years after his conversion in a Vermont revival in 1831, John Humphrey Noyes announced his achievement of perfection (sinlessness), and when he and his followers moved to Oneida, New York, in 1848, their ideological baggage included mutual improvement through education. Oneidans established adult classes for the study of astronomy, algebra, French, Greek, and Hebrew, all with the belief that knowledge was both godly and useful, that "the love of the beautiful could be made to harmonize with and quicken all kinds of manual industry," and that the community could be made "a University for the Education of the whole man."[78] Far less controversial than Noyes, Rev. John Todd, a prominent author of advice books in the antebellum period, recalled that his conversion at sixteen implanted in him "the desire for cultivating, enlarging, and disciplining the mind, and making it an instrument of usefulness."[79] Not surprisingly, Todd became a close friend of Josiah Holbrook, who lived with Todd for a period in Groton, Massachusetts.[80]

While stimulating a general desire for improvement, conversion experiences also acted in specific ways to encourage study. By introducing young men and women to the cacaphonous world of sectarianism, conversion experiences compelled them to examine the conflicting claims of rival groups and to develop skills in argument and debate.[81] Conversion experiences also encouraged a growing number of indigent young men to seek collegiate education in preparation for the ministry, often with financial aid from Protestant benevolent societies. Founded in Boston in 1815, the American Education Society was supporting 10 to 15 percent of the entire New England collegiate population by the 1840s.[82] Typically, these were young men from the backwaters of New England society who entered college at late ages. While the tendency toward late graduation was evident in colleges with ties to the Great Awakening during the eighteenth century, the proportion of young men to graduate from New England colleges at age 25 or older rose from 1800 to 1830 in response to revivals.[83]

By mid-century educated Protestants were fast outgrowing the revivals that initially had spurred inchoate impulses toward intellectual improvement. The Unitarians were the first to make self-culture an end in itself. In Unitarian thought self-culture included the unabashed quest for secular learning, which Unitarians associated with the inculcation of a disinterested spiritual elevation akin to religious belief. Self-culture became a lifelong enterprise for Unitarians and indeed continued into the afterlife; they imagined heaven as a place devoted to self-culture.[84] By the 1840s Congregational scholars at Yale, such as James Dwight Dana, George Park Fisher, James Hadley, and Noah Porter, Jr., were moving in the same direction. Where in the first quarter of the century Timothy Dwight and Lyman Beecher sought to reconcile education and revivalism, the Yale scholars substituted "the intellectual conviction gained from study for the emotional experience of the revival."[85] For these men, knowledge of the sciences or of the history of Sanskrit acquired some of the attributes of grace and imparted an elevated and disinterested outlook that Matthew Arnold in 1867 would equate with the possession of "culture."

Denominations with ingrained suspicions of learned ministers could not remain insulated from these forces for long. After the War of 1812 Methodists began to pay more attention to educating their clergymen, and the church's General Conference authorized its bishops to formulate a course of study for ministerial candidates.[86] Theology dominated the early Methodist study courses, but Methodists and Baptists alike discovered abundant reasons to found liberal arts colleges. In the three decades before the Civil War, the Methodists founded over 30 colleges in 19 states and the Baptists over 20 in 16 states.[87] Affiliated colleges created pools of potential ministers, and, more importantly, offered denominations opportunities to build ties to local communities. For example, antebellum Baptist colleges were basically local enterprises that depended on the cooperation of a few ministers, a larger number of Baptist laymen, and an even larger number of non-Baptists for whom boosterism was a more compelling motive than theology in founding colleges.[88] Whatever lingering suspicion they might have had of a learned ministry, Methodist and Baptist evangelicals copied the established format for liberal arts colleges.

These tendencies affected the West as well as the East. In 1800 there was only one college in what is now the Midwest; by 1850 there were 70, more than in any other region. Westerners relied heavily on graduates of eastern liberal arts colleges for their faculties. For example, Illinois College in Jacksonville, established in 1828, was the work of the so-called Yale Band, young men inspired by the Yale revivals of the 1820s to bring piety and literary cultivation to the West. Westerners sprinkled their almanacs with tales of Davy Crockett and other unlettered western heroes, but they bridled at being patronized by Easterners as backwoods illiterates and they wasted little time in constructing cultural institutions. Perhaps even more than in the East, such institutions in the West signified the manners appropriate to civilized society. The Cincinnati physician Daniel Drake recalled turn-of-the-century Kentucky as a virtual literary desert in which the teachers and preachers were nearly as ignorant as everyone else, but changes were already under way.[89] A subscription library was founded at Lexington in 1800 and another in Louisville in 1816.[90] A traveler on the Illinois frontier in 1817–18 observed an emerging class of physicians, lawyers, and storekeepers as well as refined mechanics and farmers who "begin the fabric of society." Men of "Education and Manners," he concluded, "were much respected."[91]

The Culture of the Medical Profession

While evangelicals were reconciling their suspicion of learning with the popular quest for refinement, leaders of the medical profession employed intellectual improvement as a tactic to woo popular support at a time of unprecedented challenges. By 1844 the followers of Samuel Thomson, the itinerant herbalist turned medical messiah, had secured the repeal of all laws regulating entry into the medical profession. The Thomsonian challenge, which fed on a mixture of radical evangelicalism and Jacksonian democracy, drove the medical profession from the barricade of protective licensing laws and into the popular forum of debate at a time when formally trained physicians lacked demonstrably superior therapies. To win respect, orthodox or "regular" doctors sought to strengthen their ties to educated laymen by encouraging the formation of broadly based cultural institutions.

The career of Daniel Drake illustrates how the acquisition of culture could serve professional as well as personal goals. Born in New Jersey in 1785, Drake was taken by his parents, poor farmers, to Kentucky at the age of three. Although he secured a medical degree from the University of Pennsylvania in 1816 (mainly to support his ambition to teach medicine in his adopted home of Cincinnati), he never attended either an academy or a college. In his youth, however, he had become an avid reader, and in maturity he made self-improvement the linchpin of his program for personal and professional advancement.

In a scathing attack on Thomsonians, *The People's Doctors* (1830), Drake attributed their success to a mixture of popular credulity and the low standards of the medical profession itself, the "gross illiteracy, superficial science, intellectual indolence, and contented mediocrity" into which "so many of our brethren have sunk." The offices of too many physicians looked as if a mob had just swept through: unlabeled medicines, greasy shelves, rusted surgical instruments, and floors stained with tobacco juice. Only by adopting a program of "intellectual improvement" would physicians achieve public respect and, perhaps more fundamentally, self-respect.[92]

Drake spoke from his own experience, for he owed his eminent position among Cincinnati physicians to his personal force, organizational skill, and literary flair rather than to evidence that he actually had cured patients. No more than other orthodox physicians of his day could he point to demonstrably superior therapies. In this context, physicians had much to gain from the acquisition of general knowledge. Reflecting on his long career in medicine, which spanned much of the nineteenth century, Dr. Samuel Gross urged that every physician know something of art, science, travel, poetry, and history, not to become "profoundly versed in any of these things," but to "appear before the world at least as a man of some culture and general information."[93] At a time when medical debates were settled more by style than substance, appearances could be extremely useful. Gross admiringly told the story of how Drake's mannered eloquence ("his whole soul would seem to be on fire") during an 1831 debate before the Philadelphia Medical Society on the doctrines of the French physiologist and anatomist F. J. V. Broussais elicited an involuntary shout of agreement from the chair.[94]

As a member of a growing yet still vulnerable profession, Drake promoted cultural institutions not only to encourage physicians toward self-improvement but to forge an alliance between physicians and laymen to promote culture in the West. From 1807 until his death in 1852, he was the prime mover behind a host of educational institutions, including the Medical College of Ohio, the Western Museum Society, and in 1814 the "School of Literature and the Arts." The last mentioned, which actually was a mutual improvement society rather than a school, reveals a great deal about cultural conditions in the Old Northwest. By blending belles lettres and science in a single society, Drake hoped to attract a wider audience for the latter, which he believed could not stand on its own feet in the West.[95]

With its broad sweep, this institution resembled the contemporary

Literary and Philosophical Society of New York (1816), whose founders included Mayor De Witt Clinton and the physician David Hosack, who had participated in nearly all the societies that were established in New York between the Revolution and the War of 1812 to advance science. Like eighteenth-century knowledge societies, the Literary and Philosophical Society drew on a wide mixture of public officials, doctors, lawyers, clergymen, merchants, and professors, and its members pledged themselves to study everything from belles lettres, history, and political economy to chemistry, natural philosophy, astronomy, navigation, husbandry, manufactures, and "all useful arts."[96] During the early nineteenth century, both the American Philosophical Society and the American Academy of Arts and Sciences widened their boundaries to include literary as well as scientific investigations, and they did so with the same objective as Drake's School of Literature and the Arts: to strengthen the educated community by broadening its base.[97]

This tactic proved successful to the extent that it gradually encouraged the formation of a class of relatively specialized societies that mixed physicians and laymen in the cause of natural knowledge. Scientific advances from the late-eighteenth to the mid-nineteenth century, represented by Lavoisier in chemistry, William Bartram and Benjamin Smith Bartram on the flora and fauna of America, and Georges Cuvier and Charles Lyell in geology, intensified interest in science without discouraging lay investigators. Cuvier's writings on paleontology, for example, had implications for the age of the earth and thereby aroused the interest of clergymen.[98] In addition, although societies that claimed all knowledge as their domain slowly gave way to more specialized societies after 1820, between 1820 and 1840 specialized societies continued to espouse a relatively broad range of objectives. The Massachusetts Historical Society (1791) and the New-York Historical Society (1804), early examples of the trend toward specialization, investigated natural knowledge as well as antiquities.[99]

The distinction between antiquities and natural knowledge gradually widened. For example, with the founding of the Boston Society for Natural History in 1830, the Massachusetts Historical Society relinquished natural history.[100] Yet none of this discouraged the involvement of amateurs in societies devoted to natural knowledge. For example, the founders of the Academy of Natural Sciences of Philadelphia originally came together in 1812 for a mixture of coterian and programmatic reasons: to occupy "their leisure occasionally, in each other's company, on subjects of Natural Sciences interesting and useful to the country and the world and in modes conducive to the general and individual satisfaction of the members, as well as to the primary object [which is] the diffusion of useful, liberal, and human knowledge."[101] Between 1817 and 1840 the Academy acquired a more formal character by starting a journal, building its library from 150 to 7,000 volumes, and developing an impressive collection of specimens: minerals, fossils, fish and reptiles, birds, shells, and plants. But all of this depended mainly on the financial and moral impetus of an amateur, William Maclure, who took up the cultivation of knowledge after his retirement from business and whose ardor for science was matched by his enthusiasm for utopian social reform.[102]

As a descriptive science, natural history remained friendly to amateur cultivators. Requiring little apparatus and readily investigated on walks through the countryside, natural history became the most popular of the scientific specialties of the antebellum period. In 1847 Yale's Benjamin Silliman, Sr., remarked on the "gratifying growth" of local natural history societies in the preceding thirty years.[103] They sprang up in all regions, in New York and Philadelphia, in Charleston and Baltimore, in Cincinnati and Louisville, and as early as 1832 in Little Rock, Arkansas Territory. The greatest concentration was in New England and the mid-Atlantic states, where they at times emerged in connection with colleges and often appeared in small towns and cities of the interior—Worcester and Lynn; Albany, Troy, Newburgh, and Buffalo; Pottsville and Media, Pennsylvania.[104]

In a nation lacking an established community of full-time scientists, local specialized societies depended on part-time cultivators of science, especially physicians. For example, in Lynn "a large number of our professional men, especially physicians," formed the Natural History Society in 1842 and collected "minerals and curiosities in every department of this science."[105] This part-time cultivation of scientific specialties was well suited to interior towns and cities, where neither population nor resources could sustain a learned society devoted to universal knowledge. It also fit the needs of physicians, who lacked a secure therapeutic base but who could point to their knowledge of science as the one clear advantage that orthodox medicine possessed over Thomsonian practitioners and later over osteopaths and chiropractors. Typically, the founders of medical sects saw themselves as prophets of new medical dispensations that would supplant all acquired scientific knowledge. While this view had a certain democratic resonance, it flew in the face of the widespread belief that science was both potentially useful and a rational affirmation of progress. Scientific investigation also harmonized with the image of the physician as a gentleman possessed of superior knowledge to benefit the public. Physicians who moved between collecting and agricultural improvement societies or who wrote reports on the causes of railroad or steamship disasters were acting out their role as public men. A remarkable report written in 1854 by Cincinnati's Dr. M. B. Wright, former Whig floor leader in the Ohio legislature and a notable reformer of Ohio's treatment of the insane, aptly depicted the relationship between the cultivation of knowledge in public settings and the elevation of the profession's status. The report stingingly dismissed the recently established American Medical Association's call for the Ohio State Medical Society to adopt its code of ethics. Squeezing all physicians into the same corset and poisoning the dignity of gentlemen, codes of ethics would never calm the acrimonious controversies that long had plagued the Ohio medical profession, Wright insisted. As gentlemen, physicians required independence from petty regulations and opportunities to express themselves through acts of rational public benevolence. Those medical societies, he concluded, "which have engaged most earnestly in scientific culture . . . are those which have excluded elaborate constitutions and by-laws, and all codes of ethics."[106]

The peculiar needs of the nineteenth-century medical profession contributed to the persistence of localism and amateur involvement in scientific organizations. True, the increasing complexity and sophistication of science posed a challenge to lay involvement, especially after 1840, when "scientists" started to replace the older term "natural philosophers" as a description of those with the specialized training necessary to penetrate the mysteries of nature and when scientists started to withdraw from educated laymen to form such institutions as the American Association for the Advancement of Science (AAAS, 1848).[107] But until the end of the century neither the professionalization of science nor the accompanying specialization significantly eroded the local societies in which physicans and other educated members of the community participated. Although the potential for conflict was ever present, popularization and professionalization were not mutually exclusive impulses in nineteenth-century medicine. More accurately, popularization in the form of reaching out to the public by lectures and joint enterprises with laymen was one of the techniques by which physicians tried to enhance their status as professionals.[108]

The developments that made knowledge useful as well as interesting for antebellum professionals affected other growing occupational groups, including merchants, printers, and teachers. In these callings intellectual improvement served as an instrument of personal advancement and, not infrequently, as a way to deflect public criticism.

Commerce and Culture

Edwin Percy Whipple was a young disciple of Emerson who established a considerable contemporary reputation as a platform lecturer and literary critic. Like Emerson, Whipple knew how to jam a lot into an hour, how to mine history and literature for epigrammatic insights ("Talent is a Cistern; Genius a Fountain"), and how to turn phrases (Whipple once said that the author of *Leaves of Grass* possessed every leaf but the fig leaf). Unlike Emerson, however, Whipple owed his early success as a lecturer and author almost entirely to a specific occupational group, merchants' clerks. Born in 1819 in Gloucester, Massachusetts, Whipple left school at fifteen, to clerk first in a Salem bank and then in a Boston brokerage. In his teens he joined the Boston Mercantile Library Association and also took part in the exercises of a literary club called the Attic Nights. "Here," a memorialist noted, "Whipple was in his element," for he could read and discourse with his young friends about Byron and Wordsworth, Goethe and Schiller, and thus gratify his taste for literature that had led him to join the Salem Athenaeum before coming to Boston.[109]

First attracting attention by reading one of his poems before the mercantile library association in 1840 and next by publishing a well-received essay on Thomas B. Macaulay in 1843, Whipple could always count on merchants and clerks to support his literary efforts. Members of the mercantile library association responded to the publication in 1843 of his first volume of essays by buying up most of the edition. When the Merchants' Exchange of Boston established a reading room and library, it named Whipple as first superintendent. As Whipple's literary career flourished, he gained entry into Boston's famed Saturday Club, where he consorted with James Russell Lowell and the senior Oliver Wendell Holmes.[110] But while literature served his career, its relation to the occupational interests of his audience is hardly clear. Put simply, his lectures had nothing to do with business or businessmen; even his lecture on "Genius" was devoid of examples of successful entrepreneurs. When he branched out beyond Boston in the late 1840s to lecture before diversified audiences throughout New England, he delivered many of the same lectures that he had originally written for the mercantile library association: "Wit and Humor"; "Charles Dickens"; "Authors in Their Relations to Life"; and "The Ludicrous Side of Life."[111]

Whipple's career underscores the danger of equating utility with practicality. He made no effort to instruct his audience in either the techniques or general principles of trade. True, the antebellum mercantile library associations offered evening classes on practical subjects like bookkeeping and stenography; arguably, these classes absorbed the demand for practical techniques and left the Whipples free to quote Lucian and Juvenal, Montaigne and Voltaire, Addison and Pope. If so, however, the demand for practical information must have been weak, for while platform lectures were thronged, the evening classes attracted only handfuls of students.[112]

Whipple's audience of clerks undoubtedly relished his "agile" and "jubilant" mind, but his appeal rested on more than his radiant wit.[113] Along with aspirants to a number of occupations and professions in antebellum America, clerks cultivated literature in part because such cultivation enjoyed the sanction of veteran tradesmen who hoped to elevate the dignity of their calling and to inculcate appropriate behavior in clerks by associating trade with literary pursuits.

The roots of this bonding of mercantile success and literary cultivation lay in the eighteenth century, when leading urban merchants took part in gentlemen's clubs alongside the lawyers and public officials with whom they had daily contacts. Merchants helped to establish the New York Society Library (1754) and they accounted for roughly two-thirds of the first 150 subscribers of the Boston Athenaeum (1807), the largest and most expensive subscription library in the United States (a share cost $300). The Athenaeum bound together the city's professional and mercantile elites, directed civic consciousness toward the advancement of literature, and reminded each new crop of merchants that the patronage of literature was a noble way to display their wealth.[114]

Brushed from the experiences of men like Charles Bulfinch, a prominent eighteenth-century Boston merchant and municipal reformer as well as the architect of the Massachusetts State House and of the mansions of Boston's Federalist elite, and Thomas Handasyd Perkins, a merchant who served as president of the Boston Athenaeum, the image of the merchant prince was employed in the second quarter of the nineteenth century to inculcate appropriate values and behavior in the thousands of young clerks who migrated to urban countinghouses from the countryside. As urban clerks began to form a distinct occupational class, leading merchants and civic officials increasingly worried about the moral perils confronting them, for by the 1820s clerks no longer boarded with their masters but instead congregated in large urban boardinghouses. The founding of mercantile library associations after 1820 was a direct response to these growing apprehensions among civic elites about the dissolute morals of young men. The diarist Philip Hone, who retired from mercantile life in 1821 to pursue the education and culture that he had never formally acquired, became one of the leading patrons of the New York Mercantile Library, which had been established in 1820, and he contributed to the erection of Clinton Hall to house the library and its governing association.[115]

The enlistment of leading merchants in the cause of intellectual cultivation intensified in the late 1830s. In 1836 the governing board of the New York Mercantile Library Association introduced annual lecture series. In the winter of 1839–40, members of the library association heard lectures on meteorology, moral philosophy, geology and the Mosaic record, the Constitution, Schiller, and Transcendentalism. Addressing the Boston Mercantile Library Association in 1843, Rev. George Putnam spoke so highly of intellectual pursuits for clerks that he confessed that "I may seem to have been addressing the members of a university."[116] Putnam need not have apologized for his hyperbole, for in 1839 the governing board of the New York Mercantile Library Association entertained a plan to establish a "merchant's college," which would include study of the Principles of Commerce; Commercial Statistics and History; Natural History, Chemistry, and Natural Philosophy; and History, "civil and literary."[117]

As the editor and publisher Freeman Hunt declared in 1839, all of this turned the New York Mercantile Library Association into something more than a "clerk's library."[118] Especially in the 1830s, merchants, including the antislavery advocate Arthur Tappan as well as Hone, contributed heavily to the association to expand its library and evening classes and in 1836 to initiate the lecture series. The lecture series appears to have had a decisive impact on membership, which rose from 600-700 in 1836 to over 5,000 by January 1840.[119] In addition, in 1839 Hunt began publication of *Hunt's Merchants' Magazine*, a trade journal permeated by calls for clerks to cultivate their minds. The onset of the panic of 1837 and subsequent depression, widely blamed on bankers and speculators, exposed merchants to virulent attacks on the trading spirit. Hone recorded many of these in his diary and they drove themselves like a lance into Hunt's side. Hunt took it on himself to preach to merchants and clerks that their character and the public's perception of them alike would be enhanced by literary cultivation. Just as a want of literary cultivation detracted from the "elevation of the mercantile character," Hunt wrote in 1840, no one on earth was worth more respect than the educated merchant, "the more if he is self-educated," who combined trade with the cultivation "of those powers which . . . shed a halo of never-ending delight around his path, and aid him both in business and duty."[120]

Neither Hunt nor lecturers before mercantile library associations could show exactly how literary cultivation would assist merchants and clerks in their business. One speaker contended improbably that merchants had to know geometry and navigation in order to guide their captains around reefs and shoals.[121] This strained invocation of the age of Bulfinch must have rung hollow when it was delivered in 1839, for even prominent merchants no longer owned or sailed the ships to which they consigned their cargoes. But clerks flocked to mercantile library associations for many reasons. Like contemporary "young men's" societies, the mercantile library associations helped newcomers adjust to urban and commercial life. In New York City merchants preferred to recruit their clerks from the interior towns of upstate New York and New England. For two dollars a year, young men from rural families could join the mercantile library association, attend its lectures, take its evening courses, and enjoy its library privileges.[122] In fact, in 1860 the New York Mercantile Library was the largest lending library in North America, and the repository of numerous novels and romances as well as non-fictional works.[123] Above all, both the library and the association embodied the expectation of employers, leading merchants, that aspirants to mercantile life would engage in self-improvement. As Franklin had well understood, whether or not an ambitious youth was actually engaged in improvement, it was desirable to be seen as so engaged. An observer of the St. Louis Mercantile Library recognized that the young businessman who passed his spare time in the library rose "especially in the regard of those whose cool heads and sound judgments have given them elevated positions in trade and commerce." These veterans were sure to note "the one who turns his hours of relaxation and pleasure to the cultivation of his mind, the improvement of his intellect, and preparation for the business of daily life."[124]

Printers and Pedagogues

The value of self-improvement for printers depended significantly on the peculiar circumstances of the newspaper business in antebellum America. After 1790 and largely (but not exclusively) in response to the rise of political parties, the number of newspapers grew geometrically. The approximately 100 newspapers in circulation in 1790 doubled by 1800, and by 1810 the United States had more newspapers relative to population than any other nation in history.[125] American newspapers continued to experience revolutionary growth and change after 1810. In the 1830s James Gordon Bennett and other urban publishing entrepreneurs introduced mass circulation penny newspapers that were as racy and exciting as they were cheap. Making use of technological innovations such as the telegraph and the steam-powered press, penny papers pioneered the modern concept of news in the form of stories about homicides and abductions, dispatched reporters to cover Congress and the Mexican War, and in sundry other ways broke with the tradition of dingy, four-page, low-circulation papers.[126] Yet the penny press carried a hidden social cost, for it contributed to the gradual severance of printing and editing. Steam presses required considerable capital outlay, which led editors to let out contracts to printers. In turn, printers underbid each other by hiring inexpensive apprentices. Thurlow Weed, who had learned his craft in the small shops of the 1810s and 1820s, complained in 1847 that "rollers and steam do the work which FRANKLIN performed. Printers now learn but half the duties which pertained to our craft in other days."[127]

As the capital outlays required to enter newspaper publishing rose toward mid-century, the tie between printing and self-improvement gradually weakened. That bond had been fused in the small shops that had turned out low-circulation partisan and sectarian papers, and it survived after mid-century mainly in towns and small cities where printers, aided by a few journeymen and apprentices, continued to edit their papers. The career of William Cooper Howells, the father of the founder of American realist fiction, highlights this older tradition. William Dean Howells wrote that his father's work was both "mechanical and intellectual." "From a quaint pride," recalled the younger Howells, "he did not like his printer's craft to be called a trade; he contended that it was a profession."[128]

Whether trade or profession, printing brought few financial rewards to the senior Howells, who was well-intentioned but impractical and inclined to unconventional political and religious speculation. With a brood that grew to seven children (William Dean was born in 1837), William Cooper Howells drifted from town to town in Ohio, at times owning the newspaper he edited, at times working as an employed editor, and interspersing his newspaper ventures with stabs at house painting, farming, and plans to become a physician. Toiling on the periphery of the changes that were transforming the newspaper business and that would lead his son to abandon printing for authorship, William Cooper Howells encountered a host of small publishing opportunities. The Ohio Valley streamed in the 1820s and 1830s with periodicals edited and printed by men but intended for a female audience and modeled on the sentimental gift books and annuals popular among genteel ladies in the East.[129] William Cooper Howells launched one such periodical, *The Gleaner*, in the late 1820s. The senior Howells was also caught up in the political and religious controversies that swirled through Jacksonian America, and when *The Gleaner* failed he brought out a journal, *The Eclectic Observer and Working Man's Advocate*, whose title disclosed his willingness to print anything and his admiration for the utopian plans of Robert Owen. Howells also plunged into the partisan press. In 1839, his fortunes at a low ebb, he scraped together enough capital to purchase a Whig paper in Hamilton, Ohio. Tiring of this venture, he sold it in the mid-1840s in order to start a Swedenborgian journal, *The Retina*. Then, discovering that publishing Swedenborgian journals in Ohio was no way to make a living, he bought back the Whig paper. His embrace of Martin Van Buren's free-soil secession from the Democratic party in 1848 effectively killed this paper, but Howells's fortunes rose with those of free-soil, and in the 1850s, after additional stops on the publishing route, he secured the editorship of a free-soil paper in Jefferson, the seat of Ashtabula county.[130]

Although Howells's failures were frequent, intensifying political and religious controversy bred the conviction among printers like Howells that there would always be a circle of readers for their views. If one circle disappeared, another could be found. Political partisanship made the newspaper business relatively easy to enter, for the parties were less interested in the newfangled mass circulation dailies than in reliable outlets for their platforms. Not infrequently, parties purchased a press a few months before a major national election, hired a room and a printer, and then, depending on the election's outcome, kept the newspaper running or sold it to the highest bidder, whose bid under the circumstances was likely to be fairly low. As long as printers wrote and edited their newspapers, they had considerable inducement to improve themselves by developing their prose styles and by amassing a fund of facts, allusions, and ideas.[131]

William Dean Howells described the printing office as his school and journalism as his university. Howells taught himself Latin, Greek, and Spanish in his spare time, the last inspired by his reading of *Don Quixote*, and he kept a diary in which he practiced the prose style of favorite authors. In addition, print shops were natural meeting places for local politicians and literati. Howells encountered his share of both during his father's peregrinations. Shop talk in Jefferson, Ohio, he recalled, "was mostly literary; we disputed about authors among ourselves, and with the village wits who dropped in and liked to stand with their backs to our stove and challenge opinion concerning Holmes and Poe, Irving and Macaulay, Pope and Byron, Dickens and Shakespeare."[132] Wherever books were scarce, newspapers became the main vendors of poetry and fiction and functioned as outlets for village versifiers as well as for established writers, and even where books were abundant newspapers often contained poetry corners.[133]

The confluence of circumstances that opened fragile opportunities for William Cooper Howells in the printing trade and that directed his son toward self-improvement can also be seen in the early career of William Lloyd Garrison. Garrison was born in Newburyport, Massachusetts, in 1805 into a family of middling but deteriorating rank. His father, Abijah, an improvident and restless mariner with an inclination to strong drink, deserted the family when William was three years old, thus forcing his spouse Fanny into a succession of moves to support her children. After a severely truncated formal education, which included three months in a grammar school, William was apprenticed first to a shoemaker in Salem, next to a merchant in Baltimore, and then to a cabinetmaker in Haverhill, Massachusetts. But William did not find a situation to his liking until 1818, when he was apprenticed to Ephraim Allen, the editor of the Newburyport *Herald*.

Allen quickly took a liking to the bright if obstinate youth, boarded him in his home, and in 1822 made him the *Herald*'s shop foreman. The *Herald* became Garrison's surrogate college. Perusing its old files, he acquired a Federalist-tainted knowledge of American history and perhaps also a familiarity with eighteenth-century polemical literature. Garrison's first publications took the form of pseudonymous letters to the *Herald* and Salem *Gazette* between 1822 and 1824 in which he styled himself an "Old Bachelor" in one instance and "Aristides" (a conservative Athenian general) in another, made knowing references to "Junius," the pen name of an eighteenth-century critic of George III, liberally employed Latin and English quotations, and displayed a mastery of the complex and convoluted sentence structure long preferred by educated gentlemen in their public discourses. In a letter to his mother written in 1823, Garrison confessed that on reading over his communications to newspapers "I feel absolutely astonished at the different subjects which I have discussed and the style in which they are written, seeing . . . I do not understand *one single rule of grammar*, and have a very inferior education."[134]

Garrison also benefited from conversations with Caleb Cushing, the son of a wealthy Newburyport merchant, recent Harvard graduate, friend of George Bancroft and Edward Everett, and contributor to Everett's *North American Review*. Cushing had returned to Newburyport in 1821 to practice law as a prelude to entering politics and then took over the editorship of the *Herald* when Allen was away. Cushing called Garrison's attention to the evils of slavery, lent him books, and encouraged him to discern the tendencies of the age by studying the rebellions in Greece and the revolutions in South America. Significantly, Garrison's early contributions to the *Herald* included articles on the South American revolutions. While still an apprentice, Garrison also associated with several poor but ambitious young men in mutual improvement sessions held in a room over the bookstore and printing office of W. and J. Gilman. His intimates in this enterprise were William Goss Crocker and Isaac Knapp, both apprentice printers at Gilman's. (Knapp later became Garrison's partner in publishing *The Liberator*.) Out of these study sessions grew a debating society called the Franklin Club, which Garrison initiated.[135]

Although by trade a printer, Garrison's real profession was to be reform; like politics, social activism became a profession in the second quarter of the nineteenth century.[136] Relying on print and public address to spread their message, reformers imparted new significance to traditional occupations, including teaching.

Demand for teachers, including female teachers (attractive in part because they worked for lower wages than males), surged after the Revolution, partly in response to the "excitement of nation building," which added a new political buttress to the cause of widespread schooling, and partly as a product of the rising rates of school enrollment that attended the development of the decentralized "district" system of public education. Starting in the late 1830s in Massachusetts and extending throughout the northern tier of states by the 1880s, the so-called common-school revival further stimulated demand for teachers. Although the common-school revival does not appear to have increased enrollment rates, it intensified the experience of schooling by lengthening terms, encouraging regular attendance, enriching the curriculum, and grading the schools by age and attainment. Graded schools required more teachers than ungraded ones and spurred the employment of female teachers under the supervision of male principals.[137]

The common-school revival is not misnamed, for its supporters brought to their task a grand conception of education as the transformation of the individual's moral and intellectual character, a virtual rebirth that would be comparable in effect to a religious conversion in a revival, and they portrayed teaching as a sacred calling, a "lesser ministry."[138] Yet the primitive conditions that prevailed in district schools in the early 1800s did little to sustain this exalted conception of education. When William A. Alcott was examined by the school committee of his native Wolcott, Connecticut, to determine his qualifications to teach, he was asked only about subjects that he would teach; the committee failed to recognize that "the sciences are a circle, and that in order to have a perfectly practical and correct view of one, it is really necessary to have a tolerable knowledge of them all."[139]

To gain an understanding of the principles of physiology and laws of health in application to education, Alcott secured a medical degree from Yale in 1826. In keeping with his earnestness he also commenced a self-conscious "literary correspondence" in the mid-1820s with his cousin A. Bronson Alcott. The Alcotts critiqued each other's literary compositions and cultivated the kind of florid style they associated with genteel discourse. "While many, perhaps most, of our youthful associates are still groping their way through the mists of ignorance, to the attainment of wealth, or to the gratification of their passions," Bronson wrote to William in 1826, "the Great Author of good has raised us from the grovelling herd, and illuminated our minds, if it be but feebly with the beams of knowledge."[140]

Alcott's language, which linked ignorance to selfishness ("the attainment of wealth," "the gratification of passion") rather than to stupidity or deprivation, underlined the disinterestedness that he and his cousin associated with teaching. The rhetoric that enveloped self-improvement and the vocation of teaching was much the same. Understandably contemporaries viewed teaching as an ideal calling for women, who were not supposed to avow personal ambition. Yet while the status of teaching as a lesser ministry attracted idealistic women to it, especially in the late eighteenth and early nineteenth centuries women faced singular obstacles in preparing themselves to do more than "keep" school. Neither the Yale medical school that William A. Alcott attended nor any contemporary college admitted women.

Although excluded by colleges, women began to discover new opportunities for gaining education beyond the rudiments in the wake of the Revolution. During the 1780s and 1790s, republican educators defended "useful" education for women, by which they meant "solid" attainments like arithmetic, geography, English composition and grammar, and history in preference to ornamental subjects like painting, piano, and needlework. A woman adept at arithmetic could help her husband keep accounts, while her knowledge of English composition and grammar would render her a more effective teacher of her children.[141]

On balance, however, the Revolution's educational legacy to women was mixed. On the one hand, republican educators urged improvements in female education, most of the academies established in the 1790s and early 1800s admitted girls as well as boys, and in the 1790s Susanna Rowson, Sarah Pierce, and a sprinkling of other educated women founded academies exclusively for girls. On the other hand, young women who attended coeducational academies were taught in separate rooms and usually for much briefer periods (often only in the summer) than boys.[142] Lacking buildings of their own, the early female academies were conducted in the homes of their principals. More fundamentally, republican educators betrayed ambivalence about female education even as they defended it. Benjamin Rush's contrast between useful and ornamental education reflected his staunch republicanism; in a republic men and women alike had to be educated to discharge the duties of their "stations." Inasmuch as virtually all educators agreed that the station of woman was to be a wife and mother, they saw no reason to endorse female intellectual incursions into the higher reaches of mathematics or natural or moral philosophy. Mathematics and natural philosophy promised to make men more inventive, but these studies threatened to deflect women from their station and, in effect, become new forms of ornamental education. For all of their blasts at ornamental education, republican educators did little to undermine the image of scholarly women as unsexed "bluestockings."[143]

The task of legitimating higher intellectual strivings by women fell to the generation of female educators born between 1785 and 1805, which included Zilpah Grant, Mary Lyon, Catharine Beecher, Emma (Hart) Willard, and her sister Almira Hart Lincoln Phelps. Born respectively in 1787 and 1793, Emma and Almira Hart each studied and then taught at a succession of recently founded coeducational or female academies in the first decade of the nineteenth century, but when Emma presented the New York state legislature with her *Plan for Improving Female Education* in 1819 (the basis for the opening two years later of the Troy Female Seminary), she scored existing academies for stressing show over substance.

Both she and her sister owed their higher education to a mixture of accident and self-teaching rather than to their experiences in academies, which taught subjects like composition, geography, French, painting, and needlework. After marrying Dr. John Willard, a Middlebury, Vermont, physician and Republican party activist in 1809, Emma began to study her husband's medical textbooks as well as those of his nephew, who lived with the Willards while attending Middlebury College. Almira joined the Willard household in 1810–11 to study geometry and moral philosophy with her sister. For all practical purposes, the college was an institution that the sisters could see (literally, for they lived across the street from it) but not touch. Middlebury officials repeatedly rebuffed Emma's requests to attend examinations so that she might observe college standards, but her proximity to the college stimulated her zeal for higher education.[144]

Emma baptized her Troy school a seminary rather than an academy, partly to deflect criticism that she was invading the male sphere of college education and partly to signify a more serious type of education—history, philosophy, mathematics, and natural sciences—than the early academies offered women. Training female teachers was one of the chief purposes of the Troy Female Seminary and of similar institutions such as the seminary that Catharine Beecher founded in Hartford in 1828, Zilpah Grant's Ipswich, Massachusetts, seminary (1828), and Mary Lyon's Mount Holyoke Seminary (1837).[145]

In mastering subjects that either were taught to women imperfectly or not at all, Emma Willard and Almira Phelps opened an avenue of female advancement beyond classroom instruction: the authorship of textbooks. Emma devised a new scheme for studying and teaching geography during her Middlebury years, while Almira read books on botany and attended lectures at the Troy Lyceum by Amos Eaton, a popularizer of science who had taught himself much of what he knew. Both of the sisters then turned their private study to profit by writing textbooks. Almira's contemporary fame rested mainly on her *Familiar Lectures on Botany* (1829), which ran through nine editions in less than a decade and which sold 275,000 copies by 1875, while Emma successfully collaborated with William C. Woodbridge on *Universal Geography* (1822). Each book evidenced a Pestalozzian approach to teaching by emphasizing induction from objects—flowers, globes, maps, and charts—over memorization. Woodbridge himself was a leading American popularizer of Pestalozzianism. Pestalozzianism and self-teaching had complementary effects. Autodidacts who despaired of existing textbooks as either patronizing or incomprehensible taught themselves subjects in much the same fashion that Pestalozzians claimed that subjects should be studied: from piece to piece, from things to words, from objects to principles.[146]

The Gender Difference

The establishment of female seminaries by no means obviated the importance of self-education for women. As was true of eighteenth-century colleges, antebellum female seminaries assumed that students would supplement their classroom instruction by self-education; in its early days Mount Holyoke Seminary required each applicant to demonstrate her knowledge of Watts's *The Improvement of the Mind*.[147] By the 1830s and

1840s advice books aimed at young women exhorted them to systematic study. Almira Phelps's *The Fireside Friend* described the contours and history of natural philosophy, chemistry, and zoology to guide her readers through the thickets of knowledge, while Margaret Coxe's *The Young Ladies' Companion* outlined a methodical strategy for mastering history, languages, geography, and the sciences.[148]

As Almira Phelps recognized, female intellectual cultivation was less controversial in 1840 than in 1800. Women were gaining access to a wider range of intellectual vocations, including teaching and authorship. Yet ideas about female education retained an underlying conservatism. Emma Willard, Almira Phelps, Catharine Beecher, Zilpah Grant, and Mary Lyon favored broadening rather than changing the sphere of women. By mid-century the limits of even an enlarged female sphere were becoming apparent. The common-school reform movement, for example, imposed subtle restraints on women by creating new executive positions for men in school administration while consigning women to the lower ranks of grade-school teaching. Increasingly, too, women found themselves less welcome as collaborators of male scientists. When Benjamin Silliman, Sr., lectured on chemistry and geology before large audiences of men and women at Boston's Lowell Institute in the late 1830s, he used essentially the same material as in classes at Yale, but the generation of American scientists that succeeded Silliman and Amos Eaton showed less interest in bringing women into partnership with male cultivators of natural knowledge. The gradual professionalization of science after 1840 bred a new conception of popular science, which sought less to widen the perimeters of the scientific community to include women than to encourage general support for science among the laity.[149]

The establishment of female seminaries in New England in the 1820s and 1830s foreshadowed the later founding of similar institutions in other regions and gradually spurred academies to offer a wider range of higher subjects (but not the classical languages) in their "ladies' departments." But opportunities for women to enter intellectual vocations lagged far behind the growth of higher schools for women, a fact that contributed to the tentative quality of arguments for the usefulness of female education and that helps to explain the preoccuption of advice books aimed at women with the character-building role of study. Advice books did not neglect the possible utility of knowledge; the poet Lydia H. Sigourney, speaking from experience (she wrote and sold her verse first to support her parents and later to help her financially pressed husband), affirmed her belief "that young ladies should make themselves mistresses of some attainment, either in art or science, by which they might secure a subsistence, should they be reduced to poverty." But Sigourney's conflation of the utility of knowledge with potential disaster was revealing, as was her connection of botany to the culture of flowers, an activity "peculiarly congenial to the feelings of our sex" and especially valuable on the "sylvan walk."[150] She and other writers of advice books stressed that it was more important for women to acquire habits of study than to amass mountains of knowledge. Whereas advice books for young men routinely warned against gambling dens, loose women, and shady business associates, those for females warned readers against themselves, against their penchant for reading novels, tolerating interruptions, and courting fashion.[151]

Differences in emphasis between advice books aimed at men and women reflected underlying differences in the male and female cultures of self-improvement. Young men who came together in literary societies had every reason to follow their noses, to pick and choose seemingly unrelated quotations, illustrations, and ideas from an eclectic assortment of texts and lectures, for there were innumerable ways for them to put such fragments of knowledge to use. In contrast, confronted by a restricted range of vocational options and by suspicion that they could never master complicated subjects, women responded by stressing systematic study and they condemned themselves for the self-indulgent literary pursuits that had proved so advantageous to men. Not surprisingly, when women began after the Civil War to dominate organizations devoted to mutual improvement, they made "culture-study" their icon.[152]

Conclusion

Economic development and political democratization shaped the popularization of knowledge in various ways, some straightforward, others tortuous. By 1815 the penetration of the market economy had brought a flourishing book trade to agricultural regions that for most of the eighteenth century had experienced few economic and cultural dealings with urban centers. In the wake of the transportation revolution, railroads helped to bring into existence a class of nationally known lyceum lecturers. In combination, commercialization and improvements in transportation contributed to the growth of the legal and medical professions. Aspirants to these professions had many incentives to engage in self-improvement, and these incentives were buttressed by the prospect of participation in public life. Political parties and reform movements used print to disseminate their platforms and thereby afforded printers both opportunities for employment and incentives for self-improvement.

All of this exemplified the pragmatic value of pursuing literature and philosophy in the antebellum era. But the quest for knowledge was more than an instrumental accommodation to new occupational opportunities. In the prevailing view, self-improvement was a disciplined and arduous undertaking that bred a certain detachment from the workaday world in those who answered its summons. Although it is not usually numbered among the antebellum reform movements, the popular pursuit of knowledge possessed close ties to temperance and school reform and it acquired some of the features of a reform movement.

Viewed as a calling, self-improvement simultaneously proved attractive to leaders of growing but vulnerable professions and occupations, who praised it as a way to spur virtue in young aspirants to law or medicine or commerce, and to women, who recognized its congruence with their "sphere" of disinterested activity. Yet while women and men alike voiced the ideal of intellectual improvement as a noble path, they differed in their approach to learning. Partly because they had to pry higher learning from a society that was indifferent or hostile to their aspirations, women came to value the mastery of subjects. In contrast, men had incomparably greater opportunities to put their knowledge to use in public forums, where appearances often counted more than substance. A plague in the eyes of authors of advice books aimed at women, superficiality could be a boon for young men.

The quest for knowledge reflected factors peculiar to time and place, and in the late nineteenth century it would wane among some of the same occupational and professional groups that had sustained it in antebellum America. For the most part, however, Americans traced the diffusion of knowledge to liberty and democracy—forces that seemed likely to become universal in their society. As we will see in the next chapter, so far from dwelling on, or even recognizing, the conditions that bounded the pursuit of knowledge, they stressed its potentially unrestricted scope.

Chapter 3

Strenuous Learning and the
Diffusion of Knowledge

Recognizing that the means of literary improvement were not widely diffused in their society, republican educators of the late eighteenth century had described schools, academies, and colleges as the primary agents of popular education. In contrast, during the nineteenth century, educators fashioned a body of ideas that accorded much greater scope to informal influences in education, in part because the spread of library companies and mutual improvement societies made it more plausible for them to identify self-education as an instrument of popular enlightenment. Heartened by the growth of voluntary associations devoted to the diffusion of knowledge, antebellum educators devised a model for acquiring education, especially liberal education, through a mixture of formal and informal influences. Although the range of informal influences included the family, workplace, and church—institutions that did not profess educational objectives—educators were primarily concerned with the complementary relationship between formal schooling and such voluntary and purposively educational activities as private reading, attendance at lectures, and participation in mutual improvement societies. They valued education acquired despite frequent interruptions, spread out over a long period of time, and gained against many if not all odds.

From one perspective, this pattern of acquiring education beyond the rudiments was no more than a practical adaptation to social conditions. In an age when children were expected to contribute to the family economy, the opportunity costs of schooling—the loss of wages while attending school—posed a formidable barrier. Most of those who sought to acquire a liberal education did so by a mixture of formal schooling and private self-education. The latter might be snatched in interludes between school and work, acquired in preparation for schooling, or pursued after brief schooling. Yet this way of gaining liberal education was more than a response to practical conditions, for it also became crystallized into an ideal, enshrined by a contemporary as "the pursuit of knowledge under difficulties." This ideal of strenuous learning promised to democratize liberal education by trimming its association with aristocracy and by emphasizing that individual persistence counted more than accidents of wealth or birth.

Viewed in one light, Benjamin Franklin and the republican educators of the late eighteenth century had already severed liberal education from its historical association with scholars and leisured gentlemen by emphasizing its value for tradesmen and (in the case of the republican educators) women. But the cultural climate in which the republican educators had framed their proposals differed significantly from that of the 1830s and 1840s, when those who publicized the pursuit of knowledge under difficulties had to plunge into an arena of popular debate about the educational requirements of a democracy and to confront skeptics, who either argued or assumed that political and industrial progress owed little to any sort of systematic quest for knowledge. It was enough, these populist skeptics contended, that children learn the rudiments in public schools and then enter the school of experience. Practical men did not require knowledge gleaned from books or lectures. Popular beliefs about the primacy of experience formed the context in which educators, scholars, moralists, and other upholders of liberal education sought to insinuate respect for learning into the public forum.

Universal Schooling and Self-Education

Republican educators of the late eighteenth century had fashioned a blueprint for a pyramidal system of schools. As theorists, they did not have to make hard-and-fast choices between different levels of education—for example, between primary and grammar schools or between grammar schools and colleges—and as a corollary they were under little pressure to choose between universal and liberal education. Yet these ideals existed in uneasy tension. Universal education would affect everyone, or at least everyone who would be in a position, if only as a voter, to influence public affairs. Whether or not it would embrace women and blacks, it would have to include all white male children, who would be taught reading, writing, and numeracy. In contrast, liberal education would enlighten youth of talent, promise, and ambition. Noah Webster and Benjamin Rush insisted that the boundaries of liberal education had to be sufficiently broad in a republic to include tradesmen, who would be instructed in the general principles pertinent to commerce, agriculture, mechanics, and government. Common sense might suggest that financially strapped new governments unable to pay their war debts were unlikely to incur new burdens by financing an extensive system of publicly supported schools at all levels, and that the plans of republican educators were wildly unrealistic. But republicans inclined to the view that, liberated from enslavement to tradition, legislatures would leap at the chance to support education. As Rush wrote in his 1786 *Plan for the Establishment of Public Schools and the Diffusion of Knowledge in Pennsylvania*:

The *present time* is peculiarly favorable to the establishment of these necessary and benevolent institutions in Pennsylvania. The minds of our people have not as yet lost the yielding texture they acquired in the heat of the late Revolution. They will *now* receive more readily than five or even three years hence new impressions and habits of all kinds. The spirit of liberty *now* pervades every part of the state. The influence of error and deception are *now* of short duration.[1]

By 1820 the issue of republican education appeared in a different light. Lacking either the will or the resources to enact the republican vision of a multitiered system of public education, legislatures came under pressure to choose between universal and liberal education. For example, Jefferson, who once had dwelled on the importance of primary schools, now responded to proposals in the Virginia assembly to cut academies and colleges off from the state's Literary Fund with a counterproposal to scrimp on primary schooling in order to leave money in the Fund for a public university.[2] At the same time, an increasing number of political leaders were moving in the opposite direction from Jefferson. In response to evidence of mounting poverty and vice, public officials, including New York's De Witt Clinton, bemoaned the absence of free primary schools. After 1813 the New York legislature appropriated funds for the Free School Society of New York City, a private, philanthropic organization originally founded in 1805 by Clinton and others to provide free schooling to pauper children. Reconstituted as the Public School Society, this organization virtually controlled education in New York City for the next three decades. Initially an offshoot of voluntarism and philanthropy, the idea of free education gradually became linked to that of tax-supported schooling, first in the platform of the so-called workingmen's parties that arose in the late 1820s and early 1830s and then in the common-school reform movement that crystallized in the late 1830s.[3]

Envisioning partisanship, ethnic divisions, and religious sectarianism as threats to social order, Horace Mann and other common-school reformers stressed the importance of common intellectual and social experiences for the children of all social classes.[4] This objective pointed reformers toward keeping children in school for longer terms each year and discouraging casual attendance, whether by the "large boys" who long had proven a disruptive presence in rural schools or by working-class truants in cities.[5] Universal education meant public support of schools for all children, but not necessarily universal attendance.[6] Basically, reformers desired more systematic and comprehensive formal schooling for children sufficiently mature to benefit from schooling but not old enough to spring at job opportunities. In practice, this meant a focus on those from eight to thirteen, the peak years of school attendance.[7] Compared to the republican educators of the 1780s and 1790s, common-school advocates paid relatively little attention to the schooling of teenagers. Whereas in 1790 Noah Webster had described the years from twelve to twenty as "the most important in life" and had asserted that influences before the age of twelve readily could be effaced, reformers imbibed the prevailing antebellum view that influences in childhood (before puberty) were nearly indelible.[8]

School reform left a trail of relatively centralized state instructional systems across the northern states between 1840 and 1880. In his biography of Mann, Jonathan Messerli observes that mid-nineteenth-century Americans "adopted a form of organization of schooling which permitted them to incorporate ever greater components of what had once been *education* into a more systematized and formal *schooling*."[9] Yet reformers' thinking left considerable scope to self-education beyond the completion of formal schooling. All of the changes in pedagogy advocated by common-school reformers—Pestalozzian "object teaching" (first the thing, then the word), the encouragement of reading for comprehension rather than merely for the ability to speak the names of words, restrictions on corporal punishment, and the fostering of a healthy spirit of "emulation" among pupils—aimed to inspire pupils with appropriate motives, so that they would later be able to guide themselves.[10] Motives became important precisely because reformers distrusted the home and workplace as self-sufficient instruments of moral or intellectual education and doubted their capacity to implant the seeds of self-control, self-direction, and self-education in each child. The very fact that school reformers discouraged casual attendance by teenagers, few of whom could afford regular attendance at school, sharpened their insistence on continuing self-education. In 1833 Robert Rantoul, Jr., Massachusetts lawyer, Jacksonian politician, and advocate of school reform, cautioned workingmen to choose their jobs and residences near "good schools, good lyceums, the beneficial influence of well educated and high-minded men in or out of the learned professions, well selected libraries, public or private, an easy supply of the best new books, [and] good newspapers."[11]

Democratic Self-Education

Before the nineteenth century, writers on education portrayed the "improvement of the mind" as an activity mainly suited to gentlemen. Locke's *Treatise on the Conduct of the Understanding* averred that only those with leisure would have the time and inclination for mental improvement. There were exceptions, but they tended only to reinforce the association of mental improvement with gentlemanly status. Eighteenth-century Americans were familiar with self-instructors, practical manuals that any literate person could read to learn some skill or "art."[12] But self-instruction of this sort lacked the ardor, dedication, and difficulty of undergoing a course of mental improvement. It is also true that both Thomas Jefferson and Benjamin Rush had venerated David Rittenhouse as an example of how arduous philosophical investigation might elevate the child of humble parents. But Jefferson and Rush tagged Rittenhouse as a genius, and hence untypical, and each employed Rittenhouse as ammunition in a debate among educated gentlemen. Jefferson invoked Rittenhouse in his *Notes on the State of Virginia*, a book he wrote to disabuse French philosophes of the notion that all species degenerated in the New World; Rush used his eulogy of Rittenhouse before the select audience of the American Philosophical Society to ridicule colleges for requiring students to learn the ancient languages.

In contrast, during the nineteenth century a mixture of college professors, school reform advocates, and liberal clergymen praised self-education as efficacious for anyone. Speaking before the Concord, Massachusetts, lyceum in 1829, the Harvard classicist C. C. Felton proclaimed: "If a whole people could be engaged at once in this magnificent object [the diffusion of knowledge], a consummation which the mind can easily comprehend, how unspeakably beautiful would be the prospect, how noble the result."[13] To many it seemed that common-school reform itself was merely a phase of the grand diffusion of knowledge; lyceums of the sort Felton addressed frequently served as rallying points for popular support of school reform.[14] School reformers themselves, who by no means thought of self-education as a sufficient species of education, favored reading rooms and libraries as "means" of self-education in adulthood. In 1841 William Ellery Channing, co-religionist and friend of Horace Mann, told the Mercantile Library Company of Philadelphia that a "tendency to universality and diffusion" of knowledge marked the age.[15] In announcing the same conclusion fifteen years earlier, Joseph Story had assumed the stance of a prophet, but by 1841 Channing was merely reciting a commonplace conclusion that he himself had advanced in his 1838 lecture on "Self-Culture" and in two lectures "On the Elevation of the Laboring Classes" that he had delivered in 1840.[16]

It is tempting to link celebrations of the diffusion of knowledge to the contemporary democratization of politics and religion, which in turn spurred the political and religious press. Channing pointed to the dissemination of print as evidence of his age's tendency "to expansion, to diffusion, to universality." "Genius sends its light into cottages," he wrote.[17] Yet the Holbrooks, Storys, Feltons, and Channings confronted their age with ambivalence. By "universality" Channing meant the growth of shared feelings, not the partisanship and sectarianism that propelled the political and religious press. "Religion is war; Christians, forsaking their one Lord, gather under various standards to gain victory for their sects. Politics are war, breaking the whole people into fierce and unscrupulous parties, which forget their country in conflicts for office and power."[18] In the thinking of Channing and other men of letters, the diffusion of knowledge differed from the angry contentiousness of the ideological marketplace, where all was challenge and response. Significantly, neither Channing nor the others compiled lists of recommended books, as Jefferson had for his friends and as any number of entrepreneurs of culture as a commodity would by the end of the nineteenth century. What mattered to Channing and the others was the process, self-improvement by mental elevation, rather than the acquisition of specific information or bodies of doctrine. To criticize their ideal of culture as vague is to miss the point, for the last thing they desired was to encourage reading as a way to strengthen the bonds of sectarian or partisan belief.

Although Channing's conception of self-culture has been called "explicitly democratic," in one respect it was profoundly conservative.[19] While portraying self-culture as universally accessible, he rejected any intimation that it would contribute to material advancement. Thus the elevation of the laboring classes through self-culture "is not an outward change of condition. It is not release from labor. It is not struggling for another rank. It is not political power."[20] For Channing books, lectures, and conversation were means of self-perfection, the elevation of the soul, rather than self-advancement. With other Unitarians, Channing believed that the value of education rose in proportion to the effort expended to acquire it. "Direct" instruction in schools would no more make one a scholar than listening to sermons would make one a Christian. Private study elevated the soul by imparting higher knowledge and by eliciting character-building effort. Channing's ideal, shared by Edward Everett, Henry Wadsworth Longfellow, and other members of Boston's Unitarian/Whig elite, was someone like Elihu Burritt, the "learned blacksmith" who taught himself over a dozen languages with so little thought of self-advancement that he turned down an invitation from Longfellow to join the Harvard faculty.[21]

Primarily rooted in theology rather than in sociology, Unitarian self-culture offered an alternative to the evangelical preoccupation with sin, repentance, and conversion. Self-culture meant steady spiritual growth to which the acquisition of secular knowledge could contribute by virtue of its disinterestedness. In flight from Calvinist gloom and doom, Unitarians thought that reading history or philosophy would dispel the morbid absorption with inner emotional states that they associated with fire-breathing revivalism, while elevating the mind and soul beyond the low and commonplace.[22] However ethereal, Unitarian self-culture embodied one of the impulses behind antebellum self-improvement, the autodidact's desire to enter a grand sphere of knowledge above partisanship and sectarianism. To elevate the soul, self-culture had to be devoid of any selfish goal. Yet the very selflessness of Unitarian self-culture restricted its popular appeal, for it was the utility of scientific and literary attainment in a growing number of professions and occupations that impelled popular self-improvement. Thus it is hardly surprising to find radical alternatives to Unitarian self-culture by mid-century. For example, Orson Fowler substituted phrenological psychology for theology, proclaimed self-improvement an exact science that would lead to material success, and even compiled a "Self-Improvement Directory Table" in which he cross-indexed 37 distinct mental faculties, ranging from amativeness and "aquativeness" (the desire for water) to causality, comparison, and memory, and told his readers how to improve each. Whereas Channing had urged the elevation of the soul through learning, Fowler struck a notably modern note by replacing the soul with discrete and measurable organs and by substituting drill and technical shortcuts (including new systems of shorthand) for intellectual cultivation.[23]

While conceptually distinct, Channing's ideal of self-culture as elevation of the spirit and Fowler's pragmatic defense of self-improvement as an aid to success converged in individuals like Isaac Mickle, Jr. (whom we met in Chapter 2). Mickle equated self-improvement with an elevated outlook, but simultaneously experimented with mental shortcuts, including a new system for solving arithmetical problems, and never doubted that he would reap material benefits from self-education. Yet self-improvement must have seemed irrelevant if not futile to many Americans, who could not ignore the innumerable examples of famous people who lacked any but practical education in the school of experience. In 1866 Samuel P. Bates, a Pennsylvania deputy school superintendent, addressed some of these concerns in his *Lectures on Mental and Moral Culture*.[24] Bates had no doubt about the value of what he called "popular education," a combination of common schools, "books and printed matter," and lyceum lectures.[25] But Bates acknowledged that a strain of popular thinking questioned the value of even this type of education. The nation was filled with successful, practical men who outstripped learned men in government and business and whose education mainly consisted of learning from experience. In Congress unlettered lions from the West, ignorant of "musty folios," matched wits with the Edward Everetts and Charles Sumners, and while "Everett and Sumner may upon occasion deliver very finished orations," in the drafting of bills and in impromptu debates "they find themselves in an assembly at least their equals."[26] Similarly, the scholar may fail in business where the practical man succeeds "because his school has been the present times."[27] Although they were strangers to the knowledge contained in books, these practical men were called in common parlance "self-educated" or "self-taught," Bates observed, and the public thrust them into the same category as a Franklin or a Nathaniel Bowditch.

Popular beliefs about the primacy of a kind of practical, nonliterate self-education drew on a variety of currents. The strain of romantic nationalism that Emerson voiced in "The American Scholar" and "Education" appealed to literati. Louisa J. Park of Boston eulogized the portrait painter Chester Harding, who enjoyed a great vogue in the 1820s:

> Most wondrous gift, from nature's self derived
> His genius of all foreign aid deprived
> Sprung up and bloomed amid our winds obscure
> And won its self-taught way to glory sure.[28]

The biographer James Parton wrote of Horace Greeley: "He escaped the schools, and so passed through childhood uncorrupt, 'his own man,' not forced upon a pattern. He was not trained up—he grew up. Like a tree he was to seek the nourishment he needed and could appropriate."[29] Often expressed in literate discourse by romantic writers, these sentiments complemented the popular undercurrent that had surfaced in the rowdy election of 1828: Andrew Jackson, the child of nature whose mind was unclouded by learning, versus John Quincy Adams, the pedant who could write but not fight.

Similar views emerged as contemporaries grappled with the educational implications of the industrial revolution; and, like the revolution itself, this grappling took place on both sides of the Atlantic. Indeed, the early industrial revolution posed a more corrosive challenge to the educational values of the literary class than did political democratization. Even after the election of 1828, men with literary attainments could still gain election to office; Quincy Adams himself was an example. But the major inventions that spurred the industrial revolution appeared to owe little to higher education. Colleges and universities had no apparent connection with the invention of the separate condenser steam engine (James Watt) or the spinning jenny (James Hargreaves and Richard Arkwright) or the automated mill (Oliver Evans). From the comments of learned contemporaries, who often described popular beliefs as a prelude to attacking them, it is clear that many if not most artisans and mechanics linked inventions to a mixture of luck, accident, and irreplicable genius. "People talk about a self-educated man as if he were a miracle," Robert Rantoul, Jr., complained. Similarly, the author of *The Modern Mechanic*, a mid-century self-instructional manual aimed at the "young workman," referred to the association between invention and accident as a common error, which was paralleled and stimulated by the boasts of inventors that "all their knowledge is original; or that they are self-taught."[30] In his frequent lectures before mechanics' associations, the Massachusetts statesman and orator Edward Everett never failed to refer to the "vague prejudice" against book learning "still afloat in the community."[31] In 1833 the *Mechanics' Magazine*, which like many specimens of the antebellum mechanics' press was edited by mechanic intellectuals, cited the "dangerous and pernicious opinion" of most artisans that literature and science were unnecessary to them.[32]

Views akin to these formed the context of Samuel Bates's *Lectures on Mental and Moral Culture*. He quickly dissociated himself from the mere scholar who disdained business. "In these matter-of-fact times we have come to deal with realities and not their semblances. We have learned to judge the culture of a man's mind, not by the number of years he has been engaged in study, but by what he is able to do—by the fruits his mind is capable of yielding." This immediately reminded Bates of Francis Bacon, and indeed of one "greater than Bacon [who] had, centuries before, declared 'by their fruits ye shall know them.'"[33] Bates next criticized the aristocratic pretensions of college graduates, but added that "liberal culture" could never be judged by the "weak and imbecilic representatives of such culture." Finally, he singled out Franklin, Nathaniel Bowditch, James Watt, and Elihu Burritt as examples of individuals who lacked extensive formal education but who cherished knowledge and who taught themselves to think philosophically.[34] Franklin's *Proposals Relating to the Education of Youth in Pennsylvania* afforded Bates a virtual feast, for he used it to show that Franklin, the exemplar of self-education, praised liberal education.[35]

Bates voiced these sentiments in lectures that he originally wrote between 1854 and 1859 for use by teachers' institutes. Most likely, his audience agreed that liberal culture mattered, but required arguments to answer local skeptics. As Bates recognized, there were many of these: farmers who sent their children to district schools to learn enough not to be cheated when they grew up, and nothing more; villagers who deprecated the "systematic and thorough culture" of physicians and who patronized folk practitioners who claimed to possess skill without education.[36] In this context, Bates's invocation of famous autodidacts who struggled to secure liberal culture in the face of obstacles was a clever and effective tactic, for it reconciled liberal culture and the work ethic. The self-taught men that Bates admired "did not despise labor."[37] In essence, Bates framed a tactically astute defense of liberal culture by celebrating those who overcame early disadvantages to acquire it.

In so contending Bates was following the argument of a book that the *North American Review* accurately described as "a favorite food of a generation of young Americans," George L. Craik's *The Pursuit of Knowledge Under Difficulties*.[38] Originally published in Britain in 1830 as part of the "Library of Entertaining Knowledge" sponsored by Henry Brougham's Society for the Diffusion of Useful Knowledge (SDUK), Craik's volume consisted of several hundred biographical sketches of individuals who persisted in their quest for literary and/or scientific knowledge despite discouraging circumstances. These included merchants who cherished learning, "literary soldiers," impoverished autodidacts, a ship painter who taught himself landscape painting, a goldsmith's apprentice who became a famed engraver, Sir Isaac Newton (for his "child-like alacrity in seizing upon whatever contributions of knowledge Nature threw at his feet"), all those who overcame "defects of the senses or other natural bodily powers," and many more. Although at one point Craik defined self-education narrowly as education without any master save "in the mere elements of reading," elsewhere he equated self-education with virtually all manifestations of the pursuit of knowledge under difficulties.[39] Craik celebrated

all, in short, who whether in humble or in high life, have pursued Knowledge with ardor, and distinctly evidenced, by the seductions they resisted, or the difficulties they encountered or overcame, for her sake, that she was the first object of their affections; and that the pursuit of her, even without any reference to either the wealth, the power, or the distinction which she might bring them, was, in their estimation, its own sufficient reward.[40]

Craik described Knowledge as a mistress in a letter to Charles Knight, a London publisher and intimate of Brougham, James Mill, Robert Owen, and other British advocates of educational reform, who edited and contributed to the Library of Entertaining Knowledge. Knight reprinted part of the letter in his preface to the 1865 edition of *The Pursuit*, to which he added correspondence in which Brougham voiced reservations about Craik's conflation of "self-exaltation" and "self-help."[41] Brougham would have preferred that Craik restrict himself to such exemplars of self-help as Franklin and the English inventors James Watt and Richard Arkwright, who used knowledge to elevate their social stations, and exclude individuals like Newton, although he taught himself mathematics, and Granville Sharp, who, although he gained fame, "was the grandson of the Archbishop of York, and could not be said to alter his station in life."[42]

Brougham did not persuade Craik to change the content of the book, but he successfully induced Craik to revise the title from Craik's proposed "The Love of Knowledge Overcoming Difficulties in Its Pursuit" (Craik also proposed "Anecdotes of the Love of Knowledge") to the final version. Not only did "the pursuit of knowledge under difficulties" become, in Knight's words, "one of the commonest forms of speech," but it was sufficiently redolent of self-help to please Brougham. At least the title did not invoke "love" as the only motive for learning. Neither did it embody the phrase "Anecdotes of Self-Taught Genius," which Brougham may have proposed and which Craik definitely abhorred as "greatly too limited."[43]

By underscoring the importance of personal initiative, the compromise title undoubtedly added to the book's popular appeal. At the same time, Craik's inclusion of individuals drawn from many social ranks gave his work a universal relevance. The degree of effort elicited by the quest for knowledge was more important for Craik than the social deprivation of those who engaged in the quest. *The Pursuit*'s reliance on biographical sketches and its freedom from exhortation happily distinguished it from William Ellery Channing's pleas that the laboring classes engage in self-culture as a kind of Unitarian duty. The call to pursue knowledge under difficulties had considerable relevance to the situation of Americans as well. In contrast to Great Britain, where mass schooling remained a highly controversial proposition even in the mid-nineteenth century, few Americans dissented from the general idea of universal education.[44] Americans increasingly enjoyed free elementary education at public expense. Far more problematic was the attainment of literary and scientific knowledge at a time when changes in the professions and some occupations were enhancing the utility of such knowledge. The opportunity costs alone of higher education were formidable, and they dictated that, if acquired at all, advanced formal education usually had to be gained intermittently, "under difficulties."

Self-Education, Formal Education

In popular usage, self-education did not necessarily involve the self-directed pursuit of literary or scientific culture. As we have seen, contemporaries sometimes applied the term to children of "nature" or to mechanics who stumbled upon inventions by a mixture of luck or accident. Educators and other representatives of the literary class in antebellum America responded to this understanding of self-education by fashioning one of their own, which emphasized the alternation of formal (schooling) and informal (purposive self-instruction) influences and which stressed that educational opportunities were within the reach of all. That the ideal of self-education favored by those attached to literary or philosophical pursuits did not exclude intermittent formal education was made clear by

Rev. Bela B. Edwards, who on the eve of the Civil War published a collection of biographies of "self-taught men."[45] As a former president of the American Education Society, a Protestant benevolent association that subsidized the collegiate education of pious but poor youth bound for the ministry, Edwards was familiar with young men jolted by religious conversions to acquire liberal education at relatively advanced ages. The tendency toward late graduation, which was evident at Princeton and other colleges with ties to the Great Awakening in the eighteenth century, continued into the nineteenth century. The proportion of young men to graduate from New England colleges at or above the age of 25 rose from 1800 to 1830; a similar tendency marked midwestern colleges after 1830.[46] Edwards pinned the hopes of evangelical Protestantism on such young men, who were eager for liberal education but who lacked means. He put their number at 100,000, the vast majority of whom were pursuing "the study of the sciences or of literature" in lyceums, by private reading, in academies, or in colleges where they were aided by benevolent societies. What all of these young men lacked was "the means of pursuing an uninterrupted course of mental improvement," for "if they have the benefit of teachers, it is only at intervals. If taught at all, they must in a great measure teach themselves."[47]

It is easy to see in Edwards's volume a concern, similar to that of Samuel Bates, to rescue liberal education from the populist charge that it unfitted individuals to live in a democracy. One counter to this accusation was to sever the acquisition of liberal education from anything that smacked of ease, leisure, or aristocracy. Edwards simultaneously detached self-education from any exclusive link to the school of experience and hitched it to liberal education outside of "regular" channels. Like George L. Craik, Edwards viewed self-education as consistent with formal education as long as the latter was sufficiently haphazard. From this perspective, liberal education acquired in an academy or college could yield immense benefits. Edwards argued that Eli Whitney's liberal education at Yale had imparted "a certain undefinable ease and self-possession" that ensured against his dismissal as "some illiterate visionary projector."[48] But although Whitney had briefly attended an academy (in fact, Leicester Academy) and graduated from Yale, by Edwards's measure Whitney was self-taught, for he spent his teen years working in his father's manufacturing shop, prepared for college partly on his own, did not enter Yale until he was 24, and graduated after his invention of the cotton gin. All of this reassured Edwards. It demonstrated that, contrary to the supposition of a noisy segment of the public "that a man must necessarily be unfitted for the higher arts of life, or the pursuit of business, by having received a liberal education," even great inventors could profit from a classical curriculum (which Whitney had pursued at Yale). At the same time, Whitney's example disclosed that the difficulty of acquiring a liberal education was no bar to attaining one. Those blessed with initiative and "genius," the latter lying "buried in our mountains and in our valleys" and merely awaiting discovery, would always come upon the means of culture. "Circumstances merely afforded the opportunity for the genius to display itself."[49]

The conditions that framed the educational experiences of Edwards's self-taught men, individuals who seem to have pried education out of the cracks, were identical to those affecting anyone desiring liberal education. "Regular" education, an uninterrupted course of mental improvement after the common grades, lay beyond the financial reach of all but a tiny fraction of the population. Further, the nature of professionalization in the antebellum era contributed to the "start-stop" character of education. Law, medicine, science, teaching, and even authorship were becoming full-time professions, but credentialing requirements had yet to acquire anything like their later importance. As the physicist Joseph Henry found out, it was still possible for someone who never had attended college to be offered a professorship in one. In this context academic degrees were less important than liberal education itself. Orators profited from learning the difference between Medusa's cauldron and Pandora's box, scientists from reconciling geology and Genesis, and authors from describing a window as a casement or a fishing pole as a piscatorial instrument.[50] The professional utility of such cultural information was derived from the latter's public display far more than from credentials that certified its possession.

Intermittent Education

The social conditions that shaped the acquisition of liberal education in antebellum America affected institutions of higher education in various ways, but most notably by restricting enrollments in colleges. Over 500 colleges were established between the Revolution and the Civil War, the number of colleges actually in operation rose from 20 in 1800 to over 200 in the 1850s, and the proportion of white males who entered college degree programs doubled between 1800 and 1860.[51] Expressed either numerically or as a proportion of white males aged fifteen to twenty, however, college enrollments were low on the eve of the Civil War. The federal census for 1850 put the number of college students at 27,821, but this figure, Colin Burke has noted, included many non-degree students, typically those enrolled in the preparatory departments that many of the new colleges felt compelled to maintain. Burke counted 9,931 enrollments in collegiate degree programs in 1850 and estimated 10,000 for 1860, in proportionate terms a rise from 0.91 percent to 1.18 percent of the white male population aged fifteen to twenty.[52]

One possible explanation for low enrollments in antebellum colleges is that young men (very few colleges admitted women before the Civil War) saw no value in liberal education. In 1827 Professor William Hooper of the University of North Carolina composed an imaginary soliloquy of a typical college student. "Of what use is all this going to be for me?" the student asks. "I am going to be a farmer or a merchant or at most a doctor, and every one knows it takes very little education to make a physician." In fact no occupation or profession in antebellum America required either a college or professional degree. Yet it is possible to view the issue of college enrollments in a different light. Burke has observed that the proportion of white males aged fifteen to twenty who were enrolled in degree programs in 1860, 1.18 percent, was not far off his estimate of the part of the total population, 2 percent, that could have afforded collegiate education. The demand for some formal liberal education may have been pronounced, but deflected away from colleges by their requirement that students complete a four-year curriculum to gain a degree. During a debate in North Carolina in the early 1820s over a proposal to establish a new college in the western part of the state, "Junius" wrote to the *Western Carolinian* to bemoan the customary requirements of four-year attendance at college, which "exclude the less opulent part of society from the field of science and throw a monopoly of learning into the hands of the rich."[53]

Junius's assumption that the less opulent part of society yearned for some formal liberal education gains force from the remarkable spread of academies between the Revolution and the Civil War. Earlier we have seen how academies began to arise toward the end of the eighteenth century in New England. Standing apart from the main development of the nineteenth-century movement to reform public education, academies were often attacked by school reformers (who hoped to substitute tax-supported public high schools for them) as vestiges of aristocratic influence in education. Yet despite such opposition academies enjoyed astounding growth in the first half of the nineteenth century. In 1850 the *American Journal of Education* reported over 6,000 academies in the states and territories, including over 800 in New York, over 500 in Pennsylvania, over 400 in Massachusetts, over 300 each in Kentucky and Virginia, and over 200 each in Connecticut, Georgia, Maryland, Missouri, North Carolina, Ohio, South Carolina, and Tennessee.[54] The federal census of 1850 reported 261,362 students enrolled in academies, a number that by 1860 had risen to 450,688. For comparison's sake, as late as 1890, when the population of the United States had risen to nearly three times its 1850 level, fewer than a quarter of a million students were enrolled in American public high schools.

One might conclude from this that provisions for secondary education shrank in the late nineteenth century, for even if we add all enrollments in private secondary schools in 1890 (many of which were still called academies) to the figure for public high school enrollments in the same year, we arrive at a modest total of 298,000 students, not much higher than the enrollment in academies in 1850. But the antebellum academies were not necessarily secondary schools. True, Jefferson had used the term "academy" to describe a class of schools between primary or "ward" schools and the state university, and this way of thinking persisted into the antebellum period. When in 1840 the North Carolina jurist and educational reformer Archibald Murphey drew up a proposal for public education, he too located academies between primary schools and the state university. The trouble in North Carolina and elsewhere was that primary schools were not always locally available, while universities tended to be distant and expensive. In practice, academies taught both the "common branches" and a rather dazzling assortment of higher subjects. For example, academies in antebellum Indiana taught some 230 subjects, ranging from zoology, aesthetics, and intellectual philosophy to filigree, tissue flowers, sociology, conchology, and archaeology. Academies also taught practical subjects like navigation, surveying, and bookkeeping; in the 1820s a class of "manual labor academies" that arose in the Northeast and then spread westward and southward taught agriculture as well as classical subjects. One academy in North Carolina compliantly promised to teach anything parents wanted taught.[55]

Chartered by the North Carolina legislature in 1802 and opened in 1805 in Louisburg, the seat of Franklin County in the north central part of the state, Franklin Academy illustrated several aspects of these institutions. As an incorporated academy, Franklin possessed a governing board, which conducted semiannual public examinations and which effectively advertised the school, but the practical burden of instruction fell on one individual, Matthew Dickinson, a Connecticut-born Yale graduate of the class of 1804. Arriving in North Carolina without property but with books and education, Dickinson quickly acquired "a very decent little estate," including a 300-acre farm, six slaves, and livestock. For this he depended directly on the profits from Franklin Academy, $1,200–1,500 a year, and indirectly on the liberal support neighborhood gentlemen afforded to literature. Edward Hooker, who graduated from Yale a year after Dickinson and who visited him in 1808, reported: "Dickinson says literature is much respected in these parts and literary men reverenced. . . . He says men of information and liberality respect literary men from principle and the rest of the community see in literary characters something so superior to themselves that they are impelled to homage."[56]

Dickinson's reputation as a man of literature brought him social cachet as well as financial rewards: when he visited Raleigh shortly after his arrival in the state, the governor invited him to dinner. Under Dickinson's guidance (he hired a Williams College graduate to assist him in

1807), Franklin Academy combined common and advanced education, and, as was true of most academies, tuition depended on whether one took the lower or higher branches. Ten dollars a year qualified a student to receive instruction in reading, writing, arithmetic, English grammar, geography, belles lettres, and rhetoric, while for an annual fee of sixteen dollars a student could study ethics, Latin, Greek, French, Italian, Hebrew, natural philosophy, navigation, surveying, astronomy, algebra, trigonometry, altimetry, longimetry, and mensuration. Hooker observed that Dickinson "has taught all branches taught in colleges, except Conic Sec[tio]ns." In effect, Franklin Academy afforded Dickinson an opportunity to transfer his Yale education to the North Carolina hill country. Not surprisingly, some students resorted to Franklin Academy as an alternative to, rather than preparation for, college. Hooker observed that Dickinson at times had as many as 90 students and of these, "20 or 30 or more [are] as large and old as himself."[57] At the time Hooker made this statement, Dickinson was 27 years old. Among these older students were twenty young men who transferred as a group from the University of North Carolina at Chapel Hill to Franklin Academy in protest against new disciplinary regulations at the former institution that required students to inform on each other.[58]

Their ambitious range of offerings inevitably exposed academies to the charge of superficiality. One critic of female academies in North Carolina complained in 1833 that "too much is attempted." The "whole encyclopedia of knowledge is embraced in the list of studies, and in the compass of two or three duodecimos; and the young lady, by the time she reaches her teens, is in danger of thinking herself grammarian, geographer, astronomer, chemist, botanist, musician, painter, and what not."[59] Such criticism was close to the mark. At the Oxford Female Academy in Granville County, North Carolina, a student who in 1840 paid $7.50 tuition could receive five months of instruction in "the Rudiments of English Education"; $10.00 purchased reading, writing, and arithmetic; $12.50, "Natural or Moral Philosophy, Chemistry, History, Rhetoric, Logic, Astronomy, Botany, Algebra, Geometry, etc." and $20.00 "Music, with use of Piano." In addition, the academy offered needlework, painting, and "Languages, etc.," "if desired." Subtract the needlework, painting, and music and add Latin, Greek, surveying, and bookkeeping, and the same could be said of North Carolina's male academies or of the male divisions of coeducational academies.[60]

Whether called "schools," "private schools," "classical schools," "literary and philosophical institutions," "collegiate institutions," or (in one North Carolina case) a "refined female college," these institutions undeniably offered superficial education. But their superficiality was merely the flip side of features that made them popular. Superficiality was less a function of the number of subjects they taught than of their short terms, three to five months, and small staffs, usually a master and a few assistants. These features kept the cost, including above all the opportunity cost, of attendance low. In contrast to colleges, academies did not have sequential curricula. Students (or their parents) paid for whatever subjects they wanted to study for a term. Nor were there set entering or leaving ages. Students attended at any age between five or six and their twenties.[61] These structural features facilitated the continuing education of autodidacts. When Silas Felton, a distant relative of Harvard's C. C. Felton, attended Leicester Academy in 1796, shortly before his twenty-first birthday, he confessed that he was "almost ignorant of the English grammar." But the publication of Franklin's autobiography in 1790 had already inspired him to embark on a program of self-education in his native Marlborough, Massachusetts. Felton's reputation for bookishness helped him to secure an appointment as the town's schoolmaster in 1795. He used his few months at the academy to master grammar, and upon returning to Marlborough he was rewarded with a salary raise.[62] Working as a sixteen-year-old apprentice cabinetmaker in Middlebury, Vermont, amid the furious election campaign of 1828, Stephen A. Douglas "formed a taste for reading, particularly political works, by being associated with a number of young men who spent their time and Sundays in reading and study." A year later he enrolled in an academy for a term, and then went on to his political career in Illinois.[63] Finally, as noted, most academies were either coeducational or exclusively female (the former was more common); thus in an age when colleges shunned female students, they provided young women with opportunities for education beyond the rudiments.

Not only did their short terms and lack of sequential curricula make academies accessible, but their very superficiality may have contributed to their popular appeal. Students in academies learned a little about a lot of subjects and studied whatever they chose. The elective system was built into the tuition structure of academies long before President Charles W. Eliot's widely publicized introduction of the system at Harvard. Some interesting parallels can be detected between the way in which academies were structured and the manner in which autodidacts taught themselves. Autodidacts and academy students alike acquired a smattering of many subjects and mixed the common branches, higher education, and practical skills in whatever combinations suited them. Self-education and academy education accorded with the notion that Americans had a penchant for shortcuts to knowledge, for a potentially useful "stock" of facts and for ideas that could be quickly grasped. In *Democracy in America* Alexis de Tocqueville identified something like this as a national trait. American democracy, he contended, bred individuals who "are full of an ambition at once aspiring and relaxed: they would fain succeed brilliantly and at once, but they would be dispensed from great efforts to attain success." American democrats were drawn to general ideas, "by aid of which they flatter themselves that they can figure very importantly at a small expense, and draw the attention of the public with very little trouble." Typically, Americans engaged in a "brief and inattentive investigation" of several objects, until "a common relation is thought to be detected." At that point, inquiry ceased, the objects were hastily arranged into a formula, and the investigator passed on to a new subject.[64]

Degree-granting colleges were by no means strangers to this propensity for the superficial. Consider the history of Canton College, which was founded in Fulton County, Illinois, in 1836 and incorporated in 1837 by the Illinois legislature. The legislature displayed some doubts about exactly what it was chartering, for it authorized the college's trustees to confer degrees (a distinctive feature of college or university status) in science, the "learned arts," and belles lettres only "as the ability of the said corporation shall increase, and they deem proper."[65] This was tentative language, but none of it seems to have affected the institution's first president, Rev. Gideon Perry, a Baptist minister who also practiced medicine and edited Canton's newspaper. One of the college's early professors, Wright Dewey, left a revealing portrait of Perry and the institution he headed. Perry, Dewey wrote to a friend in 1837, "will call it a college," might "lecture on Rhetoric & Intellectual & Moral Philosophy," and "even talks of Departments of Medicine, Law, and Divinity." Yet the "college" consisted of a single building with unfinished rooms and doubtful structural integrity (partly demolished by a windstorm in July 1843, it was never rebuilt). Its library, advertised as "choice," was not worth 50 dollars, according to Dewey. The institution claimed to offer French and the "Oriental Languages," but no one on the faculty or in the town knew enough to teach either. Dewey, who instructed three young men in Latin, was styled "Professor of the Learned Languages," a Perry-inspired conceit that Dewey viewed as a "burlesque on titles." Dewey aspired to nothing more than to make the school a prosperous academy, for "as a College it must be contemptible." Of course, Perry had grander ambitions. Although why he insisted on calling so feeble an institution a college remains a mystery, Dewey provided one hint: dazzled by titles, Perry "almost begged the degree of LL.D., from the Trustees of Canton College . . . & he is fond of the title, & uses it as much as if it were the free will offering of Oxford, Cambridge, or Gottingen."[66]

The aroma of pretension that Dewey detected in Perry could be sniffed in the air of Canton, which Dewey thought far too receptive of Perry's "puffing and blowing." Perry had attended Hamilton College in New York, but his "uncommon offhand eloquence" seemed to awe townspeople more than his literary and scientific attainments. In contrast, Dewey's understated manner led townspeople to deprecate him until they realized "that a man might know something and yet not proclaim it in the social circle, at the bedside of the sick, in public meeting, in the newspapers, or even the pulpit." In sum, the people of Canton initially kept their distance from Dewey because he did not display his learning; in contrast to the voluble and ever-active Perry, he was merely a scholar, or perhaps more accurately, merely a pedagogue.[67]

Canton College was a weak institution by any standard, but it is better classified as a less fit member of its species, the antebellum college, than as an extraordinary departure from the norm. Colin A. Burke's brief descriptions of many of the fourteen colleges that he has identified in operation in Illinois between 1800 and 1860 make them sound like Canton: McDonough College, for which "some evidence" exists that it operated as a college in the late 1830s and early 1840s and which had disappeared by 1845; Eureka College, which opened in the late 1850s and may or may not have been regarded as a college before 1860; and Monmouth College, "which may have conducted some college level work by the late 1850s."[68] Similar descriptions can be applied to most of the sixty or so Roman Catholic colleges established by the end of the Civil War.[69] In this context, the meaning of "college level" work is not always clear. Antebellum colleges widely introduced "English" or "partial" courses for students who did not want to take the classical languages and many had preparatory departments that were indistinguishable from academies. Like academies, colleges were ever stretching their curricula to lure students; before the Civil War some taught business, civil engineering, agriculture, and physical education.[70] The one clear distinction between academies and colleges was that colleges granted degrees upon completion of a prescribed course of study. This was by no means an idle or insubstantial distinction, for it enabled colleges to advertise themselves as unique institutions, and it facilitated their self-aggrandizement by opening professional schools, especially medical schools. But it was not a distinction that rested on a clear curricular difference.

Antebellum facilities for acquiring advanced education lacked the finely wrought architectural symmetry envisioned by republican educators in the eighteenth century, but they did make education beyond the elementary grades accessible. As long as institutions like Canton College could spread their wings, no one could plausibly accuse American colleges of elitism (although some did anyway). Although they did not offer degrees, academies offered a species of higher education on the principle of catch-as-catch-can. Like academies, mutual improvement societies afforded young men and women opportunities to acquire literary and scientific information. While all of these institutions allowed intermittent education, academies and mutual improvement societies were so structured as to encourage it. In turn, frequent interruptions of education were among the difficulties enumerated by Craik and hence compatible with self-education.

Does this mean that eminent Americans of the nineteenth century usually were self-educated? Inasmuch as self-education acquired a host of different and often conflicting connotations, it is idle to answer this question. What matters is that in the middle decades of the century the idea took root that the opportunities for self-education through a mixture of regular and irregular channels, for "popular education," were truly vast.[71]

In Britain during the late 1820s and early 1830s, Brougham and others, including the clergyman Thomas Dick, called for the diffusion of knowledge as a way to overcome religious bigotry and popular unrest; Brougham organized the SDUK on the assumption that existing facilities for formal and informal education were inadequate. In contrast, Americans were apt to argue that the spread of knowledge was either an accomplished fact or likely to become one in the immediate future. Even in the 1820s Joseph Story confidently described the diffusion of knowledge as already a leading feature of his age. Similarly, Channing asserted in "Self-Culture" that "in this country the mass of the people are distinguished by possessing the means of improvement, of self-culture, possessed nowhere else."[72] In his later address "On the Elevation of the Laboring Classes" he described the opportunities of laborers to attend lectures as "proof of a social revolution to which no bounds can be set, and from which too much cannot be hoped," and as "a repeal of the sentence of degradation passed by the ages on the mass of mankind."[73] Samuel P. Bates cited "the general diffusion of knowledge among us" as evidence of the wisdom of establishing common schools.[74]

These sentiments had roots in the eighteenth-century republican ideal that "the more generally knowledge is diffused among the substantial yeomanry, the more perfect will be the laws of a republic."[75] Noah Webster, who wrote these words in 1790, was quick to complain that knowledge had yet to be diffused in America, that "the *constitutions* are republican and the laws of education are *monarchical*." Despite the gap between the ideal and the reality in Webster's time, republican ideology encouraged the equation of political and educational achievement. The more secure republican political institutions appeared, the more generally diffused knowledge had become. Although the argument often spiraled into circularity—political democracy and technological wizardry were variously portrayed as causes and as effects of the diffusion of knowledge—the tendency of history seemed clear. Without ruling out additions to or refinements of the system, Samuel Bates unhesitatingly pronounced school reform a success and the diffusion of knowledge a fact. Each new library, lyceum, newspaper, and inexpensive book, every new schoolhouse, teachers' institute, and normal school sealed the victory.[76] It is revealing that where in Britain Brougham's SDUK saw itself as engaged in an uphill struggle to plant universal education in an inhospitable climate and aimed at out-of-school adults, the American Society for the Diffusion of Useful Knowledge, chartered by the New York state legislature in 1836, merely prepared and published books for common-school libraries.[77] In other words, even in the 1830s public-school supporters in New York were sufficiently confident of the success of universal education to assign the burden of diffusing knowledge to the schools. In Massachusetts Horace Mann reached the same conclusion and promoted common-school libraries as the surest way to expand the reading public.[78]

This still left room for social and public libraries and for lyceum lectures as means of acquiring culture for the out-of-school population. The popularity of lyceum lectures reinforced the confidence of educators in the triumph of the diffusion of knowledge. Typically, Samuel Bates described the ripple effect of lyceum lectures; because the speaker's voice tones and gestures affected the listener's emotions as well as mind, "the influence which one carefully-prepared lecture, pronounced by a bold, fearless orator may produce, is incalculable. It may set in motion a train of thoughts, which will modify or change the tone of life, not only of a single individual, but of a whole audience."[79]

Bates's reference to the contingent or accidental effect of random exposure to a lecture (or book or newspaper) conflicted only superficially with the school reformers' penchant for predictable outcomes, for rightly supervised common schools could be relied on to implant "character," the moral gyroscope that guided each individual through life, and a receptivity to new knowledge. Most antebellum educators approximated Horace Mann's belief in the fundamental unity of all men. As one educator wrote, "all minds have sufficient strengths to learn the highest truth."[80] Although no consensus applied this proposition to women or blacks, the very fact that female education was becoming increasingly controversial reinforced the agreement of educators on the inherent intellectual equality of white males. The majority of educators opposed full educational equality for women, but by mid-century they at least had to argue their position. In turn, it was implausible for them to reject equality for women on grounds that females lacked the same mental capacity as men and in the next breath affirm that men varied widely in inherent mental ability. In combination with widespread belief in the irresistible diffusion of knowledge, the doctrine of inherent mental equality left only one way to account for human differences in mental achievement: some individuals simply lacked the will to exploit the boundless opportunities at their feet.

Self-Education as Myth and Reality

In *Applied Sociology* (1906), Lester Frank Ward would attack this configuration of nineteenth-century beliefs and specifically debunk the wide availability of educational opportunities through informal channels. Ward was in a position to know, for "irregular education"—a pastiche of private reading, laborious self-instruction in languages, and two brief spins at an academy—constituted his own early education. Ward contended that this education on the irregular plan was shamefully inefficient and that those who puffed themselves as "self-educated," including his antagonist Herbert Spencer, had benefited from influential personal connections.[81] To Ward, the nineteenth-century celebration of the "self-taught" individual not only disguised the social advantages possessed by famous autodidacts, but also subtly excused governments from supporting more extensive provisions for formal education.

Ward's blast at self-education inspired research that undermined many of the defenses long adduced on behalf of irregular education and self-instruction.[82] Promulgated by journalists, success writers, biographers, and educators, however, belief in the efficacy of education through informal channels persisted long after the Civil War. For example, David Starr Jordan's biographical directory, *Leading American Men of Science* (1910), was a cornucopia of nineteenth-century concepts about the potency of self-education.[83] Contributors to Jordan's volume, most of whom were university graduates, subordinated the role of formal education in the lives of their subjects and instead tried to show how the single chance reading of a book or article had thrust an individual into a course of improvement that led to scientific eminence. John M. Coulter proclaimed that Asa Gray, who was a graduate of a medical school, was "one of those strong men, full of initiative, who develop in spite of lack of opportunities and contrary to the most approved principles of pedagogy." Just as Coulter played down Gray's formal education to magnify the importance of his chance reading of an article on botany, so Simon Newcomb made light of Joseph Henry's formal education at Albany Academy and emphasized instead Henry's chance reading at the age of sixteen of a book of scientific lectures.[84]

It is not difficult to discredit this preoccupation with self-instruction and random educational influences. A few years before the publication of Jordan's book, James McKeen Cattell, the head of Columbia University's psychology department, started to publish his own research into the backgrounds of American scientists, which established conclusively that scientific eminence had not been uniformly distributed throughout the nation, as one might expect had it depended mainly on chance encounters with books and plucky self-education, but was correlated with proximity to urban places and with opportunities for formal education.[85] For example, Joseph Henry certainly benefited from the fact that he grew up in Albany, in 1820 the ninth largest city in the United States. The presence of Union College in nearby Schenectady and an academy in Albany attracted those with scientific interests to the area, all to Henry's advantage.[86]

Yet although biographers who stressed their subjects' debt to self-instruction did indulge in a degree of myth-making, their descriptions of the process by which individuals acquired advanced education contained a fair amount of accuracy. True, the proportion of American scientists who by a strict standard can be classed as self-educated declined in the nineteenth century. Clark A. Elliott's *Biographical Dictionary of American Science* puts the proportion of self-taught scientists at 9.9 percent for those born before 1776, 2.2 percent for those born between 1776 and 1815, and 1.7 percent for those born from 1816 through 1867.[87] Elliott equates self-education with those who lacked formal education beyond the elementary level. It was still possible for such individuals to make a mark in antebellum America; the founder and first president of the American Association for the Advancement of Science, the meteorologist William Redfield, passed his youth as a saddler's apprentice in Connecticut and supplemented his meager formal schooling by joining a village debating society and by reading books loaned to him by a friendly physician.[88] More importantly, many of those formally educated in academies or colleges were essentially self-educated in science. For example, as an undergraduate at Yale, Benjamin Silliman, Sr., studied a classical curriculum and in his spare time read history and English literature. He then prepared for the legal profession, in 1802 was admitted to the Connecticut bar, and was immediately appointed Yale's first professor of chemistry and natural history. *After* his appointment Silliman began to study science seriously by attending medical lectures at the University of Pennsylvania, studying in the private laboratory of the Philadelphia chemist and physicist Robert Hare, and visiting leading scientific men in Britain. Similarly, Joseph Henry, on indicating in 1832 that he would accept a professorship at Princeton were it offered, described himself as "principally self-educated," although he had attended Albany Academy in New York.[89] Henry's claim was at least plausible, for he did not commence his studies at Albany Academy until he was 22, and his education there was frequently interrupted by his need to earn money.

Self-education in science took many forms besides these examples. One finds college or medical graduates who pursued fields like ichthyology, conchology, and ornithology, which were not taught in colleges or medical schools, medical graduates who taught themselves physics and made their mark in that field, college graduates who became lawyers or businessmen before turning to fields like mineralogy. The tendency of men to enter science after trying other fields continued after 1815. William Ferrel, for example, was a college graduate who is remembered as the most important figure after Laplace in the field of geophysical fluid dynamics. Yet he did not learn that the planets moved in elliptical orbits nor that there was a law of gravitation until he was 20, and he did not enter college until he was 22. He began serious scientific self-instruction at 33, wrote his first paper at 36, and first lived in a city (Nashville) at 37.[90] J. M. Gilliss, the astronomer, studied for a year at the University of Virginia, but not until he was 24. Between the ages of 15 and 23 he worked as a seaman. After leaving the University of Virginia he obtained a position with the United States Navy's Department of Charts and Instruments in Washington, and it was there that his study of astronomy commenced.[91] By the measure of college attendance, these men were not self-educated, but they hardly can be said to have moved along smooth career tracks. Much the same can be said of Henry Rowe Schoolcraft, one of the foremost ethnologists of the nineteenth century. Born in 1793 in Guilderland, New York, Schoolcraft was the son of a local glass manufacturer and grew up in the first two-story house built in Guilderland. His father bought him books in order to encourage young Schoolcraft's scientific interests. These were enough to spark a keen interest in self-improvement, and at the age of fifteen Schoolcraft started a mutual improvement club for Guilderland's youth. He prepared for Union College, but never attended. Rather, he followed his father in the glassmaking business in New York and Vermont. While in Vermont he taught himself Hebrew and German from lexicons and grammars and studied mineralogy, a field with obvious relevance to glassmaking, as a non-degree student at Middlebury College. It was only after he had abandoned glassmaking that he began to investigate ethnology. Claiming that Schoolcraft had "little means and few advantages," a memorialist described Schoolcraft as "self-dependent, self-acting, and self-taught."[92]

None of this changes the fact that the relationship between scientific eminence and formal educational attainment was strong in the nineteenth century. Of Elliott's scientists born from 1776 through 1815, 73.1 percent attended either a college or a medical school. In fact, this percentage differs little from that for scientists born before 1776: 74.2 percent. The decline in the proportion of self-educated scientists (those without formal education beyond elementary school) between the two periods was paralleled by an increase in the proportion attending academies, but college or medical school attendance held steady.[93] Nothing more maddened Lester Frank Ward, who read all of the collections of biographies he could lay his hands on, than the persistence of the belief "that one is prepared to pursue any branch of sciences with nothing but the rudiments of an education."[94] Yet the notions about scientific achievement, indeed achievement of any sort, that so exasperated Ward cannot be traced merely to the self-puffery of self-made men. Rather, they were widely entertained among nineteenth-century educators who saw the association of the pursuit of knowledge with "difficulties" as a plausible rejoinder to critics of liberal education.

Conclusion

Rather than upholding the quest for knowledge as a mark of genteel status, antebellum educators defended liberal education against an often skeptical public by emphasizing how the difficulties surrounding its pursuit would contribute to the formation of character. For any number of reasons, this way of thinking had the ring of plausibility. Americans who sought liberal education—those in academies and colleges as well as in literary societies—usually did so in the face of interruptions, which were occasioned partly by their need to earn money and partly by their penchant for the eclectic and intermittent sampling of many subjects. Inasmuch as even college and medical-school graduates engaged extensively in self-instruction, it was plausible for educators to conclude that anyone possessed of sufficient determination could acquire a liberal education, that self-education would place knowledge within the grasp of all.

In time, this way of thinking would attract critics like Lester Frank Ward, who believed not only that it exaggerated the possibilities of self-education but that it nurtured the complacent conclusion that liberal education had already been democratized. It is possible to detect another way in which their belief in the nearly limitless scope of self-education induced a kind of complacency among nineteenth-century educators. Persuaded that any enterprise so democratic in its tendency as the pursuit of knowledge had also to be useful, these educators rarely examined the practical benefits that knowledge was supposed to yield. Between 1820 and 1860 the limits of practicality would become especially evident to those who sought to popularize the very type of knowledge, science, that eighteenth-century philosophers had believed to be most useful.

Chapter 4

"The Liberal and Practical Education of the Industrial Classes"

In seeking to fashion an educational system suitable to a republic, Benjamin Rush and Noah Webster had followed Franklin's contention that education could be both liberal and useful. For every principle or law there existed a corresponding application or "art." Just as Franklin had proposed an academy to equip a youth for any trade or profession, Rush urged collegians to study the principles of commerce. Several features of this ideal, Useful Knowledge, made it attractive to republicans. It promised to bind social ranks in shared knowledge without leveling social distinctions; it would multiply inventions and conveniences, thereby contributing to the sum of human happiness; and it would trim liberal education of any exclusive association with ease or aristocracy. In essence, Useful Knowledge would reconcile genteel culture with republican principles.

This quest for Useful Knowledge persisted into the nineteenth century. In 1862 Congress passed the Morrill, or Land-Grant College, Act, which authorized the application of proceeds from the sale of public lands to colleges that would engage in "the liberal and practical education of the industrial classes in the several pursuits and professions of life."[1] This language, seemingly ambiguous in retrospect (were the land-grant colleges to teach some subjects that were liberal and others practical, or subjects simultaneously liberal and practical?), struck contemporaries as no more than a concise statement of their belief that higher knowledge, especially knowledge of science, would benefit mechanics and farmers. The framers of the Morrill Act hoped to attract the average children of average farmers and artisans into congenial institutions of higher education, and they drew on widely embraced educational and political values, including Baconianism, nationalism, and egalitarianism. Their ideal rarely encountered articulate challenge in the three decades before the Civil War, and in time the Morrill Act would become a potent symbol for those who sought to extend higher education to out-of-school adults. Even at its passage it had the character of a symbolic gesture, a dramatic commitment to opening higher education to the common people.

Yet to conclude from all of this that the Morrill Act developed smoothly from eighteenth-century ideals would miss the mark. Eighteenth-century philosophers were prone to define the domain of Useful Knowledge very broadly. For example, Jefferson made a case for the utility of Anglo-Saxon. When pressed for examples of useless knowledge, they usually cited metaphysics, a word that conjured up images of overheated speculation about the attributes of God, and the dead languages, but they did not even consistently exclude the latter from the domain of utility. For example, Benjamin Rush thought that Latin and Greek might be useful if boys were only taught to read, rather than to speak and write, these languages. In retrospect, it is easy to see that their ideal of utility was shaped by their social status as gentlemen who, in discharging the varied duties of their station, would have occasion to draw on many kinds of knowledge, and whose intellectual contacts with their social inferiors were mainly confined to conversations with philosophical mechanics.

In contrast, nineteenth-century proponents of Useful Knowledge were inclined to question the value of the knowledge of the educated, came close to equating utility with productivity, betrayed a consistent suspicion of "nonproducers"—lawyers, merchants, and speculators—and routinely lashed out at dark conspiracies allegedly aimed at the educational disfranchisement of the "industrial classes" by the infiltration of genteel subjects, those without any apparent relationship to increased productivity, into the curriculum. In contrast to the republican educators, who had viewed themselves as harbingers of progressive historical developments, in the age of Jacksonian democracy supporters of Useful Knowledge saw themselves as diehards fighting a necessary but losing struggle against the belletrists who would subordinate utility to polish and ornament.

Polish and ornament, of course, had been the staples of both the popular literary societies and colleges that proliferated in the early nineteenth century. By effectively removing the taint of leisure and aristocracy, the idea of pursuing knowledge "under difficulties" reconciled literary endeavors with democratic values. But this reconciliation failed to satisfy the antebellum proponents of Useful Knowledge, an ideal that, for all its malleability, had always stressed making science relevant to the work of artisans and farmers. In the 1820s and 1830s, this objective acquired a new urgency. Antebellum supporters of Useful Knowledge saw everywhere evidence of the nation's loosening from its republican moorings:

the speculative mania, the scramble for wealth, and the derision of honest manual work. In contrast to the republican educators of the late eighteenth century, who expected that academies and colleges would incorporate Useful Knowledge, they despaired of existing educational institutions, which appeared to be irretrievably in the grip of nonproducers. To restore dignity to work, especially the work of artisans and farmers, antebellum proponents of Useful Knowledge initially rested their hopes on an assortment of agricultural improvement societies and mechanics' institutes that would diffuse science among working adults. They turned to the idea of land-grant colleges for the children of the "industrial classes" only after experiencing a succession of frustrations in their attempts to enlist ordinary farmers and mechanics in the cause of Useful Knowledge.

The Useful Arts

Tortuous to an extreme, the road that led to the Morrill Act began with attempts to extend the influence of Useful Knowledge within the framework of eighteenth-century assumptions about social rank. In the second half of the eighteenth century, commerce, manufacture, and agriculture were thought of as "arts" in the sense that their practice required the skilled application of principles derived from the reasoned investigation of nature. Useful Knowledge did not connote tricks of the trade or chips of information pertinent to some manual or commercial activity. Rather, it referred to a body of general ideas acquired by investigation and applied to any number of situations. Like rays of the sun, science could shed light on all human activities: agriculture, manufactures, commerce, and even the fine or "polite" arts. By the same token, those in possession of scientific knowledge saw themselves as incomparably better positioned to advance the "arts" than "mere mechanicks" or "mere empiricks," the "baser sort" whose trade knowledge amounted to nothing more than tricks, "mysteries," or knacks that by definition could never be transferred from one sphere of activity to another.

Persuaded that scientific principles could be applied broadly, the educated few of the late eighteenth century established two learned societies, the American Philosophical Society (1743) and the American Academy of Arts and Sciences (1780), and a much larger number of so-called useful arts societies. The latter resembled learned societies but with comparatively more emphasis on utilitarian applications.[2] Brooke Hindle has traced this variant of the learned society to the organization usually known as the Society of Arts. Founded in London in 1754 by a Northampton drawing master named William Shipley, this society became a model for several American counterparts. Shipley himself admired Franklin and corresponded with the Charleston naturalist Alexander Garden on ways to encourage the colonial production of wine, hemp, cotton, flax, and potash. Organizations with the same general goals as the Society of Arts arose in Charleston, Virginia, and Boston during the imperial crisis of the 1760s and 1770s. As colonists adopted the tactic of nonimportation, they looked for ways to stimulate home production. Thus the "Society for the Promotion of Arts, Agriculture, and Oeconomy," founded in New York in 1764, responded explicitly to "the present deplorable State of our Trade" and, in keeping with the principle of nonimportation, announced its objectives as to "advance husbandry, promote manufactures, and suppress luxury."[3]

Societies devoted to the advance of the useful arts continued to spread after the Revolution, and like their predecessors, they were responses to specific economic conditions as much as reflections of the general idea that scientific knowledge would advance the arts. Among these were the New York Society for Promoting Useful Knowledge (1785), the New York Manufacturing Society (1789), and the New York Society for the Promotion of Agriculture, Arts, and Manufactures (1791). The overlapping titles of these societies reveal their main goal: to stimulate American production in shops and on farms and thereby to relieve dependence on Europe, and especially Britain, at a time of declining staple production and the new nation's tenuous position in international trade.

While the promoters of these organizations stressed their public benefits, they saw no compelling need to enlist broad popular participation in their activities. Useful arts societies offered the educated an opportunity to demonstrate the superior utility of their knowledge to that of artisans who understood only the tricks and mysteries of their trades. Gentlemen met in useful arts societies to read papers to each other, to publish occasional transactions, to solicit communications through the press, and to award premiums for promising experiments. To the extent that they reached out to the public, it was to encourage those enlightened people who happened to fall outside their circle of acquaintances. Useful arts societies depended on leaders capable of financing awards, such as silver plate, and whose names would command recognition outside the small circle of members. Governor George Clinton of New York was elected president of the New York Society for Promoting Useful Knowledge in 1785, while the state's chancellor, Robert R. Livingston, headed the New York Society for the Promotion of Agriculture, Arts, and Manufactures.[4] As befitted the close connections between the professions and public life in the late eighteenth century, prominent businessmen and leading physicians such as New York's Drs. Samuel Bard and Samuel Latham Mitchill also took an active part in useful arts societies. Whether public officials, businessmen, or professionals, the leaders of useful arts societies often moved freely among such organizations. For example, when the New York Society for Promoting Useful Knowledge became defunct at the end of the 1780s, Bard transferred his energies to the Society for the Promotion of Agriculture, Arts, and Manufactures. Where possible, they also joined learned societies. More than half of the charter members of the Philadelphia Society for the Promotion of Agriculture and Agricultural Reform also belonged to the American Philosophical Society.[5]

As a rule, neither the leaders nor the members of useful arts societies came from the ranks of artisans or active farmers. For example, of 26 original members of the Massachusetts Society for Promoting Agriculture (1792), only two were active farmers.[6] Typically, the agriculturalists who became active in useful arts societies were large landowners in search of alternative crops.[7] Yet allowing for the close ties in the minds of contemporaries between the cultivation of science and economic development, useful arts societies displayed a keener regard for economic development than for science as such, and they were far more numerous than the learned societies—the American Philosophical Society and the American Academy of Arts and Sciences—in which these emphases tended to be reversed. Comparatively utilitarian in their objectives and gripped by anxiety that the survival of the republic depended on finding new staples and fabricated products, the public officials, landowners, businessmen, and professionals of the useful arts societies found themselves compelled by the logic of their situation, rather than by any abstract regard for democratic education, to reach out to ever-widening circles of the public. Thus there developed a kind of progression in these societies from reading papers to soliciting communications to publishing transactions and awarding premiums. And when these devices failed to produce the desired results, it was inevitable that someone would hit upon the idea of directly appealing to practical farmers to engage in experiments.

This progression did not lead automatically to the conclusion that gentry should enlist an undifferentiated public in the cause of improvement. As late as 1823 the officers of the Massachusetts Society for Promoting Agriculture retorted to critics of their inclusion of scientific articles in the society's periodical that "knowledge must first be communicated to [educated men] and from these it will reach their less informed neighbors."[8] Yet by the 1820s this was a declining view, in large measure because of the promotional genius of Elkanah Watson, a New England businessman with far-flung entrepreneurial interests and a sentimental attachment to *"rural felicity."* This attachment induced Watson to purchase an estate in Pittsfield, Massachusetts, in 1807 and to give farming a try. But Watson, who for twenty years had longed for the pastoral retreat of husbandry, quickly found that years of city living had left him unsuited to practical farming. As he described it, "to fill up the void in an active mind" he was led to "the idea of an Agricultural Society on a plan different from all others."[9] Watson's plan was to introduce fairs to the activities of agricultural societies. In 1810 he initiated the first of the so-called Berkshire fairs, which were marked by livestock displays, orations, singing, and parades with floats containing spinning jennys and other machines. Watson also tried to interest women in agricultural improvement and home industry by staging balls and offering premiums for domestic manufactures. All of this, he hoped, would make agricultural societies popular, for "some éclat was necessary . . . so as to meet the feelings of every class of the community."[10]

Watson not only introduced new gimmicks to reach the public but also brought a new psychology to the diffusion of knowledge. Whereas his predecessors in the useful arts tradition expected benefits more or less to diffuse themselves, Watson elevated the importance of publicity. Indeed, publicity was everything for Watson; he was sure that farmers would turn naturally to books and experiments once their interest had been pricked by exhibits. Although Watson first conceived the idea of fairs before Jefferson's Embargo Act was passed at the end of 1807, the embargo's severe impact gave Watson's innovation relevance to New England's economic predicament. Watson had close ties to wool manufacturers and his favorite livestock species was the merino sheep. The compatibility of fairs with New England's quest for self-sufficiency in the pre-war and war years contributed to the appeal of fairs, and when Watson moved to New York in 1816 he carried the idea with him. Influenced by Governor De Witt Clinton, the New York legislature provided an annual fund of $10,000 to stimulate a program of premiums for the fairs held by county agricultural societies of the sort that Watson had encouraged in Massachusetts.[11]

The spread of agricultural societies on the Berkshire model stimulated the emergence of the agricultural press, especially in the 1820s, when such magazines as the *Cultivator*, the *Genessee Farmer*, and the *American Agriculturalist* sprang up to champion the application of science to agriculture.[12] By raising at least the prospect of regional crop specialization, improvements in transportation in the 1820s, symbolized by the completion of the Erie Canal in 1825, spurred interest in agricultural experimentation within a widening circle of journalists, professional men with an avocational interest in farming, and progressive farmers. For any number of reasons, most struggling farmers remained outside the circle. They were unaccustomed to obtaining ideas or information from print; no widely applicable body of principles was yet in existence; experiments were costly as well as doubtful; and the effects of the transportation revolution were not widely felt before 1830.[13] Improvement continued to be a pastime of the wealthy and educated, and some of the societies established after the War of 1812 seem more reminiscent of the older kind of useful arts society than of Watson's popular societies. For example, in 1818 a group of

gentlemen "gardeners" in New York City launched the New-York Horticultural Society and appointed the ubiquitous Samuel Latham Mitchill to
its "professorship" of botany and vegetable philosophy. Yet even this society saw fit to publish a periodical, the *New York Farmer*.

In addition, even in its embryonic stages the transportation revolution
forced gentlemen into contacts with struggling merchants and common
workmen. For example, Jesse Hawley, who first published a plan for a
canal "from the foot of Lake Erie into the Mohawk," was a merchant in
Geneva, New York, engaged in the trade of forwarding flour to the New
York City market. Forced to pay higher transportation charges when the
Mohawk River fell in the summer, Hawley in 1805 conceived the idea of
connecting Lake Erie, the Mohawk, and the Hudson by canal. His plans
were interrupted by his imprisonment for debt (caused by the failure of his
business partner), but he used his confinement to publicize the canal project through newspaper articles.[14] The canal project tossed together men
like Hawley, who possessed only a country school education, carpenters,
who suddenly had to learn how to design and build aqueducts, Elkanah
Watson, who became a valuable promoter of the canal, and polished aristocrats like the Harvard-educated Stephen Van Rensselaer and New York
City's Mayor De Witt Clinton, whose avocation was natural history.[15]
Clinton's own service on the canal commission carried him, in company
with Van Rensselaer and other public officials, on a journey through western New York in the summer of 1810. Travel conditions were wretched—
flies and mosquitoes everywhere and little protection from storms—but
Clinton found time to continue his botanical investigations, recorded his
theories about the earth's development in his commonplace book, and all
the while wrestled with the practical problems raised by the canal project.

The career of Amos Eaton illustrates how the lure of internal improvements attracted men of science as well as public officials into practical tasks. After graduation from Williams College, Eaton became a lawyer, a vocational choice that was interrupted ignominiously when in 1810
he was convicted of forgery while practicing law and acting as a land agent
in Catskill, New York. After spending four years in jail, Eaton studied science under Yale's Benjamin Silliman, Sr., for two years, taught briefly at
Williams, and became a lecturer on botany and geology in schools and
towns throughout the Northeast. A self-described "scientific peddlar," he
wrote textbooks on geology and botany and had a major influence on Almira Hart Lincoln Phelps, the sister of Emma Willard. Although Eaton
did not serve on the canal commission, he performed a geological survey
for it and bombarded it with advice on the best way to prevent the canal's
banks from washing (plant crabgrass on them). In 1826, a year after the
opening of the canal, Eaton took a party of students, including Asa Fitch
(who would become the state's entomologist) and De Witt Clinton's son

George, on a tour of the canal, a virtual traveling school of science. At each stop, notes Ronald E. Shaw, "Eaton lectured, the students studied rock formations, and the party took note of the progress of settlement."[16] The eighteen-year-old Fitch marveled at the conclusion: "How far I have been! What new ideas I have received! and how greatly my mind has been improved!" Eaton would conduct a second tour in 1830 of what by then was known as the "Rensselaer School Flotilla."[17]

Over 350 miles long, much longer in fact than any other canal in the western world, the Erie Canal boggled the minds of contemporaries (even Jefferson, who thought canals "little short of madness"), spurred interregional economic development, and inspired a host of imitations. The building of the canal propelled public officials and cultivators of science beyond the narrow perimeters of contact with the public sanctioned by eighteenth-century useful arts societies, and in a general way complemented Elkanah Watson's Berkshire societies by encouraging popular education in the relationship between work and knowledge. The canal project also underscored the meager provisions in the United States for the formal training of engineers and directly led to the opening in 1824 of the Rensselaer School (later the Rensselaer Institute and still later Rensselaer Polytechnic Institute). The school was the brainchild of Stephen Van Rensselaer, who quickly appointed Amos Eaton to its faculty—at first, Eaton *was* the faculty. Van Rensselaer envisioned an institution for "the application of science to the common purposes of life."[18] Consistent with his advanced pedagogical belief that the way to teach science was to start with practical experiments, Van Rensselaer wrote into the institute's bylaws provisions for licensing farms and shops in the Troy, New York, area "as places of the scholastic exercise for students, where the application of the sciences may be most conveniently taught."[19]

Focusing the energy of scholarly gentlemen, ambitious merchants, cultivators of science, and skilled workmen in a common cause, the transportation revolution contributed to the breakdown of the social restrictiveness and theoretical bent of the eighteenth-century useful arts societies. The emergence of the textile industry had much the same effect. Just as Francis Cabot Lowell had relied on a master mechanic to construct the power loom whose details he had memorized on a visit to England, so too the spread of cotton textile manufacture in the 1820s stimulated closer contacts between industrial capitalists and "mechanicians" (or machinists). Machinists might be drawn from any of a number of traditional crafts, including carpentry and iron working, but their relationship to industrial capitalists differed fundamentally from the old-fashioned tie between "mechanics" and their patrons. In the late 1700s and early 1800s, the term mechanic applied to a skilled workman who owned his own tools and who was either self-employed or a wage-earning journeyman. Mechanics made articles for sale to individuals who displayed little curiosity about their trade "secrets," who cared not how a clock was made as long as it kept time. In contrast, the early textile manufacturers, who often stumbled into the business by the accidents of inheritance or financial settlement and who initially knew little of machines, would give anything to find a competent machinist.[20] Thus the ties between capitalists and machinists grew close in the textile manufacture. Some manufacturers, such as John Smith Phillips and John P. Crozer in the factory village of Rockdale in southeastern Pennsylvania, learned enough about their machines to suggest improvements that machinists could then effect.[21]

Mechanics' Institutes

Permeated by the gospel of improvement—self-improvement, mutual improvement, and industrial improvement—the early factory villages were crucibles of the idea that scientific knowledge would benefit mechanics while an understanding of machines would work to the advantage of entrepreneurs. This idea had a potent impact on the emergence in the 1820s of the so-called mechanics' institutes. Mechanics' institutes blended features of the eighteenth- and early-nineteenth-century useful arts societies, especially those like the Alexandria [Virginia] Society for the Promotion of Useful Knowledge (1787) and the New England Association of Inventors and Patrons of Useful Arts (1807) that were oriented toward invention and manufacturing rather than agriculture, with features of such benevolent or mutual aid associations for master craftsmen as the General Society of Mechanics and Tradesmen of the City of New York (1785) and the Massachusetts Charitable Mechanics' Association (1795).[22] Mechanics' institutes borrowed invention and manufacturing improvement from the useful arts tradition and copied the mutual aid societies' enlistment of mechanics. Without necessarily abandoning mutual aid as an objective, they elevated the importance of mutual improvement and public outreach through their sponsorship of schools, lectures, libraries, and exhibits.

In some instances, existing mechanics' benevolent associations simply took on new functions after 1820. For example, in 1820 the General Society of Mechanics and Tradesmen of the City of New York organized a school for the children of members and a library for apprentices. Alternatively, an established mechanics' association might father a new one; established in 1829, the Portland Mechanics' Lyceum owed much to the patronage of the Maine Charitable Mechanics' Association.[23] In still other instances, wealthy and publicly spirited businessmen organized library companies in order to provide reading rooms and book collections for apprentices.[24] The Apprentices' Library of Philadelphia was the offspring of a library company rather than a mechanics' association. The moving spirits of the company, which was incorporated in 1821, included a prominent bookseller, a shoe manufacturer, a flour merchant, and an apothecary who belonged to the American Philosophical Society. All of these men were active in other Pennsylvania benevolent institutions, including the Philadelphia House of Refuge and the Pennsylvania Institution for the Deaf and Dumb.[25] Partly a response to the growing number of young men who flocked into cities in the 1820s, the founding of apprentices' libraries, most of which were quickly opened to those over the age of 21, became an appropriate charitable activity in the 1820s. Of sixteen such libraries recorded in an 1876 survey, nine were established in the single decade of the 1820s.[26] Finally, amid the general enthusiasm for mutual improvement societies and lyceums scores of new mechanics' associations were founded in the 1820s and 1830s, including the famed Franklin Institute in Philadelphia and the Maryland Institute for the Promotion of the Mechanic Arts in Baltimore. By the early 1830s, Boston was virtually bursting with mutual improvement societies, some of which were aimed directly at mechanics: the Boston Mechanics' Institution, the Boston Mechanics' Lyceum, and the Mechanic Apprentices Library Association.[27] Mechanics' institutes also spread into the West; by the 1840s Iowa contained institutes in Dubuque, Mount Pleasant, Muscatine, and Burlington.[28]

With their libraries, reading rooms, lectures, and classes, institutes served a variety of practical functions. They offered artisans and small traders congenial places to socialize, and some allowed younger members to bring their girlfriends to lectures and in some cases to have the latter's compositions read at meetings.[29] They invariably advocated temperance on grounds that were succinctly summarized by the Philadelphia workingmen's leader Stephen Simpson: "a reading and intellectual people have never been known to be *sottish*."[30] By the 1830s they were distinguished by their strident emphasis on the diffusion of scientific knowledge as well.

Although mechanics' institutes possessed American roots, part of their inspiration sprang from Britain, where in 1799 a young medical-school graduate of the University of Edinburgh, George Birkbeck, had begun to offer free lectures to Glasgow mechanics on the principles of chemistry. Birkbeck moved to London a few years later to take up the practice of medicine, but others continued his work in Glasgow, and in 1823 the Glasgow Mechanics' Institute was formally established. This became, in turn, the model for the London Mechanics' Institute, which began activities in 1824. The latter's original plan stipulated that two-thirds of the governing board were to be "working men," defined as those who made their living with their hands and who did not employ journeymen. Yet as was true of many other mechanics' institutes, the direction of the London institute fell to those several social ranks above mechanics. Birkbeck, who had never lost his interest in the education of artisans, served as the institute's "perpetual president." The institute also became the darling of middle-class reformers such as the liberal Whig politician Henry Brougham and the Benthamite James Mill, and their allies in the working-class intelligentsia, including the Charing Cross tailor Francis Place. Brougham, an indefatigable reformer whose interests included the abolition of the slave trade and Catholic emancipation, was profoundly interested in expanding the educational opportunities of the underprivileged by government support for education, the establishment of practical universities (he was among the founders of the University of London), infant schools, adult institutes, and the dissemination of inexpensive books and magazines.[31] The last mentioned of Brougham's causes took shape in 1826 with the inauguration of the Society for the Diffusion of Useful Knowledge (SDUK).[32]

Americans were familiar with Birkbeck and Brougham, borrowed some of their nomenclature by establishing societies for the diffusion of useful knowledge, and read books spun off from the British movement, including George L. Craik's *The Pursuit of Knowledge Under Difficulties.* Yet while the British institutes reinforced the activities of Americans, the movement for institutes arose more or less simultaneously in the two countries. The Quaker promoter of science, John Griscom, one of the founders of the New York Mechanic and Scientific Institute (1822), was an American equivalent of Birkbeck. The New York Mechanic and Scientific Institute may have been a model for the Glasgow Mechanics' Institute, which was certainly a model for the London Mechanics' Institute. Brougham, active in the latter, was familiar with Franklin's career and followed Franklin in equating Useful Knowledge with explanations of what the SDUK's prospectus called "the fundamental principles of some branch of science, their proofs and illustrations, their applications of practical use to the explanations of facts and appearances."[33]

The conviction that knowledge of science would make artisans more inventive was the most potent and widespread intellectual impulse behind the institutes. It united conservatives such as the Massachusetts Whig Edward Everett, who habitually lectured mechanics' associations on how the forests and quarries were bursting with "elemental principles and hidden arts and unseen adaptations to human comfort," and Jacksonian Democrats like the New York City lawyer Gulian C. Verplanck, who assured the Mechanics' Institute of New York in 1833 that even the slightest accession to natural knowledge would enhance the inventiveness of mechanics.[34] For a brief period at the end of the 1820s and in the early 1830s, it linked the British and American institutes in a common cause that was embodied in Timothy Claxton, a self-instructed London artisan who tirelessly promoted the idea of mechanics' associations in each nation.

As an apprentice whitesmith and journeyman in a London machine shop, Claxton had studied mathematics and drawing on his own, and he had constructed various mechanical contrivances. A series of lectures on chemistry and natural philosophy that he had attended in 1815 opened his eyes to the pleasures of science, and he applied for membership in a philosophical society. Rejected because he was merely a mechanic, Claxton founded a short-lived philosophical society for mechanics known as the Mechanical Institution, and then in the early 1820s journeyed to Russia to install gas lighting in a plant in St. Petersburg. By the mid-1820s he was in the United States in search of opportunity. After finding employment in a machine shop in a Methuen, Massachusetts, cotton factory, where he breathed scientific interest into a local literary society, Claxton moved to Boston in 1826 and soon established the Boston Mechanics' Institution.[35] Three years later he met Josiah Holbrook, who was in Boston to advance his ideas for practical scientific instruction. Together they founded the Boston Lyceum in 1829, and a few years later the two men combined to organize a similar institution, but one more clearly aimed at artisans, the Boston Mechanics' Lyceum.[36]

The alliance between Claxton and Holbrook was based partly on business and partly on ideology. By trade Claxton had become a maker of mechanical instruments at a time when Holbrook was searching for simple instruments with which to teach science in schools and lyceums. With Holbrook's encouragement, Claxton soon began to fabricate a range of instruments to teach science, including an extremely popular and profitable air pump. Like his fellow Yale alumnus Eli Whitney, Holbrook was fascinated by machines and enjoyed working in shops, from which he emerged so covered with grime as to astonish his friends. Like Claxton, Holbrook believed that social rank should not bar educational opportunity, that artisans deserved instruction of the same quality as that available to merchants and professional men, and that Useful Knowledge, the blend of science and craft, possessed unique potential to benefit society. Indeed, Holbrook bore some resemblance to Brougham, who was not just a promoter of popular education but also a man sufficiently versed in science to write and distribute anonymous lectures on science that were used by mechanics' institutes all over Britain.[37]

Whether derived from British or American precedents, the mechanics' institutes were spurred by the personal experiences of their architects. These were industrial capitalists, merchants, machinists, and cultivators of science who had learned to cooperate with each other in building canals or textile factories. The plan for Philadelphia's Franklin Institute "for the Promotion of the Mechanic Arts" originated with Samuel Vaughan Merrick, a young merchant who suddenly found himself in charge of a bankrupt factory and conscious of his own lack of technical knowledge.[38] Merrick quickly rounded up support from relatives, including an uncle who had studied under Joseph Priestley and another uncle who was a central figure in the American Philosophical Society.[39] Merrick's future, which included the presidency of the Pennsylvania Railroad, would be very different from that of the skilled machinists who joined the Institute, but in the heady atmosphere of the 1820s it was not difficult to persuade fabricators of every stripe, capitalists who tinkered with their machines and foremen who worked on them, of the value of union. All of the major economic developments of the early nineteenth century spurred the growth of small knots of fabricators who worked and socialized in machine shops, proved remarkably willing to share their ideas and information, and "developed a vast, mutually owned store of knowledge and experience closely akin to a body of scientific knowledge."[40] One of the mechanics who helped to found the Boston Mechanics' Institute in 1826, George W. Light, had worked as a journeyman in shops that made and repaired machines for the New England cotton textile industry, engaged in scientific experiments, taught himself mathematics, and, like Claxton, brooded over the rejection of his application for membership in a philosophical society. By the early 1830s Light was editing the *Boston Mechanic*, which he used as a forum for his notion that first principles were more valuable to mechanics than mere skill.[41]

For Light, science was not just a body of principles but a way of thinking that included "the firmest habits of mental industry, of vigilant observation of men and things, of persevering effort, of thorough inquiry, and of systematic and accurate reasoning."[42] Befitting his background in mechanic communities, Light advocated mutual improvement as the preeminent goal of mechanics' associations. Similarly, the members of a mechanics' institute in Augusta, Maine, resolved in 1841 to devote themselves to "mutual encouragement and aid in the great enterprise of mental, moral, scientific and social improvement."[43]

The career of Erastus Brigham Bigelow illustrates the close connections between mechanic communities, mutual improvement, and the conviction that science would benefit mechanics. Born in 1814 in West Boylston, Massachusetts, Bigelow was the son of Ephraim Bigelow, a farmer, wheelwright, and owner of a small factory that manufactured cotton products. Erastus performed odd jobs in his early youth, attended district school, and briefly studied at Leicester Academy. Bigelow's teacher at Leicester urged him to prepare for college, but Bigelow's father vetoed the idea and put him to work in his cotton mill. Finding the life of a mill hand distasteful, Erastus left home and went to Boston to work in a dry-goods store in the hope that he could earn enough money for college. To supplement his meager wages, he taught himself stenography and then wrote a book, *The Self-Taught Stenographer*, found a publisher in Lancaster, Massachusetts, and watched the book enjoy a profitable sale in Boston. He would later learn penmanship and then earn money as a teacher of it.

Bigelow obviously possessed a gift for turning whatever he learned to profit; his knowledge, so to speak, was always useful. But what he really craved was "general culture," a broad and comprehensive overview of relationships, and with money saved from his occupation as a teacher of penmanship and from a brief fling at manufacturing twine, he enrolled in a medical school.[44]

Bigelow was to make his mark, however, as an inventor rather than as a physician. Happening one night to sleep under a Marseilles quilt, he began to think of the slow, expensive process by which it was woven using a hand loom. Thus was stirred his interest in devising power looms to manufacture fancy products. His principal invention was a power loom for weaving coachlace, which was used in horse-drawn carriages for straps and borders and was highly useful in the age of the transportation revolution. In 1838 Erastus, his older brother Horatio Nelson Bigelow, and several others formed a corporation in the factory village section of Lancaster to manufacture coachlace.

Erastus Bigelow grew rich off coachlace and later invented a power loom to weave carpets as well. Preoccupied by inventions, he abandoned all thought of higher education. Yet his thinking about the process of invention was permeated by the same passion for a general overview of relationships that once had led him to seek higher education. Bigelow flatly dismissed the mechanics' folklore that attributed invention to accident. "One thing is certain," he wrote, "it is not chance."[45] Nor did inventions result from "suggestive circumstances." Newton did not discover the law of gravity because he saw an apple falling; at most the falling apple suggested to him a subject of inquiry. In Bigelow's conception, all inventions resulted from the inventor's gaining an overview of a subject and a vision of a desirable result. To invent the coachlace power loom, Bigelow first imagined "the character of the several motions required and the relation which they must sustain to each other in order to effect a combined result," then devised "means to produce these motions," and finally combined "these means . . . to a state of harmonious cooperation." First the hypothetical model; then the model; then the machine.[46]

The most distinctive feature of this description of the invention process lies in its emphasis on conceptualization rather than hand skill. Even the third or "practical" stage, combining the means into "harmonious cooperation," was essentially conceptual. Throughout the third stage "one must reason from what is known to what is not so—keeping in mind at the same time the necessary combinations, examining each element, not only in reference to its peculiar functions, but to its fitness, also, for becoming a part of the whole. Each position must be thus examined and reexamined, modified and re-modified, until harmony and unity are fully established." Bigelow called the final stage "practical," but it took place mainly in his mind. He prided himself on never making anything with his hands, did not even like to draw models to scale, and invariably hired draftsmen to prepare working sketches from his own crude drawings.[47]

Bigelow viewed invention as a predictable process; facts led to theories and theories to applications. Practicing what he preached, he became a benefactor of the Bigelow Mechanics' Institute, which was formed in 1846 by his brother Horatio and six others who desired "our mutual improvement" and who envisioned a course of scientific lectures, a reading room, a library, and "a repository of models and drawings of useful machines and mechanical inventions."[48]

The association of science and the mechanical arts in this statement of goals aptly illustrates Erastus Bigelow's belief that the process of invention possessed much the character of a science. But Erastus Bigelow did not write the statement; it was composed by his brother Horatio and others. Neither a mechanic nor an inventor, Horatio began his career as an overseer in his father's cotton mill and later managed the business side of Erastus's enterprises. The other founders of the Bigelow Mechanics' Institute followed a variety of occupations. A. S. Carleton worked as a paymaster in several mills. George F. Kendall and Lory F. Bancroft were in the dry-goods business. After serving an apprenticeship to a blacksmith, J. B. Parker worked in a machine shop, rose to foreman, and later started his own machine shop. It was Parker who constructed Bigelow's first coachlace loom.[49] Sanborn Worthen was a machine-shop hand who worked for Parker. Geography rather than occupation united these men; they all lived and worked in the mill village section of Lancaster. Kendall's dry-goods store in the village competed with older establishments in Lancaster. After dissolving his partnership with Kendall, Lory F. Bancroft opened his own store at which the male gossips of the town gathered on summer evenings. Only a mile square, the mill village, known as Clintonville, took its name and much of its character from Bigelow's Clinton Company.

Those who worked in and around the factories acquired an outlook that differed radically from the agricultural sections of Lancaster, and it is scarcely surprising that Horatio Nelson Bigelow was among the leaders of Clintonville's proposed secession from Lancaster. While New Englanders had been seceding from towns and forming new ones for generations, Clintonville's secession reflected the peculiar circumstances of the new factory economy. In 1848 Horatio Nelson Bigelow defended the proposed division of Lancaster in terms that underscored the self-consciousness of the mill village:

Clintonville is a manufacturing village, Lancaster proper is an agricultural town, with only such branches of the mechanic arts as are ordinarily to be found in country towns. From this difference in occupation arise different views and feelings—distinct, separate, individual wants, and interests entirely diverse. On this account alone, the inhabitants of Lancaster and Clintonville have little or nothing in common. They cannot think alike, and they have no natural sympathy with each other. And this difference of thought and feeling and consequent interest ever has [existed] and ever must exist between agricultural and manufacturing towns.[50]

The issue between Clintonville and Lancaster proper burned for another two years and was finally resolved in 1850 when the Massachusetts legislature incorporated the town of Clinton. In 1873 the Bigelow Mechanics' Institute made a gift of its library, by far its most valuable possession, to the town of Clinton.

As an extension of a self-conscious and established community of small manufacturers, businessmen, dependent merchants, and mill hands, the Bigelow Mechanics' Institute depended on a dynamic core of activists dedicated to applied science. At its establishment in 1846, the institute embodied the exchanges of opinion, information, and values that had been occurring within this core. In this respect, the Bigelow Mechanics' Institute bore some resemblance to Isaac Mickle's Washington Library Society. Drawn from various occupations, the Washington's members also coalesced in their ardor for mutual improvement. But there was a key difference. Mickle found it fairly easy to project the activities of the Washington into the cultural life of Camden by sponsoring lectures; when Mickle attended lectures, he encountered topics that complemented his society's exercises. Nothing like this occurred in Clintonville. The lectures sponsored by the Bigelow institute, delivered by Emerson, Thoreau, Edwin P. Whipple, and Horace Greeley among others, bore no relation to the technical preoccupations of its prime movers.[51] Arising at the peculiar historical moment when venture capitalists, mechanicians, and mill hands discovered their mutual interdependence, the impulse behind the society could be institutionalized only with great difficulty. Mechanicians lived primarily in a "visual and tactile" world, and neither the spoken lecture nor the printed page were of much use to them in solving practical problems.[52] In addition, most artisans lacked the education to follow lectures on science. Words like oxide and alkali meant nothing to them, and many attended lectures on science only to witness the dazzling lights and deafening explosions that accompanied demonstrations of chemistry.[53] Claxton, who feared that lectures would subvert mutual improvement, observed that even when artisans could follow lectures, the latter were apt to touch on so many subjects that "no one person can get more than a smattering of knowledge on any one subject."[54]

None of this halted the growth of mechanics' institutes, which for various reasons continued to attract support. Conservative merchants and manufacturers favored them as stitches in the fabric of paternalistic benevolence, as moral agents that would keep apprentices and journeymen from taverns and other habitats of vice. Scientists saw them as promising vehicles for investigating the relationships between natural knowledge and industrial improvement; they also used institutes as forums in which to build local reputations as lecturers. Just as the New-York Horticultural Society had appointed Columbia University's Samuel Latham Mitchill to its "professorship" of botany and vegetable philosophy, so Philadelphia's Franklin Institute established an academic faculty composed of distinguished scientists and engineers.[55] In its first winter of operation (1824), the Ohio Mechanics' Institute in Cincinnati offered a course of lectures on scientific subjects, which reflected the scientific interests of one of its principal founders.[56]

Patronage by local manufacturers and their social peers in the scientific community also marked many of the mechanics' institutes in Britain, where in 1844 one of the early historians of adult education echoed the already common complaint that the institutes attracted "persons of a higher social rank than those for whom they were designed," and where in 1861 another commentator described the British movement as a banquet laid for guests who did not come.[57] In each nation the institutes drew enough clerks and petty merchants to raise questions about their designation as "mechanics'" institutes and to prompt historians to dismiss them as little more than engines for sustaining upper-class control over workingmen and for promoting objectives, like the study of science, that were alien to the rank and file.

While clearly etched, this picture of the mechanics' institutes is not quite accurate. In both Britain and the United States, the institutes came in various sizes and shapes and displayed varying degrees of receptivity to mechanics, a word that in the 1820s included petty capitalists who sold as well as fabricated goods. Edward Everett probably was right when he said that many mechanics thought of an inventor as a genius who blazed through life "like a locomotive on a dark night, by the light of his own intuition."[58] This idea troubled Everett, for it seemed to eliminate the need for study. Everett, who was primarily responsible for discovering and publicizing Elihu Burritt, "the learned blacksmith," explicitly used his public lectures to inculcate studiousness; the message of his oft-delivered oration on Franklin's boyhood was that Benjamin owed it all to his early acquisition of studious habits and not to genius.[59] Yet on balance mechanics were more ambivalent than hostile toward science. The mechanics' press, which was the work of artisan intellectuals like Claxton and Light, was filled with little biographies of artisans who made good with the aid of studious habits and scientific knowledge. "There is hardly any trade or occupation in which useful lessons may not be learnt by studying one science or another," proclaimed the *Mechanics' Magazine and Register of Improvement and Inventions* in 1833.[60] Claxton's *Boston Mechanic* reported favorably on the progress of scientific instruction at Harvard and Yale.[61] Mechanics' journals also reprinted addresses by public figures that urged mechanics to investigate science. Thus the readers of the *Mechanics' Magazine* could peruse an address by Bishop James Madison Porter in which he told the mechanics of Easton, Pennsylvania, that every mechanic art was simply the reduction to practice of some scientific principle, that the tanner preparing his leather was a practical chemist.[62] The first issue of the *Young Mechanic* summarized the message: "Of two individuals engaged in the same department, be it what it may, the one who is most familiar with the principles of his business will always have an advantage over him who is expert only in the use of his tools."[63]

In addition, American artisans could fall back on republican traditions that were compatible with Useful Knowledge, specifically the notion that education was the ultimate guarantor of freedom and independence and a check against the degradation of labor. In New York City, artisans took pride in the Apprentices' Library, which they viewed as their own handiwork and which they praised both as a "fortress of Liberty" and as an avenue of advancement. Thomas Mercein, a baker and president of the city's General Society of Mechanics and Tradesmen, inaugurated the library by asking his audience: "Who can tell how many Franklins may be among you? Who can tell how many Rittenhouses, how many Godfreys, how many Fultons may yet spring from the Institution this day opened?"[64]

None of this means that artisans flocked to lectures on science, but in the 1820s entrepreneurs, investigators of science, and self-improving mechanics cooperated in a shared endeavor. This element of cooperation appeared and reappeared in newly industrializing communities before 1860, but by the late 1830s the ties between self-improving mechanics and other supporters of mechanics' institutes were fraying. After 1860 the institutes persisted in Britain but gradually sank into insignificance in the United States. American advocates of Useful Knowledge, the belief that knowledge of science would make artisans more productive and inventive, increasingly pinned their hopes on land-grant colleges and universities for the "industrial classes" rather than on voluntary knowledge societies in which philosophical mechanics and entrepreneurial merchants and manufacturers met to exchange ideas. This divergence between the path of Useful Knowledge in Britain and the United States cannot be explained by reference to the objectives or formal features of the institutes, which were similar in each nation. Nor can it be accounted for by the inherent tension between the social groups that coalesced to support mechanics' institutes, for these groups also were much the same in each country. British artisans may have been more class-conscious than their American counterparts, but in neither country did the institutes attract class-conscious workers; Useful Knowledge essentially was antithetical to the very notion of class.

Rather, differences between the political and cultural contexts of the British and American institutes pushed them along different tracks.

In the United States, political democratization in the 1820s and 1830s posed a distinct challenge to the institutes. In these decades the subdivision of tasks that characterized early industrialization threatened the position of self-employed artisans in the United States. In response to the widening gap between the interests of self-employed master craftsmen and small manufacturers on one side and those of journeymen wage earners on the other, sundry workingmen's parties that bore names like the Workingmen's Republican Association and the People's Party burst forth in the late 1820s. Often led by self-instructed mechanic intellectuals, these parties advocated free education, libraries, and reading rooms, but their leaders stressed political and economic knowledge rather than the diffusion of science and preferred to communicate with their followers through newspaper articles and simplified manuals rather than by elevated lectures. In a manual on political economy for mechanics, Stephen Simpson praised himself for avoiding "metaphysical refinement" and "the profound dissertations of [J. B.] Say and other writers bewildered in the fogs of Gothic institutions," while presenting merely "the elucidation of obvious principles of practical utility in equitable applications."[65] In an address to New England workingmen in 1832, the Boston "worky" leader Seth Luther traced the "great cry about the schools and lyceums and books of *sentiment,* and *taste,* and *science*" to paternalistic Waltham mill owners and cited approvingly a letter from "A Factory Hand" who ridiculed the latter for encouraging literary cultivation.[66]

The workingmen's parties never advocated the diffusion of science as a cure-all for the corrosive effects of industrialization on artisans. Institutionally and ideologically, the American workingmen kept their distance from mechanics' institutes, and the workingmen's press had virtually nothing in common with the mechanics' press. Whereas the New York *Workingmen's Advocate* attacked banks and "chartered monopolies," assailed imprisonment for debt, and called for an end to the tax exemption of church property, the *Mechanics' Magazine and Register of Inventions and Improvements* advised manufacturers on how mechanization could reduce labor costs.[67] But it was not just in the realm of institutions and ideas that the workingmen diverged from the mechanics' institutes. The workingmen took advantage of the distinctive feature of the American laboring class, their political enfranchisement, and entered politics. Indeed by the late 1830s the workingmen's parties had been sucked into the maelstrom of the American second party system and lost much of their identity as workingmen's parties. One ironic by-product of this development was to render the American mechanics' institutes less political than their British counterparts. In contrast to British mechanics, who at times challenged the conservative political economy that Brougham preached to the London Mechanics' Institute, politically inclined American mechanics were more likely to ignore the institutes altogether and to align themselves with the workingmen's distinctly political agenda.[68]

The accessibility of free schools in the United States complemented the efforts of political democracy. As noted, the British institutes succeeded in carving out a place for themselves in formal education. Originally intended for working adults, the classes that the institutes sponsored attracted the children of members, usually those between 14 and 21.[69] In a development followed elsewhere in Britain in the 1840s and 1850s, the Manchester Mechanics' Institute opened a school for girls in 1835, which taught algebra, geometry, knitting, and sewing at first and later added the French language and English literature.[70] By admitting the daughters of shopkeepers and respectable mechanics, the institutes' schools contributed to increasing the supply of female teachers and, in the absence of any state-supported system of free schools, provided relatively inexpensive elementary and secondary education for the children of the lower-middle class. In addition, many of the British institutes opened schools of design, technical rather than scientific schools that taught subjects like draftsmanship and drawing.

The American institutes began with some of the same objectives. Indeed the idea of popular education was far less controversial in the United States than in Britain, where the *Edinburgh Review*, discussing a speech by Brougham in the House of Commons, remarked in 1818 on "the murmurs and dissonant clamours with which the first proposals for communicating the blessings of Education to the great body of people was lately received."[71] Despite disagreement about the goals of popular education, few Americans questioned its value.[72] Typically, the public officials and cultivators of science who spurred the useful arts societies in the late 1700s and early 1800s advocated a broad extension of educational opportunity and looked forward to the day when municipalities and state governments would subsidize schools. Amid waxing support for universal education, mechanics' institutes also started schools. The General Society of Mechanics and Tradesmen in New York City opened a school for the children of members in 1820. The Ohio Mechanics' Institute offered to members classes in chemistry and natural philosophy. Of all of the American institutes, none made more elaborate educational provisions than the Franklin Institute, which in 1826 launched a high school whose curriculum included Greek, Latin, French, Spanish, mathematics, and the natural sciences and which was well patronized by "the best families in the cities."[73] Finally, by 1860, some of the American institutes were following the

British example of opening schools of design. Organized in 1856, the Ohio Mechanics' Institute's School of Design enrolled over 200 students at the outbreak of the Civil War.[74]

Despite these similarities, the British and American institutes developed along different lines as educational institutions, mainly because the development of state systems of public instruction in the United States undercut the role of the American institutes as schools for elementary and secondary education. Even the American institutes' schools of design suffered from public-school competition, especially after the Civil War when high schools began to introduce courses in mechanical drawing.[75] Inasmuch as public schools rarely made comprehensive provisions for instruction in drawing, some mechanics' institutes successfully retained their role as schools of drawing—today's Maryland Institute, for example, a school of fine arts, is a lineal descendant of the Maryland Institute for the Promotion of the Mechanic Arts, established in 1824. But by 1900 most of the American institutes had disappeared.

Faced with competition from the lure of democratic politics and from free schools, the American institutes gradually transformed themselves during the 1840s and 1850s into lyceum-style lecture bureaus by seeking to attract the public, men and women who vaguely associated science with progress but who had no intention of putting it to use in factories or shops. Science did not disappear from the platform of the institutes, but it was refashioned into a more popular form between 1840 and 1860. This transformation took place with the complicity of a new generation of scientists, who forged a distinctive and novel conception of the relationship between science and the public.

The early promoters of scientific instruction for workingmen had a natural affinity for lectures and self-improvement, each of which had played decisive roles in their own education. John Griscom, Sr., prominent in the founding of the New York Mechanic and Scientific Institute, claimed not to have acquired "first intelligible hints relative to those properties of matter which are taught in books of Natural Philosophy" until he stumbled at the age of seventeen across a book on geography whose introduction contained some general information on physics.[76] Several years later, while teaching school in Burlington, New Jersey, he received a copy of Lavoisier's works from a friend, along with Jane Marcet's *Conversations on Chemistry*, a British work designed primarily for women that employed an imaginary conversation to simplify scientific complexities.[77] Although Griscom eventually secured appointments teaching chemistry and natural history in the medical department of Queen's College (later Rutgers University), he never attended either a college or a medical school. Griscom taught science in part to teach himself. The same was true of Amos Eaton. Eaton studied science under Benjamin Silliman, Sr., but not until he was 40 years old. Eaton had already acquired a scientific foundation by private reading and by preparing and delivering popular lectures on science.[78] Born respectively in 1774 and 1776, Griscom and Eaton belonged to the founding generation of American science. While later generations continued to engage in self-instruction in scientific branches, they did not have to rely on such primitive methods, and they devised new goals for lectures. Whereas Griscom and Eaton taught themselves science by lecturing on it, later generations saw scientific lectures as ways to woo popular support for scientific institutions, a goal that invited address to the educated and influential segments of the public rather than to artisans.[79]

The shifting contours and objectives of the American scientific community contributed to the emerging distinction between the diffusion and the popularization of science, between the uncondensed broadcast of science as it was known by the learned and attempts to render science exciting in order to arrest the public's attention.[80] In contrast to Griscom and Eaton, who engaged in the diffusion of science, Edward Hitchcock, the geologist and president of Amherst College, exemplified the trend toward popular science. In the 1840s Hitchcock lectured in New York City and throughout New England on "The Wonders of Science Compared with the Wonders of Romance."[81] Hitchcock gave popular science a moral and even moralistic direction by seeking to demonstrate that the human passion for "thrilling realities" could be gratified more fully and safely by science than by reading fiction.[82]

Although lecturers dwelt increasingly on science as a source of inspiration, there existed a good deal of overlap between the two phases—between the diffusion and the popularization of science. Yale's Benjamin Silliman, Sr., began to lecture publicly in 1831 at New Haven's Franklin Institute. To appeal to an audience composed largely of mechanics, he stressed the practical applications of scientific principles by discoursing on pottery, porcelain, and glass.[83] But Silliman gradually became disenchanted with lecturing to mechanics, who rarely took advantage of his offers to answer questions or to display rocks or fossils.[84] In reaction, during the mid-1830s he started to lecture to fashionable audiences, which included large numbers of women. In 1838 John Amory Lowell, the trustee of the new Lowell Institute, persuaded Silliman to deliver annual courses of scientific lectures before the institute. Silliman's lectures from the mid-1830s onward were resounding successes. His audiences grew to as many as 1,500 people, while the enthusiasm of women for geology and chemistry continually amazed him.[85] But, strictly speaking, Silliman was not popularizing science. Facing negligible opportunities to acquire scientific knowledge, the women in his audience probably desired a duplication or at least a close approximation of a collegiate course. Silliman obliged them, for with some modifications his Lowell Institute lectures followed those he gave to Yale students.[86]

The impulse to diffuse science did not vanish, but it gradually lagged behind the rising interest in popular science, which itself had to compete with the general lectures of Emerson, Bayard Taylor, Edwin P. Whipple, and other lyceum performers. The shift can be seen in the history of the Maryland Institute. In 1835, at a time when the institute's membership numbered just over 700, a fire destroyed its building. After reopening in 1848, the institute quickly built its membership to over 3,000; in 1852 alone 1,000 new members joined. But this spurt in membership owed little to popular interest in the mechanic arts or to Useful Knowledge. Rather, the institute's lectures by celebrities became its drawing card: Missouri Senator Thomas Hart Benton on the geography of the trans-Mississippi West; former president John Tyler on American history; and Joseph Henry on "True Science and the Mode of Studying It." The institute's managers worried about this trend toward "disconnected addresses upon miscellaneous topics," so much so that in 1855–56 they tried to return to the pattern of serial lectures on a single subject. Three of the lecturers in that season each delivered two lectures, a series in the strict sense but a far cry from the courses of lectures that the institute had favored in the 1820s and early 1830s. Even the serial lectures of the 1850s were delivered by celebrities like Bayard Taylor and the ubiquitous Edward Everett, who spoke on the character of Washington. These lectures were popular successes; an average of over 1,500 people attended each of the fifteen lectures in the 1855–56 season. But as the institute's managers recognized, the success of the lectures resulted from their "agreeable" rather than serial character, for they embodied none of the "learned dullness" of "scientific drones." The Maryland Institute's library experienced a similar change. Books relating to science and technology comprised a steadily shrinking share of its holdings, while the proportion devoted to history, geography, and fiction rose.[87]

Other mechanics' institutes and associations followed the same pattern. In New York City, the General Society of Mechanics and Tradesmen started to sponsor lectures in 1837 and at first embraced the model of serial lectures on science. For example, in that year Professor James Renwick of Columbia University gave a course of ten lectures on natural philosophy. A year later John Torrey presented a series of fifteen lectures on "Chemistry and the Application of Science to the Business of Life," while John Griscom, Sr., gave four lectures on "The Mechanism of the Human Frame." By the 1850s, however, serial lectures had given way to single lectures, and these were broadly cultural rather than scientific. The later lectures were apt to treat virtues like heroism or portray broad social or human relationships: "Thought and Life," "Work and Labor," "Nature and

Society." While scientific subjects did not disappear from the General Society's lecture bill, the lectures of the 1850s typically were talks about science rather than expositions of scientific knowledge; they sought to present science as an engrossing field of knowledge rather than as it was investigated by cultivators of natural knowledge.[88] A more broadly cultural
tone also permeated the mechanics' press by the 1840s. By that decade
mechanics' magazines were offering their readers a fare of short stories,
poetry, exhortations to reading, and scientific pieces on exotic subjects
like the phosphorescence of the sea and waterspouts.[89]

The transformation of the mechanics' institutes in the 1840s and
1850s satisfied their sponsors, who discovered that lyceum-style lectures
were a convenient way to raise money. However, it also exacerbated a
growing complaint among a small band of fanatics for Useful Knowledge,
who saw manual workers everywhere frustrated in their quest for education by a virtual gentry conspiracy, and indirectly it contributed to the rising chorus of demands for new provisions to educate the "industrial
classes."

From Mechanics' Institutes to Land-Grant Colleges

By the late nineteenth century, some of the surviving American mechanics' institutes had developed into trade high schools, typically evening
schools serving young adult workers. But evening schools that aimed at
upgrading the technical skills of workers characterized British education
to a far greater extent than American education. Americans tended to admire the jack-of-all-trades, a person whose usefulness in a society where
new settlements were ever sprouting could scarcely be questioned, and
they recognized that demand for highly specialized craft skills could be
met by the immigration of European artisans like the Saxon pianoforte
maker who anglicized his name to Henry Steinway. Not until the 1890s
did a movement for mass vocational education start to blossom in the
United States, and this movement did not reach fruition until the decade
before American entry into World War I. Between the founding of the National Society for the Promotion of Industrial Education in 1906 and the
passage in 1917 of the Smith-Hughes Act, the nation witnessed intense
agitation for federal aid to vocational education, but even in this period
prominent figures associated with the vocational movement often contrasted the meager American provisions for vocational education with the
greener pastures in Europe.[90]

Yet a movement for a type of industrial education did spin off from
the antebellum fervor for diffusing Useful Knowledge. The striking feature of this movement was that it focused not on primary or secondary
schools but on colleges and universities. In 1862, 55 years before the pas-

sage of the Smith-Hughes Act, which committed federal funds to trade training in separate vocational secondary schools, Congress passed the Morrill (or Land-Grant College) Act. This law authorized the federal government to distribute public lands to the states for the support of colleges that would "promote the liberal and practical education of the industrial classes in the several pursuits and professions of life" by "the teaching of such branches of learning as are related to agriculture and the mechanic arts." Federal aid for industrial education, a term that covered both agriculture and the mechanic arts, did not start on the bottom of the educational ladder and work up; rather it began at the top and worked down. This reversal of what might seem the logical order would introduce a number of strains into American education by deflecting training away from job techniques and toward relatively abstract and intellectually demanding forms of technical education. In time it would propel the land-grant colleges into educational extension programs that other institutions would copy. Although the framers of the Morrill Act did not envision educational extension as a major function of these institutions, they identified, however vaguely, with the principle that colleges should become popular institutions; once established, this principle would have a life of its own.

Despite the long-term significance of the Morrill Act, the congressional debates over the proposed legislation between 1857 (when Senator Justin S. Morrill of Vermont first introduced a bill to grant over 6,000,000 acres from the public domain to the states for the establishment of colleges of agriculture and the mechanic arts) and 1862 evoked little interest in the educational issues at stake. Rather, contention in Congress sprang from conflicting constitutional interpretations and sectional interests. Democrats generally opposed the use of public lands to enhance federal power and reflexively associated land giveaways with higher tariffs (by reducing federal revenue from land sales, donations of land would increase reliance on the tariff for revenue); Whigs and Republicans were likely to support land grants for the same reasons that Democrats opposed them. In addition, Westerners (including those in the Southwest) feared that eastern speculators would seize the opening to buy the land, hold it for higher prices, and thus retard settlement. At the same time, representatives from the populous Northeast favored Morrill's bill, mainly because he proposed to distribute the land in lots of 20,000 acres (or its equivalent in scrip) for each senator and representative in Congress. Supported by a coalition of Republicans and eastern Democrats, Morrill's bill scraped past Congress in 1858, only to be vetoed early in 1859 by President James Buchanan. Buchanan's veto message focused mainly on the budget-busting and constitutional implications of the bill and touched education only in passing by warning against federal subsidies for colleges that would compete with existing colleges. Morrill then introduced a slightly modified bill in December 1861; with the departure of many southern Democrats for the Confederacy and with a Republican in the White House, the bill easily passed into law.[91]

Passage of the Morrill Act inspired little public comment, partly because of preoccupation with the war and partly because ordinary farmers and workingmen were indifferent to so-called industrial universities. Between the 1860s and 1900, the land-grant colleges compiled a dismal record of attracting students, especially students of agriculture, and they survived only by including traditional subjects in their curricula and appealing to those bound for professions like law and engineering. Even in 1900 they were a far cry from being "democracy's colleges." Indeed, their turn to educational extension programs grew out of their failure to lure students to their campus courses. Yet by 1860 several states possessed well-established and vocal lobbies for agricultural and mechanical colleges. Thirteen state legislatures petitioned Congress on behalf of Morrill's first bill. Little opposition to the idea of agricultural and mechanical colleges surfaced in the congressional debates, which focused on the federal role in education and appropriate uses of the public domain. While far from a mass movement, the campaign for the Morrill Act generated enough momentum to secure passage of Morrill's proposal twice in the face of considerable constitutional and sectional opposition.

The roots of the Morrill Act lay partly in the antebellum ideology and institutions of Useful Knowledge and specifically in the idea that farmers and mechanics would become more productive if instructed in science. Yet the foundations of this idea had been corroded long before the commencement of a serious campaign for industrial universities. By the 1840s the mechanics' institutes had ceased to be institutions for the instruction of artisans in the scientific principles relevant to their crafts; for all practical purposes the institutes no longer even espoused the diffusion of science as an objective. Further, even in the heyday of the diffusion of Useful Knowledge few had advanced the goal of universities for the industrial classes.[92] Claxton, whose aspirations for higher education had been checked by the class system in England, fluctuated between moods in which he called for mutual improvement and "a common-sense learning, a practical education which everyone can and ought to acquire," and moods in which he assured his readers that they could acquire the equivalent of a collegiate education by devoting an hour a day to study.[93] Claxton's periodical occasionally printed articles about the progress of scientific instruction at Harvard and Yale that seemed out of step with his persistent calls for mechanics to rely on their own resources and educate each other. Among colleges only the Rensselaer Institute professed higher industrial education as a goal, and by the 1830s, when the original "school" had evolved into the degree-granting institute, Rensselaer was fast becoming an engineering college. In 1835 it became the first American college to offer a degree in engineering, specifically civil engineering. Amos Eaton came to view the institute as a kind of graduate school that would rely on existing liberal arts colleges "to fashion its students as gentlemen and to provide them with the knowledge of literature and the polish of manner necessary for professional success."[94] In the late 1830s and 1840s a growing proportion of its students, at times nearly half, already held bachelors' degrees. Classroom instruction supplanted Eaton's original notion of farms and workshops as instructional centers; indeed agricultural education, prominent among Eaton's early objectives, disappeared by 1860.[95]

Thus the timing of the Morrill Act is puzzling unless we recognize that the movement to diffuse science among farmers and artisans sprang from more than a desire to enhance their productivity. It also fed on the ideology that historians have labeled producerism. At its core, producerism saw mechanics and farmers, the moral foundation of the republic, as imperiled by the machinery of finance and by social divisions that eroded their independence and mocked their calloused hands and homely manners.[96] The speculative boom and subsequent economic panic after 1815 spurred widespread anxieties among public officials and educators that intensifying social divisions were severing the nation from its republican moorings, including its quondam respect for honest manual work. In the absence of the convenient political channels formerly provided by the competition between the Federalist and Republican parties, this sentiment experienced a kind of levitation in the 1820s, when the astonishing rise of anti-Masonry disclosed deep fears of conspiracy against liberty.

Anti-Masonry quickly crystallized into a political party, and throughout the 1830s parties mediated and directed popular anxieties about threats to republican liberty. Yet the same climate that nurtured political solutions to social divisions also gave rise to a host of educational ideals and experiments that aimed at restoring social harmony by inculcating respect for producers. Along this line, it was possible to argue the value of education based on "industrial" or manual activities as a means of bonding social classes by a common experience.

Schools based on manual activities fell into two broad categories. One type aimed at inculcating simple trade skills and routinized work habits in delinquents, criminals, and paupers in reformatories and workhouses. After the Civil War some white educational missionaries would try to impose this type of industrial education on freedmen; Samuel Chapman Armstrong, the first principal of Virginia's Hampton Agricultural and Normal Institute, favored industrial education as a way to deflect freedmen from politics while instructing them in work habits.[97] Not surprisingly, black leaders resisted this type of industrial education, and middle-class whites judged it unsuitable for their own children. The other variant of manual education, evident in the manual-labor academies that spread after 1820 in the North, attracted educators who believed that some combination of academic and practical education would implant respect for work and robust health in children of privilege.

In the 1820s, the most accessible model for accomplishing this objective was the experiment, conducted at Hofwyl, the Swiss estate of Philip von Fellenberg, by Fellenberg and the educational reformer J. H. Pestalozzi. Widely reported in the United States, the Hofwyl experiment took the form of schools for different social classes in which academic and practical education would be mingled. One of the schools at Hofwyl was an academy for children of the well-to-do, which combined academic education with gardening and the mechanic arts in order to cultivate "those more expanded feelings and generous sympathies, which bind the upper and lower classes of the community, and eventually tend to exalt the condition of humanity."[98]

With its reference to the unlocking of feelings and sympathies, this description by Fellenberg points up the moral and ultimately social goals of the Hofwyl schools. Amos Eaton quickly recognized the difference between Hofwyl and the Rensselaer school. In 1828 he wrote to the *New York Farmer* to dampen its ardor for Hofwyl. Eaton contended that the shop work at Hofwyl was merely an exercise detached from scientific instruction and hence out of step with the goals of the Rensselaer school and the New-York Horticultural Society, which sponsored the *Farmer*.[99] Yet while Eaton's strictures accurately depicted the contrast between Hofwyl and Rensselaer, American educators in the 1820s generally proved more receptive to the moral rather than strictly pedagogical value of manual labor.

Sparked by Lyman Beecher and others, intensifying interest in the home missions in the 1820s reflected general concerns about challenges to liberty, including allegations of Roman Catholic designs on the West, and the specific need to harden ministerial candidates for service in the West by an emphasis on manual labor as a form of physical education. Among the experiments that proliferated in the 1820s and early 1830s, often with the support of ministers, was the "Gardiner Lyceum," actually an academy that opened in Gardiner, Maine, in 1823, and that featured a curriculum combining collegiate subjects like natural philosophy, natural history, calculus, political economy, and astronomy with carpentry, architectural drawing, and bookkeeping.[100] The Gardiner Lyceum, in turn, became a model for the school that Holbrook and the Rev. Truman Coe opened in Derby, Connecticut, in 1824. The Oneida Institute, which commenced near Utica, New York, in 1827, became the best known of these academies and inspired imitations in Pennsylvania, Tennessee, Kentucky, and

Ohio.[101] The founder of the Oneida school, Rev. George Gale, had restored his own health through manual labor and started his school with little more in mind than compelling college-bound students to exercise daily. But it was soon evident that by raising crops and working in shops students could also defray some of the cost of education. This feature appealed to Theodore Dwight Weld, the abolitionist clergyman who taught at the Oneida Institute in 1831. Fearing that the expense of education had so mounted as to render higher education "anti-republican," Weld served as the general agent for the "Society for Promoting Manual Labor in Literary Institutions" and introduced manual labor at the Lane Seminary in Cincinnati.[102]

Manual-labor academies proved attractive to evangelical Presbyterian and Congregationalist clergymen, especially to those with a burning sense of mission. The Oneida Institute nurtured more than its share of abolitionists and zealots for temperance. Mixing perfectionism and self-doubt, Weld's generation of clergymen defined its task as the moral cleansing of society rather than the mere tending of flocks.[103] The regeneration of society called for more than dedication and endurance, will and muscle. Manual labor promised to overcome the social isolation of clergymen, who feared that the newly established seminaries for training ministers produced over-refined scholars, individuals isolated from the ordinary citizens whom they hoped to influence. In this respect, the impulses behind the manual-labor academies and Hofwyl, while different, ultimately were complementary; each sought to stimulate what Fellenberg called "generous sympathies" between different social classes.

Neither the manual-labor academies nor Hofwyl aimed at social leveling, but Hofwyl did prick the educational interests of a handful of radicals who gathered in the 1820s around the British utopian Robert Owen. Owen's son, Robert Dale Owen, briefly attended one of the schools at Hofwyl in 1819. Another prominent American educator familiar with Pestalozzi's work was William Maclure. Born in Scotland in 1763 and thus eight years older than Robert Owen, Maclure moved to the United States, became an American citizen, and retired from mercantile life in Philadelphia just before the close of the eighteenth century. Maclure, who once claimed that his own classical education had left him "as ignorant as a pig of anything useful," quickly discovered the pleasures of cultivating natural knowledge upon his retirement from business—"I adopted rock-hunting as an amusement in place of deer or partridge hunting, considering mineralogy and geology as the sciences most applicable to useful practical purposes"—and became a contributor to the *Transactions* of the American Philosophical Society.[104] In 1805 Maclure visited Pestalozzi's school at Yverdon in Switzerland and there acquired the idea of Useful Knowledge as a vehicle of mass education; combining scientific instruction with practical occupations could bring education within the economic grasp of everyone.

Maclure developed these ideas in his *Opinions on Various Subjects, Dedicated to the Industrious Producers*.[105] Here he combined virulent criticism of established educational institutions with suggestions of ways to reduce the opportunity costs that effectively barred the common people from advanced schooling. Maclure saw everywhere a virtual conspiracy of ministers, lawyers, and physicians to deny knowledge to the "laborious and productive classes" by enthroning ornamental learning, especially belles lettres, at the expense of natural knowledge.[106] Thus the elite encouraged the study of rhetoric, which merely disguised the truth, and the cultivation of the imagination, that source of silly fashions. Turning to dross whatever it touched, the cultivated class even negated the value of science by transforming it into the study of ultimate causes rather than the handmaiden of utility.[107] If only teachers would learn to stress the useful applications of scientific principles, students could pass ever so swiftly through chemistry, astronomy, geology, botany, zoology, and mineralogy, for "all the literature that 99/100ths of mankind have occasion for" is "a plain, simple narrative of facts, got by evidence of the senses."[108]

Maclure combined the Baconian view of nature as a vast and orderly catalogue of facts with the Pestalozzian stress on applied knowledge and the Owenite conviction of salvation by education. The result rallied potentially conflicting ideas around the slogan "the interests of the millions requires that education shall be accessible to all."[109] At a time when science was accessible to the educated, it was relatively easy for Maclure, a self-taught geologist who earned the admiration of Silliman, to maintain that anyone could learn anything worth knowing.[110] To be sure, even Maclure disclosed occasional doubts. He did not expect collegiate education to become popular—a drawback of small consequence since colleges taught little that was useful—and in a letter to the Pestalozzian Madame Marie Duclos Fretageot in 1820 he averred that "it was impossible to give any real information to men and that the only possible means of giving useful knowledge to the world was by the education of children."[111]

After visiting Britain in 1823 and 1824 (where he first met Owen) and witnessing the recently launched British experiments with mechanics' institutes, he seems to have changed his mind. In a letter to Madame Fretageot in October 1824, Maclure counted "the mecanic institutions & cheap periodical publications for disseminating usefull knowledge thro the great mass of industrious producers" as one of the "moral improvements I saw in Britain worth the transporting across the Atlantic."[112] In the mid-1820s, Maclure embraced Owen's plan to found a utopian socialist community at New Harmony, Indiana, where he initiated several educational experiments. These included an infant school, an industrial school in which children learned trades (its pupils set and bound Maclure's *Opinions on Various Subjects*), a school for children over the age of twelve known as the "School for Adults," and the School for Manual Instruction. Announced in 1828, after all the other schools and the New Harmony community itself had collapsed, the School for Manual Instruction evolved into a mechanics' institute known as the Working Men's Institute.[113]

Maclure's contention—that established institutions of education, especially colleges and universities, educationally disfranchised manual workers by offering only an ornamental education suited to the learned professions—became a common refrain in the agricultural and mechanics' presses. Instead of providing common folk with the sort of education they desired, classical colleges flooded the country with lawyers, bankers, speculators, and demagogic politicians, in sum the nonproducers who lived off the hard work of farmers and mechanics. Jesse Buel, who in 1832 started publication of the Albany, New York, *Cultivator*, wrote of political ambition that "the mortal upon whom it fixes its fangs, abides not on the farm."[114] Attacks on classical education intensified after the Panic of 1837, which was widely blamed on speculators and other nonproducers, and permeated the mechanics' press in the 1840s. Mechanics' journals viewed as outrageous the "superior claims to power, honors and profit" advanced by "the lawyer, the professor, the speculator and many others less useful to society" than hardworking mechanics.[115] In 1846 the *Mechanics' Advocate* denounced lawyers "and the whole pack of named and nameless nothings who constitute the class of political demagogues."[116]

While these sentiments did not necessarily point to the need for colleges for the laboring classes, the very fact that so many classical colleges dotted the American landscape lent plausibility to the idea, advanced by a small number of educational visionaries in the 1840s, that the future of Useful Knowledge depended on harnessing the education of mechanics to the collegiate model. At the same time, the manifest limits of mechanics' institutes as schools for the self-instruction of workingmen gave an urgency to the experimental "farm schools" and "people's colleges" that sprang up in the 1840s and 1850s. For example, in the wake of the Panic of 1837 Harrison Howard, a self-educated carriage maker living in Lockport, New York, plunged into educational reform. Inspired partly by the distress of workers and partly by the model of manual-labor academies and Oberlin College, which had contained manual-labor features in its early days, Howard lectured extensively in the 1840s on the need for a type of college that would serve the common people and thereby bring higher education abreast of human progress. Above all, Howard believed that the reform of higher education would corrode class distinctions by enhancing the dignity of manual labor.[117]

Howard's plan for the People's College curriculum offered a smorgasbord of topics, for it was to include "Natural Philosophy, Chemistry, Geometry, Architecture, Drawing, etc., not neglecting any other branches which are taught in our best colleges and universities." Understandably, contemporaries were uncertain how the institution would benefit practical workers. An effulgent journalist proclaimed:

In this institution the student will not only read the lofty verse of Vergil's Georgics, but will reduce his rules to practice while following the "trailing-footed" oxen spoken of by Homer. The Differential and Integral Calculus will commingle with the ring of the anvil and the whir of the machine shop. The mechanic's toil will be diversified by the Histories of Tacitus or the eloquence of Cicero and Demosthenes. The elevation which mental training and intellectual power confers will be somewhat lessened by being blended with the more common and ordinary industrial occupations of everyday life, while the physical man will be correspondingly elevated, refined, and ennobled.[118]

However cloudy, Howard's vision aroused the interest of reformers and, with a boost from Horace Greeley, the proposed school secured a charter from the New York legislature in 1853. But it did not open until the end of 1860, never became more than a small academy, and is remembered mainly for two pieces of historical trivia: its president-designate actively lobbied Congress on behalf of the Morrill Act, and the New York legislature voted to make the People's College the recipient of the Morrill Act land-grant allotment in the state. But the legislature then imposed conditions that the feeble school could never meet and, ultimately, the allotment went to the newly founded Cornell University.[119]

Although of negligible long-term significance, the People's College exemplified the strain of producerist ideology that would influence the land-grant college movement in the 1850s and marks an interesting moment in the timing of the movement for industrial colleges. This movement developed less to perfect the achievements of mechanics' institutes than to respond to their failures. As long as the institutes' founders were captivated by a vision of the diffusion of science through organized provisions for self-instruction, they had little incentive to develop the case for formal higher education. By the same token, as the limits of the institutes as educational institutions became apparent, some educators turned to the collegiate model. By the 1850s a similar shift had occurred in the thought of progressive agriculturalists. Berkshire-style agricultural societies had proliferated in the 1820s in an atmosphere marked by the keen expectation that scientific agriculture was within reach. This expectation sustained its momentum into the 1840s, propelled by the work of Justus Liebig. Liebig, who in 1824 established at the University of Giessen the first school of chemical research, applied the laws of organic chemistry to farm problems. Liebig's major work, published in German in 1840 and translated in

1841 as *Chemistry in its Application to Agriculture and Physiology*, met with a ready reception in America. Agricultural periodicals opened their pages to Liebig's followers, who came as close as any Americans to being experts on agricultural improvement.[120] Liebig's own claim that the problems of farmers could be solved easily by the application of known facts contributed to the American "craze over agricultural chemistry in the 1840s and early 1850s."[121] Rising enthusiasm for scientific agriculture led to the formation of scores of new agricultural societies in the 1840s and 1850s; by the Civil War some 900 were in existence.

Yet this zeal for improvement produced disappointing results before the Civil War, mainly because the demand for reliable scientific advice exceeded the supply. In the absence of agricultural experiment stations to develop statistical controls and cost-benefit analyses, farmers were besieged by the hard-sell tactics of salesmen of unproven fertilizers and seeds and by often uncritical exhortations from agricultural editors to try new ideas. When innovations worked in one place but not in another, or simply failed to work at all, many farmers grew skeptical of scientific agriculture. Between the mid-1850s and the mid-1870s, when Connecticut introduced the first agricultural experiment station, popular support for scientific agriculture weakened.[122]

The combination of rapidly spreading agricultural societies in the 1840s and 1850s and the disappointing outcome of the initial burst of enthusiasm for Liebig and experimentation spurred those who retained faith in science to turn to the federal government for assistance. Marshall Wilder, the president of the American Pomological Society, led a group of agricultural improvers to form the United States Agricultural Society in 1852. This society not only lobbied for a cabinet-level department of agriculture but also supported the first bill for land-grant colleges that Senator Justin Morrill introduced in 1857.[123] All advocates of land-grant colleges agreed that agricultural research should be one of their major functions, and this view reflected the emerging consensus that farmers were learning little of value from their exchanges in the agricultural press.[124]

The career of Jonathan Baldwin Turner, the most important of the Midwestern supporters of Morrill's bills, illustrates the influences that came together in the 1840s and 1850s on behalf of "industrial" universities. Winton Solberg has aptly characterized Turner as "a restless visionary with a tendency to fanaticism."[125] Born in 1805 on a farm near Templeton in western Massachusetts, Turner attended Yale in the late 1820s and early 1830s, a time when ardor for revivals and the missions permeated the college. His older brother Asa was among the original members of the Yale Band, which founded Illinois College in Jacksonville as an outpost of Christianity and culture in the West. In the winter of 1832–33, Illinois College's president Edward Beecher, whose father Lyman would kindle home missionary work in *A Plea for the West* (1835), asked Yale president Jeremiah Day to send him a young instructor, and in response Day dispatched Jonathan Baldwin Turner.

Turner held the post of professor of belles lettres and literature at the college from 1834 to 1848, but his freewheeling religious views, which included an interest in spiritualism as well as a hostility to Calvinism, and his anti-slavery principles made life at the college increasingly unpleasant. After resigning his professorship in 1848, Turner devoted himself to common-school reform (long among his interests), agricultural experiments, and the idea of an "industrial" university. In a landmark address he delivered at Granville in 1851, Turner softened his early preoccupation with common-school reform and focused on the need to make higher education relevant to the common people. Distinguishing only two classes in society, the professional and the industrial, he pronounced the history of educational reform a failure because it sanctioned the assumption that improvements in mass elementary education would somehow percolate to higher education. Higher education in Illinois gave the lie to this assumption, for the state was filled with small sectarian colleges that consumed the financial resources of the state's college and seminary funds to train lawyers, physicians, and "sectarian ecclesiastics" rather than the state's manual ("industrial") workers. Thus the interests of 95 percent of the state's people, its industrial class, were sacrificed to the 5 percent in its professional class.[126]

Turner described the interests of the professional and industrial classes as cooperative rather than antagonistic, but despite his own classical education and decision to become a Congregationalist minister after moving west, his writings reveal his animus against the professional class. He blamed the latter for the pettifogging lawyers, political hacks, and sectarian bigots infesting the nation, and he hoped that the establishment of an industrial university would save young men from becoming the "starving scavengers of a learned profession."[127] At one point he even hinted that the industrial university would benignly shrink the proportion of society composed of the professional class from five to one in a hundred.[128]

Turner's frequent attacks on what Jacksonian Democrats liked to describe as nonproducers reflected well-ingrained American beliefs that drew on a mixture of republican and Jacksonian sentiments. Moreover, they accorded with his own experiences in Illinois, where his liberal religious views locked him into conflict with the conservative clergymen who dominated the state's Presbyterian synod and who in 1844 instituted an inquisition into Illinois College. His anti-slavery activities had exposed him to personal danger; in 1842 he received a warning from the Kentucky abolitionist Cassius M. Clay that slaveholders from Missouri planned to kidnap and murder him. Late in life he recollected that he was "more feeble and broken in health" at 45 than "I now am at ninety-one years of age."[129]

The industrial class in Illinois was scarcely free of pro-slavery sentiments, but Turner directed his ire at his own class, surfeited by lawyers, speculators, and conservative clergymen who feared that agitation of the slavery issue would damage the churches. Turner's loathing of speculators had roots in his own experience, for in the 1830s he had purchased a tract of land in the center of the state with the expectation that the capital would be located at the proposed town of Illiopolis. The decision to move the capital from Vandalia to Springfield instead of Illiopolis wiped out his investment.[130] The Panic of 1837 also hit Turner; for two years he had to teach without pay. Turner's disillusion with politicians fed his criticism of the professional class, to which he attributed a "chronic diarrhoea of exhortation" that he contrasted with the slow and steady mental discipline that laboring people acquired from their occupations.[131] As an opponent of slavery he had many occasions to observe the self-serving motives of politicians. Turner furiously assailed the Fugitive Slave Act of 1850 and came upon the scene as a champion of industrial universities shortly after its passage.

Primarily a publicist and agitator rather than a systematic thinker, Turner sprinkled his writings with suggestions by which the industrial university might affect the lives of most farmers and mechanics. He borrowed from agricultural societies the idea of annual exhibits or "gala-days" during which the university would throw open its doors to the public while professors and students lectured on "the divers objects and interests of their departments." Much as he had marched proudly into the West as a missionary of learning, he also expected the industrial university to train teachers of the mechanic arts and agriculture for the state's colleges, high schools, and lyceums. But perhaps the most notable of his ideas for diffusing Useful Knowledge was his contention, only half-developed, that an industrial university might have an extremely large enrollment; it would serve the people by admitting them, or at least their children, as students.

Evidence for the assertion that Turner envisioned a very large university is indirect; he never said how many students the university should admit. But he did favor a practical curriculum based on the principles of agriculture and industry and including as well such homely subjects as "the laws of courtesy and comity between neighbors" and "the principles of health and disease in the human subject, so far at least as is needful for household safety."[132] These ideas were consistent with Turner's rejection of the principle that higher education had to aim at educating public men and with his stress on the education of "any student" for "any duty." In addition, he hinted at ways to make the university accessible to young men of limited means. For example, he proposed that students be allowed to attend for whatever period they proposed, "whether three months or seven years"; that they be permitted to study whatever subjects they chose, "and to any extent, more or less"; that instruction be given in the colder months of the year, so that students could perform gainful work at home or on the premises in the warmer months; and that students be allowed to substitute work on the premises for cash payments of tuition and board.[133]

A part-time horticulturalist whose daughter remembered him as forever planting trees, Turner possessed a keen interest in scientific agriculture and in societies for agricultural improvement. A conference of such societies occasioned his Granville address. At the same time, he incorporated strains of producerist ideology into his thought and blamed the classically educated professional class rather than the industrial class for the nation's problems. His thought drew on the tradition of Useful Knowledge as well, but revealed a more explicitly democratic motif than had the manual-labor academies and the mechanics' institutes. Ultimately, the appeal of a curriculum based on agriculture and the mechanic arts lay in its inducement to the industrial class to attend college rather than in bringing the professional class into closer sympathy with the people. In Turner's eyes, a practical curriculum was essentially a means to the end of popularizing higher education. In comparison with the mechanics' institutes, none of which attempted to transform itself into a college, Turner clearly envisioned an institution of higher education, a state industrial university. The Morrill Act would stipulate that the federal land grant in each state had to be allotted to colleges, a position that differed from Turner's less by its substitution of "college" for "university"—Americans often used the words interchangeably—than by making private as well as public institutions eligible.

Turner's mixture of Useful Knowledge, scientific agriculture, democratic access, and higher education was bound to create confusion. Were the industrial class to acquire an education equivalent to that of the professional class, then such an education had to be liberal. Although it might appear an oxymoron, a liberal industrial education was precisely what Turner envisioned.[134] He used phrases like "liberal practical education" and the need for "thinking laborers and laborious thinkers," insisted that the industrial university possess "a complete philosophical, chemical, anatomical, and industrial apparatus," and did not exclude the possibility of establishing a department of classical languages.[135] The last item might appear to be inconsistent with Turner's bias against classical colleges, but it was compatible with his conviction that the elevation of labor required prestigious higher education, not trade training schools that merely duplicated apprenticeship.

Turner initially envisioned no more than an industrial university in Illinois, but circumstances led him to support a national system of industrial institutions. In the wake of his Granville address of 1851, he helped to form the Industrial League, a lobby for a state-supported industrial university. Turner and the League faced considerable opposition within the state not only from the denominational colleges but as well from teachers whose main interest lay in the establishment of a system of public common schools and attendant normal colleges. After tangling on several occasions with teachers apprehensive that the proposed university would soak up funds better spent on normal colleges, Turner pledged his support in 1856 for the establishment of a state normal university. This was no more than a tactical concession; he continued to agitate for an industrial university, and to gain public support he consciously subordinated the research features of the proposed university to its utilitarian aspects. But it was clear that the state's college and seminary funds, already bled by the denominational colleges, were inadequate to support both an industrial and a normal university. Even before his shift to support a normal university, Turner had come to recognize the necessity for federal assistance. At his urging the state legislature in 1853 instructed Senator James Shields and Congressman Elihu Washburne to introduce resolutions calling for a land grant to establish industrial universities not just in Illinois but in any state agreeable to the idea.[136]

Turner's strenuous promotion of the industrial university would later provoke a dispute over the identity of the real "father" of the Morrill Act. In 1896 the president of the University of Illinois, Edmund J. James, portrayed Morrill as little more than a front man for Turner, a view seconded by a biography of Turner by his daughter and by Turner himself in his nonagenarian recollections. The controversy over the authorship of the Land-Grant College Act lingered on until 1938, when Earle D. Ross, a learned and dispassionate historian of the land-grant schools, masterfully assessed the issues and assigned appropriate roles to all the actors: Morrill was indeed the key figure, but others contributed to the supporting cast, and of these Turner was the most voluble.[137] Yet in puncturing the exaggerated claims of Turner's adherents, Ross and others introduced a subtle bias of their own. For example, in his 1924 biography of Morrill, William Belmont Parker stressed Morrill's "eminently restrained and conservative" goals and his reluctance to pose "as a discoverer or inventor in the field of education." Parker averred that Morrill was not "proposing anything revolutionary, but a moderate, reasonable, and practical extension of the educational equipment of the country."[138] Parker's judgment, followed with some modifications by Ross, dampened the claims of Turner's backers and of Turner himself, while underscoring the role of Morrill, who blessed all participants in so noble a cause.

In reality, Morrill and Turner stumbled more or less independently on the idea of colleges for the "industrial classes," and this idea was by no means simply an extension of the "educational equipment of the country." It was conceptually distinct from the idea of higher agricultural schools that engaged in research and that fitted a small number of young men to conduct agricultural experiments. This was the usual understanding in the 1850s of the role of an agricultural college, and it was decidedly more conservative than the functions that Turner attributed to the industrial university. To be sure, the advance of scientific agriculture was on both Turner's and Morrill's list of goals of land-grant colleges. Morrill acknowledged that agricultural schools of this sort that had been founded in Europe influenced his thinking, and he believed that by encouraging short-term occupancies and frequent moves the very cheapness of public lands in the United States contributed to inefficient agriculture. But much like Turner, Morrill also stressed the need to "exalt the usefulness" of labor by opening higher education to the children of mechanics and farmers, and he criticized "literary institutions," "colleges based upon the classic plan of teaching those only destined to pursue the so-called learned professions," on grounds similar to Turner's.[139] There is little evidence that Morrill derived the idea from Turner; separated by a thousand miles, the two rarely communicated. Rather, Morrill's experience contributed to this educational philosophy. The son of a "hard-handed blacksmith" in Stratford, Vermont, Morrill had been denied his wish to attend college by his father, who had several sons, could not educate all, and chose to educate none. Thus the young Morrill had to depend on self-instruction for the refined aspects of his education. He read whatever books he could find at home, borrowed books from a local judge, and corresponded with a professor at Dartmouth for guidance in teaching himself French.[140]

Coming from different educational backgrounds, Turner and Morrill agreed that provisions for the higher education of mechanics and farmers had to be expanded to restore manual labor to dignity. Superficially, this idea resembled the contention of eighteenth-century republican educators that the study of science and its applications would render colleges more attractive to the citizenry. But in calling for a separate class of institutions for farmers and mechanics, the antebellum promoters of people's colleges and land-grant universities inadvertently betrayed their lack of confidence in the drawing power of applied science. The history of antebellum knowledge societies and colleges alike persuaded them that the prospect of literary refinement would exert a far stronger pull on those in quest of higher knowledge than would the investigation of applied science. In retrospect, it is easy to see why this was so. While literary refinement could be put to use in a variety of professions and occupations, science had little to say to

mechanics or farmers in the mid-nineteenth century. Rather than acknowledge this, Turner and Morrill sought to establish a class of institutions insulated from the attraction of literature.

Conclusion

In Jefferson's lifetime the main institutional embodiments of Useful
Knowledge were learned societies, including their useful-arts variant.
Originally organized by gentlemen, these societies were propelled first by
the embargo and then by the transportation and industrial revolutions
into an ever-widening range of contacts with the public. As gentlemen, entrepreneurs, mechanicians, and progressive farmers discovered common
interests during the 1820s and 1830s, new and more popular types of useful-arts societies—Berkshire-style agricultural improvement societies and
mechanics' institutes—arose to popularize scientific knowledge and to encourage scientific development.

The popularization of Useful Knowledge in the 1820s and 1830s deflected its advocates away from university reform, a major goal of the
eighteenth-century republican educators. Heartened by the examples of
Birkbeck, Brougham, and the SDUK, Americans looked to popular voluntary associations to stimulate economic development. Yet this was
never the sole purpose of voluntary associations, for their promoters also
hoped to dignify manual work by underscoring its relations to science. A
relatively understated objective among eighteenth-century republican educators, who by no means exclusively equated Useful Knowledge with
manual activities, the elevation of manual work became a major goal in
the nineteenth century, especially for those educators who were dismayed
by the social divisions that accompanied industrial and commercial development. From American admirers of the Hofwyl experiments in the 1820s
to agitators for land-grant colleges and industrial universities in the
1850s, a band of educational philosophers insisted that social classes be
reconciled to each other by incorporating manual labor into the curricula
of schools.

Those who in the 1820s favored manual-labor academies also puffed
mechanics' institutes and agricultural improvement societies, and a few
even hinted at the need for higher education for mechanics and farmers.
But it was not until the 1840s and 1850s, when the failure of mechanics'
institutes and agricultural improvement societies to fulfill their original
purposes became evident, that agitation for industrial universities gained
momentum.

In one sense, proponents of Useful Knowledge as a vehicle of educational and social democratization were unrepresentative of mainstream
educational currents. They had little faith in academies and colleges "of

the classical type," lyceums, or (by the 1840s) mechanics' institutes, and they often voiced contempt for the genteel culture buttressed by classical education. Yet these diehards for Useful Knowledge could tap into wellsprings—Baconianism, nationalism, and the republican emphasis on widening educational opportunity at the higher as well as lower rungs of the educational ladder—from which nearly all educators drew. The idea of tying industrial education to colleges broke with the tradition of voluntary associations as the bedrock of Useful Knowledge, but it did not spur much dissent on educational grounds.

Nor can it be said that it stimulated much support. The Morrill Act experienced a stillbirth of sorts, for in the decades after the Civil War few students enrolled in the agricultural courses of land-grant colleges; in fact, comparatively few students enrolled in land-grant colleges at all. The idea of elevating manual labor by associating it with science persisted among a small segment of educators after the Civil War, but in the 1870s mainstream colleges and such new sallies into popular education as the Chautauqua movement ignored the practical arts. Not until the early 1900s would land-grant colleges emerge as leaders of educational extension along practical lines, and they did so then in response to their woeful inability to attract resident students.

Arising in an atmosphere of disappointment with the achievements of voluntary knowledge societies and spawning new disappointments, the Morrill Act nevertheless would inspire generations of twentieth-century educators, who pointed to it not only to support widening the perimeters of higher education but also to buttress their contention that only practical education could be popular in the United States.

Chapter 5

The Homely Renaissance,
1870–1900

Extolling the newly formed American Society for the Extension of University Teaching in 1893, the prominent educator Edmund J. James predicted that university extension lectures would put "new and worthy objects of thought into the lives of people who have been content to live in intellectual sloth and barrenness." Instead of gossiping about their neighbors, Americans would sprinkle their discourse with references to Shakespeare, Copernicus, and Milton.[1]

Although he seems to have been unaware of the debt, James was merely paraphrasing the justification of lyceums that Josiah Holbrook had articulated nearly 70 years earlier. When it came to culture, the nineteenth century was full of paraphrases. James Russell Lowell's declaration in 1885 that good books admitted readers "to the company of the saint and the sage, of the wisest and wittiest at their wisest and wittiest moment" paraphrased language that Emerson had used 40 years earlier.[2] A great deal was written about books and culture during the nineteenth century, but it all had a similar ring. Literacy resembled the vote, an enfranchisement that admitted readers to the world of elevated thought and sentiment. Once enfranchised, men and women needed only to acquire a "taste" for good books, which themselves would serve as avenues to culture. Culture itself was an ideal with several components. In the century's most quoted formulation, Matthew Arnold in 1869 equated culture with the effort to make "the best that has been thought and known current everywhere, to make all men live in an atmosphere of sweetness and light."[3] Arnold used culture to signify a body of knowledge ("the best that has been thought and known") and the personal qualities elicited by the acquisition of culture. Twentieth-century critics have relished catching Arnold in little contradictions, but his contemporaries who thought of culture as a worthy goal were untroubled by loose formulations. In their eyes, its value was sufficiently evident to discourage scholastic distinctions. Educators and literati of Arnold's day linked culture to both a process of self-education that culminated in a refined outlook and to the literary masterpieces that embodied refinement, and they rarely took the trouble to argue the advantages of the "ploughing and harrowing of self by use of what the ages have transmitted to us from the work of gifted minds."[4]

The association of culture with uplifting knowledge did not significantly depend on Arnold's personal reputation. Arnold's chilly manner and his dismissal of the United States as a nation of Philistines did little for his American reputation, which fluctuated in the 1870s and 1880s before declining in the 1890s.[5] By the early 1900s culture itself was in decline as a goal of popular adult education. Long sniped at by a guerrilla band of critics, including Walt Whitman, culture gradually lost the allegiance of its own stalwarts and in the eyes of marauders and deserters alike came to connote excessive refinement and even decadence. Yet there did not exist any inherent conflict between the ideal of culture and the impulse to popularize knowledge. Rather, culture imparted a moral purpose to educational activities that otherwise might have appeared disconnected. Consistent with this moral purpose, advocates of the pursuit of culture reached out to the multitude by inventing ways to reconcile higher knowledge with mediocre interests and aptitudes. At the very time when apostles for culture within colleges and universities were adopting a siege mentality in the face of challenges from modernists of every sort, the managers of Chautauqua and other institutions of popular education in the Gilded Age were opening their lecture platforms to authorities on modern literature, political economy, sociology, and natural science, all in the name of culture. For those who would not or could not study Latin or Greek, they devised rituals redolent of classical imagery. As long as they could affirm the inspirational potential of culture, they were willing and even eager to dilute bodies of knowledge in order to disseminate culture among the many. In sum, whereas in the universities advocates of culture set themselves against the new ideals of utility and research, those who engaged in popular adult education in the 1870s and 1880s adapted modern bodies of knowledge as well as traditional subjects to the goals of culture.[6]

Culture straddled the Civil War as an organizing motif of popular education, but the feminization of culture accelerated after the war. Women predominated in all of the important institutions of popular adult education in the Gilded Age. Although foreshadowed before the war, this development transformed the methods used to disseminate culture in the 1870s and 1880s, and by the 1890s it was eroding the reputation of culture itself.

The Decline of Literary Societies

By the 1880s the literary or mutual improvement societies that had spread during the antebellum period were stagnating and in many cases facing collapse. For example, the Detroit Young Men's Society grew robustly in the three decades after its founding in 1832 and then declined swiftly after the Civil War. It held its last meeting in 1882, at which its managers announced plans to sell its collection of books, by then at least 5,000 volumes, to the Detroit Public Library.

This instance suggests that competition from new municipal free libraries overwhelmed the older social libraries of the type established by the Detroit Young Men's Society. In reality, however, the older voluntary library associations formed by upwardly mobile clerks and lawyers were declining even before municipal free libraries became abundant; the quantum leap in the number of municipal libraries in the 1890s occurred in part because male-dominated social libraries were only too eager to unload their collections. The Boston Public Library's Frederick Beecher Perkins accurately predicted in 1876 that few new social libraries would be added to the existing class of mercantile library associations and that "a decrease in their number is not improbable."[7]

Although it is possible to point to any number of competitors for the time and energy of young men, neither public libraries nor the rowing and baseball clubs that proliferated in the Gilded Age account for the decline of mutual improvement societies. Rather, these societies went into eclipse because their clients no longer saw cultural acquisition as important to their careers. The peculiar configuration of circumstances that had prompted young men before the Civil War to form literary societies and library associations gradually unraveled in the postwar period. To take one illustration, the growth of corporate business after the war sharpened demand for lawyers skilled in specialized areas of the law and contributed to the growing prominence of formal legal education. Law schools, which had played a negligible role in training lawyers before the war, gradually supplanted the tradition of learning law by clerking in law offices. This shift reduced the range of contacts between candidates for the profession and established practitioners. Such contacts had been abundant in antebellum America, when law clerks had combined their apprenticeship in law offices with attendance at court proceedings, a method of preparation that introduced them directly to veteran practitioners and to the profession's standards.[8] Mutual improvement societies of the sort that Isaac Mickle, Jr., had frequented in antebellum Camden occupied a secure place on this continuum of informal modes of preparation. In contrast, the gradual ascendancy of classroom instruction after the war reduced law candidates to the status of students facing specialized professors and undercut the importance of literary societies.

Change affected other occupations that had served in the antebellum period as pools for self-improvers. William Dean Howells often wrote about the small print shops that had played so important a role in his own self-education, but he did so nostalgically, well aware that technological changes and ever-mounting capital requirements in the newspaper business had made such shops obsolete. After the Civil War, public-school reformers continued to advocate bureaucratic centralism and the standardization of schools, but without the missionary zeal that had permeated the early common-school revival and with an increasing reliance on normal schools to train teachers.

The changes that affected printing and teaching can be detected in the late antebellum period, which also saw the erosion of the ideal of the cultured merchant. By the 1850s the calls for the pursuit of literary culture so characteristic of the early years of *Hunt's Merchants' Magazine* had disappeared from its pages. Always a defensive tactic, a way to deflect criticism of bankers and traders as bloodsucking parasites, the call to culture was giving way even before the Civil War to a new defense of business as a source of public wealth and stimulus to philanthropy. The prosperity characteristic of most of the 1850s gave plausibility to these claims, which equated the value of business with capitalism itself rather than with the private virtues of capitalists, and which thereby obviated the need for businessmen to persuade the public that their claims to leadership rested on the spiritual elevation that accompanied literary acquisition.[9]

Between 1850 and 1880 the Young Men's Christian Association, which did not attach preeminent importance to literary culture, employed prayer meetings to inculcate moral and religious values in young urban clerks. In the same years, private commercial schools gradually absorbed the role of instructing clerks in practical skills like penmanship and bookkeeping, which the mercantile library associations once had discharged.[10] In conjunction with the waning of support for literary culture among spokesmen for business, these developments stripped the mercantile library associations of many of their functions. None of this means that a generation of readers gave way to one of Philistines, that individual merchants or clerks lost their interest in culture. New literary associations continued to arise in the 1870s and 1880s, and these quickly enlisted prominent professional men and businessmen. But in contrast to the mercantile library associations, the new organizations were extremely exclusive. So exclusive was the Indianapolis Literary Club, established in 1877, that its annual election of new members was dubbed the "kitten drowning"; at one point it turned down the governor of Indiana.[11] The same was true elsewhere. The literary clubs established in Chicago after the fire in 1871 were far more exclusive than those of the pre-fire era. Societies like the Illinois Club (1873) and the Chicago Literary Club (1874) drew nearly all of their members from the ranks of prominent businessmen. Organizations like the Saracen (1876) and the Women's Club (1876) attracted society women. Although the titles of some of these clubs resembled those of antebellum literary societies, mutual improvement never became one of their major goals. Rather, these societies acted as rallying points for wealthy citizens eager to create in Chicago replicas of eastern art museums and endowed libraries.[12] In keeping with the new emphasis on cultural philanthropy, clubs became narrower in focus as well as more exclusive in membership. A growing number served special-interest groups eager to promote music or art or literature. Chicago's Apollo Music Club was formed in 1872 and its Society of Decorative Arts (a forerunner of the Art Institute) in 1877.[13]

The Popular Lecture in Transition

No less than mutual improvement societies and libraries, lyceum lectures underwent a transformation in the 1870s and 1880s that made it increasingly difficult to portray them as agents of public instruction. Yet the nature of this transformation remains open to question. In his standard history of lyceums, Carl Bode contended that in the wake of the Civil War popular lecturing became "far more commercialized and far more an entertainment than it ever had been before." "Clumsy comics" like Artemus Ward and Petroleum V. Nasby, who represented "a degree of rustic mirth which the prewar audiences would have found unseemly," supplanted serious lecturers. Bode traced much of the blame for this change to the rise in the late 1860s of commercial lyceum bureaus and to the gradual invasion of the platform by the profit motive.[14]

Many contemporaries expressed a similar view, and by the 1870s they were describing the golden age of the lyceum in the past tense. The journalist and novelist Josiah G. Holland complained that "literary jesters and mountebanks" were lowering the tone of the lyceum.[15] The reformer and editor George William Curtis remarked in 1872 that many viewed the lyceum as no more than a system of "strolling players" for the nation's amusement.[16] Commercial lecture bureaus would give the public whatever it wanted, and the public craved amusement rather than instruction. The "better class," Holland lamented, was being driven off by the buffoons who dominated the lyceum circuit.[17]

For all of the complaints about cheapening standards, however, no shortage of serious lecturers beset the lyceum after the Civil War. For example, a brigade of famous Britons paraded onto the American lecture platform in the three decades after the Civil War, including Matthew Arnold, J. A. Froude, Charles Bradlaugh, and Oscar Wilde. Critics of the late-nineteenth-century platform tended to romanticize the antebellum lyceum. They remembered the Wendell Phillipses and Ralph Waldo Emersons, but not the traveling mesmerists, phrenologists, and laughing-gas experimenters. Indeed entertainment long had been a purpose of platform lecturing, and this was true even of the antebellum lyceum's loftier manifestations. A British visitor in the 1840s described attendance at lyceum lectures as "the most fashionable amusement at Boston this year."[18] Americans long had cherished oratory less as a verbal way to communicate facts and ideas than as a source of simultaneous inspiration, education, and entertainment.

Antebellum lyceum lecturers had thought of amusement and instruction as potentially complementary rather than as necessarily antagonistic objectives. For example, in the 1840s popularizers of science routinely had portrayed nature and machines as mighty sources of sublime wonderment "for the information and amusement of the public in general."[19] The antebellum lecture had been intended as a form of high amusement and as a legitimate substitute for low amusements like the theater, the music hall, and fiction. What changed by the 1880s was the prevailing conception of morally acceptable amusement, which increasingly included the "legitimate" theater, operettas, and fiction. Imbued by "muscular Christianity," Protestant moralists also began to find ethical value in sports. Even family billiard tables and parlor games found defenders among moralists, who saw them as ways to keep young people at home and away from dance halls or worse.[20] As conceptions of legitimate amusement broadened, it became more acceptable to present instruction and entertainment as alternating phases of a single program rather than to require individual lecturers to bear the simultaneous burden of instruction and amusement. Major James B. Pond, the leading lyceum impresario of the Gilded Age, conceded that the challenge posed by the popularity of the operettas of Gilbert and Sullivan among people "who would not previously go to the theater" forced him to sponsor violinists, contraltos, humorists, and explorers in order to attract an audience.[21]

In response to these pressures, lyceum offerings became increasingly eclectic in the 1870s and 1880s. The range of institutional sponsors and attractions grew exponentially, especially in the Middle West. For example, in Indianapolis during the 1880s and 1890s the YMCA, the Chautauqua Literary and Scientific Circle, the Central Avenue Lyceum, the Indianapolis School of Oratory and Elocution, the Social Science Association, and several churches all sponsored programs. Among the performers were such standbys as Henry Ward Beecher and the temperance lecturer John B. Gough and many new faces, including Lew Wallace (the author of *Ben*

Hur), the realist George Washington Cable, the feminist Anna Dickinson, Matthew Arnold, Oscar Wilde, the Harvard College Quartet, and a "Rock Band" which accompanied a family of English balladists.[22]

Such eclectic lyceum performances in the Gilded Age reflected not only the need of sponsoring agents to compete with the growing legitimacy of the theater, but also the inventiveness of the lecturers themselves. For those who retained prejudices against the theater, for example, public reading became a morally safe way station between the stage and the crafted lecture. James Whitcomb Riley originally had intended to become an actor, but, unwilling to conform to the conventions of the stage, he added dramatic qualities to his sketches and poems and launched his career as a public reader. His readings became a sensation from Kokomo to Indianapolis, and even before he had published anything of note, they effectively established his reputation as the "Hoosier Poet." Pond and other impresarios also effectively combined diverse talents in a single program. One of Pond's most successful touring acts featured the somber Cable and the comedic Mark Twain, a combination that typified the eclectic character of the postwar lyceum.[23]

Forced to compete against an ever-expanding range of popular amusements, lyceum promoters responded by broadening their programs. This response did not put an end to serious lecturing, but it did make it difficult for contemporaries to view lyceums as vehicles for popular education. The introduction of amusements that were devoid of educational purpose stripped the fig leaf from the lyceum and exposed it to charges of mounting commercialism.

Critics of the Public

Criticism of lyceums coincided with increasingly acerbic attacks by intellectuals on the public itself. E. L. Godkin, the editor of the *Nation*, traced America's meretricious and derivative "chromo-civilization" to lyceums, small colleges, cheap newspapers, and pretentious periodicals, all of which diffused among the multitude the conviction that labor and self-denial were unnecessary components of true learning. Better a society of ignoramuses, Godkin concluded, than a "pseudo-culture" in which everyone thought himself a philosopher.[24]

Whereas antebellum apostles of popular intellectual improvement had sought to insinuate respect for learning and civility to a public that they presumed hostile to each, Godkin and other "best men" of the Gilded Age saw a public neither vulgar nor truly refined but half-educated and prone to exaggerate its competence. What this new public, the product of a half-century of superficial popularizations of knowledge, required was less exhortation to pursue knowledge under difficulties than the inculcation of respect for true culture.[25]

In the 1870s Godkin's *Nation* became a forum for intensifying criticisms of the tradition of popularization represented by lyceums. An article published in 1879, for example, complained that even serious lectures were of little value as long as they were not accompanied by study and examinations and merely featured solo exhibitions by celebrities.[26] Obviously, popular lecturing was now being judged by a new standard, and few were keener to pass judgment than a new brigade of scientific popularizers. Promoters of public interest in science complained that lecturing was too haphazard to afford instruction. If a chemist happened to be in town, the audience heard a lecture on chemistry; if an astronomer, then one on astronomy. A correspondent of the *Nation* called in 1879 for "scholarly lectures" rather than "popular dilutions," and he exhorted colleges to undertake extension lectures aimed at "the constantly increasing class of young clerks, merchants, and university graduates."[27] A few years earlier F. W. Clarke had used the new *Popular Science Monthly* to attack "scientific dabblers" and to call on the American Faradays and Huxleys to rescue the field of scientific lecturing from the half-educated.[28] E. L. Youmans, the *Monthly*'s founder and formerly a lyceum-style popularizer himself, insisted that the magazine had to make its appeal not to the half-educated but to the "generally educated classes," the graduates of the high schools, academies, and colleges. These people were "active-minded, and competent to follow connected thought in untechnical English, even if it be sometimes a little close." The *Monthly* would "enable them to carry on the work of self-instruction in science."[29]

Critics of popular lecturing wanted self-education to become more academic, and they sought to forge the institutions of popular adult education into facsimiles of formal schools. Various features of American education made this a plausible objective. Prior to the 1890s "higher education" had loose connotations. Not only were degree-granting colleges abundant, but the distinction between them and the vast number of academies, "seminaries," "collegiate institutions," and high schools was far from clear. Although at times Americans distinguished higher from secondary education, in an age when colleges often maintained preparatory departments the distinction was prone to collapse, the more so because academies and high schools offered many of the same subjects as colleges. Public high schools featured the same bewildering variety of subjects taught by antebellum academies. For example, the Boston English High School, established in 1821 for young men who did not intend to attend college, not only offered practical subjects like mensuration and surveying, but also several college-level subjects, including moral philosophy, logic, political philosophy, and astronomy. In 1823 it added courses in natural theology, evidences of Christianity, and bookkeeping. By no means was this untypical. In 1848 the public high school in Hartford offered nearly 30 subjects, actually closer to 40 if one counts American, French, English, and ancient history as separate subjects. What is striking is the extent to which academic rather than practical subjects accounted for this constant stretching of the high-school curriculum; courses in bookkeeping and surveying contributed far less to the expansion of the curriculum than did courses in natural philosophy, "intellectual philosophy," vocal music, moral science, evidences of Christianity, botany, and zoology.[30]

It was already becoming clear by the 1820s that many students desired education beyond the "common branches" but without attending colleges. The goals of these students stimulated the establishment of institutions like Boston's English High School and the founding of innumerable academies. No theory of secondary education sustained this development. Indeed, most educators who commented on it did so in a complaining spirit. They insisted that high schools (and by the 1850s even common schools) taught subjects that were too "high." They blamed the public, which demanded, as Emerson perceptively noted, that it be educated not as the state decreed but as it decreed, that it be instructed not only in the common branches but "in the languages, in science, in the useful and in the elegant arts."[31]

Gender and Culture

Several explanations come to mind to account for the growing popularity of the academic model as a basis of popular adult education after the Civil War, and these will be explored in the coming pages. But for the moment let us focus on one, the academic model's compatibility with the educational objectives of middle-class women in the third quarter of the nineteenth century.

Among the factors that shaped the educational objectives and values that middle-class women brought to women's clubs and Chautauqua in the 1870s and 1880s, two stand out, and each pointed female self-improvers toward the academic model. First, although opportunities for women to acquire higher education grew between the 1830s and the 1870s, they did so unevenly and at a pace that left most women behind men. In 1837 Oberlin became the first degree-granting college to admit women to its collegiate (as opposed to preparatory) course. State universities moved slowly toward coeducation. The University of Iowa established coeducation at its opening in 1856. Women were admitted to the normal classes of the University of Wisconsin in 1860, while the University of Michigan opened its classes to women in 1870. Starting with the opening of Vassar in 1865, elite private colleges for women sprang up in the East. Smith and Wellesley both opened in 1875 and Bryn Mawr in 1880.[32] By 1890 women made up 36 percent of all college students, whereas in 1870 they had been only 21 percent.[33] Of course there were alternatives to enrollment in degree-granting colleges. The coeducational academies and female seminaries that proliferated between 1800 and 1860 afforded women some opportunities to take advanced subjects; by 1887 the United States contained 159 "institutions for the superior instruction of women," a phrase that included academies and "collegiate institutions" as well as degree-granting colleges, and that conveys some of the looseness associated with the concept of "higher education" in the nineteenth century.[34] In addition, toward mid-century young women increasingly enrolled in public high schools, where they studied the same subjects as male students.[35] Yet these opportunities for education underscored the comparative disadvantage of women; female seminaries, coeducational academies, and public high schools alike lacked the resources and prestige of degree-granting colleges. The difference was especially felt by women who were middle-aged in the 1870s and 1880s, the backbone of the women's clubs and a sizable proportion of Chautauquans as well, for these women had come of age when opportunities for even a high-school education were less well developed. Like the woman who claimed that her Chautauqua course helped her to understand what her daughter was studying in high school, they knew what they had missed.[36]

In addition to their relative disadvantage in access to higher education, women long had lacked the same opportunities as males for mutual improvement through self-education in groups. True, antebellum women had gathered in reading circles, but these lacked the resources of the sundry literary associations and library companies formed by men. The antebellum mechanics' institutes and mercantile library associations were quasi-public bodies, not infrequently incorporated and tax-exempt.[37] In some instances, women gained access to their collections of books through male friends and relatives, and they attended lectures sponsored by young men's societies. But to note this merely emphasizes the dependence of women on benefactors. Women relied more than men on reading whatever books their families happened to possess. Not surprisingly, the recollections of antebellum women were filled with rueful laments about their disorderly and unsystematic programs of self-education, and these complaints were intensified by their lack of models of self-education.[38] Virtually all of the autodidacts whose biographies were disseminated to inspire self-improvers were males, and their achievements occurred in male spheres: mechanical invention and public life. So far from benefiting from models of self-culture, women had to struggle to overcome the prevailing deprecation of their intellects. "I found the mind of a female, if such a thing existed, was thought not worth cultivating," wrote an eighteen-year-old Maine woman in 1801.[39]

By the 1830s and 1840s, advice books that counseled young women to undertake intellectual self-improvement were presenting female intelligence in a more favorable light.[40] The experience of coeducation in antebellum high schools went far to explode belief in the intellectual inferiority of women, for the female students often outperformed their male counterparts.[41] But the rising estimate of female intelligence merely exposed another problem: what purpose was self-improvement to serve for women? Males could view self-improvement not just as an end in itself but as a way to satisfy what John Adams had called "the passion for distinction." The Transcendentalist Margaret Fuller described herself as "determined on distinction," but aside from dismissing "succès de société" as a worthwhile form of distinction, she experienced considerable difficulty in describing what it was she sought. Fuller was familiar with the protagonist of Mme. de Staël's fictional *Corinne*, who valued art and sensibility above everything.[42] But whereas men could enter intellectual vocations that were already established and expanding, it proved difficult for Fuller to translate her admiration of artistic sensitivity into a profession. Certainly her friend Emerson was little help. In a memoir of Fuller he legitimized her strenuous exercises to improve her mind on the grounds that her sole objective was self-culture. Only by asserting that Fuller lacked a desire to excel others, in effect that she lacked the very passion for distinction that she attributed to herself, could Emerson satisfy himself that she was truly "a moral person," and not merely an "overflowing genius."[43]

Told that they must not associate self-improvement with personal ambition, women faced a unique problem in organizing their self-education, for it was precisely personal ambition that long had afforded young men criteria for directing their studies, for deciding which subjects to take up or skills to cultivate and which to discard or neglect. Even such a voracious reader as Isaac Mickle, Jr., did not get lost in his reading, for Mickle knew what to look for: epigrams, quotations in foreign languages, and dramatic illustrations of political folly. Aspiring to public life, he recognized that all such gleanings were useful. But what was useful for a young woman? Until the nineteenth century, public life, the magnet for so many male self-improvers, was closed to women. Although by 1860 women could come before the public as writers and, less frequently, as speakers, their efforts at self-cultivation still lacked the range of useful applications available to men and ever threatened to dissolve into self-questioning. Advice books aimed at them revealed a near obsession with inculcating orderly and systematic habits of study, which the same books assumed could be implanted only with difficulty. These monitors typically counseled young women not to fritter away their time on novels, to be wary of reading societies that too often degenerated into idle gossip, and to cultivate the habit of closing their eyes after each sentence in order to "repeat your author's thought in your mind."[44] Yet so far from solving the problem, monitors merely indicated its scope. Eliza Ware Farrar could assign no other purpose to self-education than the cultivation of industrious habits, which became an end in itself.[45] Whereas men could avail themselves of the inherent freedom of self-education, female autodidacts were told that unstructured self-instruction threatened to dissipate their energy in wasted and futile stabs at knowledge.

The circumstances peculiar to female self-improvers affected their quest for literary culture in several ways. Although a few women attained prominence as public lecturers before and during the Civil War, including, the Grimké sisters, the suffragist Abby Kelley, and the eloquent Unionist Anna Dickinson, intellectual women usually avoided the platform. Elizabeth Palmer Peabody and Emma Willard pointedly sat when they spoke, lest they be thought of as public lecturers.[46] Margaret Fuller preferred Socratic "Conversations," a method of education as compatible with Transcendentalism as it was different from the lyceum lecture.[47] In the 1870s and 1880s women who joined study clubs had opportunities to read papers to each other; the fact that so many of the study clubs of the era were exclusively for women encouraged this type of display. But the striking feature of female self-education in the late nineteenth century was its orientation toward study rather than display. Study, specifically "culture-study," afforded women an opportunity to investigate in depth subjects that were lightly tripped over in academies and to introduce themselves to new subjects. Organizing their self-education around subjects enabled women to overcome their anxieties about the lack of order and coherence in their quest for self-improvement and at the same time to acquire an approximation of the formal education that was still more available to the other sex. If, as Ednah Dow Cheney claimed, women had long suffered from the absence of "intellectual training in thoroughness and accuracy," then the organization of self-education around curricula seemed to many the right medicine, and women's study clubs the wisest physician.[48]

Women's Clubs

A survey published in 1899 by the United States Department of Labor identified 1,283 women's clubs, their locations, dates of establishment, and stated goals.[49] In reality, the number of women's clubs was much higher. One investigator identified 1,300 women's clubs in the Midwest alone in 1906; by that year 5,000 clubs had joined the General Federation of Women's Clubs, and it has been established that these constituted only

5 to 10 percent of the total number of clubs.[50] The General Federation itself was never more than its name implies, a loose association of local organizations that arose more or less spontaneously and that marched to their own drummers. To the extent that the movement had a model, it was Sorosis, a woman's club founded in 1868 by Jane Cunningham Croly. A remarkable woman who combined motherhood with a career in journalism, Croly took offense at the exclusion of women from a dinner in honor of Charles Dickens and organized Sorosis. In the same year a group of Boston women led by Caroline Severance and Ednah Dow Cheney started the New England Woman's Club. Both Croly and Severance kept in touch with the other clubs starting up in the 1870s and 1880s, Croly became the first historian of the movement, and Sorosis was responsible for organizing the General Federation of Women's Clubs in 1890.[51]

Yet while these clubs could claim to be prototypes, neither was typical. Sorosis mainly attracted career-minded women, whereas the vast majority of clubwomen in the late nineteenth century were middle-aged, middle-class matrons without career goals. The New England Woman's Club advocated suffrage and other reforms, but the General Federation of Women's Clubs did not endorse a federal suffrage amendment until 1913. In the survey published by the Department of Labor, only one club described the advancement of suffrage as its primary goal, and only 75 of the 1,283 clubs reported their main objective as practical work in philanthropy or civic betterment. By the late 1890s a minority of clubwomen, usually those associated with large urban clubs, were trying to nudge the clubs toward interest in social issues, and one-third of the clubs in the 1899 survey announced the study of social problems as their principal objective. After 1900 this social viewpoint would push to the fore in women's clubs, but in the 1870s and 1880s the great majority of clubs described their goals as "literary studies," "the study of art, science, and literature," "mutual improvement in literature," and "self-culture." Describing the early years of the Julia L. Dumont Club of Vevay, Indiana, a member recollected "the amazing amount of study we did and I mean STUDY." Zona Gale characterized the 1880s as a decade marked by "a homely renaissance, not of learning but of study."[52]

Study took several forms. Some clubs selected a single subject for investigation. The Friends in Council of Quincy, Illinois, established in 1866, made the study of philosophy its primary purpose. In the first four months of the club's formal existence, members read William Lecky's *History of the Rise and Influence of the Spirit of Rationalism in Europe*.[53] After hearing a series of talks on the subject by a niece of Henry Ward Beecher, the Beecher Club of Portland, Maine, studied the theory of evolution.[54] Shakespeare and Browning clubs were common. Frequently, clubs that started with a single focus acquired new ones: Browning led to the study of English literature, American history to world history. In Kalamazoo, Michigan, an association established in 1852 to promote the building of a city library raised money by sponsoring lectures by Horace Greeley and Wendell Phillips, evolved in the 1860s into a reading circle for men and women, and became a women's club in the 1870s. In a typical year its topics ranged from the poetry of Sir Walter Scott to the role of literary women in history and the philosophy of John Ruskin.[55] The founders of a women's club in Dubuque wrote into their constitution provisions for several departments that would resemble those of a university.[56]

Some clubwomen found precedents for women's clubs in Periclean Athens, others in the Middle Ages, and still others in the religious study clubs that Anne Hutchinson initiated in seventeenth-century Boston.[57] This quest for precedents underscores the conservative temperament behind the movement. To establish an apostolic succession helped to disarm critics who suspected female associations of crypto-feminist intent. The introduction of social science into the study curriculum of the clubs was long retarded by its association with radicalism; one reason for the increasing acceptance of social science in the programs of women's clubs after 1900 was that, in the context of Progressive reform, the study of social issues was losing its radical connotations. Some clubwomen even worried that "club" had too many masculine associations or that it was too bold a term. Hence there arose names like the Friends in Council or the Ossoli Circle (a Knoxville club devoted to the study of Margaret Fuller Ossoli) or Sorosis, a botanical term for plants with fruit-bearing flowers and hence compatible with culture, a word that originally signified the cultivation of plants.[58]

Despite their pains to distance themselves from radicalism, women's clubs reflected the underlying restlessness that marked even conservative women in the nineteenth century and the growing tendency of middle-class women to rid themselves of male domination in activities that they perceived as legitimately within their sphere. Antebellum women had participated in mutual improvement societies, but with the exception of a small number of exclusively female clubs like the "Literary Society" for women founded at Chelsea (now Norwich), Connecticut, in 1800 and the more famous Gleaning Circle established five years later in Boston, they usually had done so as junior partners in enterprises dominated by men, who frequently read their compositions for them.[59] In contrast, the women's clubs were organized by and for women, who read their own compositions, exchanged ideas, and set their own agendas.

Whereas the allusive performances of Emerson and other paladins of the antebellum lyceum circuit had assumed a great deal of cultural information, left to their own devices women constructed study programs that attached preeminent importance to the acquisition of cultural facts, and in so doing they subtly adapted some time-honored methods of self-education to their objectives. The Cedar Falls (Iowa) Parlor Reading Circle provides a case in point. Although it was not strictly a women's club—it was, rather, merely dominated by women—this reading circle followed the path taken by some women's clubs by evolving from an earlier lyceum, the Cedar Valley Horticultural and Literary Association, which had been organized in 1859. Whereas the Horticultural and Literary Association had sponsored lectures by Emerson and Bayard Taylor, the Parlor Reading Circle, established in 1876, jettisoned lectures in favor of programs that included piano selections, readings from authors such as Dickens and Irving, and an "exercise" consisting of questions on authors. The exercise might include the reading of essays, but members usually preferred "conversations." Conversation had the approval of John Locke, Isaac Watts, and of course all Transcendentalists as a method of self-education, but in the hands of the Parlor Reading Circle it acquired the character of a school exercise in which each student recited a piece learned the night before. At a November 1882 meeting of the Circle, for example, a Major Bryant led a conversation on the reign of Charles I. According to the notes of a reporter in attendance:

Mrs. C.C. Knapp spoke of the contest between the court and John Hampden; Mrs. Abbot described Pym; Mrs. Ladd told of the attempt to establish the Anglican church in Scotland; Mrs. Ensign described the Fourth Parliament; Miss McGovern introduced Sir Henry Vane. Miss Hoagland said that the population of England at this time was about six million. Professor Bartlett [a teacher at a local normal school] brought out some strong points in the character of Thomas Wentworth, Earl of Strafford; and the Circle in general discussed Archbishop Laud.[60]

Culture-study such as this was a new and fast-flowing current in popular education during the Gilded Age. Among Chautauquans it developed into a crusade that reflected religious, philosophical, and even vocational impulses.

A Disneyland for Culture

The name of a lake in southwestern New York, Chautauqua came to signify a vast enterprise in popular self-improvement, in the words of the historian Herbert Baxter Adams "an educational Bayreuth for the people."[61] Founded in 1874 on the site of a Methodist camp meeting as a summer school for Sunday-school workers, the Chautauqua "Assembly," the legal corporation that had oversight of the grounds, empowered and supervised a host of subdivisions: the Chautauqua College of Liberal Arts (1878), the Chautauqua Literary and Scientific Circle (1878), the Teachers' Retreat (1879), and departments or schools of pedagogy, languages, music, sacred literature, and physical education. Boosted by a visit from President Grant in 1875, Chautauqua quickly became a gathering place for college professors eager to diffuse knowledge, for self-improvers in the grip of a "half-pathetic hunger for knowledge," for temperance advocates and Sunday-school officials, and for schoolteachers and librarians.[62]

For all its diversity, Chautauqua was a single movement that reflected the shifting values of late-nineteenth-century middle-class Protestantism. The cofounders of the Chautauqua Assembly, Methodist bishop John H. Vincent and Methodist manufacturer Lewis Miller, belonged to a denomination long uncongenial to the kind of experiment that Vincent and Miller started at Chautauqua.[63] The early American Methodists usually had been poor, uneducated, and unsympathetic to liberal education. Some western Methodists had opposed even Sunday schools as godless desecrations of the Sabbath.[64] As late as the 1860s, the Methodist Episcopal Church was torn by what one historian has characterized as the "holiness craze."[65] John Wesley, who founded the Methodist movement in eighteenth-century England, had preached a doctrine of holiness (sometimes called "perfection"), which stated that individuals could attain freedom from temptation as well as sin. In post–Civil War America, holiness Methodists repeatedly called for a return to the austerity of primitive Methodism, and they established huge camp meetings to advance their doctrines.

These were the very strains of Methodism that Miller and Vincent rejected. In Vincent's view, holiness Methodists "can be very trying."[66] Both Miller and Vincent drew on countervailing strains of Methodism, which also could be traced back to John Wesley. An Oxford graduate who read books on physics, mathematics, philosophy, theology, drama, and poetry, Wesley was also well versed in Arabic, French, German, and Italian. His bibliography ran to over 400 titles, including such well-known works on secular subjects as *The Complete English Dictionary*, *The Concise History of England*, and *Primitive Physick, or An Easy and Natural Method of Curing Most Diseases*. It is difficult to think of anyone in eighteenth-century Britain or America with a keener interest than Wesley in popular education through inexpensive abridgements and compendiums. In America the Methodist Episcopal Church, formally established in 1784, started its own publishing house, the Methodist Book Concern, in 1789. The Church's *Discipline* exhorted circuit riders to spend at least five hours a day in reading, and in 1818 the General Conference decreed that no itinerant could become a full member of the annual conference unless he had passed a two-year course of home study.[67]

John H. Vincent thought of the church as a large school devoted to Christian education. He preferred to think of spirituality as a growth in understanding rather than as a quality attained in the paroxysm of a conversion experience, and he acknowledged his intellectual debt to Horace

Bushnell, the Congregationalist whose *Christian Nurture* (1847) urged
Protestants to rely more on religious education in the home than on the
sensationalism of the revival. Appropriately, the one movement in which
both Vincent and Miller engaged prior to Chautauqua was reform of the
Sunday-school curriculum. That reform involved the introduction of
printed and graded lessons that could be used by different denominations
and the introduction of subjects like history and geography to assist understanding of the Bible. Wherever he served as pastor, Vincent inaugurated a class in which students, often as many adults as children, studied
the history and topography of the Holy Land. As a minister in Irvington,
New Jersey, between 1855 and 1857, Vincent organized a "Palestine
Class" in which Sunday-school teachers studied biblical history and the
geography of the Holy Land. Vincent's son aptly characterized the first
meeting at Lake Chautauqua as "no other than a gigantic Palestine
class."[68] Later, in Galena, Illinois, where he met Grant, Vincent introduced
one of the first institutes in the nation for the training of Sunday-school
teachers. Similarly, as superintendent of a Methodist Sunday school in
Canton, Ohio, Miller began graded classes and induced public-school
teachers to teach in the Sunday school. Breaking with some firmly rooted
traditions of American Methodism, each man believed that education
could cultivate piety, and both expected that Sunday-school reform would
soften denominational differences by instructing all Protestant children in
a common core of knowledge about the Holy Land.[69]

Proving themselves skillful organizers and promoters, Vincent and
Miller quietly discouraged evangelical Protestants from turning the Lake
Chautauqua ground into a camp meeting. Vincent even ordered the
grounds closed from Saturday evening to Monday morning to dissuade religious enthusiasts from wandering onto the site. At the same time, Vincent arranged for educational programs that quickly swept Chautauqua's
reputation beyond the perimeters of Sunday-school reform. Among these
was a scientific congress, held in 1876. In a way that was to become characteristic of the Chautauqua movement, the congress blended scientific
lecture-demonstrations—one professor brought three tons of equipment
from New York City—with lectures on such topics as "Bible Miracles and
Modern Science" and "Alleged Discrepancies between Science and the Bible," which reinforced the religious outlook of the audience. "All knowledge, religious or secular," Vincent proclaimed, "is sacred to him who rev-
erently surrenders himself to God, according to the divinely appointed
processes for building character."[70]

Even the physical layout of the Lake Chautauqua grounds reflected
this intermingling of education and inspiration. Vincent had a penchant
for images that associated Chautauqua with the majesty of the ancient
world. The main assembly at Lake Chautauqua contained an amphithe-

ater, a "Temple," a white-pillared "Hall in the Grove," and a hotel called the Athenaeum. A tourist could scale Chautauqua as one might scale the Acropolis. "Beyond the Point and Auditorium level," Vincent wrote, "are the terraces that run along the hillside, one above another, gardens and cottages with pathways and winding roads, leading up under welcome shadows to the higher Chautauqua—a long stretch of table land crowned now by Temple and Chapel, Pyramid, Normal Hall, Museum, and Hall of Philosophy."[71] For Vincent this physical progression symbolized the spiritual progression of a student's ascent in knowledge. "This study of the lay of the land which makes the physical Chautauqua is an allegory. There is an upper Chautauqua; and not all who visit the place see it, and not all who become Chautauquans reach it."[72]

Classical imagery was merely one way to symbolize the elevated, almost otherworldly nature of the Chautauqua experience. The Chautauqua school for teachers drew on a different tradition by calling itself the Teachers' Retreat, for the type of retreat that Vincent had in mind was the religious custom of withdrawing from the world for periods of contemplation. One of the most unusual "exercises" of the Teachers' Retreat, the Ideal Summer Trip Beyond the Sea, also illustrated Chautauqua's characteristic celebration of mind over matter. First conducted in 1878, the Ideal Trip was a summer excursion that began in, ended in, and in fact never left the tourist's mind. Vincent described it as succinctly as possible:

By the power of imagination, a party of tourists pack the delights and profits of one hundred and fifty days of travel into fifteen; and all this by the aid of conversations, lecture-lessons, class-drills, blackboard outlines, choice readings by gifted elocutionists, musical renderings by superior singers, personal reminiscences by ladies and gentlemen who have travelled widely, a library of travel, a large number of card-photographs and engravings, and by stereopticon illustrations.[73]

The Ideal Trip also illustrated Chautauqua's quest for inexpensive as well as uplifting entertainment. Improvements in transportation before the Civil War had helped to turn places like Nahant, Saratoga, and Cape May into popular watering places for the wealthy, and after 1860 summer resorts became increasingly popular among middle-class Americans. The Chautauqua Assembly also became a resort, but one distinctive for its simplicity. At first, simplicity was a matter of necessity. In the 1870s Chautauquans pitched tents. But even after the tents had disappeared by the 1890s, most Chautauquans, including Vincent, preferred to live in rustic cottages.[74] Although Chautauqua's promotional literature called attention to its resort-like attractions—Vincent wrote of "shady groves, lovely lake, fountains, lawn-tennis grounds, and roller-coaster"—Chautauqua was a Christian summer retreat, free of anything that smacked of conspicuous consumption. The historian Herbert Baxter Adams, who frequently lectured at Chautauqua, interpreted it as part of the trend in which "sensible Americans are returning to lives of greater ease, simplicity, and economy." He could have written the same about many of the so-called independent chautauquas scattered across the country, which arose in the 1880s and 1890s in imitation of the Lake Chautauqua Assembly. Like the latter, many of these were erected on the sites of former camp meetings and then, as middle-class Christians developed a taste for cultural amenities, evolved into Christian resorts that mixed simple living with lectures, concerts, and classes.[75]

The Utility of Culture-Study

Vincent depicted culture in Arnoldian terms as intercourse with great thinkers, and he thought of books as sparks that set the mind aflame. Relating the familiar story of how the sixteen-year-old Joseph Henry accidentally came upon a book of lectures on science, Vincent added his own description of Henry's reactions: "his eyes flashed, his soul was on fire, and he became the man that he was from that little book."[76]

This language drew on the Anglo-American tradition of popular self-education. Biographies of autodidacts, which long had circulated to inspire those who pursued knowledge under difficulties, consistently had portrayed the revolutionary effects of single books on individuals. This interpretive framework was rooted both in the tradition of reading the Bible, particularly in the Protestant doctrine that each individual could derive unique inspiration from the Bible, and in the experiences of autodidacts, who of necessity read whatever books fell into their hands and upon whom individual books often did make a striking impact. The belief that books would transform individuals, almost like conversion experiences, continued to attract supporters in Vincent's day. A contemporary of Vincent wrote that books "have an almost miraculous power over the mind of man. A few pages of a single volume fall, as it were by chance, under the eyes of the boy as he reads in his leisure hours. The words of the author are an inspiration to his soul. They fascinate his attention and charm his mind. The result is, the boy has a purpose in life."[77]

Although Vincent described the effects of reading as virtually miraculous, in 1878 he launched Chautauqua into an enterprise that rested on different assumptions about education. The Chautauqua Literary and Scientific Circle (C.L.S.C.) was the first major experiment in education by mail in the United States.[78] Its main predecessor in correspondence education, the Society to Encourage Studies at Home (which Anna Ticknor of Boston started in 1873), attracted a little over 7,000 students between its inception and Ticknor's death in 1896.[79] In contrast, between 1878 and 1894 some 225,000 students signed up for C.L.S.C. courses, purchased textbooks distributed through the C.L.S.C. (in many cases written specifically for Chautauquans), and joined its thousands of local circles.[80]

The Chautauqua circles were reading clubs, similar in some respects to contemporary women's clubs. Kate Kimball, the C.L.S.C.'s Executive Director, described the kaleidoscopic character of these circles: "Churches have formed rallying points for hundreds of them. Many have been organized on [a] neighborhood basis; some [have been] founded on the ruins of survivals of older literary societies. Teachers' associations, Y.M.C.A.'s, Y.W.C.A.'s, Indian schools, philanthropic institutions, army posts, mining camps, and even the prisons have contributed to the great Chautauqua constituency."[81] The "social culture" of the circles undoubtedly contributed to making the C.L.S.C. the leading correspondence school of the Gilded Age, just as the absence of this feature had restricted the impact of Anna Ticknor's Society to Encourage Studies at Home.[82] Throughout the late nineteenth century, culture-study societies relieved the drabness of life in isolated communities like Cedar Falls, Iowa, which in 1880 lacked an electric lighting plant and city water. Most Chautauqua circles arose in towns smaller than Cedar Falls, which had 3,500 inhabitants in 1880. Of the 10,000 circles that had come into existence by 1900, a quarter were located in villages of fewer than 500 people and half in places of between 500 and 3,500 inhabitants.[83] Inasmuch as few of these villages and towns possessed public libraries before 1890, the C.L.S.C.'s system of book distribution served a practical function. Further, under the direction in the 1880s of the future muckraker Ida Tarbell, the *Chautauquan*, the C.L.S.C.'s inexpensive periodical (one dollar a year), came equipped with sundry aids for study, including questions and answers after each essay and practical advice from John H. Vincent. The kind of advice Vincent offered Chautauquans revealed the distance many of them had to travel to reach gentility. Not only did he tell them how to study, but he counseled them on proper speech and manners.[84] One member of each circle should read aloud a page or two of the required reading, with others then reporting as much as they could remember. Individual circles developed their own variations on Vincent's advice. One circle, for example, organized its study of the American Revolution into twenty-minute segments, one for each year of the war.[85] The question and answer section of the *Chautauquan* stood ready to reduce the most complicated historical narratives to such digestible items as the fate of Mardonius at the Battle of Plataea or the number of ships engaged in the Battle of Salamis.[86]

Little could more drain a book or essay of its inspirational effect than to follow it with factual questions and answers. For all of Vincent's talk of the inspirational impact of single books, his pedagogical and organizational innovations encouraged a prosaic approach to education that came into its own in the 1870s and 1880s in several seemingly unrelated educational spheres. For example, manuals of self-education gradually became more explicit and detailed and less exhortatory.[87] Whereas Isaac Watts and John Locke had listed and assessed the means or instruments of learning, books like George Cary Eggleston's *How To Educate Yourself: With or Without Masters* (1872) advised readers how to study mathematics, foreign languages, the physical sciences, and political economy.[88] A journalist and novelist, Eggleston deprecated the tradition, represented by Elihu Burritt, Horace Greeley, and Franklin, of the solitary autodidact who allegedly accomplished everything by unaided efforts, and he cautioned the student not to "delude himself with the idea that he is above the need of instructors."[89]

Eggleston believed that he was addressing a male audience marked by well-defined vocational objectives. According to Eggleston, "he" studied because "an educated man can *make money* more readily and surely than an uneducated one can."[90] Describing knowledge as a worthwhile end in itself, Vincent followed a different tack, but much like Eggleston he reduced knowledge to discrete subjects to be mastered one at a time. Each man associated knowledge with the mastery of subjects taught in schools and colleges. Women may have found this approach to knowledge more congenial than the more freewheeling and display-oriented methods that characterized the antebellum literary societies. In addition, the acquisition of specific cultural facts was coming to have vocational utility in the Gilded Age. The federal civil service provides a case in point. Building on scattered precedents in the Jefferson and Jackson administrations (which mainly applied to the military service), Congress in 1853 required federal clerks in Washington to pass an examination in order to hold their jobs. This measure did not go far enough in the eyes of reformers such as Rhode Island Republican Thomas A. Jenckes, who introduced more ambitious bills in the 1860s. Jenckes, who became a recognized congressional leader of civil-service reform, advocated a system of competitive examinations along the lines of those developed in the British, French, and Prussian civil services, which would test general rather than job-specific knowledge. Jenckes's ideas bore some fruit in 1871, when Congress authorized the president to appoint a Civil Service Commission to draw up rules for examining applicants for the civil service.[91]

Nearly two decades elapsed between Jenckes's first bill and President Chester Arthur's signing into law of the Pendleton Act in 1883, which compelled examinations for only a fraction of the offices that Jenckes had in mind. Along the way, a shifting and self-replenishing coalition of congressional opponents had battered reform throughout the 1870s by the simple expedient of refusing to fund the Civil Service Commission. Yet in that decade competitive written examinations were selectively instituted. In 1873 the chief clerk of the Treasury Department administered nine separate six-hour examinations, covering arithmetic, history, government, geography, spelling, and English, to 565 candidates, including 35 to 40 women. In 1879 competitive examinations were held for the New York customshouse; President Rutherford Hayes forwarded the rules governing these examinations to collectors in other ports, and examinations were subsequently held in Boston and Philadelphia. Reform also affected the civil services of some states, especially those of New York and Massachusetts.[92]

Civil-service reform ranks among the less complete victories of nineteenth-century reformers, but it proved sufficiently controversial to split the Republican party in 1872 and periodically to embroil each party in internal struggles thereafter. Flying sparks assured public awareness of the issues involved, and indeed these issues cut to the core of educational as well as political values. The very notion of written examinations challenged long-standing assumptions about the kind of knowledge worth possessing. Virtually unknown in eighteenth-century colleges, which relied instead on daily recitations and oral commencement exercises, written examinations spread in the second and third quarters of the nineteenth century, in Britain with the stimulus of utilitarianism and in America with that of common-school reform.[93] Horace Mann preferred them because they reduced opportunities for teachers to play favorites, thereby encouraging fair competition among students, and because they were conducive to the mastery of subjects.[94] In contrast to the orations and disputations of eighteenth-century commencement exercises, no one assigned students places or parts on written examinations, which were also much longer and more detailed than oral exercises. These qualities made written examinations appealing to public-school as well as civil-service reformers, for each group valued efficiency and fairness in education and government.

By 1870 written examinations had become the dominant form of testing at all levels of American education, and by 1882 the Fairy Queen in *Iolanthe* could sing of the duke's exalted station attained by competitive examination.[95] Yet while the relationship of these developments to civil-service reform was direct, their relevance to Chautauqua was more oblique. Vincent certainly did not view Chautauqua as a gigantic vocational school, and indeed it was not. But Chautauquans could use the C.L.S.C. for whatever purpose they chose, and some had vocational objectives. Compared to the middle- and upper-class matrons who dominated the women's clubs, Chautauquans formed a diverse group, men and women, young and old. Of those who enrolled in the C.L.S.C. course in 1882, 10 percent were under 20 and only 15 percent over 40, and over the years women usually outnumbered men in the circles by five to one.[96] Many of these students intended to become or already were teachers, a vocation for which a Chautauqua education was well-suited.

Although we often think of the late nineteenth century as marked by growing stress on "credentialing," that is, by the increasing requirement that job applicants possess formal educational certificates or diplomas, teachers still did not have to possess many academic credentials, and in fact very few did. The United States Bureau of Education reported in 1887 that some 225,000 teachers were employed throughout the nation, of whom over 80 percent were female. But less than 10 percent of the teachers had ever attended a normal school.[97] The National Education Association and state boards of education were pleading for higher standards for teachers, but these standards did not require normal-school certificates or college diplomas. Rather, the usual custom was to require teachers to pass examinations set by county superintendents of education. For example, in Indiana a prospective teacher had to present the superintendent with an original composition on an American or English author in order to secure a license.[98] In addition, whether granted by state boards or county superintendents, teaching licenses were graded. The most desirable ones, which were valid for three to five years, could be obtained only upon passing an examination in the "higher branches," including "mental science," botany, entomology, physiology, history, English literature, and bookkeeping (which was "higher" because it was taught in high schools rather than in primary schools). Inasmuch as familiarity with the higher branches was also a prerequisite for teaching in high schools, where the pay was better, the incentive was clear.[99]

To help teachers prepare for examinations, several states organized teachers' reading circles. The first of these, the Ohio Teachers' Reading Circle, was established in 1883; Indiana followed in 1884, and by 1887 a quarter of the teachers in the state were enrolled in its course, which included English history, "mental science," pedagogy, and the reading of Isaac Watts's ubiquitous *On the Improvement of the Mind*.[100] By 1887 over twenty states contained such circles, which had various ties to the Chautauqua circles. In some instances local Chautauqua circles did double duty as teachers' reading circles; in other cases the activities of teachers' and Chautauqua circles ran on parallel tracks. Teachers' reading circles used many of the same books as the Chautauqua circles and often employed the *Chautauquan* as an aid to study.[101]

Implicit here was not just the question of how prospective teachers secured licenses but also what level of education would be available to them, and since most teachers were women, the level of educational opportunity afforded women by Chautauqua and similar institutions of adult education. Eager to avoid antagonizing his friends and supporters in universities, Vincent was reluctant to advertise Chautauqua as the equivalent of a college education. The Lake Chautauqua Assembly did offer academic work through its College of Liberal Arts, but at least in terms of student numbers, this was a far less important division of Chautauqua than the summer lectures and concerts or the C.L.S.C. The latter adopted a four-year cycle, and Vincent instituted "Recognition Day" as a kind of graduation for circle members who persisted through all four years, but in contrast to collegians, circle members did not proceed through a four-year sequence marked by ascending difficulty or specialization. Rather, students who enrolled, for example, in 1886 read the course prescribed for that year, which was the same course followed in 1886 by students who had enrolled in 1885. Each annual group of C.L.S.C. readings was organized around a single subject; although there were variations, a typical four-year sequence included an English, American, European, and classical year. The circles focused on history and literature, for it proved impossible to teach laboratory sciences by correspondence. Further, only a little over 10 percent of Chautauquans completed all four years, and only half even two years.[102]

All of this would seem to distance Chautauqua from collegiate education, but in reality Chautauqua's relationship to higher education was ambivalent. Vincent deeply regretted that he had never attended college, and he thought of Chautauqua as a way for others to compensate for missed opportunities for higher education. In addition, Vincent believed that college graduates could profit from Chautauqua courses. Although ill-suited to instruction in science, the C.L.S.C. offered solid programs in English literature and in history, which compared well with those in colleges. Students at the University of Virginia in the 1880s read the same textbook on Roman history used by Chautauqua circles, save for the fact that the Virginia students studied the abridged version, which had been designed for use in the English public schools.[103] In 1881 there were only eleven full-time professors of history in American colleges and universities. Harvard did not introduce a course in American history until 1883, and then assigned it to young Albert Bushnell Hart, who held the lowly rank of instructor.[104] Even at pioneering Johns Hopkins, where Herbert Baxter Adams was spearheading a new approach to the graduate study of history through seminars, undergraduate instruction resembled Chautauqua instruction. In 1897 Adams offered to teach as a summer course at the Lake Chautauqua Assembly the same course that he taught to Hopkins undergraduates. His description of the course makes it sound like the sort of brisk canter familiar to succeeding generations of college students in courses on the history of civilization, for in a semester at Hopkins he covered the history of ancient China, Japan, India, Egypt, Chaldea, Phoenicia, Israel, Greece, Rome, and early Christianity.[105]

Although distinguishable from a college, Chautauqua fell within the perimeters of higher education, still in the 1880s a loosely defined concept. In 1888 George Edgar Vincent (John H. Vincent's son) wrote to Adams to beg, without success, "a good comprehensive, popularly stated definition of the higher education."[106] With their sundry collegiate institutes, seminaries, academies, and colleges, Americans did not consistently equate higher education with degree-granting colleges and universities, and in this context it is not surprising that college graduates joined Chautauqua circles or that teachers at Virginia's Hampton Institute subscribed to Chautauqua publications.[107]

Loose boundary lines between different levels of education invited a fair amount of trespassing in the 1870s and 1880s, especially on the part of women, who took advantage of whatever opportunities crossed their paths. For example, after receiving the B.S. degree from M.I.T. in 1873, Ellen Swallow conducted the science department of Anna Ticknor's Society to Encourage Studies at Home. Swallow's correspondence with students, many of whom complained of illness, aroused her interest in the relation between diet and health, and she began to direct her graduate studies at M.I.T. toward food and nutrition. After marrying engineering professor Robert Richards, she virtually created the field of home economics, which in mature form provided women with a clearly defined niche in academic science. But in the 1870s, before her turn to home economics as a gender-typed science, she could best be described as a chemist with an interest in food and sanitation. With support from the socially prominent Boston women who organized the Women's Education Association, she started a "Woman's Laboratory" at M.I.T., where she taught schoolteachers who, like herself, were interlopers in the male-dominated world of science.[108]

The early history of summer science institutes illustrates both the scope and the limits of women's opportunities on the margins of higher education. In 1873 Harvard's Louis Agassiz and his wife Elizabeth (who would become the first president of Radcliffe College) established a zoological laboratory on Penikese Island off the Massachusetts coast. Often cited as a precedent for university summer schools, the Penikese institute was actually less a school than a circle of researchers, about one-third of whom were women eager for the kind of laboratory investigation of science that Chautauqua could never provide. Cornelia M. Clapp, a mathematics instructor at Mount Holyoke Seminary, was among Agassiz's first students at Penikese, and she later became one of the first students at the Marine Biological Laboratory, which opened in 1888 at Woods Hole, Massachusetts. A year later Clapp earned the first of her two doctorates in science, and when Mount Holyoke upgraded itself to a degree-granting college in the 1890s, she became a professor of zoology there. Clearly, she used summer institutes as springboards to full-time graduate study. These marine laboratories afforded unwonted opportunities for women. David

Starr Jordan, who taught at the Penikese institute, later took his students, including Cornelia Clapp, on walking tours in the South and in Switzerland, and when he became the president of Stanford University hired several female instructors. Aware of the possibilities for advancing women in science, the Women's Education Association helped to fund the Marine Biological Laboratory, which developed from an institute conducted in the 1880s by one of Louis Agassiz's students at Annisquam, Massachusetts. By the mid-1890s, however, male scientists fresh from the universities were chafing at the presence of women at Woods Hole; in the 50 years after 1897 only two women (Cornelia Clapp was one) were elected trustees of the Marine Biological Laboratory.[109]

Other summer institutes that sprang up in the 1880s and early 1890s also attracted women, but without posing the same challenge as Woods Hole to male domination of an academic field. For example, the Concord Summer School of Philosophy began in 1879 as a haven for perspiring philosophers who sat in contemplative silence with Bronson Alcott and caught a glimpse of Emerson on his last legs. At Concord the Hegelian William Torrey Harris edited the *Journal of Speculative Philosophy,* and Julia Ward Howe, Ednah Dow Cheney, and Elizabeth Palmer Peabody lectured on philosophy.[110] In turn, the Concord school became a model for a summer school of applied ethics at Plymouth, Massachusetts, which Felix Adler, the founder of the Ethical Culture movement, started in 1891. Adler's school attracted a luminous faculty. Henry Carter Adams, Franklin H. Giddings, Frank Taussig, and Carroll Wright lectured there on economics, while Adler led the department of ethics and a third department covered the history of religion. The first session drew over 200 students from twenty states and Canada, including clergymen, lawyers, physicians, teachers, professors, and intellectually curious women.[111] In the same year, the polymath translator and philosopher Thomas Davidson opened a school for the "culture sciences" at Farmington, Connecticut. Soon the school moved to Glenmore, a village in the heart of New York's Adirondacks. John Dewey spent much of the summer of 1892 at Glenmore lecturing on English thought in the nineteenth century, while the Harvard idealist Josiah Royce gave a series of lectures on recent tendencies in ethical philosophy.[112]

In contrast to the early science institutes, however, these schools did not hold forth the promise of catapulting women into paying instructional positions in higher education. Rather they can fairly be described as culture resorts that brought together famous educators and curious laity in relatively unstructured environments and without proclaiming the goal of female vocational advancement. The women who lectured at the Concord school were veterans of Transcendentalism, a movement that long had regarded philosophy as a legitimate female avocation. As befitted its status as an offshoot of latter-day Transcendentalism, the Concord school's participants treated lectures merely as "textbooks" for conversation.

Although summer institutes would help to inspire the university summer sessions that proliferated after 1900, the latter not only taught more subjects but, perhaps more to the point, engaged more consciously in instruction, and they lacked the freewheeling and spontaneous intellectual exchange cherished by individuals like Adler and Davidson.[113] Ultimately, summer institutes could move in one of two directions, either toward the courting of millionaires to subsidize research (Woods Hole) or toward instructing schoolteachers, mainly female, who had few prospects of rising to university teaching and whose intellectual horizons were both shaped and limited by the curricula of the schools. Making no special efforts to serve the vocational interests of teachers, the summer schools of philosophy never approximated Chautauqua's clientele and depended heavily on the charisma of their founders. Those summer institutes that specifically aimed at teachers found that they had to adjust their objectives to the average teacher, who sought summer refreshment but who lacked the ambition of a Cornelia Clapp. For example, in 1879 Homer B. Sprague founded the Martha's Vineyard Summer Institute, which initially offered classes to teachers, mainly women, on subjects ranging from botany and entomology to Latin and Greek. At the time of the founding of the Martha's Vineyard institute, Sprague was serving as headmaster of the Girls' High School in Boston, many of whose students already were engaged in teaching. Sprague, who held a Ph.D. degree and who taught in and headed both high schools and colleges in the course of his career, devised an ambitious curriculum for the Martha's Vineyard institute, but he quickly discovered that the demand for courses in Latin and Greek could never sustain the institute, and in 1888 he adjusted its curriculum to include elocution and courses on how to teach arithmetic, vocal music, penmanship, geography, and history. The effect was instantaneous. Enrollments, as low as 150 in 1887, shot up to 250 in 1888 and to 350 by 1889. In 1890 the combined total of students and instructors reached 700.[114]

Summer institutes could increase their popular appeal not only by catering to the vocational interests of schoolteachers but also by devising a lyceum-style mixture of entertainment and light instruction. The clientele of summer schools mixed a hard inner core of serious students with a soft outer core of sympathizers and camp followers. At Lake Chautauqua this distinction translated into the difference between the resident schools such as the College of Liberal Arts, the school of sacred literature, and the C.L.S.C. on one side, and on the other the "popular" or "general" program of inspirational lectures and musical entertainments. The so-called popular programme was the drawing card, "the means by which the institution secures its revenues."[115] To arouse the general audience in Chautau-qua's Amphitheater, Hjalmar Boyeson wrote, a speaker had to pour forth "his very soul in fluent and easily comprehended speech."[116]

The same division appeared at the independent chautauquas. All of the independents copied the popular program of the Lake Chautauqua Assembly, but they less consistently accompanied it with serious academic work. Like the Lake Chautauqua Assembly, the independents maintained close ties to the Sunday-school movement, the Women's Christian Temperance Union, and church organizations like Christian Endeavor and the Epworth League, but in contrast to the "mother" chautauqua, they also depended heavily on financial backing from developers eager to promote resorts. For example, the Florida Chautauqua, established in 1884, was mainly the child of businessmen who wanted to advertise De Funiak Springs in the state's western panhandle as a resort; one of its organizers was the president of the railroad that ran through De Funiak Springs. New South spokesman Henry W. Grady organized the Piedmont Chautauqua at Salt Springs, Georgia, in 1888.[117] The profit motive made the independents, which offered courses in subjects like watercoloring and photography, highly receptive to student interests. The musical tastes of some promoters of independents ran to Swiss yodelers and the Hungarian Gypsy Quartet rather than to the classical music favored by John H. Vincent. Moreover, many of the independents featured the sort of "ever popular" lecturers who would give optimism a bad name: Rev. Sam Jones on "Mother, Home, and Heaven," Rev. De Witt Talmage on "The Bright Side of Things," A. W. "Sunshine" Hawks on "Sunshine and Happiness," and Captain Jack Crawford, who was said to wrap himself in "sunshine and buckskin."[118]

On average, the independents probably fell short of the academic standards of the Lake Chautauqua Assembly; Vincent complained that some "have simply taken the name and adopted a part of the plan, usually the so-called 'popular features' which are chiefly important as a source of revenue."[119] Yet the diversity of the independents, of which there were some 200 by 1890, makes generalizations about the average risky. A few did not offer any class work.[120] But most of the independents did sponsor classes. Here again there was a distinction between institutions like the Kentucky Assembly, which restricted itself to Bible studies, normal classes, "W.C.T.U. work," and music, and the more varied classes of the Piedmont Chautauqua, which conducted summer courses in German, French, English, English literature, history, pedagogy, physics, biology, and kindergarten. One of the largest of the independents, the Bay View (Michigan) Assembly, was virtually a clone of the Lake Chautauqua Assembly. Begun as a Methodist revival campground in the mid-1870s, in the 1880s it adopted a new name, a new academic purpose, and nearly all of the subdivisions of the Lake Chautauqua Assembly. In the early 1890s Bay View initiated a correspondence school, the Bay View Reading Circle, modeled on the C.L.S.C.[121]

Like most other independents, the Bay View Assembly distinguished its popular program and class work. It was divided into an "assembly," which ran from late July to mid-August, drawing some 12,000 people a summer, and the Bay View Summer University, which closed at the same time but which began a week earlier and offered courses in nine departments that ranged from the liberal arts to business, photography, and elocution. Typically, the summer university attracted 400 to 500 students. Other independents reported similar ratios between the drawing power of the popular program and that of their classes, but it would be misleading to think of the popular program as all sunshine and fluff. At the Florida Chautauqua in 1891, the apostle of the social gospel, Washington Gladden, delivered a course of six lectures on "Labor and Property" as part of the popular program, while a Professor Felkal gave a course of four lectures on astronomy. Following the plan of university extension lectures in Britain, which were starting to come into fashion in the United States, these lecturers distributed course outlines and closed their series with examinations.[122] The distinction between sunshine optimism and inspirational lectures on the one hand and class work on the other is clearer in retrospect than it was to contemporaries, who saw culture as a talisman that would make the world a nobler and happier place to live.

The subjects taught in the independents served various clienteles, including teachers. The Florida Chautauqua held a Teachers' Normal Institute in 1887; the San Marcos (Texas) Assembly introduced a summer normal institute that covered the subjects required for teachers in the state's public schools.[123] The Michigan board of education conducted a licensing examination for teachers during the closing weeks of the Bay View Summer University.[124] Independents and other summer institutes were also convenient places for young adults to prepare for entry into normal schools, for although these essentially were subcollegiate institutions, their students often were in their twenties and thirties.[125] Courses that appealed to teachers could also attract others. At a time when art was starting to become a standard school subject, teachers could benefit from courses in oil painting or crayon drawing, but such courses could also satisfy the artistic impulses of students who lacked vocational objectives.[126] The same was true of courses on "kindergarten," a staple of the independents; Friedrich Froebel, the father of kindergartens, believed that the basic task of education was to impart to children an understanding of simple design and form. To study kindergarten methods was to investigate the relationship between evolving human nature and artistic impulses.[127] Women who were sympathizers with rather than participants in education could visit the independents as well as the Lake Chautauqua Assembly to familiarize themselves with advanced thinking about education. Especially in the 1890s, southern women made annual pilgrimages to the northern chautauquas to learn about educational reforms that they would soon implant in their own region.[128]

One notably popular subject throughout the chautauquas, elocution, nicely illustrates the range of motives and convictions that propelled middle-class women into summer cultural excursions in the late nineteenth century. John H. Vincent commissioned a textbook on elocution, and nearly all of the independents had courses on or "schools" of elocution.[129] As an "analytic" science, elocution rested on the belief that voice tones and facial gestures constituted a language of their own, which could be mastered independently of the meaning of words. Elocutionists taught how to sigh, how to control one's breath, how to gesture, how to stop stammering. Whereas in the antebellum period young men used literary societies to observe models of oratory, elocutionists chopped the art of persuasion into a multitude of little exercises. The growing popularity of elocution in the Gilded Age testified to the rejection of the older ideal that linked high achievement to inventive genius, for where geniuses were born, elocutionists were made, fabricated in schools rather than in halls of debate.[130]

To master elocution was to acquire a kind of mediocre or middling competency, for elocution did not depend on a speaker's erudition, wit, or place. It was the perfect science for those of either gender who lacked the self-confidence to achieve eloquence. It was also useful. Inasmuch as schools were starting to hire elocution specialists, teachers had an incentive to learn something about it. As individuals whose vocation required daily public presentations of the self, teachers had every incentive to improve their skill in public speaking. For women who attended the independents, it was not only useful, but immediately so, for one distinctive feature of the independents was that they afforded women some opportunities to conduct classes rather than merely to enroll in them. As early as 1878, Mrs. Abba Gould Woolson offered a course of ten public lectures on history and literature at the Martha's Vineyard Summer Institute. In addition, women lectured on American history at the National Chautauqua in Glen Echo, Maryland, and conducted classes at the Bay View Summer University, where the absence of female professors at the University of Michigan had become a sore point among the state's clubwomen.[131]

Cultural Idealism in Context

Historians have been struck by the transitional quality of the movement represented by women's clubs, the Lake Chautauqua Assembly, the

C.L.S.C., and the independent chautauquas. By the early years of the twentieth century, several of these institutions were either in decline or shifting their purpose. For example, the independent chautauquas weakened in the face of competition from university summer schools and from the so-called tent chautauquas. University summer schools grew mainly after 1900 and largely in response to demands by state and local school boards that teachers possess the baccalaureate degree. Teachers flocked to the summer sessions of universities between 1900 and 1930 in quest of academic credits, those tiny ergs, now ubiquitous, which scarcely existed in the 1870s and 1880s.[132] While university summer schools absorbed the more vocationally oriented summer chautauquans, the tent chautauquas, peripatetic cultural circuses that moved from town to town (usually on recently completed railroad tracks) with an assortment of jugglers, magicians, light instrumental music, platform sunshine, and denunciations of strong drink, extended the inspirational features of the summer chautauquas through a vast "Chautauqua belt" from the Ohio to the Rockies. The number of communities sponsoring these traveling chautauquas rose from 33 in 1904 to 10,000 by 1921. Although Charles Horner and other impresarios of the tent chautauquas described them as responses to the people's "yearning for knowledge," in reality these chautauquas lacked a clear educational motive. Their clients were the kind of people Grant Wood would paint in "American Gothic," sober country folk who could not afford a summer holiday by the shores of lake whatever but who had been led by mail-order catalogues and newspaper advertisements to crave a touch of cosmopolitanism, to savor the up-to-dateness of Kansas City.[133]

After peaking in the 1890s, the C.L.S.C. also began a slow decline. The spread of tax-supported municipal libraries in the 1890s and later undercut its function as a distributor of otherwise unavailable books; so did the Sears-Roebuck catalogue, which by 1905 devoted sixteen pages to listing books for sale by mail. In 1891 Ida Tarbell ended her eight-year association with the *Chautauquan* and, after an interlude in Paris, signed on with S. S. McClure's new magazine *McClure's*.[134] There she gained fame with her serialized biographies of Napoleon and Lincoln, later published in book form, and helped to boost *McClure's* circulation from 60,000 in the fall of 1894 to 250,000 by July 1896.[135]

Tarbell's departure might have left the *Chautauquan* unruffled had it not been for the kind of magazine she joined. *McClure's* was representative of the new periodicals of the 1890s, a category that included *Munsey's Magazine*, *Cosmopolitan*, and the *Ladies' Home Journal*. Employing the latest technology, including the process of photoengraving that drastically cut the cost of illustration, and featuring the leading writers of the day, these magazines relied on their circulation to boost advertising, and, in contrast to the venerable Gilded Age periodicals like *Scribner's*, the *Atlan-*

tic Monthly, and *Harper's*, sold for a dime rather than for 25 to 35 cents. With the exception of Frank Munsey, who was conscious of profit to the exclusion of other motives, their editors and publishers (such as McClure, John Brisben Walker of *Cosmopolitan*, and Edward Bok of the *Ladies' Home Journal*) aspired to bring fine literature to the multitude. In the process, they created breezy and attractive alternatives to the ponderous format of the *Chautauquan*.[136] By the late 1890s the *Chautauquan* had abandoned its pedagogical tone for the style of *McClure's*. Similarly, a magazine called *Modern Culture* was originally entitled *Self-Culture* and distributed among the Home University League sponsored by the *Encyclopedia Britannica*. When *Self-Culture* became *Modern Culture* in 1900, it adopted the "popularized form of magazine presentation." The same was true of the *Bay View Magazine* and the *World To-day*, each of which had started in the 1890s as an offshoot of a Chautauqua-type reading circle and then had abandoned by 1905 the reprinting of course outlines and questions and answers in favor of articles describing trips through France or visits to the sites of the ancient world.[137]

The earnest culture-study that marked the C.L.S.C. suffered not only from competition from sprightly periodicals but also from the expansion of opportunities for women to acquire higher education in prestigious universities. The descent of women on the University of Chicago after it opened in 1892 occurred so swiftly as to provoke fears that the institution would become a women's college. The same was true at Stanford, and by 1900 female students either equaled or outnumbered men at a host of state universities.[138] The proliferation of reform movements after 1900 provided women's clubs with an alternative to culture-study. In a memorable address President Sarah P. Decker told the General Federation of Women's Clubs in 1904 that Dante was dead and that women now preferred "being" to "Browning."[139] Only a minority of clubwomen became reform activists, but most shifted their focus from culture-study to the study of social issues. The women's club in Muncie, Indiana, was representative of the trend. In 1890 its entire membership engaged in the study of literature, art, music, and ancient history, but thereafter new categories started to appear on the club's study agenda: "philanthropy and civics," "sociology," and current events.[140] In effect, clubwomen became mild Progressives; by dissociating the Social Question from radicalism, Progressivism created a congenial climate for this shift of study focus. Indeed, many individuals who became prominent in Progressive reform, including Robert M. La Follette, Jane Addams, and Jacob Riis, used the institutions of popular education forged in the late nineteenth century, especially the independent chautauquas and the platform of the Lake Chautauqua Assembly, to build constituencies for reform.[141]

In theory, Arnoldian culture was by no means incompatible with engagement in activities intended to relieve social distress. Arnold himself had propagated culture as a solvent for social unrest in England. But the ideal of culture did not delineate specific roles for average individuals to play in reform movements. The cultured scholar, by implication a male, could discharge his duty toward society by disseminating ideal values in books or speeches, but for the great majority of educated persons who did not trust their ability to come before the public as writers or orators, Arnoldianism failed to spell out a plausible social role.

All of this has prompted scholars to interpret culture-study as a stage through which those excluded from the mainstream, mainly women, had to pass to build their confidence to tackle pressing social issues.[142] Yet two interpretive problems bedevil this approach. First, it is ahistorical, for just as seeds do not grasp the fact that they are germinating, few women leaped into culture-study to prepare for roles in reform movements that had yet to take shape, or to play a more active role in the established suffrage movement. No one needed a boost from culture-study to become a suffragist, and in fact the General Federation of Women's Clubs was slow to endorse a federal suffrage amendment. Second, to stress culture-study's preparatory role slights the fervent enthusiasm it aroused in the 1870s and 1880s. A participant in a Minnesota Chautauqua circle wrote that the great benefit he derived from its course was "to get his mind so filled with the higher things of life that there may be no room for anything degrading or impure."[143] Even those with overt or covert vocational goals seem to have derived inspiration from culture-study, which spurred a level of emotional commitment that matched the inspirational qualities of the summer chautauquas and that was notably missing in later experiments with instruction by mail.

One revealing illustration of the inspirational effect of culture-study lies in its permeation by ritual. When he announced the C.L.S.C. in 1878, Vincent appeared on a platform hedged by a globe, astronomical instruments, and books. C.L.S.C. classes had their own songs, banners, and pledges, and in the 1880s local circles often staged classical evenings in which members donned costumes to impersonate the Muses or Caesar Augustus. In addition, the C.L.S.C. set aside days for celebrated authors; it encouraged Bryant Days and Longfellow Days. In 1883, for example, a Chautauqua circle in Westfield, New York, celebrated Longfellow's birthday by passing the day reading "Evangeline" and by holding a supper in the evening.[144] Circles in Lockport, New York, Hiawatha, Kansas, and Media, Pennsylvania, held similar festive observances of Longfellow's birthday. Comparable rituals appeared in reading clubs that had no connection to the C.L.S.C. The Cedar Falls Parlor Reading Circle responded to Longfellow's death by festooning his portrait, snipped from an issue of a periodical, with evergreens and by placing a number of his books on a stand in front of the portrait.[145] A women's club in Kalamazoo decorated its building with stained-glass windows depicting scenes from famous works of literature and inscribed with quotations from the represented authors.[146] Matthew Arnold's tour of the United States in 1883 elicited the kind of rituals that might have accompanied visiting royalty. When Arnold spoke before the Aesthetic Society of Jersey City, the program, conducted in a local church, included an extended greeting by Mrs. Erminnie Smith, the society's president and an early member of Sorosis; the reading of "appropriate lines" from Elizabeth Browning's poetry; a quartet singing "God Save the Queen"; a speech by the chief justice of New York; sundry musical renditions; and a performance by "Mr. Lincoln, the talented elocutionist and mimic." [147]

Anthropologists usually have interpreted ritual and ceremony in the context of primitive religion; to apply these terms to the secular activities of modern industrial society poses risks. Although secular society abounds with nonreligious ceremonies and with those standardized ceremonies we call rituals, neither secular ceremony nor ritual necessarily reflects the attributes associated with religion in primitive societies. Secular rituals might survive while losing whatever role they once played in aligning participants with beliefs beyond themselves.[148] Yet these strictures cannot fairly be applied to the ceremonies of Chautauquans and clubwomen of the Gilded Age, which resembled acts of religion.[149] These were widely adopted, engaged in with great seriousness, and appear to have served as tangible embodiments of the vague but intense yearning for something higher and more ideal than daily life. Taking as axiomatic that ritual is a form of symbolic expression—"*the symbolic use of bodily movement and gesture to articulate meaning*"—we can suggest that the rituals described not only forged solidarity within study clubs but also enhanced the emotional and intellectual identification of provincial audiences with the contemporary world of high culture.[150]

In the early twentieth century, George Santayana gave this world of late-nineteenth-century cultural idealism a name: the Genteel Tradition. Like most efforts to periodize history by nomenclature, the term has produced a lot of debate, but there is little reason to stray beyond Howard Mumford Jones's concise description of the Genteel Tradition as "an operative fusion of idealism and the instinct for craftsmanship, which dominated high culture from 1865 to 1915 and which infiltrated the culture of the middle class."[151] The term "idealism" was—and remains—open to various interpretations, but here it is equated with the belief that human activity must conform to ideal types of conduct that had been aesthetically or philosophically defined, and that the artist was responsible for encouraging conformity to these ideal types. The concept of idealism was close to that of culture; together, these concepts affirmed that all progress depended on the holding of anterior ideals of perfection. Society did not advance, as Herbert Spencer argued, by material laws of which human actors scarcely were conscious; rather, the prerequisite of progress was the purposive embrace of ideas of perfection.

Idealism dominated the thinking of leading magazine editors and literary critics as well as of educators. The scandals of the Grant administration, the Great Railway Strike of 1877, and the Haymarket Riot of 1886 were so many tocsins that warned of a dangerously fragmented society, and in response the "best men" sought to unify and elevate society under the banner of culture. Their conviction that culture had to be assessed by its social effects stirred members of this alliance of the educated to communicate with and educate the public. If the Genteel Tradition had a motto, it could have been drawn from the title of the autobiography of one of its paladins, Bliss Perry (who borrowed it from Chaucer): *And Gladly Teach*. Perry was not only a professor at Harvard but a self-ordained minister to reading circles. His *A Study of Prose Fiction* (1902) told readers exactly how to contrast the types of characters in a novel and how to describe the differences in style and structure between two literary works.[152]

Long before Perry, custodians of the Genteel Tradition were turning literary journals into vehicles of popular instruction. For example, in 1873 the critic Edmund C. Stedman began to serialize in *Scribner's* chapters of what became his book *Victorian Poets*.[153] A work of criticism, *Victorian Poets* dealt with Tennyson, Swinburne, both Brownings, and Arnold among others, and thereby underscored the cosmopolitan Anglo-Americanism of the Genteel Tradition.[154] From *Victorian Poets* to his *Nature and Elements of Poetry* (1892), Stedman sought to teach the public about poetry rather than merely inspire it with a love of poetry. Following Hippolyte Taine's *History of English Literature*, translated in 1871, he tried to reverse the course of American criticism, which, as a reviewer of Taine observed, usually had consisted of masses of undigested literary information and plain gossip.[155]

Stedman and like-minded critics not only made the Victorian poets accessible to Americans but also codified American literature, particularly the New England Renaissance. During the 1870s and 1880s, when women's clubs and Chautauqua circles worshipped at the altar of Tennyson, Longfellow, Bryant, and Emerson, a combination of eastern literary critics, publishing houses, and such literary periodicals as the *Atlantic Monthly, Scribner's*, and *Harper's* created the canon of Great Names that schoolchildren for generations after had to learn.[156] Ignoring Melville, deploring Whitman, and at most tolerating Poe, the canon was insular, but it combined insularity with a sense of mission, and it exerted a cultural magnetism strong enough to pull western rebels like Twain and Hamlin Garland to New England. For those who could not make the pilgrimage, the literary periodicals of the Genteel Tradition provided a surrogate. The portrait of Longfellow that members of the Cedar Falls Parlor Reading Circle adorned at his death had been cut from the *Atlantic Monthly*, and the circle's founding had been inspired by the "Home and Society" and "Culture and Progress" sections of *Scribner's*, which Josiah G. Holland edited until his death in 1881. Through these columns, Holland attempted to uplift middle-class taste in books, furnishings, flowers, and manners. All such artifacts could become "agencies of culture."[157] Upon visiting his kinswoman Olive Chancellor, Basil Ransom, the male protagonist of Henry James's *The Bostonians* (1886), discovers "culture in Miss Chancellor's tables and sofas, in the books that were everywhere on little shelves like brackets (as if a book were a statuette), in the photographs and watercolors that covered the walls, and in the curtains that were festooned rather stiffly in the doorways."

An early biographer of Holland suggested an appropriate title for him: "The Great Apostle to the Multitude of Intelligent Americans who have Missed a College Education."[158] The same title could have been applied to John H. Vincent. Just as Vincent opened Chautauqua's platform to Unitarians and Christian evolutionists, Holland shared Henry Ward Beecher's view that Protestant denominations should concern themselves less with saving souls than with the application of religion to everyday life. Neither Vincent nor Holland had attended college; each regretted the fact and sought to make up for lost time. From our perspective they seem to have occupied positions on the periphery of American intellectual life in the Gilded Age, but many contemporaries saw them in a different light. We are more apt than they to be influenced by Whitman's view of Holland as a man good enough to tell the difference between a dime and a half-dollar but not good enough for anything else, or by William James's stinging dismissal of Chautauqua ("this order too tame, this culture too second-rate, this goodness too uninspiring").[159] Their legions of devoted followers were more likely to take note of Vincent's friendship with leading academicians, including Richard T. Ely, Herbert Baxter Adams, and William Rainey Harper, and to observe that Holland's books had "tone" (they were elegantly written), that James Russell Lowell had favorably reviewed his major poem, and that he consorted with New York's literary elite, including William Dean Howells. In sum, the lines between core and periphery seemed indistinct to many contemporaries, who engaged in rituals of culture-study as a way to align themselves with a high culture notable for its avowal of public goals and for its earnest tutoring of the public.

The Challenge to Culture

Culture never lacked critics. Literati who despaired at its methodical earnestness tried to rescue culture from the grasp of women by contending that "true" culture demanded a more strenuous and bold undertaking than joining a reading circle. William James and Rudyard Kipling, who in different ways extolled the strenuous life, numbered their experience of having been "Chautauq'd" among those they preferred to forget (on visiting Lake Chautauqua, Kipling "wrapped" himself in smoke lest he be mistaken for a missionary). In 1893 the critic Hamilton Wright Mabie pronounced the systematic pursuit of culture to be self-defeating, for "the more one really cares for it, the less he professes it; the more he comes into possession of it, the less conscious does his pursuit of it become." Like grace bestowed by Calvin's God, culture "discloses its presence" to the individual and conveys "the impression of a large and spontaneous force playing through a rich nature."[160]

By the early 1890s Chautauqua was sufficiently well established to invite pricking of its pretensions. Yet even before Chautauqua's founding, the values associated with Arnoldian culture aroused dissent. Antebellum lyceum audiences had heard Emerson question the value of book knowledge. Whitman often voiced the need for a culture rooted in rather than detached from daily life. In 1872 Charles Dudley Warner, a journalist and novelist who collaborated with Mark Twain to write *The Gilded Age*, had wondered aloud whether the intellectual values of the educated had any relevance to the working class.[161] In the same year, E. L. Youmans started the *Popular Science Monthly* to spread the materialistic doctrines of Spencer and Darwin. The Great Railway Strike preceded the organization of the C.L.S.C. by a year, and the Haymarket Riot coincided with the publication of Vincent's *The Chautauqua Movement*. The world of Chautauquans was far removed from the destabilizing forces represented by Spencer, strikes, and Haymarket, but reading circles were not barricades behind which the middle class withdrew. In the 1870s and 1880s advocates of culture saw it as a way to open rather than close doors. Missionaries for culture afforded women new opportunities for education and, as discussed in the next chapter, entertained the not entirely fatuous expectation of building a constituency for culture within the working class. Their success in popularizing culture by the end of the 1880s left them exhilarated rather than depressed at the start of the 1890s.

Conclusion

In *The Bostonians* Basil Ransom finds evidence that Boston is "a city of culture" (as he has always heard) in "accessories": the presence and display of books and furnishings. In the Gilded Age, culture still connoted a process but increasingly it was becoming a thing, whether tangible (a portrait or flower display) or intangible (a body of knowledge). Although the shift from self-culture to culture-study was gradual and never complete, it had proceeded far enough by the 1890s to provoke anguished cries from elite critics, who continued to associate culture with gentlemanly activity rather than with cultural information or mere things. Significantly, in the 1830s William Ellery Channing had urged self-culture as a process suitable for everyone, a far cry from the pronouncements of late Victorian critics.

The changing reputation of cultural acquisition reflected concerted efforts in the Gilded Age to popularize culture. For every Hamilton Wright Mabie there were a dozen Hollands and Vincents, individuals determined to construct popular constituencies for culture and ingenious at devising pedagogy for the multitude. Largely self-taught, these popularizers maintained innumerable direct contacts with the unwashed and were acutely sensitive to the importance of the building blocks of knowledge—in other words, to things. They reified culture to diffuse it. Yet their success ultimately depended less on their ingenuity as teachers than on the enthusiastic response of their followers, mainly female, who discovered in culture-study any number of actual and potential benefits: surrogate higher education, vocational preparation, social status, moral purpose, and a bonding with "the best that has been thought and known."

Chapter 6

The Decline of Culture, 1890–1900

Historians usually see the rise and fall of intellectual movements as issues decided on the battlefield of controversy. If this idea is applied to the 1890s, champions of social reform and artistic realism jousted with and ultimately dismounted knights-errant of the Genteel Tradition. Burdened by mounds of armor that had become dysfunctional in an age when strife between capital and labor, natives and immigrants, and farmers and Wall Street made clear the need for practical, realistic solutions, the vanquished knights could never rise again.

This way of looking at history gives an accurate impression of the direction of change in the 1890s. The idea that education should lift the individual beyond the material concerns of everyday life into a realm of beauty and ideal truth began to decline during this decade; by 1900 it was in retreat and by 1910 in shambles. But the battlefield analogy conveys little sense of the process of change, which engaged not only ideas but institutions and their sponsors in successive attempts to define a satisfactory relationship between intellectuals and the public.[1] Experiments in popular education during the 1870s and 1880s, most notably Chautauqua, did little to upset the notion that the pursuit of culture could form a common ground between intellectuals and the public. At the start of the 1890s, even the daring realist novelist George Washington Cable pinned his hopes for the elevation of the masses on a network of "home culture" clubs (little Chautauqua-style reading circles that would fill idle hours with noble thoughts), and after opening Hull House in 1889 Jane Addams spent a decade disseminating what she called "college-type culture" to immigrants. She engaged lecturers from the University of Chicago, hung reproductions of masterpieces on the settlement's walls, and earned a favorable notice from Herbert Baxter Adams, who favored art to uplift "Italians and other foreign-born, with whom it is not always easy to converse."[2]

This is not the usual image of Addams, the pluralist and activist who doubted the value of mere "mental accumulations" and who started a settlement house to overcome her feelings of dispirited passivity.[3] Yet her decade-long dalliance with Arnoldian culture is understandable on several counts. It suited her genteel education at Illinois' Rockford Female Seminary and her respect for Matthew Arnold, whose grave she visited on a European tour in the 1880s. In addition, owing to William Rainey Harper, a Chautauquan who became its first president and who initiated its extension program, the University of Chicago was able to provide Addams with a steady flow of lecturers. Some of these buried their subjects under dry facts and abstruse hypotheses, but others had acquired a knack for popular lecturing and their presentations inspired passionate involvement from Hull House audiences. Slavic immigrants had no trouble relating a lecture on European capitals and their social significance to the feud between Austria-Hungary and its Slavic subjects; Greeks were pleased to see reproductions of the Acropolis, and Italians to meet Americans who valued something other than money.[4]

Addams gradually abandoned Arnoldian culture in favor of "socialized education," which she defined as "education addressed to the client's immediate situation."[5] In this respect she typified the trend, but her evolution occurred in stages and without any hint that culture was unpopular among poorly educated immigrants. In Addams's case, the shift from Arnoldian culture coincided with her changing focus from immigrants to their children and her realization that to encourage immigrants to cherish their European culture only widened the distance between them and their Americanized offspring.[6] Others who employed culture as the basis of popular education in the 1890s reached the same destination as Addams: socialized education addressed to immediate situations rather than the diffusion of ideal culture. Like Addams, their transit took place in stages and by a process of trial and error. Like Addams, they initially saw no incompatibility between culture and addressing the Social Question; in fact, they were sure that culture would establish a common ground between social classes. Like Addams, they abandoned culture when their experiences within institutions to diffuse it persuaded them that culture, while popular at some level, failed to establish such a common ground.

In one respect, Addams differed from most apostles of culture in the 1890s: she entered the decade with at least a half-articulated sense of culture's vulnerability to the charge that it patronized its clients, that it rested on the scholar's superiority to everyone else. Most apostles outside the social settlements, specifically those who mounted campaigns in the 1890s for university extension and public libraries, started with no such reservations. Paradoxically, many of them jettisoned culture more swiftly than did Addams.

University Extension

University extension began to come into fashion in the United States toward the end of the 1880s. In the antebellum era, professors such as Louis Agassiz and Benjamin Silliman, Sr., had frequently lectured in public on scientific topics, and in the 1860s Andrew Dickson White, future president of Cornell but then a young instructor in history at the University of Michigan, lectured in a number of Michigan towns "to spread the interests of the university."[7] But none of this amounted to a concerted movement for university extension. The extension movement that arose at the end of the 1880s owed less to these precedents than to the twin examples of Chautauqua and the British university extension movement.

During the 1880s prominent academic figures such as Richard T. Ely and Herbert Baxter Adams developed close ties with the Chautauqua movement. Although Ely acquired a reputation as a radical in some quarters, his brew of social concern with deep religious conviction made him a welcome lecturer at the Lake Chautauqua Assembly, where he attracted, among others, the future muckraker Ida Tarbell. The Chautauqua circles were no less familiar with Ely's name. He originally composed his *Introduction to Political Economy* as part of the C.L.S.C.'s required reading program. As a graduate student at the universities of Göttingen, Heidelberg, and Berlin, Adams had come to admire the German system of state support for adult education and, upon returning to the United States, he settled on the Chautauqua model as a promising substitute for state sponsorship of adult education. Adams even called Chautauqua a "folk moot," just as he found the "germs" of fabled New England democracy in the moots of the primitive Aryo-Teutons who inhabited the Black Forest in the days of Tacitus.[8] Chautauqua had already taken tentative steps toward university extension. John H. Vincent had successfully hammered "the best that has been thought and known" into a series of discrete subjects that could be studied by masses of earnest autodidacts. Despite Vincent's frequent disclaimers of any intention to offer the equivalent of a university education, the Chautauqua Assembly briefly incorporated itself as a university, in part to offer extension courses and academic degrees to the more persistent members of the Chautauqua circles.[9] Chautauqua's success in attracting students impressed contemporaries as "striking testimony to what economists call 'an effective demand' upon the part of the general public for a liberal education."[10]

The inspiration for university extension also sprang from the apparent success of British universities in planting the field of extension lectures during the 1870s and 1880s. Starting in 1867, James Stuart of Cambridge University began to offer lectures to audiences of women, and by 1873, when Cambridge undertook formal sponsorship of extramural classes, Stuart had developed the procedures that were to characterize British university extension for the next half century: lecture series on announced topics; the issuance of formal syllabi; discussion; the writing of essays (undertaken to provide women too shy or nervous to speak in public with a way to express themselves), and examinations.[11]

Cambridge's considerable success with extension classes—by 1875 the university had enrolled some 17,000 students in extension classes held at local centers throughout the nation—inspired similar experiments elsewhere in Britain. The London Society for the Extension of University Teaching, formed in 1877, enrolled 6,000 students by 1887. At Oxford University, Michael Sadler developed an extension program whose enrollments rivaled those of Cambridge by the late 1880s. It was not long before full-time extension lecturers, the so-called staff lecturers, came to dominate the movement in Britain. Several of these staff lecturers, including Richard G. Moulton, W. Hudson Shaw, and Hilaire Belloc, came to America during the 1890s to lecture under the auspices of one or more of the major American pioneers of university extension.

The models of the British extension movement and Chautauqua propelled the American extension movement of the 1890s toward the study of culture in the form of literature, history, economics, natural science, and the fine arts. Neither vocational education nor what later became known as public service formed components of university extension during the 1890s. In addition, the Americans borrowed from Britain the model of lecture courses, with printed syllabi and homework to supplement the lectures. Few American advocates of university extension wanted to emulate the unsystematic lyceum lectures of an earlier time. The Americans also copied the British movement's reliance on localism and voluntarism. In both countries the minimal definition of university extension, the offering of off-campus lectures by professors, took hold. Neither the British nor the Americans expected universities to provide significant financial or administrative support for these lectures. In the late 1880s, for example, New York's state librarian, Melvil Dewey, devised a plan for "university extension" under the auspices of his library. Similarly, Herbert Baxter Adams remembered his student days at the University of Heidelberg, where professors occasionally secured special rooms as book deposits for the exclusive use of their advanced seminar students. He urged American public librarians to "set apart special rooms where classes and clubs can meet under competent direction for special use of books," and he contended that "every great public library should become, in its own field, a people's university, the highest of high schools in the community."[12]

Though little came of these schemes, a combination of local centers and independent sponsoring organizations guided extension in both countries. In essence, civic, labor, or church groups were expected to invite university lecturers, pay their expenses and fees, and arrange for their accommodation. The assumption that local centers would drive extension had American roots in the practice of antebellum lyceums and in the more recent spread of Chautauqua circles and women's clubs. Adams, who frequently lectured before such organizations, interpreted Chautauqua's growth as incontrovertible proof that demand for culture-study was surging through American society and would sustain local initiatives. He contended that public support for extension would corrode voluntarism. "Not a dollar should be granted to localities or institutions to enable them to enjoy academic lectures," he insisted.[13]

In keeping with this de-emphasis on direct public or university involvement, private and independent societies took the lead in coordinating extension lectures. In America the most important of these was the Philadelphia Society for the Extension of University Teaching, founded in 1890. The brainchild of William Pepper, the provost of the University of Pennsylvania, this society arranged for several colleges in the area and the University of Pennsylvania to provide lecturers for interested local centers. An intimate friend of Philadelphia's civic and business leaders, Pepper saw the society as a way to enhance his university's image, particularly among the business and professional elite, but he was careful to keep the society administratively apart from the university.[14]

The Philadelphia Society quickly gained support from the ubiquitous Adams, who recognized that Dewey's efforts to construct an extension program around the state library in New York were having difficulty getting off the ground. Additional encouragement for the Philadelphia Society's efforts sprang from Richard G. Moulton, the most popular extension lecturer in England and a man who stated flatly that "university extension has nothing to do with universities."[15] The son of a Methodist circuit rider, Moulton stood foursquare in the same tradition of educational evangelism occupied by John H. Vincent. Much like James Stuart of Cambridge, Moulton believed that popular demand for higher learning beyond the universities would outstrip the ability or interest of universities to respond. While Stuart struggled to overcome inertial resistance to popularization at Cambridge, Moulton transited the Atlantic to become a stalwart supporter of the Philadelphia Society.[16]

Under the sponsorship of the Philadelphia Society, university extension spread swiftly in the Philadelphia area. Existing institutions, including YMCAs, YWCAs, civic clubs, and an occasional workingmen's group, became the local centers that petitioned the society for lecturers. Often, in fact, these local centers negotiated directly with professors. In these cases the Philadelphia Society undertook to print syllabi and make travel arrangements. Since universities in the area did not directly support extension, Pepper, who served as first president of the society, spent much of his time soliciting support from his wealthy friends. During its first year of operations, 1890–91, the Philadelphia Society arranged for 40 courses in 23 local centers (most in Pennsylvania, New Jersey, and Delaware); the 290 lectures sponsored that year drew 55,000 people. Exhilarated by its success, the society changed its name in December 1890 to the American Society for the Extension of University Teaching (ASEUT). Although it never became a truly national organization, ASEUT remained the most important component of the American extension movement during the 1890s.[17]

In contrast to Philadelphia, Baltimore lacked an independent society to coordinate university extension lectures. But The Johns Hopkins University, opened in 1876, contained a core of professors who, like Herbert Baxter Adams, were dedicated to bridging the gap between academic intellectuals and the public. Its newness deprived Johns Hopkins of the cushion of public support that generations of collegiate graduates provided for older, well-established institutions.[18] These characteristics of the university stimulated Adams, his colleague Richard T. Ely, and such students of theirs as Frederick Jackson Turner, Charles McLean Andrews, and E. W. Bemis to actively cultivate ties to the community by offering extension courses. Since Johns Hopkins University provided no direct subsidy for their efforts, its extension-oriented faculty depended on initiatives from voluntary associations. Chautauqua circles in the Baltimore area, teachers' associations, and the YMCA all provided students for extension courses.[19]

Despite the original assumption that universities would shun direct sponsorship of extension courses, several universities began to take an interest in off-campus instruction during the 1890s. In contrast to well-established eastern colleges and universities, midwestern universities increasingly saw extension as a way to establish their public usefulness and gain sympathy from legislatures and/or civic leaders. William Rainey Harper, the Hebrew and classical scholar who left the Yale faculty and Chautauqua's College of Liberal Arts to accept the presidency of the newly founded University of Chicago in 1892, led Chicago to establish an extension division that offered both lecture and correspondence courses, which quickly absorbed the work of an ASEUT-type independent society founded in the Chicago area in 1891.

As late as 1900, when enthusiasm elsewhere for extension was lagging, Herbert Baxter Adams saw potential in Chicago's extension programs for the development of "a vast academic and national alliance" that would bind educated men and women everywhere together in the cause of good.[20] In 1898 Chicago's extension lecture courses alone attracted an aggregate attendance of 30,000 in 92 local centers. Its correspondence courses extended the university's reach far beyond the Chicago area. Harper's experiences at Chautauqua, particularly his familiarity with the C.L.S.C., led him to cherish correspondence courses as an outstanding method of popular education.[21] Annie M. McLean, who supervised Chicago's correspondence program in sociology, reported that between 1893 and 1923 the university enrolled 32,000 students in its correspondence courses in sociology. The clientele of Chicago's correspondence courses was far more diverse than that of Chautauqua-style reading circles; whereas the latter remained overwhelmingly middle-class and female, the former included gardeners, cigar-makers, department-store managers, college professors, farmers, nurses, druggists, postal clerks, priests, teachers, truant officers, secretaries, cashiers, engineers, and housewives.[22]

Just as Harper brought Chautauqua's inspiration to the University of Chicago, Richard T. Ely carried it to the University of Wisconsin. When Ely left Johns Hopkins for Wisconsin in 1892, he had already established himself as a leading exponent of the new currents in American economic thought that castigated the abuses wrought by unrestrained capitalism. His *Social Aspects of Christianity* (1889) had become a best-seller; indeed his gift for mixing academic economics and religious inspiration had made him a darling of audiences at the Chautauqua Assembly and at many of the independent chautauquas. Lured from Johns Hopkins by President Thomas C. Chamberlin of Wisconsin, Ely agreed to direct Wisconsin's extension activities in return for a free hand in shaping the university's projected department of civics, sociology, and historical science.[23] Even before Ely's arrival, Madison had become the site of the Lake Monona Assembly, an independent chautauqua at which Washington Gladden and William Graham Sumner vigorously debated their sharply clashing approaches to economic issues, while Adams's former student, Frederick Jackson Turner, frequently delivered public lecture courses in the Madison area.[24]

In addition to his fame and energy, Ely brought two graduate students to Wisconsin, Lyman Powell and F. W. Speirs. While Powell organized local centers throughout the state, Speirs supervised the extension program at the People's Institute in Milwaukee, an institution that grew out of philanthropic efforts to quiet labor unrest in that city by instructing workers in the value of self-culture. As in the East, local centers formed the spine of extension during the 1890s. As the historian of Wisconsin's extension programs has noted, "the local mainstays of extension were the teachers and church and social clubs whose members made house-to-house ticket sales and opened their homes to the teachers."[25]

In all of the universities where extension took root in the 1890s, its success depended on the dedication of regular faculty members. Extension divisions had yet to emerge as self-sustaining bureaucracies engaged in carving out spheres of activity apart from those of the faculty. University extension demanded professors eager to become apostles of culture. The Chautauqua-Johns Hopkins axis provided many of these ambassadors, including Harper, Adams, Ely, Turner, and Bemis. These scholars were not averse to using extension to build support for their campus departments.[26] But extension also sparked abundant idealism as "essentially a missionary enterprise" that "can be carried on only in a missionary spirit."[27]

Despite the enthusiasm that it aroused, the extension movement of the 1890s fell far short of expectations. By the mid-1890s interest in extension had waned at all of the midwestern universities save the University of Chicago, and by the late 1890s ASEUT had retrenched its activities to the vicinity of Philadelphia. Still national in name, it had become local rather than even regional in scope. In a lengthy report of "educational extension" published in 1900, Adams pronounced a virtual obituary on the movement. Most advocates of university extension would have agreed with George E. Vincent's assertion in 1904 that "university extension dealing with culture studies, not with professional pursuits, cannot be made permanently self-sustaining."[28]

Few movements to have swept across the American educational landscape left more unfulfilled expectations than university extension of the 1890s. Although the idea of university extension was revived in the United States after 1905, extension no longer stressed the diffusion of culture through popular instruction in academic subjects like history, literature, economics, and the natural sciences. Rather, vocational courses and a variety of activities that answered to the name "public service" thrust their way toward the center of extension offerings. Academic intellectuals gradually lost interest in the movement; the new leaders were more likely to be professional administrators whose jobs depended on their ability to attract students to off-campus courses. These were individuals who viewed higher education from the boiler room rather than from the bridge. Compared to the university extension movement of the 1890s, the revived movement was far more prone to take its cues from the perceived interests of clients rather than from the university curriculum.

The reorientation of extension programs during the early twentieth century sprang from various sources, but it depended initially on the conviction that to tie extension to the diffusion of academic subjects would severely restrict its impact. Under pressure from legislatures to prove their worth, state universities opted for high-yield service and vocational programs that offered virtually no scope to leading academic intellectuals. The latter, in turn, had quickly become disillusioned by the long hours demanded by work in the field of extension. Herbert Baxter Adams cited the vast distances separating local centers, the difficulty of attracting faculty members to a life dominated by railroad schedules, and the greater importance attached by professors and presidents to on-campus instruction.[29] As an exhausted and chastened Frederick Jackson Turner concluded, he needed less extension and more *"intension."*[30] The lukewarm public response to extension, Adams added, offered little inducement for professors to surmount these obstacles.

Much of this was true. Unlike the lyceum lecturers of the 1840s and 1850s, university professors of the 1890s did not depend on off-campus lecturing for their livelihoods. Professors had only to glance at the grueling burden imposed on ASEUT staff lecturers to realize how exhausting a serious commitment to extension could become. For example, one ASEUT staff lecturer traveled 20,000 miles in a single year and spoke before 34,000 people.[31] By the late 1890s, in addition, public interest in extension courses was definitely waning. The format, borrowed from Britain, of lectures followed by course work proved cumbersome and unattractive. Only a quarter to a third of those who signed up for lectures stayed for course work and less than 1 percent of these did enough course work to secure certificates.[32] Because most universities did not offer academic credit for extension courses, students had little incentive to complete them. For example, teachers who sought to continue their studies increasingly preferred to take on-campus summer courses for credit rather than to patronize extension courses. As early as 1891 Charles McLean Andrews, a student of Adams's who was briefly caught up in the latter's enthusiasm for university extension, doubted whether extension would do more than prick popular interest in academic subjects. It was one thing, Andrews observed, to train students in a school, quite another matter to train listeners at a lecture.[33]

In retrospect, it is easy to see how Adams and Ely were beguiled by the Chautauqua model. Venturing into upstate New York for what amounted to paid summer vacations, they had gathered the fruits of Chautauqua without much toil. Neither man understood how many hours John H. Vincent and Ida Tarbell had worked to make Chautauqua a popular success. Rather, Adams's description of Chautauqua as a folk moot imputed an inevitability to its growth, as if it flourished merely as a by-product of self-enacting historical laws. In reality, the Chautauqua Assembly and the sundry independent chautauquas had always taken care to complement their serious course work with the drawing card of the "popular programme." Similarly, the Chautauqua circles made abundant provision for "social culture," including parlor rituals and neighborly fellowship. More broadly, the Chautauqua circles, women's clubs, independent chautauquas, and the Lake Chautauqua Assembly allowed women to participate as organizers, lecturers, and study leaders. University extension failed to duplicate these peripheral but important features of culture-study. Not a single woman lectured under the auspices of university extension during the 1890s.

University Extension and the Working Class

The obstacles confronting university extension were far more formidable than its advocates realized. Writing in 1899, Adams echoed a consensus that lukewarm public response had corroded the will of academics to continue extension along academic and cultural lines.

Yet the pattern of public response to university extension was more complex than Adams intimated. In numerical terms, enrollments in American extension classes approximated those in England. For example, in 1892–93 the three English extension syndicates reported 51,000 students, compared to a combined figure of 56,601 students in extension classes sponsored by ASEUT and the University of Chicago.[34] On both sides of the Atlantic some students were counted more than once, and hence these figures are not precise measures of actual attendance. But they convey the general picture. Midwestern extension lectures, which were not under ASEUT's control, also drew respectable numbers in the 1890s. The onset of a severe economic depression in 1893 stimulated popular interest in economic issues and guaranteed a warm reception for extension lecturers. By 1896, for example, Wisconsin had acquired a reputation as a fine field for extension courses.[35] Women's clubs and business and professional associations brought extension lecturers to places like Kenosha, Ashland, and River Falls. A young economics instructor at Lawrence University in Appleton, Wisconsin, was astonished that local newspapers wanted to report the discussions of his economics seminar. In 1893–94, when some 9,000 people took extension courses in the state, Frederick Jackson Turner described extension work in Wisconsin as "astonishingly popular."[36]

So far as attendance figures are concerned, the university extension movement in America was at least as successful as its British counterpart. American professors, it is true, were often dismayed by the failure of students to complete their courses or to do their assignments, but the British faced the same problem.[37] Where the two nations differed was in their response to the problems surrounding university extension. American university extension shifted after 1900 to vocational and public service activities, while British extension retained its orientation toward academic subjects, especially history, literature, and economics. Further, British extension strengthened its ties to the working class after 1900; one of the major goals of extension in Britain became the training of a working-class intelligentsia. The establishment of the Workers' Educational Association (WEA) in 1903 contributed mightily to cooperation between British universities and trade unions. In contrast, while a number of experiments with "workers' education" arose in the United States from 1900 to 1930, they had only sporadic ties to universities. In America the people meant the public, not the masses or the workers.

This fundamental difference between the American and British movements informs the reasons for the American retreat from academic culture as the basis for extension. Adams and others attributed the retreat to a lukewarm public response, but in reality attendance at American extension lectures did not level off until the very end of the 1890s. Considerable evidence indicates that the interest of leading academic intellectuals in the extension movement waned even before public apathy became a problem. Magazines aimed at general readers, which contained numerous articles on extension in the early 1890s, virtually ignored the topic thereafter.[38] Similarly, Adams's students and associates at Johns Hopkins wrote prolifically about the movement until 1893–94, and thereafter next to nothing.[39] Measured by his writings, even Adams's interest flagged after 1893. Aside from his general survey of educational extension at the end of the decade, in which he dismissed extension as a lost cause, he ceased to chronicle the movement after 1893.

All of this prompts a closer look at the roots of the diminishing zeal for university extension. Flagging interest in extension has to be understood within the context of the expectations of the founders of the movement. Unquestionably, those expectations were diverse. But extension contained a vigorous corps of professors for whom one goal was paramount: to provide universities with access to the working class and to bring their personal influence to bear on the Social Question (the gap between the social classes). Although this social motive virtually disappeared after 1895, it glowed in the early 1890s, and nowhere more brightly than at Johns Hopkins.

During the 1890s the Hopkins department that Adams headed swelled with earnest young men eager to influence the working class. Like Adams, many of these were devout if not orthodox Protestants who saw extension as an arm of the social gospel. One of Adams's students, Edmund Kimball Alden, began in the 1890s to chronicle "progressive methods of church work" embodied in the various "tabernacles" and "people's palaces" that arose in the 1880s and 1890s in connection with urban churches. For example, the Berkeley Temple in Boston offered courses in elocution, German, stenography, millinery, dressmaking, mechanical drawing, and current events, all as part of its church work. In Jersey City a "People's Palace" attached to a church on the edge of a slum contained a gymnasium, museum, and even soda fountains as part of an effort to com-

pete with the saloon culture. Alden viewed Chautauqua, university extension, and progressive or "institutional" church work as part of a single impulse to focus the energies of the educated on social issues. Russell Con-
well, the Baptist minister whose "Acres of Diamonds" speech became one
of the most popular public addresses of the century, started a "Temple
College" (later Temple University) alongside his church in Philadelphia.[40]

Adams also sympathized with the idea of the institutional church and
used his pen to advertise its accomplishments.[41] He attended one such
church in Baltimore, the Associate Congregational, which maintained
various clubs and literary societies. Hopkins professors frequently lectured at this church on such academic topics as "Workingmen during the
Middle Ages," while church-sponsored social clubs sought to reach
"newsboys and street waifs."[42] Adams knew of many others, including the
Rev. W. S. Rainsford's St. George's Episcopal Church in New York City.
From a five-story Memorial House next to his church, Rainsford conducted institutional work on a grand scale. The Memorial House contained departments for distributing clothing and groceries to the poor as
well as rooms for classes in the skilled trades like plumbing, carpentry, and
printing.[43]

Adams's own interest in the social role of the churches had been
aroused at least as early as 1889, when his student Albert Shaw delivered
a paper on "Popular Education in London" before Adams's seminar at
Johns Hopkins. Shaw described the work of the prototypical People's Palace, opened in London's East End in 1887 by Queen Victoria. The palace
incarnated the ideas of the novelist Walter Besant, whose popular *All Sorts
and Conditions of Men* (1882) had envisioned a "Palace of Delight" for
the downtrodden of the East End, a magnificent building filled with noble
rooms, statutes, tapestries, a library, gymnasium, and classrooms.[44] The
actual building, whose construction owed a great deal to the organizational efforts of Besant and to philanthropy, was only a little less grand. It
included baths, a gymnasium, a library, a concert hall that sat 4,000 people, and classrooms. Richard T. Ely, who visited the palace in the summer
of 1887, saw it as a happy substitute for the gin palaces frequented by the
masses, while Adams, after listening to Shaw's paper, concluded that England was far ahead of America in devising democratic means for the education of the masses.[45]

In the same paper, Shaw described Quintin Hogg's Polytechnic Institute in London. In 1864, just after he left Eton, Hogg began a school for
street waifs in the London slums near Charing Cross. At first Hogg's primary concern was to wash and clothe his charges and to tutor them in correct behavior, but Hogg gradually expanded his methods to include technical education. Increasingly, too, he focused on the "better class" of
boys—upwardly striving youth of the lower middle class. In 1882 Hogg

purchased the Royal Polytechnic Institution in Regent Street, a building formerly devoted to scientific exhibits but used by Hogg as a center for educational and social activities that included a debating club and savings bank as well as classes for instruction. Keeping the name "Polytechnic," he increased the latter's membership to 7,000 young men and women in its first month of operation and to 12,000 by 1889.[46]

Like Thomas Hughes, the author of *Tom Brown's School Days* and a founder of Christian Socialism in England, Hogg typified the muscular, outgoing Christianity that attracted many upper-class Englishmen in the late nineteenth century. A friend once gibed to Hogg, "I hear you can talk of nothing but football and religion."[47] As the Social Question loomed increasingly large in the thinking of the educated classes of both countries, criticism mounted of the exclusive focus of the churches on personal salvation. Demands were intensified that they address the social and educational as well as spiritual needs of society. Both the "institutional" churches and the YMCA reflected the impulse of social Christianity. Each stressed harmonious cooperation between the classes rather than an exacerbation of class conflict. For example, Hogg hoped to imbue the working class with the same moral values as the upper class in order to encourage cooperation. By leaving many decisions relating to the Polytechnic's management to members' committees, he believed that working youth would develop the same esprit de corps that had characterized his football club at Eton. Education promised to bridge the gap between classes not only by providing technical instruction to equip working youth for the skilled trades but also by giving gentlemen an opportunity for personal contact with the lower class. Shaw noted approvingly that distinguished scholars in literature, history, and science had been invited to advise the educational programs of the People's Palace, which gradually became mainly an educational institution and in the twentieth century a branch of the University of London.

All this was consistent with Matthew Arnold's belief that those who sought culture had to take the downtrodden of East London with them.[48] During the late 1880s and early 1890s, Adams, Ely, and their followers also hoped to bring their influence directly to bear on the working class. Although Ely had already argued for an increased regulatory role for the state, philanthropic experiments like the People's Palace that enhanced contact between the classes attracted him. In many respects, the idea of scholars uplifting the public by personally imparting knowledge had deeper roots in American than in British tradition. The experience of the antebellum lyceums had been widely interpreted as evidence of a public hunger for enlightenment, while memories of Franklin and other self-improving artisans, kept aglow by generations of enthusiasts for popular education, helped to buttress the belief that even the poor could be inspired by scholarly ideals. Unaccustomed to think of the United States as marked by the same depth of class division as England, Americans had long thought of scholars and workers as part of the same public. This assumption, in turn, nurtured paternalistic ideals of uplift and continued to encourage experiments to diffuse knowledge. University extension, Adams predicted, would break down the antagonism between the classes and the masses and would harmonize the highest interests of capital and labor.[49]

The labor upheavals of the 1870s and 1880s did nothing to corrode the conviction of reform-minded professors that the quest for knowledge had deep social roots. While recognizing the sharpening of class divisions, Ely saw no signs of a diminishing educational interest among workingmen. He devoted an entire chapter of his *The Labor Movement in America* to "The Educational Value of Labor Organizations."[50] Not only had workingmen consistently supported public education, he affirmed, but labor organizations themselves served as virtual "schools of political science" in which working people learned to speak and to think. It delighted Ely that a Baltimore barber craved a copy of his *Recent American Socialism,* that the Journeymen Bricklayer's Union of Baltimore spent $1,000 stocking its library, and that workers in Massachusetts testified to the educational uplift that attended their membership in labor organizations. Ely never doubted that self-instruction would encourage temperance among workers, but he contended that the true value of self-instruction lay in the development among workers of a keener awareness of the public issues that affected them. One heard many disparaging remarks in Baltimore about The Johns Hopkins University, Ely said, but not from workers. Rather, it was the small-scale employers—corner grocers and retail liquor merchants—whose pursuit of gain left them with no time for culture and hostile toward universities.[51]

Although Ely exaggerated the extent of self-instruction among workers, the failure of the railway strike in 1877 did prompt labor organizations to stress the value of education. In particular, the Knights of Labor attached immense importance to the education of workers throughout North America. Terence V. Powderly, the eloquent Grand Master Workman of the Knights, envisioned the organization as a gigantic school to teach workers the value of forming producers' and consumers' cooperatives, the wisdom of arbitrating labor disputes, the self-destructive potential of strikes, and the need for temperance.[52] A Canadian Knight described the order's local assemblies throughout North America as "the schools of teaching the people to remedy the mistakes of the past."[53] The bitter aftertaste of the failed strikes of the 1870s confirmed the belief of Powderly and his lieutenants that labor needed a general reshaping of its outlook, while the proceedings of the Knights' annual meetings contained calls for "reading rooms in every village."[54] Cooperation and arbitration by no means exhausted the fund of strategies that workers had to comprehend as alternatives to the "thraldom" of the wage system. For example, Powderly combined his endorsement of cooperation with a keen interest in land reform and, while never a strict single-taxer, he supported Henry George in the New York City mayoralty election of 1886.[55]

The structure of the Knights guaranteed a wide diffusion of its leaders' ideas about the industrial system. All local assemblies of the Knights had to purchase the *Journal of United Labor*, which contained abundant material on political economy.[56] Many of the local assemblies also subscribed to *John Swinton's Paper*, a terse and accurately named newspaper that Swinton, a sometime physician, journalist, and editor, launched in 1883. Book notices in Swinton's paper trumpeted the writings of Henry George and urged workers to become "readers, thinkers."[57] As the first genuinely national labor organization in the United States, the Knights inevitably acquired an eclectic ideology that exposed workers to a wealth of new solutions to industrial strife: cooperation, arbitration, insurance, Georgism, even Edward Bellamy's nationalism. All of this was a far cry from the stolid self-culture advocated by William Ellery Channing and Elihu Burritt in the pre–Civil War era, just as it stood at several leagues' distance from the practical "pure and simple unionism" that Samuel Gompers would later impose on the American Federation of Labor. The Knights had much to offer workers in the way of intellectual fare; local assemblies often turned themselves into little schools and stocked their libraries with "works on economical subjects."[58]

Historians often have portrayed the Knights as a throwback, an organization doomed by its opposition to strikes and the wage system to be bypassed by more "realistic" labor organizations, particularly the American Federation of Labor.[59] Yet in the 1880s divisions that would later become sharp remained blurred in outline. Eclectic in its ideology and absorptive in its structure, the Knights brought together strange bedfellows. For example, P. J. McGuire, an Irish-American firebrand who built the Brotherhood of Carpenters and Joiners into a major union, has often been viewed as a radical forerunner of "Big Bill" Haywood. Yet for much of the 1880s McGuire advocated the liquidation of unions into the Knights.[60] Education formed one of the links between McGuire and the Knights. McGuire saw unions as schools to train workers for leadership after the collapse of capitalism and kept the Brotherhood's journal, the *Carpenter*, well-stocked with weighty articles on history, philosophy, and trade unionism. For the better part of a year during the 1880s, he devoted an entire page of each issue to a serialized history of the world. Under McGuire's editorship, the *Carpenter* was filled with advertisements that offered carpenters discounts on the works of Plato, John Ruskin, and other philosophers.[61] At the other extreme, the Knights also gained the approval of Edmund J. James, well remembered as the president of two major universities, Northwestern (1902–4) and the University of Illinois (1904–20), and as a pioneer of business education in universities. Between 1883 and 1895, while serving as professor of public administration at the University of Pennsylvania's Wharton School of Finance and Economy, James devoted part of his time to ASEUT, over which he presided from 1891 to 1895. For all of his interest in educating better businessmen, James found time in 1888 to cooperate with George E. McNeill (a former president of the Boston Eight-Hour League), Powderly, and Henry George as a coauthor of *The Labor Movement: The Problem of To-Day*.[62] James's contribution to the volume, a piece on "Recent Labor Legislation" in Europe, expressed approval for both unions and ameliorative efforts in the form of savings banks, mechanics' institutes, libraries, and schools.[63] Social Christianity propelled men like James to think that the cooperative ideal would prevail if only scholars guided the education of workers.

Much like the Knights, the Patrons of Husbandry—or Grange as it was commonly called—saw self-improvement as a fundamental component of any program to uplift the laboring classes. Along with the experience of the Knights, the example of the Grange went far to convince professors that the workers would rally to the cause of popular education. The cooperative ideal provided an important link between the Grange and the Knights and stimulated ardor for education in each.[64] The Grange and the later Farmers' Alliance rested many of their hopes for rural America on the establishment of farmers' cooperatives and recognized that the success of the latter depended on a more intelligent farming population.[65] One of the most important institutions of the Grange, for example, was the lecture hour. Jennie Buell wrote in 1921, "There are thousands of men and women who joined the Grange in early youth, and who now, though grown, aged and feeble, still attend the meetings in the spirit of students at college—open-minded and eager to participate in its intellectual activities. Such members justify the claim that the Grange is clearly entitled to rank among educational institutions. It is, in fact, a school out of school."[66]

Lectures before the Grange covered a range of topics from crop rotation to home beautification, but as agricultural unrest intensified in the 1880s and 1890s, political and economic issues—gold and silver, greenbacks and specie, corporations and banks—came to the fore of local lecture hours. Commenting on the increasingly political and economic orientation of Grange educational programs, C. S. Walker wrote in 1894, "These associations are themselves efficient schools, giving to their faithful members training in public speaking, in writing and reading, in thinking and in administration. As a result of twenty-six years of this work, the

Grange has become a national university, employing hundreds of teachers, college educated as well as self-taught, who stimulate thought and lend inspiration to their fellows."[67]

The educational activities of the Grange provided intellectual stimulation for farm women as well as men. Women commonly held the position of lecturer, the person responsible for arranging the lecture hour's program. The programs themselves contained not only talks on farm topics but poetic recitations and essays delivered by farm women before admiring neighbors. Much like Chautauqua circles, the Grange's meetings were suffused by rituals in which women acted the roles of the goddesses Pomona, Flora, and Ceres. Michigan's Mary Ann Mayo described the Grange as the rural equivalent of the women's clubs, with the difference that the former was not limited to women but brought them together with men on terms of equality. Mrs. Mayo's good friend Jennie Buell, who was an editorial assistant for the organ of the Michigan State Grange, was also a Chautauqua agent, and on at least one occasion she arranged to have Mrs. Mayo speak at a joint meeting of Grangers and Chautauquans.[68]

In *The Labor Movement in America*, Ely praised the Grange for encouraging farmers to read and to take more newspapers. Instances of local granges that started libraries delighted him and reassured him that the flame of temperance, that perennial by-product of reading, would spread throughout the nation.[69] Ely saw education as one of the two main links between the Knights and the Grange. The other was cooperation. Inspired by Robert Owen, the Co-operative Movement rose to prominence in Britain in the 1840s, when the Equitable Pioneers Co-operative Society in Rochdale (usually known simply as Rochdale) came into existence. With a cooperative store as its base, Rochdale grew swiftly, soon devoted a portion of its profits to education, started its own library, lecture series, and classes, and became a model for similar cooperatives throughout industrial areas. By the 1880s cooperatives dotted the industrial regions of Yorkshire and Lancashire and provided the universities with their principal source of worker-students at extension lectures.[70] Familiar with Rochdale, Ely saw cooperatives for producers and consumers as a way to reduce the waste of resources imposed by competitive capitalism and as "a practical application of Christianity to business."[71]

Ely acknowledged that the history of cooperatives in America was disheartening, that the ground was "strewn with fragments of wrecks."[72] The problem, however, lay not in the cooperative ideal but in the failure of intelligent citizens to interest themselves in the affairs of laboring people. Nowhere in the civilized world "have the laborers, as such, been so isolated as in the large industrial centres of the United States." Both in Germany and in England "many of the most brilliant and renowned and highest-minded men of our times have been heart and soul with the laborers in all their aspirations and struggles," but "such has not been the case in the United States."[73] In effect, Ely was not merely recording the progress of labor but extending an invitation to the scholarly and contemplative class to address workers, while simultaneously reassuring the educated that labor would respond eagerly to guidance from above. Interpreting socialism as a grand movement toward cooperation among classes, Ely acted during the 1880s as a mediator between the middle-class, Christian public and the strange and disturbing movements that were sprouting among workers. In essence, he argued that the middle class had little to fear from labor as long as it allowed a pricking of its own social conscience.

By stressing the cooperative and educational features of the Knights of Labor, he tried to reassure his audience that labor's demands deserved a respectful hearing. Yet nowhere did Ely endorse either socialism or trade unions or the actual practices of local assemblies of the Knights. He conceded, for example, that "individual knights and individual assemblies have been guilty of outrageous conduct with reference to their employers, the general public, and their fellow-workingmen."[74] Similarly, he alerted his readers to the presence of violence-prone and anti-Christian factions among the socialists and anarchists; on these factions he blamed the Haymarket bombing of May 1886. All of this was lamentable, but not inevitable. Just as he detected a new moral earnestness within the middle class, he portrayed the Knights, unions, and socialism as comparable steps toward a "closer union of social factors."[75] Such was the direction of evolutionary change. Indeed, Ely implied that the growing harmony among social classes would eliminate the need for the very labor movement he described.[76]

Ely sympathized with the Knights and the Grange, but his academic position offered him no direct way to address the laboring classes. University extension was a promising approach, but it required local centers that would simultaneously attract workers and professors. Herbert Baxter Adams, who knew far less than Ely about labor movements but who shared his goal of class harmony, pinned many of his hopes for reaching laborers on the Workingmen's Institute of Canton, an industrial district of Baltimore with a population of 4,000 to 5,000 workers, mainly of Welsh origin. Rev. J. Wynne Jones, an admirer of William Ellery Channing's addresses to workingmen in the late 1830s and of Thomas Hughes's Workingmen's College (established in London in 1854), organized the Canton Institute in the fall of 1879. Jones saw the institute as the beginning "of an intellectual solar system having the Johns Hopkins University as the central light and source of learning." In Jones's eyes, the institute would be "the first little satellite, and others should be formed until there was a perfect ring of them in the 'Belt' district, and each one could communicate light to others."[77]

Several members of the Hopkins faculty had taken a keen interest in the Canton Institute nearly a decade before Adams's interest in extension was piqued. President Daniel Coit Gilman of Hopkins envisioned the institute as a center for lectures, musical performances, a library and reading room, and evening classes, and he estimated that the city could support four or five such institutes. Canton soon had a circulating library, reading room, and concerts, while distinguished Hopkins professors, including the botanist H. N. Martin and the physicist Ira Remsen, lectured on such topics as "Some Uses of Plants," "The Air We Breathe," and "The Light We Use." In 1887 Adams started his own work in extension. Twelve Hopkins lecturers (Adams called them the "twelve apostles") toured three working-class neighborhoods in Baltimore. Adams himself spoke on "The Educational Movement Among Workingmen in England and America." Others in Adams's little band included two men who would become famous historians, Charles McLean Andrews and J. Franklin Jameson.[78]

For all of the enthusiasm that it generated among Hopkins professors, the Canton Institute failed to arouse much interest among workers once the glow of newness had worn off. Academic lectures, Adams had to confess, "failed to reach the working class."[79] From this failure Adams drew a more general conclusion: the "zeal of university men to attempt to lecture to workingmen as such, or indeed to any 'class of people,' was mistaken." Whatever future university extension might have, it "should be for citizens without regard to their occupation."[80]

At the very least, the timing of university extension was unfortunate. Ely and others viewed the Knights of Labor and the Farmers' Alliance as evidence of the quest for self-improvement among workers, but the Knights were unraveling even as university extension was taking shape. In the same year that Ely published *The Labor Movement in America*, Samuel Gompers assumed the presidency of the American Federation of Labor, then a minor labor organization that had just been renamed from the earlier Federation of Organized Trades and Labor Unions. A self-taught intellectual who read Marx, Gompers nevertheless distrusted both socialism and "those self-appointed preceptors to the Labor movement known as intellectuals," accepted the wage system and the strike, and pushed labor orthodoxy back to its original position that the public school provided sufficient intellectual enfranchisement.[81] When first organized in 1881, the Federation of Organized Trades and Labor Unions proclaimed in its constitution that "the history of wage-earners in all countries is but the history of constant struggle and misery engendered by ignorance and disunion." When the Federation was reorganized in 1886 as the AFL, this sentence and all other references to education were struck from its constitution.[82]

Farm protest was also taking a form at the turn of the 1890s that distanced it from Ely's brand of Christian socialism. In the 1880s, disaffected southern Grangers established the Agricultural Wheel and then the Farmers' Alliance. Between 1887 and 1894, the Alliance carried the message of purchasing cooperatives throughout the South. By 1889 it was moving into Missouri and Kansas and soon into Nebraska and the Dakotas. The Alliance was attempting to construct "some variety of cooperative commonwealth," but there was a crucial difference between Ely's conception of cooperation and that of the Alliance. Ely expected that the capitalists themselves would become progressively more cooperative, but the Alliance owed its growth not only to its calls for self-help in the form of cooperative stores but also to its burgeoning political agenda, which included higher taxes on railroads and the sub-treasury plan unveiled in 1889 by Charles W. Macune, an acidulous critic of Rochdale-type stores and an advocate of state marketing cooperatives. In Macune's conception, sub-treasuries would operate as federally subsidized warehouses in which farmers could store their crops before sale, while waiting for their price to rise. Meanwhile, sub-treasuries would loan farmers money. Addressing the needs of credit-starved farmers, especially in the South, the sub-treasury scheme became a major plank of the emerging Populist movement; it signaled the shift of farm insurgents toward political solutions and away from the earnest self-improvement so close to the hearts of the Grange and academic intellectuals.[83]

These developments coincided with a conservative backlash that forced reform-minded academics to reassess their own commitment to popular education. Ely himself became the focal point of a celebrated case at the University of Wisconsin in 1894. In that year a pugnacious regent of the university, Oliver E. Wells, published a letter in the *Nation* assailing Ely for teachings and practices that provided "a sort of moral justification for attacks on life and property."[84] Wells charged that Ely had counseled and entertained a strike organizer during a printers' strike in Madison in 1893, that he had threatened to take business away from a printing firm unless it unionized its shop, and that he was at heart a socialist who disguised his radicalism with the glittering generalities and "metaphysical statements" favored by academics. A month later Ely spoke before Bishop Vincent and a hushed crowd in the Chautauqua Amphitheater and vigorously rebutted the charges. The outcome was an inquiry by the university's Board of Regents, which exonerated Ely.[85]

Ely's was one among several cases in which activist professors were charged with stepping beyond the legitimate boundaries of their position. In 1886 the economist Henry Carter Adams was dismissed from Cornell University for a pro-labor speech that antagonized a wealthy benefactor of the university. In 1895 Edward Bemis, a former student of Herbert Baxter Adams, lost his job at the University of Chicago. Depending on whom one believes, Bemis was forced out either because he was an incompetent lecturer in the university's extension division or because he advocated the municipal ownership of utilities. Pro-labor views also caused the economist John R. Commons to be eased out of his professorship at Indiana University and then forced out of one at Syracuse University.[86]

No case caused more of a stir than that of Edward A. Ross. Raised in "the tight little intellectual world" of midwestern Presbyterianism, Republicanism, protectionism, and capitalism, Ross pursued graduate study in Germany, earned a Ph.D. in economics at Johns Hopkins, and won professorships at Indiana, Cornell, and Stanford. Along the way he shed most of the ideologies in which he had been raised, acquired a feisty and combative temperament, puffed free silver, and roasted uncontrolled capitalism. At Stanford he clashed with Mrs. Leland Stanford—the widow of the founder, "Mother of the University," and an equally combative person who stood at the opposite pole from Ross on many economic and political issues.

The beginning of Ross's undoing came during the summer of 1896 when he propounded his free-silver ideas to a group of students in Chicago amid one of the most tense election campaigns in American history. Thrilled to find a prominent academician in favor of free silver, the Democratic National Committee printed Ross's speech in the form of a 60-page pamphlet, liberally illustrated with cartoons. Sixty thousand copies of the pamphlet, *Honest Dollars*, were distributed during the campaign, and upon his return to California in August, Ross found himself in demand as a popular lecturer. This was not a new role, for at Indiana and Cornell he had often given extension lectures on current economic issues. Nor was it an unwelcome role, for Ross's experiences as an extension lecturer convinced him "that the general public hungers for a candid consideration of current problems, and that the prudent course for the economist who proposes to challenge the invisible capitalist control is to win all the attention he can for his views."[87] In fact, Ross drew more attention than he wanted. *Honest Dollars* incurred Mrs. Stanford's wrath and Ross began to realize that "a single, careless off-hand reply to a question asked in an 'open forum' following an extension lecture" might give his enemies the opening they sought to paint him as a dangerous man. In response, Ross began to dilute his public speeches with qualifiers and to read from drafts to the point where friends wondered what had come over him.[88] All to no avail, for when Ross spoke before a mass meeting opposing Oriental immigration a few years later, Mrs. Stanford forced his resignation from the faculty.

Most likely, university extension would have fared poorly among wage earners without additional blows from the changing agendas of labor and farm protest or the conservatism of university trustees. Local assemblies of the Knights often were beehives of mutual improvement and self-education, but as Jane Addams would note, workers liked their economics spiced with partisanship and relevance, qualities missing from the oblique and academic titles of the lectures delivered by Adams's little band of "apostles": "Labor in Japan," "Slave Labor in Ancient Greece," "Labor and Manufactures in the United States One Hundred Years Ago." At the very least, workers desired inspirational lectures. Adams ruefully observed that ministers who delivered inspirational biographies of heroes of the Bible or the Reformation seemed to make a far greater impact on popular audiences than did professors.[89]

Patronizing and dry lectures undoubtedly alienated many listeners. Much the same problem existed in England, where it proved difficult to attract workers to extension courses. English university extension was far less successful in reaching the working class than in evoking a warm response from the middle class. Even in the industrial areas of Lancashire and Yorkshire, workers dominated only about a quarter of the local centers affiliated with Oxford's extension program, and in the south of England, workers had no more than a negligible interest in university extension.[90] It took over two decades of painful and often frustrating efforts by universities to cultivate their ties to workers before the WEA came into existence.

However tenuous their ties to workers, the English universities nonetheless kept at it until the dividends (in the form of the WEA) began to arrive, while their American counterparts flatly rejected the notion of aiming extension at any social class. Of the possible explanations for this pronounced difference in the paths taken by university extension in the two nations, we can safely dismiss at least one. English promoters of university extension were no more radical or sympathetic to the working class than were the architects of university extension in the United States. The impulse behind university extension in both countries rarely moved beyond Christian Socialism, the type of socialism that celebrated cooperation between social classes and that viewed class conflict as neither desirable nor inevitable. In both countries advocates of extension sympathized with worker cooperatives, which they viewed as ways to restore self-help, temperance, and independence to mechanics. The founding of the Fabian Society in 1884 would lead to the gradual introduction of Marxism and other forms of continental socialism into mainstream academic thought in Britain, but this development did not have a significant impact on university extension. Christian Socialism continued to impel the latter. Even the WEA owed its origin to a Christian Socialist, Albert Mansbridge, rather than to any of the miscellaneous and more radical forms of socialism embraced by Fabianism. Although the Fabians included free compulsory schooling and government-financed scholarships up to the university level in their program, education never occupied the same position of prominence in Fabian thought that it held for Christian Socialists.[91]

Although the impulse behind extension in Britain and America was much the same, the Americans faced several distinctive obstacles. Their recollection of Benjamin Franklin and Elihu Burritt, the "learned blacksmith," induced a kind of complacency among American intellectuals eager to reach the working class. George E. Vincent recalled that at ASEUT's first meeting, "few of the speakers suggested doubts or difficulties. The general feeling seemed to be that university extension was peculiarly adapted to the great democracy and would quickly triumph."[92] Ely blandly construed the intellectual strivings of the workers in the 1880s as the latest manifestation of an enduring tradition of popular self-instruction in America. Similarly, Adams's writings sought to unveil a popular tradition of autodidacticism from the mechanics' institutes and lyceums to Chautauqua and university extension. Indeed, Adams was virtually the first historian of adult education in America. By establishing historical precedents for their activities, Ely and Adams buttressed their confidence in their ultimate success and mitigated opposition within universities.

In contrast to the Americans, the British apostles of university extension took class differences as deeply ingrained. As Christian Socialists, they wanted to bridge the gap between classes, but Britain lacked any equivalent to the American antebellum lyceums, which had drawn a mixture of professionals, merchants, middle-class women, farmers, and mechanics to public lectures. So segmented by class were Britain's educational traditions that even Christian Socialists could not doubt their depth. The British extension movement would prove far more persistent in courting the workers because its leaders knew it had to be.

In isolated instances, however, intellectuals in the United States actively cultivated the higher education of workers. This was especially true in the needle trades. By the 1920s Jewish workers would form the backbone of the contemporary movement for "workers' education," while sweatshops would glow in the memory of Morris Hillquit and other leaders as little universities in which workers debated socialism and anarchism while they stitched and threaded. But in reality, most of the Jews who fled Russia in the wake of the pogroms following the assassination of the Czar Alexander II in 1881 were too religious to follow the lead of secular intellectuals. By tracing the root of injustice to abstractions like capitalism and the state, socialism and anarchism encouraged a speculative cast of mind, but these creeds were not self-propagating. In the mid-1880s Abraham Cahan, the immigrant writer and journalist, helped to organize the Russian Labor Lyceum to disseminate socialism among Russian-speaking Jews, a Russian-Jewish Workers' *Verein* for lectures in Yiddish, and the Yiddish press to propagate socialism. Respectively a teacher's son who became a lawyer and a storekeeper's son who became a teacher, Hillquit and Cahan represented the middle social rank of the Jewish migration.[93] More representative of the bottom rank was Abraham Bisno, a poor tailor with a penchant for socialism and union activism. In 1888 Bisno and some of his friends organized the Workingman's Educational Society in Chicago, where they debated the merits of socialism and anarchism in "fever heat." Along the way, Bisno, although illiterate in English, acquired a knowledge of Darwin, Marx, Spencer, and Malthus that would later astound Jane Addams and Ellen Gates Starr at Hull House, and they obligingly struggled to teach Bisno the basic skills he lacked, specifically the ability to read and write English. While Bisno impressed settlement workers with his knowledge of ideologies, he left a positive impression on the rank and file in the needle trades by his readiness to picket and court arrest. By serving as springboards to unions as well as forums for socialism, Jewish educational clubs of the sort Bisno had founded complemented the work of the articulate Cahans and Hillquits and contributed to the formation of a reliable Jewish clientele for lectures and forums.[94]

This Jewish audience was urban and mainly centered in New York City. Permeated by ideological fervor, it was a far cry from Chautauqua, but non-Jewish intellectuals occasionally tapped into it. For example, in 1898 Thomas Davidson, the Scottish free-lance philosopher who earlier had organized a summer institute of the "culture-sciences," began to lecture under the auspices of New York City's People's Institute, recently founded by Columbia University's Charles Sprague Smith. Smith wanted to open the church to the workers, but the church he had in mind was Protestant, while Davidson's listeners were "nearly all Jews." Davidson himself defied labels; he once declared that he was too much a socialist to be an anarchist and too much an anarchist to be a socialist. Mainly he was an educator with a Channingesque faith in the "elevation" of the working class; he desired "to give them such an outlook upon life as would lift their lives out of narrowness and sordidness, and give them ideal aims."[95]

This avowal of culture seemed ill-suited to his audience; his friends predicted that he would be drowned by disputatious Jews, and one auditor pointedly asked Davidson what possible relevance knowledge of history and philosophy could have for people who worked ten or more hours a day. A fair question, he acknowledged, but Davidson recognized that the ideological biases of his listeners worked to his advantage, for they arrived at his lectures with an ingrained, if not informed, interest in history and sociology. He described a sphere for himself by questioning their assumptions in a Socratic manner and by volunteering to offer follow-up classes in which he laid out a range of cultural information—biographies, maps, definitions—so that his listeners could better comprehend their own ideologies. This proved to be an effective tactic, for many in Davidson's audience probably recognized the same gap that Bisno saw between heady opinion and meager knowledge.[96]

There were other instances of successful lecture series that aimed at serious adult education. In the 1890s Henry M. Leipziger, a British-born Jewish school official in New York City, started a small lecture program under the auspices of the city's school board. After 1900 Leipziger's "People's University" developed into a major enterprise; in 1909 alone he arranged for some 5,500 lectures in 175 school and other centers, and by 1914–15 aggregate attendance had risen to over one million people. In contrast to Davidson, Leipziger did not target Jewish radicals; rather, he conceived of the lecture series as a kind of surrogate secondary school for those who left school between the ages of fourteen and twenty.[97]

Preferring his status as a roving ambassador of enlightenment, Davidson turned down offers to teach in universities, while Leipziger worked within a school rather than a university bureaucracy. Owing in large measure to New York's huge Jewish population, efforts to address working-class concerns through educational extension persisted in the city, but without significant support from universities. In the absence of such support, Davidson's "Bread Winner's College" dissolved at his death in 1900. Conceived as an experiment in continuing education for early school leavers, Leipziger's People's University was already being undercut by growing secondary-school enrollments at the time of his death in 1917. In much the same way, the occasional ASEUT lecturer who built a following outside of the social mainstream lacked any device for institutionalizing his success. The British-born ASEUT staffer Hudson Shaw attracted African-Americans by the hundreds to his lectures on English history, but he did so by virtue of his charisma and open-mindedness rather than because of any support from universities. Lyman P. Powell, who organized extension work in Milwaukee on behalf of the University of Wisconsin, identified this reliance on charismatic lecturers as part of the problem and urged greater attention to planning and system in order to secure automatic results. After 1905, it is true, university extension would reemerge in a radically different and more systematic form. Writing in 1901, however, Powell did not envision a significant future for university extension; rather, he was more impressed by the possibilities of diffusing knowledge through the extension of library services.[98]

Libraries and the Public

Since the days of Benjamin Franklin, advocates of self-improvement had viewed libraries as key instruments for the diffusion of knowledge. An address to the public, printed in the *Connecticut Courant* in 1774 on behalf of a proposed subscription library, observed that the utility of such libraries and "their smiling Aspect on the interests of Society, Virtue, and

Religion are too manifest to be denied."[99] During the nineteenth century, philanthropists from Peter Cooper to Enoch Pratt and Andrew Carnegie viewed the library as an indispensable means of self-improvement. Even the parsimonious John Jacob Astor bequeathed $400,000 to found a library in New York City. Carnegie, wealthier and more generous than Astor, made libraries his favorite charity. An ardent autodidact who remembered fondly the days when a gentleman in Allegheny, Pennsylvania, allowed him and other working lads to use his library, Carnegie gave $50,000,000 for the construction of library buildings and dreamed of covering the nation with them.

Contemporaries were so convinced of the value of libraries that they spoke of their goals only in general and vague terms. Even Carnegie, whose "gospel of wealth" rested on the idea that the rich had an obligation actively and scientifically to administer the distribution of their wealth, never explained exactly what libraries were supposed to accomplish.[100] Rather, he contented himself with broad assertions that the library would contribute to character and success. There was no mental sloppiness here, merely a reflection of the general conviction that fine literature was valuable (and, by implication, libraries too) for self-evident reasons.

Librarians who espoused the broad objective of Arnoldian culture did not ignore the practical benefits of reading. Particularly when seeking financial support, they pointed to the tangible social effects of free libraries. For example, when the directors of the Lowell, Massachusetts, library asked their city council for financial aid in 1865, they drew an explicit connection between books and the prevention of crime and vice: "Let the library be free to all, and then, perhaps, there will be one young man less in the place where intoxicating drinks are found. . . . Make the library free to all and then, perhaps, there will be one young woman less to fall from the path of purity and goodness down to that depth of degradation and misery to which only a woman can fall."[101]

Libraries would not only save youth from plummeting into the "dangerous classes" but also diffuse knowledge and encourage salutary recreation. These goals were not alternatives to culture so much as complements of it. As a prominent leader in the library movement wrote in 1895: "But neither the supply of recreative reading nor the better equipment of men for their work or for social and civic duties represents the highest and best influence of the library. That may be summed up in the single word *culture*. No word so well describes the influence of the diffusion of good reading among the people in giving tone and character to their intellectual life."[102]

These words underscore the broad public functions that contemporaries still assigned to the pursuit of culture. Literary culture was not merely a way to fill up idle hours. Rather, a widening quest for culture would have an immediate impact on the amelioration of social problems. Libraries, particularly free libraries, would save the multitude from "wasted and ruined lives."[103] As George Ticknor, the Boston Brahmin who became the moving spirit behind the establishment of the Boston Public Library in 1852, wrote to Edward Everett, free public libraries would extend the nurturing influences of schools into maturity "by the self-culture that results from reading."[104]

Twentieth-century critics have often found it difficult to comprehend the public functions that Victorians associated with culture, which they have dismissed not only as inconsequential "sweetness and light" but also as elitist. This association between culture and elitism gains force from the undeniable fact that the most articulate proponents of the ideal of culture, including those who became prominent in the movement for public libraries, had conservative social philosophies. Suspicious of Jacksonian democracy, they sympathized with rule by an elite of the "best men." They viewed social distinctions as necessary and ineradicable, feared both the unruly rabble and the crass nouveaux riches, and saw popular education as an antidote to anarchy.

Austere, lonely, and even reclusive individuals, the Victorians were uncomfortable unless talking to other men of letters, and sometimes uncomfortable even then. Ticknor, described by a sympathetic biographer as a "neo-Federalist," was representative of the type, a man who feared the despotism of the ignorant majority.[105] Justin Winsor, the first president of the American Library Association, was born to wealth, became a man of letters, and mingled at Boston's famed Saturday Evening Club with Edward Everett Hale, Oliver Wendell Holmes, Sr., and Francis Parkman.[106] A difficult friend at best, he was a man one might address but never speak to.[107] His social views resembled Ticknor's; indeed, Winsor frankly compared the public library to a derrick lifting the inert masses. Similarly, Winsor's contemporary William Frederick Poole, first director of the Chicago Public Library, complained about the stench left by working-class readers and told his assistants not to distribute books to those with unclean hands.[108]

The personalities of Winsor and Poole virtually guaranteed a tension between their elitist social preferences and their desire to bring good reading to the multitude. Possessing an almost physical attraction to books, Poole resisted both the decimal system of classification devised by Melvil Dewey and the stack system on grounds that each would cut readers off from the presence of books.[109] First as librarian of an exclusive Yale literary society and later as an assistant in the Boston Athenaeum, the nation's most illustrious proprietary library, Poole had developed a love of browsing, which he encouraged at the Chicago Public Library. When in 1887 he left the latter to head the newly established Newberry Library, a reference rather than a lending library, the Chicago *Times* attributed his move to a desire for a "more secluded field of effort."[110] Drawing on an elite and gentlemanly clientele, the Newberry presented Poole with none of the drawbacks of contact with the masses that he had experienced at the Chicago Public Library.

With attitudes like these, it is small wonder that the mid-Victorian founders of the library movement have become easy targets for revisionist historians of American libraries.[111] Yet Ticknor, Winsor, and Poole all had imaginative and, for their day, advanced ideas about library administration. Ticknor believed that the popularity of libraries was a fair test of their success. Unlike the Astor Library in New York City, whose establishment led Ticknor to fear that Boston might lose its cultural as well as economic hegemony to its brash rival to the south, the Boston Public Library became essentially a circulating rather than a scholarly reference library. This was just what Ticknor wanted, for he believed that popular taste could be uplifted by good reading. To this end it was important for the library to have several copies of the most popular works, even if the latter turned out to be fiction or other forms of "the pleasantest literature of the day."[112] Light fiction would lead readers to better books, Ticknor argued, not in every case but in enough to justify the purchase of multiple copies. Like a good teacher, the librarian could then make himself superfluous. The appetite for good books, "once formed, will take care of itself. It will, in the great majority of cases, demand better and better books."[113]

Winsor articulated a similar conception of the library's role. At least at the beginning, Winsor recognized, not all readers would crave elevating literature. "A spurns as trash what elevates B, who looks down on the highest reading C is capable of, and so on till you get to the mere jingle that amuses the half idiot, who is happy because he can understand something about the cauterwauling of the roofs."[114] But Winsor did not conclude that libraries would best serve the public by catering to its diverse needs and tastes:

It is by no means to be inferred that, however we take things, we must leave them as we find them. Librarians do not do their whole duty unless they strive to elevate the taste of their readers, and this they can do, not by refusing to put within their reach the books which the masses of readers want, but by inducing the habit of frequenting the library, by giving readers such books as they ask for and then helping them in the choice of books, conducting them, say from the ordinary society novel to the historical novel, and then to the proofs and illustrations of the events or periods commemorated in the more readable of the historians. Multitudes of readers need only be put in this path to follow it.[115]

Far from challenging the ideal of culture, Winsor was illustrating its flexibility and his own unshakable confidence in the tendency of books to elevate character. As Poole put it, the masses have little in the way of literary culture but, "as a rule, people read books of a higher intellectual and moral standard than their own, and hence are benefitted by reading. As their tastes improve, they read better books."[116]

For decades autobiographies and manuals of self-instruction had popularized the notion that single books could transform the lives of even the humble. In this climate of opinion it was natural to ascribe the most remarkable social changes to free libraries. Belief in the elevating effect of reading stimulated plans to make libraries accessible to the masses. After becoming superintendent of the Boston Public Library in 1868, Winsor increased its circulation within a decade by nearly tenfold.[117] Winsor quickly concluded that the library had to serve not merely the "professedly bookish" but also the "pastime readers" who comprised, according to Winsor, three-fourths of the library's patrons.[118] President Charles William Eliot of Harvard commented that Winsor was the first librarian he had ever seen who strove to ensure that the library's books were used, even if they were used up.[119] Similarly, in Chicago it was William Frederick Poole who insisted that the library first purchase popular works (specifically to form the taste for reading among the people) and only later add scholarly and technical works, and it was Poole who as head of the Cincinnati Public Library before coming to Chicago became the first librarian in a major city to open reading rooms on Sunday.[120]

Public libraries became one of the means by which men of letters sought to buttress their cultural leadership in the Gilded Age. Only by a broad diffusion of popular refinement could the scholarly elite hope to influence society. Inevitably a tension arose between the belletristic literary proclivities of librarians and their missionary impulse to diffuse culture. Yet as long as the leaders of the library movement could persuade themselves of the library's potential to elevate reading tastes, they were able to hold their twin goals of refinement and popularization in balance.

Ironically, in their effort to diffuse culture, the library elite fastened onto a new conception of the public library, specifically the tax-supported library, which would ultimately undermine their confidence in the social value of popularizing culture.

The Transformation of the Public Library

Before the closing decades of the nineteenth century, few libraries were public in the sense of being supported by taxes and open free of charge to residents of their locales. The term "public library" merely signified the opposite of a privately owned collection of books kept in someone's house. Public libraries took various forms. Some were subscription libraries, which charged all users a fee. Others operated as joint-stock companies (or "proprietary" libraries), but these frequently allowed nonshareholders access for a fee. Whether subscription or proprietary, public libraries were often attached to clubs or societies that permitted members to use their book collections. These "social libraries" often amassed huge collections. On the eve of the Civil War, the largest lending library in the United States was that of the New York's Young Men's Mercantile Library Association. Charles Coffin Jewett, the librarian of the Smithsonian Institution, nicely captured the varied features of public libraries when he defined them in 1850 as "libraries which are accessible—either without restriction, or upon condition with which all can easily comply—to every person who wishes to use them for their appropriate purpose."[121]

By 1876, when Winsor, Poole, and others organized the American Library Association, an alternative definition of a public library as one that was both free and tax-supported had sprung into existence. The basis for this new definition was laid during the third quarter of the century, first in New England, then in the Middle West, and finally in the Far West, as states began to pass laws enabling municipalities to tax their residents for the support of free libraries. New Hampshire led the way in 1849, followed by Massachusetts in 1851, Maine in 1854, and Vermont in 1865. Between 1868 and 1875 Ohio, Wisconsin, Connecticut, Iowa, Indiana, Illinois, and Texas all passed similar enabling acts.[122] But these laws had only slight impact, for no state actually gave financial assistance to municipal libraries, and few municipalities started free libraries. At a memorable convention of librarians held in 1876 as part of the Centennial Exposition, only 30 of the 103 persons in attendance represented tax-supported libraries.[123] The next decade witnessed a vigorous growth of the public library movement, but one that was regionally unbalanced to an extreme. As late as 1887 Massachusetts contained 176 of the 424 free tax-supported libraries in the United States, while in the same year New England accounted for 280 of the 424.[124]

One reason for the slow growth of tax-supported libraries lay in the persistence of subscription and proprietary libraries, which many contemporaries viewed as adequate to meet the needs of the reading public. A federal survey in 1887 that recorded tax-supported libraries, for example, also listed 341 libraries attached to clubs and associations ranging from fraternal lodges and churches to Henry George clubs and the "Society for the Relief of the Crippled and Ruptured." Another 452 libraries fell under the rubric of corporate lending libraries open to subscribers. Most of the libraries of young men's associations and institutes, mercantile associations, and mechanics' societies were included in this classification, which was distinguished from the former classification "by the greater freedom in conditions for the use of their contents." Allowing for this difference, both of these categories fit the term "social libraries." Combining the two categories yields a figure of 793 social libraries in 1887, but because the survey excluded libraries with fewer than 1,000 volumes, the actual number of social libraries undoubtedly was much larger. Compared to tax-supported free libraries, moreover, the social libraries were more evenly distributed throughout the nation. The southern and western states contained only 20 of the 424 tax-supported free libraries, but 138 of the 793 social libraries.[125]

In either their proprietary or subscription forms, social libraries appeared to satisfy the interests of the reading public and thereby to obviate the need for tax-supported libraries. When in 1850 Charles Coffin Jewett described social libraries as public, his intent was not to offer a controversial or extravagant assessment but to express what then seemed obvious: social libraries offered ample opportunities to those with a taste for reading. Yet Jewett's position would never satisfy the leaders of the American Library Association, for Winsor and Poole envisioned the library's clientele as not merely the reading public but the potential reading public as well—the young men and women of modest circumstances who might be induced to take up reading by the presence of tax-supported free libraries, but who might feel intimidated if expected to join a club or literary society to obtain books.[126]

Throughout the third quarter of the nineteenth century, the positions represented by Jewett on the one hand and by Winsor and Poole on the other coexisted, but by 1875 the manifest decline of the literary associations that in the antebellum period had sustained the larger social libraries was swinging the balance toward advocates of tax-supported libraries. The social libraries founded after 1860 lacked the broad embrace of the antebellum mercantile and mechanics' library associations; instead, they served the narrower constituencies of churches, trade associations, reform clubs, and philanthropy (e.g., the "Society for the Relief of the Crippled and Ruptured"). One common pattern was for proprietary or subscription libraries in decline to donate or sell their collections to newly formed municipal libraries. Seventeen of the first 25 free libraries established in Massachusetts absorbed one or more social libraries. Elsewhere, too, social libraries suffered from the decline of the literary societies that had given them birth.[127] This was true not only in cities like Buffalo and Detroit but in such smaller locales as Evansville, Indiana; Owatonna, Minnesota; Peoria, Illinois; and Beverly, Massachusetts.[128]

As the names of many a public library attested, philanthropy also stimulated the spread of free libraries. Some philanthropists like New York's James Lenox and Chicago's James Crerar were bibliophiles who endowed libraries to perpetuate their collections. Others like John Jacob Astor in New York and Enoch Pratt in Baltimore were self-made men who in varying measure envisioned free libraries as agencies of popular self-instruction. Whereas in the 1820s and 1830s wealthy business leaders had contributed money to mercantile library associations, by the 1870s and 1880s they were channeling their philanthropy toward the public. Andrew Carnegie typified the trend, for none could match his zeal for popular education. Wedded to the doctrine of self-help, Carnegie insisted that, while he would provide the buildings, communities themselves had to raise money for books. Thus the hundreds of Carnegie libraries established between 1886 and 1919 were both endowed and municipal free libraries.

The same mixture of endowment and municipal self-help characterized the less conspicuous efforts of small-town philanthropists across the northern tier of states, efforts that antedated Carnegie's philanthropy by several decades. Much like the Carnegie libraries, these small benefactions involved close cooperation between philanthropists and municipal authorities. For example, in 1859 Dr. John Green of Worcester, Massachusetts, gave his city 7,000 volumes for use as a free reference library.[129] A year later the city, in accordance with the terms of the gift, erected a library building. In the village of Sturbridge, Massachusetts, a library association donated 400 volumes to the town on condition that the latter would appropriate $100 annually to maintain and increase the collection.[130] In Northbridge, Massachusetts, a private bequest in 1844 became the basis of a library maintained in ensuing years by subscription. In 1876 the subscribers voted to make the library free if the town would support it by an appropriation of $200 a year.[131]

A sign of the times was the increasingly active role of women in library philanthropy. Shortly after moving to Carlisle, Massachusetts, in 1870, Mrs. Lydia Patten, the wife of a minister, organized a subscription library, which the town took over in 1872. In 1894 a bequest from Mrs. Joanna Gleason enabled the town to construct the building for its library.[132] Similarly, in 1894 Susan B. Clay bequeathed a library building to Jaffrey, New Hampshire, to house the collection that the town had been supporting with appropriations for a decade.[133] In addition, women's clubs frequently started their own libraries and then, once they had demonstrated their ability to manage important enterprises, turned them over to municipalities. While women sometimes gloated over the failure of male-dominated social libraries, they had neither the resources nor the inclination to create a permanently self-sustaining world of female libraries. Women's clubs in several states instead lobbied state legislatures to expand the taxing powers of townships to embrace support for free libraries.[134] Partly as a result of their efforts, the number of tax-supported free libraries in Indiana leaped from 57 in 1899 to 213 by 1920.[135]

The lending libraries with diversified collections that were established throughout the northern tier of states in the 1880s and especially in the 1890s usually were either endowed or tax-supported, and the former tended to turn quickly into the latter. For example, in New York 54 of 78 new libraries (other than libraries associated with academic institutions) launched in the 1890s were tax-supported. In Minnesota, 13 of 14 new libraries in the 1890s were tax-supported; in Ohio, 20 of 22; in Michigan, 6 of 7; in Indiana, 22 of 24; in Iowa, 22 of 25.[136] Enabling acts by state legislatures contributed to the development of municipal tax-supported free libraries, but as a prominent librarian observed in 1895, "whatever legislation may anywhere be proposed, it appears certain that no State will adopt and carry out generous legal provision for its public libraries until their benefits have in a measure been experienced."[137] In other words, the impetus for tax-supported libraries had to spring from communities themselves. Although the steady rise of tax support for libraries facilitated the purchase of books—more volumes were added to American libraries between 1895 and 1900 than were held by all libraries in the United States in 1875—it was intensifying popular demand for library services that undergirded the movement for tax support. In particular, the women's clubs and Chautauqua circles of the Gilded Age forged major constituencies for free library services. In the absence of public libraries (in the modern sense), literary women had discovered alternative ways to gain access to books. But in the long run, tax-supported libraries possessed clear and unarguable advantages.[138]

Between 1890 and 1910 the public library movement developed a self-sustaining momentum. The establishment of public libraries in some towns stimulated demand for them in neighboring towns. State governments, which prior to 1890 had confined their support of public libraries to the passage of laws enabling municipalities to tax citizens for their support, began to establish state library commissions to record progress and promote new libraries. Wisconsin's Free Library Commission, established in 1891 and dominated by the state's growing number of professional librarians, endorsed library philanthropy but agitated specifically for tax-supported municipal libraries.[139] In 1890 Massachusetts offered $100 worth of books to any town that established a free library for the first time. As a result, the proportion of municipalities in Massachusetts that possessed free libraries rose from two-thirds in 1890 to nearly 100 percent in 1901.[140] In 1901 California made it obligatory for municipalities to establish public libraries upon petition by 25 percent of their voters.[141] Traveling libraries also came into fashion. State officials mailed crates of books to far-flung communities. The Michigan legislature, for example, passed a law in 1895 that provided for the mailing by the state library of 50-book collections to local groups for a modest annual fee. Often housed in Grange halls, these book collections contributed to what one contemporary called "the marked growth of library sentiment" at a time when twenty cities in the state were either building or about to build public libraries.[142] No politician could ignore the impact of these traveling libraries. From July 1902 through June 1904, the Michigan state library sent and received 11,600 letters about traveling libraries. The public's interest in the latter helped to convince legislators of a swelling demand for public libraries, which would ultimately render traveling libraries unnecessary.[143]

Despite the library movement's successes in the 1890s, pronounced regional differences persisted. New England, which had slightly more than half of all public libraries (52.8 percent) in 1876, still possessed nearly half (45.8 percent) in 1900.[144] As late as 1934 expenditures for public libraries in Massachusetts, by then considerably lower than those in New York, still exceeded the combined expenditures in all southern states.[145] Equally striking were differences within regions and within states.[146] In addition to these geographical differences in the distribution of public libraries, the proportion of the public that used libraries was much narrower than the public pronouncements by librarians indicated. Several studies have shown that over the last 40 years a relatively small number of ardent readers has consistently accounted for a disproportionate share of the circulation of public libraries. David I. Macleod's research on the users of Carnegie libraries in Wisconsin indicates that the same was true during the early 1900s. Macleod notes that "only a fraction used the library extensively." Library users were far more likely to be women than men and to be drawn from the professional and business rather than working classes.[147]

Most contemporaries, however, projected the image of a book-thirsty public virtually battering down the library's doors. In 1897, for example, A. L. Peck, the librarian of the Gloversville, New York, Free Library, described how the community's expectations soared in anticipation of the opening of the library. Townspeople averred that the free library would not only make abundant reading available but would drive the saloons out of business. Indeed Peck found that he could not get the library's books unpacked and shelved fast enough. With every delay the public moaned that he really intended to read all of the books himself before opening the doors.[148] John Cotton Dana, who in the 1890s had pioneered advertising by libraries, greeted the twentieth century with the assertion that the popular demand for books would soon render advertising unnecessary.[149]

Several factors help to explain such optimism. The idea that the public thirsted for knowledge, preached for decades by supporters of lyceums and chautauquas as well as libraries, had deep roots. Further, the opening of new libraries, a familiar occurrence between 1890 and 1910, often produced an initial spurt of demand for books. In effect, demand that had been pent up by the absence of free libraries suddenly found an outlet.[150] It was tempting and plausible for librarians to view this surge as the beginnings of a wider growth rather than as a result of the satisfaction of limited demand.

At the opening of the twentieth century, R. R. Bowker expressed the triumphant mood of many librarians as he recorded the achievements of the preceding quarter of a century. Although in 1876 the United States had fewer than 3,700 libraries with 300 or more volumes, it contained at least 8,000 and perhaps as many as 10,000 such libraries in 1901. In the eight years before 1901, the traveling library system had spread into 42 states. Seventeen states had established library commissions. Individual libraries had experienced spectacular gains in circulation. And only seven years old, the Philadelphia Free Library had just recorded an annual circulation of 1,758,851 volumes. No longer the skipper of a dory, the modern library head resembled "the commander of a huge steamer" or "the commodore of a great fleet" as he presided over a huge building, catalog and shelf departments, and multiple branch libraries.[151]

The Purpose of the Public Library

The apparently irresistible momentum of the public-library movement spurred a gradual reassessment of the goals of libraries. Envisioning culture as an anodyne for social unrest, the early leaders of the American Library Association repeatedly had affirmed that, once formed, the taste for reading would lead the public toward fine literature, which in turn would elevate morality. With their irrepressible confidence that popular taste could be elevated, the American Library Association's old guard— Winsor, Poole, Samuel S. Green, and Charles Ammi Cutter—consistently advocated a policy of generous inclusion of fiction. As men of letters accustomed to converse with their peers, these men confidently viewed novel-reading as a passing phase in the developmental cycle. "I have never met a person of much literary culture," Poole reminisced, "who would not confess that at some period in his life, usually in his youth, he had read novels exclusively." Poole's experience convinced him that, as long as this youthful craving for novels was satisfied, that person "passes safely out into broader fields of study, and this craving never returns to him in its original form."[152]

Poole was voicing both a conviction and a clever tactic, for opponents of tax-supported libraries often contended that revenue would be misappropriated if spent to gratify recreational preferences (light novels); those eager to read novels could join circulating or social libraries. The counterargument, that mediocre and even bad books would breed a taste for better ones, committed the advocates of tax-supported libraries to the role of wise counselors who would guide their communities' taste in reading, and it made popular uplift a fair test of the library's effectiveness. Yet the policy of including fiction revealed the conflict between catering to and elevating popular taste, for at some point the consumption of fiction, at least cheap fiction, was supposed to wither away as the public rose to higher fare. Public librarians in major cities took heart from circulation figures that showed a drop of a few percentage points in the annual circulation of novels, although the same figures revealed a continued preponderance of fiction. In 1878, for example, the Indianapolis public library proudly reported that its circulation of fiction had dropped from 80 percent to 72 percent.[153]

Unreconciled to the preponderance of fiction in circulation figures, many librarians campaigned against purchasing various types of fiction.[154] Their targets included stories about crime ("Newgate" fiction) as well as the domestic fiction of writers like Mrs. E. D. E. N. Southworth, Augusta Jane Evans Wilson, Caroline Lee Hentz, and other authors of novels about and essentially for women.[155] Yet the effects of this campaign were more cathartic than tangible. Public libraries continued to stock fiction, and by the 1890s Young Turks in the library movement like John Cotton Dana, who had flirted with socialism and the ideas of Henry George, were ridiculing paternalism. By temperament a gadfly, Dana startled the doyens of librarianship by flatly defending amusement as a major goal of reading and by ridiculing the sacred names of the Genteel Tradition. "Browning and Dante, and the gossip of dead royalty, are well enough in their way and at the proper time and place," he wrote, "but a wide diffusion of knowledge and common sense about business, money, credit, transportation, and trade, would do more than anything else to set the world on the high road to that general diffusion of well-to-do-ness which is the first essential of all progress."[156]

The economic depression that commenced in 1893 contributed to the intensity of attacks on the position of paternalists who sought to use purchasing policies to guide public taste. As the depression deepened and unemployed workers (called "boarders" by municipal librarians) flocked into the reading rooms of urban libraries, a growing number of librarians insisted that libraries stock whatever books refreshed the downtrodden. Tessa Kelso of the Los Angeles Public Library numbered the ability of libraries "to add to the fast diminishing store of human pleasure" as a sufficient justification for their existence. Even were the library to become no more than "the recognized loafing centre of the city," Kelso affirmed, "its existence on that score would be justified."[157]

Forged amid the depression, the defense of public libraries for promoting recreation gained most of its adherents after the return of prosperity. Unorthodox when voiced in 1894, Kelso's opinion became the standard response of a segment of the profession between 1895 and 1910. "If a book enables a sufferer to forget pain, a tired worker his cares, or a woman her household worries," contended John Ballinger, an advocate of recreational reading, "why the trouble about the exact place on the literary plane of the book which refreshes the spirit?"[158]

Nothing in the defense of recreational reading involved an embrace of the new literary currents typified by Stephen Crane, Frank Norris, and Theodore Dreiser; "genteel" continued to be a fair description of the literary preferences of most articulate public librarians. Even John Cotton Dana, perhaps the best known nemesis of cultural paternalists, insisted in 1898 that "the millions of novels issued from the hundreds of public libraries in this country, were . . . a serious evil to the public and a perversion of the true mission of the library."[159]

What one detects in librarians' debates over fiction during the 1890s and early 1900s is less a triumph of libertarianism over restrictiveness or of naturalism over the Genteel Tradition than an emerging disillusion among younger librarians that popular literary taste could be uplifted. After 1890 defenses of recreative reading were more likely to view recreation as its own justification, regardless of whether readers experienced the kind of gradual elevation of literary sensibility predicted by the genteel leadership of the American Library Association in the 1870s and 1880s. "The librarian has always been told at school and library conventions that people are hungry for knowledge," Agnes Hill of the Bridgeport Public Library wrote in 1902. "Now people in general are not hungry for knowledge," she countered. The library faced a public that, "apart from what it offers in recreation," was indifferent to it. Librarians could save themselves a lot of wasted motion, she concluded, if they began by conceding that "people with a taste for the highest literature are few and far between."[160] Hill expressed a kind of bureaucratic relativism, a belief that, whatever literary preferences or ideals librarians might avow, these could not form the basis of the library's policies. Armed with such attitudes, librarians increasingly resisted outside interference. For example, during the 1890s "reading committees" often advised librarians about which books to purchase. In a widely cited attack on paternalism, Lindsay Swift of the Boston Public Library assailed these committees, partly because they were dominated by upper-class women whose ideas about literature led them to dismiss anything that smacked of Third Avenue or the South End, and partly because the mere existence of reading committees challenged the autonomy of librarians.[161]

Swift's opposition to outside interference in the selection and purchasing of fiction by public librarians underscores the librarians' growing professionalism in the 1890s and early 1900s. The genteel leaders of the American Library Association in the 1870s and 1880s saw themselves as men of letters rather than as technicians skilled in the science of dispensing books to the public. Although quite capable of running efficient libraries, these men never allowed their identity to be submerged by professional librarianship. Both Winsor and Poole served as presidents of the American Historical Association as well as of the American Library Association, and each is remembered for works of scholarship—Winsor for his history of Boston, and Poole for his well-thumbed index to periodical literature.

In contrast, Melvil Dewey, who became the foremost figure in American public librarianship during the 1890s and early 1900s, represented a new emphasis on the professional education of librarians and a preoccupation with technical administration. Dewey's mania for efficiency led him to devise his famed decimal system to speed the location of books and to standardize their classification. In many ways, Dewey was the antithesis of the man of letters. He filled his communications to professional journals with phonetically spelled words—"thot," "hav," "giv," and even "Melvil Dui"—that pained the older generation. An advocate of professional education for librarians, Dewey headed Columbia University's School of Library Economy, the first school of library science in the nation, at its opening in 1886. A student of Dewey's reminisced, "What Dewey taught was not the love of books, either for their literary content or for their physical properties, but how to administer a library and how to care for the needs of those who would know and use books. He was not a great student or scholar nor a great bibliographer, but he was what might be called a great mechanician."[162] In 1897 Dewey told librarians to view their calling as a high-grade business and to "look after the working details, have things go smoothly, and let people get their own meat or poison."[163]

Dewey also championed librarianship as a profession for women, many of whom entered the newly established schools of library science. Dee Garrison has suggested that the feminization of librarianship in the 1890s contributed to the weakening of the position of Winsor and Poole that popular taste could be elevated, for women may have been less assertive than men in censuring popular taste and more subservient to the wishes of the library's clients.[164] Yet the feminization of librarianship may merely have substituted maternalism for paternalism, particularly in small-town libraries where librarians long continued to try to uplift the reading tastes of their neighbors and their neighbors' children.[165]

Although professionalization provided librarians with a terminology for articulating the growing attitude of bureaucratic relativism—their self-image as efficient managers of book distribution—professionalization did not compel librarians to become relativists or to abandon the traditional goal of moral uplift. No one was more committed than Melvil Dewey to transforming librarianship into a school-taught science, yet Dewey's assessment of paternalism changed in the 1890s, *after* his zeal for professionalism had developed. As late as 1888, two years after he had been chosen to head the first school of library science in the United States, Dewey described the cultural role of the public library in terms indistinguishable from those of Winsor and Poole. The schools, he wrote, "give the chisel; the libraries the marble; there can be no statues without both." Initially at least, Dewey saw no inconsistency between the professionalization of librarianship and his conception of the library as a "people's university." Fiction and humor belonged in libraries, but merely as "the embroidery and not the web," he declared.[166]

Like the shifting contours of the debate over immoral fiction, Dewey's move away from a missionary conception of the library's role has to be set within an institutional rather than strictly professional context. More than any other factor, the growth of public libraries during the 1890s, which brought librarians into unprecedented contact with the public, undermined the idea of uplifting public taste. Librarians found it difficult to escape the conclusion that the public used libraries primarily to acquire recent fiction. This pattern was particularly evident in small-town libraries, which circulated little but fiction.[167] Yet even in the larger towns and cities, the spread of public libraries exposed librarians to the reality of a public that viewed libraries primarily as inexpensive places to acquire recent novels. Increasingly, the real test of a librarian lay in the ability to justify public expenditures by displaying rising circulation figures. An exasperated librarian in Pennsylvania described the typical response of the authorities to his complaints about the low level of public literary taste as an injunction "above all things [to] make the library popular." Inasmuch as "all classes are taxed for the library's purpose," ran the trustees' argument, "all classes of reading ought to be represented."[168]

Not all public librarians accepted this popularity-at-any-price criterion. Most remained wedded to conservative ideals of literary excellence and continued to hope that the public would prefer history and science to fiction. "Mission" continued to occupy a privileged position in the lexicon of public librarians. In 1901 R. R. Bowker described the librarian as "the typical home missionary of the time."[169] But direct experience with the public bred, if not contempt, then caution about the chances of influencing taste. Observing that the public resisted advice and demanded what its tax dollars had paid for, a librarian concluded that the only way to influence popular reading was to make certain that the library's shelves contained books on topics of current interest such as Venezuela and Cuba.[170]

For decades supporters of public libraries had described them as major improvements on the old social libraries, equally a means of culture while far more accessible to the multitude. In reality, it proved difficult to transfer the ideology of self-culture from social to public libraries; indeed the more successful the public-library movement became, the more apparent the difficulty. Compared to social libraries, public libraries lacked an intimate relationship to their users. By virtue of their historic ties to mutual improvement societies, social libraries had served a clientele that could be presumed interested in self-improvement. Literary societies had always attracted a core of self-improvers, who could act as models for their less earnest members. In contrast, public libraries lacked a select membership; indeed they lacked members as such. Rather, they served an "average reader" whose very identity remained a mystery. Patrons appeared from nowhere and disappeared to nowhere. Public librarians found, too, that they were judged by their ability to serve diverse constituencies. In 1906 Lindsay Swift wistfully compared the status of proprietary and public librarians. "The proprietary librarian," he wrote, "fortunately is not called upon to assume the complicated role of a high-class janitor, caterer, or department-store manager; he may still walk in the fear of God and not of a board of aldermen, loving and knowing and cherishing his books, courteous and helpful of his constituents." Proprietary libraries were happily free of the embarrassments of catering to "the caprices and necessities of the whole mass of citizens," Swift added, for "these happy institutions, having a fairly homogenous body of constituents, can do practically as they please."[171]

If librarians could no longer play the role of learned counselors guiding popular taste, what mission remained for them? During the early 1900s public librarians developed a variety of new conceptions of their mission. One approach, evident even in the 1890s, emphasized the library's duty to children. Ticknor's generation had often spoken of saving youth from wasted lives, but by "youth" paternalists had meant out-of-school teenagers rather than the little ones to whom libraries increasingly catered. During the 1890s urban libraries began to extend borrowing privileges to children under ten and to open children's rooms staffed by trained professionals.[172] Josephus N. Larned of Buffalo, one of the leaders of the profession, noted in 1907 that, while libraries had long existed in harmony with the public schools, the tendency of the times was toward intimate cooperation.[173] Indeed the more that librarians came to doubt whether popular literary taste was capable of elevation, the more plausible it seemed to focus on instilling in children an appreciation of fine literature. Appropriately, during the early 1900s articles on the relations between public schools and libraries began to clog professional journals. What marked these articles was less a general exhortation to encourage the young to read than specific advice about how to coordinate school assignments and the library's services. By 1910 Louis R. Wilson could proclaim that "the library's first duty, obviously, is to the child."[174]

This transfer of interest from adults to children was part of a broader tendency that saw public libraries redefine their educative role between 1890 and 1910. Whereas Ticknor's generation had construed education as a phase of culture, a process of elevating taste and outlook, after 1890 librarians gradually moved toward a conception of education as the provision of specific services to subpopulations. Like department stores, libraries would offer something for everyone, particularly information for specific occupational groups. To facilitate this kind of education, librarians began to departmentalize libraries by subjects. In 1895 the Boston Public Library allocated a group of shelves to books on the fine and industrial arts. In 1913 William H. Brett established nine subject departments within a single room of the temporary quarters of the Cleveland Public Library. The idea of subject departments marked a break with the prevailing practice of dividing books into those kept on reference shelves and those allowed to circulate. As Joseph Wheeler of the Los Angeles Public Library contended in 1914, it was immaterial whether books were read at home or in the library. What mattered was that "the reader secure all the literature on his subject . . . without loss of energy or time."[175] Small-town librarians also became infected by the criterion of utility. One described in 1909 how she boosted her library's circulation by stocking books on Persian rugs after a salesman had come to town.[176] By 1924 William S. Learned of the Carnegie Foundation could describe the ideal public library as a virtual service station for subpopulations: motorists seeking road maps for their annual holiday, electricians in search of manuals on wiring, clergymen looking for up-to-date books on theology.[177]

The Old and the New

In 1915 the novelist and short-story writer Katherine Fullerton Gerould described "the Extirpation of Culture," which she identified with the decline of Matthew Arnold's reputation twenty years earlier. Gerould's timing of the decline, the mid-1890s, is consistent with the argument of this chapter, but her comments provoked a minor storm of dissent from those who pointed to libraries crammed with readers, symphony orchestras springing up in midwestern cities, and ever-lengthening lines to obtain opera tickets.[178]

Gerould's critics had a point. In the Arnoldian sense of the best that had been thought and known, culture did not suddenly go out of fashion in the mid-1890s. Although precise measurement is impossible, the proportion of the public interested in serious literature, music, and art most likely has widened in the twentieth century.[179] Yet her critics also missed *the* point. In the 1870s the architects of Chautauqua and the public-library movement had assumed that fine literature and art were suited to all classes. By the turn of the century, however, this confidence in the universal suitability of culture had weakened notably. Even as libraries opened neighborhood branches, symphonies spread to new cities, and art museums started docent programs, all such efforts at the diffusion of culture were now aimed either at children or at adults with a taste for culture. Popular educators had concluded that the "public" was merely the sum of discrete publics, each with its own peculiar experiences and proclivities and each requiring a different kind of education.

In 1898 the educator and reformer Vida Scudder averred that "in any community there are fewer people to respond to an intellectual than to a moral stimulus."[180] The trouble with Arnold, she added, was that he thought social change depended on prior understanding, a view that comforted the indolent who languidly pursued understanding without intending to take action. Scudder's generation saw the beginnings of a redefinition of culture, which attempted to associate the word with activities and nonreflective beliefs. As early as 1871, the British anthropologist Edward B. Tylor had framed the modern anthropological definition of culture as the "complex whole" that included "knowledge, belief, custom, art, law, morals, and any other capabilities and habits acquired by man as a member of society."[181] Rooted in human "capabilities," Tylor's conception was decidedly less ethereal than Arnold's, from which it diverged most fundamentally by according primacy to a vast range of human activities. Arnold had insisted that culture would spur action, but Tylor's formulation was essentially descriptive rather than prescriptive. His definition did not enter British or American dictionaries or encyclopedias for more than a half century, and throughout the first two decades of the twentieth century Progressives still equated culture with uplift. But at the same time, Progressive reformers began to associate culture with daily activities, a tactic that worked against attempts to harness it to lectures and that, in the long run, would erode culture's traditional association with moral uplift.[182]

Conclusion

Although the ideal of culture had come under attack within universities from advocates of such rival ideals as research and utility, it continued to arouse the enthusiasm of those engaged in popular adult education at the start of the 1890s. In contrast to research and utility, access to culture required neither scholarly nor technical knowledge. Rather, it called for little more than sympathy with fine literature and a desire for refinement, qualities that educators thought were widely diffused if imperfectly satisfied. For decades promotional literature had puffed the accomplishments of the self-taught, elevated the antebellum lyceum to legendary status, and portrayed a literate public that anyone could enter. The familiarity of idealistic professors and librarians with Chautauqua and its promotional literature (which exaggerated Chautauqua's appeal across class lines) reinforced this image of an expanding public eager for knowledge. So did their interpretation of the Knights of Labor, the Grange, and the Farmers' Alliance.

The initial optimism spurred by all of these factors collapsed in the face of new experience. Professors discovered that, while by no means indifferent to knowledge, workers cared little about academic expositions of subjects. Advocates of tax-supported libraries stumbled across a reading public that fit none of the conceptions of the public derived from decades of experience with social libraries. Missionaries who initially had seen the diffusion of culture limited only by their own dedication and administrative skills came to question their most basic assumptions, and they began to move away from culture toward types of education aimed at immediate situations and everyday experiences.

The language employed by educators disguised the abruptness and depth of this change. For example, by the end of the century John Dewey was starting to describe ways to make work an instrument of culture, by which he meant the individual's understanding of work's social and economic relations. Although more grounded in everyday experience than Arnoldian culture, Dewey's conception by no means equated culture with experience; culture still involved the attainment of broad understanding. Despite this superficial resemblance, however, the change was truly momentous. At some level, all of the nineteenth-century missionaries of culture had assumed an underlying congruence between their goals and those of the public. They saw their task as incorporating the unwashed into this culturally striving public by widening access to the means of culture. This missionary enterprise was rooted in local outposts, in Elkanah Watson's agricultural fairs that would stimulate farmers to read, in "lyceum villages," "circles," and "local centers" from which culture would "radiate." Widening the circle of culture required the personal presence of its emissaries, for example as lecturers, and it was antithetical to bureaucracy, which would obstruct the personal influence that missionaries valued. In contrast, Dewey and others who sought to ground culture in such experiences as work, parenting, or consuming no longer addressed the culturally striving public. Rather, they wrote about "society," a faceless and amorphous entity composed of diverse subpopulations about which little was known.[183] No longer dedicated to imparting a way of life, social educators of the twentieth century would try to tailor specific types of knowledge to the educational interests of those diverse subpopulations. They necessarily would come to rely on bureaucracy, for now they would have to identify prospective students, discover their "reading interests" and "educational needs," and guide them to appropriate courses.

Chapter 7

From Useful Knowledge to
Job Improvement, 1870–1930

Between 1900 and 1925, educators in flight from Arnoldian culture and imbued with the values of Progressive reform groped toward a new conception of culture grounded in the experience of work. John Dewey, the most influential of these educators, did not maintain that work in itself was educative. Without a systematic effort on the part of the public schools to teach the relationships among types of work and between work and such social institutions as the family and neighborhood, work became "isolated, selfish and individualistic."[1] But if taught with regard to the historical background of present conditions of work, and with the aim of imparting initiative and intelligence in dealing with agencies of production and work's political and civic associations, vocations would give individuals "a sort of social education by necessity, since everyone must learn to adapt himself to other individuals and to whole communities."[2]

In the 1920s Dewey used "culture" in the anthropological sense as equivalent to social customs, beliefs, and dispositions, but before World War I he employed the word normatively to denote a "habit of mind which perceives and estimates all matters with reference to their bearing on social values and aims."[3] In this respect, culture became an appropriate aim of education, a view shared by Matthew Arnold. But Dewey criticized Arnold for relying on history and literature as the primary means of culture and for neglecting "manual and industrial" activities. In Dewey's eyes, Arnoldianism's fatal flaw lay in its irrelevance to modern industrial society. Any conception of culture that ignored urban and industrial development could never become democratic in a society distinguished above all by swift urbanization and industrialization.

Yet Dewey also acknowledged that Arnold spoke for a type of culture that had deep popular roots in the United States. In one of his more arresting insights, Dewey recognized Arnold's paradoxical kinship to the pioneer spirit in America. Coming from countries with "traditions of culture and 'learning,'" pioneers naturally looked to schools "to keep alive these transplanted ideals in the midst of their struggle with nature." Like Arnold, they equated education with "the storing up of historical facts and the acquiring of the knowledge and the literature of the past."[4]

In his effort to link education to work, Dewey urged his contemporaries to think in more democratic ways about culture. Yet his dismissal of Arnoldianism deflected Dewey from time-tested methods of popularizing knowledge. From Josiah Holbrook in the 1820s to Herbert Baxter Adams in the 1890s, scholars who came before the public as missionaries for popular intellectual improvement had implicitly forwarded the idea that by identifying and encouraging local clienteles eager to improve themselves, the scholarly class would progressively widen the perimeter of sympathy for knowledge and for the moral qualities elicited by its pursuit. Dewey could never accept this approach to popularization—in part because of its association with the idea of culture as elevation beyond experience, and in part because it rested on the assumption that what the public most required was to become more like scholars, to learn to share their intellectual refinement. Dewey was a pluralist to the extent that he sought to make culture relevant to the diverse situations of life; in turn, this objective inclined him to view education as a process of adaptation rather than as a progressive mastery of a body of information or ideas. But in rejecting Arnoldianism, Dewey and his followers encountered a problem that defied an easy solution. Having jettisoned the enterprise of guiding local clienteles already eager for the mental elevation promised by Arnoldian culture, Deweyans struggled to attach educational agendas to the objectives of people who lacked any apparent interest in those agendas.

The history of early-twentieth-century initiatives in vocational education illustrates the difficulty that educators such as Dewey faced when they abandoned the original approach toward "diffusing" knowledge. Historians have described the vocational education movement primarily as an attempt to reform the curriculum of the public schools, but between 1890 and 1930 the main demand for organized vocational education came neither from parents nor schoolchildren but from young working adults who flocked in astonishing numbers to proprietary schools that offered a mixture of classroom and correspondence instruction. Inexplicably, historians have ignored this development, but early-twentieth-century public educators were aware of it and responded to it with ambivalence. On the one hand, the surge of adult interest in vocational courses persuaded them that schools could teach vocations and indeed would have to if they were to prevent juveniles from dropping out. On the other hand, adult demand mainly took the form of enrollment in courses that promised immediate dividends in the form of job-specific skills rather than any broad integration of culture and experience. Recognizing that demand for vocational education arose primarily among working adults and outside of public education positions us to understand the major dispute that developed among vocational educators in the Progressive era: the conflict between Deweyans, who wanted to make productive activity the basis for social education, and the so-called efficiency educators, who preferred pure and simple trade training in job-specific skills. Historians have cast this as a clash between educational liberals and narrow utilitarians, but at a more basic level the conflict engaged rival conceptions of the appropriate age group for vocational education. Viewing the contemporary practice of vocations as antithetical to his conception of culture, Dewey focused on the education of "future workers." He wrote mainly about small children, next to nothing about teenagers, and just enough about adult job-training programs to indicate his disdain for them. In contrast, the efficiency educators wrote mainly about teenagers, and they drew inspiration from programs established to train adult workers. Their goal was to make vocational education in secondary schools more similar to adult training programs.

Dewey's focus on educating young children reveals just how harshly time had dealt with the hoary ideal of Useful Knowledge. In the 1820s and 1830s the promoters of mechanics' institutes, who shared Dewey's general objective of making work the basis of education, had aimed their educational message at adults, and in the 1860s the framers of the Morrill Act had identified colleges as the instruments for dignifying work by tying it to scientific understanding. But the ideological impulse behind both the mechanics' institutes and the Morrill Act, Useful Knowledge, was moribund by 1900. It had left a residue of academicism, encouraged a detachment of education from the lives of working people, and indirectly stimulated the rise of proprietary schools offering job-specific training. In sum, Dewey's preference for educating small children about the relationships between individual production and the larger society reflected both the dominant position of job-specific types of vocational education for teenagers and young adults in his day and the decay of the one tradition, Useful Knowledge, that had addressed the integration of work and knowledge for those old enough to hold jobs.

Useful Knowledge and the Corporate Revolution

In the Civil War era, Justin Morrill and Jonathan Baldwin Turner had expected land-grant colleges to attract the children of farmers and mechanics by offering scientific instruction relevant to the "industrial classes." The trouble was that few such sciences existed. Ordinary farmers remained skeptical of the claims of agricultural science; as late as 1890 more was known about the relative endurance of different metals under stress than about the potential of different seeds to grow corn.[5] Land-grant colleges at times tried to enhance the stature of agricultural science by harnessing it to more traditional subjects. Florida State University, for example, created a professorship of agriculture, horticulture, and Greek.[6] But such ploys could not disguise their inability to attract sizable numbers of students into their agricultural courses. The Morrill Act had appealed to spokesmen for agricultural interests as a gesture of concern for farmers, but the law failed to inspire much enthusiasm among the class that it was supposed to benefit. Initially, blame for low enrollments fell on the practice, employed in several states, of designating traditional liberal arts colleges or universities for the Morrill endowment. In the 1850s Evan Pugh, who rose from the blacksmith's forge to become the first president of Pennsylvania State University, had contended that the establishment of independent agricultural and mechanical colleges would alone ensure the attendance of working people, and this argument enjoyed a good deal of currency in the 1870s as an explanation for the failure of land-grant universities to attract students. But the situation did not improve even when independent agricultural and mechanical colleges became more prevalent.

To take one of many examples, in the early 1870s the University of Mississippi, the recipient of the Morrill endowment in that state, introduced a course in agricultural science. It attracted only a handful of students, however, and in reaction the state legislature chartered the Agricultural and Mechanical College of Mississippi (now Mississippi State University) in 1878. But little actually changed. Most students continued to avoid the agricultural course, and many of those who took it eventually abandoned agriculture. A particular source of embarrassment to the college was the fact that the son of its president enrolled at Harvard Law School after graduation.[7]

The mechanic arts fared better in the land-grant colleges. In contrast to agricultural science, still in the fetal stage in the 1870s, the mechanic arts could be related to a well-developed academic discipline, engineering. Engineering departments became the core of most land-grant institutions and easily outgrew their agricultural counterparts. But engineering triumphed in a form that distanced it from Useful Knowledge. Whereas Justin Morrill envisioned the mechanic arts as encompassing little more than the mechanical operations ancillary to running a farm in the middle of the nineteenth century, courses in mechanical and electrical engineering multiplied in colleges and universities after 1870, often in response to industrial demand. In the 1870s and 1880s, conflicts broke out within several engineering colleges between advocates of shop-based instruction, which stressed application to practice, and proponents of higher mathematics and the sciences. When the dust settled, supporters of a curriculum based on mathematics and science were in control of most American engineering colleges. At Cornell, for example, Robert Thurston, whose background lay in the engineering corps of the navy rather than in shop work, reorganized the curriculum along scientific lines in the 1880s and successfully scuttled a provision to allow credit toward entrance into the engineering school (the Sibley College of the Mechanic Arts) for shop experience.[8]

The triumph of academic engineering was part of a larger development in which universities established ties to corporations. Favored by an ever-expanding home market, American corporations introduced high-speed machinery in the 1870s and 1880s in the manufacture of matches, cigarettes, and soap; in the refining of oil and the milling of flour; and in the fabrication of a wide range of metal products. What distinguished American industry from its European counterpart, however, was less the introduction of new machines than the emphasis that Americans placed on the organization of work. Whereas in Europe the skilled machinist made his company's product, his American counterpart was more likely to design or set up a semi-automatic machine for less skilled workers to operate.[9]

These developments spurred demand for university-trained engineers. In contrast to shop-trained mechanics, whose knowledge of the workings of machines rested on a mixture of intuition and experience, engineering graduates had the mathematical knowledge—algebra, geometry, and calculus—to understand the theory of steam engines and other machines. While always desirable, a knowledge of theoretical mechanics became more important after 1870, as machinery spread beyond its traditional bases in the textile and shoe industries into new realms of production. In addition, engineering colleges taught a broad range of specialties to enable their graduates to respond to the fast-changing requirements of business. By 1914 the student of mechanical engineering at M.I.T. had to take heat engineering, boiler design, electrical engineering, machine design, factory construction, hydraulics, power-plant design, refrigeration, and heating ventilation. In 1918 a Carnegie Foundation report found their curricula "congested beyond endurance."[10]

Engineering colleges were also convenient places to transmit new technology, especially that of electricity. In 1876 Thomas A. Edison opened a research laboratory, the famed "invention factory," at Menlo Park, New Jersey. There and later in his laboratories at Orange, he hired university-trained engineers to assist his work. These laboratories foreshadowed the massive research laboratories established by General Electric and Westinghouse in the mid-1890s, which in turn hired large numbers of engineering graduates. In 1906 over 80 percent of the members of the American Institute of Electrical Engineers held college degrees, and well over half of these worked as salaried engineers, mainly for General Electric and Westinghouse. Nationally, the proportion of engineers to have graduated from engineering colleges rose from one out of nine in 1870 to one out of two by 1918.[11]

Industrial growth also stimulated the demand for managers to devise and implement incentive plans for workers, forecast sales, perform market analysis, decide on the best way to finance expansion, and comprehend the relationships between raw materials, production, marketing, and sales. Colleges and universities taught none of this. Even the handful of university business schools established before 1900 taught business more as a liberal art than as a technical skill by teaching such subjects as English literature; logic; ethics; Roman history; the constitutional histories of Germany, Switzerland, and England; sociology; the art of newspaper making; "economic botany"; and "the history of commerce in all countries and at every age."[12] Yet the very comprehensiveness of such curricula—the University of Pennsylvania's Wharton School of Finance and Economy taught 52 subjects and the University of California's business school even more—made it as plausible for business schools as for engineering colleges to advertise the ability of their graduates to think broadly and flexibly and thereby facilitated the increasing movement of graduates into managerial positions. In a sense, the same was true of graduates of liberal arts colleges, for the traditional defense of liberal education, that it encouraged a wide outlook, acquired new resonance at the end of the nineteenth century. Not all corporate leaders leaped at the opportunity to hire graduates. Henry Ford, for example, preferred to recruit his executives from within his organization. But overall the reputation of college graduates soared in board rooms at the end of the century. Even those corporate leaders who wondered about the cash value of academic subjects could find reassurance about the moral value of college "life" in the strenuous extracurricular activities—sports, clubs, and student government—that became so prominent in the closing decades of the century and that promised to inculcate such useful qualities as competitiveness, decision-making, and an ability to work within organizations.[13]

Even as higher education expanded its ties to business, it distanced itself from anything that smacked of on-the-job training. Engineering colleges concentrated on teaching science, mathematics, and a wide range of engineering specialties, all as preludes to productive work. Modeling themselves on university law and medical schools, which were fast severing their ties to professional offices, collegiate business schools disdained the "mere arts of the counting room" and sought to develop a curriculum "which it would be worth the while of a future business man to complete before he took up the actual work of the counting-house, bank, the insurance office, the railway office, and so forth, in the same sense in which it would be worth the while of the physician to take the medical course or the lawyer to take the legal course."[14]

Contemporaries praised general professional education in formal schools as more conducive to upward mobility. Defending the American approach to educating engineers first in theory and then in practice, Thomas C. Clarke reminded the American Society of Civil Engineers in 1874 that the British system, with its stress on apprenticeship, reflected the persistence of personal patronage in Britain, a society in which one's "chance of future employment depends on being personally known to some engineer in large practice."[15] In contrast, by establishing the primacy of comprehensive and theoretical education over practice, Americans afforded able young men who lacked such personal connections an opportunity to enter the engineering profession. Yet while higher education established its relevance to the corporate revolution, few young people could afford either the tuition or the opportunity costs of this sort of education. In 1890 only 1.8 percent of the population aged 18 to 24 attended college (including collegiate or university professional schools). This proportion doubled between 1890 and 1918, but as late as 1944 less than 7 percent of the 18 to 24 age group was enrolled in higher education.

All of this reminds us of the problems inherent in the Morrill Act's goal of harnessing practical and higher education in democratic universities. In contrast to Justin Morrill, leading university presidents of the late nineteenth century saw practical utility and higher education as fundamentally incompatible. Cornell's president, Andrew Dickson White, quietly interred Ezra Cornell's call for university-connected factories that would teach students to become self-supporting, while Harvard's Charles William Eliot dampened any notion that Harvard educate practical workers. At Johns Hopkins, Daniel Coit Gilman pursued a similar course by promoting a research-oriented institution while simultaneously campaigning for an elaborate, differentiated, and hierarchical system of lower schools to produce middle-level technicians and ordinary mechanics.[16]

This notion of a middling type of technical education, one positioned between higher professional schools and narrow on-the-job training, would long appeal to American educators; in the second quarter of the twentieth century junior colleges would try to carve a niche for themselves as institutions specializing in the training of "semi-professionals." But to the extent that such technical institutions engaged in trade training, they failed to inspire much interest in the public or among educators before 1900. Sub-university institutions for trade-oriented technical education developed only slowly in the United States. As late as 1907 Arthur Jones of Columbia University observed that American teenagers, while more likely than their European counterparts to attend secondary schools, were less likely to enroll in trade schools.[17]

Various factors account for this retarded growth of technical instruction in the United States. Lacking European traditions of craftsmanship and a well-ingrained apprenticeship system, Americans long had been accustomed to acquiring trade skills on the job. In addition, the corporate revolution spurred demand for workers at the higher and lower rather than the middle rungs of the ladder, for college graduates at one end and for unskilled machine tenders at the other rather than for middling "technicians." Finally, the tradition of Useful Knowledge was fundamentally antithetical to any kind of trade training detached from higher science. The goal of Useful Knowledge was to produce philosophical mechanics like Benjamin Franklin and David Rittenhouse, individuals who refused to rest content with the mastery of craft techniques and who pried into the secrets of nature. This was an old-fashioned image—by 1890 Useful Knowledge's heroes had been dead for a century—but traces of it lingered in movements like manual training, which aroused far more interest than trade education in the 1870s and 1880s.

Manual training was the brainchild of Calvin Woodward, the dean of Washington University's O'Fallon Polytechnic Institute. In the 1870s Woodward became alarmed by the inability of his students to handle tools, and in response he devised a curriculum based on a graded sequence of shop exercises for the St. Louis Manual Training School, the nation's first shop-oriented technical preparatory school. As a preparatory school for the Polytechnic Institute, the St. Louis Manual Training School did not pretend to teach trades. Woodward insisted that manual training's purpose "is not to make mechanics."[18] Indeed, the idea of teaching trades in any schools struck him as an absurdity, for it was both expensive and difficult to teach all of the crafts of a locale in a school, while teaching only a few would overstock individual trades.[19] Rather, he envisioned manual training as a way to develop his students' comprehension of the principles of science by first instructing them in the mastery of tools and mechanical processes.

Much like Jonathan Baldwin Turner and Justin Morrill, he also believed that the nation was overstocked with greedy lawyers and speculators. Just as Morrill praised farmers as men who "do not produce, vend, or consume luxuries" and as sober workmen who "go untouched by all epidemical speculations," Woodward averred that "the good workman is much less frequently reduced to want than those who live by their wits."[20] In the eyes of both men, manual workers formed a saving remnant in a nation where "the distant possibilities of affluence through speculation or the shrewd management of the labor of others, the large salary or the enormous professional fee of the occasional professional man, drew the infatuated crowd as the song of the fabled Siren did the voyagers of old." In sum, manual training would restore respect for labor and dampen "the ambition to be rich."[21]

Contrary to Woodward's hopes, most graduates of the St. Louis Manual Training School avoided manual occupations, a sign that by the 1870s those who could afford to prolong their education into their teen years aspired to become more than mechanics.[22] Nor did Woodward's ideas arouse much enthusiasm among engineering deans and faculties, most of whom believed that engineering graduates could acquire adequate practical experience on the job and that preparatory schools should not distract students from science by stressing instruction in the handling of tools. In the early 1880s he shifted his focus from reforming collegiate preparatory education to transforming public elementary education, and he won an ardent following among public-school educators who favored simplified manual training, usually in the form of woodworking, as a way to teach urban children some of the skills and values associated with rural life. But public-school educators were no more interested than Woodward in trade training. Beginning as an attempt to break down the academicism of the engineering colleges, manual training ended by accentuating the academicism of the public schools.[23]

Here and there, some trade schools sprang up between the cracks of American education. The 1880s witnessed the establishment of a number of high schools devoted to trade training, and throughout the second half of the nineteenth century a type of school known as the technical institute enjoyed a modest growth. Among the latter were the Polytechnic Institute of Brooklyn (1855), Cooper Union's evening classes (1859), the Pratt Institute (1887), the Drexel Institute (1891), and the Carnegie Technical Schools of Pittsburgh (1905). Many of these functioned wholly or partly as continuation schools for students with previous work experience. In 1902, for example, the average age of the students in one such institute, the Springfield (Massachusetts) Evening School of Trades, was 23.7, and half of the students were over 24. Typically, teachers in the technical institutes possessed industrial experience.[24]

Technical institutes drew on various sources. Some were survivors of antebellum mechanics' institutes, others arose in response to local demand for a particular type of technician, and still others were lengthened shadows of individual philanthropists, usually self-made men who preferred to endow schools for workmen rather than colleges for the wealthy. Opened in 1859, the Cooper Union for the Advancement of Science and Art illustrates the philanthropic motive and also the slow process by which this type of school fought its way through the tradition of Useful Knowledge before arriving at practical trade training.

Inspired and supported by Peter Cooper, a New York financier and inventor, the Union was partly intended as a night school for artisans, but Cooper accorded little attention to anything so pedestrian as classroom instruction. Instead, he envisioned a grand institution for "science," a concept he applied to society as well as to nature and which he equated not only with the development of harmonious laws but with the spiritual elevation of the working class. The creed of William Ellery Channing was among the influences that steered the mature Cooper to Unitarianism, while his prolonged involvement with Cyrus West Field in the laying of the Atlantic cable convinced Cooper of the utility of science. The laying of the cable had nearly destroyed Cooper's fortune, and for a period it did wreck his reputation, but he recognized that most of this grief could have been averted had more been known in the 1850s about electrical charges and insulation.

Yet Cooper had little understanding of the relationship between science and technology. With little formal schooling and little inclination for reading books, he was accustomed to acquire his ideas and information in unrelated patches pieced together from conversations, tinkering, and visits to museums. In his mind, science amounted to the belief that these patches were threaded together by rational and progressive laws. His beneficence toward Cooper Union gave him an opportunity to afford others the chance to grasp his intuitive understanding of the universe. His original plans for the Union included a museum, a cosmorama containing pictures of foreign cities and other noteworthy sites (to be glimpsed through holes to enhance the effect of illumination), "conversation parlours," where workmen in the various trades might meet amid portraits of Washington, Franklin, and Lafayette to exchange ideas, and a balustraded roof garden for concerts and vistas.[25]

Traces of several influences are evident in Cooper's educational plans: Useful Knowledge, with its assertion that trade training without science was beneath the dignity of schools and workers alike; romantic naturalism; the Unitarian equation of knowledge with grace; and the mechanics' institutes, with their stress on evening instruction of workers. Indeed, Cooper envisioned as much an institution for the intellectual and spiritual refreshment of the public as a school for workers. If any single event contributed to the early fame of the Union, it was Abraham Lincoln's address there during the 1860 presidential campaign, which foreshadowed the Union's future role as a public forum. In contrast, the Union's development as a school for workers was retarded by Cooper's blithe disregard for education as a process. Rather than ruminating on types of instruction that might profit tired artisans and clerks, Cooper proposed a polytechnic school to produce "engineers, architects and mechanics" and then sought to induce Columbia University to conduct the school within the Union's walls.[26] Columbia did not accept the invitation, and the Union established two principal evening divisions, a School of Science and a School of Art, each of which granted certificates rather than college degrees. But while students flocked to the evening classes in the 1870s and 1880s—annual enrollment in the Gilded Age averaged 3,000 to 4,000—most lacked the background to pursue scientific studies. As a result, very few students in the School of Science persisted to certificates. Far different was the School of Art's experience with classes in mechanical drawing, which proved highly popular. Requiring little preparatory education and much in demand by employers, skill in mechanical drawing was an avenue to advancement in a variety of occupations.[27]

Cooper's original plans had not disregarded drawing, which was taught in the Union's early School of Design. But in the initial conception this was to have been an art school for women rather than a school for male workers eager for advancement. That drawing was stressed at all merely reflected the insistence of an early director of the school that women should learn to draw before they started to paint.[28] The rise of mechanical drawing, a practical and vocationally useful subject, occurred in a series of almost accidental steps. Yet this ascendancy of mechanical drawing contributed to the Union's emergence as a technical institute, a type of school whose students valued the mastery of specific, marketable skills more than the completion of sequential courses of study. This orientation toward skill-specific study hindered the forging of a sense of solidarity among technical institutes.[29] Even the name technical institute did not come into fashion until the 1920s, and in the late nineteenth century neither the trade high schools, of which fewer than twenty had been established by 1890, nor the technical institutes posed a serious challenge to the ascendancy of the manual training movement.

As interstitial institutions without a shared ideology or sense of purpose, technical institutes also encountered difficulties in competing with engineering colleges. In 1930 there were only 37 technical institutes in the United States, compared to 150 engineering colleges. In quest of the prestige attached to the collegiate degree, many technical institutes turned one or more of their subdivisions into colleges. For example, the day schools of the Drexel Institute began to grant degrees in 1915. The Armour Institute in Chicago, which started in 1893 with both vocational and collegiate departments, gradually discontinued the former. The Carnegie Technical Schools of Pittsburgh, which originally included a School of Applied Science, a School for Apprentices and Journeymen, a School of Applied Design, and a Vocational School for Women, were reorganized in 1915 into the Carnegie Institute of Technology, a degree-granting college. Just as manual training loomed larger in the minds of educators than trade training, the model of the college proved far more alluring to Americans than that of the technical institute. While only a small fraction of Americans attended college in the nineteenth century, Americans established colleges at a dizzying pace. In 1850 the United States contained over 200 colleges, and while many of these were "poor, little, half-starved" institutions, their number alone encouraged the belief that engineering education could be harnessed to the collegiate model. In contrast, possessing only a handful of universities, Britain gravitated to the model of the technical institute. In 1897 nearly 300,000 British students attended technical classes sponsored by the Department of Science and Art of the Committee of the (Privy) Council on Education, and of these nearly 200,000 attended in the evening.[30]

In sum, during the 1870s and 1880s the corporate revolution forged new bonds between higher education and the higher levels of business enterprise. The framers of the Morrill Act had envisioned an intimate relationship between theory and practice, between higher science and the ordinary trades, but by 1890 few educators shared their confidence. The spirit of the Morrill Act persisted in the manual training movement, but not the substance, for the kinds of shop exercises that Woodward envisioned as handmaidens to classroom scientific instruction bore no relation to trade training. By 1890 Americans were pioneering new methods of higher professional education, but provisions for sub-university technical or trade instruction remained comparatively meager.

In contrast, between 1890 and the Great Depression a vast industry of part-time vocational institutions developed in the United States, including correspondence and corporation schools and evening colleges. Aided by passage of the Smith-Hughes Act in 1917, vocational education also invaded public schools in these years, but proprietary schools spearheaded its development. Enrollments in proprietary commercial schools, which arose in the 1870s and 1880s to train office workers in bookkeeping, typing, penmanship, and stenography, leaped from 6,500 in 1871, to over 90,000 by 1892, and to nearly 300,000 by 1918.[31] By the early 1900s the nation's leading correspondence school was enrolling 100,000 new students each year, mainly in technical courses. Casting loose from their evangelical moorings, the YMCA and (to a lesser extent) the YWCA entered the field of evening vocational instruction. One reason for this early ascendancy of private and proprietary schools lay in the source of demand for vocational education, which sprang less from the teenagers who might have enrolled in vocational high schools than from working adults in their twenties, who were impelled by the vision of "job improvement," the prospect of a fatter pay envelope, and the possibility of "getting to the other side of the desk." Deterred by opportunity costs from full-time schooling, young working adults flocked to part-time schools. Although some public-school systems maintained evening schools at the turn of the century, for the most part these were not vocational schools. For all practical purposes, the only place to obtain part-time vocational instruction in 1900 was in a private, fee-financed school. By definition, all of the correspondence schools were part-time, and even the proprietary commercial schools that relied on classroom instruction, many of which had originated as day schools, quickly became dependent on evening students. While enrollments in the day classes of proprietary commercial schools rose 15.7 percent between 1900 and 1917, those in evening classes leaped 560 percent.[32]

The Rise of Correspondence Schools

Although the Chautauqua Literary and Scientific Circle had been the first major organization in America to employ instruction by mail, between 1890 and 1930 proprietary correspondence schools spearheaded a shift away from Chautauqua's cultural focus and toward vocational subjects. By 1910 over 200 proprietary correspondence schools offered instruction in an astonishing range of topics. For example, the Home Correspondence School of Springfield, Massachusetts, had departments specializing in academic preparatory, commercial, normal, agricultural, and civil-service subjects. The American Farmers' School in Minneapolis claimed to be the "only school in the world exclusively devoted to teaching farming by mail."[33] The Moody Bible Institute in Chicago offered correspondence courses in missions, the Bible, and even prophecy.[34] Fly-by-night correspondence schools found a profitable business in peripheral medical areas like chiropractic and osteopathy.[35] In Ohio a man claiming to hold the degrees of M.D. and D.O. (Doctor of Osteopathy) advertised a ready-to-mail textbook and diploma in osteopathy for $25; a former sailor advertised a similar service in New York City for $100. A professor at New York University commented in 1916 that correspondence schools had persuaded Americans that any occupation—detective, executive, musician, whatever—could be learned by mail.[36]

Several sources fed the movement for instruction by mail. The prevailing success ideology encouraged a correspondence student in Nebraska, who related how the motto "Pick out your peak and climb it" guided his efforts to become an embalmer.[37] The advertisements of correspondence schools projected the familiar images of famed autodidacts from Franklin to Lincoln. The novels of Horatio Alger, Jr., advanced a complementary image of street waifs who rose to respectability by a mixture of honesty, diligence, luck, and education, by "study at home in long winter evenings" that would qualify eager lads for "posts of higher responsibility, and with a larger compensation."[38] In fact, the rise of correspondence schools coincided with the proliferation of state licensing requirements in a wide variety of occupations. As was true of teachers and librarians who took correspondence courses through the Chautauqua Literary and Scientific Circle, embalmers, plumbers, electricians, and mining inspectors did not have to obtain academic credentials to secure licenses; rather, they had to pass tests that measured their grasp of specific bodies of knowledge. Correspondence schools were well suited to this type of instruction. Despite their occasional claims to the contrary, proprietary correspondence schools could not confer recognized degrees, but they could teach useful facts.[39]

The growth of correspondence schools also coincided with the quantum leap in public-high-school enrollments from under 250,000 in 1890 to over 4,000,000 by 1930. But each successive surge in school enrollments left an army of stragglers, those too old to attend or too poor to persist beyond a few grades, and these stragglers, in turn, sought surrogates for the education denied them. Miss Iona Cunningham of Concordia, Kansas, found herself in her early twenties faced by the need to become self-supporting. Keenly sensitive to her lack of a high-school diploma, she enrolled in English and bookkeeping courses through the American School of Correspondence, founded in 1907.[40] Peter Ackerman, a Dutch immigrant, enrolled in the same school after failing to adjust to an American high school.[41] Ackerman did not indicate the reasons for his failure, but other correspondence students pointed to the impersonality of the correspondence method as a positive advantage, for correspondence students could not be embarrassed by their race, gender, ignorance, or their inability to speak fluent English.

Correspondence schools preached the relationship between education and success, but little would have come of such exhortations had these institutions failed to satisfy customers. Although occasionally prone to fraud and always characterized by brazen advertising, correspondence schools pioneered innovative educational methods and forged close and mutually beneficial ties to major corporations. These aspects of correspondence schools can be glimpsed through the activities of the most famous one, the International Correspondence Schools of Scranton, Pennsylvania (ICS).

ICS originated in the 1880s in a column of a Pennsylvania mining paper that miners used to exchange information about the causes of accidents. In time, the popularity of the column persuaded the paper's editor to start a mining school by mail, and in 1891 this school, headquartered at Scranton, became ICS. In ICS's early days virtually all of its students were coal miners, typically men in their mid- to late twenties who hoped to qualify as mine inspectors or foremen by passing the state's licensing examinations. Few possessed the knowledge of arithmetical fractions necessary to calculate the flow of air through mine passages, or the ability to identify the different gases encountered in mines. With families to support, most were too busy or too embarrassed by their ignorance to attend night schools. The composite picture of these early students drawn in 1906 by ICS's president was close to the mark: a young head of household studying at home, with the kitchen table as his desk and with one hand rocking the cradle to quiet the baby.[42]

ICS grew slowly until the mid-1890s; by the end of 1893 it had enrolled some 3,000 students, mainly miners. Gradually, however, ICS devised new tactics to broaden its base. It began to employ salesmen, 1,200 covering 800 national "routes" by 1906, to canvass "prospects" and to engage in "inspirational" advertising and solicitation. By 1916 ICS's advertising budget exceeded $2,000,000. In this respect it did not differ from other correspondence schools, all of which engaged in massive advertising campaigns. Lee Galloway, a professor of commerce at New York University, reported in 1916 that one New York advertising school paid its salesmen annually an amount equal to the annual income of the nation's largest commercial day school. Advertising on this scale helped to popularize the idea that any human activity required specialized training—"Muscles at Twenty, Brains at Forty"—and that correspondence schools represented an effective way to acquire training. This is precisely what ICS meant by inspirational advertising: the encouragement of a desire for self-improvement rather than the mere announcement of the availability of a course.[43]

Yet advertising brought ICS some problems, for, as its president conceded in 1906, three-fourths of its students were recruited from the ranks of "careless or indifferent persons."[44] Indifferent students posed a financial challenge to the company, for ICS sold its courses on the installment plan. It could not retrieve the cost of its textbooks and staff from the three- to five-dollar monthly remittances of students unless those students persisted. ICS's answer was to follow up its advertising with "*inspirational solicitation*," the canvassing and re-canvassing of prospects by field agents. Even with re-canvassing, over 85 percent of ICS's students failed to complete the course for which they had enrolled. This is hardly surprising, for courses took anywhere from three to thirteen years to complete. But ICS broke its courses into "subjects"; as many as 30 or 40 subjects might compose a course.[45] Half of its students failed to complete a single subject, but the remaining half, on average, completed three subjects and stayed with ICS for a year.[46] This was long enough for ICS to turn a profit, the more so because enrollments leaped in the late 1890s. In 1898 over 38,000 new students enrolled; the number doubled in the following year. In the early 1900s, 100,000 new students were signing up each year. By 1910 cumulative enrollments stood at over 1,000,000, and by 1930 ICS could claim over 4,000,000 alumni.[47] An expansion of its offerings accompanied the leap in enrollments. By 1906 ICS contained 31 divisions (or "schools"). While there were schools of advertising, window trimming, and language, technical divisions always predominated: civil engineering, metal mining, navigation, plumbing and heating, sheet-metal work, steam and marine engineering, structural engineering, and telephone and telegraph engineering.[48]

No proprietary, endowed, or public institution in the annals of American education ever achieved such a dramatic increase in enrollments over so short a span of years. ICS's growth reflected the fact that, even as traditional skills like blacksmithing and cooperage were in decline, new ones were coming to the fore. The introduction of electricity into factories stimulated demand for wiremen and dynamo operators. Typewriters and automobiles required skilled persons to repair them.[49] The trade high schools of the 1880s and 1890s usually did not offer instruction in skills associated with advanced technology; rather, they focused on traditional skills like stonecutting, plumbing, carpentry, plastering, blacksmithing, and tailoring.[50] The difficulty and expense of recreating factory conditions within a school restricted the growth of trade high schools and help to explain the preference of public-school educators for the relative simplicity and cheapness of manual training. In addition, opportunity costs restricted enrollments in all forms of full-time secondary education.

ICS was different. Its students could not leave their jobs or families to attend institutes or colleges, and the vast majority lacked a firm elementary education. Ninety percent of its enrollees could not work fractions and began their studies with arithmetic. ICS not only reduced the opportunity costs of education essentially to nil, but its specially prepared textbooks assumed nothing beyond the ability of its clients to read simple English. Assuming literacy but not numeracy, ICS's profusely illustrated textbooks explained simple arithmetical terms and concepts before proceeding to difficult ones. In this respect ICS overcame a problem that long had plagued attempts to instruct mechanics through print: the tendency to talk over the heads of readers.[51] In addition, ICS's students could study whatever they chose. In 1906 ICS offered 500 different subjects. Typically, a student might complete arithmetic, geometrical drawing, and mechanical drawing; arithmetic, mensuration, and mine ventilation; or blow-piping, assaying, and mineralogy. Rather than a comprehensive education, ICS students aimed to upgrade specific skills to secure minor promotions. For example, depending on the horsepower of the steam engine one wished to operate, a student could take any of three steam-engineering courses. In effect, ICS was conducted as a kind of educational automat; it chopped fields of technical knowledge into discrete pieces. For identification purposes, ICS attached a letter or combination of letters to each course. The letter N, for example, signified Sanitary Plumbing and Gas-Fitting; NB, Complete Coal Mining; NC, Metal Mining; NF, Short

Coal Mining; NH, Metal Prospecting; NI, Complete Metallurgy; NJ, Hydro-Metallurgy; NK, Smelting; NL, Milling; and NN, Ocean Navigation.[52]

One striking feature of ICS's student body lay in the predominance of native-born young men. This statement is based on inference. No detailed studies of the characteristics of correspondence students were conducted until after 1920, and even then the studies focused on students in university-sponsored home-study courses. But in 1905, ICS published a list of all of its graduates and of students who had completed a third or more of the course for which they had signed up. This list contained 54,500 names, culled from the larger group of 650,000 students for whom ICS had records. The list, in other words, was biased toward persistent students.[53] The list contained last names, usually the first and middle initial, and an address. The only first names that appeared were female. If the use of initials instead of given names was a way to distinguish genders, then over 95 percent of those listed were men, a fact that is hardly surprising in view of ICS's technical orientation. ICS reported that its typical student was a male in his mid-20s. Nor is it surprising that metropolitan areas and industrial cities like Bethlehem, Pennsylvania, and Troy, New York, provided a disproportionate share of ICS's students. What is striking, however, is the proportion of northern European and especially English names on the list. In Boston, for example, only 11 of 186 names were Irish; in Chicago, fewer than 25 of 1,200 names were Slavic; in New York City, only 12 of 1,200 names were Italian or East European.

Undoubtedly, many foreign-born workers lacked the facility with written English that even the simplest ICS courses required. But ICS's appeal to the native-born rested on more than a shared language. At a time when foreign-born workers were flooding the manual trades, ICS's magazine, succinctly entitled *Ambition*, told native-born young men that they could rise from the "yoke" of unskilled labor to the "other side of the desk"—to the sphere of supervisory positions.[54] Many native-born parents in the early 1900s were pushing their children toward high schools and white-collar work. In contrast, ICS drew its clients from the ranks of those unable to afford prolonged education but eager to acquire the respectability associated with the possession of a valuable skill.[55] In reality, ICS could not change the rules of the game, for major corporations were increasingly prone to hire their managers from the ranks of high-school and college graduates rather than from the shop floor. But ICS's students could benefit from the school's close ties to corporate management to secure small promotions. This relationship can be viewed clearly in the railroad industry, for railroad corporations recognized correspondence schools like ICS (which by 1906 had contracts for discounted instruction with 164 railroad corporations) and the School of Railway Signaling by referring their employees to correspondence courses, by deducting tuition fees through payrolls, and by using enrollment in correspondence schools as a basis for promotion.

Several features of correspondence schools, all of them related to prevailing theories of scientific management, made them attractive to railroad executives. Among the first industries to employ salaried middle- and top-level managers, the railroads by 1860 had created the organizational methods that other industries would soon imitate. In addition, by 1890 the subdivision of manual tasks had come to characterize routine work in the industry. J. Shirley Eaton, who served as the chief statistician of the Lehigh Valley Railroad and who in 1909 wrote an exhaustive report on education in the industry, described how "the area of skill which was formerly called a trade has been cut up into minute subdivisions, some of which can be learned in a very short time, and do not require the maturity and breadth of view in the operator which the trade as a whole required."[56] Eaton recognized that the correspondence method was ideally suited to such an industry, for the former "is definite, specific, even arbitrary, never speculative": "A principle is stated in no more general terms than may be necessary to embrace all its phases in the limited area of the particular course where it occurs. A special skill has been developed in opening up a subject to untrained minds by simple description, definition, and diagram. The avowed purpose is to fit the worker to a standard mold."[57] The general superintendent of the Union Pacific Railroad extolled the correspondence method for a similar reason. He praised the continuation school started by the Union Pacific in 1909, which employed correspondence techniques, for pruning from mechanical engineering subdivisions like marine and hydraulic engineering that were irrelevant to railroads, and for "teaching only that which is applicable to railroads, and particularly to the Union Pacific, using our standards, rules, and specifications."[58]

Although they engaged in highly specialized instruction, correspondence schools explicitly resisted the notion, advanced by some advocates of scientific management, that modern industrial conditions had rendered skills obsolete. In this respect, correspondence schools resembled the movement for corporation schools, which gained momentum in the first decade of the twentieth century and which was embodied in the establishment in 1913 of the National Association of Corporation Schools (NACS).

Corporation schools usually began with modest efforts to familiarize all employees with the techniques of the ablest ones. The educational program of the National Cash Register Company (NCR) provides a case in point. The first American patent for a cash register was issued in 1879. Five years later John H. Patterson acquired a controlling interest in the fledgling NCR and set to work to raise the company's sales. As Patterson recognized, cash registers faced considerable skepticism and even hostility, for they were new, expensive, and extremely unpopular among store clerks, many of whom had long been accustomed to pilfering from the cash box. In 1886 Patterson called together five of his sales agents for an informal exchange of techniques. A sharp increase in the sales of cash registers between 1885 and 1890 prompted Patterson to place his company's educational efforts on a more formal basis, and in 1894 he opened a school next to the company's headquarters in Dayton. Patterson even constructed model butcher, drug, and grocery stores, complete with dummy merchandise, so that students of salesmanship could learn in a realistic setting. Patterson flatly rejected the idea that salesmen were born as well as the notion that fast talkers necessarily made good salesmen. Rather, he viewed salesmanship as a practical science that developed from the ability of salesmen to understand the distinctive needs of their customers. Among NCR's favorite slogans was the statement that "There is in every company store a need which, when uncovered, will lead to the sale of a National cash register." By the same token, Patterson thought of salesmanship as a highly specialized activity. He refused to allow his salesmen to carry screwdrivers on their trips, lest their tinkering with broken cash registers distract their attention from sales. Instead, he established a separate school for repairmen.[59]

Corporate schools had close ties to the contemporary movement for corporate paternalism or "industrial betterment," which aimed to quiet worker unrest and reduce labor turnover by improving conditions in the workplace. For example, Patterson established a model welfare plan between 1904 and 1915 for his employees at NCR, including hot meals, visiting nurses, dental clinics, baths on company time, and paid vacations. Supporters of profit sharing also inclined to the idea of corporation schools. Charles Steinmetz, the German-born inventor who became the first president of the NACS, embraced profit sharing as a logical extension of the socialism that he had espoused as a youth in Germany; Steinmetz continued to think of himself as a socialist of sorts even as he drew his $100,000-a-year salary as director of General Electric's educational programs.[60] One of the objectives shared by the movements for industrial betterment, profit sharing, and corporation schools was to reduce labor turnover by stimulating worker loyalty to their companies.[61]

As an independent school, ICS could never coordinate its programs with management as precisely as did the corporation schools, but, wherever possible, ICS sought to ingratiate itself with employers by stressing its potential for reducing turnover. The president of ICS claimed:

Our greatest service to industry is in bringing a man through the ranks where he is employed. Our first aim is to assist men with initiative to qualify for advancement, and usually this can be accomplished most effectively with the confidence of the employer and by cooperating with him in solving his training problems. Our close relations with employers would not be cordial if we promised other positions to students. The student grows up in the industry as a rule and is not transplanted to some other industry.[62]

ICS possessed advantages that corporate schools could not duplicate. Corporation schools tended to be restricted to large firms in relatively new industries like railroading, machine tools, and electrical machinery.[63] They were also useful for training white-collar workers, but only in the large companies that could afford to maintain them. Corporate schools could never fulfill the job-improvement ambitions of workers for small companies. In addition, manual workers tended to resist company schools as a threat to their traditional control over the number, rate of advancement, and training of new workers. In the 1880s some railroads started shop-based "apprenticeship schools" that aimed to shorten the period of apprenticeship and thereby to increase the number of skilled workers. But this approach was open to the objection, as Eaton recognized, that "the competitive earning power of the present journeymen in the trade would be jeopardized. It would be the same effect as the disorganization following on the introduction of a labor saving machine."[64] Eaton bluntly identified the opposition to apprenticeship schools as rooted in the traditional autonomy of the shop and as permeated by "medieval conditions of prejudice, distrust, and bigotry."[65] Compared to these schools, ICS had the advantage of institutional detachment from the corporation. Foremen might grumble about executives who encouraged workers to bypass the shop's control over training by taking ICS courses, but ICS formed a less proximate target than intramural apprenticeship schools. By the same token, ICS appealed primarily to workers in their mid-twenties whose interests did not necessarily coincide with those of the shop veterans. As Eaton recognized, shop customs that restricted the number of apprentices and rewarded seniority indirectly penalized youthful workers. By opening the way to training workers for promotion independently of the shop, ICS could serve the interests of young workers as well as those of management.

The Cash Value of Education

In contrast to the land-grant colleges and the manual-training movement, which never aroused grassroots interest, popular demand for vocational training propelled part-time schools in the 1890s and early 1900s. Inasmuch as corporations engaged in all sorts of hidden and overt persuasion to induce workers to take courses, it may seem naive to refer to "demand" for vocational education. Yet there really is no better word to describe the surge of public interest in taking courses. Bosses nudged their workers into courses and advertisements painted glowing portraits of promotions and raises, but individual workers made the decision to enroll. To be sure, correspondence schools spent a large proportion of their budgets on advertising, but adults enrolled in vocational courses even when they were not advertised. The YMCA provides a case in point. As late as 1860 only four associations in North America offered classroom instruction, and these had a total of only 60 students, most of whom were preparing for the ministry. In response to calls from members, a number of associations began to offer evening classes in commercial subjects during the 1880s. Evening classes proved highly popular and spread beyond business education; by the 1920s some twenty associations were conducting evening law schools and 75 maintained evening schools of automotive repair. But initially the national leadership of the YMCA, far from encouraging vocational work, was embarrassed by it and sought to deflect attention from it.[66]

At least in the case of the YMCA, vocational education arose without the benefit of advertising and directly in response to the aspirations of members. The fundamental motive behind this and indeed nearly all forms of adult vocational education in the late nineteenth century can be summarized by the phrase "job improvement." Yet the existence of this motive is less striking than the form it took. Americans long had aspired to better jobs, but had not identified vocational instruction as a significant avenue of advancement. For example, the antebellum mercantile library associations taught classes in bookkeeping and stenography, but they were not as well attended as the lyceum-style lectures that these associations sponsored. Similarly, the antebellum mechanics' institutes neither attached any special importance to classroom instruction nor aroused widespread interest among manual workers.

Thus the success of ICS contrasted sharply with the history of worker indifference to trade instruction. One factor that eroded this indifference was the rise of new technologies. Provisions for the vocational training of adults first arose in industries affected by inventions. At a time when manual training schools and private trade high schools (neither of which aimed at out-of-school adults) ignored new technologies, corporation schools and proprietary schools, each driven by the profit motive, were quick to adapt to teaching the new skills required by a swiftly changing economy. This was true not only of the schools maintained by General Electric, Westinghouse, and other corporate goliaths, but also of ICS and the proprietary commercial schools, which spread rapidly in the wake of the invention of the typewriter in the 1870s.

Yet this kind of explanation, which portrays changes in schooling as driven by changes in the workplace, can only be carried so far, for by subdividing job tasks the advanced stages of industrialization seemingly negated the value of mass vocational education. Manufacturers concentrated such skilled tasks as the repair and maintenance of machines in the hands of a small number of well-paid machinists and then hired unskilled workers to tend the machines.[67] Corporations hired more office workers and then relentlessly subdivided their job descriptions. Thus the growth of popular demand for vocational education at a time when the skill requirements of many occupations were declining presents some puzzling features. The likeliest explanation for intensifying demand for vocational education lies in the burgeoning conviction among both educators and working adults that education paid—for everyone involved.

Evidence of the cash value of vocational education arose from many sources. Quantum leaps in the number of professional schools of law, engineering, business, pharmacy, and medicine in the late nineteenth century testified to the perceived value of formal vocational training and sent signals that ricocheted through American education. In addition, firms that established their own schools for apprentices or that farmed out training programs to ICS had every incentive to advance workers who completed their courses, for the reduction of labor turnover was among the major goals of such schools.

Such instances of apparently successful vocational programs would have been less widely publicized had it not been for the promotional efforts of public-school educators and their allies in university schools of education between 1900 and 1920. In these decades an increasingly influential corps of educators began to argue that secondary education would become for the twentieth century what elementary education had been for the nineteenth: a universal experience that would forge shared values and "social solidarity" among young people of diverse ethnic and class origins. Employing this argument, the landmark "Cardinal Principles of Secondary Education," a 1918 report of a committee of the National Education Association, urged compulsory high-school attendance to age eighteen.[68] In the eyes of Clarence Kingsley, principal author of "Cardinal Principles," vocational education was less an end in itself than a way to induce young people to persist longer in school, and hence it seemed a necessary correlative of the prolongation of education. It also seemed a plausible means, for the astonishing growth of proprietary schools between 1890 and 1910 encouraged educators to argue that a vast reservoir of popular demand for vocational courses existed.

All of this reversed the bias of those nineteenth-century educators who had contended that the "self-taught" individual would outstrip one "college-bred." The antebellum school reformers had described the economic benefits of education only in very general terms; they had written more about the value of educated workers to employers than about the cash value of schooling to workers themselves; and they had not stressed raising educational attainment (or years of schooling completed). As late as 1873, Massachusetts had simultaneously increased the number of weeks that children were required to attend school each year and dropped the age limit of compulsory schooling from 14 to 12.[69] In making their case for prolonged education, early-twentieth-century educators had to overcome the ingrained belief that teenagers, especially boys, should enter the school of life as quickly as possible. To this end they seized on every shard of evidence that vocational courses paid.

In turn, much of this evidence emerged from contemporary studies of the benefits of corporate training programs and proprietary schools, for as late as 1910 public schools themselves engaged in relatively little vocational education. Scholars recently have shown that public-school persistence in the late nineteenth and early twentieth centuries did yield cash benefits; those who persisted longer in public schools during the late nineteenth and early twentieth centuries were more likely than non-persisters with similar social-class and ethnic characteristics to gain entry to prestigious occupations. But in the 1910s most of the available evidence for the economic value of education came from the records of corporate training programs and the publicity of proprietary schools. By 1917, when A. Caswell Ellis of the University of Texas summarized the case for the "money value" of education, he could cite over 100 books and articles, many pertaining to corporate and proprietary schools, which purported to show that each increment of education would yield cash benefits to individuals as well as to society. These investigations formed a pool educators drew from in their quest for federal and state aid to vocational education and for the prolongation of formal education into the teen years.[70] Although as late as 1910 public-school vocational education was little more than a fly on the elephant of proprietary education, by 1920 the economic argument had become the primary rationale for formal education in the United States.[71]

While a consensus developed among educators about the value of vocational education as a way to encourage persistence in school, disagreements abounded over the type of vocational education required. At one end of the spectrum, Dewey and other liberal Progressives wanted vocational education to inculcate a broad understanding of industrial relationships; at the other end, a combative corps of educators saw vocationalism as a way to enhance the productivity of everyone, even unskilled workers. In the middle of the spectrum, many educators contended that schools could impart vocational skills that would enable young people to bypass the dismal swamp of unskilled jobs, the so-called dead-end jobs, and secure more favorable initial employment.[72]

The Conflict over Continuing Education

Behind these conflicts over the breadth of vocational education lurked a more fundamental issue: whether vocational education should be a preparation for work or a supplement to it. Nineteenth-century phrases like "irregular education" and "the pursuit of knowledge under difficulties" described a cluster of experiences and values that were loosely threaded by the intermingling of work and formal education. Academy students interspersed brief periods of formal education with longer periods of gainful employment. Not infrequently, students enrolled in college after working in shops or on farms. The professional preparation of lawyers might include attendance at law lectures as well as clerking in a law office and fraternizing with veteran practitioners on court circuits. Physicians often acquired medical degrees after they had commenced practice. For much of the nineteenth century, a mixture of weak apprenticeship traditions, popular individualism, and the high opportunity costs of full-time schooling sustained a type of education based on the principle of catch-as-catch-can. In this configuration of experiences and values, education was not necessarily a prelude to work; rather, it was sought in interludes and was more extensive (spread out over a period of years) than intensive. Contemporaries praised the alternation between work and school for instilling flexibility and adaptability. Emerson lauded the plucky lad "who teams it, farms it, peddles, keeps a school, preaches, edits a newspaper, goes to Congress, buys a township, and always, like a cat, falls on his feet."[73] As late as 1884 Edward Everett Hale worried that urban children who passed each day in school would lose any sense of affiliation with the "great organism" of society, while manual-training educators tried to introduce "natural activities associated with productive work into the artificial world of the classroom."[74]

In proposing that children alternate between school and work on a daily basis, Hale foreshadowed the meaning that the term "continuation school" would acquire by World War I. But in 1900 a continuation school usually meant an evening or correspondence school for working adults. When in 1907 Arthur J. Jones described continuation schools in the United States, his main examples were institutions like Cooper Union, the Springfield Evening School of Trades, the evening classes of the YMCA and YWCA, and ICS.[75] Fourteen years later Paul Douglas cited Jones's monograph and added that "he did not mention the type of school that we now regard as 'the continuation school.'"[76] What Douglas had in mind was a part-time public school that required four to eight hours a week of attendance by those aged fourteen to sixteen who no longer attended full-time school.

Although in the nineteenth century some urban school systems had maintained evening continuation schools for children who had ceased to attend full-time schools, educators accorded little attention to such schools before the second decade of the twentieth century, and Edward Everett Hale's call in 1884 for "half-time" schools aroused negligible interest among schoolmen. Born in 1822, Hale was out of step with the younger generation of public educators, who viewed full-time schooling to age fourteen as morally safe (the best way to keep children off increasingly dangerous city streets) and who saw manual training as a sufficient concession to those who, like Hale, worried about the insulation of urban children from nature. After 1900, in contrast, the idea of half-time schooling won a more attentive following among educators. The turning point came in 1910, with the American lecture tour of Dr. George Kirchensteiner of Munich. Kirchensteiner punctured misguided American enthusiasm for German trade schools by pointing out that Germany relied mainly on apprenticeship, supplemented by a few hours a week in public continuation schools, to train its workers. Kirchensteiner visited the United States under the auspices of the National Society for the Promotion of Industrial Education (NSPIE), an organization formed in 1906 to promote federal aid to vocational education in the public schools. The NSPIE was the primary institutional mover behind the passage of the Smith-Hughes Act in 1917, which stipulated that at least one-third of the appropriations it authorized had to be spent on public continuation schools.

The support of an influential segment of American educators for public continuation schools is a little perplexing at first glance, for the German system rested on a foundation of apprenticeship that was largely missing in the United States. But by 1910 most educators were eager to extend schooling to the age of sixteen, and they perceived continuation schools as a feasible first step, a way to extend the benefits of education to those over fourteen who otherwise would not attend school at all. In addition, these schools fitted nicely into the thinking of the so-called efficiency educators, notably David Snedden and Charles Prosser, who favored part-time schooling on philosophical grounds. The NSPIE encompassed a variety of viewpoints, and its membership included Jane Addams and Samuel Gompers as well as small businessmen associated with the National Association of Manufacturers. But Prosser became its dominant voice and he virtually wrote the Smith-Hughes Act.

Prosser and Snedden shared an attachment to Frederick Winslow Taylor's philosophy of scientific management, which welcomed the subdivision of work tasks as a basis for increasing productivity.[77] Each favored "real" vocational education, which they contrasted with the broad socializing and acculturating objectives that educators had associated with manual training. In their eyes, Dewey and like-minded educators who spoke of inculcating "industrial intelligence" were "parlor philosophers" who dwelled amid airy abstractions and who failed to comprehend or respect the bracing world of work. Accusing their antagonists of a sentimental attachment to the age of craftsmanship, Prosser and Charles R. Allen contended in *Vocational Education in a Democracy* that the traditional crafts such as smithing, butchery, and tailoring were few in number, had never employed more than a fraction of the pre-industrial workforce, and in any event survived under the industrial order. Now these crafts were joined by new occupations, which required greater intelligence and employed vast numbers. More intelligence was needed to oversee 80 electrical looms in a textile plant than to operate four water-powered looms in days of yore. Discovery and invention were ever producing new machines and processes for which workers required specialized training; doubters had only to look at the correspondence schools, Prosser and Allen argued, to see that Americans by the millions craved job-specific instruction.[78]

Ultimately the differences between the efficiency educators and Dewey went beyond conflicting assessments of broad industrial education. For all of their talk of scientific management, Prosser, Snedden, and Allen were throwbacks to the world of nineteenth-century individualism and success ideology. Their ideal was the eager youth who left school at an early age to start a working career in a shop or factory, shifted from job to job, and acquired new skills in the process. Whereas Dewey and most liberal Progressives interpreted labor turnover as evidence of the failure of the schools to equip youth with industrial understanding, Prosser argued that the "tremendous" shifting of workers from job to job often was the "best thing." Dewey's industrial intelligence was a chimera, for intelligence was always specific rather than general; a knowledge of one process did not lead to the learning of others.[79] Real training could be acquired only under real conditions, by a kind of "mental seeing" of the materials that the worker was being paid to manipulate. "Here we have the true explanation for the accomplishments of the 'self-made man,' " Prosser and Allen wrote, the man "who without the benefit of college or high school education displays what is to the academic an amazing ability to establish and carry on great enterprises sometimes of widely varying character. Somehow, in his experiences with real situations and real facts, he has hit upon ways of thinking which have proved successful and which he has developed into habits of thinking—an asset valuable to him in all undertakings."[80] This statement left little room for any sort of formal schooling.

Prosser wrote support for public continuation schools into the Smith-Hughes Act, but neither he nor Snedden appear to have expected much from them. In theory, continuation schools would supplement skills acquired on the job, but inasmuch as all educators agreed that fourteen- and fifteen-year-old school dropouts began at the lowest and least-skilled jobs, continuation schools would have little to supplement. Here again the differences between Germany and the United States were crucial. German continuation schools mainly addressed the general education of apprentices. In the absence of a well-grounded system of apprenticeship in the United States, some American educators who supported continuation schools hoped that they would engage in "trade extension," that is, vocational education, but most public continuation schools ignored it.[81]

American entry into World War I and the subsequent mass training of defense workers provided the efficiency educators with a more attractive model for industrial education: systematic job training conducted by supervisors on work sites. During the war Charles R. Allen, Prosser's occasional collaborator, oversaw the training of shipyard instructors under the auspices of the Emergency Fleet Corporation of the United States Shipping Board. According to Allen, the only way to train the mass of skilled and semiskilled workers required in the shipyards was to instruct veteran workers to educate green hands. To accomplish this, the worker-instructors themselves had to be taught how to analyze their own trades into a number of discrete tasks, each of which could then be taught to new workers. The most efficient training would be the narrowest. Typically, Allen thought it inadvisable to teach any worker more than he needed to know. "Under good instructional conditions," he argued, "the industrial instructor will not waste any time instructing a man in anything that he will not actually need to use and apply in the work for which he is being trained."[82] Similarly, Snedden painted a glowing future in which publicly supported job-training facilities would be skillfully positioned along the path of every working adult in order to ease job transitions.[83]

Wartime conditions made this a plausible position. Neither trade high schools nor public continuation schools contributed in any significant way to the training of defense workers in World War I. The experience of organizations like the Emergency Fleet Corporation and the United States Training Service, the latter instituted in 1918 within the Department of Labor, established beyond a reasonable doubt that, by employing the principle of subdivision described by Allen, skilled foremen could transform unskilled workers into efficient manipulators of tools in a few days or, at most, weeks. Such training was narrow in the sense that neophytes did not learn to operate the full range of tools used in plants, but the students speedily mastered those to which they were assigned. The war also demonstrated that the United States did not have a shortage of skilled workers. To the extent that the nation experienced a manpower problem, it lay in the shortage of unskilled candidates for training in specific industries. Yet none of this had much effect on educational thought, and in fact the same lesson had to be learned all over again in World War II. The Training Service was disbanded at the war's conclusion. The Federal Board of Vocational Education, established to administer the Smith-

Hughes Act, continued to urge efficient trade training in the schools, and the 1920s witnessed a new surge of support for public-school vocational education along a broad spectrum of educational opinion.[84]

Although the efficiency educators wrapped themselves in the flag of hardheaded realism, their antagonists who called for full-time schooling and delayed entry into the job market were more in tune with historical developments. During the debate over continuing education, public-high-school enrollments were exploding under the feet of educators. The proportion of seventeen-year-olds to graduate from full-time high schools rose from 3.5 percent in 1890, to 7.4 percent in 1907, and to over 25 percent by 1926. In contrast, public continuation schools proved a disappointment in the 1920s and declined sharply in the 1930s. The Federal Board of Vocational Education encountered chronic difficulty in finding enough continuation schools to fund. Most educators wanted to prolong full-time schooling on moral and social grounds, and increasingly young people stayed longer in school.[85]

A sign of how old-fashioned the efficiency educators were lay in their failure to comprehend the expanding role of high-school diplomas as passports to white-collar work. As one respondent to a survey of manual workers in San Jose, California, expressed it, "my brother George, sure he made it, but he got the breaks. He went to high school; he's got the white-collar job."[86] Wedded to a variant of nineteenth-century producerist ideology as well as to Taylorism, Prosser and Snedden were suspicious of office work and clerical occupations, and in defining "vocational" to include industrial, agricultural, and home-economics education, the Smith-Hughes Act excluded commercial education. It did so at the very time when the demand for commercial training was leaping forward in response to the continuing expansion of office work in the American economy.

By spurring the coordination and organization of work, the corporate revolution contributed mightily to the growth of office work. While reducing demand for skilled craftsmen, scientific management summoned into existence a huge class of clerks and timekeepers to ensure that the flow of raw materials to workers would not be interrupted. In addition, as manufacturers began to devise incentive systems to reward productive workers (an offshoot of Taylorism), they became more dependent on maintaining complete and accurate cost records, and hence more dependent on clerks. Similarly, whereas as late as the 1890s a corporate sales department typically included only a sales manager, salesmen, and a stenographer, by the 1920s most sales departments of sizable businesses engaged in market analysis.[87] As the keeping of accurate records became indispensable to sales operations, venerable white-collar occupations like bookkeeping experienced subdivision into specialties: invoice clerk, journal clerk, ledger clerk, machine bookkeeper, cashier, and accountant. The economist Paul H. Douglas estimated that the ratio of clerical workers to all workers in manufacturing dropped from one in thirteen in the decade 1890–99 to one in seven by 1924.[88] Inasmuch as the work of clerks and bookkeepers traditionally had been associated with middle-class status, the growth of office work appeared to create new opportunities for entry into the middle class. Douglas observed that in the 1890s the clerical class was virtually "a separate, non-competing group." The machinist's son or daughter "did not ordinarily become a white-collar worker, for the very good reason that a machinist was seldom able to send his children far enough through school to qualify them for any office jobs." In contrast, by the 1920s the manual worker, "with more dollars in his Saturday-night envelope," prolonged his children's education in order to graduate them into the white-collar class.[89]

Unlike the manual trades, whose multiplicity made them difficult to teach in a classroom format, office work proved highly compatible with full-time schooling. Commercial courses in bookkeeping and stenography began to invade public high schools in the 1890s, and they enjoyed considerable popularity among both parents and students. Enrollments in the commercial curricula of public high schools rose from 161,250 in 1914 to 430,975 in 1924; during the same period enrollments in proprietary commercial day and evening schools declined from a peak of 336,032 in 1920 to 188,363 in 1924.[90]

In sum, the preoccupation of the efficiency educators with job-specific training fell victim in the 1920s to their failure to define a plausible role for public schools in vocational education and to the simultaneous surge of parental and student interest in high-school commercial courses. Inasmuch as Prosser and Snedden had espoused part-time schooling as a moral ideal as well as a practical necessity, it might appear that the hoary tradition of alternating schooling and work was effectively supplanted in the 1920s by the new ideal of schooling as a self-sufficient preparation for work. So far as the public schools are concerned, this generalization holds up. Although the spread of commercial education in secondary schools owed little to Dewey's ideal of inculcating broad industrial understanding, commercial education reconciled practicality and full-time schooling in ways that the efficiency educators would not have thought possible. Yet in 1925 as in 1900, vocational education flourished principally outside of the public schools, specifically in the proprietary correspondence schools and among adults.

The Persistence of Correspondence Schools

While the growth of commercial courses in public high schools in the 1920s thinned the clientele of the proprietary schools that relied on classroom instruction, enrollments in correspondence schools continued to surge, so much so that investigators had a hard time keeping track of the number of these schools. In 1926 J. S. Noffsinger, who undertook a major study of correspondence schools on behalf of the recently founded American Association for Adult Education, put the number of proprietary correspondence schools at between 300 and 350 and estimated that at least a quarter of these had been founded since the start of the decade. In 1925 alone correspondence schools enrolled 1,750,000 to 2,000,000 new students, a number four times that of the resident students in all colleges and universities.[91] Noffsinger also found that 80 percent of correspondence students avowed vocational goals, while 15 percent recorded "personal efficiency" (memory training, public speaking, applied psychology, physical training, diet) and a meager 5 percent liberal education as their objectives.[92]

The question that naturally arises is how this shadowy empire of correspondence schools fits into the picture of rising full-time enrollments in high schools and as well into the national pattern of heightened emphasis on educational credentials. Noffsinger provided some clues on this count, for his evidence made it clear that high schools and correspondence schools were not competing for the same students. According to Noffsinger, the average age of correspondence students in the mid-1920s was 26, with half between the ages of 25 and 30, and 10 percent over the age of 40. Nor is it likely that correspondence students were seeking some credential comparable to a high school diploma. True, many correspondence schools offered fancy diplomas to students who had completed their courses. But perhaps as many as 90 percent of correspondence-school students never completed the course for which they paid.

Although some correspondence students enrolled with Mittyesque motives to become movie stars or private detectives, their high attrition rates can be explained on other grounds. An ICS executive observed in 1906 that "many students enroll for the purpose of studying certain subjects that will enable them to pass an examination, such as for a license for mine foreman, for engineer, etc. They do not care whether they complete the course or not, provided they get the information they need."[93] This explanation becomes more plausible in view of one of the most surprising conclusions turned up by Noffsinger. On the basis of a sample of over 100,000 students in over nineteen proprietary correspondence schools, he concluded that 83.5 percent had persisted in school at least until the eighth grade, more than half had attended high school, and 14 percent had attended college.[94] These findings are consistent with those of economist Stuart Chase, who in 1933 reported that at ICS, still the leading correspondence school with some 200,000 active students, 84 percent had persisted at least until the eighth grade and 46 percent had attended high school.[95] For comparative purposes, assessments of the famous alpha and beta intelligence tests administered to army recruits in World War I disclosed that only 49 percent of the recruits had persisted until the eighth grade and that 23 percent had attended high school.[96] Since most of Noffsinger's correspondence students had completed their formal schooling well before 1926, these figures from tests conducted in 1917 and 1918 represent a fair benchmark. Although we lack comparable data for the early 1900s, by the 1920s enrollees in proprietary correspondence schools possessed above-average levels of educational attainment.

By 1920 it had become possible to secure university credits through correspondence courses, but most correspondence students gravitated to the proprietary schools, which offered neither credits nor recognized academic certificates and which were not, as a rule, cheaper than university courses. A fair surmise from this is that a sizable segment of the public equated the slogan "education pays" with the proposition that knowledge paid rather than with the proposition, cherished and increasingly publicized by schoolmen, that school persistence, or educational attainment, carried financial rewards that were independent of knowledge acquired. To put it a little differently, most correspondence students seem to have assumed that they already possessed adequate levels of educational attainment and that their principal requirement was the acquisition of job-specific knowledge.

True, by 1920 public schools also purported to teach technical trades, but for various reasons the spread of vocational education in public schools did little to impair the flow of students into correspondence schools. Previous high-school attendance by students in proprietary correspondence schools exceeded the national norm, but nearly half of the proprietary students had not attended high schools, where nearly all public-school vocational instruction took place. In addition, despite Smith-Hughes appropriations, the ability of high schools to teach technical trades continued to be restricted by equipment costs, by the inherent difficulty of teaching trades that were both numerous and unrelated to each other, and by the rise in the 1920s of credentialing requirements for teachers, specifically the stipulation that high-school teachers hold baccalaureate degrees.[97] This requirement made it increasingly difficult for school systems to hire electricians, auto mechanics, and similar technical specialists as trade instructors. To the dismay of the efficiency educators, high schools responded to these problems by attending more to vocational guidance and to courses in the "industrial arts" that described industry in general rather than taught marketable trade skills.[98]

Some public-school systems did conduct vocational programs in the 1920s as part of their evening classes, but these did not compete seriously with the proprietary correspondence schools. Enrollments in public-school evening classes leaped from 135,000 in 1910 to nearly 650,000 in

1916, declined during World War I, and then rose again to nearly 1,000,000 by 1924. But public-school evening classes were not primarily devoted to trade training. Much of their growth between 1910 and 1916 resulted from their Americanization classes for immigrants, a motif still evident in the 1920s despite the drive for immigration restriction. In addition, evening classes provided general education for grade-school dropouts and opportunities for those who left high school to study toward diplomas. In the 1920s some public evening schools began to make provision for trade training. Only Buffalo, Gary, and a few other urban systems did so in any large-scale manner, however, and even these programs were restricted by local unions. For example, in Buffalo public evening classes in specific trades were open only to workers actively engaged in those trades.[99]

The problems that confronted commercial education in the public schools were only a little less daunting. It was easy to teach typing or stenography in a classroom, but public schools lacked the breadth of proprietary correspondence schools. Whereas public schools invariably taught entry-level office skills, some of the proprietary schools, including the Alexander Hamilton Institute and Pace and Pace, offered courses in accountancy, management, and salesmanship.[100] Instruction by mail permitted the hiring of a small number of instructors with highly specialized skills, each of whom then taught a huge number of students. In the early 1930s ICS had a student-faculty ratio of 200:1.[101] In contrast, vocational education in public high schools and in proprietary classroom schools entailed expenses for the construction, rental, and maintenance of buildings, and for the hiring of instructors to teach only the relatively small number of students who could fit into a room. This may explain why the proprietary commercial schools that relied on classroom instruction declined in the 1920s in the face of competition from the commercial courses in public high schools, while the proprietary correspondence schools continued to grow. Not only did the correspondence schools advertise advanced business subjects, but they also offered many subjects that public schools did not even pretend to teach, including photography, Morse code, radio technology, electrical refrigeration (by the 1930s, air-conditioning), hotel and restaurant administration, and even candy-making.[102]

Critics complained that correspondence schools were expensive. On the basis of independent investigations, Noffsinger and Chase arrived at similar cost figures of $10 to $300 per course, with the mode of $40. Since correspondence schools eliminated the opportunity costs of education, however, they retained decisive advantages over full-time public schools and, in general, their price per course was lower than that of proprietary schools which sold classroom instruction.[103] Correspondence schools also overcame the geographical limitations of proprietary classroom schools.

Most of the latter were located in large cities.[104] Noffsinger found that correspondence students were disproportionately drawn from places of 2,500 to 25,000 inhabitants (23.2 percent of the correspondence students versus 15.6 percent of the population) and as well from places with between 25,000 and 100,000 inhabitants (16.2 percent of the students versus 9.8 percent of the population).[105] The likeliest explanation for this phenomenon is that intermediately sized communities possessed sufficiently complex local occupational structures to nurture the job-improvement motive and, at the same time, relatively meager provisions for acquiring specialized trade instruction in classrooms.

Enrollment at ICS reached its peak in 1920 and leveled off for the rest of the decade. The Depression would undercut nearly all forms of part-time vocational education, but throughout the 1920s ICS enrollment remained steady and other correspondence schools grew. True, by the 1920s the opposing model of vocational education, which stressed schooling as a full-time and self-sufficient preparation for employment, had acquired immense prestige within higher education and as well the allegiance of most public-school educators. In view of this, it is plausible to interpret the kind of job-specific, helter-skelter training afforded by correspondence schools as a historical anachronism, doomed to be bypassed by the more progressive model of full-time schooling. But contemporaries can easily be excused for not grasping this point. When Stuart Chase listed competitors for ICS, he not only included other proprietary schools but also universities, which were offering their own correspondence courses. Between 1890 and 1930 higher education sorted out its own role in the sphere of popular vocational instruction. In the process, colleges and universities absorbed proprietary law schools, opened evening business schools, taught stenography, plumbing, auto repair, in fact nearly anything, and they taught these subjects on work sites as well as through the mail. To foreshadow the main theme of the next chapter, although reformers of university professional education sought to render it more theoretical and abstract, the older practice-oriented model persisted within universities in a sometimes conflicting but often congruent relationship with the new theoretical model.

Conclusion

Most historians have stressed the role of public education in the rise of organized vocational education. In the usual chronology, the private trade high schools of the 1880s and 1890s foreshadowed extensive provisions for vocational education in public schools between 1900 and the 1920s. The rise of vocational education in the public schools provoked a split in the 1910s between advocates of broad vocational education

(Dewey) and efficiency educators (Snedden and Prosser), who favored narrow trade training in separate vocational high schools.

Throughout the period from the 1890s to the 1920s, however, the bulk of organized vocational education in the United States was conducted in proprietary schools, which mainly targeted employed adults. Proprietary schools, especially those specializing in correspondence instruction, pioneered simplified methods of mass vocational training and attracted clients in astounding numbers. Their success depended not only on their advertising and marketing proficiency but also on the public's increasing association of specialized skill with middle-class status and on the close ties between leading correspondence schools and corporations. At a more fundamental level, correspondence schools benefited from the fact that they were motivated by profit and carried none of the ideological baggage of Useful Knowledge. Like parking meters, to keep running they relied on small infusions of money from their clients; in turn, their clients demanded small and specific infusions of knowledge, not a liberal education or a comprehensive understanding of the relationship between their jobs and social forces.

The growth of correspondence schools helped to persuade public schoolmen that demand for vocational education was virtually bottomless and strengthened their determination to introduce vocationalism into the public schools. Inasmuch as correspondence instruction was narrow and "never speculative," it posed a challenge to public educators and contributed to their division over broad vocational education versus narrow trade training. Although advocates of trade training, the efficiency educators, gained a major victory with the passage of the Smith-Hughes Act in 1917, they were never really comfortable with the idea of separate trade high schools, for no trade high school could ever duplicate the conditions of employment. Heartened by the effectiveness of governmental training programs during World War I, the efficiency educators hoped that, in the long run, public vocational schools attached to each work site would train adults.

While nothing came of this expectation, the model of continuing education—trade training acquired after departure from public school and as a supplement to, rather than preparation for, work—remained the dominant form of organized vocational education in the United States throughout the 1920s. Although the widespread introduction of commercial education into public high schools in the 1920s successfully challenged those proprietary schools that specialized in classroom instruction, correspondence schools were still thriving on the eve of the Depression.

Chapter 8

Higher Education and the Challenge of Job Improvement

In Frank Norris's novel *McTeague* (1899), McTeague receives a letter from city hall informing him that his lack of a diploma from a dental school disqualifies him from practicing his profession. McTeague, who learned dentistry from a traveling charlatan, is dumbfounded, but Trina, his wife, bluntly tells him that he can no longer call himself a doctor. McTeague protests, "What do you mean, Trina? Ain't I a dentist? Ain't I a doctor? Look at my sign and the gold tooth you gave me. Why, I've been practising nearly twelve years." But Trina persists. Without a diploma, McTeague can not continue to treat patients. McTeague asks, "What's that—a diploma?" "I don't know exactly," Trina responds. "It's a kind of paper that—that—oh, Mac, we're ruined."

Having plotted a lurid demise for McTeague, Norris arranged for his protagonist to abandon his practice compliantly. In reality, someone in McTeague's predicament probably would have searched for an evening school that awarded diplomas with minimal pain. Such schools were legion in the early 1900s, and they offered education not only for the traditional professions but also for occupations that were fast rising to professional status. Their existence posed both a challenge to and an opportunity for established colleges and universities.

From republican educators in the late eighteenth century to proponents of Useful Knowledge in the nineteenth, a strain of American educational thought had long affirmed that colleges and universities were appropriate settings for the study of what the Morrill Act had termed "the several pursuits and professions of life." In contrast to the British, who as late as 1900 equated liberal education with knowledge pursued for its own sake and without thought of material gain, Americans inclined to the view that liberal and practical education could be synthesized, or, put differently, that a liberal education could also be practical. Such a reconciliation could occur on any of several grounds. Land-grant colleges sought to teach the science of agriculture even as they struggled to discover a sound scientific basis for farming. Reforms introduced at Harvard's professional schools in the 1870s rested on the conviction that law and medicine were sciences worthy of investigation in a university. By affording students an overview of all fields of engineering, engineering colleges in the 1880s and 1890s advanced still another meaning of liberal education, the comprehensive and broad introduction of a student to the range of specialties in the field. The Wharton School of Economy and Finance and other early collegiate business schools sought to elevate commerce to the status of a liberal art by teaching its historical, moral, and political as well as economic relationships.

In turn, the tendency of Americans to blend liberal and practical education led them to baptize many occupations as professions founded on scientific principles. By upgrading occupations into professions, Americans facilitated their introduction into the curriculum of higher education. Although advocates of Arnoldian culture continued to scrap with defenders of vocational utility in American universities long after 1900, the latter's triumph was a foregone conclusion by that date. Indeed, boosted by Useful Knowledge's moral commitment to the elevation of the dignity of work, vocationalism invaded American universities more swiftly than the public high schools, which only turned to vocational education after 1900.

Yet all of this carried a price, for the integration of liberal and practical education committed educators to the cumbersome and expensive model of education as a preparation for, rather than supplement to, work. To study the scientific, historical, and moral foundations or relationships of a profession or trade was time-consuming and imposed high opportunity costs. Rooted mainly in proprietary schools, the alternative model of vocational education, which stressed education as a continuing supplement to work rather than as a self-sufficient preparation for it, made up in popular appeal what it lacked in prestige, for it was relatively inexpensive and attuned to the educational goals of working adults.

Colleges were free to ignore this alternative model, but for various reasons they were reluctant to do so. Although nineteenth-century professional schools are usually viewed as training grounds for the practice of law or medicine, for much of the century, in reality, lawyers and physicians had been more likely to enter practice directly from apprenticeship and to attend lecture courses, if at all, only later. The same was true of many of the occupations that in the late nineteenth and early twentieth centuries were struggling toward professional status and university recognition. As late as 1920 a Carnegie Foundation study reported that most students in western normal schools were "drawn intermittently from the active pursuit of the practice [teaching] for which the schools were expected to prepare them."[1] Characteristically, the Carnegie Foundation deplored the practice of allowing students to enter normal schools at any time during the year and at any age. Teaching such students, who ranged in age from 15 to 50, the report argued, was like discussing a play with an audience of which half had missed the first two acts. Yet such atavisms persisted in many fields. In addition, like their counterparts in the public schools, university administrators recognized surging popular demand for vocationally useful education, as evidenced by the growth of proprietary education in the 1890s and early 1900s. State universities eager to raise their profiles and to deflect public criticism of their cloistered ways; municipal universities, which saw themselves as urban equivalents of the land-grant colleges; and private urban universities seeking ties to local business communities alike spearheaded attempts to tap popular demand for accessible forms of vocational education.

In seeking to accommodate popular interest in vocational education, universities found themselves drawn into a thicket of issues relating to academic standards. New boundary lines were crisscrossing American education, just as they were dividing the economy. In the 1870s the economist Francis A. Walker sounded a distinctly modern note when he ridiculed the idea that all young people competed for all jobs; instead, he emphasized the segmentation of the economy into self-contained layers and the difficulty of vertical movement from one layer to the next.[2] The drawing of comparable boundary lines in education and the forging of a distinction between higher and lower forms of vocational education were among the major tasks that educators confronted in the Progressive era.

Higher education's movement toward vocationalism—toward educating students for specific occupations—spurred innumerable issues, but among the most revealing was whether colleges should award credit for subjects below the "college grade." This proved a thornier issue than whether colleges should offer vocational courses, in part because of uncertainties surrounding the notion of "college grade." As late as 1890 no consensus existed in the United States on so seemingly simple an issue as the definition of a college. Many colleges maintained so-called preparatory departments, and standards varied widely among colleges. In 1893 the *Educational Review* characterized half of the colleges in the nation as "secondary schools giving more or less instruction of the collegiate grade."[3] Starting in the late 1880s, regional accrediting associations brought increasing coherence to collegiate admissions requirements by inducing individual colleges to state clearly the subjects and levels that they expected students to have studied, but this still left open the definition of a college. By 1910 a definition had taken shape, but mainly as the result of a sequence of historical accidents. With the widening use of the elective system after 1870, some colleges began to devise internal systems of "units" or "credits" to establish equivalencies between the "work" generated by different students taking different subjects. In order to implement Andrew Carnegie's gift of $10,000,000 for pensions for "college" teachers, the Carnegie Foundation for the Advancement of Teaching (CFAT) in 1909 defined a college as a four-year liberal arts and sciences institution that employed at least six full-time professors and required not less than four years of high-school preparation. In turn, the CFAT borrowed the notion of an academic unit or credit to measure satisfactory preparation for college. Thus a college was defined as an institution that required candidates for admission to have completed at least fourteen units (these became widely known as Carnegie units) of high-school work. To acquire a unit, a student had to study a major subject for a year, which was defined as five 40- to 60-minute periods stretched out over 36 to 40 weeks.[4]

This brief detour into the origin of Carnegie units discloses the sometimes eccentric character of boundary drawing in early-twentieth-century American education. The notion of academic credits played a major role in defining "college-grade" work, just as the development of clearly defined collegiate admissions requirements sharpened the distinction between higher and secondary education, and all of this would contribute to etching the contours of vocational education. Yet the chief promoters of clarity in collegiate admissions standards, notably presidents Charles W. Eliot of Harvard and Nicholas Murray Butler of Columbia, did not believe that either high schools or colleges should teach vocations; the Carnegie units owed their origin to the practical requirements of administering a bequest. Trial and error marked the process by which colleges and universities reconciled popular demand with their conception of the activities appropriate to higher education.

The following pages describe the process by which colleges and universities sought to reconcile popular demand for vocationally useful education with their evolving conception of what constituted appropriate behavior for institutions of higher education. Law, business, engineering, and teaching, the four fields that form the focus of this chapter, were all affected by keen public interest, and each was actually or potentially compatible with university-level instruction.

A different pattern unfolded in each of these fields. In legal education, the tradition of law-office instruction, supplemented in some cases by attendance at a law school, started to collapse after 1870, but less because of competition from elite university law schools than in the face of competition from part-time, usually evening, law schools. Whether these were proprietary schools or appended to universities, universities could not afford the luxury of ignoring these institutions, which mainly catered to adults who worked by day in occupations other than law and who aspired to enter the legal profession by taking night courses. In the closing decades of the nineteenth century, several universities took over proprietary law schools and then struggled to reconcile the traditions of these adopted institutions with new ideas about the appropriate content of university legal training. Business education developed along a different track, for while proprietary business schools abounded in 1900, in contrast to proprietary law schools these were rarely affiliated with colleges or universities. Rather, the latter opened their own evening business schools and then used them as a basis for devising a full-time undergraduate business curriculum.

Whereas urban, usually private, universities spearheaded evening instruction in law and business, so-called engineering extension emerged primarily at land-grant colleges and universities, which simultaneously were developing ambitious programs in agricultural extension. In view of the land-grant colleges' charter commitment to agriculture and the mechanic arts, these developments are unsurprising. What is striking is how unreceptive the land-grant colleges proved toward engineering extension and how quickly they subordinated it to a limited type of extension, the continuing education of schoolteachers, that formed no significant part of their original mission.

Despite differing patterns of development in each field, one general conclusion stands out. A number of universities entered vocational and professional extension education with the loudly proclaimed objective of democratizing higher education. Gradually, however, a mixture of internal and external pressures propelled them toward types of extension education that can fairly be described as marginal in that they bore little relationship to the desire of working adults to move up the occupational ladder.

The Rise and Fall of the Evening Law School

At the start of the 1890s, the nation's nine night law schools contained only 1,192 students, a third of whom (403) attended the six full-time law schools. These modest numbers reflected the reality that most would-be lawyers continued to be trained in law offices rather than in law schools. But law-office instruction had started to decline even before 1890, and in the four decades after 1890 university and independent law schools absorbed many of the functions traditionally discharged by law offices. While both full-time and part-time (usually evening) law schools grew swiftly in these decades, part-time schools experienced the most striking growth. Alfred Z. Reed, a Carnegie Foundation staffer who conducted two major studies of American legal education in the 1920s, estimated that in 1926 the nation's 25,477 part-time law students constituted 57 percent of all law students.[5]

Full-time education in a law school, especially one attached to a university, had several advantages. Schools of this sort could hire career law professors and offer instruction in specialized areas that the corporate revolution spawned. But these schools were expensive. Although few law schools in 1900 required college graduation as a prerequisite to enrollment, the opportunity costs of full-time attendance for two or three years of legal education were formidable. The combination of the decline of law office instruction, the expense of full-time formal education, and the widening demand for legal education opened an avenue for part-time law schools.

Part-time law schools began to proliferate after the Civil War, either as independent schools or as branches of universities or colleges. They offered courses at hours when self-supporting workers could attend—early in the morning, during the lunch hour, late in the afternoon, or (most commonly) at night. What is most striking about the part-time law students of the Gilded Age is that they studied law while otherwise engaged. It had not been unusual in the antebellum period for young men to switch from occupations to professions or to acquire professional training by a mixture of practice and part-time schooling. But part-time schools in the 1870s and 1880s served self-supporting workers who intended to become lawyers but who were not employed as legal clerks. For example, Columbian (now George Washington) University's law school, which opened in Washington, D.C., in 1865, drew its students primarily from the federal bureaucracy. A trustees' report observed the presence in the city of "many young men with college degrees or literary backgrounds, working in the government, but with much time on their hands and looking forward to the law."[6] In 1895 only 10 of 82 Columbian students were clerking in law offices. Most of the remainder were employed as patent examiners, clerks of congressmen, or in the federal civil service.[7] Columbian had no difficulty attracting students, a fact evidenced by the decision in the 1870s of Georgetown and National universities to start their own part-time schools. This kind of legal education would stir criticism in the twentieth century, less because students and faculty gave only part of their time to law school than because students gave "only part of their time to any sort of legal training."[8] Yet this new approach to studying law reflected a dynamic impulse, the aspiration of young men who lacked personal connections in the legal profession to enter it with a boost from formal professional training. Formal legal training did not become more important after the Civil War because states suddenly began to require law degrees for entry into practice—in fact, none did—but heightened ambitions and new opportunities for legal practice were conspiring to forge new routes into the profession.

In one respect, Columbian was unusual, for virtually all of its students were native-born males. Most part-time schools catered to a different clientele. A few schools served women. Examples included the Portia Law School in Boston (1908) and the Cambridge Law School for Women (1915). The latter was started by Joseph Beale, a Harvard law graduate and former dean of the University of Chicago's law school, in direct response to Harvard's repeated refusal to admit women to its law school. Part-time formal education was virtually the only route into legal practice that was open to women, for the major law schools generally refused to admit them, while law offices rarely accepted them as clerks. There were exceptions, but they tended only to prove the rule. For example, Ellen Spencer Mussey, one of the co-founders in 1899 of the Washington College of Law, a part-time school serving both sexes, learned law in an office, but as a clerk to her husband. The other founder, Emma Gillett, who along with Mussey had been rejected by Columbian on grounds of gender, had attended Howard University's part-time law school. Part-time law schools contributed significantly to the rise in the number of female lawyers in the United States from 5 in 1870 to over 1,000 in 1900.[9]

While part-time schools opened opportunities to women, by the early 1900s these schools drew the bulk of their students from the ranks of urban immigrant males. The dean of the John Marshall Law School commented in 1918 that "the ancient and modern chosen people"—the Jews and the Irish—predominated in Chicago's evening schools.[10] In 1915 the dean of the University of Wisconsin's law school noted that the class rolls of evening schools in the large cities contained "a very large proportion of foreign names. Emigrants and sons of emigrants, remembering the respectable standing of the advocate in their own home, count the title as a badge of distinction."[11]

Mounting pressure for inexpensive legal education stimulated the growth not only of part-time law schools in general but of proprietary law schools in particular. Proprietary law schools (fee-financed and owned by their professors) antedated the Civil War. The most famous of these schools, Tapping Reeve's law school in Litchfield, Connecticut, was in operation from 1784 to 1833. Reeve's school and other antebellum schools like it developed out of law-office instruction; a gifted practitioner-teacher would take on scores of apprentices in his office and then lease a building and conduct a school. In contrast, most of the proprietary law schools that emerged in the early 1900s did not arise directly from law-office instruction. Rather, some grew out of classes in business law offered by proprietary commercial schools. Others began as cram schools for bar examinations. Still others began as YMCA law schools, either as schools directly sponsored by the association or as cram schools that merely leased rooms from the association.[12] Whatever their origin, these proprietary schools lacked university affiliation and functioned exclusively as part-time schools. By 1927–28 such institutions made up a third of all American law schools, up from a fifth in 1909–10 and a quarter in 1919–20.

Even as they flourished, part-time law schools became a target of the American Bar Association (ABA) and the American Association of Law Schools (AALS), an organization founded in 1900 to represent the interests of the elite, full-time university law schools. Both organizations embodied a movement to raise professional standards that gained momentum after the Civil War, but the movement proceeded obliquely by focusing on the issue of legal education rather than on the imposition of rigorous central examinations for would-be lawyers. The legal profession lacked the incentive that had led the medical profession in the late nineteenth century to insist on state examining boards as a way to control homeopaths, botanic practitioners, chiropractors, and osteopaths. Without any equivalent of these medical sects, the legal profession as a whole downplayed the importance of bar examinations, while the legal elite, represented by the ABA and AALS, focused on raising educational standards.[13]

The AALS led the way. Although the ABA established a committee on legal education in 1892, Alfred Z. Reed observed in 1928 that "most of the changes that have occurred during the last thirty years have been initiated by law school men, for the purpose of promoting standards in which they had already come to believe."[14] The leading law schools had come, in turn, to view legal education as a prelude to practice. Their idea of raising standards was to lengthen the period of legal education. For example, in 1900 the AALS voted that starting in 1905 its members had to offer a three-year course, and in 1909 it ruled that member institutions offering evening instruction had to require four years' work for the degree. The Committee on Legal Education of the ABA lent hortatory support to the movement, for example by approving in 1907 "the action of certain night schools in making their course one of four years."[15] As this statement indicates, some part-time schools did lengthen their course to four years. But most part-time law schools dropped out of the AALS rather than adopt the four-year requirement.[16]

Various motives impelled the attack on part-time schools. Anti-immigrant and anti-Semitic biases tinged the debate over part-time schools in both the AALS and ABA. The dean of the University of Wisconsin law school warned in 1915 that the immigrants who congregated in night schools viewed the Code of Ethics with uncomprehending eyes. "It is this class of lawyers who cause Grievance Committees of Bar Associations the most trouble."[17] In 1921 a furious debate in the ABA's Section of Legal Education over a proposal to require two years of college for admission to law school produced sneering references to the "influx of foreigners" and "an uneducated mass of men who have no conception of our constitutional government."[18]

The composite image of the graduates of evening law schools included ambulance chasing and scrounging around the police courts for clients. Inevitably, low ethical standards became part of the image. Although impossible to substantiate, the idea that evening-school graduates inclined to unethical practices was taken for granted by many elite lawyers. H. S. Drinker, Jr., a leading Philadelphia lawyer, argued that part-time graduates who cut corners were merely acting out their role in a kind of familial saga. Time and again, Drinker found, "these fellows that came out of the gutter, and were catapulted into the law, have done the worst things, and did not know they were doing wrong. They were merely following the same methods their fathers had been using in selling shoe-strings and other merchandise."[19] P. J. Wickser, the Secretary to the New York Board of Law Examiners, blamed the snobbery of penthouse lawyers for the low ethical standards of the profession's underclass:

One element of our Bar, for reasons which are easy to understand, simply will have nothing to do with another element of our Bar. It instinctively dislikes the element in question, has no respect for it, and would as leave avoid even standing alongside of one of its members in the subway. The so-called inferior element knows that it is despised by the superior element with the result that the inferior element freely participates in all kinds of nefarious practices because it gets into a 'don't-give-a-damn' frame of mind.[20]

Yet the assault on part-time law schools was fought primarily over the issue of their educational standards rather than the ethics or ethnicity of their graduates. By no means were educational standards merely a veil for ethnic or class bias. Bias scarcely needed any sort of veil in the 1920s, a decade in which pressures for immigration restriction culminated. At the core of the debate over standards lay the case method of instruction. Introduced by Christopher C. Langdell after he became dean of the Harvard law school in 1870, the case method aimed to model law on the natural sciences. Langdell thought that law could be investigated in scientific fashion through the analysis of appellate decisions, much as laboratory experiments enabled physicists to construct the laws of motion. The case method promised to cut through the morass of judicial opinion to the essential principles of the law, which Langdell confidently believed to be few in number.

The case method became the standard at leading university law schools by the second decade of the twentieth century. Even those who suspected that Langdell had underestimated the number and complexity of legal principles recognized the method's suitability to the format of a law school. Whereas law offices seemed suited to instructing clerks in the techniques of drafting documents and in the precedents and statutes appropriate to a particular jurisdiction, law schools could perform the higher function of teaching students to think as lawyers—to identify, manipulate, and apply legal principles regardless of where they practiced. The case method spawned related characteristics that came to be associated with the image of an elite law school. For example, the method depended on the presence of a large law library containing a considerable number of state and national law reports and statutes, many in duplicate. It also required professors and students with nimble minds, for instruction proceeded on the Socratic method. One way to secure better students was to require that applicants for law school present college credits. The University of Wisconsin College of Law, which aligned itself with the AALS's recommendations and with the Harvard model in the first decade of the twentieth century, began in 1906 to require that law students present two years of college credits or the equivalent.[21]

As the standards of legal education rose, practices that had passed without challenge for generations encountered new opposition. For example, for much of the nineteenth century proprietary law schools sparked little criticism from professors at university law schools, and for good reason. Just as the proprietary law schools represented a simple extension of law office training, so too the university law schools themselves often possessed close ties to proprietary schools. For example, in the 1820s Yale established its law school by absorbing a local proprietary school, appointing its owner to a vacant professorship, and listing the proprietary school's students in its catalogue as Yale students. These alliances continued even as law office training began to decline after the Civil War, for sinking proprietary schools often were eager to be salvaged by universities. The Blackstone Law School, established in Denver in 1888, contracted in 1892 to become the law faculty of the University of Denver. Even after affiliating with the university, Blackstone retained some of its proprietary features: its professors continued to be paid by fees, and until the 1920s they owned the books in the school's library.[22]

Wedded to the case method and to the idea of law as a science, leaders of the ABA and the AALS could scarcely have reacted favorably to the independent schools or to the part-time education with which the latter were associated. Typically, these proprietary enterprises had small staffs that were composed of practicing lawyers rather than career teachers. They focused mainly on schooling their students in the intricacies of the laws of the states in which they were located. They were totally dependent on student fees, and they could raise their standards only at the price of losing revenue. The independent schools were not cheapened versions of elite schools so much as antitheses of the direction that elite education was taking.

Although out of step with elite law schools, evening schools were neither victims of an all-powerful legal oligarchy nor without influential friends. The history of Boston's Suffolk Law School provides a case in point. This institution was the brainchild of the ambitious and enterprising Gleason Archer. While still a student at Boston University's law school, Archer began in the fall of 1905 to advertise for law students of his own. The first person to answer his advertisement, a Norwegian house painter with "very faulty" English, asked Gleason directly, "Can you learn me anything?" Another student confided to Archer that he could not attend Boston's well-known evening law school, the YMCA law school, because his job left him too exhausted for more than a night or two of study a week. As a newcomer to the evening-school enterprise, Archer had to settle for the most disadvantaged students; the tuition that he charged, $45 a year, made his school among the cheapest in the nation.[23]

During the first decade of its existence, Archer's school overcame a variety of tribulations. Recognizing that "no man in this age of the world could hope to accomplish much with an institution named after himself, unless he belonged to the aristocracy of wealth," Archer changed the institution's name from the Archer School of Law to the Suffolk School of Law (and later to the Suffolk Law School). He also opened his own law firm, built the school's faculty to five (including his brother and his law partner), and squelched a student uprising. The cause of the uprising underscored the fragile status of enterprises like Archer's. Some students became enraged upon learning that Archer would not personally teach them and upon hearing that they would have to purchase textbooks.

Quickly overcome, this student mutiny proved the least of Archer's headaches, for he soon became embroiled in controversy with what he would later call the "educational octopus." In a controversial move, the state legislature in 1904 had empowered the YMCA school to grant law degrees. Six years later, the Massachusetts Bar Examiners ruled that evening students could take the bar examination only on condition that they held a high-school diploma or passed the entrance examination for the state normal schools. The bar examiners refused to allow graduates of evening high schools to take the examination, but made an exception for graduates of the YMCA's evening high school.[24] Archer had long suspected that the examiners enjoyed a cozy relationship with the YMCA school (the chairman of the examiners served on the latter's faculty), and now he had definitive evidence of a conspiracy to destroy his school.

In desperation Archer introduced a cram course for the state normal-school examinations, only to find that his students who sat for the examination were never informed of the results.[25] In 1911 Archer took a new tack by initiating a day school. As he expected, the day school attracted no more than a handful of students, but it served its purposes. As long as Suffolk enrolled even five day students, the public could no longer assume that all Suffolk lawyers had obtained their education in the evening. The addition of day students also assured the public that "the school was prospering, for only the prosperous can be expected to add new departments."[26] In reality, by 1911 the school had fewer than 40 students and was on the verge of collapse. At this point Archer conceived the idea of incorporating the school and petitioning for the power to grant degrees. Only in this way could he effectively rival the YMCA law school.

Dragging on for three years before it succeeded in 1914, Archer's campaign for a charter and degree-granting authority encountered opposition from both Harvard University's president, A. Lawrence Lowell, and the Massachusetts Board of Education (then headed by David Snedden). Each argued against empowering an unendowed, unaffiliated proprietary school to grant degrees.[27] Archer railed against the "arrogant sons of Harvard" and the "dyed-in-the-wool aristocracy" that seemed to be on the verge of strangling his institution. Behind their facade of public service, Harvard men had only contempt for the "cart horses," their term for the "children of the working man."[28] One of Archer's legislative allies, former mayor Martin Lomasney, urged the legislature to frustrate any insidious scheme to "make a trust of legal education in Massachusetts."[29]

For all of his denunciations of aristocrats, Archer conceded that his "chief opponent" all along was the YMCA law school.[30] The latter served the same clients as Archer, working people too poor to attend full-time law school. Further, although Archer portrayed himself as a nearly helpless victim of the octopus's tentacles, his close ties to the Democratic party and the latter's sweep of the state elections in 1913 ensured his triumph. Suffolk was incorporated in 1914 as a degree-granting law school. Almost immediately, its enrollment leaped fivefold.

As Archer's experiences indicate, proprietary law schools had a good deal of resiliency. New proprietary schools continued to open in the 1920s, with the result that the AALS actually contained a smaller proportion of the nation's law schools in 1928 than it had in 1920.[31] Bar requirements and law school standards remained on separate tracks. As late as 1927 no state required attendance at a law school as a prerequisite for admission to the bar.[32]

In the 1920s, however, the tide began to change, in part because both the ABA and the AALS started to shift their tactics toward the notion of reform from the bottom up rather than from the top down. In 1922, for example, the AALS amended its constitution to allow evening law schools to qualify for membership by meeting various conditions. Refined and strengthened in 1923 and 1924, these conditions aimed at "equivalence" between full-time and part-time study through the requirement that part-time students attend school for 160 weeks distributed over not less than four years.[33] The AALS had not abandoned its bias against part-time schools, for full-time students were required to be in residence for only 90 weeks (without stipulation as to the number of years in residence). But the way had been eased for part-time members. The ABA moved in the same direction and increasingly pressured states to elevate bar requirements. By 1930 four states required attendance at a law school, and in the same year the ABA sponsored a new organization, the National Conference of Bar Examiners, which sought to persuade bar examiners to devise exams that resembled those of the better law schools. In addition, by 1932 seventeen states required two years of prelegal college education, up from six in 1928.[34]

Had it not been for the Depression, many part-time schools might have continued to ignore the standards of the major law associations. But the Depression struck part-time schools especially hard. As opportunities for legal practice shrank, fewer individuals were willing to undergo the ordeal of acquiring legal education at night. Elite law schools held their own; between 1928 and 1935 the number of students at law schools approved by the ABA (the ABA's list of approved schools differed little from the membership of the AALS) rose by 5,000. But the number at unapproved (mostly part-time) schools dropped by 10,000.[35] The number of exclusively part-time (often proprietary) schools declined from 65 in 1936–37 to 38 in 1956–57.[36]

Before the Depression undercut their position, proprietary law schools and the idea of part-time legal education benefited from the support of legislatures, which perceived each as a way to democratize access to the legal profession. In contrast, leading universities displayed little sympathy for either the proprietary school or part-time education. For all the talk of democratizing higher education through university extension in the early 1900s, the extension movement ignored legal education. For example, at the very time when the University of Wisconsin was reviving its extension programs, the university's law school was moving to raise its standards in a way that discouraged part-time students. Deans at university law schools took their cues from the practices at elite law schools rather than from their own institutions' resident advocates of extension.

The Emerging Profession of Business

In contrast to lawyers, businessmen did not claim professional status during the nineteenth century, and it would be a considerable exaggeration to say that even in 1930 businessmen thought of themselves as professional in the same sense as lawyers or physicians. What can be said is that, starting in the late nineteenth century, a small number of educators and philanthropists began to call for higher business education, less as a way to transmit bodies of technical knowledge than as a means of associating business with the liberal intellectual values that properly marked education for the learned professions. Joseph Wharton did not expect the school that he sponsored in Philadelphia to train specialized professionals to manage the ever-expanding subdivisions of the modern corporation; rather, his aim was to encourage the education of commercial and industrial leaders marked by a broad outlook and a keen awareness of their public responsibilities.[37] With their numerous courses describing the relationships between different forms of trade to each other, to history, and to the public, the early curricula of the Wharton School of Finance and Economy and the University of Chicago's College of Commerce and Politics were compatible with this goal. From the 1890s to the 1920s, university presidents like Edmund J. James and A. Lawrence Lowell baptized business a profession, but less, one suspects, from a clear conception of a profession than out of a desire to hitch higher education to the rising star of corporate enterprise—and philanthropy.[38] The rise of proprietary business schools in the late nineteenth century, some of which called themselves colleges, made it all the more necessary for universities to emphasize the elevated and general features of the kind of business education that they offered and to stress that business education, properly approached, would resemble more familiar kinds of professional education.

The idea of higher education for business encountered stiff opposition from some faculty members, who saw "higher business education" as an oxymoron, but this was not the main problem. Rather, the most daunting task was to devise a type of business education that would attract students. The broad and descriptive curricula of the collegiate business schools established before 1900 were open to the obvious objection that few students would delay entry into business in order to learn its history or to sample branches that they might never practice. The Wharton School enrolled only 528 students between 1892 and 1898, and at the close of 1900 only seven colleges or universities had started schools or departments of business.[39]

This picture would change after 1900 as universities turned to a different model, the evening business college that served self-supporting workers rather than undergraduates. For example, the average age of the students at New York University's School of Commerce, Accounts, and Finance, established in 1900 as an evening school, was 30. Similarly, in 1908 Northwestern University opened an evening business college in downtown Chicago rather than on its Evanston campus. All of Northwestern's business courses were offered at night to workers in the city's financial institutions; in 1916 the average age of Northwestern's business students was 25. Unlike Wharton and similar full-time business colleges, evening collegiate business schools experienced no difficulty in attracting students. Northwestern's business enrollments, for example, rose from 255 in 1908–9 to over 1,000 by 1917–18. Other universities that launched evening business colleges experienced similar success. In 1917–18 New York University's commerce school enrolled nearly 3,500 students, more than five times the number of students in its college of liberal arts. A decade later evening business enrollments exceeded day business enrollments in seven of the eight universities that had established both evening and day business schools.[40]

In contrast to the proprietary schools, which sought an immediate financial return in the form of student fees, the universities were more interested in establishing their reputations among leading businessmen in the expectation of long-term dividends, including "important benefactions from men who are attracted by definite and visible results."[41] But to show results they had to draw tuition-paying students from the ranks of working adults. In the years before World War I, Northwestern's evening-school tuition was $75–$100 annually, close to the average *monthly* salary of its students.[42] And while the universities looked to long-term benefits, the students expected fast results. Although the collegiate business schools taught banking, brokerage, insurance, and commercial law, their courses in accountancy proved to be the most attractive to students and drove much of the evening enterprise.

The corporate revolution gradually fashioned a distinction between bookkeeping and accountancy that was clear conceptually if not always verbally. What the Wharton School taught as accountancy in the early 1880s was actually bookkeeping, a mercantile art developed during the Renaissance and refined between the sixteenth and nineteenth centuries. Bookkeeping was adequate for describing the operations of an economy based on commercial exchange, but it proved unsuitable to the industrial and corporate economy of the late nineteenth century. Whereas bookkeepers recorded the profit or loss from an individual sale, industrialists bought items that they did not sell and carried fixed costs that did not lend themselves to the traditional recording methods of double-entry bookkeeping.[43]

The problem of cost accounting was recognized in the nineteenth century, but until the rise of scientific management at the end of the century, industrialists showed more interest in cutting specific costs than in the daunting task of measuring overall costs. The revolution in management techniques that accompanied industrial growth in the United States between 1870 and 1900 stimulated interest in cost accounting as well as in many other forms of accounting that had been made necessary by the increasing sophistication of financial institutions. Increasingly, accountants distinguished themselves from "mere" bookkeepers, the world's Bob Cratchits, and insisted that they be accorded professional status. Starting with New York in 1896, one state after another began to regulate entry into the new profession of "certified" public accountancy by establishing examinations and licensing procedures. By 1923 all states and the District of Columbia regulated accountancy.

The rise of certified public accountancy stimulated the growth of evening business schools attached to universities. New York State, for example, entrusted the administration of its accountancy examination to New York University. The latter's School of Commerce, Accounts, and Finance, established in 1900, initially functioned mainly to train bookkeepers and other office workers for the new examinations.[44] Similarly, the great majority of Northwestern's evening business students studied accountancy.[45] This is not to say that universities started business colleges in order to teach accountancy or merely to attract fee-paying students. Fundamentally, university officials wanted to establish ties to local business communities, which they saw not only as potentially fruitful sources of benefactions but also as progressive social forces. Historians have often described the process by which universities expanded their research facilities to bring themselves into conformity with modernizing social and cultural currents. Universities could also modernize themselves by absorbing economic and social activities traditionally outside of their perimeters. Accountancy was well suited to this tactic, for by 1900 it consisted of a useful and demanding body of knowledge that had become sufficiently standardized to allow examination by state-sponsored boards.[46]

Although accountancy demanded an understanding of the modern business corporation and strove to establish generally applicable principles, few university professors in 1900 were equipped to teach the subject. Rather, universities relied on moonlighting CPAs from established urban firms to carry the instructional load. One of the axioms that floated around business schools in the early 1900s was that those who knew accountancy could not teach it, and those who could teach it did not know it. A former student at New York University's school recalled the pedagogical methods of his accountancy instructor who, like all the school's other accountancy teachers in the early 1900s, was a practicing accountant:

He gathered a number of C.P.A. problems—that was the basis of the whole thing in the early years; and he worked out his own solutions on a piece of paper which he kept in the lower left-hand drawer of his desk, filed away with the problems. A few minutes before six o'clock in the evening he would rush into his office and reach down and pull out a problem and put it in his pocket and rush up to Washington Square and meet his class at a quarter of eight—and this is no exaggeration, it's a fact—we were just as likely to have Problem 17 to-night and Problem 17 next Wednesday night as anything else. There was absolutely no order to it. He picked the first one which came to his hand, plastered the solution on the board, and we sat there like a lot of dummies and copied the solution.[47]

The rise of accountancy had conflicting effects on part-time higher education in business. In the short run, accountancy sustained evening collegiate business schools. Before the 1920s most instructors trained in accountancy could only teach in the evening, for they practiced their profession by day. At the same time, the shortage of competent instructors restricted the capacity of universities located outside of major cities to teach accountancy at all. The correspondence and off-campus lecture courses of university extension divisions consisted mainly of subjects like bookkeeping and stenography, which were the staples of the proprietary business schools and the public high schools, rather than accountancy.

In the long run, the introduction of accountancy into the business curriculum subtly worked against evening colleges. As the first business subject with an analytic or theoretical body of knowledge, accountancy whetted the appetite of business faculties to make higher business education more abstract, more a science. Only in this way could business attain the level of the learned professions like law and medicine. The elevation of business to professional status had been an objective of Edmund J. James and other promoters of higher business education in the late nineteenth century, but James and his cohorts had been forced to resort to the introduction of subjects like history and ethics in order to achieve their goal. Accountancy promised much more, but few educators viewed evening colleges as compatible with proper professional education. Charles Waldo Haskins, the dean of New York University's School of Commerce, Accounts, and Finance and one of the most prominent business educators before his death in 1903, averred that "it will be conceded without argument that banking education has in mind the training for a calling or profession of men who are not yet prepared to engage actively in work."[48] In reality, whether studying banking, accountancy, or insurance, all of the students in the school that Haskins headed did work. But this did not deter Haskins from associating true professional education with full-time training prior to the advent of work. Evening students were vulnerable to the fatal objection that they chose courses at random and failed to pursue a broad curriculum of study. Some collegiate business schools contrived incentives for evening students to embark on programs of extensive study. For example, Northwestern University established a three-to-four-year program leading to a "Diploma in Commerce," a certificate rather than an academic degree. But this innovation changed nothing, for Northwestern's business students ignored the certificate program and continued their pattern of ad hoc selectivity.[49]

By the 1920s most business educators had come to view the undergraduate (in some universities the graduate) school of business as a viable and preferable alternative to evening business colleges. In 1931 James H. S. Brossard could describe the commercial day course as "the basic development," the one "implied ordinarily when the term collegiate school of business" was used. The evening school, in contrast, "has its distinctive clientele, with its own particular needs and demands."[50]

Various factors stimulated the growth of undergraduate schools or departments of business. Although not nearly as spectacular as the rise in high-school enrollments, college enrollments also accelerated in the 1920s. The proportion of the population aged 18 to 24 to attend institutions of higher education rose from 1.8 percent in 1890, to 3.6 percent in 1918, and to 7.1 percent by 1928. The growing number of undergraduates formed a pool from which business faculties could recruit full-time day students. This development affected the proprietary and YMCA evening commercial schools as well as the colleges. Squeezed between expanding enrollments in the commercial courses of public high schools and the surge in college enrollments, many of the proprietary and YMCA institutions found themselves pinched for students and began to convert themselves into degree-granting colleges and junior colleges. Although the proprietary correspondence schools continued to grow until the Depression, the tide was turning against most forms of part-time instruction.[51]

Full-time business schools also benefited from their compatibility with the long-standing objective of business educators to elevate their field to the status of a learned profession. As early as 1909, for example, Northwestern's business dean, Willard Hotchkiss, proposed the establishment of a full-time undergraduate program on the university's Evanston campus. Rebuffed by the trustees on several occasions, Hotchkiss resigned in frustration in 1917, but two years later the university introduced an undergraduate degree program in business. Throughout the debate neither Hotchkiss nor his opponents suggested that the university's primary obligation lay with its evening students. The latter were useful as a way to maintain the university's profile with Chicago's business leaders, but all parties looked forward to the day when Northwestern could concentrate its energies on undergraduate business students. The only issue between Hotchkiss and the trustees was timing. The trustees initially were skeptical that enough undergraduates could be attracted to commerce to sustain a school in Evanston. Walter Dill Scott, who began his career at Northwestern in the psychology department before becoming a professor of advertising in the school of commerce in 1909, warned that full-time schools at other institutions had met with indifferent success. Although Northwestern's Chicago evening students outnumbered its Evanston undergraduates in the 1920s by a factor of ten, the undergraduate school of commerce at Evanston survived by vigorously recruiting students from other departments, at times with threats that students who failed to enroll faced a bleak occupational future.[52]

Ultimately, undergraduate and graduate instruction in business meshed more readily with the concept of the business school as an institution devoted to broad and interpretive inquiry rather than a mere trade school. Possessing far more theoretical ballast than the bookkeeping courses of the proprietary schools, accountancy was a step in the right direction. But the preparation of office workers in evening classes for the CPA examination seemed an unpromising basis for the sort of research programs in accountancy that some university officials envisioned. In addition, new subjects were constantly coming to the fore. The growing popularity of applied psychology as an academic discipline made it possible to consider advertising an academic field. Although the New York University School of Commerce, Accounts, and Finance offered a few scattered lectures on advertising as early as 1906, the subject attained a more permanent footing in 1910 when the Advertising Men's League established a group of evening courses for advertising executives. Harry L. Hollingworth, a distinguished psychologist at Columbia University, taught one of these, a course on advertising psychology. Another, on advertising display, was taught by Frank Parsons of the New York School of Fine and Applied Art.[53] In a sense, the evening school functioned as a convenient place to try out subjects whose academic credentials were cloudy. Once these subjects had acquired a kind of innocence by association with established academic disciplines (e.g., psychology), it became easier to transfer them to the undergraduate commerce college that New York University started in 1912. The more subjects that made the transition, the easier it became to establish full-fledged degree programs, and even post-graduate programs. By 1917, 200 students at New York University were working toward the degree of Master of Business Administration.

A change in the nature of the business faculty also encouraged a gradual downgrading of the importance of evening schools. While the growth of undergraduate schools of commerce did not draw students away from evening schools—the two types of school did not compete for the same students—undergraduate schools could survive only if full-time professors of business could be found to carry on day instruction. To find and employ full-time professors was one of the main problems that confronted business schools in the 1920s. In 1929 L. C. Marshall listed as qualifications of an ideal professor of business training in psychology, psychiatry, physiology, economics, law, quantitative methods, and industrial management. Marshall conceded that most business professors fell far short of the mark, but he stressed that the future of business education lay in the hands of academically trained Ph.D.'s rather than practitioners. As undergraduate schools of business took root, they followed Marshall's prescription to the extent of drawing their faculties primarily from economics departments or from their own graduates rather than from business. Professional organizations for teachers of business multiplied in the 1920s. For example, in 1926 the recently established American Association of University Instructors in Accounting began to publish *The Accounting Review*; this association usually held its annual meetings in conjunction with those of the American Economic Association.[54] The professionalization of business education, in turn, accelerated the expansion of the business curriculum. At the Wharton School the number of courses addressing different subjects rose from 28 in 1890–91 to 118 by 1930.[55] In the same year the New York University School of Commerce, Accounts, and Finance offered 213 different undergraduate courses, an extreme example of a general national trend.

Specialization to this extent posed a challenge to the concept of the business school as an agent of general education. A professor of business organization at Ohio State University complained that the drive for specialization fostered "an era of water-tight compartment instruction in business subjects."[56] With their courses leading to the CPA examination, evening schools also encouraged specialization. But it proved much easier to harness specialization to the goal of broad education in undergraduate business schools than in evening schools. Most undergraduates took the view that their decision to study business was itself a sufficient genuflection to specialization, and, accordingly, tended to sample a wide range of business courses. In effect, they gave themselves a general education. The preference of undergraduates for a broad approach to business education also facilitated the introduction of the case method into full-time collegiate business schools. Originating at the Harvard Business School in the 1910s, the case method gradually came into use in the 1920s at leading collegiate business schools like those of Northwestern and the University of Chicago. While casebooks made their way into business classes more slowly than into law schools, prominent business educators had little difficulty grasping the connection between the case method and the elevation of business to the rank of a liberal profession.

Arising primarily as spontaneous adaptations to popular professional aspirations, evening colleges of law and business suffered from their lack of legitimacy in the sense that they could not invoke any body of educational principle that sanctioned lowering standards in order to make higher education more accessible. Even as evening colleges were sprouting, collegiate administrators were clarifying their notion of the components of higher standards of professional education. In their eyes, a high-quality law or business school inculcated broad principles and generally applicable bodies of professional knowledge, not the specific techniques and locally applicable knowledge of the evening schools.

In theory, the land-grant colleges should have found it easier than urban universities to engage in extension work that fulfilled the occupational and professional aspirations of employees in evening or off-campus programs. In contrast to the urban universities that opened evening colleges, the land-grant colleges inherited a democratic mission to educate the "industrial classes." During the first two decades of the twentieth century, the land-grant colleges plunged into university extension. Yet land-grant administrators were not free of concern over standards and, perhaps more important, they were ambivalent about if not antithetical to "job improvement." The framers of the Morrill Act had idealized the plodding farmer or mechanic, not the urban hustler prying his way into commerce or the professions with the aid of a quick course. This mission pointed the land-grant colleges toward agricultural extension, toward earnest but largely unsuccessful experiments with extension work in the "mechanic arts," and ultimately toward the most secure haven of all, the credentialing of schoolteachers.

The Rebirth of University Extension

The perceived failure of the university extension movement of the 1890s did not dampen the interest of university officials in raising the public profiles of their institutions. Rather, as enthusiasm for culturally oriented extension programs waned in the mid-1890s, university leaders began to search for alternatives. One promising line of attack lay in the off-campus programs for farmers, the so-called farmers' institutes, that a sprinkling of universities commenced in the 1880s.

While they assumed various shapes, farmers' institutes were basically "short courses" lasting from a few days to a week in which university agronomists traveled to agricultural locales to give short lectures and exhibits on scientific farming. Comparable road shows engaging agricultural editors and gentlemen farmers had existed before the Civil War, but universities entered the field only in the 1880s and then in direct response to legislative criticism of their failure to attract students into their campus agricultural courses. For example, the University of Wisconsin launched its farmers' institutes in the mid-1880s, at the very time when the state legislature was seriously contemplating removing the college of agriculture from the Madison campus and establishing an independent agricultural college.[57]

In Wisconsin the farmers' institutes helped farmers to reduce their reliance on grain production, which suffered from a skittish market, and encouraged a new emphasis on the dairy industry. In Minnesota the institutes aided farmers to become better businessmen by teaching them how to calculate the return on their investment; farmers learned to stop borrowing money at 6 percent to run farms that returned only 5 percent. The value of the institutes to the universities equaled their importance to farmers.[58] The institutes blunted public criticism of the land-grant universities by providing tangible evidence of the latter's commitment to popular welfare. Wisconsin's president, Thomas Chamberlin, praised the institutes' accomplishments in high-flown language that foreshadowed the rhetoric of the university extension movement in the twentieth century: "Scholarship for the sake of scholarship is simply refined selfishness. Scholarship for the sake of the state and the people is refined patriotism."[59] When Charles Van Hise, who became president of the University of Wisconsin in 1903, proposed three years later to revive Wisconsin's extension program, he cited the farmers' institutes as an example of inexpensive, geographically dispersed, and popular extension work. Van Hise's admiration for the institutes reflected, in turn, the influence of Charles McCarthy, a reform-minded Rhode Islander who had obtained a Ph.D. in history from the university (under the direction of Frederick Jackson Turner) before becoming the chief of the state's legislative reference bureau. In a memorandum to Van Hise in 1906, McCarthy wrote:

The short courses of the Agricultural Department and its form of university extension—the Farmers' Institutes—seem to be very popular and seem to the average man to be nearer to him in every way than the rest of the University. In casual conversation I have tried to seek information as to the state of public opinion on the question of extension of other branches of the university work in the same way. I have been astonished at the enthusiasm expressed for any project of this kind by all. I feel that no work could so interest the people of your state in the University than some work of this sort.[60]

McCarthy saw the revival of university extension and the funneling of university experts into public affairs as integral components of Wisconsin's Progressive approach to reform. The university's interest, which McCarthy invariably portrayed as disinterested and benign, would counter the corrosive influence of corporate lobbies and guard the machinery of government from "the invasion of the corrupting force and might of concentrated wealth."[61] Much like Frederick W. Taylor, who believed that a scientific standard of work could be established, McCarthy envisioned the university as a fount of nonpartisan, scientific solutions to policy questions. Theodore Roosevelt praised McCarthy's *The Wisconsin Idea* as a book that "every reformer, just at this time, should have in his hands."[62]

McCarthy and Van Hise were instrumental in bringing to Wisconsin two men who would dominate its extension work for decades: William H. Lighty and Louis Reber. A Cornell graduate who had absorbed President Andrew Dickson White's belief that universities should teach whatever students wanted to learn, Lighty had become active in the Ethical Culture movement and worked as assistant director of educational programs at Self-Culture Hall, a St. Louis settlement house, before accepting an appointment as the University of Wisconsin's director of correspondence courses in 1906.[63] Lighty's job shift symbolized the transition that many other educators made from Channingesque ideals of self-culture through moral and spiritual uplift (ideals that pervaded the Ethical movement) to practical self-advancement. His experiences in St. Louis had convinced Lighty that Ethical Culturists spent too much time debating their purpose, while neglecting the diffusion of practical education.[64] Reber, who in 1907 left the deanship of the engineering school of Pennsylvania State College to become "Director of Extension" at Wisconsin, shared Lighty's practical inclinations and accepted the necessity of making vocational correspondence work the foundation of the university's revived extension programs.[65]

Lighty and Reber benefited from McCarthy's close ties to Wisconsin's small manufacturers, who could not afford to sponsor their own training programs and who in 1907 lobbied successfully for a state appropriation to underwrite the cost of vocationally oriented extension. All three men contended that, by improving the skills and earnings of workers, extension work would quiet the socialist agitation then fermenting across the state. "Efficiency" in the form of vocational education would yield public benefit as well as private gain.[66] Like McCarthy, Lighty believed that the success of agricultural extension had demonstrated the ability of universities to encourage "a real democracy of learning."[67] The achievements of the private correspondence schools, in addition, convinced the three men that university vocational courses would never lack takers. McCarthy estimated in 1906 that 35,000 Wisconsinites were already enrolled in private correspondence courses.[68]

Aware that the farmers' institutes had spread the university's influence to remote agricultural areas, Reber and Lighty hoped that technical courses, or "engineering extension," would reach the state's manual workers. But reach them to what purpose? The farmers' institutes exemplified the benefits of diffusing expert knowledge, but they had never made the encouragement of social mobility a major goal. Whereas the concept of Useful Knowledge had extolled the mechanic whose liberal education enabled him to control and direct industrial operations, agricultural extension's watchword was efficiency. In *The Wisconsin Idea*, McCarthy interpreted reform to include opening avenues of upward movement to workers, but he took pains to reassure his readers, including industrial educators, that the university would not compete with trade training in the public schools. Rather, by cooperating with industrial education, the university would elevate trade instruction to the plane of moral betterment. He approvingly cited a state report on industrial education, issued in 1911, for casting trade training in the larger mold of civic education; workers would become better citizens through instruction in civics and sanitation.[69] McCarthy's poorly concealed desire to avoid offending public-school educators and the university's own engineering faculty clouded his conception of the university's role in industrial education. While hinting that the university might instruct a few extraordinarily alert workers in advanced techniques, he contented himself in the main with platitudes about civic and moral betterment.

Reber and Lighty could not afford such sentimentalism; they had to attract paying customers. The same was true of the field agents whom Lighty hired to enroll students in correspondence courses offered by the university. In 1919 one of these agents received arrestingly blunt advice from another agent: "If you want to be on the job next year, take it from your Uncle Dudley that you have to deliver the goods."[70] To deliver the "goods," Reber and Lighty worked closely with associations of employers, who not only helped their workers pay for courses but who also made available rooms where instructors and workers could meet. By 1919 some 2,000 students were enrolled in technical courses at the university's evening branch in Milwaukee. Meanwhile, university-sponsored correspondence courses, whose adaptability to the multiplicity of technical specialties had already been demonstrated by the International Correspondence Schools (ICS), carried the Wisconsin Idea to less populated parts of the state.

Yet even in Wisconsin, which had the most ambitious technical extension program in the nation, engineering extension failed to attain the prominence of agricultural extension. The university, which had to compete in a market already dominated by ICS, was placed in the demeaning position of copying ICS's courses. For example, Reber made a study of ICS's methods before assuming his duties at Wisconsin, while Lighty often wrote to proprietary schools, impersonating a prospective student, in order to obtain their instructional materials.[71] At times, ICS's resources left the university's field agents standing, or at least walking; in La Crosse, Wisconsin, it was the ICS agent, not the university's representative, who first used an automobile to visit students.[72]

To compete with ICS and similar proprietary schools, Wisconsin, Pennsylvania State, Iowa State, and other pioneers of engineering extension introduced non-credit courses in such practical subjects as plumbing, automobile repair, and house painting. But most workers who desired to upgrade their skills—piano tuners who aspired to learn the operation of player pianos, printers who needed instruction in the matching of colors—bypassed engineering extension in favor of ICS, the evening courses of trade schools, or on-the-job training. For their part, engineering professors usually avoided extension work and resented the adoption of "engineering" to describe courses of "a purely vocational or trade character."[73]

Such disdain contrasted with the support that university agronomists gave to agricultural extension. Several factors accounted for the difference. First, although farmers had assailed universities in the 1880s for failing to attend to their needs, neither mechanics nor trade unions organized to demand technical instruction. Reflecting the long-standing fear of labor leaders that technical education would multiply the number of skilled workers and reduce wages, unions remained indifferent to engineering extension. To the extent that universities encountered external pressures to develop technical education courses, these pressures sprang from manufacturers, especially from small manufacturers who lacked the resources to train their own employees, but the steady expansion of technical instruction in the public schools tended to weaken even this source of pressure. For example, in 1909 the mere suggestion of a plan to create a statewide system of public vocational schools in Wisconsin induced the Milwaukee Merchants and Manufacturers Association to withdraw its support from a bill to subsidize the University of Wisconsin's Extension Division with $150,000.[74]

In addition, engineering extension and other forms of nonagricultural vocational extension raised the issue of academic standards. Farmers who attended "short courses" on seed selection or soil conservation were not students in the conventional sense, for they neither sought diplomas nor studied. In contrast, engineering extension enrolled real students in courses that in some instances carried academic credit. In general, universities did not allow credit for courses in auto repair or plumbing, but professors continued to be outraged by extension officials who described courses in practical occupational skills as forms of engineering. Ira Howerth, who left the University of Chicago in 1912 to assume the directorship of the University of California at Berkeley's extension division, lost his job in 1917, in large measure because he had tried to use extension to teach occupational skills. Two years later the position he had held was abolished; in its place the university established an advisory board of university extension, which made tranquil relations with the faculty its priority.[75]

Even extension courses in calculus or hydraulic engineering raised the standards issue, for engineering extension relied heavily on the correspondence method. Education by mail became a logical recourse because "engineering" encompassed a vast number of specialties; few towns or even small cities contained enough individuals interested in any single specialty to sustain lecture courses. Originating in profit-hungry proprietary schools, the correspondence method lay under an ever-thickening cloud of suspicion, for even reputable correspondence schools like ICS engaged in brazen advertising and many correspondence schools were far less reputable than ICS. Universities gradually adopted the term "home study" to distinguish their correspondence courses from the proprietary version, but engineering faculties, which were better established and less in need of resident students than agricultural faculties, never reconciled themselves to instruction by mail.[76]

These factors severely retarded the development of engineering extension, which received no federal assistance and negligible support from state governments. By the mid-1920s only a handful of universities, notably Wisconsin and Penn State, could boast of well-established programs.[77] The modest impact of engineering extension dismayed advocates of what C. R. Mann, a prominent engineering educator, described in 1919 as the "American spirit" in education. In a combative and stimulating history of engineering education, Mann identified two antagonistic forces. On one side were the practical men who respected knowledge, overcame the gaps in their own educations, and energetically promoted the popularization of learning. The heroes who crowded Mann's pantheon included Franklin, Peter Cooper, Evan Pugh, and Jonathan Baldwin Turner, who condemned liberal-arts colleges for producing sophistical debaters rather than "real men who can discharge the hard side of every single duty."[78] On the other side were men of science like Joseph Henry, who had warned that agricultural education would turn the Smithsonian Institution into a cow pasture, and the wealthy benefactors of institutions like Harvard's Lawrence Scientific School and Yale's Sheffield School, men "who were eager to put science to use, but who lacked practical experience with industrial production."[79] While Mann enthusiastically supported engineering extension, he conceded that the movement had failed to prosper, "largely because of the vague sentiment among engineering-school faculties that work of this sort was not of college grade and therefore outside the scope of their activities."[80]

According to Mann, the "American spirit" in education was embodied not only in the doctrine that practical experience would stimulate a desire for theoretical knowledge, but also in the belief that an educational system stressing classroom instruction as a prelude to work would never afford useful education to a vast majority. It troubled him that a principle so obviously compatible with American character as the "Turner principle" (that knowledge is best acquired by setting every man "to earnest and constant thought about the things he daily does, sees, and handles") had so long eluded American educators. At the same time, he took comfort from the federal government's organization of the mass training of technical workers during World War I, the more so because colleges had participated in some of these programs. Mann hoped that this experience would forge a foundation for the postwar participation by higher education in training technical workers, but nothing of the sort developed. Even during the war, the universities accorded less attention to training technical workers than to an assortment of public-service roles, including funneling government propaganda on "war aims" to the citizenry, training Red Cross workers, and launching publicity campaigns to warn soldiers about the dangers of venereal disease.[81]

In 1919 the president of the University of Wisconsin described this shift toward public service as "not so much an education as the amelioration of life by the direct application of knowledge."[82] Adoption of the service goal (described in Chapter 9) enabled extension divisions to avoid conflict with resident engineering faculties and with the increasing number of trade courses in the public schools. To remove any lingering doubts about the purity of their motives, directors of university extension divisions adopted a distinctive nomenclature. Rather than take over the title of an existing subdivision of the university and then add "extension," extension deans invented a nomenclature by establishing "bureaus of correspondence," "lyceum methods," "class teaching," and "visual instruction." In 1919 Walton S. Bittner, the associate director of Indiana University's extension service, described this terminology as signifying "methods of teaching and propaganda," and he stressed that this sort of classification arose as a deliberate alternative to organizing extension around academic subjects.

Bittner's definition of a "true" university encompassed myriad unrelated activities, "with both open gates and cloistered laboratories, both practical itinerant messengers and theoretical, isolated servants." Thus "a short course for Boy Scout Masters may be held on the same campus where a learned conference of sociologists is discussing the theory of mob psychology."[83] Ultimately, this conception of a university served the interests of both research and public relations. Lighty recognized that the University of Wisconsin's extension program prompted the state legislature to treat the entire university, including its laboratories, with greater generosity.[84]

By 1920 university extension no longer had a clear connection to what had been known in the 1890s as "the extension of university teaching," for neither its goals nor its teachers were those of the university. Yet there is one notable exception to this generalization, for extension divisions gradually discovered a plausible instructional role: teaching teachers. This enterprise, which would reach vast proportions in the 1920s, had not formed part of Charles McCarthy's original conception of extension's vocational mission, but it proved appealing to extension directors not only because of the evident demand for it but because it nicely skirted the issue of standards as well.

University Extension and the Teaching Profession

When counting their blessings, extension officials pointed with pride to their programs in agricultural extension and prayed that engineering extension would come upon better times. These were the forms of extension most easily reconciled with the heritage of Useful Knowledge. Yet by the 1920s approximately 60 percent of those enrolled in extension credit courses in universities were teachers.[85] While agriculture had become the basis for the non-credit, non-degree side of extension, the teaching profession formed the foundation for extension courses that bore academic credit. This was particularly true in the decade after World War I. Between 1917–18 and 1927–28, teachers contributed significantly to the expansion of enrollments in extension classes from 32,800 to 196,451. In the same period, enrollments in the correspondence courses offered through extension divisions rose from 5,378 to 88,890. Nor do these figures tell the whole story, for by 1926 an additional 50,000 students were enrolled in the extension courses of teachers' colleges.[86]

Enrollments in university summer schools also soared in the decade after 1917, from 78,059 to 239,570. "The invaders," a contemporary noted, "stream across the Yard at Harvard; they file from Teachers College to the Library at Columbia; they pour into Hutchinson and Noyes Halls at Chicago; they pause to hear the chimes of the Library Tower at Cornell; they sit on the Oak Knoll at Minnesota; in the cool of evening they stroll across the serpentine brick walls that Thomas Jefferson built at the University of Virginia."[87] The majority of these "invaders" were teachers. In 1931, 273,148 of the nation's 425,100 summer students were taking courses in education.[88] Women made up a majority of all summer students (over 60 percent between 1917–18 and 1927–28), hardly surprising in view of the numerical domination of the teaching profession by women.

As a child of Chautauqua, William Rainey Harper was a natural candidate to initiate a summer session at the University of Chicago in 1892. At their inception in the 1890s, university summer schools afforded women relief from the drudgery of school-keeping or housekeeping and opportunities for intellectual stimulation in an uncommonly free atmosphere.[89] These features of summer schools persisted, but only in the face of counterpressures generated by the revolution in credentialing requirements for the teaching profession between 1900 and 1930. By the latter year, the acquisition of the baccalaureate degree in order to renew or upgrade their certificates (or licenses) had become one of the main objectives of summer students. As the authors of a major study of the education of teachers observed in 1933, "The prescription of the baccalaureate degree as a basis for the certification of some groups of teachers has determined one of the chief purposes of the summer sessions in universities, colleges, and teachers' colleges."[90]

Then as now, summer schools also attracted undergraduates who were either accelerating or making up failed courses. The same was true of extension courses, with the added twist that high-school students frequently enrolled in extension courses in order to prepare themselves for university admission. In effect, the industry that contributed most to the sustenance of university extension in the 1920s was education itself.

The pioneers of the revival of university extension after 1906 had not envisioned the teaching profession as a major source of extension students. But between 1890 and 1930 a number of convolutions within their profession stimulated the interest of teachers in acquiring college credits through so-called in-service (continuing) education.

In deference to the growing conviction that education was a science worthy of study in universities, several leading universities established chairs of pedagogy in the 1880s. This development would have had little impact on the vast majority of teachers had it not been for the dramatic growth of the American public high school. More than any other single factor, the rise of the high school sparked among teachers the drive for higher educational credentials.

The sharp rise in enrollments in public high schools from less than a quarter of a million in 1890 to nearly 4,000,000 in 1926 created a vast number of new teaching and supervisory positions. High schools were in a position to choose their teachers, and they usually preferred those with college credits if not degrees. The implication did not escape teachers or extension divisions. For example, in 1898 Columbia University's Teachers College began to extend academic credit for extension courses taught on Saturday mornings to the city's schoolteachers, a move that coincided with a ruling by the city's board of education that teachers seeking licenses entitling them to teach in high schools would have to present evidence of having taken advanced courses.[91] Another sign of the times lay in the movement to upgrade normal schools into teachers' colleges. In 1890 the vast majority of American normal schools based their three- or four-year curriculum on the graduation requirements of elementary schools; normal schools expected their students to have mastered reading, writing, spelling, geography, grammar, and arithmetic. The normal-school program itself consisted mainly of courses in the history and science of education.[92] In effect, normal schools were secondary schools that specialized in professional training. This situation would soon change.

In the colonial era and early 1800s, the awarding of certificates (or licenses) for teachers had been a local responsibility. As state governments established boards of education in the middle of the nineteenth century, the authority for certifying teachers shifted gradually to the state level, but states rarely exercised their authority before the 1880s. For example, only in the late 1880s did New York and Massachusetts centralize the drawing up of examinations for certification. By 1898 state officials alone made up examinations for teachers in 21 states, but in only four states did these officials grade the examinations. The trend toward centralization continued during the next two decades. By 1919 state authorities set examinations in 43 states and graded them in all but ten states.[93]

Along with centralization, the certificates themselves became increasingly diverse, ranging from life certificates that were valid in any public school, to renewable five-year (or less) certificates, to temporary, non-renewable licenses. By 1921 New York state offered fourteen different certificates; teachers in Michigan, Delaware, and California could qualify for any of fifteen separate certificates. The lowest-grade certificates were easily obtainable; as late as 1919 only eleven states (up from one in 1911) required teachers who secured the lowest certificates to be high-school graduates.[94] Many states still issued "emergency" certificates to virtually anyone. In 1924 a 46-year-old widow who had returned to teaching after her husband's death implored the state superintendent of public instruction to give her a certificate "without 'Emergency' written on it for I just can't pass those awful examinations."[95] Thus few were barred from entering the profession. But the diversification of certificates effectively raised standards for those seeking the most desirable teaching and supervisory positions. In 1919, 28 states required would-be high-school teachers to obtain special certificates, either by examination or, more commonly, by presenting evidence of college work.[96] Even those who held low-grade certificates were starting to feel pressure in the 1920s to upgrade their skills.[97]

Although the forces that elevated the importance of the baccalaureate degree for teachers were in motion before World War I, the scaling down of defense industries at the conclusion of the war sent large numbers of men and women to find new employment. In addition, the general prosperity of the 1920s, rising high-school enrollments, and improving teachers' salaries made teaching an increasingly attractive profession.[98] Summer-school enrollments nearly doubled between 1917–18 and 1921–22. Elementary-school enrollments failed to grow at anything like the pace of secondary enrollments in the 1920s, but the increasing number of courses in music and art (by-products of the educational reforms of the early 1900s) and the introduction of school nurses, visiting teachers, and various educational specialists all contributed directly to the demand for better-trained teachers and indirectly to the growth of summer and extension courses.[99] In many states the advancement of teachers had come to depend on their acquisition of university credits; those who acquired more credits earned more money. Extension courses were not only more convenient but usually cheaper than regular campus-based courses; in 1926 the president of Ypsilanti (Michigan) State Teachers College calculated that the credit-hour cost of extension work was less than a third that of residential university work.[100]

The upgrading of normal schools into teachers' colleges, the rise of summer schools, and the marked expansion of university extension all reflected the extent to which the acquisition of college credits was coming to have vocational value for teachers. Leaders of the teaching profession portrayed the entire movement in positive terms: upgrading opened avenues of professional "usefulness" and "advancement." To a degree, this was true. If they accomplished nothing else, the educational reforms of the Progressive era greatly increased the number of supervisory positions in the public-school systems. The measurement of educational credentials represented a clear-cut and reasonably fair way to allocate desirable positions. Yet in practice the allocation of teaching and supervisory positions did not necessarily proceed on fair principles. No matter how many educational credentials they amassed, women rarely secured supervisory positions. By the 1920s women were making their way into high-school teaching positions, but even then they were disproportionately relegated to fields like home economics.

In addition, the line between "advancement" and compulsion was often a fine one. In 1928 Lorine Pruette complained about the tyranny of "compulsory" summer school: "And so they come in increasingly swarming hordes, these pathetic seekers after—what? Knowledge, wisdom, technical information? No. They come to hold their jobs. They come because they dare not stay away."[101] Pruette's rhetoric carried her away ("Slave looks at slave and wonders what will make them free"), but she had a point. School boards in the 1920s increasingly required teachers to secure college credits in order to continue in their positions.[102] Even enthusiastic supporters of university extension recognized the vocational orientation of most students. As Alfred Hall-Quest, a former ASEUT staff lecturer who conducted a major investigation of university extension in the mid-1920s, observed:

At first glance it may be difficult to account for the popularity of courses in romance languages, history, and mathematics, but many of these are pursued by teachers and students interested in either a college degree, or in greater fitness for service in their fields. . . . In other words, one might rightly conclude that the demand for the most popular courses is chiefly vocational in the sense that they contribute to the attainment of some business or professional career.[103]

By the late 1920s, moreover, the supply of teachers was exceeding demand, especially in metropolitan areas. Inevitably, as competition for jobs intensified, so did the quest for credentials. Merely to march in place, teachers had to work continually for academic credits. The National Survey of the Education of Teachers reported in 1933 that "competition among teachers will probably increase the demand for professional courses as long as an oversupply of certified teachers exists."[104]

A few educators questioned the pedagogical value of both extension and summer courses, especially the latter. One educator doubted whether students could absorb a semester's material in six weeks. The size of summer sessions also caused dismay. In the summer of 1927, Columbia University enrolled 13,500 students, a number that exceeded the size of its enrollment during the regular academic year. Inevitably, summer schools relied on lecture courses and "machine methods."[105] In particular, the overcrowding of schools of education in urban and state universities caused anxiety: "Upon them during June, July and August each year is poured such a horde of college and high school teachers, superintendents, principals and supervisors as would 'clog the works' of any but the largest schools."[106] From the standpoint of those close to the extension movement, however, the descent of teachers into extension and summer courses in the 1920s was a blessing, for the education of teachers allowed a marriage between vocational and academic objectives. Administrators could now sidestep the challenge that engineering extension had posed: whether university credit should be allowed for work below university grade. The kind of people taking extension and summer courses in the 1920s wanted the genuine article, subjects (and credits) as close as possible to the regular offerings of universities.

In a more general way, the influx of teachers into extension courses blunted the edge of extension's claim to represent a radical alternative to the university's entrenched academic values. Between 1910 and 1920 some educators and commentators on education had advanced this claim. In 1917, for example, a writer in the *New Republic* argued that "education cannot be given merely by plumping great chunks of knowledge down on people in the shape of lecture courses, no matter how logically and truthfully such courses may be presented."[107] Reed College's William T. Foster warned in 1915 against interpreting the slogan "carrying the university to the state" to mean that courses designed for college students should be taught to those who did not intend to go to college.[108] The ideal for these educators was a kind of Deweyan Progressivism that viewed ideas as weapons of change and knowledge as a creative adaptation to environment. On the other side, conservatives cautioned against extension's "do-everything–reach-everybody ecstasy." Some of these conservatives were university presidents and deans who saw extension as permeated by "an atmosphere of bluster and pretense that has left a rather disagreeable odor in the university air."[109] Others were extension officials like Columbia's James Egbert, who had become in 1910 the university's director of the summer session and of extension teaching. Egbert related that he had often experienced more than his share of "the uplifted brow and questioning shrug which follow reference to extension teaching." His response was to urge extension to trim its sails by making "the class instruction of the established curriculum" its model.[110] Although both sides of the debate put forth plausible arguments, the domination of extension classes by teachers tended to settle the controversy on the side of the conservatives, for teachers wanted the extension curriculum to approximate the regular university curriculum as closely as possible. By the 1920s universities had discovered the comforting truth that they could discharge their "outreach" mission without abandoning or even modifying their academic standards.

Conclusion

Taking the long view, we can identify several distinct ways in which higher education reached out to working adults in the course of the nineteenth century. Starting early in the century and persisting (but with weakening momentum) into the twentieth century, colleges and universities enrolled older students who glided intermittently between school and work: farm youth who enrolled in academies or colleges when in their mid-twenties; lawyers or physicians who first served apprenticeships and only later attended a course of professional lectures; teachers who secured appointments in schools and later enrolled in a normal school.

Elite educators of the late nineteenth and early twentieth centuries condemned this kind of discontinuous education, and they devised an alternative way to accommodate intensifying popular demand for vocational education. Borrowing from techniques forged in the late 1880s by university agricultural departments, they established separately administered evening colleges and extension divisions for the public. In this way they simultaneously could raise standards for resident students and experiment with new courses for nonresidents. This type of bureaucratic specialization diverged from the 1890s movement to "extend university teaching" not only by its explicit vocational orientation but also by its rejection of any literal projection of the university to the people.

The fact that the new model of extension originated in agricultural departments, which had been among the least successful subdivisions of universities when it came to attracting students, highlights the close relationship between post-1900 university extension and the institutional agendas of university deans and presidents. For the most part, these officials lacked the missionary impulse that had characterized the university extension movement of the early 1890s, which had owed very little to university administration and which had sprung from the idealism of professors more than from institutional priorities. Although post-1900 administrators talked of educational democracy, they saw extension mainly as a way to protect universities from public criticism by accommodating, or at least by appearing to accommodate, popular demand for vocationally useful courses. In turn, this weakening of the missionary impulse imparted a certain neutrality and flexibility to university extension and it led extension divisions in myriad new directions—for example, by turning them into testing grounds for subjects like business or journalism whose acceptance in the regular curriculum was still controversial, and by briefly encouraging universities to "extend" their engineering programs by offering courses on popular mechanics.

It is easy to disparage the vocational extension endeavor of the Progressive era. With their right hand, universities raised their standards, while with their left they sanctioned courses on window display for store clerks and troop leadership for scoutmasters. They assailed proprietary correspondence schools and then copied their methods. When confronted by faculty opposition to teaching law or engineering in evening classes or off-campus facilities, they scrounged for marginal activities that were unrelated to the extension of university teaching. Gradually, they redefined the democratization of education to mean serving the public rather than teaching it.

Accurate if harsh, this assessment leaves open the question of whether university extension denied major segments of the public access to the kinds of education that they craved but could not afford. The shape of extension resulted from trial and error, which included a continuing assessment by extension officials of the flow of public demand for education. Although extension divisions at a number of public universities were receiving modest legislative appropriations by 1915, extension divisions were expected to become essentially self-supporting. This did not mean that each activity within extension had to generate revenue. Community welfare activities, which became prominent after 1910 and form the subject of the next chapter, produced no revenue. Nor did luncheon or after-dinner talks by professors to women's clubs and similar civic organizations. Rather, extension divisions depended primarily on their correspondence courses and off-campus lecture courses.[111] Arthur Klein, the executive secretary of the National University Extension Association, stated flatly in 1919 that "purely cultural subjects are not popular; the work is too difficult and requires too much hard work to attract the aimless habitué of the reading circle and women's literary society."[112] Wisconsin's Lighty voiced similar views. Perhaps Klein and Lighty simply failed to detect demand for cultural extension courses; Klein's reflexive association of culture with aimlessness (and women) might have deterred him from looking. But Lighty certainly did look. He dispatched staffers to every part of the state in search of "good future prospects" for extension courses.[113] Discouraging reports from these agents about the demand for courses on history or literature contributed to Lighty's decision to emphasize engineering extension.[114]

Lighty and other extension officials could not escape the fact that between 1890 and 1910 opportunities for the voluntary private study of cultural subjects had expanded enormously. Readers could purchase books from the Sears, Roebuck catalogue or borrow them from new public libraries. A few universities tried to accommodate the "aimless habitué." When he became the president of the University of Minnesota in 1911, George Edgar Vincent organized Minnesota's General Extension Division and introduced "University Weeks" around the state.[115] In the tradition of Chautauqua's "popular programme," the university sponsored plays, lectures, concerts, and debates on successive evenings. In 1913 Columbia University opened its Institute of Arts and Sciences, a "general catch-all and cultural grab bag" that mixed lectures, concerts, and dramatic performances.[116] But each of these experiments reflected an unusual circumstance: in one case, a university president who literally had grown up at Chautauqua; in the other, a metropolitan university.

For the most part, extension directors and university presidents did not seek to arouse public interest in cultural or academic subjects or to raise the public's intellectual horizons. As long as teachers were crowding academic courses taught through extension or in summer schools, and as long as swiftly rising high-school enrollments were expanding the pool of potential college students, it was safer for universities to offer short courses on window display than to try to twist academic subjects into a popular format. The latter smacked of disregarding academic integrity. One extension official noted ruefully that a certain Dr. W. presented himself one day in Indianapolis and without difficulty attracted 800 fee-paying students to a course of lectures on psychology, which advised students how to banish poverty and despair from their lives and gain health and happiness. In contrast, Indiana University, which had offered various psychology courses over five successive years for adult audiences in Indianapolis, never had enrolled more than 50 students in a course.[117]

Extension divisions encountered some of the same problems when they offered vocational courses. Yet it is unlikely that universities could have dented ICS's clientele under any conditions. Inspired by job-improvement motives, public interest in the acquisition of formal vocational or professional education was intense throughout the Progressive era, but that interest was only intermittently directed toward amassing college credits or degrees. Business students who enrolled in the downtown branches of universities showed negligible interest in securing college degrees, even when shortcuts were available. The blue-collar workers who enrolled in ICS courses did not see any advantage in taking a correspondence course merely because a university happened to sponsor it. All of this contributed to the meager results of vocational extension in the Progressive era, which by 1920 were widely perceived as disappointing, and indirectly it encouraged extension divisions, especially after 1910, to veer away from utilitarian vocationalism and toward community welfare activities.

Chapter 9

Educating the Public, 1900–1925

Historians usually equate progressive education with a series of (sometimes conflicting) innovations in elementary and secondary schools: learning by doing, the child-centered school, the school study of occupations, and functionally specialized school bureaucracies. All of these were components of Progressive-era educational reform, but Progressives did not restrict education to schooling.[1] Envisioning reform as an outgrowth of an enlightened citizenry, they turned reform movements into educational campaigns, crusades for "educating the public." Educating the public meant teaching citizens to think more rationally and scientifically about their jobs, their health, the raising of their children, and community issues. This type of education aimed at directly changing popular attitudes rather than at popular instruction in science as a body of unimpeachable facts and principles. Most Progressive reformers implicitly accepted John Dewey's criticism of Matthew Arnold for treating science as a mere repository of great laws and discoveries rather than as a refinement of everyday experience.[2]

Progressive reformers attached negligible importance to books and lectures as means of popular instruction, mainly because these had failed to influence the very people—dirt farmers and urban immigrants—whose behavior seemed most in need of change, and they frequently used "education" and "propaganda" interchangeably. But reformers were innocent of propaganda's pejorative connotations (gradually acquired after 1920), and they devised innovative programs of popular instruction that contemporaries unhesitatingly pronounced educational. Several features of Progressivism itself pointed reformers toward campaigns that relied on new

modes of popular education. Lacking a clearly identifiable regional or occupational constituency, the backing of a powerful administrative state to
command compliance with reform, and an exclusive attachment to any
political party; feeling committed to myriad scientific solutions to a broad
spectrum of problems; inheriting traditions of evangelical advocacy but
not wedded to ecclesiastical institutions; and addressing diverse constituencies that evinced little desire for the gentrification afforded by culture-
study, Progressives became educational innovators by necessity. It was important for Progressives not only to gain the public's general assent to reform and its support at the ballot box but also to implant in the public
their own spirited commitment to ameliorative change and to induce the
public to accept and even yearn for the advice of trained experts.[3]

The Psychic Factors

The sociologist Lester Frank Ward laid some of the groundwork for
this outlook by identifying the role of "psychic factors" in social progress.[4] This notion, which took various forms in the writings of Ward and
other early sociologists, boiled down to the assertion that society was a
"mental" rather than merely physical or mechanical system.[5] George Edgar Vincent, the son of Chautauqua's cofounder and a student of Albion
Small, the University of Chicago sociologist, described society as a "vast
psychic organism."[6] Belief in the primacy of psychic factors appealed to
sociologists as the basis for meliorist and progressive evolution. In contrast to the harsh conflict for survival that marked the world of nature,
humanity's spiritual and mental development yielded benign results—not
only inventions and conveniences, but also the increased humaneness evident in the care of children, the abolition of slavery, and the protection of
the weak. Further, to Progressive sociologists this mental development appeared to be "racial" or social, rooted in an evolving "social intellect"
rather than in a few remarkable individuals. As Ward put it, "the individual has reigned long enough." The time had come for society to imagine
itself as an individual, with a single conscious, progressive intellect and
will.[7]

While Progressive sociologists expressed confidence in the direction
of change, they did not trust evolutionary laws to enact themselves. Planning and rational intervention were necessary accelerants of evolution. On
the one hand, evolution made rational planning possible, for the social intellect was becoming more rational; on the other hand, intervention in the
social process was necessary, for pockets of resistance to progress were
formed by vestigial ignorance and individualism. For his part, Ward insisted that "the universal diffusion of the maximum amount of the most
important knowledge" would speed the evolution of the psychic factors.[8]

But by 1900 this phrasing, redolent of Henry Brougham and the Society for the Diffusion of Useful Knowledge, had an old-fashioned ring. Born in 1841, Ward was a generation older than the individuals who shaped American social thought in the Progressive era, and in his youth he had had comparatively little formal education. "Roaming wildly over the boundless prairies of northern Iowa in the fifties," he recollected,

Interested in every animal, bird, insect, and flower I saw, but not knowing what Science was, scarcely having ever heard of zoology, ornithology, entomology, or botany, without a single book on any of those subjects, and not knowing a person in the world who could give me the slightest information with regard to them, what chance was there of my becoming a naturalist? It was twenty years before I found my opportunity, and then it was almost too late. A clear view of a congenial field is the one fundamental circumstance in any one's field.[9]

Although Ward later compensated for his early disadvantages by securing three degrees in evening college, his experiences left him with a passionate regard for an orderly presentation of information and ideas, the diffusion of knowledge, which he viewed as a species of reform and as an end in itself. In contrast, the other sociologists possessed abundant formal education and viewed the diffusion of knowledge less as an end in itself than as a handmaiden of reform. With few exceptions they were born within a decade on either side of 1860 in small towns or small cities. A high proportion had some contact with the Protestant ministry. Small, William Graham Sumner, George E. Vincent, Edward C. Hayes, James P. Lichtenberger, Ulysses G. Weatherly, and John L. Gillen had at one time in their careers been ministers. Some of these men, including Small and Vincent, had fathers who were ministers. Although never themselves ministers, Franklin H. Giddings and W. I. Thomas also had fathers in the ministry.[10]

The religious backgrounds of these men imbued most of them with a strong sense of social obligation, a belief that the scholar, like the minister, had public responsibilities. The movement from small towns to cities like Chicago and New York riveted their attention on urban problems and gave focus to what otherwise might have been inchoate impulses to do good. Sociology provided them with an academic discipline that was both theoretical and practical, and neither in moderation. The theoretical quality of sociology, which was replete with jaw-twisting and bloodless terms like "heterogeneity," "telesis," and "maladjustment," placed the field in an empyrean above the contentious forum of popular economics. It was scarcely accidental that Mrs. Stanford allowed E. A. Ross to remain at Stanford as a member of the sociology department after she had kicked him out of her economics department. Yet the early sociologists had a keen interest in social change. With their potent ethical convictions, the founders of American sociology viewed themselves as architects rather than mere students of change. Albion Small affirmed that the ultimate justification of sociology would lie in its contribution to social reform, while Charles A. Ellwood described education as the "method through which the various factors in progress, especially the psychic factors, may work."[11]

The question, of course, was how all of this was supposed to occur, for sociologists were few in number and were not disposed to engage in direct political agitation. The experiences of academic social scientists in the 1890s, especially those of economists, dampened the willingness of university professors to expose themselves to political crossfire by maintaining high profiles on public issues. The combustible political atmosphere of the 1890s singed both iconoclasts like Richard T. Ely and such conservatives as the University of Chicago's monometallist J. Lawrence Laughlin. Laughlin was rudely pushed into the dunce's corner by the popular economist William Hope Harvey in his best-seller *Coin's Financial School* and then pilloried by academic economists for an excess of "vulgar illustrations and similes" when he tried to reply to Harvey.[12] After his near dismissal from the Stanford faculty, Ross wrote *Social Control* (1901), in which he advocated that social scientists assume the role of social engineers whose task was to influence national and regional political leaders to initiate wise legislation.[13] Ross's "sociologist" would not preach abroad the secret of control "with allegory and parable, with bold face and scare headlines"; rather, he will address "those who administer the moral capacity of society—teachers, clergymen, editors, law-makers, and judges, who wield the instruments of control."[14] Although Ross did not explicitly draw the connection, his notion of social scientists as experts who counseled established political leaders effectively sidestepped the political arena and promised to protect academic intellectuals from perilous embroilments over hotly contested issues.

By the 1930s Ross's position would become the dominant view among academic sociologists.[15] But as heirs to Protestant evangelicalism and to the missionary spirit that had infused popular education in the nineteenth century, many members of the founding generation of American sociologists sought to mediate their influence through the public rather than through political elites, which in 1900 or 1910 could not be presumed to be sympathetic to reform. Encouragement of popular education was one way to accomplish this result. But popular education of what sort? At the end of the 1880s, idealistic professors had turned to educational extension as a way to address the Social Question by facilitating personal contacts among the social classes. The perceived failure of this approach quickened the search for alternative forms of educational extension after 1900. In turn, this search was conducted within the framework of the Progressive social scientists' conceptualization of social issues as a mosaic of interdependent causes and effects that in its totality was beyond the comprehension of ordinary citizens. Albion Small justified sociology for its sensitivity to patterns of "vortex causation," where each social situation resulted from "causal factors that run in on that center from every point of the compass," while Dewey ruled out any such thing as sheer self-activity "because all activity takes place in a medium, in a situation, and with reference to its conditions."[16]

From this perspective, traditional conceptions of the diffusion of knowledge were inappropriate because they aimed at a general individual empowerment or "self-activity." Although Dewey favorably reviewed *The Psychic Factors in Civilization* and accepted Ward's contention that knowledge was increasing and that intelligence would solve social problems, Dewey's writings reveal his quest for a type of education that would immediately integrate knowledge with specific experience.[17] On this score Ward's formulation was unsatisfactory, for he did not make clear how individuals confronted by specific problems would benefit from "the universal diffusion of the maximum amount of the most important knowledge." The real questions seemed to be which individuals under what conditions and with what kind of knowledge. As befitted one who had acquired far more formal schooling than Ward, Dewey did not reverence book knowledge. Although Dewey believed that education had to convey ideas and information, the knowledge contained in books struck him as too detached from the learner's experience. Others agreed. In *The Promise of American Life* (1909), Herbert Croly argued that the nation's schooling had to consist "chiefly in experimental action aimed at the realization of collective purpose," and concluded that "the national school is not a lecture hall or a library."[18]

By the early 1900s, Jane Addams could not have agreed more with Dewey's belief that life itself had to be made educative. Earlier I noted Addams's initial efforts to implant Arnoldian culture at Hull House. When she and her friend Ellen Gates Starr decided that art exhibits were vulnerable to the charge of encouraging passivity and failing to integrate culture with experience, they turned to education in artistic skills. Several of Hull House's residents who also belonged to the Chicago Arts and Crafts Society used the settlement's studio to encourage handicrafts, to which Addams attributed "restorative power."[19] Addams also started to stress the potential of drama to inject force into moral truths that sounded hollow and platitudinous from the lectern, and she vividly recollected her own exhilaration at witnessing the passion play at Oberammergau on a fine summer day in 1900. The residents of Hull House conducted a little theater, which presented a range of dramatic productions, from "Snow White" for the youngest to plays in Yiddish and English staged by the Young People's Socialist League.

Although Addams retained her attachment to drama as a vehicle of moral instruction, she conceded that the kind of moral epiphany she experienced at Oberammergau "comes only in rare moments," and she came to doubt whether moral drama would ever compete with the five-cent theaters that showed slides depicting lurid tales. Extending similar doubts to education in art, she feared that promising skills would be extinguished when the young entered factory work, and she told the poignant story of a Bohemian girl who, hoping to support her family, ruined her voice in a six-month vaudeville tour. If society could offer nothing more to poor but talented youth than vaudeville, then art would devour its offspring. Ultimately, her idea of socialized education left little room for art and less for culture, for she came to prefer trade instruction, gym classes, and even military drill.[20]

The key to Addams's gradual shift away from culture as a basis of popular education lay in her recognition that culture was irrelevant, or damaging, to the children of immigrants rather than to immigrants themselves.[21] Even the folk dramas and passion plays that inspired immigrants failed to satisfy their Americanized children. She recalled "a play written by an Italian playwright of our neighborhood, which depicted the insolent break between Americanized sons and old country parents so touchingly that it moved to tears all the older Italians in the audience."[22] Newly gained artistic skills also threatened to sever young people from their parents. In this respect, Addams was representative of those reformers who concluded that the socialization and Americanization of children had to take precedence over other educational goals.

Yet Progressives approached reform with a sense of urgency that led them to explore ways to enlist the adult public as well in its own betterment. They customarily described this enlistment as an educational process, but as one aimed at those who could not be presumed either to comprehend the philosophy behind reform or necessarily to sympathize with reform. What was required was a model of education that would act directly on feelings and stir impulses to action, even if this meant eliminating the middleman of intellectual understanding. Addams's experiences at Hull House in the 1890s and early 1900s probably retarded her ability to devise alternatives to Arnoldian culture, which was viable, if not altogether satisfactory, in the peculiar setting of a social settlement and a nearby elite university. The model of popular education that would win the allegiance of a wide spectrum of Progressive reformers did not originate in metropolises, where reflective reformers, elite universities, and immigrant intellectuals threatened to give culture a new lease on life, but rather in depressed agricultural regions, where it did not have to compete with residual Arnoldianism. In turn, this model was absorbed by the newly revived extension divisions of state universities, which either had ignored the university extension movement of the 1890s or had concluded that it did not serve their institutional goals.

The Extension Revival

Charles Van Hise, who served as president of the University of Wisconsin from 1903 to 1918 and who gained legislative funding for its extension division, had worked alongside Lester Frank Ward in the 1880s as a member of the United States Geological Survey, then headed by the legendary John Wesley Powell. Both Van Hise and Ward were impressed by Powell's objective of using scientists on the survey to protect the public's interest in the utilization of western resources. "Major Powell," Ward wrote, "was very liberal in his ideas of official duty. . . . With him it was all for science and the public good."[23]

In the late nineteenth century, the relationship between science and the public good seemed axiomatic to Ward and others, but doubts were arising about the best way to popularize science. Sharing the widespread criticism that lyceum-style popularization was too haphazard, E. L. Youmans had intended the *Popular Science Monthly*, started in 1872, for the educated public, for those who could follow an instructive rather than merely diverting type of popularization. Yet Youmans himself quickly came under attack from the astronomer Simon Newcomb for his failure to impart to the public any sense of the activities of scientists. In Newcomb's view, even the educated public was prone to lapse into the belief that science was a treasure trove of discoveries by geniuses who lacked specialized training, and hence that it did not require public financial support. It rankled Newcomb that even after the Civil War the public continued to confuse genuine scientific associations, those composed of trained investigators, with broadly based mutual-improvement clubs.[24]

When first voiced in 1874, Newcomb's attack on Youmans aroused little interest, in part because, despite Herbert Spencer's often difficult language, comprehension of the evolutionary naturalism that Youmans expounded in the *Monthly*'s pages did not require prior mastery of a specialized vocabulary. Like Youmans, Spencer was essentially self-taught in science, while both Darwin and Thomas Huxley wrote in a readily accessible style. Between the mid-1870s and the early 1900s, however, several factors undermined the kind of popularization that Youmans favored. No major scientific development subsequent to natural selection could be as easily understood by educated laity. In addition, scientific societies of the sort long familiar to Americans, those mixing amateur investigation and mutual improvement, declined in the late nineteenth century, especially after 1890. The experience of San Diego's Society of Natural History was

representative of the trend. As late as the 1880s, when San Diego's population numbered around 2,000, the society attracted a range of "clergymen, lawyers, teachers, business men [and] working men" to its meetings.
"Everybody came," C. R. Orcutt recalled in 1912, "bringing a rock or a
shell or a bird or some object curious or rare, contributing to its little museum and rousing discussion." In contrast, by 1912, when San Diego's
population had swelled to nearly 50,000, the society barely drew enough
members to elect its officers.[25]

Complementing the disappointment of university extension in the
1890s, underlying changes in the organized pursuit of knowledge formed
part of the context in which university extension divisions sought to define
a new relationship to the public after 1900. At Wisconsin, Charles Mc-
Carthy included vocational education in his list of worthy extension activities, but vocationalism was a dubious foundation upon which to erect the
edifice of extension. Proprietary schools and public schools either occupied or were fast encompassing the field of formal vocational training.
Not surprisingly, McCarthy envisioned extension's role in vocational education as that of a coordinating agency. In practice, many universities
sponsored job-training programs during the Progressive period, but in so
doing they risked antagonizing resident faculties and, in any event, they
found it difficult to reconcile "job improvement" with broader public objectives. Frederick Jackson Turner warned universities against promoting
"individual advancement alone."[26]

In this context, many extension officials latched onto the alternative
goal of public service. Advocates of the "service function" of universities
routinely described their objectives in high-sounding language. For example, in 1915 Van Hise portrayed public service as an ideal that unified
all activities of the university. "In a broad sense the idea of culture, the idea
of vocation, and the idea of research," he told the National University Extension Association (an umbrella organization of universities committed
to new approaches to extension) "are held and developed in order that an
institution may perform public service."[27] Yet Van Hise and others were
well aware that public-service activities also spruced up the university's
image and that citizens who felt that the university took an interest in the
public welfare were likely to support legislative appropriations for laboratories, libraries, and faculty salaries.

As an instrument of public relations, university extension's value
rested partly on its direct impact on legislators, the precise goal of Mc-
Carthy's Legislative Reference Bureau in Madison. In addition, extension
had to reach the public directly, "every fireside" in McCarthy's words,
while remaining within realistic perimeters. The realities of higher education in the early twentieth century included the fact that professors gained
prominence by research rather than by public service, that the effort to

model university extension along British and Chautauquan lines in the 1890s had been judged a sorry example of "the aristocratic influence of education," and that an increasing number of professors were convinced that the public could not follow complex trains of thought.[28] In a trenchant criticism of Lester Frank Ward's belief that everyone should be given the opportunity to acquire all knowledge, the psychologist E. L. Thorndike insisted that most people "can learn particular habits of dealing with the physical environment, but cannot learn the general principles of science."[29]

Buffeted by conflicting influences—their desire to influence the public directly and their conviction that the public could not understand the complex reasoning of experts—Progressive advocates of popular education shifted their focus from intellectual elevation to habit formation and the manipulation of popular values. As one contemporary expressed it, the goals of education "are that it should arrest attention, excite curiosity, create and hold interest, stimulate desire, and compel action, sacrifice, and competent effort."[30] Arnoldian culture no longer promised any of this. In 1915, at the first meeting of the National University Extension Association, R. G. Moulton, famed veteran of the British extension movement and the American Society for the Extension of University Teaching, made a plea for "the humanities in university extension," but significantly his speech was the last on a three-day program, and the only one that participants did not discuss, for all were leaving to catch trains.[31]

The revival of university extension was driven by developments in the field of agricultural extension, not by culture or the humanities. Around the turn of the century, a new and ultimately effective form of agricultural extension began to emerge. The groundwork was laid by the Hatch Act of 1887, which authorized the establishment of "agricultural experiment stations" attached to the agricultural departments of the land-grant colleges "in order to aid in acquiring and diffusing among the people of the United States useful and practical information on subjects connected with agriculture." In the 1890s the agricultural stations tried to fulfill their mission of diffusing information by mailing circulars to farmers; in 1897 alone they dispatched these to over 500,000 different rural addresses.[32] In addition, Penn State and a few other universities started correspondence courses for farmers in the 1890s, while university-sponsored farmers' institutes dispatched lecturers to agricultural areas. This was an improvement over the continuing dismal performance of colleges in attracting students to courses in agriculture (fewer than 4,000 students nationally in 1897), but it left advocates of agricultural extension uneasy. Printed circulars could only influence farmers who could read and, perhaps more to the point, who chose to believe what they read. In addition, as late as 1890 only a quarter of Americans had mail delivered to their doors; rural home delivery did not start until 1896, and it suffered from nagging restrictions until the early 1900s.[33] Some agricultural improvers looked to the day when secondary schools would teach agriculture, and in 1917 agricultural education in high schools would become one of the main beneficiaries of the Smith-Hughes Act. But in the early years of the twentieth century, the most attractive model (attractive in part because it originated in the South and directly affected poorly educated farmers traditionally resistant to innovation) arose from the work of Seaman A. Knapp.

In 1903 Knapp, an employee of the United States Department of Agriculture (USDA), launched the so-called Farmers Cooperative Demonstration Work in Texas. At that time Knapp was approaching his seventieth birthday and in the course of a varied career he had been a teacher; Methodist minister; superintendent of a state school for the blind (a point not missed by admirers of his extension methods); and bank president, as well as a farmer; agricultural editor; professor at, and president of, Iowa Agricultural College; and authority on rice culture. Knapp's interest in rice culture secured his appointment by the USDA as an "agricultural explorer," in which capacity he had toured Japan in 1898 and 1899 in search of superior rice seed.[34]

Knapp's varied experiences in agriculture had left him with a deep suspicion of existing forms of agricultural extension. The agricultural press and farmers' institutes alike failed to reach the average farmer. USDA officials shared many of Knapp's reservations about the customary forms of extension, and even before the USDA appointed Knapp its Special Agent for the Promotion of Agriculture in the South in 1902, the department had started to conduct model "demonstration" farms so that farmers could see for themselves the value of new methods and, in the South, crop diversification. Knapp's contribution was not to invent the notion of a demonstration but to turn the farmer into the actual demonstrator. With funds raised from local businessmen, Knapp arranged to indemnify farmers who tried his methods on a corner of their land if the experiment failed. Thus the farmer could directly test the value of Knapp's advice and retain any profits that he made from the experiment. At the very time when John Dewey was constructing his educational philosophy around learning by doing, Knapp discovered that farmers learned new methods only when they assumed responsibility for the experiment. In Knapp's thinking, even the indemnity fund operated mainly as a psychological rather than financial stimulus, for if the farmer failed, his friends and neighbors were the losers.[35]

Aided by the Rockefeller Foundation's General Education Board, which spent nearly $1,000,000 from 1906 to 1911 to publicize it, demonstration work spread throughout the lower South, and, reflecting the legacy of freedmen's education during Reconstruction, demonstration methods proved effective among black as well as poor white farmers. Freedmen's education had consisted in part of agricultural and mechanical training, and the schools that white missionaries had established for blacks in the postwar South had routinely conducted evening classes for working adults.[36] At Alabama's Tuskegee Institute, Booker T. Washington, who had studied at the Hampton Agricultural and Mechanical Institute under Samuel Chapman Armstrong, introduced both industrial education and extension programs in the early 1890s, all in the name of subordinating blacks' quest for political equality to economic gains. In 1906 Thomas Monroe Campbell, a recent Tuskegee graduate, became the first African-American extension agent employed by the USDA. Riding a mule wagon, the so-called moveable school, Campbell exhibited purebred hogs, milk-testing gear, and improved cultivators.[37] Along with Hampton Institute, Tuskegee became a major center of extension work among blacks during the Progressive era, and in this respect it reflected the spirit of Booker T. Washington, whose interest in finding new ways to instruct the uneducated paralleled Knapp's. Suited to the needs of poor and often illiterate farmers, demonstration work became the first extensive program of popular education to achieve greater success in the South than in the North.

Crusty and dogmatic, Knapp suspected any kind of demonstration based merely on the exhibition by professors or agents of superior methods. Yet it was this type of demonstration in which Campbell and many white agents engaged. Traveling exhibits were especially useful for showing off improved livestock species, and they acquired some of the features of demonstrations when agents helped farmers build dipping vats to rid cattle of ticks.[38]

It was also possible to combine exhibits with attempts to improve rural home life by a kind of friendly visiting. Booker T. Washington, who began to conduct farmers' institutes at Tuskegee in the early 1890s, often made impromptu Sunday visits to black homes, where he preached the importance of growing vegetables and canning fruits and where he exhorted farm women to attend more to their clothing and appearance. For Washington, extension work was inseparable from racial advancement; as a local hero among black farmers in Macon County, Alabama, the seat of Tuskegee, Washington deflected suspicion engendered by the inherent intrusiveness of these visits. In contrast, what became known as home demonstration work developed more slowly among white farmers and initially focused mainly on children. After 1905, Knapp's agents began to note that farm children were less resistant to new ideas than their parents. Knapp embraced the idea of home demonstrations in which agents encouraged boys to form corn clubs and girls and their mothers to establish canning clubs—in part because it proved almost instantly popular and in part because it was compatible with his contempt for classroom instruction. Moreover, it created a new profession for women, that of home demonstration agent. Advocates of domestic science from Catharine Beecher to Ellen Swallow Richards had relied on the same methods as proponents of scientific agriculture, print and lectures, to disseminate their ideas. Home demonstration work, which initially drew its agents mainly from the ranks of rural teachers, marked a new approach to popularization, one that directly employed women in practical, ameliorative work and that in no way required them to become authors or public speakers.[39]

Demonstration techniques also influenced northern agriculture, but not before encountering hostility from the land-grant colleges. Northern land-grant colleges already had their farmers' institutes and correspondence courses for farmers.[40] Addressing a more literate farm population than that of the South and having been persuaded of the effectiveness of their established extension programs, they initially resisted Knapp's rather strident dismissal of forms of extension that did not rely on the farmer as the primary demonstrator. In addition, the issues confronting agriculture in the North were more varied than in the South, where Knapp concentrated almost entirely on crop diversification and on reducing the ravages of the boll weevil. But with some modifications, demonstration work infiltrated northern agriculture after 1900. A key figure was William J. Spillman, a USDA agricultural scientist who was managing government farms in the South at the same time that Knapp was hitting upon the demonstration method. When it became clear that Spillman's model farms were having less impact than Knapp on southern agriculture, Spillman redirected his attention toward farm management, including such largely ignored matters as cost accounting. As head of the USDA's Office of Farm Management after 1905, Spillman worked with the land-grant colleges to send agents to assess the needs of northern farmers. The land-grant colleges proved more receptive to Spillman than to Knapp, in part because the kind of advice that Spillman offered to farmers was broader and more sophisticated than Knapp's and more in tune with their status as academic institutions. By outlining a less threatening and dogmatic form of demonstration work, Spillman was able to woo the land-grant colleges to the value of a system of agents who directly engaged farmers in the field.[41]

As part of their quest for more flexible forms of demonstration work, the northern land-grant colleges, with a spur from James J. Hill and other railroad executives, also experimented with so-called demonstration trains. At Iowa State College, the agronomist Perry Holden found himself in the thick of arguments over whether the results of experiments in growing corn that were conducted on the college's experimental farms could be applied by farmers who lacked comparable equipment and resources. This was a critical issue, for the argument that Holden had to confront—

that most farmers were unable to utilize the fruits of science—had long be-deviled efforts to popularize scientific agriculture. Holden's answer was to use railroads to carry exhibits to remote counties. In 1902 he organized the first "seed-corn gospel train"; by 1911, 71 demonstration trains were in operation in 28 states and drew nearly 1,000,000 spectators to their ex-hibits. On his tours Holden carried boxes of seeds and demonstrated their different capacities to farmers.[42]

Demonstration trains were both popular and controversial. Knapp re-peatedly attacked these and similar corruptions of the pure farmer-as-demonstrator method. After Knapp's death in 1911, his son Bradford car-ried on the war and the long struggle that led up to Congress's passage in 1914 of the Smith-Lever Act. This act pitted the spirit of Seaman A. Knapp against the modifications introduced by William J. Spillman, spokesmen for the South against northern methods, and, to a degree, Democrats against Republicans; it also prohibited appropriations for demonstration trains. But Spillman's modifications and Seaman A. Knapp's blessing of home demonstration work contributed to the acceptance of a wider mean-ing of demonstration work than Knapp had originally sanctioned. The ev-ident popularity of home demonstration work made it appealing to all sides, while the fact that it was conducted mainly by women, and espe-cially after 1910 by graduates of recently founded university home eco-nomics departments, probably softened the opposition of the land-grant colleges to the general idea of demonstration work.[43] The Smith-Lever Act, which established the Agricultural Extension Service under the joint supervision of the land-grant colleges and the USDA, did not specifically incorporate the suggestion of Knapp's followers that three-fourths of all appropriations be spent on field demonstrations, nor did it embody Knapp's original definition of a demonstration. Nevertheless, Smith-Lever marked a victory for demonstrations as the basis of agricultural extension. For example, it prohibited appropriations for building or repairing college buildings, and it severely restricted appropriations for publications.[44]

The Agricultural Extension Service ranged over a vast terrain: teach-ing farmers how to calculate their production costs, promoting herd-im-provement associations, persuading farmers to grow more pasture crops, and winning farmers' cooperation in pest-control and "grow healthy chicks" campaigns. Whether in the pure and simple form originally de-vised by Knapp, which one contemporary called "ridiculously simple," or in its more varied and sophisticated versions, the demonstration method broke radically with traditional forms of popularization.[45] At no point did it require farmers to understand science. Deprecating the influence of print and oratory, Knapp claimed not to care whether farmers planted by the cycles of the moon, so long as they used his methods.[46] In this respect, the demonstration method resembled the ideology of vocational education that was coming into fashion in the early 1900s. Like Knapp, Charles Prosser sought to train workers to apply scientific principles that they neither devised nor necessarily understood. Vocational educators and scientific agriculturalists alike aimed to influence the will, even at the risk of bypassing the intellect.

Agricultural scientists also hoped that demonstrations and exhibits of applied science would enhance the influence of experts by engendering a self-sustaining enthusiasm for scientific solutions, by turning the farmer "into a stronger advocate of the solution recommended."[47] Like Progressive sociologists who advocated a harnessing of the "psychic factors" in civilization to the cause of reform, Progressive promoters of agricultural extension saw the demonstration method as a way to instill scientific attitudes in farmers. In 1927 Charles J. Galpin, a pioneer rural sociologist, claimed that "the great characteristic of rural life in the ten-year period 1917–27 is the evident revolution in the human mind, whereby science has entered as the habitual guide, displacing the blind guides." As Galpin saw it, scientific hogpens and barns were merely forerunners of sanitary houses; scientific feeding of cattle and hogs would lead to scientific feeding of the family ("had not the human mind come already to share with the hog in the values of protein and vitamin?"); determined efforts to eradicate the corn borer "are simply indices of the energy which will be expended in eradicating the parasites which at present feed upon rural societies."[48]

Demonstration work aroused considerable interest among reformers outside of agriculture, who were attracted by its unrivaled ability to extend the influence of experts to the unlettered and by the fact that it carved out new public roles for women as well. In the latter respect, it was vastly superior to Arnoldian culture. Chautauqua had sanctioned female intellectual endeavors and prepared women to teach, but only in the classroom. In contrast, home demonstration work, which aptly illustrated Dewey's stress on the primacy of immediate situations in the learning experience, blended the roles of teachers and reformers by sanctioning friendly visiting by experts in the name of social betterment. In different ways, Lester Frank Ward and Jane Addams had reconciled pure and applied sociology, but after 1910 most academic intellectuals, mainly males, came to assign themselves the more theoretical aspects of social science, while they contended that women were especially suited to applied sociology, to social work.[49] This mixture of respect for expertness, the diffusion of knowledge by demonstrations, and gender typing also marked the movements for health and parent education that arose between 1900 and 1930.

Health and Parent Education

Contemporary advocates of public health employed many of the same techniques as agronomists to arouse popular support for preventive health measures. At times, the same trains that carried agricultural exhibits bore health displays as well. In other instances, state health boards independently conducted their own trains. For example, in 1910 the Louisiana State Board of Health borrowed a train from a railroad company to carry exhibits throughout the state. In each town inspectors departed from the train long enough to score unsanitary buildings and to publicize their findings in local newspapers.[50] A reliance on publicity also characterized the many state and national societies that sprang up between 1900 and 1920 to combat specific disorders. Efforts to reach the public through mass education became a feature of organizations as diverse as the National Tuberculosis Association (1904), the Society for Mental Hygiene (1914), and even the National Society for the Study and Correction of Speech Disorders (1912) and the American Posture League (1913); and they also characterized the burgeoning university home-economics departments. Flora Rose, who worked with Martha Van Rensselaer to establish Cornell University's department (later school) of home economics, recollected that she planned nothing less than to save the world by nutrition.[51]

The stress on publicity that marked public health campaigns in the Progressive era followed a succession of medical breakthroughs that enhanced the authority of the medical profession. The advent of antiseptic surgery in the late nineteenth century, Robert Koch's isolation of a pure culture of the tubercle bacillus in 1882, Wilhelm Röntgen's discovery of X-rays in 1895, and Walter Reed's demonstration (made known in 1901) that a type of mosquito transmitted yellow fever were so many harbingers of a new era of scientific medicine. Reed's work had an especially dramatic impact on Americans. The efforts of French engineers under Ferdinand de Lesseps to construct an isthmian canal had been devastated by yellow fever, which in the single month of October 1884 had killed 654 canal workers. The new understanding of the disease's transmission yielded startling results. The last fatal case of yellow fever in the Canal Zone occurred in 1906; by the time the United States completed construction of the canal in 1914, the death rate from all diseases in Panama was below that of any American state or city.[52]

The medical breakthroughs of the late nineteenth and early twentieth centuries were the work of scientists who isolated themselves in laboratories and experiment stations. The bacteriological revolution had the potential to dampen enthusiasm for popular health campaigns. The identification of bacilli and viruses (efforts to distinguish the two were under way by 1920) discredited the cherished theory of nineteenth-century sanitarians that "miasms," emanations from decaying animal and vegetable matter, caused diseases. At the turn of the century Charles W. Chapin, the health commissioner of Providence, Rhode Island, attacked the traditional "filth theory" of disease for its failure to distinguish "dangerous dirt from dirt not dangerous."[53] Reed's experiments in Havana demonstrated that no amount of exposure to the clothing of yellow fever victims could inflict the disease. In practice, however, even as sanitarians distanced themselves from the miasm theory after 1870, they heightened their emphasis on personal and household hygiene. Throughout the Gilded Age, popular health writers incorporated the germ theory into their general indictment of bad air and foul water.[54] The discovery of the bacilli that caused specific diseases did not impair the association of household filth with disease, in part because, save for some relatively rare diseases like rabies, effective vaccines, which might have obviated the need for popular health campaigns, did not quickly become available; fruitful efforts to develop a vaccine against yellow fever, for example, were not begun until the 1930s.[55]

To encourage both household and personal hygiene, Progressive reformers deemphasized the diffusion of advice through print and instead stressed demonstrations and exhibits. The anti-hookworm campaign, one of the most notable public-health successes of the era, provides a case in point. Long recognized in Europe as a lassitude-inducing disease caused by an intestinal parasite that entered the body through the skin, hookworm began to attract American attention after the Spanish-American War. Public-health officials who followed American troops into Puerto Rico discovered that the disease affected a large part of the island's population; estimates ranged as high as 90 percent. Soon public-health physicians such as Dr. Charles Wardell and Dr. Charles Stiles discovered extensive evidence of the disease in the American South, and in 1909 John D. Rockefeller donated $1 million to be spent over a five-year period to overcome the disease. The Rockefeller Sanitary Commission for the Eradication of Hookworm Disease flooded the South with advertisements and motion pictures promising medicines "that will change you from a tired, indolent, despondent kind of man to one who goes about his work with a vim and a rush, always finding pleasures in everything."[56]

More important than advertisements in combating the disease were the dispensaries that were established in southern states with Rockefeller support. In these dispensaries physicians made microscopic examinations of excreta to determine the hookworm's presence, distributed printed cards describing the disease, and handed out thymol and Epsom salts, which proved effective and inexpensive remedies. In various ways the dispensaries served as demonstration projects; indeed they were often described by contemporaries as demonstrations rather than as hospitals.[57] Before the dispensaries could demonstrate the ease with which the disease could be cured, they had to show by microscopic examinations its presence on a vast scale.[58] The contention was controversial. Northerners had long traced the laziness of southerners to the after-effects of slavery, while southerners had been reluctant to accept the notion that laziness was a leading feature of their society. Now it became possible to explain why laziness characterized southerners, while removing any blame from the white South. In addition, the dispensaries were established in public places such as schoolhouses or in tents in encampments that resembled camp meetings. Physicians acted like circuit riders, moving from dispensary to dispensary at appointed times and treating patients who lined up outside their doors. All of this made the dispensary extremely visible. Walter Hines Page, a trustee of the General Education Board and friend of Knapp, praised the "value of the dispensary as an educational agency and the value with which this demonstration method gets its hold upon the people."[59] In sum, the dispensaries did not merely cure patients. They also persuaded southerners to become patients, to recognize that they were diseased, and to take rudimentary precautions like covering their feet (preferably with shoes) on their next trip to the privy.

The same emphasis on demonstrations, exhibits, popular participation, and an alliance among physicians, educators, and reform-oriented health workers also characterized the movement against tuberculosis. By 1900 medical scientists knew the cause but had yet to develop a specific therapy for tuberculosis; they had also not found a way to induce immunity. Each disease struck hardest at the poor, but tuberculosis, far deadlier than hookworm, primarily ravaged the people of cities, particularly large cities.[60] In 1900 the death rate from tuberculosis was more than 50 percent higher in cities of 8,000 or more than in rural areas, while cities of 500,000 had the highest death rates. Measures and facilities for combating this "white plague" were, at best, meager. Most health boards in 1900 did not require the registration of tuberculosis cases and nowhere in the nation was registration enforced.[61] Sanatoriums for treating "consumptives" were far beyond the financial reach of the poor. In 1904 only 8,000 beds were available throughout the country for the treatment of tuberculosis patients, at a time when tuberculosis claimed 40,000 lives in the eleven states that required registration.

The meager facilities for treating tubercular patients reflected more than public fatalism. As late as the 1890s, some well-known physicians like Philadelphia's S. Weir Mitchell and Owen J. Wister dismissed the idea that tuberculosis was infectious, while many physicians still argued for the disease's transmission by heredity. By 1904, when the National Tuberculosis Association was founded, advocates of hereditary transmission were in full retreat, and the first statistics compiled on the distribution of the disease revealed that its incidence rose in supposedly healthy areas of the West as soon as patients congregated there. The demonstration that tuberculosis was infectious stimulated both the movement to arouse public awareness of the need for personal hygiene and avoidance of exposure to the sputum of tubercular patients, and the enlistment of leading physicians, including Richard C. Cabot of Massachusetts General Hospital and Johns Hopkins's William H. Welch and William Osler, in public health campaigns.[62]

Yet physicians like Cabot, Welch, and Osler were exceptional, for the medical profession as a whole distanced itself from public health. Much of the burden of this work was instead carried first by laymen and lay women and later by graduates of recently established schools of social work and nursing. Trained as a nurse and lacking Jane Addams's early allegiance to Arnoldian culture, Lillian Wald began her Henry Street Visiting Nurse Association on New York's lower East Side in 1893. Wald also inspired the city to establish its Bureau of Child Hygiene. The bureau's first director, the physician S. Josephine Baker, shared the view of settlement workers that the problem of the urban child was "more of a socio-economic than a medical problem."[63] This statement was open to various interpretations, including a search for alternatives to capitalism, but for the most part social workers and socially minded physicians construed it as a sanction for educational campaigns aimed at personal and household hygiene. The Baby Health Stations established by Baker's Bureau of Child Hygiene were accurately described as "educational preventoria," for while they began as community-based centers in which mothers could purchase inexpensive pasteurized milk, they were soon offering hygienic advice on baby and child care. On their missions to homes, public-health nurses extended their role as teachers of the poor by offering instruction in diet, clothing, exercise, and the care of breasts and teeth.[64] Similarly, Edward T. Devine (who had studied economics under Simon Nelson Patten and Edmund J. James at the University of Pennsylvania and served in the 1890s as a staff lecturer for the American Society for the Extension of University Teaching before turning to social work) gradually came to equate the latter with improvements in public health. When the National Tuberculosis Association was formed in 1904, Devine joined such leading public-health physicians as Lawrence A. Flick and Herman Biggs on its board, and in *Misery and Its Causes* (1909) he devoted more attention to ill health than to unemployment as a cause of poverty.[65]

During its early years, the National Tuberculosis Association relied heavily on exhibits to arouse popular enthusiasm for the anti-tuberculosis movement. Originating at international conferences in Europe, exhibits combined photography and lantern slides showing unsanitary conditions and desirable sanatoriums with tables and charts displaying comparative death rates.[66] In the winter of 1905–6, a traveling exhibit sponsored by the National Tuberculosis Association drew hundreds of thousands of spectators in major American cities. Other measures included the inauguration in 1910 of "Tuberculosis Sunday," on which clergymen delivered addresses on the disease and, later, Tuberculosis Week. State associations complemented the work of the national. The Michigan Anti-Tuberculosis Association successfully lobbied the University of Michigan to commit the resources of its extension division, revived in 1911, to an anti-tuberculosis campaign.[67]

This stress on publicity that characterized the anti-tuberculosis movement showed the commitment of reformers and public-health officers to employ every weapon in the still meager arsenal of measures against the disease. Yet even when specific therapies were available, for example, the typhoid vaccine, Progressive reformers inclined toward medical extravaganzas that attracted as much public attention as possible. As a southern reformer put it in 1915, the attitude toward the public-health movement "must be more than an attitude of assent. It must be a crusade. With the zeal of Peter the Hermit, and the sanity of Paul the apostle, we must build the walls of prevention stronger than the assaults of disease."[68]

A mixture of ideological and occupational considerations led reformers to embrace the notion of a crusade against disease. The religious terminology that marked advocacy of public health during the Progressive period reflected the evangelical heritage of many social reformers. At the same time, the preference of Progressive reformers for broad-ranging health crusades grew out of their quest for suitable social roles to play. What C. E. A. Winslow called the "new public health" gave women in the emerging professions of nursing and social work and laymen like Devine an opportunity to act independently of physicians in health movements that stressed education and social uplift as part of preventive public health.

Efforts to improve infant care through "parent education" revealed how publicity skills developed in public-health crusades proved readily transferable to other problems. The movement for parent education that developed between 1910 and 1930 followed the contours of the drive to popularize health and possessed close ties to the methods of agricultural extension as well. As late as 1900 the propositions that the care of pregnant mothers should be left to physicians and that physicians alone should supervise births were still on the periphery of American thought. Both immigrants and rural villagers continued to depend on midwives. Most Americans, in addition, viewed child rearing as an acquired art rather than as a science. Organizations like the Society for the Study of Child Nature (established in 1888 and later known as the Child Study Association of

America) and the National Congress of Parents and Teachers (established during the 1890s) spoke for the idea of scientific child rearing, but these organizations lacked influence beyond the perimeters of the urban middle class.

Several developments between 1900 and 1920 pointed to growing federal and state involvement in the cause of child welfare: the first White House conference on child welfare (1909), the United States Children's Bureau (1913), the system of county home-demonstration agents supported by the Smith-Lever Act of 1914, vocational education courses in homemaking funded by the Smith-Hughes Act of 1917, and programs for parent education by the U. S. Public Health Service (initiated in 1918). While all of this underscores the widespread interest of Progressives in child welfare, a basic division developed within the movement after 1900. In the 1880s and 1890s, middle-class mothers dominated the child-study clubs, engaging in discussions of *Emile* and other classics of pedagogy and occasionally inviting lecturers like the psychologist G. Stanley Hall. These mothers assumed that the clubs would acquire and diffuse knowledge among their members and encourage the formation of other clubs. Gradually, however, research and popularization underwent a separation. Research became the task of centers or "stations" for child study. Just as the Hatch Act of 1887 subsidized agricultural experiment stations at the land-grant colleges, child-research stations arose as subdivisions of universities. The University of Iowa established one such center in 1911, and by the 1920s similar centers had emerged at Cornell, Yale, and the universities of Minnesota and California.

The psychologists who dominated these centers defined their task as the discovery of principles and facts relating to child development. In contrast to the period after 1930, when the psycho-social development of the child became the overriding concern of child research, investigators in the 1910s and 1920s focused on physical development as a way to improve the health of children. These investigators drew support from public-health doctors associated with the Children's Bureau, child-guidance experts attached to state departments of education, and an assortment of specialists in home economics, but, regardless of the source of interest, the focus remained on health. This preoccupation with the physical aspects of child development nurtured, in turn, a relatively simple conception of popular education. Magazines like *Infant Care* (published by the Children's Bureau) and *Parents' Magazine* (founded in 1926 and subsidized by the Laura Spelman Rockefeller Memorial) would disseminate the unarguable principles and unimpeachable facts discovered by professionals.[69] University extension divisions also sowed advice on child welfare by furnishing newspapers with articles on infant hygiene and by supporting the child-welfare activities of women's clubs with speakers and exhibits.[70]

In 1921 child advocates received an enormous boost when Congress passed the Sheppard-Towner Maternity- and Infancy-Care Act. Jeanette Rankin, the only female member of Congress, had introduced a bill in 1918 based on a proposal made by Julia Lathrop, the head of the Children's Bureau, to provide public protection for maternity and infancy. Rankin's bill called for instruction of expectant mothers in pre-and post-natal care, and this idea became a feature of the Sheppard-Towner Act, which provided matching funds for instruction in the hygiene of maternity and infancy through a program of child care conferences, pamphlet distribution, public health nurses, and visiting nurses.[71] University extension divisions along with sympathetic organizations like the League of Women Voters, the General Federation of Women's Clubs, and state education and hygiene boards cooperated in the diffusion of information. Although nothing in the Sheppard-Towner Act restricted funds to rural areas, in fact rural areas received disproportionate attention, and extension divisions were well situated by virtue of their commitment to rural revitalization to play a key role. Knapp had taught the importance of simplicity, and his message was reflected in devices like "diet cards" distributed en masse to pregnant mothers in rural areas.[72]

Forging a Community

Broadly speaking, one function of demonstrations and exhibits was both to rally public support for the idea that science could contribute tangibly to social betterment and to enhance popular regard for such institutions as extension divisions and health boards that represented science to the public. Not infrequently, Progressives redefined social issues—for example, intemperance, prostitution, and juvenile delinquency—as problems that resulted from the absence of effective social policies rather than from personal depravity and that were susceptible to scientific solutions.[73] In addition, Progressives employed popular education to encourage feelings of identification with the social group or community. In an extended account of the Rockefeller commission's work, Walter Hines Page underscored some of the communal benefits of the demonstration that Progressives found so appealing:

And the effect of this health campaign on the sick is not the whole story. It brings into play the best qualities of the well. It makes men and women charitable in their judgments and helpful in their impulses and actions. The neighbors whom they had blamed or despised have been—only sick. It brings a new community-spirit. It is the duty of the whole community to cure the sick and to prevent the disease. Well, if this disease, why not others? It brings a new conception of sanitation—sanitation which must involve the conduct not only of the individual but of the whole neighborhood. It brings a new idea of education, too. The school is becoming a centre of health-knowledge. It brings a new duty—at least a specific duty—to the church: the hookworm stands in the way to salvation; and if the hookworm, why not other results of bad sanitation? And a new form of political activity, of course, comes to many a rural community when it spends its first health-money for compelling the use of sanitary privies.[74]

As the sociologist J. F. Steiner observed in 1928, Progressive sociologists and social workers possessed an "enthusiastic and somewhat blind allegiance to the community as a kind of magic talisman of value in dealing with social problems."[75]

This attachment of Progressives to the ideal of community sprang from several of their basic convictions: that the civil unrest embodied in such upheavals as the Haymarket Riot and the Pullman and Homestead strikes had revealed a society dangerously fragmented along class and ethnic lines, that political partisanship merely exacerbated social fragmentation, and that the feeling or affection of social identification (or "loyalty") could be cultivated and strengthened. Jane Addams's conception of the settlement house, John Dewey's idea of the school as an agent of socialization, the social psychologist Charles Horton Cooley's ideal of the social self, and the innumerable community studies that Progressives used as both techniques of social investigation and as ways to identify vital communities in the cities—all of these illustrated the Progressives' commitment to molding more intimate communal ties among Americans.

These twin goals of Progressive-style popular education—the enhancement of the public's receptivity to scientific solutions and the intensification of feelings of community—frequently overlapped. Progressive social workers were uncomfortable with the word "individualism" and preferred instead terms like "community," "cooperation," "socialization," and "interdependence." Although sincere in their belief that community had weakened under modern conditions, Progressives not infrequently ignored or denigrated vibrant community institutions (for example, rural evangelical churches) that seemed unlikely vehicles of reform. When they spoke of a "true" community, they meant not merely a neighborly one but also, and more fundamentally, a community that would accept their definition of its problem, their proposed solution, and themselves as agents of ameliorative change. Progressive social workers were often on the margins of power—ministers, former ministers, and women—without political constituencies and in flight from the roles traditionally associated with the pulpit, the schoolmarm, and the lady bountiful. Part of the genius of Progressivism lay in the forging of new social roles and new intellectual occupations, such as psychiatric social worker, civic-league president, and recreation-association official. All of these occupations demanded clients who had to be led, or educated, to desire the social services offered.

Reformers so wedded to the ideal of community and consensus inevitably produced a formal movement for "community education" that flourished after 1910. Community education took various forms, but a unifying thread was the education of adults for keener participation in the affairs of the community. Community education was a phase in the general shift from Ward's theoretical consideration of egalitarianism "to specific investigations of both sociologists and social workers for the purpose of ascertaining the efficacy of different techniques in modifying social behavior."[76] Through community councils and the use of schools and churches as "social centers," Progressives tried to forge the kind of social loyalties which they thought had weakened under modern conditions. In *Community Organization* (1921), the prominent educator Joseph Kinmont Hart outlined the central themes of the movement.[77] Like most Progressives, Hart thought of community along the lines suggested during the late nineteenth century by the German sociologist Ferdinand Tönnies. In Tönnies's concept of *Gemeinschaft*, a community was less a place than a way of life marked by intimate, face-to-face relationships. Most American sociologists (and Tönnies himself) identified *Gemeinschaft* with the small town, where the boundaries of personal loyalties tended to approach those of the town itself.[78] In contrast, sociologists argued, with the growth of cities loyalties tend to be fragmented along class, sectarian, or partisan lines. As Hart put it, social life "becomes a sort of mosaic patchwork instead of a unified experience."[79] What was needed was a true community, which Hart sometimes described as a place but more often as a social ideal, a construct of the "social imagination of individuals."[80] The task of education was to produce "a more thoroughgoing social understanding."[81]

Hart was familiar with the adult-education movement in Britain, but he drew few ideas from it. In Britain adult education still focused on academic subjects and aimed to provide working-class intellectuals with a substitute for the Oxford or Cambridge education that they had missed. In contrast, Hart wanted to produce a sensitive and magnanimous citizen rather than an intellectual; accordingly, he made the acquisition of knowledge less important than the inculcation of attitudes and behavior. In the kind of adult education he envisioned, the classroom played little if any role. Rather, the key agency of education was to be the community council, a group of approximately fifteen persons who would represent the interests of the whole community rather than some fragment of it. Unlike city councillors, members of the community council were not to think of themselves as representatives of voting blocks but as a deliberative elite of men and women with some training in social science. "They should not *represent*—they should *know*; they should not be propagandists or partisans, they should be, just as far as possible, scientists in their fields."[82] Their task was to organize the public against a host of evils: poverty, war, injustice, the breakdown of families, ugly houses, cheap billboards, and even jazz.[83] To the argument that there already existed city councillors and other municipal officials to accomplish these goals, Hart retorted that no change would occur until individuals were induced to seek the good life. Negative ordinances were not the answer. For example, an effective program of public health depended on "such a reorganization of the whole attitude of the community towards the value of life as will make health contagious and disease a sort of disgrace."[84] What adults needed was not legislation but a new kind of education.

Although the primary focus of Hart and other Progressive sociologists and educators was the urban community, Progressives identified the same kind of fragmentation in rural areas that they saw in cities. The most visible manifestation of the rural social problem lay in the steady flow of farmers from the land. During the 1870s, half of the gainfully employed workers in the United States engaged in farming; by the 1920s, the proportion was less than a quarter. Each passing decade marked a new decline; from 42.5 percent in 1890, to 37.7 percent in 1900, to 30.7 percent in 1910.[85] After 1900 there were several organized responses to this trend. The Presbyterian Board of Home Missions, for example, established a Department of Church and Country Life in 1910. The Federal Council of Churches and the Young Men's Christian Association began to take an interest in the problems of rural churches and rural schools. The United States Bureau of Education established a Division of Rural Education.[86] But the event that galvanized the Country Life movement was President Theodore Roosevelt's appointment of the Commission on Country Life in 1908.

Much like the founders of academic sociology, the leadership of both the Commission on Country Life and the broader Country Life movement that emerged in the wake of its report was composed mainly of men from rural or small-town midwestern backgrounds who had fallen under the influence of the social gospel. Most of the leaders were educators or journalists with little recent experience in agriculture but with a keen interest in scientific agriculture.[87] The commission's chairman, Liberty Hyde Bailey, was an internationally known horticulturist and dean of the New York State College of Agriculture at Cornell University. His coworker, Kenyon L. Butterfield, was president of the Massachusetts State College of Agriculture and a rural sociologist.

More representative of the rank and file than of the leadership was Charles J. Galpin, another rural sociologist and the author of *The Social Anatomy of an Agricultural Community* (1911), a book that spurred a number of rural and community surveys.[88] For Galpin there was little distinction between sociology and social work. With many of the early rural sociologists, he engaged in practical activities indistinguishable from those of demonstration agents: furnishing programs for meetings of rural organizations, organizing classes and conferences for country leaders, and promoting recreational activities.[89] The son of a Baptist minister, Galpin grew up in Michigan, only twenty miles from the home of Liberty Hyde Bailey. Although he was a graduate of Colgate and briefly studied philosophy at Harvard, Galpin had no training in sociology and became a rural sociologist mainly by accident. While working in Madison, Wisconsin, as an assistant in a church of which his brother was pastor, Galpin was asked to teach a course in rural social problems in the University of Wisconsin College of Agriculture. Extension lecturing quickly became one of his major activities. In an autobiography appropriately entitled *My Drift into Rural Sociology*, he recalled those early days:

With stereopticon, lantern slides, and a gas tank for places without electricity, I earnestly plugged for better things in rural life. My theory was simple: show farm people what other people have done, and constantly praise farm people for what they are doing. . . . I ballyhooed like any circus barker for consolidated schools, social centers, farmers' clubs, farm and town cooperative effort, county fairs, play days for county schools, school district self-surveys, church interest and social improvement, country-life conferences.[90]

By whatever route these men entered rural social work, they carried with them a keen interest in both science and its applications. For example, Bailey's reputation as a horticulturist rested in part on his ability to link the study of horticulture to biology, but he viewed the application of science as no less important than science itself.[91] Appropriately, he searched for ways to make education in practical science more effective. When he arrived at Cornell, he found that agricultural education consisted of formal lectures followed by a virtual parade of professors and students to visit the university's farm and observe the hired hands at work. Bailey quickly changed this, substituting indoor and outdoor laboratories in which professors and students worked together to set up experiments and apply principles.[92] Both Bailey and Seaman A. Knapp hoped that the effective application of science to agriculture would make the latter more profitable and thereby staunch the hemorrhaging of population from the land.

Yet a crucial difference separated the two men, for Knapp's goals both began and ended with the raising of farm income. As he wrote in 1906:

Every highway in the country might be made as good as a Roman road, with a free delivery mailbox and a telephone at every crossing, and a box stuffed with newspapers; you might hold a Farmer's Institute at every third house and establish an agricultural college on every section of land in the United States: and the flow of young men from the country to the city would not be arrested in the least, so long as the earning capacity of the average city laborer, or clerk, or professional man, is at least five fold what the same talent can command in the country.[93]

In contrast, Bailey and other Country Life Progressives denied that making agriculture more profitable was a sufficient answer to the problems of rural America, for they were simultaneously concerned with the quality of rural life. They viewed rural America as suffering from a spiritual hollowness. Farmers did not cooperate enough with other farmers. Their churches and schools were too small and isolated, their opportunities for recreation too limited. It was not enough to make farming more profitable: rural culture had to be revitalized. Consolidated schools, consolidated churches, and rural festivals would intensify feelings of belonging to a community.[94] Wisely crafted federal and state laws could contribute to desirable change by advancing better roads, scientific agriculture, and rural free delivery. But in the eyes of Country Life Progressives, their essential task was to induce rural people to see the world as they perceived it, to think more scientifically about their problems, and ultimately to embrace change without prodding. As Liberty Hyde Bailey wrote to Theodore Roosevelt in 1909, "Our feeling is that a general extension campaign is needed to arouse the whole people, and that bills for specific kinds of institutions will come as they are needed."[95]

Country Life Progressives received a boost from the Smith-Lever Act's establishment in 1914 of the Agricultural Extension Service. Although the service's immediate objective was to raise farm productivity and profitability, home demonstration work provided an opening for rural social workers whose primary allegiance was to community building rather than to production.[96] By the fall of 1916, 420 southern counties had home demonstration agents. In Anson County, North Carolina, for example, a demonstration agent started a small canning club in 1913. The movement spread so rapidly that the major problem became finding enough cans to keep the clubs active, a problem that was solved by donations from local businessmen. From lessons for girls in canning and preserving, demonstration agents broadened the agenda to include the improvement of schools and school grounds. By 1916 the county had eleven "community clubs" devoted to "the improvement of school buildings and grounds, better roads, campaigns against flies and other insects, study of food, and social life for old and young."[97]

Home demonstration work sought more than to render farmers' wives more efficient homemakers. It aimed also to organize farm women and youth to overcome their presumed indifference to cooperation. The real purpose of corn and tomato clubs, proclaimed a speaker before the Southern Sociological Congress in 1915, was not instruction in growing better corn and tomatoes; that was "little more than a byproduct." Rather, the value of these clubs was that they "have furnished wholesome, happy cooperation—in other words, recreation. The clubs have broken down the isolation that is the curse of rural America."[98] Others described the values of home demonstration agents as to " 'organize and cooperate.' Isolated existence is doomed and it is time that we take our places among members of social groups."[99]

At the root of these calls for cooperation lay the belief of most Progressives that atomistic individualism plagued rural America to a greater degree than urban America. Progressives often imputed to urban immigrants a natural love of community; Edward A. Ross, the Progressive sociologist, described the southern Europeans who crowded into American cities as "less individualistic" and as "more gregarious and dependent" than northern Europeans.[100] In contrast, Progressives usually described farm people, especially those in the South, as marked by a dauntless individualism. For example, John C. Campbell's *The Southern Highlander and His Homeland*, one of several studies of southern mountain people that appeared during the early 1900s, identified the dominant trait of southern highlanders as "independence raised to the fourth power."[101]

Improved schools, particularly consolidated schools, became a major means by which Progressives tried to engender strong feelings of community in rural areas. Home demonstration workers shared this goal with the School Improvement Leagues that proliferated in southern states to mobilize public opinion on behalf of educational reform. These campaigns enlisted large numbers of women, who formed the backbone of the School Improvement Leagues. Inheriting strong traditions of evangelical advocacy and lacking direct legislative or administrative power, women became vigorous supporters of social betterment. Progressives often contended that the School Improvement Leagues helped to create a collective consciousness among rural women by making possible "the intermingling of women from all sections of the State."[102] Edgar Gardner Murphy described women as "the agents of the community."[103] The leagues themselves sought to beautify schools by painting them and by planting grass in their yards. The beautified schoolhouse was to be a demonstration of the advantages of progress, one that would appeal as much to the imagination as to the reason. Once they were made attractive, rural schools would become central institutions for the entire community, magnets that would draw rural people out of their individualistic isolation and enable them to recognize their ties to each other. Rural Progressives specifically sought to overcome localism by the encouragement of consolidated schools firmly under county control. As late as 1906, for example, Kentucky had over 8,000 school districts, each of which set its own standards. Progressives hoped that consolidated schools would counter this fragmentation by drawing students from relatively large areas. Children from the villages and hollows would meet children from the towns, play with them on athletic teams, and build lasting friendships. Above all, the viewpoint of the townspeople, whom Progressives saw as the modernizing force in rural America, would rub off on the rural children.[104]

The consolidated school was to be an agent of "socialization," a word that Progressives used not only in its narrow sense of teaching children to play and to cooperate with other children but also in the broader sense of inducing rural people to identify with modernizing forces emanating from towns and cities. Consolidated churches also appealed to Progressives. Uncomfortable with the narrowness of the social allegiances of farmers and convinced that the isolation and individualism of rural life bred demoralization, rural Progressives favored closing small, sparsely attended country churches and advocated mergers to form larger churches that would draw parishioners from a wider area, expose rural people to a broader community, and adopt the social gospel. The ideal country church, in the words of one stalwart of the Country Life movement, was to be a "social experiment station," replete with social clubs and community-betterment projects rather than narrowing doctrines.[105] Much like the consolidated school, the consolidated church would act as a funnel for Progressive influence in rural areas. Farmers could reasonably contend, of course, that they already had a community, that they cooperated to maintain rural schools and the Baptist church. But these were not the forms of community with which Progressives identified. Rather, they preferred to talk of the "larger" community, by which they meant feelings of solidarity between rural people and townspeople, the true agents of modernization. President Edward K. Graham of the University of North Carolina, who was unsurpassed in his ardor for university extension and who spoke glowingly of a new "cooperative socialism" and "constructive materialism" as alternatives to Matthew Arnold's ideal of culture, equated these democratic manifestations of "true culture" with harmony between farmers and townspeople and with the ascendancy of booster values. This boosterism was evidenced by the creation of town slogans, by electric "Welcome" signs across Main Street, and by civic committees of every sort.[106]

The motive of community building also permeated Progressive-era campaigns against illiteracy in the rural South. As late as 1911 Michael Sadler, a leading figure in university extension in Britain, could cite the relative American indifference to illiteracy as a major difference between adult education in the United States and Britain, where a variety of Sunday schools and so-called ragged schools long had targeted illiteracy.[107] In contrast, most nineteenth-century American educators had assumed that the inevitable spread of free public schools would banish illiteracy. The main exception to this generalization actually reinforces it. Both white missionaries and black educators in the Reconstruction South found their classes thronged by freedmen of all ages eager to learn to read in order to comprehend the Bible, labor contracts, or ballots, but the freedmen's quest for the rudiments was readily attributed to the effects of slavery and did little to jar the belief of educators that the American population's level of educational attainment was high and ever-rising.[108]

In the same year that Sadler underscored the relative indifference of American educators to illiteracy, Cora Wilson Stewart, the school superintendent of Rowan county in eastern Kentucky's feud-ridden mountain region, initiated the "moonlight schools" (so-called because they met in public schoolhouses at night) for adult illiterates. In the absence of any textbooks for adult illiterates, Stewart edited a simple newspaper for her students, and she secured support from Kentucky's governor, who expanded the program statewide in 1914. Under a variety of names—moonlight schools, lay-by schools, community schools, and schools for grownups—schools for adult illiterates quickly spread to South and North Carolina, Mississippi, Georgia, Oklahoma, and New Mexico, and much like cooperative demonstration work these schools gradually made their way north. New York began adult literacy programs for the foreign-born in 1917, and Pennsylvania followed a year later. The eradication of illiteracy became a plank in the platform of each major party in 1920.[109]

Crusading against illiteracy appealed to Cora Wilson Stewart not only for its promise to emancipate the victims of ignorance and facilitate the diffusion of printed health charts and guides in rural communities, but also as a way to promote rural community spirit. Sounding much like other rural Progressives, she was pleased to record the growth of "good-roads clubs, fruit clubs, agricultural clubs, home economics clubs and Sunday schools" in the wake of the moonlight schools. All of this pointed to "a whetted desire for cooperative activity where individualism and stagnation had prevailed."[110]

Seeking to forge a collective consciousness and to enhance feelings of community identification, Progressives displayed remarkable inventiveness in rallying support for their goals. Although pamphlets and exhibits might effectively popularize new ideas about health and child care, they could not spark the kind of emotional affiliations that reformers sought to arouse. A far more promising technique of mass education, in the eyes of many Progressive reformers, was the theater.

This was an age when the theater as well as the school were thought to have educational potential. Led by men such as George Pierce Baker, Alfred Arvold, and Frederick H. Koch, universities began to introduce courses in playwriting. By 1929 over 150 colleges and universities offered courses in the writing and production of plays, and several, including Northwestern and the universities of North Carolina, North Dakota, Minnesota, Oregon, and Utah, sent their players on tour.[111] The belief that drama could intensify community consciousness formed an important component of this enterprise. For example, Alfred Arvold, who headed the Public Discussion and Social Service Department at the North Dakota Agricultural College in Fargo, had his cast perform social surveys of the communities that they visited.[112] Similarly, university extension divisions mailed "package libraries" of drama in an effort to teach farmers how to stage pageants and harvest festivals. In December 1916 the playwright Percy MacKaye described drama as a "new method of community building," "a dynamic, cooperative means of education in community aims."[113] Elsewhere MacKaye spoke of "sociological theatres," and he explicitly described community theater as a phase of the "Wisconsin Idea."[114] "It is only through the drama," MacKaye argued, "that reform can be made spectacular enough to interest the nervous, restless people of today."[115] Community theater was an agent of "the movement of social reorganization led by the social scientist."[116]

In Progressive thought "community drama" had two distinct meanings. On one level, it referred to the sponsorship of a play; a community theater was one owned and operated by amateurs. Louise Burleigh, who had studied drama at Radcliffe under George Pierce Baker before becoming an ardent organizer and advocate of community theaters, equated democracy with opportunity for the many rather than for the few. Although we often view Progressives as dazzled by the image of bureaucracy, Burleigh explicitly contrasted community theater with bureaucracy and equated the latter with professional actors, profit-hungry producers, and booking syndicates that purchased efficiency and polish at the price of broad popular participation. Too often, she argued, the theater merely reinforced American commercialism and capitalism by separating individuals into specialized roles instead of uniting "all classes into a unified community."[117] The true community theater was to be found not on Broadway but in local neighborhoods. Her examples of community theaters included the Neighborhood Playhouse, an offshoot of the Henry Street Settlement in New York City, the Hull House Playhouse in Chicago, the Vagabond Players in Baltimore, and the Provincetown Players.[118]

Burleigh's community theater was a first cousin of the Little Theater, a movement for experimental drama which included Stanislavsky's Moscow Art Theater (1897), Germany's Kleinestheater (1902), Dublin's Abbey Theater (1904), France's Théâtre-Libre (1887), and the experimental theaters launched in Copenhagen and Stockholm by August Strindberg. In the United States Philadelphia, Indianapolis, Madison, Wisconsin, and other cities became centers of the Little Theater movement by 1915.[119] All Little Theaters aimed at subordinating commercial to artistic goals and, at least initially, most provided ample scope for amateurs. But not all met the second criterion of community theater, the idea that the play had to be redolent of the life of the people of a community, an expression of their common values and traditions. In particular, historical pageants appealed to Progressives as ways to dramatize communal values and their own reformist agendas.

Although a historical pageant was staged as early as 1888 in Marietta, Ohio, the main growth of the genre came after the staging in 1905 of a successful pageant in Sherburne, England, by Louis Parker. Between 1905 and 1913 at least 46 pageants were produced in fifteen American states.[120] These included the Pageant of Wisconsin, the Pageant of the Northwest, "The Pageant and Masque of St. Louis" by MacKaye and Thomas Wood Stevens, and MacKaye's "Caliban of the Yellow Sands." Whatever its subject, the pageant was a kind of dramatized epic, a succession of episodes (not acts, for there was no interval or curtain) illustrating some grand theme drawn from history and/or myth, often local history and myth. Yet this description scarcely conveys the complexity and indeed confusion that marked many pageants, for, as in an epic, plot continuity was subordinated to the representation of picturesque incidents. Adding to the complexity was the tendency to link the pageant with a masque—that is, a dramatized allegory in which the actors personified abstract ideas such as education, science, the Renaissance, or (as in "The Pageant and Masque of St. Louis") the growth of a metropolis.[121]

Although blended into a single production, a masque and pageant were distinct forms and might have separate authors. MacKaye, the most important American playwright to become associated with the movement, wrote the masque but not the pageant of the St. Louis production. Compared to the English, Americans paid a great deal of attention to the masque. In the St. Louis production, for example, the masque and pageant were of equal length. The reasons for this are open to speculation, but two contemporary students provided an intriguing clue when they noted that Americans were less familiar than the English with their local history and needed the allegory of the masque to give it meaning. A related possibility is that, here as elsewhere, Americans were uneasy with art for its own sake and strove to associate it with edification through allegories.[122] Masques also made it possible to preach an explicit reformist message. "The Pageant and Masque of St. Louis" (1914) culminated in the triumph of the people over the kind of municipal corruption that Lincoln Steffens had exposed in *The Shame of the Cities* (1904).[123]

Pageants appealed to local civic officials as a way to impress socially diverse audiences with a coherent vision of their community's past. Typically, pageants distilled a town's past, present, and future into two hours of dramatic sketches that reenacted familiar scenes from the town's history. Most plots deemphasized conflict in favor of harmonious growth. As David Glassberg has observed, "Pageant plots depicted expansion in the scale of social life from primarily local to regional and national relations as a nearly organic process, smoothly unfolding from forest primeval to city beautiful."[124] For example, when Schenectady, New York, staged a pageant celebrating its history in 1927, the "First Settler" appeared in the finale to bestow approval on the "Spirits of Life" representing the city's main employer, the General Electric Company.[125]

Pageants were appealing partly because they celebrated the common historical achievements of the populace and partly because of the extraordinary amount of social cooperation needed to stage one. They had to be amateur productions, for no city had enough professional actors to fill their innumerable roles. "The Pageant and Masque of St. Louis," for example, had a cast of 7,500 and played before an audience of 150,000. "Caliban of the Yellow Sands" was incredibly complicated. Viewing a rehearsal in the stadium of the City College of New York, Burleigh conceded that few of the thousands of actors had any conception of the relationship of their roles to others in the production. The action took place, more or less simultaneously, on four separate stages and purported to trace the "waxing and waning of the life of Dramatic Art from primitive barbaric times to the verge of the living present."[126] Drawing its main characters (but not its theme) from *The Tempest*, the play was a celebration of the education of mankind by the arts, especially the drama, and was written to commemorate the three hundredth anniversary of Shakespeare's death. Despite innumerable stumbles and reverses, Caliban rises from brutality to spirituality. This theme, stated reductively as the importance of education and growth, accounted for part of its appeal to Burleigh. So did the fact that "the work was done not easily, but with an effort, and because of the sacrifice and the difficulty which they represented, the pictures were strung one after the other upon the spirit of fellowship as beads hang upon a silken thread. Underneath and through the medley throbbed the inspiration of a great cooperative feeling."[127]

The Progressive Surge

Agricultural extension, health education, community theater, and other forms of popular education arose before World War I, but war mobilization boosted all of these and propelled them into the 1920s. University extension provides a case in point. America's entry into World War I stimulated the expansion of service-oriented university extension and solidified the equation of education and publicity. Walton Bittner of Indiana University wrote in 1919 that "the propaganda to win the war was actually a wholesale adoption of educational extension methods. All the instruments and devices laboriously created or appropriated by the university extension movement during the last decade were utilized to mobilize public opinion and to teach the soldiers, sailors, and industrial fighters, and to train them in the practical techniques necessary to make their blows effective against the opposing forces."[128]

University extension played many roles on the home front. State universities furnished speakers on behalf of war bonds and the Red Cross, displayed motion pictures and lantern slides on the war and war effort, and gave emergency courses on subjects like "military French," camouflage, food conservation, automobile repair, and typing. Extension divisions also cooperated with various governmental agencies and railroad companies to run demonstration trains in support of the war effort. For example, the Pennsylvania State College of Agriculture, the Pennsylvania Food Administration, and the Pennsylvania Railroad cooperated to run a demonstration train from which experts gave lessons on baking bread with wheat substitutes and on canning and drying fruits and vegetables.[129] In gratitude, the federal government in 1918 created the Federal Division of Educational Extension to coordinate the activities of the various state university extension divisions.[130] A breathless paragraph in a United States Bureau of Education report issued in the mid-1920s summarized the range of extension's service activities:

general information service, including the answering of inquiries and questions of various groups and individuals throughout the State; women's club work; conducting high school debating leagues; high-school athletic associations; school and community drama service; school and community music service; contests in literary and other events; school service, especially rural service; welfare weekends; the conducting of Good Roads essay contests; health service; special fair exhibits; workers' education; technical service; library extension service other than package library service; debate and public discussion outside of, or in addition to, high-school service in this line; government research or municipal reference bureau; service to women's clubs in assisting in the organization and extension of activities; play and recreation service; community institutes; community center aids; surveys (economic, social, and school); short graduate medical courses; assistance in community organization and improvement; assistance in problems of rural economy and sociology; surveys, information, etc. on community and industrial relations; high-school visitation; music extension; fostering bible study in schools; forestry extension service; engineering extension service; citizenship education; retail salesmanship; including short courses and institutes on business.[131]

Thinking Versus Doing

Progressives responded eagerly to wartime opportunities to organize the home front and had little time or incentive to analyze the differences between education and propaganda. Propaganda in a strict sense merely meant to propagate the truth, and hence it could be construed as no more than a fast-acting form of education. Obviously, it was one thing to raise human interests to the level of knowledge, another to raise them merely to the level of activity.[132] In his formal treatises on education Dewey related interests to knowledge, and in *Experience and Education* (1938) he explicitly attacked the notion, which he attributed to runaway Progressivism, that feelings and activities were themselves educative.[133] Yet all Progressives affirmed that education had to be measured by its effects on behavior, and many distrusted the traditional means of education, books and lectures, as too remote and unpredictable in their impact.

The Progressive era marked a low point in the history of the popularization of science; by substituting propaganda and publicity for instruction, Progressives, especially those who engaged in extension or outreach activities, sought to induce the public to accept the results of science and implicitly to identify with the cause of science rather than to understand it. This is not what Lester Frank Ward had in mind when he called for the universal diffusion of universal knowledge, but it is a fair description of the uses to which reformers put science.

Set within a broad historical framework, the Progressive approach to educating the public was merely the final act of a drama that had commenced in the 1830s and 1840s, when popularizers began to reduce science to a succession of wonders—a chaste, mildly edifying form of amusement—in order to arrest popular attention. By the Civil War, serious investigators of science were well on the road to severing their ties with the public by establishing such professional associations as the Association of American Geologists and the American Association for the Advancement of Science. To be sure, there were countercurrents. Laymen continued to participate in scientific activities until the end of the nineteenth century, and in sharp contrast to the antics of popular phrenological lecturers before the Civil War, E. L. Youmans turned the *Popular Science Monthly* into a serious forum for the discussion of evolutionary naturalism during the Gilded Age. But these countercurrents had played themselves out by 1900. Lay participation in scientific societies declined toward the end of the nineteenth century, a development that coincided with the monopolization of most scientific fields by the universities. In the world of academic research there was little room for a self-taught popularizer like Youmans. The evolutionary naturalism that Youmans disseminated, in addition, aroused far less controversy after 1900 than in the 1870s and 1880s. Inasmuch as the major documents of evolutionary naturalism, the writings of Darwin, Huxley, and (to a lesser degree) Spencer, were written in language accessible to the educated lay public, the waning of debate over evolution worked against Youmans's kind of popularization. By 1920 the *Popular Science Monthly* had become a popular mechanics' journal.

As heirs to these developments, Progressive reformers could not escape their implications. At the same time, Progressives had their own reasons for devising their peculiar form of popularization. In contrast to Youmans, they were not trying to reach merely the educated public, which Youmans defined as lay people who had acquired a smattering of science in academies and colleges. Rather, Progressives sought to influence dirt farmers and urban immigrants. In addition, as reformers, Progressives did not value the popularization of science as an end in itself but as a means of changing behavior. Their definition of appropriate behavior included respect for the findings of science rather than comprehension of scientific reasoning. Finally, the tendency of Progressive reformers to merge education and propaganda in outreach programs gained force from the confluence of historical circumstances under which Progressivism arose. One such circumstance was the combination of renewed faith in science in the wake of the medical advances of the late nineteenth century and dismay at the ineffectiveness of traditional methods of popularization. The fact that Progressivism coincided with the explosion of secondary-school enrollments and notable increases in collegiate enrollments between 1900 and 1920 weakened pressure for the diffusion of knowledge by print. By assigning knowledge to the schools, Progressives could concentrate on reform. The other circumstance grew out of the fragility of reform itself. The governmental bureaucracies that in time would gain the power to impose ameliorating change were still in their infancies. For example, the Pure Food and Drug Act of 1906, the product of a typically Progressive coalition of scientists, muckrakers, professional reformers, and educators, did not ban impure food and drugs. Rather, it merely demanded truth in labeling and its success hinged on an alert and discriminating public.[134] This climate of intense commitment to reform and (as yet) unobtrusive bureaucracy was conducive to a type of popular education that verged on propaganda.

After 1920, when the term "adult education" became the preferred description for activities formerly covered by educational extension and popular education, "educating the public" became one of the recognized forms of adult education. By 1930, to institute a program of adult education in a town or county meant to encourage local civic agencies—school and health boards, the League of Women Voters, chambers of commerce, and church groups—to cooperate in inducing the public "to find and apply intelligent solutions to the problems of common life."[135] Once acquired, this meaning of community adult education persisted. In the 1950s the Ford Foundation sought to encourage local forums in which citizens discussed philosophical questions, only to come up against this well-ingrained equation of adult education with the coordination and propagation of social services.[136]

A Comparative View

The Progressive era saw a widening distance between university extension in the United States and Britain. The differences between the two can be traced to dissimilarities in the nature of reform, universities, and culture.

In 1909 Oxford University formally instituted a joint committee of university members and representatives of the Workers' Educational Association (WEA) to plan tutorial classes, which qualified for government grants on condition that the course last at least three years and meet the standard of university honors work, which included the frequent writing of essays. The tutorial classes embodied the ideal, shared by socialists such as R. H. Tawney, a legendary figure in British adult education, and liberals such as Albert Mansbridge, of empowering workers by providing the working class's talented tenth with an elite education. Intellectually serious, this approach to adult education envisioned nothing less than the transfer of the don's knowledge to the manual worker, the extension of university teaching.[137]

The British model was both ambitious and rigid, and its limitations became increasingly evident by the 1920s, when the tutorial classes began to attract a growing number of middle-class employees—teachers, social workers, and clerks—and as well middle-class women, both housewives and employees. As the clientele of British university extension became more heterogeneous, governmental regulations were rewritten to allow support for "terminal" and "short" courses (respectively, 24 and 12 weeks), and for courses on subjects like public speaking, music, and literature, which were not related in any obvious way to the achievement of equality for manual workers. By the 1930s traditionalists, who wanted to adhere to the university honors standard and to revive manual-worker domination of university adult education, found themselves under attack by modernists, who hoped that adult education would accommodate the diverse interests of an increasingly variegated clientele.[138]

Yet even as the British made concessions, they continued to seek the extension of university education. Their terminal and short courses were much longer than their American counterparts. When the Americans said short, they really meant short—a few days or a week at most. In addition, the Americans were far more equivocal than the British about whether university extension should involve the extension of a genuine university education. Part of the difference arose from the American perception that higher education was relatively accessible in the United States, and consequently less in need of extension. Although they encompassed only a small fraction of the population, American colleges and universities were open to a wide variety of individuals. More fundamentally, however, Americans were uncertain of the meaning of a university education. They had to devise measurements like the Carnegie units and academic credits (the latter were unknown in Britain until relatively recently) to distinguish secondary and higher education and to establish distinctions between collegiate and sub-collegiate work.

Additionally, in Britain liberal education remained a relatively unitary and cohesive concept; it signified education pursued for its own sake rather than for some trade or professional preparation. In contrast, marked by a history of ambivalent attitudes toward cultured leadership, Americans long had displayed equivocal attitudes toward this kind of education. By the early twentieth century, Americans were substituting terms like "the humanities" or "general education" for liberal education. To put it differently, in the American scheme subjects such as business, law, or engineering could qualify as liberal if instruction was sufficiently general (covering all aspects of the field) or adequately analytical. Americans used university extension to mold new shapes for higher education, to test the waters for new subjects before welcoming them into the curriculum. They also used it to buttress the cultural authority of leadership, specifically, to win popular approval for the value of expert knowledge. Whereas the British assumed influence as a quality of leadership, Americans grappled for ways to enhance the influence of leadership.

The British format inclined to brittleness, the American to formlessness. Yet each had its benefits: in one case, a clear sense of purpose; in the other, flexibility. The contrasting qualities would continue to shape the development of university adult education in each nation. For example, the British have continued to debate how to make liberal education relevant to the interests of working adults. For the most part, this was not a significant concern of Americans in the first two decades of the twentieth century, but it did arouse intense interest for a period in the 1920s, when critics of the banality of American higher education would seek to revive liberal education in the popular forum.

Conclusion

For much of the nineteenth century, popularizing knowledge had meant reducing refined knowledge to morsels that could be readily ingested by those sufficiently educated to desire refinement but insufficiently educated to acquire it on their own. With its reliance on lectures and print, this diffusion of the "means of culture" had played itself out by 1900; the institutions that it had spawned persisted, but its erstwhile missionary zeal disintegrated.

Progressive reformers devised new approaches to popularization, less because they aimed at social reform as such—the diffusion of knowledge had always sought to improve the public's behavior—than because they redefined the nature of the reform enterprise. Disaggregating the Social Question into myriad specific problems and recasting those problems in terms that invited scientific solutions, Progressives forged new approaches to popular education in order to encourage public receptivity to their solutions. At the very least, this objective meant inducing people to follow expert advice. It also meant finding ways to render this acceptance of advice self-sustaining, so that individuals would almost instinctively define their problems in much the same way that reformers did. Cooperative demonstration work would not merely raise crop yields but would persuade dirt farmers to follow expert advice about their health and general welfare—to recognize, for example, that they were sick rather than lazy.

For all of their particularism, Progressives envisioned popular education as something more than the sum of its parts. Education had to aim not only at hitherto neglected subpopulations but also at the building of communities of individuals who might never be led to desire general knowledge of science but who could become enthusiasts for the general reform of society along scientific lines.

Much like their predecessors in the history of the diffusion of knowledge, Progressive reformers also envisioned knowledge as the basis for forging a community founded on mutual understanding between the public and themselves. But by targeting populations that could not be presumed sympathetic to acquiring knowledge, Progressives found it necessary to rely far more than their predecessors on publicity and bureaucracy—in other words, on new means of educational extension that often conflicted with the Progressives' call for spontaneous community.

Chapter 10

The Electric Fire of Thought

Using reform movements as instruments of popular education appealed to social thinkers who no longer believed that intellectual cultivation in the vein of Matthew Arnold could form either a basis for understanding between social classes or a springboard for participation in reform. Yet even the most sour critics of what Chautauquans and clubwomen of the 1880s had innocently called culture-study had to acknowledge that the exponential growth of high-school and college enrollments between 1890 and 1920 was widening the market for books and periodicals that catered to literary tastes. By the 1920s a minor industry of counsellors had arisen to continue the work, undertaken in the 1870s by Josiah G. Holland, of guiding an eager if not always informed public toward familiarity with fine literature, modern philosophy, and the latest trends in science. The executive officers of this industry ranged from President Charles W. Eliot of Harvard, whose Five-Foot Shelf of "Harvard Classics" turned into an extraordinarily successful publishing venture between 1910 and 1930, to the editorial board of the Book-of-the-Month Club, which was founded in 1926 by a New York advertising executive, to an obscure newspaperman, Jesse Lee Bennett, who reminded his readers in 1924 that the liberally educated usually employed the technically educated.[1]

While the popular quest for culture persisted, it also changed, in part by becoming increasingly private. Whereas John H. Vincent had stressed the "social culture" of Chautauqua circles, by 1920 President Eliot and other counsellors of the culture-seeking public were promising that a liberal education could be acquired in a mere fifteen minutes a day in the privacy of one's home. The spread of libraries and inexpensive compendiums of knowledge contributed to this trend, which was reinforced by the decline of culture as a public cause, as a mission that aimed at remaking society. By the 1920s the quest for culture had become almost exclusively what it long had been in part: a means of personal growth rather than the foundation of a social crusade.[2]

Shifts in the prevailing conception of liberal education complemented these changes. Matthew Arnold's description of culture as a process of elevation into an "atmosphere" of sweetness and light had given the pursuit of culture a bad name among liberal educators, who by 1910 faced intense competition from advocates of professional and technical education in wooing the best and brightest youth. In response, university advocates of liberal education began to talk more of breadth than elevation, to stress liberal education's inculcation of an ability to grasp relations among sundry objects of thought rather than to transcend the workaday world. In addition, during the 1920s middle-class Americans increasingly associated liberal education with the nurturing of unique, creative personalities. As Warren Susman suggested, personality became the twentieth century's substitute for what the nineteenth century had called character. More was at stake here than a shift in terminology, for the adjectives that modified personality—stunning, creative, forceful, dominant—invariably possessed connotations of self-expression rather than self-restraint.[3]

The new language that enveloped liberal education in the 1920s at once yielded dividends and carried a price. Far more than Arnoldian culture, this language reconciled liberal education with a hedonistic consumer society, but it also thrust liberal education into competition with all the other means of getting ahead in the world or of refashioning individual personality. In *Middletown* (1929), the Lynds documented the more instrumental and eclectic approach to cultural acquisition that was in full bloom by the 1920s. Not only did Middletown's female literary societies now have to compete with a host of bridge and bowling clubs, but even the literary clubs were abandoning the consecutive study of a single subject for a variety of brief topical discussions: Hull House, the Panama Canal, the Bible, and the "wonders of radio." Secure in their possession of the ballot, clubwomen no longer required complicated rationales for discussing civic affairs, and they no longer attached much importance to systematic study of any sort. Only one literary society continued the study-club tradition by devoting as many as four months to the exploration of subjects like the history of Mesopotamian architecture, and even this club did so in part to deter the social climbers who were invading all the other clubs. Social climbing in Middletown seems to have been part of a more complex impulse that led men and women alike to search for ways to enhance their personal appeal, for example by enrolling in practical psychology courses where they chanted in unison: "I am relaxing, relaxing, relaxed. . . . I am wholly passive—Universal Mind has taken possession of me. . . . Knowledge is Power. I desire Knowledge. I have Knowledge."[4]

The knowledge sought here was not that of Mesopotamian architecture but self-knowledge. Popularizations of Freud in the 1920s promised just this quality. Bruce Barton, the indefatigable popularizer of everything from big business to Jesus Christ, assured his readers that "once you begin to study the Mr. Hyde about you—the unconscious selves of men and women—you find that you have opened a whole new universe of interest and practical value."[5] This language spoke to both the hopes and anxieties of the middle-class public of the 1920s, which felt a certain sense of entrapment by life. Whereas Victorians had juxtaposed success and failure, their descendants worried about failure within success, about becoming mired in a comfortable but lifeless job or social setting. In the 1920s the success-oriented *American Magazine*, which employed a star-studded galaxy of writers from H. G. Wells and F. Scott Fitzgerald to Bruce Barton, preached one fundamental message: life could be turned around at any age and by any number of means. Its pages included advertisements for President Eliot's Five-Foot Shelf that promised purchasers "the broad viewpoint and the culture that are the tools of success in modern life," but these were nudged on every side by blurbs for correspondence schools and sales-training programs.

Packaged and sold, culture had been a commodity since the early days of Chautauqua, but now it became a commodity without a social message. Yet the privatization of culture did not stop a vocal band of intellectuals in the 1920s from trying to reconcile it with public values. The herd-like conformity and hysterical red-baiting that had surfaced in the aftermath of the Great War bred disillusion among intellectuals. Concluding that the adult public was beyond hope and that popularization corrupted education, some preferred to educate adult elites in schools and bureaus of municipal research, which they envisioned as avenues for directly communicating with policymakers.[6] But most of those attracted into the field newly labeled adult education were heartened by evidence of popular interest in culture. It did not interest these intellectuals that correspondence schools and evening colleges of law and business were reaching their zenith, that public schools were offering evening vocational courses, that teachers were flooding extension courses, or that agricultural extension was becoming a colossal enterprise.[7] Rather, the Red Scare, the revitalization of the Ku Klux Klan, and the Scopes trial persuaded them that the public most needed education in critical thinking. They interpreted popular strivings for cultural acquisition as a likely foundation for promoting their values, and they sought to forge a variety of alternative popular institutions of adult education, including the New School for Social Research and a variety of labor colleges and folk schools.

The agendas of the public in quest of liberal education and of alienated intellectuals committed to critical thinking partially converged. Possessing a higher formal educational attainment than Chautauquans of the 1880s, adults who engaged in the voluntary quest for liberal education in the 1920s were comparatively uninterested in systematic academic expositions of subjects, and were more inclined to seek a general understanding of social and political relationships in order to enhance their social standing. Yet the fit between the public's quest for culture and the intellectuals' search for alternatives to the Progressive era's techniques for diffusing knowledge was far from perfect. Conflict between the goals of the public and those of intellectuals, which permeated a great deal of adult education in the 1920s, can be traced in the newly founded American Association for Adult Education (AAAE).

The American Association for Adult Education

After the death of Andrew Carnegie in 1919, the Carnegie Corporation of New York began to reorder its philanthropic priorities and define a new role for itself in the burgeoning field that increasingly was known as adult education. In 1924 the corporation summoned its first conference on the education of adults and in the next ten years made grants totaling just under $3,000,000 to organizations that engaged in adult education. The 1924 conference resulted in the establishment two years later of the American Association for Adult Education, which acted both as a "clearinghouse" for ideas and as a consultant to the corporation. Its organ, the *Journal of Adult Education*, bestrode the field to such an extent that few individuals or organizations of any prominence did not appear in its pages. Carnegie munificence assisted the publication of more than a score of important studies on topics ranging from university extension to libraries and correspondence schools, the use of leisure and the habits of readers, community drama and parent education.[8]

Despite the diversity that would characterize adult education in the 1920s, the Carnegie Corporation initially approached the subject with focused and fairly narrow goals. In place of Andrew Carnegie's encouragement of popular self-improvement through libraries, the corporation saw adult education as a way to facilitate communication among experts in different fields. During the war the corporation had helped to fund the National Research Council, a subdivision of the National Academy of Sciences that had been organized to facilitate communication between science and industry. After the war it subsidized the Institute of Economics, established in 1922 to ascertain and disseminate economic truths. Running through both organizations was a conviction that new agencies were needed to carry the fruits of research swiftly to the public.[9] This priority reflected the influence of Henry S. Pritchett, who headed the Carnegie Foundation for the Advancement of Teaching between 1906 and 1930. Pritchett was profoundly interested in what might be called the relations of science: science and applied science; science and the humanities; science and public opinion. Trained as an astronomer, he believed that scientific studies could develop a humanistic outlook as fully as history or literature, and that neither science nor technology could flourish without the other. As president of the Massachusetts Institute of Technology between 1900 and 1906, he tried to merge science and applied science by inducing (unsuccessfully) the Lawrence Scientific School at Harvard to join with M.I.T. Later, as head of the Carnegie Foundation for the Advancement of Teaching, he sponsored Abraham Flexner's earth-moving *Report on Medical Education in the United States and Canada* (1910). Flexner was not a physician and initially thought that Pritchett had confused him with his brother Simon (who worked at the Rockefeller Institute for Medical Research), but Pritchett quickly explained that he wanted a study that would reach the public, not merely the profession, and that Abraham was his man.[10] Still later, while serving as an interim head of the Carnegie Corporation, Pritchett gave $7 million to the National Academy of Sciences to create the National Research Council.[11]

Pritchett shared Abraham Flexner's criticism of American education as superficial. In the eyes of both, public schools tried to do too much too quickly for too many. Rather than encompassing a smattering of all knowledge, they believed that mass education should focus on the molding of mental discipline and habits in order to equip individuals for self-education in maturity. Organized adult education could play several roles in this enterprise, including the forging of contacts among experts in different fields and the encouragement of the diffusion of factual knowledge through libraries and popular magazines. When Frederick Paul Keppel, a former dean of Columbia College, became president of the Carnegie Corporation in 1923, he inherited this agenda and subsidized the publication of William S. Learned's *The American Public Library and the Diffusion of Knowledge*, which portrayed the ideal public library as a service station for the distribution of printed vocational knowledge.[12]

Yet Keppel quickly recognized that Pritchett's agenda failed to provide an active role for the public at a time of burgeoning popular interest in adult education. Keppel estimated in 1926 that at least five times as many adults were pursuing some form of educational study as the total of all degree candidates in the nation's colleges and universities. These included the 1,500,000 *new* students enrolling each year in correspondence schools, the 1,000,000 students in public-school evening or continuation classes, 150,000 students in university extension classes, 100,000 in Y.M.C.A. classes, and nearly 100,000 in Y.W.C.A. courses.[13]

Keppel's recognition of the magnitude and diversity of adult education dissuaded the AAAE from trying to dictate the movement's direction. As noted, the AAAE described itself as a clearinghouse, not a headquarters. Yet Keppel's deference to the multiplicity of interests within the organization could not conceal his dissatisfaction with some forms of adult education. For example, although it became fashionable in the 1920s for directors of public libraries to describe themselves as engaged in "library adult education," Keppel doubted that libraries could become educational institutions, for they had no control over what their patrons read. More significantly, Keppel had ill-disguised contempt for correspondence schools. The invitation lists for the Cleveland conference on adult education in 1925 and for follow-up conferences in the next year did not include a single representative of correspondence schools. On the other hand, these lists did include a host of public-school officials, university-extension directors, and representatives of unorthodox types of adult education that either first flourished or first arose after the war: Alvin Johnson, the director of the New School for Social Research; the Columbia historians Charles A. Beard and James Harvey Robinson, both of whom joined the original faculty of the New School; Everett Dean Martin, the director of the People's Institute in New York City; the philosopher Scott Buchanan, also connected with the People's Institute; Spencer Miller, Jr., the secretary of the Workers' Education Bureau; and Will Durant, on the eve of his fame as author of *The Story of Philosophy* and in 1926 the director of the Labor Temple School in New York City.[14]

Although it would be difficult to summarize in a single sentence what was unorthodox about these schools, all of them shared an aversion to vocationalism. By 1920 the passage of the Smith-Hughes Act, with its focus on job training, and the continued expansion of the private correspondence schools, with their Algerine devotion to job improvement, had seriously weakened the appeal of vocational education to reformers. Keppel maintained close ties to extension divisions and to adult educators in the public schools (in other words, to institutions with strong vocational leanings), but he also pointed to the Workers' Educational Association in Britain as evidence that "this overwhelming emphasis on the vocational in our adult education isn't inevitable."[15] He lamented as well the ingrained disposition of the universities to allot less than their best to extension activities and the fact that "this whole vast movement has grown up outside our best educational traditions and leadership, and so without the guidance and control by which it might have profited."[16] As a foundation executive loath to make waves, Keppel tried to avoid conflict within the field of adult education. But after the war, a host of leading American scholars and intellectuals assailed the philistinism of Progressive-style popular education as part of their broader indictment of American education at all levels. These critics turned to alternative ideals, specifically what James Harvey Robinson called the "humanizing" of knowledge, and to such institutions as the New School for Social Research.

The New School Intellectuals

Whereas Herbert Baxter Adams and his cohorts in the 1890s hoped to leaven the popular mind by the extension of university teaching, Robinson and his colleagues at the New School for Social Research, including Thorstein Veblen and Charles A. Beard, distrusted the established American universities, with their fat endowments, business-dominated boards, and listless undergraduates. On October 8, 1917, Robinson resigned his professorship at Columbia University in protest against the university's controversial dismissal of two anti-war professors, the distinguished psychologist James McKeen Cattell and an assistant professor of comparative literature, Henry Wadsworth Longfellow Dana. Beard exited soon after. Both Robinson and Beard were familiar with Thorstein Veblen's scathing *The Higher Learning in America,* published in 1919 but completed in manuscript by 1910. The dismissals of Cattell and Dana seemed to bear out Veblen's contention that university executives, in Columbia's case President Nicholas Murray Butler (who orchestrated the dismissals), were at the service of business-controlled boards of trustees. Robinson, Beard, and Veblen (who moved from the University of Missouri) then joined the faculty of the New School for Social Research. Opening early in 1919 in six brownstone mansions in New York's Chelsea district, the New School was the brainchild of Herbert Croly, the founder and editor of the *New Republic* and long an advocate of an independent institute devoted to research in the social sciences. The school was also a beneficiary of the philanthropy of Dorothy Whitney Straight, heir to the Whitney fortune and with her husband Willard a frequenter of *New Republic* intellectual circles.[17]

The intellectuals who taught at the New School in the early 1920s— Robinson, Beard, Veblen, the philosopher Horace Kallen, the anthropologist Alexander Goldenweiser, and the economist Wesley Mitchell— shared in what Morton White has called the "revolt against formalism."[18] Strongly influenced by John Dewey's instrumentalist philosophy, they sought to relate ideas to pressing issues in society and politics. For example, Robinson had already become the chief spokesman for the "new history." In his book of that title published in 1912, he flayed historians for filling their accounts with dynastic struggles and royal pedigrees while ignoring the social and economic forces that shaped public events.[19]

In 1912, Robinson still envisioned the public-school curriculum as the place to introduce the new history. But World War I and its aftermath led him to doubt whether public education could be reformed. The killing or maiming worldwide of some 15,000,000 young men, the disappointment of the Versailles Treaty, the hysteria of the Red Scare, and the repression of dissent at Columbia and other universities convinced him that mankind was experiencing a catastrophic failure of intelligence. Remarkable for its science and technology, American society nevertheless produced leaders who could not utter a coherent sentence about the League of Nations or distinguish between the ideas of Jane Addams and Trotsky. In *The Mind in the Making* (1921), Robinson insisted that the times called for a "thorough reconstruction of our mind."[20] Schools and colleges themselves reflected the sorry state of national intelligence. School boards that trembled at the thought of displeasing capitalists might introduce Progressive-style courses in citizenship, but these would be shorn of any controversial features that might spur critical thought. In effect, he nominated himself to illuminate the popular mind. *The Mind in the Making* drew upon history, anthropology, and psychology to demolish the confident positivism of Lester Frank Ward and other nineteenth-century cosmologists who thought they saw a smooth evolution of civilization's psychic factors. Rather, Robinson contended, intellectual progress had ever been the work of the creative few, while the average person "is ever prone to find excuses for slipping back into older habits."[21]

In *The Humanizing of Knowledge* (1923), Robinson reaffirmed his belief that the "*supreme problem of our age*" was to close the gap between the scientific outlook, which had so vastly augmented human knowledge, and the inherent conservatism of the popular mind.[22] The early 1920s had yielded more evidence of the magnitude of the task, for now state legislatures and school boards, having routed the Bolshevik menace, were dismissing teachers who dared to defend Darwin. But the main contribution of *The Humanizing of Knowledge* was to advocate a new conception of popularization. In *The New History*, Robinson had dismissed the usual sort of popularization, the felicitous narration of past events by men of letters. *The Mind in the Making* sought less to dramatize historical events and personalities than to illuminate a single issue. By 1923 it was clear to Robinson that the key to all successful popularization lay in beginning with some critical public need and in drawing on academic subjects to point the way toward answers.[23] In this way popularization would educate rather than divert. Indeed by 1923 Robinson had abandoned *The New History*'s call for an improved school curriculum. Now he contended that the only effective type of instruction was that which addressed adults rather than children and which therefore occurred outside of conventional educational institutions.

Other members of the New School's original faculty shared one or more of Robinson's basic tenets. Beard's *An Economic Interpretation of the Constitution* (1913) not only underscored the economic motives of the founding fathers but also treated history as a social science relevant to modern issues. Mitchell tried to bring economics down from theory to the investigation of the workings of economic institutions and to ground economics on precise statistical observation. Kallen's philosophy drew on Dewey's instrumentalism, while his ideas about education owed a great deal to Veblen and to Upton Sinclair's scathing indictments of American colleges and public schools in *The Goose-Step* (1922) and *The Goslings* (1924). In 1925 Kallen portrayed the entrapment of American education during and after the war as the result of a one-two punch: first came the super-patriots—the Key Men of America, the Sentinels of Liberty, and the Klan—at once fanning and exploiting wartime fears; then, with the American mind rendered "psychopathic," reactionary businessmen moved swiftly to identify unionism with Bolshevism and to infiltrate school committees and boards of trustees.[24] Common to virtually all of the New School's faculty was a view of learning as a combustion process: materials from history, economics, sociology, or philosophy had to touch off an explosion at the point where the student grasped the relation between academic knowledge and social issues.[25] Thought, Beard proclaimed, was "electric fire."[26]

Yet the school's faculty divided over the balance between research and teaching. Croly envisioned the New School as an American counterpart to France's École des Sciences Politiques, as an institute that would conduct socially valuable research while training leaders in business, government, labor, and education.[27] This conception was akin to Henry S. Pritchett's notion of adult education as the communication of expert knowledge to the public. Croly's view also was in the vein of Walter Lippmann's *Drift and Mastery* (1914), a blueprint for organizing society along rational and scientific lines by training elites to overcome their prejudices and work together.[28] This conception of the New School envisioned little scope for students. Indeed some of Croly's projects dismissed students altogether; at one point he planned a labor research institute that would sell its services to unions. Mitchell's research interests also overrode his concern for teaching; even while serving on the New School faculty, he began his long career as director of research of the National Bureau of Economic Research, and in 1927 he became chairman of the Social Science Research Council. Of Veblen's interest in teaching, the less said the better; by 1925 he was refusing to teach at all and was forced off the faculty.

The basic problem with the idea of turning the New School into some amalgam of a think tank and a "school" in which experts communicated the latest science to policymakers was that the institution barely subsisted in its early years on annual grants from Dorothy Straight. Research was not self-financing and, in the absence of an endowment, the school needed to attract fee-paying students. Robinson's insistence that the school instruct an unselected student body through courses was considerably more practical and also in tune with his stance in *The Mind in the Making* that a reconstruction of the popular mind alone could save the world from chaos.[29]

The conflict between research and teaching boiled over in 1922, when Alvin Johnson, an editor of the *New Republic* and until then a relatively inactive member of the New School's board, engineered a compromise. Sharing Robinson's belief that wartime propaganda had exposed the public to "torrents of emotion-bearing catchwords," Johnson's compromise maintained a nominal role for research while fundamentally emphasizing teaching.[30] The New School's lecture courses had already proven popular; registrations had risen from 348 in 1919–20 to nearly 800 in 1923–24. But Croly thought that lectures would turn the institution into a "one-horse Chautauqua" and severed his ties to the school.[31] Mitchell, whose heart was in research, resigned from the faculty in 1924, and a year later Johnson fired Veblen. More surprising were the resignations in 1922 of Beard and Robinson, for these two, and especially Robinson, approved in theory of Johnson's stress on teaching. But Robinson had little use for even the rudimentary bureaucracy that the New School required to coordinate its fund-raising and feared that the institution was becoming too much like the Columbia University that he had resigned from in 1917.[32]

The departure of the school's original faculty accelerated a shift, favored by Johnson, to part-time lecturers who were paid on a fee basis rather than by salary. The change was not only financially advantageous to the school but pedagogically sound, for New York City was filled with needy intellectuals who, while lacking the scholarly stature of Robinson or Beard, had gained valuable experience in instructing adults at neighborhood cultural centers. Everett Dean Martin and Eduard C. Lindeman, each active in the AAAE, were representative of the New School's staffers of the mid-to-late 1920s.

A sometime Congregationalist and Unitarian minister and frequent socialist soapboxer, Martin occasionally held teaching positions in universities but spent most of his career in institutes established by disaffected academics. Between 1917 and 1938 he served as assistant director and then director of the People's Institute. Founded in 1897 by Columbia University's Charles Sprague Smith, who hoped to make higher education relevant to the working class, the People's Institute gradually shed its social-gospel ties and evolved into an adult forum with some resemblance to Cooper Union and to the New School. At the People's Institute Martin regularly drew from 800 to 1,200 auditors to his Friday evening lecture courses. These consisted of 24 to 48 related lectures on a single subject. As one contemporary noted, "The subject is not easy to label, as it does not lend itself to rigid college departmentalization. It cannot be called patly psychology, sociology, or philosophy. All these fields may be traversed, and sometimes others. What Mr. Martin does is to interrelate those divisions of knowledge to their application to the problem he is discussing for the year."[33]

Martin's emphasis on relationships permeated the offerings of the New School in the late 1920s. New School courses typically contained "and" in their titles: psychology and personality development; economics and labor. They also stressed the relevance of liberal education to contemporary problems. As one of the school's bulletins expressed it in 1930, adult education had to concern itself with the League of Nations rather than with the Amphyctionic League or the Holy Alliance, with Stravinsky and Bartok rather than Bach and Beethoven.[34] Even after Robinson's secession from the school, Martin's preoccupation with relevant and interdisciplinary courses continued to gain ground, while the ideal of social research retreated.

Martin also preferred education by discussion. The philosopher Scott Buchanan, who served as the assistant director of the People's Institute, related how the lectures (held at Cooper Union) were often followed by prolonged discussion. Martin and Buchanan found this a congenial format, for each believed that adult education had to proceed by Socratic dialogue. As Mortimer Adler, a close friend of Buchanan, wrote in 1927: "One cannot tell another how to think; he can simply tell the other how he thinks himself."[35] Buchanan was a link between the adult-education movement of the 1920s and Adler's later campaign for education by Great Books. The description that Adler applied to Buchanan depicted Martin as well: "His mind was constantly searching for analogies that would reveal the unifying similarities among comparatively dissimilar and conflicting things."[36] While lectures could draw these analogies, it seemed to Buchanan and Martin alike that they would arise more spontaneously and genuinely from the give-and-take of discussion.

Eduard C. Lindeman resembled Martin in many ways. Born in 1885 into a large and poor family headed by a Danish immigrant, Lindeman worked in his youth as a riveter in shipyards, a farm laborer, and a miner in the salt mines of his native St. Claire, Michigan. He did not enter the Michigan State Agricultural College (now Michigan State University) until he was 21. In the mid-1920s Lindeman said that his youthful experiences of work and strikes led him to see college as detached and unreal.

Perhaps, but while at Michigan State Lindeman played an active role in campus affairs, managing the football team and directing the campus chapter of the YMCA. Upon graduation in 1911 he engaged in a fairly conventional sequence of reform activities: assistant to the pastor of the Congregationalist church in Lansing, charged with youth work; organizer of clubs for farm youth through the extension division of Michigan State; worker for the American Recreation Association and the War Camp Community Service; and secretary of the American Country Life Association.

At this period Lindeman shared the Progressive enthusiasm for encouragement of community cooperation as a solution for social problems. As his biographer noted, "Lindeman's concern for community action was great. He wanted to understand better how one could help communities determine their own fate and how experts and citizens could work together."[37] While teaching at the North Carolina College for Women in Greensboro, he wrote a brief book, *The Community* (1921), which sought to distill principles and techniques for community organization from his experiences in Michigan.[38] An unexpected dividend of authorship was his meeting Mary Parker Follett, a prominent advocate of Progressive causes and the author of *The New State* (1918), a book promoting the abandonment of political parties and the substitution of self-governing neighborhood groups. Follett rescued Lindeman from Greensboro, where his family's social contacts with blacks had made his position increasingly uncomfortable, and introduced him to Herbert Croly and Dorothy Straight of the *New Republic*. Lindeman's circle of acquaintances and friends quickly expanded to include Dewey, Beard, Robinson, Veblen, Wesley C. Mitchell, Edmund Wilson, and Robert MacIver.[39]

Lindeman's first profession had been social work, an interest he continued during the 1920s by lecturing at the New York School of Social Work. Yet he was becoming increasingly critical of many of the Progressive assumptions that guided the first generation of professional social workers. In 1924 he flayed several recent studies in a savage review published in the *Survey*. Of Augustus W. Hayes's *Rural Community Organization*, he wrote: "the unit of rural civilization finally discovered: unconvincing"; on H. N. Morse and Edmund deS. Brunner's *The Town and Country Church in the United States*, "how long can a social institution live after death? A partial answer to this question of institutional pathology"; on John J. Dillon's *Organized Cooperation*, "the Freudian wish of a market director whose directions were not followed"; on the proceedings of a Country Life conference, "education without consulting the patients"; on O. M. Kile's *The Farm Bureau Movement*, "how the farmers have imitated chambers of commerce."[40]

Lindeman's exposure to the Country Life movement left him with a sense of its banality and flaccidity. By the mid-1920s it was becoming clear that the introduction of rural free delivery, consolidated schools, and the automobile would not make rural life more attractive or stem the flow to the cities. Rather, they were merely making villagers aware of what they were missing. Throughout rural America, Lindeman wrote in 1927, "gasoline stations seem to grow up on every corner as naturally as the toadstool emerges from warm humus." The symbols of beauty that now blazoned forth from the sides of barns read "Hot-dogs, Balloon Tires, Lucky Strikes, History While You Ride at Thirty Miles An Hour, Ask Dad—He Knows, and That Schoolgirl Complexion." While urbanites tried to resurrect folk-dancing, the farmer and his wife wanted to go to the movies.[41]

The problem was not merely that the magnet of the city exerted an irresistible pull. The movement to instill scientific attitudes in farmers while simultaneously inducing them to preserve their rural heritage had aimed at altering their attitudes without actually educating them. It was like feeding people intravenously; farmers were supposed to gain sustenance without ever being conscious of it. By the mid-1920s Lindeman had come to recognize the fallacy: "We did not distinguish between education and propaganda." He added, "Since I was among the worst of these sociological sinners . . . , I do not hesitate to recognize the fallacy and short-sightedness of this program."[42]

Others in the 1920s were discovering the same distinction. The founders of what became known in the 1920s as public relations, Ivy Lee and E. L. Bernays, worked their way from journalism into publicity work even before World War I, but initially neither saw himself as manipulating public opinion by twisting facts. Even if he did not always practice it, Lee professed a creed of full disclosure, "Accuracy, Authenticity, Interest"—the public be informed rather than damned. Bernays's first venture after his graduation from Cornell University in 1912 was to produce a play, *Damaged Goods*, which sought to raise public consciousness about syphilis. In keeping with this Progressive objective, he raised money by establishing a sociological fund committee to attract contributions from leading reformers.[43] By the mid-1920s much had changed. By then, Lee's numerous and lucrative face-lifts on corporations had earned him the sobriquet "Poison Ivy" from Upton Sinclair. In 1922 Walter Lippmann, chastened by his experience as a wartime propagandist with the military intelligence branch of the U.S. Army, stressed in *Public Opinion* that the mental "pictures" of reality, themselves products of the observer's class and culture, distorted the public's understanding of events. "The facts we see depend on where we are placed, and the habits of our eyes," he wrote.[44] A year later Bernays, who had worked for George Creel's Committee on Public Information during the war, staked out in his *Crystallizing Public Opinion* a position similar to Lippmann's.[45]

Lippmann had laid an epistemological mine field for educators. His own conception of education hinged on "an independent expert organization for making the unseen facts intelligible to those who have to make the decisions."[46] Such an organization would position itself between the private citizen and the "vast environment in which he is entangled."[47] Lippmann gave several examples of the kind of organization that he had in mind: "the bureaus of municipal research, the legislative reference libraries, the specialized lobbies of corporations and trade unions," and the philanthropic foundations.[48] Yet Robinson had implied in *The Mind in the Making* that the public might be brought to recognize its biases and under the right conditions reconstruct its own mind. Lindeman adopted this view, which left scope for adult education. Progressives had erred in assuming that by turning farmers into scientific agronomists they would make them into rationalists; in reality, farmers might adopt modern conveniences like electric light bulbs and still smother their minds with Fundamentalism.[49] But education might still succeed if it detached itself from the tentacles of conservative capitalism, super-patriotism, and narrow religion.

As practitioners of adult education, Lindeman and Martin adopted the approach to humanizing knowledge that Robinson had sketched out. Lindeman's *The Meaning of Adult Education* and Martin's *The Meaning of Liberal Education*, each of which appeared in 1926, took positions akin to Robinson's on the failure of schools and colleges to educate young people into adults capable of critical thinking, on the view of education as a process of acquiring intelligence rather than bodies of knowledge, and on the vapidity of Progressive-style extension. The field of popular education was awash in propaganda and had become a forum for crusaders with narrow causes like teaching farmers to fertilize crops and inculcating workers with loyalty to their companies. The task of adult education, Martin contended, was to revitalize liberal education to enable the individual "to take a richer and more significant view of his experiences, to place himself above and not within the system of his beliefs."[50]

Martin and Lindeman advocated popular liberal education oriented toward such "burning issues" as capital versus labor and Fundamentalism versus modernism. This was a far cry from Arnoldian culture, but just as Chautauqua had been sustained by the cultural strivings of middle-class women in the late nineteenth century, so the New School intellectuals were buoyed by evidence of popular interest in serious, issue-oriented books.

The Humanizing of Knowledge

James Steel Smith has aptly called the period from the end of the Great War until the Depression "the day of the popularizers." Histories like H. G. Wells's *The Outline of History* (1921), Hendrik Van Loon's *Story of*

Mankind (1921), James Harvey Robinson's *The Mind in the Making* (1921), Claude Bowers's *Jefferson and Hamilton: The Struggle for Democracy in America* (1925), Charles and Mary Beard's *Rise of American Civilization* (1927), Vernon Louis Parrington's *Main Currents of American Thought* (1927-30), and Will Durant's *The Story of Philosophy* (1926); popularizations of science, including Arthur Thomson's *Outline of Science* (1922), Paul De Kruif's *Microbe Hunters* (1926), and Bertrand Russell's *The ABC of Atoms* and *The ABC of Relativity* (1925); and the ubiquitous Little Blue Books published by Emanuel Haldeman-Julius—all of these works enjoyed remarkable sales as popularizations of knowledge aimed at the general reader. "Never has the attempt to popularize," Smith has observed, "appeared so intense and vigorous and so spectacular in the response."[51]

Perhaps, but assessments of the scope and intensity of popularization are risky. The popularization of knowledge had become well established long before the 1920s. Chautauquans had read textbooks, studied subjects, taken quizzes, and assured themselves all the while that they were acquiring culture. Although Chautauqua as an organized movement declined after 1900, the approach to popular education that it represented persisted. Published in 1909, the Harvard Classics (the Five-Foot Shelf) traced the development of civilization through readings of the greats, came equipped with course outlines for further study, and enjoyed a sale of 350,000 sets (over 17,000,000 separate volumes) over the next two decades. Much like Bishop Vincent at Chautauqua, President Eliot's enterprise rested on an apparent incongruity: by ponderously working his way through a list of books, the autodidact would acquire "a liberal frame of mind or way of thinking."[52]

Conditions in the 1920s nurtured a different approach to popularization. Not everyone had become a reader, but the increase in high-school and college enrollments pointed to a more self-assured public. In their study of *The Reading Interests of Adults* (1929), William S. Gray and Ruth Munroe concluded that "college people read decidedly more books than any other group, those having a high-school education read a medium amount, and those having a grade-school education only read very few books."[53] Gray and Munroe found that college and high-school graduates also brought a more serious purpose to their reading than did grade-school graduates; those with education beyond the elementary grades were far more likely to read to acquire information and ideas rather than merely to fill up spare time.[54]

Rising levels of educational attainment helped to create a market for serious popularizations, which also reflected new cultural currents. Popularizations of science fed on discoveries like that of the x-ray and diphtheria antitoxin, and on popular fiction. De Kruif's *Microbe Hunters* appeared the year after Sinclair Lewis's *Arrowsmith* (which it resembled in portraying the scientist as a lonely explorer, a prophet without honor who defies the odds) and in the same year as the first American science-fiction magazine, *Amazing Stories. Microbe Hunters* was itself a collection of amazing stories; the search for microbes and antitoxins was one of "insane paradoxes."[55] The cultural climate of the 1920s was also receptive to historical popularizations. Wells remarked in the introduction to the 1931 edition of *The Outline of History* that at the close of the Great War people felt the urge "to 'get the hang' of world affairs as a whole."[56] Even the scientific popularizers like De Kruif and Russell strove to present the big picture, the relationship between science and human progress, rather than a simple account of recent developments in medicine or physics. Robinson, who greatly admired Wells, neatly compressed this quest for understanding in his phrase "the humanizing of knowledge." For Robinson and many contemporary intellectuals, the ideal setting for humanizing knowledge was informal, a "new" school or a cultural center marked by rousing debates and by exchanges between audience and lecturer, a kind of intellectual free-for-all. In these settings lecturers learned to stay on their toes and make their subject interesting; otherwise, the audience would walk out. No one learned this lesson better than Will Durant.

Born in 1885 in North Adams, Massachusetts, Durant was raised a devout Catholic and intended to become a priest. But while attending a Jesuit college in Jersey City, he found his faith slipping away. Although he entered a seminary after graduation, he soon cut his ties to the church, moved to New York City, taught at an anarchist school in Greenwich Village (where his future wife and collaborator Ariel was one of his students), and in 1913 entered Columbia University as a graduate student in philosophy. Durant's doctoral dissertation, published in 1916 as *Philosophy and the Social Problem*, foreshadowed the issue that would preoccupy Robinson in *The Mind in the Making*—how to bring understanding of social science abreast of knowledge of natural science. Durant approvingly quoted Lester Frank Ward's assertion that "in politics we are still savages" and, in the vein of Ward's call for "sociocracy," he urged scholars to organize a "Society for Social Research" that would gather the best brains to study the social problem, assemble unassailable facts and principles, and disseminate correct information through the press. Durant hoped that, directly or indirectly, these reports might reach a million voters, who would form a kind of truth lobby to keep politicians from straying into emotional rhetoric.[57]

When *Philosophy and the Social Problem* was reissued in 1927, Durant reaffirmed his belief in the Society for Social Research as the "logical first step in the reconstruction of modern philosophy."[58] But Durant's fame owed nothing to this book, which sold only 100 copies in its first edition, and everything to *The Story of Philosophy*. The roots of his publishing success lay less in his graduate study than in his experiences as a lecturer at various neighborhood cultural centers, including the Labor Temple, an adult education and social-service center founded in 1910 by Presbyterian social gospelers. Durant lectured 30 to 40 times a year at the temple from 1914 to 1927. By the 1920s he dominated its educational program, discoursing on philosophy, biology, psychology, the history of art, music, sociology, and the history of science.[59]

Although founded by Protestants, the Labor Temple exemplified the intellectual concerns and the cut-and-slash debating style of the Jewish immigrants who dominated its audience. Neither the detached culture-study of Chautauquans nor the vestiges of Protestant gentility at social settlements characterized the educational clubs frequented by Jewish immigrants. Abraham Bisno, the Russian-born tailor-intellectual, benefited from his association with settlement workers, who taught him to read and write English, but at close quarters his relationship with them turned tense and abrasive. During one of his visits, Bisno attacked a liberal Episcopalian clergyman who believed that the poor were victimized but who also affirmed that religion was their true recourse. As Bisno recognized, the language of his attack, appropriate in the debates of the Workingmen's Educational Society, led the settlement workers to conclude that he was boorish and ill-bred, and he "felt that they might be right."[60]

As a lapsed Catholic, Durant adapted much more smoothly than settlement workers to the style of self-taught Jewish intellectuals, and in fact he married the daughter of Jewish immigrants. The predominantly Jewish audiences attracted to his Labor Temple lectures relished his penchant for debate and dramatization. In 1921 he induced the famed trial lawyer Clarence Darrow to debate him on the subject "Is Progress Real?" He also had a knack for attracting lecturers with dramatic flair to the Temple's staff. Ariel introduced him to John Cowper Powys, a British philosopher whose *The Meaning of Culture* would become a best-seller in the early 1930s. "There was something theatrical about John in those early days of our friendship," Durant wrote. "His wearing of his scholar's robe when he lectured may have been a strategem to arouse a curiosity that would alert attention."[61] Soon Durant and Powys were dueling before an appreciative audience over the question "Who Are the Ten Greatest Authors?"

Durant's years at the Labor Temple not only sharpened his skill at dramatizing ideas but introduced him to Emanuel Haldeman-Julius as well. The self-taught son of a Jewish bookbinder from Philadelphia, Emanuel Julius moved to Girard, Kansas, in 1915 to take over the editorship of a socialist paper and a year later married Marcet Haldeman, a niece of Jane Addams. In 1920 Haldeman-Julius, as he was known after his marriage, began to publish the Little Blue Books. These were paperbacks with standard lengths of 32, 64, 96, or 128 pages. Regardless of their length, they sold for a nickel. The Little Blue Books ranged over several fields. Many were self-help manuals: how to conquer stupidity; how to get a liberal education; how to enjoy reading. Others were self-instructors in foreign languages. Still others were either reprints of classics or brief scholarly guides to ancient and modern literature. By January 1, 1928, Haldeman-Julius had 1,260 different titles in the series; in 1927 he sold over 20,000,000 Little Blue Books. When he published a brief history of the enterprise in 1928, he could truthfully entitle it *The First Hundred Million.*[62]

Haldeman-Julius discovered Durant in 1922, while the latter was lecturing on Plato at the Labor Temple, and subsequently induced him to publish the lecture as one of the Little Blue Books.[63] Between 1923 and 1925 Haldeman-Julius brought out ten other Durant lectures as Little Blue Books and then proposed that, with suitable connecting tissue, these eleven booklets would make an excellent history of philosophy. It was Haldeman-Julius who made the first contact with the publisher, Simon and Schuster, and who arranged with Durant to divide the royalties. Durant later terminated this arrangement with a pre-publication buy-out of Haldeman-Julius's share for $500.

Clearly, Durant benefited from the friendly shove by Haldeman-Julius, but while Durant may have needed an impresario, he scarcely required a scriptwriter. In his years at the Labor Temple he had developed a genius for popularizing difficult subjects without trivializing them. *The Story of Philosophy* was both a solid account of the history of philosophy and a readable narrative of the lives of famed philosophers. While it is impossible to identify with certitude the specific qualities of *The Story of Philosophy* that appealed to individual readers, there can be little doubt about the qualities that distinguished the book as a superior popularization. In contrast to James Harvey Robinson, who in *The Mind in the Making* could never decide whether he was talking to the public or about it, Durant often used "we" and "our" to suggest an experience of investigation that he shared with his readers, and he was not above appealing to a lay audience by distancing himself from philosophically abstruse concepts. This was especially true of his incursions into the "maelstrom of metaphysics." Because Durant ignored the medieval scholastics, whom he thought deserved treatment as theologians rather than as philosophers, critics at times blasted him for ignoring metaphysics. Actually, he did not dismiss metaphysics at all, but he approached it gingerly and with apologies to the reader. For example, of Spinoza he wrote:

Again, the modern student will stumble and grumble over the terminology of Spinoza. Writing in Latin, he was compelled to express his essentially modern thought in medieval and scholastic terms; there was no other language of philosophy which would then have been understood. So he uses the term *substance* where we should write *reality* or *essence*; *perfect* when we should write *complete*; *ideal* for our *object*; *objectively* for *subjectively*, and *formally* for *objectively*.[64]

One subject that Durant did slight was epistemology, which he thought was best left to psychology and "has kidnapped modern philosophy and well nigh ruined it." He described his own task as reawakening an understanding of philosophy as "the synthetic interpretation of all experience rather than an analytic description of the mode and process of experience itself."[65] As the synthetic interpretation of experience, philosophy is related to human concerns. The book's subtitle, *The Lives and Opinions of the Greater Philosophers*, suggests his preoccupation with integrating life and thought. Again, his comments on Spinoza are revealing: "After all, as we perceive, Spinoza's philosophy was an attempt to love even a world in which he was outcast and alone; again, like Job, he typified his people, and asked how it could be that even the just man, like the chosen people, should suffer persecution and exile and every desolation."[66]

One effect of Durant's method of integrating biography, cultural history, and the history of philosophy was to make his book very long, nearly 600 pages. By way of comparison, Clement C. J. Webb's *A History of Philosophy*, which one critic of Durant judged a superior popularization, traversed the history of philosophy in 250 pages, but at the cost of the biographical and cultural background that distinguished Durant's book.[67] Webb's history, which appeared in a British series coedited by Gilbert Murray and entitled the "Home University Library of Modern Knowledge," was an excellent example of a more traditional type of popularization, the lucid digest. It provided a useful vademecum for students and valuable review for graduates, but it lacked the breadth and human interest to lure many readers who did not already have a good reason for studying philosophy. Further, in striking contrast to Durant, who devoted nearly half of *The Story of Philosophy* to the period from Schopenhauer to Dewey, Webb gave short shrift to post-Kantian philosophy. In sum, Webb provided a clear digest of a university philosophy course; Durant sought to induce his readers to agree that philosophy was "the front trench in the siege of truth."[68]

Durant unhesitatingly labeled *The Story of Philosophy* "an attempt to humanize knowledge," an enterprise that led him to inject human interest into his sketches of philosophers, to search for underlying principles that threaded the history of European civilization, and to try to relate knowledge to his readers' experience.[69] Although Dewey had a greater impact than Robinson on him, Durant frequently lectured at the New School, and he and Ariel often attended the lectures of Everett Dean Martin, who taught at Cooper Union and the New School. But the fame that Durant gained from *The Story of Philosophy* gradually weakened his ties to the

New York world of neighborhood cultural centers. In February 1927, he resigned as director of the Labor Temple School, and for the remainder of the decade he occupied himself with transcontinental lecture tours, interviews, magazine articles, and his work on new books. Success brought him wealth and a softer intellectual profile; the fiery exchanges of the Labor Temple gave way to high-fee magazine articles on "The Ten Greatest Thinkers."[70] His politics also shifted from the militant socialism of his student and Labor Temple days to a skeptical liberalism. His "mental autobiography," *Transition* (1927), ended with a sentimental chronicle of the birth of his first child ("I Became a Daddy") and the suggestion that familial bliss could be an anodyne for the restlessness of modern man.[71] Durant continued his career as a popularizer, but without the intensity or urgency that characterized Wells or Robinson. When in October 1927 Durant debated Bertrand Russell on "Is Democracy a Failure?" the *New York Times* found it odd that Russell, whose *Principia Mathematica* had sold little more than 100 copies, avowed more faith in the common people than Durant, whose *The Story of Philosophy* had already sold 200,000 copies.[72]

Durant's career exposed a latent tension between the humanizing of knowledge and the popularization of culture. Robinson retained enough of his early Progressivism to insist that knowledge produce more than personal enlightenment and cultural refinement, that it influence the way in which individuals responded to social issues. In some of their utterances Martin and Lindeman took the same position, but less consistently. Like the parlor game in which a story is told around the room, experiencing a slight change at each passage until it is scarcely the same story, Lindeman's successive thrusts at defining liberal adult education progressively distanced him from Robinson. Adult education would "put meaning into the whole of life." It would cultivate "individuality, uniqueness, difference." At one point Lindeman argued that even recreation in the form of hobbies and pastimes, if reflected upon and suitably interpreted, had educative value. Adult education, indeed, "will have justified itself if it does nothing more than make adults happier in their hours of leisure."[73]

Lindeman's problems in defining adult education partly reflected the shifting sands beneath his feet, for with the departure of the New School's original faculty, its social-science profile weakened. By the mid-1920s courses in literature, art, and psychology were multiplying in response to the interests of its predominately female students, and by 1927 the New School no longer described itself as devoted to social reform. Rather, it would offer "whatever seriously interests persons of mature intelligence."[74] This user orientation, endemic to most forms of adult education, was intensified by the Progressive educational values that permeated New School intellectuals, specifically by the Progressive goal of integrating learning and living. Whether disillusioned or merely chastened by their wartime and postwar experiences, the New School intellectuals affirmed this fundamental but amorphous Progressive tenet, which could justify such diverse foci as vocational education, social research, critical thinking, and personal fulfillment.

However blurred the contours of the ideal of integrating learning and living, intellectuals of the 1920s united in opposition to most traditional forms of popular education. Viewing education as a voluntary quest for understanding the modern predicament, they dismissed all external motives for learning, including the job-improvement motif of vocational education and the credit-driven and credential-oriented courses that extension divisions offered for schoolteachers. So far from identifying with the kind of self-improvement represented by culture-study in women's clubs and Chautauqua, they shared the complaint of *Main Street*'s Carol Kennicott that the members of Thanatopsis, the women's study club in Gopher Prairie, ignored most of "the really stirring ideas that are springing up today."[75] Indeed they engaged in a virtual Kulturkampf against Chautauqua, which in their minds was less a place or even a movement than an image that evoked prudery, Puritanism, Bryan, and Fundamentalism. In 1922 Robert M. Lovett derided Chautauqua as an example of the American "superstitious faith in education." Better that our fathers had died, he averred, "their intellectual thirst unsatisfied, than that they had left this legacy of mental soft drinks for their children."[76] Even old-fashioned customs like reading aloud, Robert Molloy wrote in 1930, appall "our modern intelligentsia," who "are afraid to do anything similar to the Middletown Ladies Club."[77]

The task that New School intellectuals and, more broadly, the 1920s intelligentsia confronted was to establish ties to a public that they viewed with a strange mixture of bemusement, distrust, contempt, and expectation. Rejecting the traditional manifestations of popular cultural striving, they looked for new ones. The success enjoyed by popularizers like Wells and Durant suggested that a portion of the public was ready for the message of intellectuals, but the outline of this emerging public was still indistinct. Although the middle-class quest for culture was changing in the 1920s, it still had too many associations with women and Chautauqua to satisfy the New School intellectuals, who saw the developing movement for workers' education as an especially promising vehicle for extending their influence.[78] In 1926 Lindeman described workers' education as "already the most vital sector of the adult-education movement."[79] Yet workers' education and the free-lance intellectuals attracted to it from the New School sprang from different sources and would soon evolve in different directions.

Workers' Education

Most of the intellectuals connected in the 1920s with the New School leaned to the political left, but prior to 1919 only Charles A. Beard had envisioned the education of workers as a mainstay of popular education beyond the schools. After graduating from DePauw University in 1898, Beard studied at Oxford, and with the aid of another American, Walter Vrooman, founded Ruskin Hall as a workers' college at Oxford. But when Beard returned to America in 1902 to take up graduate study at Columbia, he temporarily put agitation and reform behind him.[80]

That Beard did not even consider establishing an American equivalent to Ruskin Hall testifies to the difficulty Americans had identifying worthwhile missions for labor colleges in the United States. In Britain Beard had been aroused not only by the writings of John Ruskin but by Keir Hardie's efforts to convert trade unions to the idea of a Labour Party. Beard and Vrooman saw Ruskin Hall as a place to prepare working-class elites for the new responsibilities that would accompany labor's growing political power.[81] To most Americans, the prospect of workers gaining political power seemed sufficiently remote in the early 1900s to discourage many organized efforts at labor education. The interest of university professors like Herbert Baxter Adams and Richard T. Ely in addressing workingmen through university extension had evaporated by the mid-1890s. After 1900 most extension lecturers defined their target as the public rather than workers. Under the leadership of Samuel Gompers, the American Federation of Labor evinced little interest in workers' education before 1900 and remained wedded to the view, well-entrenched even before the Civil War, that the public schools and the ballot box sufficiently provided for the intellectual and political enfranchisement of the American worker. Gompers's well-publicized hostility to intellectuals in the union movement rested on his belief that socialism, anarchism, and other ideologies threatened to subordinate trade unionism to abstract and doomed causes.

Here and there, the AFL sanctioned modest gestures toward workers' education. In 1902 it established an educational department, and in 1914 it endorsed the Training School for Women Organizers, established by the Women's Trade Union League.[82] But neither of these actions marked a significant change of Gompers's views. He endorsed workers' education only to ensure a directing role for the AFL; his support for the Training School for Women Organizers reflected the fact that the latter's goal, stated in its title, was his own. Any form of workers' education beyond the public schools could justify itself only to the extent that it turned workers into better unionists.

Socialism proved a far more receptive environment for the idea of advanced education for workers than had Gompers's pure and simple unionism. Eugene V. Debs, the perennial standard-bearer of the Socialist party and himself an autodidact, frequently portrayed socialism as a school in its own right. Debs liked to claim that he ran for president not to win but "to teach social consciousness."[83] Debs did not translate his general sympathy for advanced education into any specific labor college, but Jewish immigrants in the needle trades blended socialism, education, and union activism. In some instances, immigrant self-improvement societies gave rise to unions; in others, unions in the needle trades supported educational clubs.[84] In 1890, for example, a cloakmakers' union in New York City founded the Cloakmakers Educational Club, which propagated socialism and taught its members to read and write English.[85] In these early enterprises, the line between unionism and socialism tended to blur. Viewing unions as convenient and promising sources of recruits to their cause, socialists equated workers' education with the introduction of union members to the writings of Marx, Bakunin, and Darwin, while union activists saw socialist-dominated education clubs as an opportunity to sign up dues-paying members.[86] Jewish workers in the needle trades also provided a disproportionate number of the students at the avowedly socialist Rand School for Social Science, which opened in 1906 on the basis of a trust fund established by Mrs. Carrie Rand and her daughter Carrie Rand Herron, the second wife of the radical social gospeler George Herron.

Located in New York City, the Rand School attracted a lively faculty that included Scott Nearing, a learned and cosmopolitan socialist whose lectures Will and Ariel Durant frequently attended in the early 1920s. But at its inception in 1906, the Rand School was something of an anomaly, for it was the only institution of any note established between the collapse of the early university extension movement and World War I to offer advanced education specifically to the working class. As late as 1914, the cause of organized workers' education aroused hostility from the AFL and only mild interest among socialists. This would soon change.

Widespread interest among trade unions in workers' education developed during World War I in response to a variety of factors. Not surprisingly, the International Ladies Garment Workers' Union (ILGWU) led the way. Two well-publicized strikes by garment workers in New York City, known in union lore as the "uprising of the twenty thousand" in 1909 and the "great revolt of 1910," resulted in the so-called Protocol of Peace, a collective bargaining agreement between labor and management in the needle trades. The Protocol and the tragic fire at the Triangle Shirtwaist Company in 1911, in which 146 workers (most of them female) perished, spurred the growth of the ILGWU from 66,000 members in 1911 to around 90,000 by 1914 and aroused concern within the "International" about the lack of understanding of collective bargaining on the part of the new members, mainly women with little experience in union activity.[87]

At the same time fissures between moderates and radicals within the ILGWU's leadership, widened by disagreements over the best way to enforce the protocol, intensified the interest of moderates in education. The ILGWU's 1914 convention resolved "to dwell particularly upon the more solid and preparatory work of education and not to devote much time to the mere superficial forms of agitation and propaganda."[88] As part of this accent on education for good unionism, the ILGWU reached an agreement in the winter of 1917–18 with the New York City Board of Education whereby four "Unity Centres" and a "Workers' University" were established in several of the city's public schools.

The ILGWU's educational program evidenced the diverse goals that the union attached to education: to encourage intellectual and spiritual self-improvement, to keep female workers interested in their union, and to train leaders of both sexes for their duties as union officers. The Unity Centres offered instruction in English, hygiene, economics, history, applied psychology, and music appreciation and sponsored dances and excursions, while the harder-core Workers' University centered its courses on labor problems, industrial economics, and American government and history.[89]

The ILGWU's leadership sought to sever workers' education from socialist "propaganda," but socialists continued to gravitate to education as a way to enhance their influence in union affairs. Fannia Cohn, who had a history of radical affiliations in her native Russia before her emigration to the United States in 1904, became the executive director of the ILGWU's educational department in 1918. Cohn viewed workers' education as a movement "for special education in subjects which will enable the workers to accomplish their special job, which is to change economic and social conditions so that those who produce shall own the product of their labor."[90] Socialists continued to occupy high positions in the ILGWU; Morris Hillquit, one of the founders of the Socialist Party of America, served as the International's general counsel from 1913 until his death in 1933.

The ILGWU's provisions for education spurred a few imitations during the war. The Amalgamated Clothing Workers of America, formed in 1914 by a secession from the ILGWU and the AFL, established labor colleges in Rochester and Baltimore in 1918. But these institutions merely reinforced the already evident association between predominantly Jewish garment workers and education. Then, in the three years following the Armistice, the cause of workers' education began to surge beyond the perimeters of the needle trades. The year 1921 witnessed the opening of the Bryn Mawr Summer School for Women Workers, the Boston Trade Union College, and the Brookwood Labor College in Katonah, New York. In the same year the University of California organized its first extension classes for workers, and a year earlier Amherst College drafted a plan for classes for laborers. In 1925 the University of Wisconsin launched a summer school for women workers, largely in imitation of Bryn Mawr's school. During the early 1920s periodicals like the *Nation*, the *New Republic*, and the *Survey* eagerly followed the movement, which also attracted the attention of mainstream education journals like *School and Society* and the *Educational Review*.[91]

Several, often conflicting, impulses shaped this burst of educational activity. In 1919, President M. Carey Thomas of Bryn Mawr rejoiced at the recent enfranchisement of British women, realized "that American women would soon be politically free," and contemplated "the next great social advance." That advance, it seemed to Thomas, would bring equal opportunity to the manual workers of the world, and "I realized that the first steps on the path to the sunrise might well be taken by college women who, themselves just emerging from the wilderness, know best of all as women living under fortunate conditions what it means to be denied access to things of the intellect and spirit."[92] Comparably idealistic motives also influenced the establishment of the Boston Trade Union College. "It was a lofty and religious time," Horace Kallen recollected: "Almost, as I think of some of the early conferences which the young professors from Harvard and Wellesley and Tufts, who had contributed to the making of the Boston Trade Union College, held in the house where Henry Wadsworth Longfellow wrote 'The Village Blacksmith,' I recapture something of the exalted mood of service in which the Boston enterprise was launched."[93]

Kallen's description, evoking an image of earnest scholars eager to reach downtrodden workers, reminds one of the Johns Hopkins "apostles" whom Herbert Baxter Adams led into working-class neighborhoods in Baltimore in the late 1880s. The faculty of the Boston Trade Union College featured several leading scholars, including Roscoe Pound, Frank Taussig, and Felix Frankfurter of Harvard, as well as Henry Wadsworth Longfellow Dana (Cattell's co-victim in the Columbia Purge of 1917) of Amherst. University professors would continue to contribute to workers' education in the years between 1920 and World War II, but at no point did they dominate the movement. In addition, they often blurred the line between workers' education and the burgeoning field of industrial relations.[94]

The striking feature of workers' education after World War I was not the interest of university professors but the growing prominence of trade unions. For example, unions in Boston picked the faculty of that city's trade union college. Similarly, the government of the Bryn Mawr Summer School rested with a joint administrative committee, which was composed of representatives of the college, alumnae, and women workers. The first committee contained eight representatives of the college and an equal number of representatives of women workers. Among the latter were such union activists as Rose Schneiderman, vice president of the Women's Trade Union League and a former ILGWU organizer, and Agnes Nestor, vice president of the International Glove Workers' Union and president of the Womens' Trade Union League.[95]

During the 1920s the balance on the joint administrative committee between representatives of the college and those of labor shifted in favor of the latter, who gained the right to elect the college's representatives. In 1928 the Bryn Mawr Summer School became part of a venture known as the Affiliated School for Workers, which included summer schools for workers launched in the 1920s by the University of Wisconsin and Barnard College. Partly in response to the directors' recognition that it had become "increasingly difficult to be loyal to two such different institutions as an academic college and the labor movement," the school severed its ties with Bryn Mawr in 1938 and moved to New York state, where it became the Hudson Shore Labor School.[96] The same trend affected the University of Wisconsin's Summer School for Women Workers. The school's founder, Alice Corl, described her goals in terms that harmonized with middle-class educational ideals: "greater culture," "hunger to live more abundantly," and an "expanded outlook on life." Organized labor, which played a role in planning the school, gradually came to dominate it, and by the 1930s most of the students were trade unionists who viewed the institution as a way to advance specific union objectives.[97]

While the trend between 1920 and 1940 was toward union domination of workers' education, this general tendency contained several conflicting currents. In the early 1920s trade unionists did not present a united front on the purpose or scope of workers' education. On one side, Gompers and the AFL leadership approached the movement with a mixture of suspicion and tactical accommodation. On the other, radical unionists, often socialists, saw education as a way to advance "social reconstruction," industrial unionism, and other leftist causes.

Conservatives and radicals within the trade-union movement greeted the 1920s with fundamentally different assessments of existing educational institutions. Whereas Gompers continued to view the public schools as the foundation of workers' education, radicals were gripped increasingly by dismay at nearly all established forms of education. For James Maurer, a veteran of the Knights of Labor and the Populist movement who became an ardent socialist and head of the Pennsylvania Federation of Trades, public education had fallen into the hands of flag-waving super-patriots. Maurer related how the same schools that eagerly invited representatives of the American Legion to address students routinely shunned labor spokesmen. Even the arithmetic texts used in schools subtly revealed the hand of conservative, anti-union interests. Students asked to calculate the profit percentage of an employer who sold a pair of shoes for $5.25 while paying the shoemaker $5 received a mixture of misinformation and bias, for an individual shoemaker no longer made an entire shoe and employers certainly expected more than a 5 percent return on their investment. "From the time of the first preparedness parade to the present," Maurer concluded in 1922, "there have been outrages committed on our rights."[98] The publication of Upton Sinclair's *The Goose-Step* and *The Goslings* popularized labor's indictment of American education. Sinclair portrayed universities from the Ivy League to midwestern cow colleges as ensnared by hyperthyroid patriots, business interests, and pious Protestants, all bent on suppressing Bolshevism. His depiction of public elementary and secondary education was no less gloomy: "It is the thesis of the business men who run our education system that the schools are factories, and the children raw material, to be turned out thoroughly standardized, of the same size and shape, like biscuits or sausages."[99]

For Sinclair and for the intellectuals associated with the New School for Social Research, the anti-union tendencies of the public schools were merely part of a tapestry of imposed conformity and the repression of dissent, while for Maurer and other radical trade unionists, the schools' anti-unionism was the paramount issue. As Maurer recognized, the anti-union mood arose during the war initially in response to labor's indifference and occasional hostility to preparedness. The war in general and preparedness in particular had split the American union movement. Gompers viewed support for the war as labor's price for its continued expansion; in fact, the AFL nearly doubled its membership between 1916 and 1920. But Gompers's ardent pro-war stand antagonized trade unionists like Maurer and Hillquit, who had socialist and anti-war allegiances. By the war's end, Gompers was also under attack from non-socialists within the AFL, less because of his stand on the war than because of his opposition to industrial unionism, health insurance, and unemployment insurance. Gompers's conservatism at a time of growing militancy within his federation jeopardized his grip of the AFL. In 1921 John L. Lewis of the United Mine Workers became the first candidate in nearly 30 years to make a serious run against Gompers for the federation's presidency.[100]

In sum, workers' education arose not only in response to flag-waving patriots in the schools but also within the context of unprecedented challenges to the conservative leadership of the AFL. The controversies that divided the AFL and that embroiled its relations with the political left between 1918 and 1921 both stimulated the movement for workers' education and turned it into a battleground between rival factions. In 1922 Matthew Woll, vice president of the AFL, told a conference on workers' education that trade unionism itself was a school superior to any college, an utterance that seemed to negate the need for labor colleges.[101] Yet at the same time the AFL, so far from ignoring formal workers' education, was trying to take it over. The Workers' Education Bureau of America (WEB) provides a case in point. Established in 1921 by a mixture of conservative AFL unionists, more radical unionists associated with the Amalgamated Clothing Workers, socialists, liberal reformers, and AFL radicals (including Maurer and Fannia Cohn), the WEB was to serve as a clearinghouse for information about the movement, a laboratory for textbooks used in labor colleges, and a registry for teachers. In 1922 the AFL successfully restricted membership in the WEB to its own affiliates and to those of the four railroad brotherhoods. In their hearts Gompers and Woll probably hoped that the entire movement would evaporate, but while it lasted, they seemed determined to keep an eye on it. In his introduction to the published proceedings of the first National Conference on Workers' Education, sponsored by the WEB and convened in 1921 at the New School for Social Research, Gompers advanced six recommendations to the conference, five of which pertained to textbooks used in labor colleges. For his part, Woll in the mid-1920s would lead an AFL-sponsored investigation of left-wing infiltration of the Brookwood Labor College.[102]

Whereas Gompers and Woll infiltrated workers' education to disarm the movement of its radical potential, socialists had higher expectations. Ironically, at the very time that the Socialist party was breaking up, a number of socialists were persuading themselves that the workers were gaining power and that a crisis between capital and labor would occur within their generation or the next. Most American socialists had greeted the Russian Revolution with enthusiasm, and even after the secession of leftists from the Socialist party in 1919, socialists continued to invoke the "splendid example set by our comrades in Russia."[103] Socialists were also inspired by the example of the British Labour Party, whose gradualist tactics and keen interest in workers' education seemed well suited to American conditions. Even when most American socialists turned against the Bolsheviks in the mid-1920s, several socialist leaders, including Maurer and Norman Thomas, continued to defend the Russians.[104] In sum, a number of prominent socialists in the 1920s thought that the working classes of the world were approaching the successful conclusion of their long struggle for power and that workers' education could serve as the midwife of the workers' age.

Try as he might to keep workers' education under the AFL's aegis, Gompers faced an uphill struggle. Indeed workers' education was a loose cannon on the deck of the labor movement, a cause into which sundry intellectual factions that were either associated with or sympathetic to labor could read whatever goals they chose. J. B. Salutsky of the Amalgamated Clothing Workers of America talked of educating "thinking proletarians"; John Brophy of the United Mine Workers hoped to educate workers to understand the need for nationalizing the railroads; Norman Thomas saw education as a way to radicalize labor by teaching workers that the minerals of the earth belonged to everyone and not just to the coal operators; Gompers and Woll envisioned more instruction in pure and simple unionism; and a sizable faction within the movement, including the sponsors of the Bryn Mawr Summer School for Women Workers, espoused the liberal education of workers as an end in itself.[105]

These differences in the conception of labor education's goals had the potential to tear apart the movement, but in the early 1920s workers' education maintained a semblance of unity, in part because its different wings did not conflict sharply over the issue of curriculum. While love of learning for its own sake scarcely permeated the American working class, it did influence the Jewish garment workers, whom a contemporary called the "Jewish backbone" of labor colleges.[106] The same Jewish workers who enrolled in courses in music appreciation and literature also evinced an interest in social science as part of their quest for an understanding of labor's predicament. "Culture" and "burning issues," in other words, did not conflict in the labor curriculum. Most worker-students at labor colleges subscribed to culture as a valuable goal that did not clash with more radical objectives.

The experience of the Bryn Mawr Summer School illustrates the point. Few of its early students were academically prepared for higher education. The vast majority had not gone beyond the eighth grade, and a steadily rising proportion were foreign-born.[107] Instructors who distributed long reading lists quickly found that the students became discouraged and did none of the reading. Unaccustomed to listening to lectures, students let their attention wander in class. In response the faculty scaled down assignments to three or four pages a week per subject and introduced discussions and visual aids. The results were gratifying and even electrifying. The students themselves demanded a course on music appreciation and found ways to relate academic subjects to their experience. They viewed psychology as a way to interpret their personal problems and praised economics for teaching them the relation between their jobs and society. Students frequently made connections that startled their instructors. Introduced in a science class to the concept of evolution, one student commented that "it just shows you can afford to wait," for "what's the labor movement to a hundred thousand years?"[108] One of the school's instructors described the students' conviction that "education was a process by which one gained almost secret and mysterious power to accomplish one's will in the world."[109]

This breadth of interest on the part of worker-students helped to harmonize workers' education with the objectives of the New School intellectuals. Robinson's *The Humanizing of Knowledge* was published in a series entitled the Workers' Bookshelf. The series' editorial board included Fannia Cohn, Matthew Woll, and WEB director Spencer Miller, Jr., as well as Beard and John R. Commons. Nor did the AFL, which by 1923 controlled the WEB, oppose the mixture of literature and social science that marked the curricula of workers' colleges. In 1925, for example, the WEB recommended a labor curriculum that included history, economics, psychology, public speaking, sociology, literature, English, and health—all subjects that had formed the curriculum of the ILGWU's Workers' University.[110] The social sciences, especially when taught from a labor perspective (as the WEB recommended), had considerable potential to radicalize workers, but this potential does not appear to have disturbed Gompers and Woll. As long as the AFL dominated the WEB and could keep labor colleges from meddling in union policies, Gompers and Woll were curiously indifferent to the content of workers' education.

The institution that ultimately would shatter the AFL's assumption that it had domesticated labor education was the Brookwood Labor College. At the end of World War I, two pacifists, William and Helen Fincke, started a preparatory school near Katonah, New York, and in 1921 converted the school into a college for working adults. Several factors contributed to Brookwood's unique position among labor colleges. Although the AFL provided it with a subsidy and with most of its students, Brookwood had no formal affiliation with the AFL; indeed it was the only postwar labor college unaffiliated with a union, college, or university. Brookwood's distinctiveness also owed a great deal to A. J. Muste, its director from 1921 to 1933. Born in the Netherlands in 1885, Muste came to the United States in 1891, became a Dutch Reformed and later a Congregationalist minister, and embraced pacifism. Muste's admiration for Eugene V. Debs led him to socialism, but it was his participation in the 1919 strike of textile workers in Lawrence, Massachusetts, that radicalized Muste. Joining the picket lines and enduring a beating and a jailing (for "disturbing the peace"), Muste increasingly grew critical of the AFL, whose affiliate, the United Textile Workers, denounced the Lawrence strike. In the wake of the strike, Muste served as the general secretary of the newly formed and militant Amalgamated Textile Workers (ATW), familiarized himself with the ATW's experimental workers' classes in Passaic, New Jersey, and shortly before the ATW's collapse, accepted an invitation to head Brookwood.[111]

Muste's varied experiences and allegiances made it relatively easy for him to address diverse constituencies: liberal intellectuals, socialists, and radical unionists. In the early 1920s, Brookwood secured the endorsement of Progressive educators (led by Dewey), pro-labor social scientists, and union radicals like Maurer and Brophy. Curiously, the school's early relations with the AFL were not marked by open antagonism. In 1924 Muste, who was not without a devious streak, respectfully observed the deaths of both Gompers and Lenin and a year later that of Debs.[112] For its part, the AFL left Brookwood alone in the early 1920s, partly because Brookwood lacked formal trade-union affiliation and partly because the AFL's control of the WEB made Gompers and Woll complacent about their ability to check subversive tendencies in workers' education.[113]

The honeymoon was brief, for in 1926 William Green, Gompers' successor, started an inquiry into the politics of Arthur Calhoun, the social historian who was Brookwood's resident Marxist. In 1928 the AFL's annual convention adopted a report of an investigating committee, chaired by Woll, that sharply criticized communist influence at Brookwood and called for the withdrawal of financial support for the college by all AFL affiliates. A year later AFL partisans dissolved Brookwood's membership in the WEB and vacated Muste's position on the WEB's executive committee. At the same time, Muste found himself embroiled in controversy within his school. At issue was whether the college should hold firm in its commitment to education or, as Muste preferred by the early 1930s, devote itself to training strike organizers. By 1933, when Muste resigned from the school under fire for his activism, Brookwood was in the throes of a financial crisis and suffering from declining enrollments that would force the institution's closing in 1937.[114]

The eruptions at Brookwood reinforced the AFL's distrust of independent ventures in workers' education and led it to a renewed emphasis on education for good unionism. The onset of the Depression intensified the stress on education for unionism. While the ILGWU and the Amalgamated Clothing Workers continued to espouse "social reconstruction" as a legitimate goal of workers' education, the new industrial unions that arose in the 1930s primarily envisioned education as a way to train union staffers. "The goal of assimilating raw recruits," Florence Schneider noted in 1941, "has made education in the new groups almost entirely pragmatic."[115] For example, the educational department of the United Automobile Workers (UAW) emphasized "training for trade union service" in order to obtain "a sufficient proportion of the membership to man the organization, take care of the interests of the men in the shops, and protect contractual relations with the employers."[116] Even the collegiate experiments like the Bryn Mawr Summer School felt the pressure. From a roughly equal division between union and non-union students in its early days, the school's student body was two-thirds unionized in 1934 and 84 percent unionized by 1938.[117] In two parallel and related trends, the students increasingly were union activists—in 1937 more than half of the trade unionists admitted to the school held office within their organizations—and were drawn from industrial rather than craft unions.[118]

It would be unfair to fault Lindeman and other New School intellectuals, who in the early 1920s pinned their hopes on workers' education as a vehicle for disseminating the "electric fire" of thought, for failing to predict the direction that workers' education would take in the 1930s. Yet even in the mid-1920s some warning signals could be detected, and these prompted Alvin Johnson, the most (and perhaps the only) hardheaded figure associated with the New School, to caution that unions, having little use for intellectuals, would quickly set them to licking stamps.[119] Had other New School intellectuals followed the dynamics within unionism and socialism that generated workers' education, they would have recognized that few of those drawn to the movement shared their objective of making the public more critical and open-minded. Instead, most New School intellectuals treated workers' education as a kind of epiphany.

While publicizing workers' education, the New School intellectuals played only a minor role in it and did not even follow it closely. In contrast, their quest for purely voluntary forms of education led them to an almost unrestrained enthusiasm for the so-called folk schools.

Folk Schools

References to these schools abound in the literature of the adult-education movement during the 1920s. Lindeman began *The Meaning of Adult Education* with an account of his discovery of them on a visit to his father's homeland in 1920. In Denmark he found a "cultural oasis," a nation both free of the catastrophic nationalism that had wrecked Europe and sustained by its folk high schools. The indefatigable Progressive author Joseph Kinmont Hart, also a lecturer at the New School, described them as "the light from the North."[120] But the most influential account was that of Frederic C. Howe, a forceful spokesman for the small-is-better side of Progressivism. The spirit of Henry George and of Cleveland's reform mayor Tom Johnson infused Howe, and almost everything about Denmark appealed to him. The opening words of *Denmark: A Cooperative Commonwealth* were "Denmark is a little country," but its subtitle identified its real appeal for Howe. The cooperatives, in which farmers joined together to control their own marketing and banking and to produce and buy everything from chocolate to cigars, were the basis of Danish agriculture. Economic cooperatives laid the basis for other types of cooperation. Widely diffused land ownership made this "team play" possible, but Howe thought that the real explanation for Denmark's success lay in education, especially in the folk high schools.[121]

The folk high schools had been inspired by a nineteenth-century Lutheran bishop, N. F. S. Grundtvig. Grundtvig was a romantic Danish nationalist who, in the wake of Denmark's loss of Schleswig-Holstein to Prussia, wanted schools to emphasize the Danish language and lore in order to instill patriotism in those bound for the professions or bureaucracy. This national outlook would be acquired by mingling with the folk. What emerged from Grundtvig's influence and from other forces were schools for young adults aged 18 to 30 that made little use of textbooks or examinations and emphasized instead instruction by the spoken word. Although many of these folk schools were supported by the state, they lacked a standard curriculum. Some taught cultural subjects such as literature and history, others emphasized horticulture and agriculture, and many mixed the two. For Howe the great appeal of these schools was their control by farmers. They were devices by which a farm population could teach itself whatever it wanted, without meddling by an alien, urban bureaucracy. Teachers depended not on credentials but on charisma; students attended by choice during the slack season. "Accustomed as we are to political supervision of education and inflexible standards of what shall be taught and what the pupil shall know at the completion of each grade, the freedom of these schools seems quite incomprehensible," Howe wrote.[122]

In the United States, Danish-Americans established a scattering of folk high schools, mainly to resist assimilation, but the folk high schools principally appealed to Progressives like Hart and Howe, who saw them as ways to unify educational and economic experiences.[123] Although they were described in a United States Bureau of Education bulletin as early as 1914, it was not accidental that interest in them swelled during the 1920s among intellectuals who were equally disillusioned by the narrow vocationalism of the Smith-Hughes Act and by the preoccupation of the Agricultural Extension Service (established by the Smith-Lever Act) with raising farm production. At a time when the Scopes trial seemed to puncture the expectation that teaching farmers better ways to grow crops would turn them into rationalists, former Country Life Progressives were despairing at the Extension Service's subordination of cultural values to more efficient production.[124]

Even the most ardent admirers of Danish folk schools recognized the difficulty of transplanting them to America. The 1920s did witness several experiments modeled on the Danish schools, including the Poconos People's College near Henryville, Pennsylvania, the Waddington People's College at Wheeling, West Virginia, a school in Ashland, Michigan, and the Highlander Folk School in Monteagle, Tennessee. There were direct links between the founders of these schools and the Danish schools. Hart, for example, was associated with the Ashland school. Lindeman lectured at the Pocono People's College. The latter's founder, S. A. Mathiasen, visited Denmark before establishing his own folk school. Donald West, one of the founders of Highlander, visited Denmark in 1931. But it was impossible to transport to America some basic features of the Danish schools. American educators attracted to Danish models had no interest in Danish nationalism and no desire in the wake of the Red Scare to promote American nationalism. Nor were they really interested in farmers' cooperatives, a cause that had attracted support from agrarian radicals in the late nineteenth century and later from Progressives but which by the 1920s seemed too closely tied to the interests of large, commercial farmers to attract much enthusiasm from reformers.

Aside from their promise to blend culture and work, the most attractive aspect of the Danish schools to Americans was their informality; their absence of credits, academic subjects, and examinations; and their direct appeal to the interests of students. The Ashland school, for example, was aimed at young workers over age eighteen "who are seriously trying to find themselves and the meaning of life."[125] A contemporary described Mathiasen's goal as "the humanizing of knowledge for ordinary folk."[126] Although describing itself as a college, the Pocono school was not a college in any ordinary sense. Most students were between the ages of 20 and 25. In line with its efforts to translate knowledge into non-scholastic terms, the school featured informal lectures and conversations rather than formal classroom study. "Students' suggestions are sought and generally followed. . . . The lecturer himself is subject to interruption and challenge at any time."[127] A typical class included a migratory worker who had been a Wobbly and was now a communist, a young woman with a master's degree and a vague leaning toward social service, a Jewish office worker with a passion for learning, a Catholic woman of 30 with a recently acquired interest in ideas, a shop mechanic from a Pennsylvania industrial town, and some young men and women from farm villages. The topic was "escape," and the students clashed over whether religion and communism were merely escapes. Not surprisingly, "the debate extends far over the hour and finally adjourns inconclusively."[128]

The Pocono People's College obviously embodied the goal of Lindeman and other New School intellectuals of using adult education as a way to inculcate critical thinking. While it drew on Dewey's idea that learning had to be integrated with experience, the experiences were essentially private rather than public. Its ideal was to produce students who could give a rational account of why they held their beliefs. Almost by definition, it was not trying to construct a movement, and its structure virtually guaranteed that it would be small. Although located in a rural area, it had no economic program to offer farmers; it was, indeed, antithetical to programs and ideologies. While Pocono aimed at working adults, it was a day school with three-month sessions. The antebellum academies had been able to attract farm youth during the slack season, but few working young men and women in the twentieth century could take three months off from a job. Even by the standards of experimental schools it had trouble attracting students. A contemporary reported that its largest single enrollment in a three-month session was sixteen full-time students.[129]

The most celebrated and durable of the folk schools, the Highlander Folk School in Monteagle, Tennessee, pursued a different strategy. Founded in 1932 by Myles Horton and Donald West, Highlander became active first in the labor movement and later in civil rights. Before the revocation of its charter in 1961 by the state of Tennessee (for alleged communist influence), it served as a magnet for southern radicals. It offered courses for union officials, helped to organize and support strikers, and directly attacked the southern caste system. Revived and renamed the Highlander Education and Research Center, it plunged into programs to benefit the poor of Appalachia in the late 1960s.

Both Horton and West were born in Tennessee in 1905 and each had graduated from Cumberland University. Horton then spent a year privately reading the works of William James and John Dewey and fell under the influence of Eduard C. Lindeman. After advanced study at Vanderbilt, the University of Chicago, and the Union Theological Seminary, where Reinhold Niebuhr introduced him to a radical strain of social Christianity, West visited Denmark to study its folk schools.[130]

Although Highlander was founded explicitly as a folk school rather than as a workers' college, its early history revealed the limitations of folk schools in the American setting. Fearing that Highlander would become just another short-lived utopian venture, Horton hoped that the school would sink enduring roots in the neighborhood around Monteagle, and its staff encouraged dances and songfests for the surrounding community. Zilphia Johnson, who married Horton in 1935 and who is credited with teaching "We Shall Overcome" (Highlander's theme song) to Pete Seeger, directed the school's musical activities. But the school's folk festivals were awkward and unsuccessful, and both West and Myles Horton encouraged broader contacts with the labor movement. A generation younger than Lindeman and coming on the scene in the early years of the Depression, each man saw education as a way to accelerate the transfer of power to workers rather than to merely prepare them for the ultimate assumption of power. Highlander's economics courses, for example, took their material directly from strikes rather than textbooks. During the 1930s the school's staff—which included Elizabeth Hawes, a Vassar College and Brookwood alumna who became a southern organizer for the Amalgamated Clothing Workers, and James Dombrowski, a former graduate assistant to Niebuhr—directly supported strikes by southern textile workers by mailing out strike materials and by traveling back and forth between the school and strike locations.[131]

As Highlander became better known, it attracted a growing number of activists in the movement for industrial unionism and, after the founding in 1935 of the Congress of Industrial Organizations (CIO), Highlander began to sponsor workshops for individual unions that wanted their members to learn such concrete skills as how to mediate grievances from the rank and file, make posters, and use parliamentary procedures.[132] Myles Horton, however, never fully reconciled himself to the idea of Highlander as a school for CIO organizers. In the early 1950s he became the educational director of the United Packing House Workers of America in the hope of encouraging broader educational interests among the rank and file, but he soon resigned in despair. By then the CIO had severed its ties with Highlander on grounds of the school's alleged communist influence.[133]

Highlander's history illustrates the comparative advantage of workers' schools over folk schools, for the workers' schools could replenish their student bodies from the ranks of union activists. Yet Highlander, Brookwood, and the Bryn Mawr Summer School all paid a price for their growing identification with activism. In their early days, these institutions had acted as incubators for "enthusiasts and missionaries" in the labor movement.[134] The broad conception of workers' education shared by the founders of these schools could accommodate advocacy of industrial unionism, especially when industrial unionism was little more than an alluring image on the labor horizon. Some tension existed from the start between workers' education and the emerging adult-education movement. The WEB declined to affiliate with the AAAE, partly because of the latter's taint by Carnegie money. But AAAE leaders like Lindeman and Martin viewed workers' education as a promising form of adult education in the 1920s, while the curricula of the residential labor colleges addressed many of the "burning issues" that preoccupied New School intellectuals. As industrial unionism became a reality in the 1930s, it contributed to the constriction of workers' education by engendering a preoccupation with training union officials. By the mid-1930s the movements for adult education and workers' education were far apart.

Hilda W. Smith, one of the few figures to bridge the workers' education movement in the 1920s and 1930s, reluctantly recognized this tendency. After serving for over a decade as director of the Bryn Mawr Summer School, Smith became a specialist in workers' education under the Federal Emergency Relief Administration (FERA) in 1933. The forerunner of the Works Progress Administration (WPA), FERA put unemployed teachers to work in sundry adult education activities, including classes for workers. By November 1937, 3 percent of the students registered in WPA classes were enrolled in a workers' education program. Although a minor component of the WPA, workers' education remained controversial and federal officials tiptoed around the program. Smith kept searching for signs of cultural and philosophical vitality in the WPA's workers' program, but she conceded in 1935 that union officials had little interest in relating cultural expression to the economic lives of workers and were preoccupied by "the bread and butter struggle and the need for recognition of the union."[135]

If anything, Smith understated the opposition of union leaders to efforts to nudge workers' education away from bread-and-butter union issues. A 1939 study of the WPA educational program averred that "any attempt to subordinate the workers' education program to the adult education program as a whole is likely to result in the withdrawal of the cooperation of organized labor."[136] Part of this hostility to general adult education arose from the rivalry between the AFL and the CIO in the late 1930s, for each feared that the other would capture federal programs and turn them into propaganda forums for its philosophy. For the most part, unions preferred to conduct their own educational programs, which could easily be kept on a safe and narrow course. In addition, unions distrusted public-school officials, who in most states administered WPA educational appropriations. In the South, school officials subordinated workers' education to literacy programs and elsewhere turned it into a service for informing workers about new federal legislation affecting labor. As several critics noted, the distribution of information had little to do with education. In 1939 the WPA's workers' education program was removed from its Division of Education Projects and relocated in its Professional and Service Projects Division under the new title of the Workers' Service Project.[137]

Eager to debunk the popular mind and often contemptuous of old-fashioned institutions of popular education like Chautauqua, 1920s intellectuals fastened on labor and folk schools as part of their quest for relevance. But workers' education proved difficult to harness to the values of liberal intellectuals, who relished debate and open-mindedness as ends in themselves. Liberals defined the problem of their age as an excess of uncritical popular belief and tried to inculcate skeptical attitudes in the public. In contrast, trade unionists turned to workers' education either to radicalize the working class or to enhance its loyalty to unions, not to encourage suspended judgment for its own sake.

Although the divisions between liberal intellectuals and trade unionists ran deep, the former maintained a paternalistic interest in workers' education into the 1930s, partly because workers' education seemed such a fine illustration of the integration of learning and living and the devotion of knowledge to problem-solving. Nevertheless, the ties between liberals and unionists weakened steadily.

Conclusion

In retrospect, the intellectuals of the 1920s might be faulted for their criticism of the established non-profit institutions of adult education—

specifically university extension, the evening classes of the public schools, women's clubs, and Chautauqua. By pledging themselves to experimental and unorthodox institutions—the New School and the labor and folk colleges—intellectuals inevitably restricted their impact. Having defined the reconstruction of the popular mind as an urgent national problem, they then selected local and even eccentric means for addressing the problem. In reality, none of the established institutions of adult education held much promise of serving the objectives that intellectuals valued. Neither the service or vocational programs of university extension, nor the evening classes for adult immigrants, nor the genteel reformism of the women's clubs, nor the job improvement motif of the correspondence schools accorded with the agenda of intellectuals in the age of the Red Scare and the Scopes trial.

By distancing themselves from the established institutions of adult education, intellectuals also positioned themselves outside the popular quest for educational credentials. One of the problems with the word education, Beard declared in 1930, was that it connoted "grades, classes, subjects, points, credits, degrees," all objectionable as extrinsic forces that disturbed the purity of voluntary learning.[138] Their contempt for credentialing propelled intellectuals toward the instruction of those who already possessed as much formal education and as many degrees and credits as they desired. For example, in the 1919–24 period 80 percent of the students in the New School had attended college and 60 percent held college degrees. While these proportions dipped modestly between 1925 and 1930 (to 72 percent and 52 percent, respectively), the New School was basically an institution for the further education of the educated.[139] This was precisely the sort of institution that Beard and Robinson desired; their experiences at Columbia had persuaded them that elite institutions were failing to educate students who were academically prepared to learn.

In a somewhat different manner, the AAAE reinforced this emphasis on adult education for the educated. Frederick P. Keppel hoped to nudge adult education away from the preoccupation with job improvement and credentials that marked correspondence schools and university extension in the 1920s. At a time when the motto "Education Pays" seemed to have greater relevance than ever before, to reject the cash value of education was to dismiss the educational goal of much of the population.

Yet on balance intellectuals were more ambivalent than settled on the issue of democratizing education. They *did* want to democratize knowledge; their problem was that they could not accept established educational institutions as agents of democratization. One reason for the enthusiasm with which liberal intellectuals greeted workers' education lay in the latter's promise to tap a potentially large segment of the public that desired knowledge for its own sake. Events would quickly underscore the naivety of this view, but in the early 1920s it seemed plausible and necessary.

It is possible to detect in the 1920s the glimmerings of another way to link non-pecuniary educational values with adult education: the notion of education for some mixture of leisure and self-realization. A. J. Muste observed in 1926 that adults who attended classes or lectures were motivated not only by intellectual curiosity but by a quest for "emotional release, advice on personal problems, and inspiration to idealistic living."[140] In a similar view, Lindeman hinted in 1926 that adult education might justify itself if it did no more than help adults occupy their leisure. The onset of the Depression would afford abundant opportunities to test this view.

Chapter 11

The Art of Living

Most of the initiatives in adult education that began in the 1920s persisted into the 1930s, but with widely varying appeal. Gradually, the Depression created a climate more conducive to some forms of adult education than to others. In the course of the 1930s, adult education veered away from the attempts of New School intellectuals to make it an instrument for undermining conformity and intolerance. With the support of New Deal relief agencies, especially the Works Progress Administration, adult educators encouraged individuals to participate in community associations that mixed education, amateur artistic creativity, recreation, and sociability. In other words, adult education became more therapeutic and civic than intellectual and individual, a way to assist people to feel better about themselves and their communities rather than an instrument for encouraging social criticism. Indeed, in the 1930s many educators scaled down their expectations of the public's capacity for serious intellectual exchange and even for serious reading. Although these developments provoked despair among the acerbic social critics who had latched onto the movement in the 1920s, they encouraged others, including a growing number of public-school educators, who avowed that voluntary associations within residential communities would fulfill the expectations funneled in the preceding decade into folk schools.

The Discovery of Mediocrity

In the early years of the Great Depression, Americans crowded libraries and attended forums in order to understand the roots of the catastrophe. The Lynds noted that the per capita circulation of Middletown's public libraries doubled between 1929 and 1933.[1] In addition, forums for the discussion of public affairs proliferated in the early 1930s. In 1932 John W. Studebaker, school superintendent in Des Moines, Iowa, secured a grant from the Carnegie Corporation (administered through the AAAE) to finance an experimental program of forums, which were designed to encourage "open-mindedness" and "critical thinking."[2] In the first six months of their operation (January-July 1933), the Des Moines forums reported attendance of 48,000 (in a city of 144,000) at public discussions of the federal debt, tariffs, the New Deal, and the future of democracy. More than a score of towns from Daytona Beach to Loma Linda initiated forums modeled on the Des Moines experiment.

Especially in places without ingrained traditions of unionism, forums afforded convenient and apparently innocuous platforms for speakers with left-of-center views, "little nurseries of revolution" in the eyes of their detractors. Studebaker capitalized on the widening appeal of forums to gain appointment as United States Commissioner of Education in 1934.[3]

Despite popular patronage of forums and a variety of informal adult institutes throughout the 1930s, the intellectuals who in the 1920s had defined the broad philosophical goals for adult education that were represented by the humanizing of knowledge and by the labor and folk schools gradually lowered their expectations in the 1930s. At the same time, inspired by the manifest seriousness and intellectual questing of a widening segment of the public, public-school educators raised their expectations for adult education beyond its association with Americanization and rudimentary literacy. Increasingly, educators in the 1930s directed their attention to what George E. Vincent called in 1933 "the great masses of mediocre people."[4] "Having begun in America with the frankly remedial effort to give the immigrant a few words of English and a muddled but highly emotionalized 'Americanism,' " wrote Columbia's Lyman Bryson in 1933, "and leaping thence to the opposite pole and trying to dissolve the mental stasis of the privileged, we are now coming to realize that the greater problem lies in between."[5]

What might be called the discovery of mediocrity emerged only slowly in the field of adult education. Although by 1930 educators had acquired several decades of experience with teaching adults through university extension, most extension students in credit courses were either schoolteachers or college students with above-average educational attainment. In addition, the preoccupation in the early 1920s with debunking the popular mind of its prejudices and the great expectations that surrounded workers' education in the same period encouraged the assumption among intellectuals that most Americans had the capacity for intellectually sophisticated education and required only stimulation and guidance by scholars. In this context educators equated uneducated people with illiterates—mainly recent immigrants and southern mountaineers. While conceding that these people required special pedagogy, they made fairly complacent assumptions about the educability of the norm.

By the late 1920s this complacency was being corroded by several forces. The experience of educating workers in summer schools quickly pointed up the problem of teaching individuals who, while technically literate, were unaccustomed to getting either their ideas or information from books. The very fact that, despite their control by unions, the most notable labor colleges of the 1920s sprang up under collegiate auspices and were decidedly more academic than the workers' educational clubs of the 1880s and 1890s ensured that the deficiencies of their students would not escape educators. In addition, it gradually became clear that the shortcomings of students in labor colleges did not differ markedly from those of the public at large.

Evidence of the limited scholastic attainment of average Americans began to surface in World War I, when leading psychologists, notably Robert Yerkes and Lewis Terman, persuaded the army to administer newfangled intelligence tests to recruits. Much has been written about the biases of these tests and the racist conclusions that some social scientists drew from them. In reality, by the mid-1920s academicians and schoolmen alike were distancing themselves from some of the more extreme conclusions, including the notion that the average American had the intelligence of a thirteen-year-old. But one conclusion, stumbled upon almost accidentally, endured. Investigation of a representative sample of upwards of 80,000 recruits revealed that of every 1,000 native-born recruits who entered the first grade, only 490 persisted until the eighth grade, 230 entered high school, 95 graduated from high school, and a mere 10 graduated from college. Carl Brigham, a Princeton University psychologist who in 1923 reviewed the results of the intelligence tests, described these statistics as "startling," and indeed they did puncture prevailing assumptions.[6] The picture that emerged from this snapshot of the native-born population's educational attainment conflicted sharply with the optimistic assessment of attainment that most observers had drawn from decades of expanding school populations. The more children attended school, the wider the educational gap between the generations became. Sampling nearly 9,000 high-school students in 1930, Charles Judd found that only half of their parents had persisted beyond elementary school.[7] As Lyman Bryson was quick to observe, even this conclusion overstated the national levels of educational attainment.[8]

This growing recognition of the public's limited educational attainment coincided with several investigations into the reading habits of adults. In different ways, William S. Gray and Ruth Munroe's *The Reading Interests and Habits of Adults* (1929) and Louis R. Wilson's *The Geography of Reading* (1938) questioned whether the technical acquisition of literacy enfranchised Americans to read serious books. The Gray-Munroe study demonstrated the wide gap between the reading habits of urban and rural dwellers, men and women, farm owners and tenants, salesmen and manual workers, and high-school graduates and nongraduates. While most Americans read the newspapers, often they read only the sports pages and the funnies, and far fewer read books than newspapers.[9] In sum, the Gray-Munroe study underscored deep and possibly persistent gender, class, occupational, and educational correlatives of reading.

Wilson, a towering figure in the library profession who served as librarian of the University of North Carolina from 1901 to 1932 and then as dean of the University of Chicago's graduate school of library science, amassed data to reveal huge differences among and even within regions. For example, he devised a measure called "library development," a composite of the percent of the population in each state residing in local library districts, per capita expenditures on public libraries, per capita circulation of public libraries, and volumes per capita possessed by public libraries. Accounting for five of the six states heading the library development list, New England vastly outstripped the South (Alabama, Georgia, Mississippi, West Virginia, and Arkansas ranked forty-fourth through forty-eighth).[10] Wilson also underscored differences within states. In Illinois nearly all of the counties with low levels of library development were in the southern half of the state, the part originally settled by southerners.[11] Finally, Wilson identified a strong correlation between library development and such related measures as the distribution of Book-of-the-Month Club subscriptions, the circulation of national magazines and daily newspapers, the presence of women's clubs, the ownership of telephones and radios, the value of farm and manufactured products, and even per capita life-insurance policies. Wherever library resources were abundant, bookstores, magazines, newspapers, radios, movies, telephones, and school enrollments flourished.[12]

As a southerner born and educated in North Carolina, Wilson possessed a keen sensitivity to the role of culture (in the anthropological sense)—"attitudes and ideas" that conditioned what and how much people read. He acknowledged that even if one controlled for wealth and education, southerners had never been as accustomed as New Englanders to acquiring ideas and information from print. Had he pursued the argument, Wilson might have been led to the position, later advanced by W. Lloyd Warner and Paul S. Lunt, that "library development" itself reflected deeply seated cultural attitudes rather than mere mechanistic determinants like wealth and urbanization.[13] But as a professional librarian, he drew back from this conclusion, with its fatalistic implications about the prospects of overcoming regional differences, and predictably pleaded for more and better libraries. For their part, Gray and Munroe betrayed no significant doubts about the benefits to be gained from improved library administration and from school programs aimed at implanting the habit of reading early in life.

Yet while they steered away from cultural determinism, all of these investigators amassed evidence of the stark divisions that characterized the reading public. In a general way Americans long had known that educated people read more and better books than the uneducated and that some regions were better served by libraries than others. But it was only in the 1890s and early 1900s that studies of the users of libraries started to proliferate as an offshoot of the public-library movement. The Gray-Munroe bibliography listed 150 of these studies, many of them conducted by local librarians who canvassed their patrons. Similarly, Wilson's investigation of the "geography" of reading, which had circulated in manuscript for several years before its publication in 1938, synthesized numerous studies from the 1910s and 1920s. Financially supported by the AAAE and the American Library Association, these books helped to convince educators that despite generations of rhetoric about the triumph of universal education and the ever-expanding reading public, the United States was far from being an intellectual democracy.

In the 1930s this conclusion became intertwined with a sharpening awareness that most Americans lacked the reading skills to master serious books, even the supposedly popular books of the 1920s like Wells's *The Outline of History.* In 1935 the historian Percy W. Bidwell wondered whether such books were really popular: "Who reads them? Men and women who buy the 'quality magazines' and who patronize the little theaters. The mass of people never see them. And why? The style is not popular enough; such books can be read easily by only about ten percent of our adult population."[14] In the same year, William S. Gray and Bernice Leary published a major and widely cited study of the reading ability of 1,690 persons drawn from several selected subgroups: parent-teacher associations, adults in evening elementary schools, blacks (both teenagers and adults) studying in programs conducted by Florida Agricultural and Mechanical College, whites from the southern Appalachians, adults (mainly white) from villages and rural areas of Illinois, and black adults from northern cities.[15] As the authors acknowledged, the sample was defective in many ways. Since they were not testing children in school, they had to depend on volunteers, who may well have been among the abler readers within each group. Whatever the limitations of their study, their conclusion provided adult educators with some rules of thumb: only one-sixth of the adults tested were able to read with the degree of proficiency normally achieved by high-school graduates, and at least one-third had not "acquired sufficient skill to enable them to engage intelligently in adult reading activities."[16]

Gray and Leary devoted most of their study to identifying those structural elements of print that influenced reading ability as measured by the scores of the sample on different paragraphs. In other words, they pinpointed the paragraphs on which their subjects scored poorly and then analyzed them "for the occurrence of elements of expression that may bear some relation to difficulty."[17] In turn, they derived these elements of difficulty from the suggestions of adult-school directors, English teachers, and the growing body of professional studies of children's reading.[18] Among the variables that determined the ease or difficulty of reading were sentence length in words and syllables, the percentage of words that other tests had revealed were unknown by 90 percent of sixth-graders, and the number of infinitive and prepositional phrases. In ranking the variables, Gray and Leary simply correlated the score of their subjects on each section of the test with the frequency with which a specific variable appeared in that section. In this way the authors were able to establish criteria for predicting the ease or difficulty of any passage and, armed with their "predicted index of difficulty," they then analyzed 350 books in demand in bookshops and libraries.

There was a certain cruel irony in the result, for some of the so-called popular books of the 1920s and early 1930s that attempted to make complex ideas or events intelligible and exciting for the "average" reader fell into the most-difficult-to-read category. These included Robinson's *The Mind in the Making*, Frederick Lewis Allen's *Only Yesterday*, James Truslow Adams's *The Epic of America*, and Hendrik W. Van Loon's *The Story of Mankind*.[19] The net effect of these investigations of popular reading was to throw into question the assumption of 1920s' intellectuals that the principal failure of public education arose from its domination by superpatriots and reactionary capitalists who conspired to douse intellectual curiosity. From the perspective of the 1930s, the main limitation of public education sprang from the fact that many adults had persisted only through the early grades and consequently lacked the foundation to continue to educate themselves.

These investigations into the limitations of the public's reading ability provoked various reactions. In the early 1930s Lyman Bryson, who had entered adult education from the direction of newspaper work, experimented at Columbia University with rewriting books in simple language for those with limited education, and he then collaborated with Charles A. Beard and Morse Cartwright (of the AAAE) on the editorial board of the People's Library, published by Macmillan.[20] Gradually, however, Bryson made his way into a medium that did not depend even on simplifications of print: radio broadcasting. In 1938 he joined the Columbia Broadcasting System, becoming chair of its Adult Education Board and eventually director of its educational activities.

One program for which Bryson worked behind the scenes at CBS was "Invitation to Learning." First aired in 1940, "Invitation to Learning" was the most scholarly of several radio book programs of the late 1930s and 1940s; others included the National Broadcasting Company's "Swift Hour," hosted by Yale's William Lyon Phelps, and "Town Crier," hosted by Alexander Woollcott. Bryson averred in 1947 that the "ordinary fellow" who might not read difficult books could profit from hearing them discussed and explained. But which books? Woollcott made his mark by discussing recent books and their authors. In contrast, the inspiration for "Invitation to Learning" sprang from Stringfellow Barr, a colleague of Mortimer Adler's at the People's Institute in the 1920s and, with Scott Buchanan (another veteran of the People's Institute), the cofounder in 1937 of the "great books" curriculum at Annapolis's St. John's College. But radio book programs became popular to the extent that they subordinated textual analysis of classics to the personalities of their hosts. The evolution of "Invitation to Learning" after its first season, Joan S. Rubin has observed, "entailed a gradual acceptance, and even defense, of the program's potential to replace, rather than stimulate, reading 'great books.'"[21]

Such concessions to popular taste were nothing new. Chautauqua had demonstrated the possibility of mingling education for earnest autodidacts with light programming. Still, much had changed between the 1890s and 1930s. At Chautauqua, John H. Vincent had invoked essentially religious motives for secular study; knowledge of literature or science would lead to better understanding of divine works. In contrast, by the 1930s decades of political reform had established the primacy of social objectives for voluntary learning. In the decade of the Red Scare and Scopes trial, intellectuals had identified reform with the reconstruction of the popular mind, but amid the Depression their focus shifted to a model of reform through social engineering and central planning that constricted the role of the public. In 1933 George E. Vincent reflected on the conflicting emotions that he had experienced by virtue of his upbringing amid "the almost evangelical enthusiasm of education for everybody" at Chautauqua and his later career as a student at Yale and young faculty member at the University of Chicago. At Yale and Chicago he had encountered "the feeling of academic exclusiveness" and the attitude that the only important task of education was to identify the truly talented persons and give them the opportunity to learn. Confessing that his tendency to see both sides of the question had disturbed his peace of mind, Vincent wrestled with whether democracy necessarily meant offering advanced education to the multitude. He resolved the issue on the side of the multitude, but only by distancing himself from the evangelical fervor of his Chautauquan boyhood. All that popular education could accomplish, he averred, "is that we may develop enough sagacity in a sufficiently large number of our people to enable them to choose from among the well-educated superior persons representatives and specialists who can be trusted."[22]

Vincent was by no means alone in advocating popular education as an aid to the public's choice of experts. In their widely cited investigation, *Leisure: A Suburban Study*, the sociologists George A. Lundberg, Mirra Komarovsky, and Mary Alice McInerny claimed that adult education would accomplish much merely by convincing the public of its inadequacy to address political issues and of the need to defer to experts in civic as much as scientific matters.[23] To be sure, something like this had been implicit in the original conception of the New School for Social Research and earlier in Walter Lippmann's *Drift and Mastery*. By the early 1920s, the results of World War I intelligence tests already had created a sensation. But intellectuals of the New School variety saw the humanizing of knowledge as the best way to address urgent social issues, and by definition this objective led them to enlist the public in their plans for postwar social reconstruction. Buoyed by the popularity of serious books in the 1920s and by their image of workers' education as a vehicle for extending their ideals to commoners, they ignored the implications of intelligence testing. Developments by the 1930s had shattered their optimism and provoked a new look at the public's intellectual capacity. In the 1930s a broad range of educators and social critics rallied around the proposition that, while much of the public lacked the ability to profit from books like *The Mind in the Making* and the intellectual doggedness to examine and reexamine their basic assumptions, adult education might still achieve valuable personal and social results by helping ordinary Americans fill up the vast reservoir of leisure time.

The New Leisure

In the late nineteenth and early twentieth centuries, utopian novelists, apostles of the gospel of abundance, and critics of the work ethic and success myth voiced the idea that modern technology would culminate in an age of mass leisure. Many of these expectations focused on the length of the work week, which had declined gradually in the second half of the nineteenth century and which had then fallen sharply between 1900 and 1920. Organized labor long had trumpeted the shorter work week, less from a preference for leisure than from a conviction that a shorter week would raise wages and encourage employment.[24] Most professional economists played a different variation on the theme throughout the 1920s by arguing that technological advances would create a future marked by different kinds of work rather than less work and that ways would have to be found to stimulate consumption (and hence production) of the nonessential consumer goods that had become so abundant.[25] But in contrast to labor leaders and economists who looked to a reorganization of work, a consensus developed in the 1920s along a broad spectrum of psychologists, sociologists, educators, and professional recreation workers that in the future individuals would have far more disposable time and that they would require education for leisure.[26] Typically, the report of the committee of social scientists that President Herbert Hoover assembled in the fall of 1929 called attention to the "gradual shortening of the working day and the general lightening of the burden of excessive toil" that "have brought in their train an increasing amount of leisure and a demand for improved means of enjoyment."[27]

The Depression intensified interest in leisure, most obviously by imposing the forced leisure of unemployment on millions of workers, more subtly by reviving a debate that had waxed on and off for decades over the implications of technology for work. The essential paradox of the Depression—the presence of unemployment and misery amid vast productive capacity—pointed social critics and economic planners toward the idea that American society stood less in need of economic growth than a reallocation of work: more men working fewer hours and women retreating from the workplace to housewifery.[28]

The redistribution of work hinged on the idea that the American economy had already achieved the status of mature abundance and would experience little growth in its productive capacity. In *The Economy of Abundance* (1934), Stuart Chase traced the dawn of abundance to the closing decades of the nineteenth century. After 1870 the "curve of invention" became the dominating force in economic life, and by 1880 energy drawn from coal, oil, and water performed the bulk of economic work. By 1920 the American economy could produce more than the public could consume.[29] In the train of abundance came technological unemployment, a trend that Chase had identified in a series of 1920s' articles that formed his book *Men and Machines*, published on the eve of the Depression.[30] Chase viewed the Depression as the culmination of economic forces long in motion rather than as an aberration. Had it not been for the World War, the Depression might have struck as early as 1914. Had it not been for the nation's overinvestment in capital goods in the 1920s—the construction of skyscrapers and factories that stood half empty—it certainly would have occurred before 1929.[31] In its frenzied quest for profits, capitalism had created an artificial prosperity in the 1920s, but now its time had run out. The American industrial and agricultural plant had been built to the point where it could provide for about twice the active demand for consumers' goods.[32] Barring another world war, Chase averred, neither demand for goods nor employment was likely to revive, for "population in western civilization is approaching its peak," and backward nations were building their own factories and energy systems.[33]

Like Thorstein Veblen, Chase in the 1920s had predicted an economic downturn in the wake of overproduction. The Depression itself neither surprised nor demoralized Chase, for he had often contended in the 1920s that Americans could live happily with less. That they would have to live with less, he did not doubt, for barring another war, he saw no prospects for a return to full employment. That they could live with less, he was certain. All they had to do was to stop throwing their money away on motor cars, amusement parks, and motion pictures and learn to enjoy the inexpensive pleasures of boating, camping, and the outdoors that would restore "psychic equilibrium" to American civilization.[34]

Ideas about the appropriate forms of leisure blended in the 1930s with mounting concern over the perils and prospects of middle age. Chase's essay "Fired at Forty" (1931) described a growing tendency of plant managers to lay off men over forty. "With mergers daily cracking about us like sky bombs," he wondered, "who is sure that his job is not one of the overhead costs which the merger is so often inaugurated to reduce?"[35] While intensified by the Depression, the shelving of middle-aged workers to make way for younger blood had been on the rise at least since the 1890s. For example, the widespread introduction of linotype machines in printing in the 1890s led employers to prefer supposedly more alert and adaptable young workers. The shorter work week of the early 1900s accelerated the displacement of mature workers from the economy, as employers sought young and vigorous workers who could meet the accelerated production schedules required by the shorter work week. A formidable body of medical literature sprang up between 1880 and 1930 to link burnout to the nerve-wracking complexity of modern machinery.[36]

Between 1890 and the late 1920s the preponderance of opinion among psychologists supported the proposition that old dogs could not learn new tricks. In the *Principles of Psychology* (1890) William James contended that "disinterested curiosity"—curiosity extending beyond one's line of work—virtually disappeared after the age of 25, when "the mental grooves and channels [are] set, the power of assimilation gone."[37] In 1905 William Osler, chief physician at the Johns Hopkins University Hospital, offered an only slightly more optimistic assessment when he proclaimed that the "effective, moving, vitalizing work of the world is done between the ages of twenty-five and forty."[38] These opinions harmonized with the views of Lester Frank Ward and other social scientists, who explicitly rejected the old-fashioned belief, rooted in the autodidactic traditions of the nineteenth century, that with the right mixture of pluck and luck, anyone could learn anything, anytime.

As late as 1927, the psychologist H. L. Hollingworth concluded that mental decline began in the late twenties, but even as Hollingworth was writing, E. L. Thorndike and his associates at Columbia University were conducting the experiments that would reverse pessimism about adult learning.[39] Published in 1928 as *Adult Learning*, Thorndike's investigations painted a very different picture. Nobody under 45, Thorndike claimed, "should restrain himself from trying to learn anything because of a belief that he is too old to be able to learn it."[40] Teachers of adults should expect them to learn at nearly the same rate and manner as fifteen- to twenty-year-olds. Although Thorndike conceded that those over 55 experienced a severe decline in their ability to learn, learning ability did not show significant atrophy before that age. Further, Thorndike was reluctant to attribute any slippages in learning capacity to aging itself. Like muscles that grow weak from inactivity, adults might lose their learning ability simply because they stopped trying to learn. Without dismissing the possibility that declining learning ability late in life had a physiological basis, Thorndike suggested that "if we keep on learning we may lose less of our ability to learn."[41]

Those who read the fine print would have identified some of the limitations of Thorndike's study. His conclusions were not based on longitudinal investigations, but on cross-sectional analyses of different age groups. Moreover, his "ability to learn" was an abstraction based on investigations of selected groups of subjects engaged in different types of learning.[42] Still, Thorndike and his associates investigated a very wide range of skills and abilities: driving automobiles, learning to sail a boat, writing wrong-handed, understanding mathematics, typing, even learning nonsense syllables, and their influence on education of adults was pronounced. According to two contemporary investigators of popular reading taste, Thorndike "renewed the faith of many who had considered people beyond thirty or forty years of age to be too old to learn anything new efficiently."[43] After Thorndike, wrote the historian James Truslow Adams in 1944, "those who had thought of the efforts of adults to increase their knowledge as harmless dilettantism were suddenly forced to face the facts, which pointed straight to the possible enormous increase in the capacity of the individual."[44]

It remained for Walter B. Pitkin, a Columbia University professor of psychology and journalism and a dogged composer of inspirational books, to fasten the tie between the new leisure and self-improvement in middle age. In his best-selling *Life Begins at Forty* (1932), Pitkin blithely sentenced young men to the drudgery of running farms and tending machines, dismissed the gospel of work as the "after-stench of rotten quackery," reassured the middle-aged that their creative powers were just beginning to blossom ("not a man in a million under forty is worth listening to, except for gag lines and clowning"), and urged the over-forties to relish travel and study ("experimenting and studying just for fun after forty lead to many of the most interesting ways of using leisure"). Like many inspirational books, *Life Begins at Forty* was filled with contradictions. On some pages Pitkin described diminishing economic opportunities for the middle-aged; on others he assured them that they could readily turn their experience to managing great corporations. But these contradictions probably added to the book's popular appeal by underscoring the possibilities open to over-forties at a time when the onset of middle age was provoking widespread anxiety.[45]

Chase and Pitkin made the leisure revolution seem natural, inevitable, and enduring. They also contributed to the intensifying debate over the quality of leisure. Would Americans waste their newly acquired leisure on such passive recreations as attending ball games, amusement parks, and motion pictures, or would they employ leisure as a means of self-improvement? Traditionally, self-culture manuals had extolled travel and communion with nature as appropriate activities for the wealthy and praised reading as suitable for everyone. While these refrains persisted into the 1930s, what distinguished the decade was the growing emphasis on the mass acquisition of amateur artistic skills.

Adult Education and the Arts

The fine arts played little role either in the thinking of the founding faculty of the New School for Social Research or in the Carnegie Corporation's initial conception of adult education. Gradually, however, the focus of adult educators shifted toward the arts, and in the late 1920s and early 1930s the Carnegie Corporation sponsored several major studies of American art, architecture, music, and theater. These included Robert L. Duffus's *The American Renaissance* (1928), Frederick P. Keppel and Duffus's *The Arts in American Life* (1933), and Kenneth Macgowan's classic *Footlights Across America* (1929). Programmatic as well as descriptive, all of these books assessed the level of popular interest in art and called implicitly or explicitly for national and regional planning to integrate art into leisure. *The Arts in American Life* was one in a series of monographs published under the auspices of the President's Research Committee on Social Trends for use in its report *Recent Social Trends in the United States*, which itself was a planning document. Macgowan called for a national organization of local theaters to give direction to a movement that was by definition decentralized.[46]

In addition, these studies were counter-polemics of a sort, responses to the drumbeat of 1920s' criticism of the suffocating effect of Puritanism on the arts in America. Their authors set out to demonstrate that America, and even mid-America, was a far cry from H. L. Mencken's Sahara of the beaux arts. For example, Keppel and Duffus traced the development of art education from modest beginnings in the 1870s under Charles Eliot Norton at Harvard. By the 1920s scores of colleges and universities had introduced art majors, public schools were actively teaching the arts, and independent art schools were affiliating with colleges in order to meet the schools' demand for certified art teachers.[47] New art museums were constantly opening, and through their docent programs museums had established themselves as educational institutions.[48] Aided by a Carnegie grant, Macgowan traveled over 14,000 miles to visit and study local theater groups that sprouted in the most unlikely places. Duffus identified the beginnings of an American Renaissance of popular craftsmanship as well as of art instruction.[49]

Yet all of the authors had to confront evidence that conflicted with their optimism. During the Progressive era, museums had extended their hours and introduced lectures as part of a deliberate effort to reach a broader public. Successful in the short run, outreach programs soon reached a point of diminishing returns, or so it seemed from the available evidence. Attendance at major art museums fluctuated within a modest range during the 1920s, and one consultant to the Carnegie Corporation concluded that "if it be true that there is now a wider interest in art than formerly, it appears not to have centered about the art museums."[50]

This soberingly flat arc of museum attendance was not the only sign of public apathy. As Keppel and Duffus recognized, the Lynds' study of Middletown challenged the optimism of educators about the diffusion of art and indeed of any form of high culture. The portrait of American culture drawn by the Lynds pointed to a decline since the 1890s in the integration of culture and daily life. In the 1880s and 1890s Middletown's bankers, lawyers, physicians, and merchants had come together in the Literary and Scientific Association to hear papers on "What Is Mind," "The Relation of Science to Morality," and "The Relativity of Knowledge." By the 1920s they assembled instead at the Rotary Club to listen to talks on "Making and Selling High-Tension Insulators." Men had virtually ceased to engage in organized study groups; by the mid-1920s only twelve men were numbered among the 710 members of Middletown's adult study groups.[51] The female study clubs also encountered change, for by the 1920s they engaged more in the discussion of current events than in the study of art or literature and, perhaps more important, they had to compete with a host of recreational clubs devoted to such activities as bridge, dancing, and bowling. While the number of Middletown's study clubs merely doubled between 1890 and 1920, its recreational clubs increased tenfold.[52] Residents of Middletown did not seem to exhibit a spontaneous interest in either literature or art by the 1920s. The number of art volumes in the city's public library had increased twenty-fold since the 1890s, and the public high school now taught art, but art "seems somehow to drop out of the picture between the time boys and girls sketch in their high school classes and the time they become immersed in the usual activities of Middletown's adults."[53]

Rather than the absence of the "means" of culture, the lack of spontaneous popular participation in artistic activities seemed to mark the Middletown of the 1920s. Whereas in the 1890s the members of the Art Students' League rented a studio and criticized each other's sketches, by the 1920s the league had become just a "fashionable club" whose members listened to papers on Japanese prints or Renaissance art.[54] The same pattern affected music. Serenading, solo singing, and church choirs all had atrophied since the 1890s.[55] Not that the townspeople ignored music; they listened to it all the time on the phonograph and radio. But "thirty years ago diffusion of musical knowledge was entirely in the handicraft stage; today it has entered the machine stage."[56] In the realm of culture, Middletown residents had shifted from participatory activity to passive spectatorship. Golf outings where men put together business deals and bridge games where women gossiped had become the natural leisure pursuits of the city's residents.

By identifying the drying-up of popular artistic participation in a mid-American city, the Lynds challenged the optimism of educators, who nevertheless continued to affirm that popular cultural pursuits were expanding rather than contracting. One area seemingly marked by growth was the local or "community" theater, which educators interpreted as evidence of a grass-roots cultural democracy and as a bastion of creative amateurism in an age of professionalism and machine-made culture. Thus Macgowan wrote in 1929:

About fifteen years ago the professional theater began slowly and unobtrusively committing suicide in that rather inclusive portion of the United States known as the Road. At the same time, a number of fanatical amateurs took to the notion that they might be Belascoes or Barrymores without invading Broadway. It was a happy coincidence, this emergence of amateurs in Madison, Evanston, Ypsilanti, and Indianapolis as the professionals withdrew.[57]

Macgowan's reference to amateurism revealed one connotation of local theater. But what Macgowan preferred to call local theater and what most others described as little theater encompassed diverse strands, including a strain of professionalism that would conflict with educational objectives. The first American little theaters mushroomed in 1912, catalyzed by the American tour in 1911 of the Irish Players associated with Dublin's famed Abbey Theatre.[58] The American little theaters reacted against the Broadway commercial theater's enshrinement of profit, presentations of long-running shows that destroyed repertory, typecasting that checked the development of actors, and hostility toward experimentation.[59] Just as the Abbey Theatre of Synge and Yeats symbolized an Irish renaissance, the little theater in America represented a quest for a national, distinctively American drama.

The rise of the little theater coincided with the maturing of university drama departments and troupes. In 1912 Harvard's George Pierce Baker turned his playwriting course, English 47 (the first such course in an American university), into the 47 Workshop, a theatrical laboratory. Baker's students and assistants included Louise Burleigh, author and advocate of community pageants in the Progressive era, Hallie Flanagan, who would head the Federal Theatre Project in the 1930s, and the indefatigable "proff" Frederick Koch, who in 1918 founded the Carolina Playmakers, a company of drama students at the University of North Carolina. Although Koch himself wrote a pageant, *Raleigh: The Shepherd of the Ocean*, and his student Paul Green authored the long- (and still-) running pageant *The Lost Colony*, Koch is best remembered for his encouragement of "folk plays," dramas with the "legends, superstitions, customs, environmental differences, and the vernacular of the common people."[60] Dramas like Green's *In Abraham's Bosom*, Lula Vollmer and Hatcher Hughes's *Sun-Up* and *Hell Bent for Heaven*, Dorothy and DuBose Heyward's *Porgy*, and Roark Bradford's *Green Pastures* were, in Koch's words, "earth-rooted in the life of our common humanity."[61]

Koch labored to build little theater on the foundation of native (especially folk) themes and local talent. The University of North Carolina's extension division contained a bureau of community drama that encouraged the production of plays in schools and "little places in the state."[62] In 1935 a grant from the Rockefeller Foundation enabled the extension division to add a traveling instructor in drama to its staff "for help in play making among potential leaders and amateur actors behind the mountains."[63] The Carolina Playmakers toured the state each year, and after 1923 the Carolina Dramatic Association held an annual festival to which amateur theatrical clubs, including many from high schools and some from black colleges like Shaw in Raleigh, submitted plays.[64]

This ideal of original plays addressing rural folk life and relying on amateur casts appealed to those who saw drama as an educational and social force, for it promised to school communities into a self-sustaining enthusiasm for drama and to overcome the passivity and spectatorship inherent in movie-going. While high-school and college clubs had the most direct relationship to educational theater, many advocates of the amateur stage saw it as a fount of intellectual and psychological benefits for the entire community. Local theaters that gave as many people as possible a chance to act connected "the person to the group through the community effort which is demanded in even such simple terms as giving a cue or getting from one place to another on the stage."[65]

Yet maximum feasible participation was by no means a necessary component of little theater. Hostility to the subordination of drama to profit and not amateurism as such was the unifying feature of little theater. Repertory theaters like Eva Le Gallienne's Civic Repertory Theater in New York City and the Hedgerow Theater in suburban Philadelphia, both founded in the 1920s as part of the little-theater movement, relied not only on professional actors but on foreign plays as well, for many American playwrights were still dazzled by the vision of Broadway hits. Macgowan recounted how little theaters were driven by and at times succumbed to the logic of professionalism. Starting in whatever auditoriums they could find, those that attracted audiences soon rented or constructed larger playhouses; by then mired in debt, they turned to hired directors or a core of professional actors to raise the standard of performance and attract larger audiences.[66] When the business manager of the Pasadena Community Playhouse (est. 1917) sent a questionnaire to 600 local theater groups in 1929, the replies indicated that "surprisingly few groups stressed what is theoretically the basis of community theater—giving as many people as possible an opportunity for self-expression." More common were replies that listed "the encouragement of original drama" and "good plays by professionals" as objectives.[67]

This is not to say that little theaters automatically turned themselves into professional companies. The Pasadena questionnaire elicited replies from only 45 of the 600 companies circularized, and these were probably the larger and more successful ones that could employ secretaries to answer mail. (So many little theater companies started in the 1920s and 1930s that it was difficult to keep track of them. Clarence Perry recorded 789 such groups listed in the magazine *Drama* from October 1925 to May 1929, and 231 new groups listed between May 1929 and June 1931.[68] Macgowan counted just over 1,000 in 1929, but each man conceded that his estimate was too low.) Yet little theaters did experience considerable tension between amateurism and professionalism, and this tension would significantly affect the work of the Federal Theatre Project (FTP) in the 1930s.

In January 1934 Harry Hopkins, President Franklin D. Roosevelt's "minister of relief," set aside a portion of Civil Works Administration funds for projects employing out-of-work theatrical personnel. To aid in planning the projects, Hopkins called upon Hallie Flanagan, the much-acclaimed director of the Vassar College Experimental Theater. Officially installed as National Director of the Federal Theatre Project in August 1935—by then the FTP had become a division of the new Works Progress Administration (WPA)—Flanagan applied her extraordinary energy to realizing the vision, which she shared with her mentor George Pierce Baker, of a national theater organized locally and regionally to arouse and educate the American people.[69]

Flanagan had to confront myriad obstacles, including bureaucratic red tape, the hostility of the commercial theater, the suspicion of Actors' Equity Association that the Federal Theatre would lure audiences from viable productions that already employed actors, and finally and most destructively the 1938 inquisition by the House Committee on Un-American Activities into the FTP's alleged communist leanings.[70] Although she dealt resourcefully with these challenges, Flanagan failed to achieve the goal of a regionally decentralized national theater. The FTP scored its major successes in metropolitan areas. For example, in 1936 it sponsored the simultaneous production of Sinclair Lewis's anti-fascist *It Can't Happen Here* in New York, Los Angeles, Chicago, Denver, San Francisco, Detroit, and Cleveland; touring companies carried Lewis's controversial play to smaller cities. But even before the FTP fell to the congressional axe in 1939, it had failed to spread deep roots into the hinterland. Outside of large cities its local bases were firm only in those states like Iowa, Wisconsin, and North Carolina where ambitious university departments of drama had established a high standard in local community theater. The FTP was irrelevant to those community theaters that had sprouted since 1920 and that still relied on amateurs, for the project aimed at out-of-town professionals. While some amateurs did find theatrical employment through the FTP, these instances created headaches for Flanagan, who was far more committed to high-quality productions of socially relevant plays than to amateurism as such.

Efforts by the project to reach isolated areas through touring productions also ran afoul of an administrative problem: workers who had registered for relief in one area could be transferred and remain on relief.[71] Thus, as Jane De Hart Mathews records: "Hallie Flanagan, who had intended to create strong regional and community centers, found herself in charge of three huge metropolitan projects [New York, Chicago, and Los Angeles] and many small, often weak units in towns and cities. The foundation stones for a regionally centered national theater had, in short, been dumped in three large piles with a few pebbles scattered about elsewhere."[72]

Despite the FTP's limited impact on local and regional drama, amateur playwriting thrived in the 1930s, aided by the extension divisions of the state agricultural colleges. While Frederick Koch had some influence on the latter, Alfred Arvold exerted a more direct and potent impact. The founder of the Little Country Theatre in Fargo, North Dakota, and of the Dakota Playmakers, Arvold already had acquired a formidable reputation by 1920 as a promoter of rural pageants, harvest festivals, and plays about prairie life. By using the extension division of the North Dakota Agricultural College to mail plays to inquiring farm groups—what Arvold called "intellectual rural free delivery"—he established a pattern that other universities would follow in the 1920s and 1930s. Whereas Koch primarily valued carefully crafted folk plays, Arvold considered theater "more in a sociological sense than in a literary or art sense."[73] In practice, this meant the encouragement of home-talent plays that explicitly urged rural people to stay on the farm, the promotion of village beautification through "lilac festivals," and historical pageants that gave special prominence to the elderly, who carried local history in their memories.

Essentially conservative, Arvold's influence was a far cry from the FTP, for the latter, while scarcely that hotbed of communism alleged by J. Parnell Thomas and Martin Dies of the House Un-American Activities Committee, had liberal-left leanings. Arvold's orientation was basically that of Country Life Progressivism, which was embodied in the rural social workers and sociologists who long had sought to pry the Agricultural Extension Service from its preoccupation with the economics of farming and to point it toward the revival of rural culture. By making it clear that overproduction rather than lack of efficiency cursed the farmer, the Depression indirectly boosted Country Life Progressivism, which met with an increasingly friendly reception in the extension divisions of the land-grant colleges. A. M. Drummond, the director of Cornell's University Theatre, worked closely with Cornell's land-grant colleges of agriculture and home economics to encourage home-talent plays.[74] By the 1930s extension divisions were adding specialists in recreation, who usually were attached to departments of rural sociology.[75] Although recreation specialists were not experts on drama, they saw home-talent plays as one way to achieve their goals of community cooperation and the combating of rural isolation. These objectives, familiar to Progressive reformers before 1920, continued in the 1920s and 1930s in the form of efforts to make the surviving farmers' institutes serve recreational and communal objectives. For example, in 1930 a farmers' institute in Alexandria, Ohio, adopted an agenda of community goals that included better church attendance, wholesome recreation, rural electrification, the removal of sign boards, the landscaping of public buildings, the attraction of industry, and the proper celebration of Memorial Day. Five years later Alexandria's citizens celebrated these accomplishments with "A Rural Dramatic Festival and Home Coming," which included the staging of Gilbert and Sullivan's *Trial by Jury*, a colorful outdoor pageant illustrating the value of drama in the country-church program, art exhibits, and the display of agricultural products.[76]

As these examples indicate, amateur drama often took forms that were unsophisticated. One amateur group in a small Wisconsin village, eager to select the right play for its opening performance, asked the Wisconsin Dramatic Guild for information about a play by an Irishman that had something to do with love under trees, which these local thespians believed would be especially appropriate for their village, known as it as for its lovely trees.[77] If these villagers concluded (as they were advised) that Eugene O'Neill's *Desire Under the Elms* was too demanding for a first attempt, they could have turned to one of the plays composed by the Stewart brothers of Fairfield, Iowa, who in 1926 formed the Universal Producing Company to assist amateurs in staging plays. R. R. Stewart, Universal's general manager, established a simple criterion for the company's plays: that the parts be numerous and very short so that as many as possible, typically around a hundred people, could obtain roles. The Stewarts marketed their plays to Ladies' Aid societies, Rotary clubs, American Legion posts, scouting troops, and other organizations that either wanted to put on a play for their own sake or to stage a benefit performance. In addition to scripts, Universal provided acting coaches, costumes, and a national network of salesmen to stimulate local interest. As business grew, R. R. Stewart "employed a playwright—a university girl—just as he would employ a stenographer, [and] assigned her to a studio to hammer out vehicles for the nation's amateur talent."[78]

As professionals in the business of promoting amateurism, the Stewarts kept their scripts topical: flappers in the 1920s, the Depression in the 1930s. *The World's All Right*, an upbeat "anti-depression comedy" that required virtually no props, began with a parade of tots, and featured lyrics set to familiar tunes, was little more than a cornpone version of *It's a Wonderful Life*, but, along with a few other Stewart staples, it was in demand. By 1934 Universal was booked to produce more than 3,000 performances, about ten shows a weeknight across the nation, employed 225 coaches and a swarm of salesmen, and billed itself as the largest producer of amateur theatricals in the world. Between 1928 and 1934 more than 1,000,000 amateur actors appeared in casts of its productions, which played to more than 6,000,000 people. What the International Correspondence Schools had been to vocational education, Universal was to amateur theatricals.[79]

Contemporaries eager to inspire communities through Good Theater tended to count all manifestations of the amateur impulse as art. In their survey of "everyman's drama" sponsored by the AAAE, Jean Carter and Jess Ogden did not cite Universal but they offered estimates of the scope of amateur drama that resembled Universal's body count: 300,000 theatrical groups and upward of 1,000,000 spectators a year.[80] Undoubtedly, one reason for the FTP's failure to fulfill Hallie Flanagan's dream of a national theater rooted in local and regional theater was that much provincial amateurism was so rankly amateur. Yet despite its range from the artistically significant to the ludicrous, amateur drama impressed educators in the 1930s as an important pedagogical force. The support for folk plays, pageants, and the FTP given by some segments of the public helped to establish a climate in which almost any form of amateurism seemed educationally valuable. Educators affirmed that the worthy use of leisure was as important as vocational preparation, perhaps even more so now that the future seemed to promise little economic growth. Amateur theatricals, by the same token, seemed an excellent way to fill up leisure time. The "worthy use of leisure," proclaimed a textbook used in college courses, "cannot easily be taught through formal instruction"; rather, "it must be achieved through active participation in leisure pursuits."[81] Hence popular avocations had immense educational significance:

Adult education must not be confined to the few but to the many, and it needs to be more informal and avocational in nature, in which adults may pursue their hobbies and their interests and find fulfillment for their talents. There are many adults who have hidden talents in the sciences and arts who have not had the opportunity to develop them—in fact, in some cases they may have been suppressed in their school days [when] vocation and not avocation was the emphasis.[82]

From Vocations to Avocations

Throughout the 1930s, inspirational books assailed the stress on success characteristic of the 1920s and urged Americans to cultivate the fine art of leisure. Typically, Marjorie Barstow Greenbie's *The Arts of Leisure* contrasted Thoreau, the noble loafer, with Babbitt, the hollow booster. What Babbitt lacked was the will to follow his instinctive desires consistently, to enjoy the pleasures of life without regard to their impact on his bourgeois reputation. Psychic health required only that each person do something for its own sake and in response to the promptings of the spirit. "There should be some art, some knowledge, some well doing, which has no personal end, something that is its own sure and certain reward. For some, very simple hobbies serve this end; and in this way they do work of lasting good and glory. . . . It only matters that in this avocational activity, whatever it is, the spirit is wholly free."[83]

Heightened interest in both serious intellectual issues and amateur artistic performance compelled established institutions of adult education to adapt to new demands from their patrons. As unemployment rose and as the public mood became more sober in the early 1930s, vocational courses lost much of their former appeal for adults, the ideal of job improvement went into hibernation, and enrollments in proprietary schools and evening colleges of law and business plummeted. The YMCA, one of the pioneers of adult vocational education back in the 1880s, began to recast its educational programs to satisfy new interests. Thomas H. Nelson, an association executive, noted in 1933 a definite rise of interest among association students in "controversial issues of political, economic, and social life."[84] Increasingly, local YMCAs began to offer lectures and discussions on "How the Scientist Looks at Life," "The Meaning of Current Political Events," and "The Art of Living."[85] While some association officials did not welcome discussion of controversial public events, Nelson observed that the constituencies of local Y's demanded it. Just as the association's leadership initially resisted vocational education in the 1880s, only to be swept along by popular demand, so too it acquiesced in the 1930s to the heightened concern of its constituents with burning issues.

In addition to organizing programs on public events, the association found itself besieged in the 1930s by growing pressure for lectures on the "art of living" and forced to recognize "a rapid growth in the Association of dramatic societies, little theaters, art clubs, music groups, writers' clubs, and hobby groups." In contrast to the Chautauquans' quest for cultural information in the late nineteenth century, the association's clients were propelled by "a more articulate desire for expression in the realm of the artistic." Nelson observed that

Some wanted to paint pictures, some to write stories, some to produce and participate in plays—or in musical programs; others found their self-expression in craftsmanship or in pursuit of hobbies. Still others sought the artistry of delightful fellowship in recreation, home, or social groups. Here were desires that differed much from the gaining of new knowledges and skills for some utilitarian purpose.[86]

"Everyone tried to fit in and be well liked," Warren Susman wrote of the 1930s.[87] To feel better meant not just to cultivate one's own personality but to develop sensitivity to others, even if only for appearance's sake. The odyssey of Dale Carnegie indicates the direction of change. After graduating from college in 1908, Carnegie sold course books for the International Correspondence Schools, then began to teach public speaking in YMCA evening classes, made his reputation with *The Art of Public Speaking* (1915) (which was something more than a standard elocution manual in that it told speakers how to overcome their fears of performing in public), and initiated his own venture in proprietary education: the highly successful Dale Carnegie courses. With the publication in 1936 of *How To Win Friends and Influence People,* Carnegie shifted his attention from individual to group therapy: since everyone wanted to feel important, the way to success lay in making others feel important.[88] In the same year Henry C. Link, a psychologist who after World War I had advised employers how to raise profits by boosting the morale of their employees, addressed a different public in his *The Return to Religion*: those who could not pinpoint the source of their unhappiness. In most cases, Link contended, self-absorption was the culprit; people mistakenly assumed that they could improve their personalities "by intellectual concentration on themselves."[89] Much like Carnegie, Link exhorted readers to cultivate social skills. Indeed he attributed religious significance to dancing and bridge; the listless, inattentive bridge player was "thoroughly selfish in his disregard for the pleasures of three people."[90]

Link's attribution of ethical and religious significance to dancing and bridge highlighted the decade's tendency to attach higher importance to recreations that required active engagement in a group. Typically, Link urged his readers to take dancing lessons rather than merely to dance, for lessons compelled "a man to make physical contact, not with one woman but with many women."[91] While his association of bridge with religion was extreme, a growing number of educators praised neighborhood adult centers, which mingled recreation and education in ways that emphasized participation as an end in itself. Adult institutes or adult schools included venerable institutions like Cooper Union and the Lowell Institute; several "people's institutes" or "people's universities" (New York City's People's Institute became a department of Cooper Union in 1934); summer adult institutes such as the Summer Institute for Social Progress in Wellesley, Massachusetts, and the Summer Institute of Euthenics conducted by Vassar College; religiously affiliated adult centers, including the Jewish People's Institute in Chicago and the School for Adult Jewish Education in New York; the New School for Social Research; and a number of neighborhood or community adult centers, such as the Poppenheim Institute, a free evening school open to residents of College Point, New York; and the Maplewood, New Jersey, adult school.[92]

Adult schools or institutes differed from the adult classes long maintained by public-school systems. Historically, the latter had served three distinct functions: educating young people compelled to drop out of the regular day classes of the schools, teaching immigrants to read and write English, and providing rudimentary vocational education. Except for the immigrants, students in public-school adult classes usually were in their late teens or early twenties and belatedly were completing their primary or secondary education. In contrast, students in the adult schools typically were in their thirties and forties. They had little interest in securing certificates and diplomas—in fact many were college graduates—and they were motivated far less by job improvement than by eagerness to understand world and national affairs, to work out personal problems, to find new ways to express themselves, and to become socially more acceptable.[93]

With a few exceptions, adult schools did not offer credit for their courses, and in this respect they differed as much from university extension as from the public-school adult classes. Depression-era adult schools were usually established in well-heeled suburbs like Hastings-on-Hudson, New York, and Radburn and Maplewood in New Jersey, and they exemplified 1930s ideals of community planning and rational leisure.

The ideal of the suburb as a felicitous blend of town and country had fascinated Americans since the days of Andrew Jackson Downing and Frederick Law Olmsted and had also gained support from the English reformer Ebenezer Howard, whose conception of garden cities called for communal ownership of land by residents, balanced factory and residential development, and a mixture of social classes. Yet as the automobile stimulated unprecedented suburban growth in the 1920s, it was becoming clear to city planners and social critics that suburbs, while well-stocked with social organizations for children, were not true communities. Few workers could afford to own the automobiles upon which suburban living depended, and few factory owners saw economic benefits in relocating to suburbs. Not only were suburbs mainly populated by the middle and upper-middle classes, but even these residents experienced a kind of fragmentation of their personalities. In 1925 Harlan Paul Douglass complained about the suburban "tendency toward divided personality" exemplified by the husband so depleted by commuting and work that, once slumped down at home, he would rarely budge. "It is not good for a boy to know his father habitually in such moods," Douglass warned.[94] Once idealized as conducive to a freer expression of moral and spiritual energy than the harried life of big cities, suburbs now seemed to encourage introversion and snobbery.[95]

Amid this drumbeat of criticism of the suburban "wilderness," some social critics and town planners tried to revitalize the suburban ideal. "A crowded world," Douglass insisted, "must be either suburban or savage."[96] One especially influential organization, the Regional Planning Association of America (RPAA), was founded in 1923 and brought together the architects Henry Wright and Clarence Stein, the economist Stuart Chase, the reform-minded land developer Alexander Bing, and the young architectural critic Lewis Mumford to consider alternatives to the suburban trend. Out of the RPAA's deliberations, Stein, Wright, and Bing devised a plan for a model satellite town near Fairlawn, New Jersey, which was about to be brought closer to New York City by the completion of the George Washington Bridge. Construction of Radburn began in 1928, and the first of its projected 25,000 residents moved in in 1929.[97]

Radburn's planners permitted individual home ownership, a departure from Howard's garden-city concept, but otherwise retained the spacious interior parks and informal curvilinear street patterns associated with the suburban ideal. Above all, Radburn encouraged "the happiness of community living."[98] To overcome the privatism characteristic of most suburbs, Radburn's planners divided the town into three villages, each with its own elementary school, and each village into 35- to 40-acre "superblocks," in which houses faced away from the street and toward interior parks. Provision for recreational and cultural activities also loomed large in the Radburn plan, which sought to check the child-centeredness of most suburbs by the encouragement of enrichment programs for adults. To supplement municipal taxes, the incorporated Radburn Association imposed charges on homeowners in order to finance a program of education and recreation for adults. Although lacking direct administrative functions, a Radburn citizens' association communicated the educational and recreational preferences of residents to the Radburn Association.

Severely depopulating the town before it was even half completed, the Depression blighted Radburn's development. But homeowners who managed to hold their jobs and meet their mortgage payments did participate during the early 1930s in a host of adult-education activities, including a choral singing group; a little theater called the Radburn Players that staged two major productions a year; and discussion courses on American politics, modern literature, child study, music appreciation, psychology in everyday life, home decoration, and handicrafts.[99] These courses epitomized the kind of voluntary learning favored by adult educators of the 1920s and 1930s. Decisions about course offerings were based on residents' responses to questionnaires. None of the courses required homework, nor did they carry academic credit. Like most students in adult schools during the 1930s, Radburn's residents had as much formal education as they wanted. Nearly 90 percent of the adult men and three-fourths of the adult women in Radburn had received part of their education in institutions of higher learning.[100] Although scarcely a typical suburb, Radburn partly fulfilled the prediction made by Harlan Paul Douglass in 1925:

The reorganized suburb . . . will have its theaters, its galleries. Out of the more closely associated lives of its people, and away from the over-specialization and professionalism of the city, may spring up forms of amateur expressions of the creative arts. In the semi-independent community one may hope for more singing and dancing, more painting of pictures and writing of books with and for one's neighbors, and with less dependence upon high-priced specialists and geniuses.[101]

J. Keith Torbert, the director of the adult school in Maplewood, New Jersey, and author of perhaps the first manual for conducting such schools, described their student bodies as "comparatively unchanging" from year to year.[102] Compelled to cater to persisting students, partly dependent on student fees, and lacking the spur of job improvement, adult schools had to satisfy the wishes of their clients or go under. Torbert's prescription of "education plus recreation" fairly describes how most of these schools maintained their appeal. Torbert's own school in Maplewood of-

fered 24 courses in its 1935–36 season.[103] "Economic Forum" attracted
the largest number of registrants, followed closely by "American Literature." Adult-school directors customarily classified these subjects (along
with chemistry and astronomy) as "cultural activities," which they distinguished from avocational and/or hobby courses. Torbert noted that writing, public speaking, and piano instruction fell into a gray area of "partly
cultural" activities. In Maplewood, attendance at the economic forum
and registration in American literature revealed the strong appeal of cultural knowledge, but of the 1,542 total registrations, the great majority
were in courses that actively engaged participants in the mastery of some
skill. Judging from the popularity of word usage, elocution, and diction
classes, a popularity that surprised the directors of adult schools, many of
the enrollees were eager to improve the way in which they presented themselves in daily life. Piano, pottery, wood carving, photography, drawing,
and sketching also attracted large enrollments. In addition, academic-
sounding subjects were deftly personalized. In at least one adult school,
the course in economics taught homeowners how to avoid foreclosures on
their mortgages. Psychology typically became "Understanding our Children" or "Towards Successful Marriage" or "The Art and Science of Effective Living."[104]

The Maplewood adult school was unusual in one respect: it did not
appear to offer contract bridge, ballroom dancing, or tap dancing (unless
these were included under the rubric "gymnasium"). But Torbert and
other directors were well aware of the issue. One director commented that
he had filled three sections of tap dancing and might fill twelve. Torbert
advised newly established adult schools to avoid these subjects, lest they
dominate the curriculum and give the wrong impression about the
school's purpose. He also warned directors to schedule bridge and dancing classes during interludes in the regular program so that students "who
find it difficult to choose between French, for example, and bridge" could
take both.[105]

Torbert's advice disclosed the eclectic interests of participants in adult
schools. This eclecticism reflected more than the idiosyncracies of individual students, for adult-school courses were bound up with middle-class
culture in the 1930s. This was true not only of forums on the economy or
world affairs but even of contract bridge. In *Middletown in Transition*, the
Lynds observed that within the middle class the practice of entertaining
friends at home supplanted taking them to dinner at the club. Hostesses
uncomfortable with banter or repartee for its own sake found bridge "the
universal social solvent."[106] Courses on parenting, which might appear under titles ranging from "Character Education" to "Psychology and Parent
Education," also reflected middle-class culture. Although traceable to the
late nineteenth century and by no means confined to the middle class, par-

ent education in adult schools, informal suburban discussion groups, or study clubs of the 1930s stressed the relationship between successful parenting and adult self-fulfillment. Jean Carter, a prominent adult educator who investigated the national movement for parent education on an AAAE grant, noted how orchestras, choruses, and hobby classes had become integral to parent education: "Children grow best in an atmosphere of growth, and parents must themselves keep growing if they are to create this atmosphere. Parent education may, therefore, have as its task the educating of the adult to follow his or her adult interests and thus to keep growing as a person in order to avoid shrinking into a mere parent."[107] Carter related how one mother in a discussion group at a select private school confessed that she really wanted to resume her study of music but had not done so "for my family's sake." In response, the discussion leader advised: "For your family's sake, you *should* resume your study of music."[108]

These currents converged in places like Maplewood and Radburn and, with aid from the New Deal, spread beyond them. Despite its fiscal travails, Radburn became one of the models for the so-called greenbelt towns, whose construction was subsidized by the Resettlement Administration, a New Deal agency established at the prompting of Rexford Tugwell in 1935. Construction of towns like Greenbelt, Maryland, Greenhills, Ohio, and Greendale, Wisconsin, provided work relief for the unemployed, but the towns themselves attracted relatively affluent, well-educated, and community-conscious residents. Joseph L. Arnold notes that almost every adult in Greenbelt belonged to at least one organization or committee, and a political scientist from the University of Maryland who visited Greenbelt in the winter of 1938–39 concluded that the town's residents were "over-stimulated" and had organized more groups than they had time for.[109]

With their propensity to fit adult education into their dizzying pace of activities, Radburn and the greenbelt towns embodied the Progressive ideal of education as a direct stimulus to community cooperation. While the impact of these planned communities was necessarily restricted, the concept of adult education as a blend of cultural and recreational activities received a boost in the mid-1930s from the Works Progress Administration's Division of Education Projects.

The Works Progress Administration and Adult Education

In May 1933 Congress passed the Federal Emergency Relief Act, which appropriated $500,000,000 for the newly established Federal Emergency Relief Administration (FERA). Harry Hopkins, who headed

FERA and later the Works Progress Administration (WPA), brought to his job the experience that he had acquired directing New York state's relief program in 1932. In New York, Hopkins revealed his preference for work relief over the dole and for finding public projects that would allow professional and semi-professional workers to maintain their skills rather than learn new ones.[110] Through its "emergency education program," FERA created jobs for unemployed teachers to instruct unemployed and needy adults. By focusing on adult students, the emergency education program intended to rehabilitate unemployed workers as well as find jobs for teachers.

The emergency education program was housed in FERA's Division of Education Projects, which passed intact to the WPA when the latter supplanted FERA in 1935. Commencing with the employment of rural teachers thrown out of work by rural school closings, the Division of Education Projects enjoyed swift growth. Within a year of its establishment in September 1933, the Division embraced programs for literacy education, the vocational training of unemployed adults, the vocational rehabilitation of handicapped adults, the general education of unemployed and other needy adults, and workers' education. A team of investigators of emergency educational programs observed in 1939, "Thus almost inadvertently the education program developed as an essential part of the relief program, and the way was prepared not only for the selective relief of a special group of unemployed persons—namely the teachers—but also for the provision of economic, cultural, and social rehabilitation for unemployed workers in general."[111]

The Division of Education Projects' role as a relief organization colored its educational history in several ways. While federal and state officials often stated the now familiar justifications for one or another branch of adult education, their fundamental goal was to employ teachers and to identify pools of students. In its early days the division expected to recruit most of its students from the ranks of unemployed manual workers and it made vocational education and vocational rehabilitation two of its main subdivisions, or "points." But vocational education failed to attain the prominence envisioned for it—partly because other New Deal agencies, especially the Civilian Conservation Corps (CCC), absorbed some of the demand for vocational courses, and partly because the Depression discouraged public interest in vocational education. In March 1937, when the WPA employed some 40,000 teachers to instruct over 2,000,000 students, only just over 10 percent of the students (206,297 out of 2,020,310) were registered in vocational courses. A slightly larger number of students, 241,048, were enrolled in literacy and naturalization classes in the same month. Especially in the South, WPA programs made significant incursions on illiteracy among blacks. But the striking development was in the field of "education for avocational and leisure-time activities." In March 1937 over a quarter of all WPA students, 646,770, fell into this category.[112]

What was becoming known as avocational education made its way into the WPA by a circuitous route. One of the early subdivisions of the Division of Education Projects was "general adult education," which FERA originally conceived as encompassing adult education in subjects taught both in secondary schools and colleges: history, economics, English literature, foreign languages, and science. By encouraging young people to prolong their education into high school, the Depression indirectly stimulated this type of academic instruction. The steep rise in public-high-school enrollments in the 1930s undercut one of the traditional constituencies of the adult classes maintained by public-school systems, namely early school leavers who enrolled in night courses to finish their elementary education. Urban school officials reported an increasing number of high-school graduates in their adult classes during the 1930s.[113] Many of these students hoped to enter college when their finances permitted and took adult classes in academic subjects as an approximation of a college freshman course. In 1934-35 FERA encouraged this objective by establishing a number of "emergency junior colleges," that is, post-secondary classes for high-school graduates. One study revealed that most enrollees in emergency junior colleges possessed some work experience and were looking for a cheap way to start their collegiate education.[114]

Emergency junior colleges proved highly controversial and underscored the risks that FERA and the Division of Education Projects faced whenever they stumbled into the preserve of established educational institutions.[115] In addition, both FERA and the Division of Education Projects often aroused opposition from public-school officials, who saw their programs as potential threats to their own adult classes. While in some cities municipal budget cuts forced the suspension of these classes until the WPA took them over and ran them with federal funds, more commonly school boards continued to fund adult classes at reduced levels and thereby kept alive the possibility of conflict with the WPA. The political pressures that engulfed the WPA and that led the Division of Education Projects to employ many individuals who previously had never held a teaching position intensified the opposition of local and state school officialdom.[116]

Since the WPA's Division of Education Projects was primarily a relief measure, the federal government had an incentive to avoid conflict with school officials in the interests of maximizing employment. The simplest way to accomplish this goal was for the WPA to allow public-school officials to concentrate the Division of Education Projects' programs in fields neglected by public education. For example, early in its history the division started a program of nursery schools for the children of unemployed and needy adults. This decision to fund preschools rather than kindergartens was taken explicitly to avoid conflict with public kindergartens. The same logic applied to avocational education, which was not a significant component of public-school adult classes in the mid-1930s. As the decade wore on, federal and local officials avoided flare-ups by focusing WPA programs on popular subjects that would employ as teachers as many individuals as possible. Irene Freuder, a German teacher in California, complained in 1935 that WPA and local officials had adopted a rule that no Division of Education Projects class could be continued if its average attendance fell below ten students. She observed that in effect this rule reduced all WPA courses to a recreational level. German-language instruction suffered because it was thought too "high brow" to attract many students.[117]

Typically, the WPA educational programs subordinated traditional academic education to handicrafts, dramatics, nature study, creative writing, music, and art. This trend gained momentum after the National Recreation Association proposed in March 1935 the organization of relief employment in the field of public recreation. In July an executive order established the WPA's Community Organization for Leisure, which a month later became the Division of Recreation Projects.[118] A WPA survey noted that this division conducted a program "in which the line between education and recreation is vague and indefinite. The work includes arts and crafts, drama, music, lectures and discussion groups, literary and cultural appreciation, swimming, athletics, sports and group play."[119] In many states the same WPA official supervised both divisions.[120]

Spanning the spectrum from literacy and naturalization to hobby and handicraft classes, adult education understandably struck contemporaries as disjointed. Former Amherst College president Alexander Meiklejohn complained in 1934 of its "vast complementation of classes" bound together "by no dominating ideas or purposes."[121] To those like Meiklejohn who wanted adult education to concentrate on making the great books of the social sciences and humanities relevant to adults in the modern world, the developments within adult education in the 1930s were profoundly disheartening. As a work-relief program, the WPA was antithetical to the philosophies that traditionally had prompted initiatives in popular education. "The classes belong to the people," wrote the WPA's educational director in St. Paul. "They get what they want; if they don't get it nothing compels them to stay."[122]

Yet sympathizers with progressive education could reconcile Depression-era adult education with some cherished doctrines. Nearly all of the different connotations of progressive education could be related to one or another of the forms of adult education. The terrain of adult education revealed traces of vocational education, evidence of education as a way to stimulate involvement in community affairs, and above all the principle that education should address the common situations of life. The Depression itself tended to encourage forms of adult education with which followers of John Dewey could sympathize. Just as the Depression blunted the idea that the farm problem was essentially one of inadequate production—and thereby afforded Country Life Progressives new opportunities to promote their distinctive emphasis on rural community development—it effectively undercut the public-continuation schools favored by the efficiency educators of the 1910s, notably Charles Prosser, who had inspired the Smith-Hughes Act and whose obsession with job-specific training long had been anathema to Deweyans. The swirl of popular demand for job-specific training and job improvement had quieted Dewey's early calls for making work relevant to culture, but by the 1930s progressive educators could plausibly portray learning a vocation as merely part of the fabric of the abundant life.

Some of the more dogmatic critics and educators of the 1930s insisted on linking all vocational activities to new patterns of living. For example, in 1936 Ralph Borsodi, a social critic and ardent Jeffersonian, started the School for Living in Suffern, New York, where urbanites could learn spinning, weaving, canning, cooking, carpentry, masonry, farm economics, and animal husbandry, and also imbibe Borsodi's belief in the value of simple living on subsistence homesteads. While Borsodi's rigid insistence on subsistence farming as the sole answer to the blare of city living drew fire from Lewis Mumford and other critics, his School for Living was consistent with the trend toward the integration of learning and living in a relatively small and manageable community, whether a cluster of homesteaders, a suburb, or a neighborhood cultural center. This ideal rallied social planners as diverse as Borsodi, Mumford, Tugwell, and Arthur Morgan (the director of the Tennessee Valley Authority), who introduced adult classes to stimulate a "community ethic" in the river's region.[123]

In the eyes of many progressive educators of the 1930s, adult education seemed the ideal means of integrating learning and living—in part because the processes of social and economic life had become so complicated "that the knowledge, attitudes, and skill needed to handle them cannot be adequately mastered in the brief period of childhood and youth," and in part because adult education was "so much less hampered by vested interests and traditions than are other branches of education."[124] Such educators equated democratic education with keeping opportunity "continuously open" to the mass of people, but the opportunity they envisioned was to acquire at any age a useful skill rather than to gain access in maturity to the formal educational opportunities missed in youth.[125]

Adult education might have aimed more consciously at the have-nots and made second-chance education its main goal. In fact, the middle-class hue of adult education troubled some educators; adult schools in places like Radburn and Maplewood obviously were not for the underclass, and with their stress on leisure and recreation, neither were the WPA classes.[126] Some critics within the adult-education movement complained that adult education's focus on leisure robbed it of its potential to encourage the public to think critically.[127]

For various reasons, however, educators saw little value in directing adult education toward rectifying inequalities in education. The latter objective would have entailed modeling adult education on the established educational system, which even those who assailed the preoccupation with leisure associated with narrowness and rigidity. In addition, for more than a century American educators had assumed that equal opportunity was actually or potentially (and imminently) a hallmark of American education. By the second quarter of the twentieth century, state universities and land-grant colleges had gained the veneration that educators once had accorded to the common school as embodiments of democracy in higher education, outposts of opportunity for those who could profit from a collegiate education. Moreover, in the 1930s a broad spectrum of educators concluded from the Depression that the proportion of young people enrolled in colleges and universities already was sufficiently high; larger enrollments in colleges and universities would merely add more professionals to the unemployment lines. In sum, higher education was as democratic as it needed to become. Future expansion of the system of formal education would come in secondary schools and (in the eyes of a small number of dedicated visionaries) in junior colleges, rather than in the established institutions of higher education.[128]

Progressives, of course, had displayed ambivalence toward the notion of educational extension; even before the 1930s, university extension had not necessarily meant extending university education to have-nots. More often it meant the provision of assorted educational services to as many as possible, a view highly compatible with 1930s-style adult education.

Conclusion

Summonses to adapt education to the swiftly changing requirements of adults had been implicit in the reaction against Arnoldianism and in Dewey's philosophy of integrating culture and work, and explicit in the post-1900 university extension movement and the Agricultural Extension Service. Efforts to infiltrate this type of education into the public schools under such rubrics as vocational education and home economics persisted into the 1930s, but without inspiring such high expectations as before 1920. In the 1930s progressive educators indifferent to or disillusioned by the direction of public-school education increasingly looked to adult education as the most hopeful forum for grounding education in experience.

By the eve of World War II, adult education had achieved a status at once vast and marginal. Its marginality was the product of several factors, not the least being its self-conscious detachment from established institutions of education. If adult education was to be equated with the provision of intellectual services to meet the varied needs of citizens, then it hardly required the baggage of diplomas and degrees; rather, it would depend on the timely offering of immediately useful (but not necessarily vocational) types of knowledge in small and spontaneous settings. True, there remained the danger of a drowning accident whenever education swam so close to the rapids of life, for the goal of integrating learning and living could lead to the conflation of education with publicity, disconnected chips of information, or narrow techniques. The Progressive-era approach to "educating the public" had encountered all of these problems, but they did not trouble adult educators in the 1930s, when the experience of adult institutes and WPA classes pointed to a sizable public eager to attempt more abundant living.

Yet the direction of adult education in the 1930s did dampen the interest of the intellectuals. In the 1920s a mixture of people—reformers determined to find new soil for seeds that would not grow elsewhere, clergymen and former theology students with an inclination toward the social gospel, and academic refuseniks like Beard and Robinson—had looked to adult education as an oasis of voluntarism. By the end of the 1930s, however, most of the scholars and critics who had brought independent reputations to the field had departed. Figures like Beard and Robinson professed an alternative vision of what education might accomplish, but little in their writings supported the kind of adult education entrenched in WPA classes or adult institutes. Beard himself welcomed the growth of Western Civilization courses in colleges as a sign that higher education was finally becoming more interdisciplinary and relevant to modern intellectual dilemmas.[129] For its part, adult education showed little sign of becoming more academic in any sense and safely could be left to other hands.

As adult education ceased to arouse the interests of social critics, it became exclusively what it long had been in part, a minor bureaucracy within state and local education departments, university extension divisions, and collegiate schools of education. The career of the *Journal of Adult Education* exemplified the nature and timing of the change. In 1941 the Carnegie Corporation withdrew its financial support from the *Journal*, which ceased publication after its October issue. The corporation redirected its aid to the Institute of Adult Education, which was attached to Columbia's Teachers College and which devoted itself to preparing in-structural materials and training teachers and directors of adult-education programs.[130] In 1942 the *Adult Education Journal* began publication as a successor of sorts to the *Journal of Adult Education*, and in 1950 the former was merged with the *Adult Education Bulletin*, published by the National Education Association's Department of Adult Education, into the new *Adult Education*.[131] But the *Adult Education Bulletin* and *Adult Education* were merely chronological rather than spiritual descendants of the *Journal of Adult Education*. Dominated by "news from the adult education field" and short reports by professional adult educators, they were little more than published bulletin boards.

Adult educators took heart from their newly acquired professionalism, which assured their position as a star, albeit a relatively dim one, in the galaxy of educational specialties that included curriculum and instruction, special education, and other fields taught in schools of education. As was true of these other specialties, the key to professional status for adult education lay in its growing preoccupation with methodology rather than content. Inasmuch as the main goal of adult education in the wake of the WPA was to stimulate the interest of adults in education and to induce them to attend classes, regardless of what they were studying, adult education inevitably became preoccupied with methods, especially the need for informality and maximum participation on the part of students.[132] By 1940, 51 institutions of higher education offered training in adult education, and four conferred doctoral degrees in the field.[133]

Yet the description of adult education as a marginal professional field does not do justice to its long-term impact. The ideals associated in the 1930s with adult education continued to attract support from educators long after 1940. Among these ideals were those of education available to all and of education as a community enterprise founded on the expressed and anticipated needs of residents of a residential community. After World War II these ideals would shape the development of the American community college.

Chapter 12

The Learning Society

As an inmate of the Norfolk, Massachusetts, Prison Colony in the late 1940s, Malcolm X became an insatiable reader. He devoured books by Will Durant, Arnold Toynbee, H. G. Wells, and Gregor Mendel, as well as by black writers like W. E. B. Du Bois and Carter G. Woodson. When later asked by an innocent journalist to identify his alma mater, Malcolm bluntly responded: "Books."

It may seem odd to describe so revolutionary a figure as Malcolm X as old-fashioned, but several traditional features marked his self-education. In the manner of nineteenth-century autodidacts, Malcolm availed himself of the "means" of culture, specifically a library bequeathed to the prison. He read by the corridor light when his cell light was switched off, so often that upon his release he needed glasses. Since the book collection he explored was tilted toward history and religion, he became something of an authority on these fields, while remaining ignorant of others. He looked up words that he did not understand, and in this respect his elementary and higher education were of a single piece. As was true of nineteenth-century autodidacts, individual books had a revolutionary impact on him, and, collectively, books led him to understand that Malcolm Little, well-known pimp and hustler, was more accurately a victim, a member of that vast class of the oppressed and a brother of all non-whites. Although it led him to a cosmic understanding, Malcolm's self-education was never free of self-interest. He commenced it out of envy, one of the cardinal sins, rather than love of knowledge for its own sake. He could not love what he did not know, but he could recognize that the "celebrities" among the black inmates were the "walking encyclopedias" to whose conversation even the white jailers listened. As was true of Benjamin Franklin, Malcolm's education proved useful. Not only did it make him one of the celebrities, but it pleased the authorities (for "an inmate was smiled upon if he demonstrated an unusually intense interest in books"), increased his self-confidence in writing to his idol, Elijah Muhammad, and later helped him to dazzle audiences at Harvard.[1]

To describe the education of Malcolm X as old-fashioned is not to say that this type of experience has disappeared. Many of its components persist. Adults still freely seek education, not only to acquire specific skills but also to enhance their general understanding, and they are impelled by a mixture of disinterested and self-interested motives. Many of them still engage in "self-directed learning projects," an awkward twentieth-century approximation of "self-culture." Those with extensive formal schooling continue to be fascinated by the occasional self-taught prodigy. Just as Thomas Jefferson lionized David Rittenhouse and Edward Everett publicized Elihu Burritt, the "learned blacksmith," so too Eric Sevareid introduced Eric Hoffer, the sometime migrant worker and longshoreman turned philosopher, author, and Berkeley lecturer, to a national television audience in 1967. Yet most adults who have sought further education during the last half-century have depended far more than Malcolm X or Hoffer on educational institutions, and far more than their predecessors in the 1930s on institutions of higher education. Malcolm X showed little interest in the classes taught in his prison by instructors from nearby colleges, and he scorned the idea of acquiring a college degree. What seemed an empty status symbol in his eyes, however, was far from empty in the eyes of an increasing number of Americans after 1945.

A Postwar Profile

Starting with the flood of veterans into colleges and universities after World War II, the period since 1945 has witnessed a succession of surges in adult course enrollments. For example, during the span of less than a decade from the mid-1960s to the early 1970s, participation by adults in organized educational activities rose at more than twice the rate of their increase in population.[2] Although adult education continues to thrive in a great variety of settings, institutions of higher education, including two-year colleges, have absorbed much of the adult education carried on in the 1930s in public-school evening classes and in WPA classes. Especially since 1970, established colleges and universities have also made incursions into the realm of "nontraditional" adult education, which in the 1920s and 1930s was the preserve of such anti-universities as the New School, Brookwood, and Highlander. By the end of the 1970s, higher education (including community colleges) had become the leading provider of adult education in the United States.[3]

Other providers of adult education have not fled the field. In the 1950s and 1960s, enrollments in proprietary schools grew at a slower rate than collegiate enrollments, but then leaped forward in the 1970s and 1980s.[4] Business corporations have vastly increased their role in adult education; employer training programs constitute a $40-60 billion-a-year business in themselves. But both proprietary schools and corporations increasingly have had to define their relationship to higher education. Community colleges, for example, now present the proprietary schools with much stiffer competition in the market for vocational training than did colleges and universities in the 1920s. In contrast, corporate and higher education have enjoyed a symbiotic rather than antagonistic relationship. While the sponsors of corporate training programs have come into conflict with colleges and universities over a number of issues, corporate education has contributed to the expanding role of higher education, for business corporations have often contracted their training programs out to colleges. The same has been true of the military, which has sponsored a vast range of adult educational programs for service personnel.

These successive surges in adult course enrollments repeatedly have caught educators off guard. Just as few in the nineteenth century expected that a summer institute for Sunday-school workers would blossom into the Chautauqua movement or that a column in a newspaper read by miners would act as the springboard for the International Correspondence Schools, few educators expected that millions of veterans would take advantage of the G.I. Bill to enter college, attached much significance to the persistence of older students in colleges in the 1950s and 1960s, or predicted the remarkable development of college entry and reentry by older students in the 1970s and 1980s.

This record of failed forecasting in the postwar era resulted from several factors. Educational planners were stunned by the eagerness of veterans to enter colleges in the late 1940s, in part because educators' experiences during the 1920s and 1930s had led them to expect that older students would seek either job improvement through proprietary schools or such avocational skills as learning to restore furniture, play bridge, or speak French. More generally, those inclined to view education as a tactical adaptation to changing conditions rather than as a process of self-elevation assumed that adults would enroll in courses to acquire relatively narrow, situation-specific skills or bodies of knowledge. This outlook, which permeated progressive education between the wars, assigned relatively little importance to colleges and universities, which were deemed suitable only for the small fraction of the population interested in liberal or advanced professional education.

The surge of veterans into colleges after 1945, plausibly attributable to the extraordinary effects of the war, did little to jar these assumptions. Further, the caution and pessimism spawned by the Depression pushed educators and social scientists to conclude that most people would choose their life work in late youth or early adulthood and, if possible, stick to it. By the early 1950s a consensus among social scientists portrayed career choice as a process that began in adolescence and terminated by the mid-20s. From this perspective, it was practically unthinkable that affluent and settled adults would quit good jobs out of boredom or frustration and start anew in different fields.[5]

In reality, such career shifts have become increasingly common. For many Americans the achievement of job security has bred a desire for new challenges rather than for more security. Both the spread of pension benefits and earlier access to them have contributed to this growing penchant among the affluent to change careers. Changes in the work ethic have had a complementary effect since the 1960s. Buttressed by the end of the military draft in 1973, attitudes toward discontinuous schooling have become more relaxed and tolerant; in effect, dropping out has been decriminalized. In addition, the rise of the women's movement in the late 1960s and 1970s enhanced the effects of demographic changes: earlier marriages and lower fertility that led to empty nests, and higher divorce rates that encouraged decisions to start and restart careers.[6]

It would be misleading to think that adults who go back to school have done so only to advance their careers. They have also sought the emotional and intellectual satisfaction that comes with mastering a course of study and testing themselves in a competitive academic environment, and in many cases they have sought to begin or continue their general education. In sum, the vocational and psychosocial benefits of education have blended in the minds of students. What is most striking is the extent to which those seeking this mixture of benefits have identified colleges and universities as the likeliest avenues. Traditionally, nonprofit institutions of formal education played only a minor role in training students for vocations; correspondence schools and other proprietary ventures had flourished between the 1890s and 1920s because neither high schools nor colleges had taught a sufficiently broad and accessible range of vocational courses to accommodate demand. In contrast, since 1945 higher education has become increasingly vocational in orientation, and as the economic value of a college degree has become more evident, the prestige of higher education has risen among all age groups.[7] Whether the value of a college education lies in the new skills it imparts or merely in the academic credentials it distributes, higher education has come to be seen as a passport to success and self-fulfillment.

One factor that has made successive generations more inclined to value higher education has been the gradual advance of educational attainment at lower rungs of the academic ladder. Between 1910 and 1986, the median number of years of formal schooling completed by the entire population aged 25 or over rose from 8.1 to 12.9.[8] Those with higher levels of educational attainment have not failed to recognize the value of educational credentials and, reluctant to return to already attained educational levels, they have sought additional credentials at higher levels. As John W. C. Johnstone and Ramon Rivera noted in 1965, "Participation in adult education is probably as much affected by formal schooling as practically any other type of social behavior one might think of."[9]

Most of the 50 percent increase between 1910 and 1986 in the median number of years of schooling completed by those aged 25 or over was accomplished between 1940 and 1970 (8.6 to 12.2 years). In turn, the seeds of developments after 1940 were planted in the 1930s, when a combination of hard times and restrictive policies undercut the position of teenagers in the labor market and encouraged them to complete high school; the proportion of seventeen-year-olds to graduate from high school rose from 29.0 percent in 1929–30 to 50.8 percent in 1939–40.[10] This jump of 22 percentage points exceeded the combined increase of the 1910s and 1920s, decades also notable for leaps in high-school graduation rates. In retrospect, we can see that the growth of graduation rates in the 1930s resembled a delayed-action bomb. In the late 1930s educators used it as an argument for new measures, especially the expansion of junior colleges, to increase average educational attainment even more. In World War II military personnel started using their off-duty hours to take college-level courses, and after the war their eagerness to enroll in colleges under the G.I. Bill surprised nearly everyone. The experience of World War II directly led to a fundamental reversal of estimates about the proportion of the population that could benefit from higher education, spurred new conceptions of educational development and testing, and stimulated the rise of community colleges. Inasmuch as many veterans also sent their children to college, the G.I. Bill helped to make college education a normal expectation for a broad segment of the public. In effect, the war experience contributed to making the growth of collegiate enrollments self-sustaining. When blacks and women in the 1960s and 1970s demanded full participation in American society, wider access to higher education became one of their main objectives.

The Depression and the Junior College

Despite the great expansion of American colleges between 1915 and 1930, most educators and social critics of the 1930s did not see comparable potential for the future. The Depression decade, it is true, witnessed a general rise in the educational attainment of children of lower socioeconomic groups as well as a more socially diverse collegiate population.[11] But while the Depression stimulated secondary-school enrollments, hard times did not produce a corresponding rise in enrollments in four-year colleges. From 1890 to 1930 collegiate enrollments had registered an absolute decline only once, in the war year of 1918. As the economy plummeted in the early 1930s, so did college enrollments, which declined absolutely in 1932–33 and again in 1933–34. In the middle of the decade, Columbia University's Lyman Bryson predicted that collegiate enrollments would never return to their 1929 peak.[12] In fact, enrollments rebounded modestly in the late 1930s; in 1930, 7.2 percent of the 18–24 age group was enrolled in college, a figure that dropped to 6.6 percent in 1934 and then rose to 9.1 percent by 1940.[13] But this represented a notably slower rate of increase than in any previous decade after 1890. Teenagers who could not find jobs persisted longer in secondary schools, but college was another matter. Amid the economic gloom of the early 1930s, families drained savings earmarked for their children's higher education. The majority of collegians in the 1930s still attended private institutions, with all of their stated and hidden costs, and even state universities, including those of California and Wisconsin, introduced tuition charges for the first time in the 1930s.[14]

The slow growth of four-year college enrollments in the 1930s was by no means the sole factor that dampened expectations about the future expansion of higher education. The post-1890 expansion had coincided with the widespread introduction of practical subjects into the collegiate curriculum, and by the 1920s it was plausible for educators who reflexively associated practical education with popular appeal to conclude that the rising number of engineering and business majors was spearheading the overall growth of collegiate enrollments. But in the mid-1930s, enrollment declines were sharpest in such professional fields as engineering and business. The lesson of the Depression appeared to be that investment in professional and technical education ran the risk of overstocking the market with unemployable specialists.[15] Further, while liberal-arts enrollments did not slump as sharply as those in professional and vocational curricula and recovered much more swiftly, few expected a surge in liberal-arts enrollments in the foreseeable future. By the 1930s the belief that only practical education could become truly popular burdened nearly all educators, even the ones who criticized vocationalism. As late as 1944, Robert Maynard Hutchins of the University of Chicago, perhaps the most acidulous critic of vocationalism and specialization in American higher education, warned that the Servicemen's Readjustment Act of 1944 (the G.I. Bill) would turn universities into "educational hobo jungles," for Hutchins was sure that the veterans would flock to vocational courses.[16]

This climate of opinion dampened but did not extinguish expectations of expansion. Administrators at state universities continued to call for wider access to higher education. But the striking feature of the 1930s lay in the extent to which junior colleges began to be envisioned as the pioneers of future growth.

Junior colleges emerged out of several coincidental but essentially unrelated developments. As American educators became more familiar with the German educational system in the late nineteenth century, they recognized that the German gymnasium afforded two years of secondary education beyond the American high school; in effect, it seemed to encompass the first two years of the American college. At a time when elite universities were upgrading their graduate and professional schools, William Rainey Harper ("the Father of the Junior College"), Nicholas Murray Butler, and David Starr Jordan asserted that junior colleges could take over the task of general liberal education—the first two years of a university college—and thereby enable universities to concentrate on graduate and professional education.[17] Harper tried to induce a number of struggling midwestern four-year colleges to turn themselves into two-year junior colleges by promising that their graduates could enter the University of Chicago as juniors without examination.[18]

With a few exceptions, however, junior colleges did not arise in response to Harper's recommendation that weak four-year colleges transform themselves. More commonly, public high schools added on two years of course work, not in response to Harper but to accommodate local pressure for cheap and accessible post-secondary education. Starting from bases in California and other western and southern states, junior colleges spread throughout the nation in the inter-war years and enjoyed swelling enrollments. The number of junior-college students rose tenfold between World War I and the mid-1920s and then nearly tripled between 1929 and 1938.[19] The rise in junior-college enrollments between 1929 and 1939, 65 percent, was especially striking in view of stagnating four-year-college enrollments in the same period. Yet even in 1935 junior-college enrollments, then a little over 120,000, formed only a tenth of those of four-year colleges.[20] Further, junior colleges did not enjoy much prestige. In the 1930s roughly three out of four of them were still housed in public high schools, and their heads were usually called principals rather than deans.

Despite conflicting objectives, American educators of the 1930s came to assign a distinctive democratic mission to junior colleges. In essence, junior colleges complemented the evolving agendas of two potentially antagonistic groups; one, highbrow, the other, middlebrow; one insistent in its demands for standards and hierarchy, and the other wedded to the establishment of average institutions for average people.

Both groups found a voice in the Carnegie Foundation for the Advancement of Teaching (CFAT). CFAT president Henry S. Pritchett and its key staffer, William S. Learned, maintained in the 1920s and 1930s that the primary task of American higher education was to raise its standards and to clarify the relationships among its sundry components. Neither Pritchett nor Learned opposed outreach or expansion by higher education, but each saw colleges corrupting themselves by an indiscriminate eagerness to enroll students in practical courses. In the thinking of these CFAT planners, different levels of higher education should serve different constituencies. Learned, who bemoaned the "bane of the average" in American education, thought that the refinement of tests for measuring student achievement and aptitude and the sorting out of different missions for different levels would liberate elite universities from catering to mediocre students with crassly commercial goals.[21]

In 1932 an extremely influential CFAT study, *State Higher Education in California*, drew out the implications of this preference for differentiation by calling upon the state's public junior colleges to transform themselves from college-transfer institutions into terminal, mainly vocational, schools.[22] In this scheme, junior colleges would become capstones of secondary education rather than preludes to higher education. At the time, the majority of junior-college students were enrolled in college-transfer curricula, but the "terminal function" already had become well ingrained in the minds of junior-college advocates, in fact more deeply rooted in the minds of educators than students. As early as 1926 Frank W. Thomas, the president of Fresno State Teachers College, described the terminal function as "perhaps the peculiar province" of junior colleges, the linchpin of their "popularizing function," even though "it is frequently stated by junior college principals that their students show very little interest in terminal courses."[23] Walter C. Eells, an important investigator and advocate of the junior-college movement, observed in 1941 that even before there was evidence that parents or students desired a practical or terminal junior-college curriculum, the movement's leaders hoped to subordinate college preparatory to terminal studies.[24]

The roots of this bias toward terminal education can be traced to the formative epoch of American secondary education between 1890 and 1920. This period was marked not only by the emerging ideal of mass secondary education and the widespread introduction of vocational education into public high schools, but also by the general divorce of public secondary education from elite university leadership. Whereas in 1893 the famous report of the Committee of Ten, chaired by President Charles W. Eliot of Harvard, had virtually ignored subjects like manual training and bookkeeping, the *Cardinal Principles of Secondary Education* of 1918 was redolent of the new creed of socialized education. Rather than taking the familiar universe of academic subjects as its starting point, the *Cardinal Principles* approached curriculum by identifying the distinctive needs and tasks of young people in modern society: health, "command of fundamental processes," home membership, vocation, citizenship, worthy use of leisure, and ethical character.[25]

In conjunction with the Carnegie units, the *Cardinal Principles* not only sharpened the line between high schools and colleges but widened the distance. The growing gap between secondary and higher education was evident in the differences between the composition of the Committee of Ten and that of the Commission on the Reorganization of Secondary Education, which authored the *Cardinal Principles*. Whereas the former had been dominated by college presidents and professors, the latter did not include any university representatives from academic fields; with one exception, all of its members who were employed by colleges or universities were professors of education, and the sole exception, Edward O. Sisson, had been a professor of education before becoming president of the University of Minnesota.[26] In this respect the commission's membership ratified a change evident by 1911. As calls for a more practical high-school curriculum mounted, figures like presidents Eliot of Harvard and Nicholas Murray Butler of Columbia bemoaned the ascendancy of the Philistines and severed their ties with the National Education Association. Butler might plausibly have cited Sisson as an example of the disagreeable tendency of the NEA, for in 1908 Sisson complained that the typical high-school teacher had become "too absorbed in the intellectual aspects of his particular subject."[27]

The views of the *Cardinal Principles of Secondary Education* met with a warm reception among public-school administrators and aroused support from professors in university schools of education and from officials of municipal universities. Of these, professors of education played the key role in popularizing the terminal function of junior colleges. In fact, nearly all of the major writers on the junior-college movement taught in schools of education.[28] Much like the junior colleges themselves, which usually were described as institutions of "post-secondary" rather than higher education, schools of education had an ambivalent relationship to their parent universities. Professors of education often met with a chilly reception within universities, in large measure because they seemed more interested in the process rather than the content of education, and they responded to intra-university criticism by strengthening their ties to public-school bureaucracies.

In the 1920s and 1930s, schools of education became outposts within universities of the values of progressive education, especially the notion that curricula be organized around explicit social objectives. Professors who specialized in education rather than in economics, physics, or history were determined to bring junior colleges into line with the promotion of "effective social behavior."[29] Social education led not only to a preference for vocational studies but to an anti-elitism that verged on anti-intellectualism. Kramer Rohfleisch, a history and political science instructor at California's Santa Ana Junior College, observed in 1941 that some advocates of terminal education "feel a certain sense of failure when their graduates return from state universities with outstanding scholastic records. They feel, apparently, that they have neglected the interests of the vast majority of students."[30] At the same time, those in the universities and foundations who desired higher education to become more rather than less elite welcomed suggestions that junior colleges focus on terminal vocational programs, which promised to rid universities of indifferent or incapable students.

Throughout the 1930s the majority of junior-college students continued to enroll in college-transfer programs, but the promoters of junior colleges initiated several studies that indicated that, while most junior-college students expected to attend four-year colleges, their expectations often went unfulfilled. By 1941 these two studies had resulted in "universally quoted statistics" proving that 75 to 80 percent of all junior-college students were terminal in fact, while only 34 percent were enrolled in terminal curricula.[31] From these data it became possible to conclude by 1940 that post-secondary education was the scene of a monumental mismatch between students with practical and terminal objectives and colleges with liberal goals.[32]

Despite their proliferation, junior colleges were still marginal institutions in the 1930s, ever in search of new ideas about their "mission." An educator could establish a reputation in junior-college circles merely by describing a new mission for these institutions, as long as it did not read "college preparatory." In a broad sense, terminal education qualified as a mission, but it was a hollow shell in itself. To give substance to the notion of terminal education, junior-college officials and advocates rallied around education for "semiprofessional" fields, those below the level of university professional schools and above high-school vocational courses. The movement's leaders compiled lists of technical or semiprofessional occupations as targets for their vocational courses: technical illustrators, draftsmen, dancing teachers, sports instructors, radio operators, photographers, and many others. In general, "semiprofession" connoted more genteel work than "skilled trade," and hence it appealed to parents who would make "frantic efforts" to "avoid raising their sons and daughters as artisans or craftsmen."[33]

Education for the semiprofessions was more a slogan than an idea with substantive content. No junior-college advocate could give a coherent account of why semiprofessions required two years of post-secondary education rather than four, one, or no years, even as they insisted that semiprofessions were "middle-level occupations between the trade level and the professional level for which two years of college education are necessary and sufficient."[34] Some promising semiprofessions simply disappeared from beneath the feet of the junior colleges. For example, in the 1920s junior-college spokesmen heralded optometry and pharmacy as semiprofessions that they were best suited to teach, but by the late 1930s they conceded that these had been absorbed by other institutions. Rather than track a moving target, they fell back to the position that semiprofessions were any occupations that junior colleges taught.[35]

The idea of education for the semiprofessions was related to several evolving bodies of economic and social thought in the 1930s. In *The Industrial Discipline* (1933) and subsequent writings, the New Deal braintruster Rexford Tugwell questioned whether the enlightened consumption of leisure was a self-sufficient educational goal and whether leisure itself was the tendency of historical development. Accordingly, he called for "adult retraining" to fit people for new kinds of work, whether as managers or as providers of education, health, or recreation.[36] Tugwell's views, which after 1934 weaned most prominent educators from their initial enthusiasm for educating Americans to consume leisure, complemented the work of economists, including Frank W. Taussig and Richard T. Ely. They contended in the 1930s that vocational education could reduce competition for the lower grades of employment by raising skill levels, while simultaneously intensifying competition for the higher grades by increasing the pool of skilled workers. The effect would be to narrow class differences by funneling wages toward the middle.[37] Vocational educators of the Progressive era occasionally had hinted at something like this, but the framers of the Smith-Hughes Act were more concerned with the productivity and "efficiency" of individual workers than with reducing wage inequalities. In the peculiar circumstance of the 1930s, when a nation with immense productive capacity was yet marked by unemployment and social inequality, the ideas of Taussig and Ely appealed to educators more than those of Charles Prosser and David Snedden, the Progressive-era stalwarts of social efficiency.

Occupational training still ran the risk of overstocking skilled trades and professions, but in the 1930s educators and sociologists took the position that an appropriate, community-based system of occupational guidance counseling and job placement would reduce the risk of misdirected training. Although the phrase "vocational guidance" had come into fashion before 1920, the Smith-Hughes Act had ignored guidance counseling, largely in response to Prosser's belief that "real" vocational education would obviate the need for guidance. Equip a lad with skills and he would take care of himself. In contrast, the Depression kindled interest in guidance as a solvent for the problem of unemployed youth between the ages of 16 and 25. By drying up employment for those in their early teens, the Depression encouraged persistence in school and redirected the attention of educators from adolescents to young adults. Increasing enrollments by those aged 16 to 25 in high-school evening classes and in WPA courses seemed to indicate a desperate hunger for job training and guidance by those who had left school only to thrash about in the job market. Two books by Howard M. Bell, *Youth Tell Their Story* (1938) and *Matching Youth and Jobs* (1940), each based on surveys conducted by the American Youth Commission of the American Council on Education, gave added substance to the argument that some combination of job retraining and guidance would reduce unemployment.[38]

One implication of Bell's position was to redefine the "youth problem." Whereas Progressives had focused on early school leavers between the ages of thirteen and sixteen, the New Deal targeted older teenagers and young adults. In 1935 President Roosevelt established the National Youth Administration (NYA) as an autonomous division of the WPA in order to afford part-time work for students aged 16 to 24 (the age threshold was raised in 1936 to 18) and for youth of families on relief. In combination with the WPA's classes, the NYA aroused the interest of public educators in programs of vocational and avocational adjustment for an extended age group.[39] Bell did not assign junior colleges a role in occupational adjustment, but the authors of *Education and Economic Well-Being in American Democracy* (1940), an influential report by the Educational Policies Commission of the National Education Association, used Bell's data and cited Taussig and other economists in defense of raising the average level of schooling in the United States to fourteen years. To reach this object, the commission proposed that elementary education be reduced to six years, while secondary education, reorganized into a four-year "junior high school" and a four-year "senior high school," be lengthened to eight years. This proposal was substantively if not verbally compatible with the idea of junior colleges as extensions of four-year high schools, for the commission's description of the last two years of the senior high school resembled contemporary depictions of junior colleges.[40]

Even in the late 1930s, various features of junior colleges limited their appeal to those educators who hoped to raise the average level of educational attainment without relying on four-year colleges. Enrollments in junior colleges were still only a fraction of those in four-year colleges and were clustered in a few states, notably California, Texas, and Florida. In addition, for all the talk of their terminal function and education for the semiprofessions, most junior colleges were too small to engage in specialized instruction. A few developed reputations for programs in fields like aviation, costume design, or interior decorating, but these were the exceptions. Vocational education in a junior college usually meant taking a course in "business," which consisted of low-level office skills like typing, stenography, and bookkeeping. To qualify for federal funds under the George-Deen Act of 1936, which opened commercial or "distributive" education to Smith-Hughes appropriations, junior colleges had to specify that any vocational course which they offered was "less-than-college-grade." The U.S. Office of Education interpreted this to include vocational courses that did not lead to degrees and that were open to nongraduates of high schools. The latter stipulation virtually invited junior colleges to admit adults to their courses, for students who entered junior colleges directly from secondary schools by definition had graduated. Thus continuing or adult students filtered into junior colleges, which in 1938 enrolled some 20,000 "special and adult" students. This was only a fraction of adult enrollments in the 1930s, most of which were absorbed by WPA classes and public-school evening classes, but it was enough to implant the notion that junior colleges might develop a distinctive mission of serving adults and indeed entire communities.[41] In 1941 William C. Bagley of Columbia University's Teachers College described the junior college and adult education as "the two most important and promising present-day movements in American education."[42]

It took World War II to elevate adult education into a major junior-college activity. By 1944 over 193,000 "special and adult" students were enrolled in junior colleges. From 15 percent of total enrollments in 1938, these students accounted for nearly 60 percent by 1944.[43] As marginal institutions in search of new student pools and faced with the loss of teenagers to the draft, junior colleges adapted swiftly to training workers for defense industries and for civil defense. For example, the Sacramento Junior College began to offer courses to train men and women for work in shipyards and airplane factories.[44] In many junior colleges, the categories of special and adult students overshadowed all others during the war. This was especially true in California, where defense industries and military bases helped the state to increase its share of national junior-college enrollments from 37 percent in 1940 to 51 percent in 1944. In 1944, 73 percent of all California junior-college students fell into the special and adult category.[45]

Although junior colleges made only a peripheral contribution to training defense workers during the war, wartime mobilization boosted them in various ways.[46] Most defense workers were trained directly on the job through the government's Training Within Industry (TWI) program, a subdivision of the War Mobilization Commission (WMC).[47] In addition to TWI, the WMC established training centers in several states, complete with tools and machinery for educating workers. Although less important than TWI, these centers indirectly benefited junior colleges, for when the WMC was abolished near the end of the war, its equipment was declared surplus and transferred on request to public junior colleges.[48] Thus wartime mobilization ultimately nourished the resources of junior colleges. Stimulated by their experience during the war, junior colleges also embraced adult education as an integral component of their mission. Starting in the war and continuing into the 1950s, junior colleges absorbed many of the evening classes that had been taught in public schools during the interwar years.[49] As individuals ever on the lookout for new pools of students, few junior-college officials could ignore the role of adult students in increasing junior-college enrollments from around 100,000 in 1935 to 325,000 in 1942.[50] Soaring adult enrollments, in turn, reinforced the idea of junior colleges as providers of educational services for all residents of a locale, in other words, as "community colleges." In the 1940s the terms "community colleges" and "junior colleges" sometimes were used interchangeably, or combined into the awkward "community junior college," but "community college" was becoming the preferred description. All community colleges were junior colleges. For a junior college to establish itself as a community college, however, it would have to serve a wider clientele than recent high-school graduates and operate over an "extended day" from 8:00 A.M. to 10:00 P.M. The watchwords of the community college were "service to the local community" and education as a "lifelong process" necessitated by the "complexity" of modern society and the growth of leisure. Above all, community colleges would educate as many adults as young people.[51]

The G.I. Bill and Higher Education for American Democracy

In 1940 the Educational Policies Commission's report on *Education and Economic Well-Being in American Democracy* designated longer secondary education in eight-year junior and senior high schools as the vehicle for prolonging the average period of schooling in the United States. The growth of junior-college enrollments during World War II encouraged a different conclusion, namely that junior colleges would carry democracy into higher education. In 1943 the National Resources Planning Board, which originated in the early New Deal as the National Planning Board under the Public Works Administration, projected only a 25 percent increase in postwar enrollments in degree-granting colleges over the 1940 base, while proposing a 600 percent increase in postwar junior college enrollments over the same base, and more than a fivefold increase in appropriations for junior colleges. All of this was to be accomplished not only in the name of democratic access to education, but as an instrument of "manpower readjustment" as well. Advocates of manpower readjustment envisioned educational institutions as both training grounds and holding places. The prolongation of education would delay labor market entry and thereby check unemployment in the wake of postwar demobilization. The same thinking lay behind the Servicemen's Readjustment Act of 1944, the G.I. Bill.

The educational title of the G.I. Bill provided federal support (tuition, fees, books, supplies, and a modest subsistence allowance) for one year of schooling for veterans who were not over 25 on entering the armed forces and who had served at least 90 days. These veterans could also receive additional schooling equal to the time they had spent on active duty beyond 90 days. Veterans who entered the service beyond the age of 25 were limited to one year of schooling (unless they could demonstrate that the war had interrupted their education), but this restriction was removed by an amendment to the bill in December 1945.[52]

At a time when nearly everyone recognized that wartime spending had ended the Depression and feared that postwar spending cuts might revive unemployment, the G.I. Bill promised to remove some veterans from the labor market at the war's close. Concern that unemployed veterans might fall prey to political extremists (as in Europe after World War I) contributed to Congress's unanimous approval of the bill. So did Depression-shaped images of war heroes selling apples on street corners. It was less clear to contemporaries that the bill would democratize higher education. Some university presidents and professors, including Harvard's James Bryant Conant, worried that an influx of veterans would dilute academic standards. Almost all colleges, however, smoothed the way for veterans by modifying their admissions requirements to admit by examination veterans who had not graduated from high school and by providing refresher and remedial courses where necessary. But in 1945 few educators expected an avalanche of veterans to enroll under the bill's provisions. In March 1945, Earl McGrath, a World War II veteran and a dean at the University of Buffalo (and later U.S. Commissioner of Education), analyzed three wartime studies of veterans' attitudes toward higher education and concluded that in no coming academic year would more than 150,000 veterans become full-time students in colleges and universities. In view of the decline of enrollments in degree programs offered by American colleges and universities between 1940 and 1944, it did not appear that the G.I. Bill would accomplish much more than restoration of the slight upward curve in enrollments between 1936 and 1940.[53]

In reality, veterans flooded into institutions of higher education. In 1946 and again in 1947, over a million veterans enrolled in colleges and universities under the G.I. Bill; nearly a million enrolled in each of the next two years. In the peak year of 1947, veterans accounted for almost half of all enrollments in higher education. This surge of veteran enrollments fed the huge increase in total enrollments in higher education from 1,364,815 in 1939 to 2,281,298 in 1950.[54] On the whole, veterans distinguished themselves as mature and academically successful students. Benjamin Fine, the education editor of the *New York Times*, toured campuses in the East and Midwest in the fall of 1947 and reported that veterans "are hogging the honor rolls and the Dean's lists." Several studies conducted in 1946 and 1947 sustained Fine's assessment.[55]

Although the surge of veterans into colleges caught most planners off guard, the near doubling during the 1930s of the proportion of seventeen-year-olds to graduate from high school had prepared the way. Graduates who intended to attend college found their plans thwarted when the draft age was dropped from 21 to 18 in the wake of Pearl Harbor. Those who did not plan to go to college after graduating from high school but who subsequently resolved to continue their education rejected any thought of returning to high schools to take evening classes. Rather, they looked to higher education, the more so because many enlistees were assigned to college campuses during the war to take specialized military courses.[56] In addition, the postwar veteran surge was foreshadowed by the wartime experience of the United States Armed Forces Institute (USAFI), the main coordinating body for a vast range of wartime educational programs.

Organized in February 1943, the USAFI absorbed the earlier Army Institute and cooperated with the Navy and Marine Corps (each of which continued to maintain independent educational programs) in coordinating correspondence courses and classroom instruction on bases around the world. The reach of the USAFI was truly astonishing; course materials were even mailed to American POW's held in Europe and Japan. Instant universities were established on bases from the Aleutians to the Philippines; GI's at Guantanamo named theirs "SNAF-U." In fact, GI's did more than name their schools, for they controlled much of their content. During World War I the military had made few overt efforts at educating service personnel, and at the start of World War II the USAFI's forerunners were quartered in the Morale Division of the Adjutant General's Office. The shift from building morale, an accepted military function by 1918, to diffusing knowledge occurred in large measure because so many soldiers by the 1940s wanted to devote their off-duty hours to teaching and learning. In effect, offering educational services came to be seen as a way to keep soldiers content and hence to build their morale.[57]

During the war some two million service personnel made use of courses distributed by the USAFI and by the U.S. Navy, Coast Guard, and Marine Corps. Enrollment was voluntary and cheap; after 1943 enlisted personnel paid only two dollars at their first registration in USAFI courses. Courses were sometimes related to military activities, but most often they were not. Most classroom instruction was offered by service personnel, not necessarily officers but educated individuals of any rank who taught whatever they knew. A base in West Africa offered Hebrew, advanced

Spanish, Fantu (a local dialect), physics, and abnormal psychology. Many enrollees took technical and vocational courses, but these did not predominate. Late in 1943 the USAFI, which initially had purchased all of its correspondence courses from proprietary schools, responded to demand for a broad range of high-school and college-level courses by obtaining courses from universities.[58]

As it expanded the range of its offerings, the USAFI received a growing number of inquiries about college-entrance requirements, and it had to devise a policy for enrollees who lacked high-school diplomas but who wanted to take college-level courses. The solution was the General Education Development (GED) test, which sought to ascertain whether a prospective enrollee had acquired the equivalent of a high-school education, less in terms of factual knowledge than in terms of ability to think clearly. Although not administered to civilians until after the war, the GED test would have a significant influence on American secondary education by enabling high-school dropouts to resume their formal schooling at a higher level.[59]

The GED test should also be viewed as one among several innovations of World War II that aimed at flexible testing. The army alpha tests during World War I had stimulated school testing for IQ in the 1920s, but by the late 1920s and 1930s such testing had come under fire from two directions. In keeping with its objective of sorting students into different levels of the educational system, the CFAT sponsored a study by William S. Learned and Ben Wood; begun in the early days of the Depression and published on the eve of World War II, *The Student and His Knowledge* sought to measure achievement, or knowledge, rather than mere aptitude. Specifically, Learned and Wood wanted to determine whether students at a given grade level possessed adequate knowledge to advance to the next grade level. Learned concluded that the nation needed a standardized testing system, so that students could be examined and reexamined at each stage. His calls would lead to the incorporation of the Educational Testing Service in 1947. But an alternative approach to mental testing developed in the 1930s. The so-called Eight-Year Study, which the Progressive Education Association (PEA) commenced in 1933, pioneered the use of tests to measure competence to learn a body of material within a specified period of time, with little regard to the sorting of students into different levels of the educational system. Broadly speaking, the PEA approach to testing struck a blow against hierarchy and standardization; much like the earlier *Cardinal Principles of Secondary Education*, it sought to liberate secondary schools from domination by the values of elite colleges.[60]

Experience with mental testing during World War II undermined Learned's assumption that relatively few Americans were intellectually fit for college. During the war the Army administered the Army General

Classification Test (AGCT) to some ten millon inductees. Inasmuch as the AGCT data gave the distribution of scores by the highest year of schooling each individual had completed at the time of induction, it became possible to assess the relationship between test scores and education levels. Walter V. Bingham, a pioneer of psychometrics who headed the Army testing program, concluded in 1946 that the tests revealed "a vast pool of talent now only partly drawn upon."[61]

The wartime testing conducted by the Army Air Force (AAF) Aviation Psychology Program buttressed conclusions even more favorable to mass higher education, especially when the latter permitted specialization. Forced to train aviators quickly, the AAF drew on research conducted between the wars by Leon L. Thurstone, who questioned the widely held notion of a general, undifferentiated human intelligence. Isolating fully 27 separate aptitudes, AAF psychologists discovered that pilots, navigators, bombardiers, and flight engineers each required different combinations of aptitudes. The AAF tests achieved impressive results in the form of high correlations between test scores and graduation from flight school, accident rates, and promotions.[62]

Published assessments of the AAF results coincided with and partly influenced the widely cited 1947 report of the President's Commission on Higher Education. Drafted by George F. Zook, the president of the American Council on Education, *Higher Education for American Democracy* briefly traced the expansion of the American educational enterprise since the turn of the century, noted the "unprecedented peak" of collegiate enrollments in 1947, urged greater federal appropriations for higher education, and concluded that "we shall aim at making higher education equally available to all young people, as we now do education in the elementary and high schools."[63] Additionally, the Zook commission proposed making education through the second year of college available without cost to all Americans who could not afford otherwise to attend college.[64] The Zook commission, which was strongly influenced by the AGCT data, affirmed that 49 percent of the population had the "mental ability" to complete the first two years of college, and that 32 percent were capable of completing additional years of schooling.[65]

These proposals established *Higher Education for American Democracy* as a landmark in the history of American education. Breaking completely with Depression-bred doubts about the value of expanding significantly the proportion of the population enrolled in colleges and universities, the report predicted that at least 4,600,000 young people should be enrolled in colleges and universities by 1960.[66] Although stated as a goal, the 4,600,000 figure was at least partly a prediction, for the commission called attention to the beginnings of the baby boom as well as to the unexpected hordes of veterans who enrolled in colleges and universities under the G.I. Bill. In addition, the commission was influenced by new currents in mental testing, which pointed to the conclusion that a much higher proportion of the population than previously supposed might benefit from higher education.

In calling for federal aid to public higher education and a geometric expansion of higher education, and in also attacking racial and gender discrimination in higher education, *Higher Education for American Democracy* was a farsighted and humane document. Yet the report had some curious features that speak pages about the configuration of forces within education committed to educational democracy. Although written in the peak year of veteran enrollments, the report actually paid very little attention to the G.I. Bill and its effects. Aside from a few brief references early in the report to the role of veterans in widening the avenue to higher education, the commission generally skirted the subject of veterans. One plausible explanation for this slight was that the commission's interests focused on long-term expansion, while everyone conceded that veterans would have no more than a short-term impact on higher education. But one suspects that the real reason was rather that the educational preferences of the veterans ran counter to the direction that the commission hoped American higher education would take.

For the most part, returning veterans enrolled in prestigious four-year colleges and universities and primarily pursued liberal arts rather than vocational curricula. In the fall of 1948, when the majority of non-veterans enrolled in public institutions, the majority of veterans entered private colleges and universities, institutions where the traditions of liberal education were strongly ingrained.[67] Some veterans enrolled in junior colleges and teachers' colleges, but usually because they could not get into more prestigious institutions, and even in the teachers' colleges they took liberal arts rather than teacher-preparation programs. For its part, the commission exhibited a pronounced bias against private colleges and specifically recommended that all federal aid be channeled to public institutions.[68] Above all, *Higher Education for American Democracy* focused on community colleges as the spearheads of the future expansion of higher education. It called for making education through the fourteenth grade (in other words, through the first two years of college) universal in the same sense that high-school education had become universal, and it identified community colleges as the institutions most likely to accept the burden of democratizing higher education.

The Zook commission boosted community colleges not only by associating them with the increasingly popular cause of democracy in higher education but also by assigning them significant responsibilities for adult education. Although at one point *Higher Education for American Democracy* called upon all colleges and universities to become true community colleges by taking adult education seriously, most of its expectations for adult education focused on community colleges. It urged these institutions to serve as centers of learning for their surrounding communities and to gear their programs to local wishes. Citing one public junior college with a daytime enrollment of 3,000 and a late afternoon and evening enrollment of 25,000, the commission encouraged community colleges to adopt a mixture of recreational and vocational programs: workshops in painting or singing or playwriting ("for fun"), refresher courses on child psychology and journalism, and Spanish courses for sales personnel, bellboys, and waiters in regions visited by Latin Americans.[69]

The values that permeated *Higher Education for American Democracy* had both distant and proximate sources. As described by the Zook commission, community colleges bore some resemblance to antebellum academies. Let it quickly be added that Zook and other members of the commission would have balked at this comparison. Since the days of Horace Mann, public schoolmen had dismissed academies as enclaves of aristocratic privilege. But this dismissal, while close to the mark as a description of academies by the end of the nineteenth century, misconstrued the antebellum academies, which were local, nonresidential, quasi-public institutions and which offered a broad assortment of liberal and vocational courses. With academic terms structured around the farming seasons, minimal attention to sequential curricula, no degrees, and essentially no admission requirements, academies afforded some students the opportunity to acquire primary education, others a preparation for college, and still others a self-sufficient facsimile of a liberal education as well as useful occupational skills. No academy would have imagined itself as engaged in adult education, but academy students often were young adults who attended school between interludes of work.

Since Zook and his colleagues paid no heed to academies and probably knew little if anything about them, the foregoing comparison may seem irrelevant. Yet it is possible to piece together from the antebellum academies, lyceums, and countless small colleges a configuration of popular attitudes about education that took shape before the Civil War and persisted into the twentieth century. These attitudes include a propensity to load the curriculum with innumerable subjects, a sometimes hilarious tolerance of superficiality, a desire for inexpensive, locally accessible, and locally responsive institutions of higher education, and the belief that higher education should be both liberal and practical.

These were not the values of leading universities during the Progressive era, when public-school educators experienced increasing alienation from the mainstream of higher education. But Progressive sympathizers with these values garrisoned a few outposts in higher education, including university extension and municipal universities.[70] As president of the University of Akron between 1926 and 1933, Zook had nudged the university toward greater involvement in its locale. The values that Zook brought to Akron were highly compatible with the image that community colleges projected. Although he never taught in or headed a junior college, Zook had inspired the organization in 1920 of the American Association of Junior Colleges and later, as president of the University of Akron, he had served on the CFAT commission that authored *State Higher Education in California*, the so-called Magna Charta of junior colleges.[71] While decades of self-promotion contributed to their designation as democracy's vanguard, the junior colleges owed more to the congruence between the image they projected and the values of an influential segment of educators.

From Adult to Continuing Education

Although the Zook commission identified the vocational education of adults as a legitimate objective of community colleges, it more frequently associated adult education with "community education," a shaggy fabric of noncredit programs aimed at the leisured. Shaped by Depression-era forums and WPA classes, community education included a range of activities from musical and dramatic performances to forums and lectures, arts and crafts, and courses in recreational skills.[72] Progressive educators long had found public benefit in community education, less on the grounds that it encouraged intellectuality or aestheticism than on the principle that to bring citizens together in a common purpose was in itself desirable.

With the onset of World War II, the WPA classes had ceased and the public forums popular in the 1930s had been redirected toward homefront preparedness ("Let's Talk About Milk Production for a World at War"). But in the late 1940s and early 1950s, informal adult education received a powerful boost from an interlocking directorate of intellectuals and elite business leaders. Walter Paepcke, a Chicago paper manufacturer, was a key figure in forging this alliance of commerce and culture. Paepcke and his wife, Elizabeth, not only cherished the arts but each recognized as well the compatibility between modern art and spare and compelling industrial designs. In the late 1940s Walter Paepcke began to gather refugee intellectuals, American philosophers (notably Robert Maynard Hutchins and Mortimer Adler), and business leaders at the former mining town of Aspen, Colorado. There he organized a cultural festival, held in June 1949 to commemorate the bicentennial of the birth of Goethe. Crowned by lectures by Albert Schweitzer and the Spanish philosopher José Ortega y Gasset, the festival led to the establishment of the Aspen Institute of Humanistic Studies. Paepcke saw this institute as an embodiment of his long-standing goal to slay Babbittry; Hutchins and Adler perceived it as a way, in the postwar world, to encourage intellectual unity on the foundation of the reasoned analysis of moral values.[73]

Hutchins and Adler long had believed that only mass adult education could rescue civilization from the twin snares of positivism, which dismissed ethical issues as unresolvable, and the mass culture that Ortega y Gasset had flayed in *The Revolt of the Masses* (1930) as hedonistic and shallow. As a summer haven for intellectuals and executives, however, the Aspen Institute lacked a popular foundation. Drawing on several precedents, Hutchins and Adler fashioned Great Books courses for adults during the 1940s. These forerunners of the Great Books publishing venture of the 1950s were originally offered through the extension arm of the University of Chicago and after 1947 through the independent Great Books Foundation.[74] But the invitation-only Great Books courses had only a modest popular impact beyond the perimeters of Chicago businessmen and their spouses.[75] To popularize liberal education, which he envisioned as no less than a means of saving the world, Hutchins seized upon the opportunity afforded by the reorganization and endowment of the Ford Foundation to become its associate director in 1951. His influence quickly became evident in the foundation's decision to establish a subsidiary foundation in the same year, the Fund for Adult Education (FAE).

In the early 1950s the FAE sought to construct a broad base for humanistic adult education by seeding grants in designated "test cities," including Akron; Memphis; Bridgeport; Kansas City; San Bernardino, California; Little Rock; and Niagara Falls. For the most part, these were cities that could not be presumed sympathetic to liberal adult education through the informal discussion groups on which the FAE insisted. Typically, FAE officials contacted leading citizens and encouraged them to form adult-education councils composed of representatives of church, welfare, labor, business, and women's organizations, who would then arouse public sentiment and spur attendance at discussions of materials packaged by the FAE around broad humanistic themes: the Jeffersonian Heritage, Human Freedom, the Ways of Mankind.[76]

In the eyes of the FAE, the purpose of the enterprise was to teach people *how* rather than *what* to think and to engender in communities a self-sustaining popular commitment to critical thinking. The former objective was consistent with the goals of the New School intellectuals in the 1920s, but the latter, which stressed media saturation of communities with advertising for deep thinking, marked a new tactic. Partly because it aimed at building a popular base, the FAE did not encourage colleges to take the lead in organizing discussion groups. Although local participants in Great Books discussion groups at times stimulated their communities to apply for FAE support, the discussion groups aided by the FAE were not Great

Books clubs. Rather, discussion groups drew on brief typescripts, films, and lecturers supplied by the FAE, which saw its role as priming the pump.

But the pump did not stay primed for long. By the mid-1950s, when the FAE was ready to withdraw from active support, local disputes were developing between advocates of the humanistic education and public officials who perceived adult-education councils as useful only to the extent that they spurred public interest in such issues as youth and delinquency, problems of the aged, and regional planning. In 1955, for example, Elwood Street, a Bridgeport official, pleaded with John Osman of the FAE to sanction a scheme whereby the adult education council would become the educational division of the community chest. In Street's conception, the division would use Ford funds targeted for discussion groups to promote public awareness of local social issues, an objective that he described as compatible with adult liberal education "broadly conceived." Adhering to the more rigid and ambitious FAE standard, Osman dismissed the proposal as beyond the pale of liberal education.[77]

When it ceased operations in 1961, the FAE had relatively little to show for its decade of experiment with popular adult education. By then the movement for liberally educating the adult public through discussion groups or sales of Great Books was losing momentum.[78] Hutchins's own interests were shifting toward the study of civil liberties; in 1954 he became president of the Ford Foundation's Fund for the Republic, and between 1959 and 1974 he served as president of the Ford Foundation's Center for the Study of Democratic Institutions in Santa Barbara. In one respect, this was a logical progression, for the FAE's commitment to open discussion had reflected more than the postwar search for the intellectual foundations of a liberal society. On the local level the FAE had encouraged an oblique attack on McCarthyism by sponsoring discussion groups on press censorship and intolerance. In turn, the waning of McCarthyism contributed to the unraveling of the rationale for discussion groups.

In a few instances, local colleges absorbed the kind of adult programming favored by the FAE. For example, the Adult Education Foundation of Akron established an Institute of Civic Affairs at the University of Akron when Ford support dried up in the mid-1950s.[79] But the agendas of colleges were gradually shifting away from this kind of adult education and toward the enrollment of older students in formal courses. Marked by a self-perception as a "democratic community service" and by open admissions and low cost, community colleges were proving attractive to older students in the 1950s and 1960s. Jesse Bogue recalled giving a commencement address in 1952 at a community college where the average age of the graduates was 30.[80] Leland L. Medsker reported that in 1960, 47 percent of the regular day students in a sample of over 13,000 junior college students were age 23 or over, and 28 percent were 26 or over.[81] The conclusion of the Korean War brought a new batch of veterans into colleges, and the declining age of marriage in the 1950s probably contributed to delayed college entry.[82] Similar trends were evident in four-year colleges, which recorded a 47 percent increase between 1953 and 1957 in the number of students aged 25 to 34.[83] But community colleges were more receptive than four-year colleges to older students who attended part-time and without planning to obtain degrees. Usually classified as "special and adult" (or as "adult" or "special"), these students accounted for 35 percent of all community-college students in 1948 and 60 percent in 1953–54. Some institutions were composed mainly of such students.[84] For example, California's Long Beach City College, a community college, registered 39,915 students in 1954–55, of whom 23,955 were classified as special.[85] The trend continued into the 1960s; in 1966 the *Junior College Directory* reported 486,975 part-time students and 424,676 full-time students in American junior colleges.[86]

Special students in community colleges ran the gamut from high-school dropouts (most states required public junior colleges to accept students regardless of whether they had acquired high-school diplomas) to college graduates. The flexible structure of community colleges virtually invited attendance by special students. Ever in search of new student pools, community colleges were less likely than four-year institutions to resent the administrative burden of part-time students. Further, students who were returning to school and were insecure about their academic qualifications probably felt more comfortable in community colleges, which had sketchy general education requirements even for full-time students (and none for part-timers), low standards, and a self-image as institutions for the academically underprivileged. Community colleges were also inexpensive. Students could, and in most instances had to, live at home while attending.

A significant expansion of the vocational offerings of community colleges enhanced their appeal to older students in the 1960s. Community colleges continued to advance their role in education for the semiprofessions, a term that had the right ring for those who returned to school to qualify for better jobs. By the mid-1960s community colleges were introducing courses in police and fire science and in hotel and food technology, which offered at least a verbal reconciliation between student aspirations and local occupational structures. In addition, increases in the average size of community colleges (enrollments in public two-year colleges doubled between 1960 and 1965 while the number of such colleges increased by 20 percent) made possible more specialized vocational offerings. Vocational courses formerly available only on a pilot or experimental basis now were integrated into full-time occupational or career curricula, which led in many cases to the Associate in Arts (A.A.) degree.[87] In 1963, passage of the Vocational Education Act opened the faucet of federal funding for occupational courses in community colleges (and other institutions) and specifically freed community colleges of the sundry restrictions of the Smith-Hughes Act's heritage. The confluence of these circumstances pushed the proportion of community-college students enrolled in occupational curricula from one-quarter to one-third during the 1960s.[88]

The inherited lexicon of community-college terminology imperfectly reflected the increasing diversity of their students.[89] Both the early pioneers of junior colleges and the Zook commission had favored adult education, which they usually had equated with education for leisure. By the 1960s, however, it was clear that community colleges were attracting considerable numbers of students beyond the normal college years of 18 to 21 into their academic or vocational curricula. The distinguishing characteristics of these students were that they were mainly male, attended part-time, and were more likely than full-time day students to take vocational courses. An indeterminable number of them hoped to acquire the A.A. degree, which by the late 1960s could be obtained through vocational curricula (as noted, full vocational curricula were becoming the norm) as well as through the traditional college-transfer curriculum. Although in some community colleges these part-time students took courses through divisions of adult education, they did not fit the inherited image of participants in adult education/community education. In response, community-college officials increasingly insisted on distinguishing their "continuing" from their "adult" students. This was partly a self-serving distinction, for state legislatures often balked at subsidizing anything labeled adult education, with its residual associations from the 1930s of classes in bridge and tap dancing. But the distinction rested on a genuine, if not always crisp, difference between (mainly) young men in their twenties, often veterans and with families to support, who sought either to secure the A.A. en route to college transfer or, increasingly, to complete vocational curricula, and those in mid-life and beyond who expected little more from education than the satisfaction of personal interests.

In the early 1960s colleges of all varieties faced the task of absorbing the postwar baby boomers. Swelling enrollments affected all kinds of colleges, but community colleges achieved the fastest growth rate. Providing for one student in every six in 1955, they enrolled three in every ten by 1970.[90] Nearly all of this increase occurred in public community colleges, which by 1970 enrolled 95 percent of all two-year college students.[91] Degree-credit enrollment in community colleges more than tripled in the 1960s and, partly in response to the growing number of eighteen-year-olds in the population, in 1966 the number of full-time students in community colleges surpassed that of part-time students for the first time in the decade.[92] Collectively, these factors strengthened the preference of community-college officials to forge their evening programs into parallels of their day curricula on the principle that evening students should complete regular academic or vocational curricula.

Community colleges thought of themselves as islands of innovation, but their preoccupation with raising enrollments and securing funding encouraged them to confine their innovations to vocational programs and to community education. Beyond their valued contribution to the body count, older students who enrolled for credit attracted no special attention and rarely were studied.[93] Nor can it be said that four-year colleges in the 1950s and 1960s viewed adult students as constituting a special class with distinctive needs. By the end of the 1960s, much of the innovative spirit that had permeated adult education in the interwar years had left the movement. Yet one significant exception to this generalization has to be recorded. At the start of the 1960s a handful of institutions—mainly state universities with strong extension traditions, elite women's colleges, and coeducational private universities with separate women's colleges—began to introduce special centers or institutes for women returning to college. For example, in 1960 the University of Minnesota launched its Minnesota Plan for the Continuing Education of Women. A year later the Radcliffe Institute for Independent Study opened, and in 1962 Sarah Lawrence College initiated its Center for Continuing Education. By the mid-1960s there were roughly 100 continuing education programs for women (CEW) in the United States.[94]

As the title of the Radcliffe Institute suggests, it and some of the other CEW programs were originally conceived as opportunities for career women to advance their knowledge and skills, but CEW centers quickly attracted women afflicted by what Betty Friedan would call in *The Feminine Mystique* (1963) "the problem that has no name"—the dissatisfaction of educated women with their exclusive role as parents or housewives. Middle-aged women who had left college to marry, or who now aspired to degrees beyond the baccalaureate, used the institutes for guidance and counseling as well as for seminars in which they explored the role of women in sundry academic disciplines.[95]

Arising in leading four-year colleges and universities rather than in community colleges and designed as experiments with restricted clienteles, CEW centers nevertheless foreshadowed the surge of college reentry by middle-class women in the 1970s, and this surge has affected community colleges more than any other tier of American education.

The Revolution of the 1970s

Rising initially in the early 1960s, gaining momentum in the early 1970s, cresting in the late 1970s, and still showing few signs of receding, a wave of interest in "lifelong learning" has swept across American education. There had been waves earlier in American history: Josiah Holbrook and his lyceums in the 1820s, John H. Vincent and Chautauqua in the 1870s and 1880s, Progressive-style university extension after 1900, and the "humanizing of knowledge" in the 1920s. While each wave has differed in contour from its predecessor, one common feature has been the emergence during each period of a new clientele for voluntary learning.

Significant improvements in the quality of educational statistics since 1970 make it possible to sketch the features of the new clients of the 1970s and 1980s. As the postwar baby boom matured and then receded, the proportion of eighteen-year-olds in the population started to decline, provoking fears by the early 1970s that colleges would run out of students. In reality, enrollments soared in the 1970s, mainly because of entry by students older than age 21.[96]

Increasing enrollments by females spearheaded this rise in older students. Throughout the 1950s and 1960s, males predominated in all age groups in colleges and especially among students beyond the age of 21. With their strong vocational bent and receptivity to part-time students, community colleges were practically male bastions in these years; in the 1960s males outnumbered females in these institutions by at least two to one.[97] The shift in the 1970s was remarkable. As late as 1974 men still outnumbered women among collegians aged 14 to 34, but during the next five years, while the number of men remained unchanged, the number of women rose by one-fourth. Nearly half of this increase in female enrollment took place in two-year colleges, and it was most pronounced among the older age groups. From 1972 to 1979 the number of female collegians aged 25–34 rose 127 percent (compared to 15.1 percent for males), while the number of females aged 35 and over increased 119 percent (compared to 33 percent for males). In 1979 just over one-fourth of all college students aged 14 to 34 were enrolled in community colleges, but nearly half of the 25- to 34-year-olds were. Although the rate of increase in collegiate enrollment slackened in the 1980s, these trends persisted, and, as in the 1970s, community colleges and women accounted disproportionately for the growth. In 1987 undergraduate male students slightly outnumbered females in four-year colleges, while in two-year colleges undergraduate women outnumbered men by nearly three to two, and by nearly two to one among students age 25 or over.

"Nontraditional," which became the term of choice to describe new students in the 1970s, encompassed collegians who were poor, black, Hispanic, female, or older. For the most part, these were discrete rather than overlapping groups. While predominantly female, collegians who enrolled at the age of 25, 30, or beyond were not drawn disproportionately from the academically or economically disadvantaged population. Studies have consistently shown that participation in organized adult education of any sort correlates positively with previous educational attainment, and this generalization applies to the older collegians of the 1970s and 1980s. In the late 1960s, two-thirds of the students who entered college beyond the age of 21 were in college for the first time, but by 1971 half of those entering beyond 21, and by 1978 over 70 percent, already had attended college.[98] The rising educational attainment of older college entrants resulted in large measure from the influx of older women, who constituted only 29 percent of college entrants over 21 in 1966 but 57 percent by 1978.[99] In contrast, black students, who composed 20 percent of all 18- to 19-year-olds in community colleges in 1987, constituted only 10 percent of those aged 25 or over.

The media has publicized instances of grandmothers who return to college to secure the baccalaureate, but few of the graying collegians of the 1970s and 1980s were elderly. In 1987 less than 1 percent of collegians aged 25 or over were 65 or over, and only 6 percent were 50 or over; more than half were 30 to 44. Older female collegians had a higher rate of concurrent labor-force participation than comparably aged non-collegians (the older, the higher), and they were less likely to be married and living with their spouses. These facts help to explain why so high a proportion of older female collegians entered two-year colleges. Older collegians who were in the labor force rather than supported by spouses would find community colleges cheaper (in terms of cost per credit-hour) than even public four-year colleges, more conveniently located, and highly receptive to part-time students.[100]

The rising enrollment of working adults fed the growth in the proportion of part-time students (defined as those who carry less than 75 percent of what a given institution considers a full-time credit load) in higher education. Between 1970 and 1991 part-time enrollments in all institutions of higher education increased at more than three times the rate of full-time enrollments and made up nearly half of all enrollments by 1991. In 1991 community colleges enrolled 57 percent of all part-time students in higher education, compared to 42 percent in four-year institutions. Within community colleges the proportion of part-time students enrolled in credit courses rose from 48 percent of all enrollments in 1970, to 62 percent in 1979, and to 67 percent by 1987.[101] As women have increased their labor-force participation and as the number of two-income families has risen, women have come to outnumber men among part-time students; there are nearly twice as many women as men among part-time students aged 35 and over.

The Paper Chase

While set within the context of demographic change, the phenomenon of college reentry in the 1970s and 1980s cannot be explained merely by the aging of the population. Both the size of the pool and the rate of enrollment increased among older students, who enrolled primarily to acquire degrees in such fields as business, engineering, health, and computer science.[102] Even in community colleges most stated degree intentions. The Current Population Survey reported in 1979 that two-thirds of all part-time students in community colleges sought at least the A.A. degree; still others sought vocational certificates, and only 29.2 percent listed their intention as "no degree." While the survey did not control for age in responses to this particular item, the confluence of two facts—the high proportion of students aged 25 and over who enrolled part-time, and the high proportion of part-time students who avowed degree intentions—suggests widespread degree aspirations even among older community-college students.[103]

Anyone who browses through the educational supplements of the *New York Times* or *Washington Post* is likely to reach the same conclusion without having to wind through tortuous statistical paths. Whereas in the 1950s and 1960s advertisements described opportunities for mastering effective speaking, real-estate brokerage, and other discrete skills or bodies of knowledge, now most describe degree programs.

The increasing prominence of degree programs and the academic credentials they impart has resulted from the conjunction of bureaucratization, professionalization, and the expansion of higher education. The key word here is "conjunction," for in itself bureaucratization does not dictate any single method for selecting and rewarding merit. For decades the merit system of the nation's largest bureaucracy, the federal government, relied on tests rather than on academic credentials. The authors of the Pendleton Act of 1883 established competitive examinations rather than educational qualifications as the basis for entry into the classified segment of the bureaucracy (the segment controlled by merit rather than political patronage). They did so explicitly to counter critics who argued that the restriction of patronage would nurture an undemocratic, British-style civil service, dominated by the American equivalents of Oxonians and Cantabrigians. With some exceptions, examinations continued to dominate entry and promotion in the federal (as well as state and municipal) civil services for the next half-century, while business corporations displayed a near obsession with intelligence and personality tests well into the 1950s. Within the context of their time, the strategies of self-improvers who joined home-study clubs in the age of Chautauqua or who took Dale Carnegie courses in the 1940s and 1950s were plausible responses to the selection procedures of both governments and businesses.[104]

The emphasis on academic credentials rather than examinations was initially propelled by the governmental and corporate quest for experts and professionals, an offshoot of the movement for scientific management during the late nineteenth and early twentieth centuries. In contrast to candidates who presented themselves for examinations, experts and professionals claimed status based on ascription by insisting that their credentials demonstrated their competence. Governmental and corporate bureaucracies accepted this claim by exempting professionals from competitive examinations, by allowing them lateral entry at higher rungs, and by deferring their certification to professional associations and indirectly to universities.[105]

These developments occurred slowly. Not until the 1920s and 1930s did the scientific-management movement shift from identifying and training efficient workers for routine jobs (the world of Charles Prosser and David Snedden) to the recruitment of higher-ups. The federal civil service, which started to exempt experts from competitive examinations in the 1890s, did not actively recruit university graduates until the 1930s, and it did so then less to fill slots with experts than to lure future managers from the ranks of elite collegians. At each step the federal bureaucracy tried to maintain the appearance of conformity to the established merit system. When it began in the 1890s to certify rather than examine experts, it called its certification procedures "non-assembled examinations," and when in the 1930s it sought university graduates for future management posts, it claimed that it was recruiting professionals in public administration.[106] Regardless, the direction of change was clear; experts and professionals formed the entering wedge for employees whose entry and future prospects depended on their academic credentials more than on their performance on examinations.

Eager to strengthen their ties to influential bureaucracies, universities have encouraged these developments (which also have impacted state and municipal bureaucracies) by introducing programs oriented toward the marginal professions like city planning, public administration, school administration, librarianship, and social work. The cementing of the bond between higher education and the professions has not appreciably altered the relative prestige ranking of the latter, but it has contributed to the internal stratification of the professions on the basis of academic credentials. In addition, it has encouraged a vast extension of credentialism, both laterally across the spectrum of universities and downwardly to the junior colleges. This extension has been spurred to a significant extent by the marginal professions themselves, for in these professions academic credentials are not merely sought but cherished. Marginal professionals are far more likely than doctors or lawyers to work for bureaucracies as salaried employees. Lacking clients as such, their claims to professional status are best evidenced by their credentials rather than by their ability to extract fees for services, which was a valid measure of professional status in the nineteenth century but in twentieth-century bureaucracies is known as extortion.[107]

The forging of bonds between the professions and the bureaucracies has helped to popularize the expectation of a career, a hierarchical sequence of related jobs through which individuals move in a predictable fashion.[108] Outside of the commissioned officers corps of the military, careers were rare in the nineteenth century, but with the bureaucratization of both government and business in the twentieth century they have become the objective of middle-class Americans, so much so that having a career is now a plausible criterion of middle-class status.[109] Careers depend on bureaucratically structured workplaces, which are unparalleled in their capacity to generate sequences of related jobs. And careers have come to depend on the possession of educational certificates, a process initially driven by the desire of bureaucracies to hire experts but gradually widened to include collegians, even liberal-arts graduates, who were likely candidates for promotion up career ladders.

None of this would have occurred without the complicity of bureaucracies outside of the university. Regardless of the rate at which universities churned out credentialed job applicants, governments and corporations could have decided to make do with fewer highly credentialed employees. But any proclivities in this direction have been checked by several factors. Bureaucratic professionals have a vested interest in maintaining the primacy of credentials (the basis of their own positions), and the legislated rules of merit that have governed public bureaucracies mandate more or less rigid hiring and promotion procedures in the name of fairness. In addition, within bureaucracies departments inevitably acquire a measure of independence from the central command. For example, in large, highly departmentalized corporations in the private sector, which have been as prone as government bureaucracies to use educational attainment as a basis for selecting employees, departmental managers typically write job descriptions with less regard for the requirements of the corporation than for those of their departments, which they see as ends in themselves. In addition, these managers routinely use educational attainment as a convenient if unexamined predictor of efficiency.[110]

Long valued by men, academic credentials have become increasingly vital for women who hope to break out of gender-segregated occupations. The experience of "Janet Klein," an employee of a multinational corporation, is representative. After leaving secretarial school, she took a variety of company training courses and even a Dale Carnegie course, but at the age of 38 she had come to recognize that to obtain a management position in 1978 "I'm going to have to get that degree."[111]

During the 1950s an increasing number of older, married women entered the labor force, but without any discernible impact on gender segregation.[112] As late as 1970, about 60 percent of all women in the labor force worked in occupations in which women formed a majority of at least 80 percent. Gender segregation declined modestly in the 1970s and precipitously in the 1980s, a development that should be viewed as an effect rather than cause of higher educational attainment by women. Although educational attainment by both men and women has risen since the early 1900s, the G.I. Bill widened the gender gap in higher education by encouraging males to think of college as a normal experience. As late as 1967, when the pool of high-school graduates was evenly divided between men and women, 71 percent of male graduates entered college, compared to only 52 percent of female graduates.[113] As demands for equality of occupational opportunity mounted throughout the 1970s, women who earlier had bypassed college or dropped out now elected to secure the baccalaureate. By 1984 the percentage of women aged 24 to 29 to have attended at least one year of college was virtually the same as that of men.[114]

Rising educational attainment by women in the 1970s and 1980s coincided with their push into formerly gender-segregated academic fields and contributed significantly to their drive into formerly segregated occupations. Educational attainment was coming to have a significant impact not only on the occupational trajectories of women but on their entire life course. For example, in 1950 women with higher educational attainment had their first child at about the same age as those with lower attainment, but by 1980 highly educated women were delaying motherhood. Women increasingly mixed education, motherhood, and work, activities that once had been sequential or incompatible.[115]

The same advertisements that trumpet degree programs emphasize the enhancement of self-esteem that comes with academic achievement as well as the job-improvement motive. Recent studies have indicated that diverse motives, self-fulfillment as well as job improvement, push older Americans toward college reentry. For example, the late 1970s found Margaret Greenson of Santa Fe "feeling angry almost all of the time at my children and my husband. It was as if everybody else was entitled to do what they wanted except Mother." Although dissatisfied with her work as a bookkeeper, she did not want a better job. Rather, tired of making sacrifices for her husband and four children, she accepted an income reduction, worked part-time in a museum, and enrolled in a home-study course through the University of Maryland in order to nourish "the fifth kid, me."[116] While education has long promised psychosocial as well as economic benefits for adults, older Americans, especially women, increasingly have sought to boost their self-esteem by the relatively solitary experience of testing themselves in an academic environment rather than by social participation in the sort of adult institutes that proliferated in the 1930s.[117]

A fair question is whether this quest for self-fulfillment represents a new motive, or a new name for an old one. Women who joined literary societies and Chautauqua circles in the nineteenth century did so not only to master bodies of knowledge but also to push their intellectual horizons beyond the kitchen. The prevailing doctrine that women were morally superior to men made it difficult for Victorian women to acknowledge self-interested goals, but just as they found vocational applications for cultural information, so too they derived personal emotional benefits from the challenge of study. By casting study as an elevated calling that required detachment from the workaday world, Arnoldian culture legitimized the intellectual ambitions of women in a cultural climate that was unreceptive to their avowal of self-interest. In contrast, under the label of self-fulfillment, the assertion of self-interested motives acquired new sanction in the 1970s and 1980s. Indeed, such assertion virtually became a mark of moral triumph, a victory over the cowardly "bottling up" of motives.

While self-interest is scarcely a new motive, an increasing proportion of the population has acknowledged its legitimacy and has possessed the resources and will "to define and enact possibilities of feeling and mind as freely and as fully as possible." Postwar affluence and successive assaults on the legal and philosophical bases of racial and gender inequality have laid the foundation for this "democratization of personhood."[118] As more Americans acted out their wish for further education, colleges and universities began in the 1970s to make it easier for older students to acquire degrees. The boldest experiments saw institutions like Minnesota Metropolitan State College (now Metropolitan State University), Empire State College in New York, the Community College of Vermont, and a score or so of others award credit for varying combinations of unusual learning methods, including previous experience, instruction in geographically dispersed adult centers, individualized learning contracts between instructors and students, and the acquisition of competencies in broadly defined interdisciplinary fields.[119] Introduced by Connecticut's Wesleyan University in 1953, the interdisciplinary Masters of Liberal Studies (MLS) degree has become extremely popular among older students; the number of MLS programs rose from 12 in 1975 to 120 in 1990.[120] In addition, hundreds of colleges and universities, ranging from struggling Catholic women's colleges to Johns Hopkins, have opened satellite campuses adjacent to major metropolitan areas.

Many obstacles continue to confront reentry students, including the fact that criteria for awarding federal, state, and private student aid long have discriminated against part-time students. Not infrequently, part-time students have been unaware of even those grants for which they do qualify.[121] In addition, a high proportion of older students who attended community colleges stated their intention to secure degrees, and then did not acquire the A.A. or a subsequent baccalaureate. The proportion of students who transferred to four-year colleges, which had hovered at around one-third between 1945 and 1970, declined in the 1970s.[122] Throughout the 1970s and 1980s, only about 9 percent of community-college students even secured the A.A. degree (the prerequisite for transfer) or an occupational certificate.[123] Older community-college students may have had weaker degree intentions than their counterparts in four-year colleges, but we cannot assume this. Older women, who gravitated in disproportionate numbers to two-year rather than four-year colleges, may have chosen the former because they were less expensive (studies indicate that women attach more importance than men to cost in choosing colleges), and not because these women had weak degree intentions. What is clear is that the institutional atmosphere of community colleges, never very hospitable to college transfer, became almost antithetical to transfer during the 1970s—partly because federal funding was making it possible for community colleges to offer a greater variety of vocational programs, and partly because community colleges were attracting younger students who indeed were educationally and socially disadvantaged and who probably did have weak degree intentions.[124]

A question that naturally arises is whether this enormous growth of higher education has benefited either students or society. Until the late 1960s few educators or economists questioned either the individual or public value of investment in education. In this respect they were much like other twentieth-century Americans, who have assigned to education the same roles that their nineteenth-century ancestors accorded the frontier: a source of opportunity and a solvent of class differences. Economists who in the 1950s and early 1960s hammered together the planks of human-capital theory affirmed that the long-term benefits or rate of return from an individual's investment in education were superior to other forms of investment. In addition, these economists contended that education would increase the skills and hence the productivity of the work force, and that a more equal distribution of education would lead to a more equal distribution of income. Thus investment in education would lead to social as well as personal benefits.

The human-capital approach owed much of its appeal in the 1960s to a particular historical circumstance: the keen demand of corporations, research laboratories, and university faculties in the 1950s and 1960s for a degreed work force. At a time when those with advanced levels of educational attainment quickly found employment suited to their education, it was plausible to argue that the supply of degreed workers was determined by genuine demand for the skills acquired in the process of attaining degrees, and that increases in supply as a consequence of personal and public investment in education would facilitate economic growth. Then in the late 1960s and early 1970s several developments provoked a reassessment of the human-capital approach to evaluating education. Despite an ever-expanding stock of degreed workers, worker productivity began to decline, differences in income distribution failed to shrink, and the market for Ph.D.'s started to buckle. In this context, books like Ivar Berg's *Education and Jobs: The Great Training Robbery* challenged the idea that society necessarily derived benefits from the expansion of education. Berg found no evidence that workers with high levels of educational attainment were more productive than those with lower levels.

In a similar vein, Douglas Adkins crisply distinguished a "technogenic" model, in which the increasing stock of degreed workers is determined by the expansion of the nation's productive activities, from a "sociogenic" model, in which the growth of the supply of degreed workers reflects intergenerational values and beliefs about education and develops independently of the labor market. Although Adkins acknowledged the explanatory power of the technogenic model when applied to the 1950s, for the 1970s he cast his ballot for the rival sociogenic model. In turn, the sociogenic model led to the conclusion, developed by Lester Thurow and others, that academic credentials were not mere by-products of an educational process whose real value rested in the skills it imparted and the genuine economic demand it met, but were themselves the principal benefit of education. Education, Thurow argued, is a good investment for individuals but for essentially defensive reasons, "not because it would raise people's incomes above what they would have been if no one had increased his education, but because it raises their incomes above what they would have been if others acquire an education and they do not."[125]

The Knowledge Industry

A key prop of Thurow's argument is that skills required for jobs inhere more in the jobs than in individuals. Most training occurs after an individual secures a position. Faced with an excess of applicants with high levels of educational attainment, employers use attainment, evidenced by credentials, mainly as a quick and largely unexamined screening device to assess "trainability." One piece of evidence that appears to support this view is the colossal amount spent each year by American industry on training programs.

Company training programs have taken various shapes. Companies at times have cooperated with institutions of higher education to train their workers. For example, in the early 1980s General Motors arranged with 45 community colleges across the nation to retrain its dealer-based auto mechanics in new automotive technology.[126] Such training is "customized" in the sense that it is employer-specific; two-thirds of all such courses are offered at job sites.[127] In these fast-proliferating alliances between business and community colleges, companies are the senior partners. They donate state-of-the-art equipment, afford community colleges the opportunity to count paid company employees as part-time students, train faculty to instruct workers, and thereby dodge the costs of adding to their own training centers staff for whom they might have no future use.[128]

The requirements of corporate training often have worked to blur the lines between colleges and companies. In at least one instance, a proprietary school has turned itself into a college; in the 1970s Scranton's ICS was accredited by the Middle States Association of Schools and Colleges to award the A.A. degree. In other instances, companies have launched colleges. In 1979 Massachusetts incorporated the Wang Institute of Graduate Studies, which granted a master's degree in software engineering and drew students from several of the major computer engineering firms, including Apple, Digital, and Hewlett-Packard as well as Wang.[129] Twelve corporations have started the National Technological University, based in Fort Collins, Colorado, which beams engineering courses by satellite to corporate classrooms.[130] In the murky world of proprietary education, there has arisen a class of fee-financed institutions that offer degrees for suspiciously brief attendance periods (one night a week).[131]

Despite all of this, the bulk (60 to 80 percent) of corporate training in the 1980s was conducted within companies. In 1980 AT&T alone spent $1.7 billion to run 12,000 courses a day in 1,300 locations for 20,000 to 30,000 employees. Depending on whether one includes the cost of diverting employees from their regular duties to training sessions, annual corporate training expenditures in the 1980s either nearly equalled or greatly exceeded the annual expenditures of all colleges and universities (including community colleges) on all of their educational programs, a figure that stood at just over $60 billion at the start of the 1980s.[132]

The training of middle- and higher-level managers has been a major preoccupation of corporate schools since the 1930s, when the famous experiments at Western Electric's Hawthorne Works pointed to an understanding of human relationships as the key to increasing worker productivity. Elton Mayo, then a professor at the Harvard Business School and a consultant on the Hawthorne project, gave wide publicity to the significance of the experiments in his *Human Relations of an Industrial Civilization* (1933).[133] In the next half-century, various theories about the education of managers rose and fell. In the 1920s the Bell System's Chester Barnard arranged with the University of Pennsylvania for special humanities courses for young executives, an approach that Bell would return to in the 1950s.[134] More typically, corporate training courses came to bear the label of the exact quality sought, such as "Human Relations" or "Creative Thinking." The shift from humanities to human-relations and creative-thinking courses indicates both the tendency of corporations to stress immediate results in their training programs and the apprehension of managers enrolled in humanities courses that their grades would determine their advancement within the corporation. In response to intensifying foreign competition, the tendency in recent years has been for corporations to prune their training programs of any education that does not contribute directly to their strategic agenda—material that would be "nice to know" but that cannot pass the test of cost analysis.[135]

Even as they have emphasized immediate results, corporate training programs have adapted to new demands for specialized knowledge. In particular, the computer revolution has spurred company-based engineering programs. The automation of the banking industry has also contributed to the growth of company-based technical programs for a range of workers from keyboard operators upward. Corporate technical education may well surpass management training as the number of knowledge-intensive industries grows, or, alternatively, attention devoted to training sales personnel in fast-proliferating product lines may exceed that accorded to management and technical training.

As was true in the late nineteenth century, corporate training programs have flourished in industries marked by new technologies. Although high schools and colleges are far more receptive to vocational education now than in 1900, they have always been cumbersome instruments for teaching these technologies (which may explain why corporations have spent so much money on their own instructional programs). The field of management education has also spurred a good deal of acrimony between universities and corporations, which frequently complain that graduates of university business schools lack "real world" techniques. These conflicts have long been implicit in the very notion of vocational education. Vocational courses made their way into universities in the early 1900s with the promise that they would offer more abstract and/or general instruction than did the proprietary schools. To the extent that corporations now demand highly specific training, even in such "soft" skills as problem-solving or creative thinking, the tension has become more explicit. Yet for all the tension between university professional and vocational courses on one side and corporate training programs on the other, the two have often cooperated. Corporations that invest considerable sums to train their workers in company-specific techniques are by no means reluctant to hire college graduates, and universities at least profess to teach the general skills that businesses claim they want: the ability to think clearly, to communicate ideas effectively, and to work well with others. In this respect little has changed since the late nineteenth century, when business leaders, who for decades had derided collegians as unfitted for the world of affairs, began simultaneously to raise their estimate of college graduates and to launch their own training programs.

None of this proves that the public benefits of investment in education exceed those of alternative investments. Opinion on this issue swings back and forth; lately, human-capital theory has been making a comeback in response to the widespread fear that, compared to its foreign competitors, the American work force is inadequately educated.[136] So far as the personal benefits of investment in education are concerned, even the most acidulous critics of human-capital theory have not doubted the value of credentials to their possessors. The growth of corporate training underscores the importance of academic credentials for individual advancement, for entry to training programs depends significantly on educational attainment. College graduates become management trainees, secretaries with high-school diplomas are taught software systems, and noncredentialed workers at Domino's Pizza are given instruction in literacy, as well as in how to make pizza dough, through videodiscs.[137] Similarly, when companies contract with colleges for training programs, they are attentive to rankings within higher education. Graduate business schools train managers; community colleges train auto mechanics.

While it has been fashionable during the last few decades to compare the credentialing role of higher education to a treadmill, a good case can be made that the expansion of higher education since World War II and the growth of continuing education in colleges and universities have opened avenues for economic mobility *and* self-fulfillment that would have remained closed in the absence of these developments. If we compare the situation now with that earlier in the twentieth century, when proprietary schools dominated the job-improvement market, some significant differences come to light. Whether collegiate courses turn their students into more productive workers, they are widely perceived as paying economic dividends. This perception has contributed mightily to the growth of higher education, which in turn has opened opportunities for acquiring credentials of undeniable value in the job market. To be economically valuable, a credential does not have to be job-related. If the cash value of higher education depends significantly on simply the acquisition of a credential, degrees in such fields as Liberal Studies may well have the same potential for advancing the student's subsequent career as a more explicitly job-related degree. The popularity of the MLS degree among older students suggests that many reentry students see the issue in just this way.

Working adults who seek degrees in business and other vocationally oriented subjects also have benefited from the increasing centrality of academic credentials in the marketplace. In the early 1900s universities marginalized their evening business colleges in part because evening students chose courses at random, rarely sought degrees, and hence conflicted with the self-image of universities as institutions of broad education.[138] In contrast, the spread of credentialing has pushed working adults into degree programs, which in no sense are marginal activities of universities.

While perhaps arbitrary, credentials themselves are not inherently restricted by race, class, or gender. In fact, during the last few decades gaps between the educational attainment of men and women and that of whites and blacks have steadily narrowed.[139] They probably would narrow more were community colleges less ambivalent about whether they were engaging in higher education (recall the conflict between their "terminal" and "transfer" functions) and were they to become more successful at inducing students to transfer to four-year institutions. Further, since higher education has proclaimed the democratization of economic opportunity as one of its goals, it can fairly be judged (and funded) by the measure of its success in achieving this goal. The same can hardly be said of corporations, whose ability to raise capital depends entirely on the expectations of shareholders and financial institutions about their profitability. When corporations allocate resources to training programs, they do so mainly on the basis of their anticipated contribution to the bottom line, and in practice corporate expenditures on training have been heavily skewed toward the upper part of the employee ladder, toward management, and advanced-technical, training.[140]

If we take the long view, we can also see that over the course of the twentieth century the gap between job improvement and adult education has narrowed. In the first quarter of the century, job improvement meant proprietary schools, while adult education came to be embodied in such institutions and movements as the New School, workers' education, folk schools, adult institutes, WPA classes, community education, forums, Dale Carnegie classes, Great Books clubs, handicrafts, hobbies, and various other means of encouraging self-realization, general understanding, and the fruitful use of leisure. In its early days the American Association for Adult Education tried to sharpen the boundary between job improvement and adult education and to encourage nonvocational tendencies in the latter. The Depression strengthened the association between adult education and personal therapy and eroded interest in vocationalism. As late as the 1960s, community colleges maintained a sharp distinction between their vocational programs, which attracted many adults, and what they called adult education. While this distinction persists, developments since 1970 have tended to blur it. Whether they enroll in vocational programs, college reentry students (and older students who have entered college for the first time) have mingled vocational and nonvocational motives, and they have done so in the setting of institutions that are far more receptive to this mingling of motives than were the proprietary schools of the 1910s and 1920s.

Adult Education Under Siege

Professional adult educators have been challenged by developments since the early 1970s, mainly because their heritage of suspicion toward educational formalism has clashed with the growing preference of adults for formal education. As heirs to several strains of progressive education, professional adult educators have favored the integration of learning and living. Such integration can take any number of forms, but for many adult educators the ideal setting is an informal discussion or encounter group and the main goal of education is to alter behavior.[141] Of the sundry leaders associated with adult education in the 1920s, the one with the most pronounced influence on the development of adult education after 1940 was Eduard C. Lindeman, who in 1926 had stated flatly that "the approach to adult education will be via the route of situations, not subjects."[142]

Lindeman's preference for situations over subjects underscored the New School intellectuals' emphasis on adult education as a way to sharpen the public's awareness of burning issues. But Lindeman was not above justifying adult education merely on grounds that it made people happy, and this aspect of Lindeman's legacy has persisted in the literature of those professional adult educators who have preferred to evaluate adult education by its contribution to the satisfaction of "felt needs" and by the extent to which it renders learning "a joyful, wholly fulfilling experience in self-actualization."[143] Some adult educators have contended that all adult education is a form of psychological therapy. The theory of group dynamics espoused by the psychologist Kurt Lewin was long in vogue among adult educators; it is still not uncommon to encounter such jaw-twisters as "transactional modes" in the literature of adult education.[144] While many professionals have distanced themselves from a purely therapeutic conception of adult education, most still define adult education as a world of its own, an educational oasis of voluntarism and innovation that contrasts with the deadening "ritual" of classroom instruction.[145]

In contrast to these expectations, the explosion of continuing education in the last two decades has been driven by credit-seeking students who seek to master bodies of knowledge, usually within classrooms. Even innovations have become more technological than pedagogical. Video cameras and satellite dishes make it possible to transmit images around the world, but the image is that of a professor lecturing from a podium. Almost 90 percent of adult students in higher education take classes and study on their institution's main campus, and 83 percent are taught by full-time faculty members.[146] To the dismay of veteran adult educators, many of the newer students seem to prefer the traditional format of classroom instruction, so that they can quickly digest chunks of necessary information and master new skills. The same has often been the case even in noncredit university courses. The number of registrations in such courses more than doubled between 1968 and 1976, and by 1979 enrollments in noncredit courses for adults continuing their education stood at over 12,000,000. More than half of these were in community colleges, and nearly a third fell under the rubric of continuing professional education (CPE).[147] Starting in the health professions (medicine, dentistry, nursing, pharmacy, optometry, clinical psychology), and expanding into areas like public accountancy, law, real estate, social work, and nursing-home administration, there has developed a virtual educational subindustry to accommodate those professionals compelled by state mandates to undergo continuing education for relicensure.[148] By 1988 48 states mandated continuing education for CPAs, 39 for pharmacists, 45 for nursing-home administrators, 26 for veterinarians, and 29 for real-estate brokers.[149]

The parallel development of the knowledge industry and CPE have put a strain on older conceptions of adult education as a joyous and therapeutic activity and have compelled adult-education professionals to sharpen the verbal distinction between adult and continuing education. Yet they have subsumed both adult and continuing education under the category of "lifelong learning," a rallying cry with a global ring that came into fashion in the 1970s. From this perspective, society gains if as many individuals as possible annually engage in self-conscious learning activities, whatever they might be. In this situation, Malcolm Knowles has written, "The development of a race of human beings who are capable of approaching their full potentiality would then be possible, and the consequences in terms of the political, social, and cultural implications of our civilization would be incalculable."[150] One is reminded of the statement by Harvard's C. C. Felton in 1829 that an "unspeakably beautiful" result would spring from the engagement of the whole people in study and the diffusion of knowledge.[151]

Whether issued in the 1820s or 1970s, such statements underscore the American association of knowledge with personal fulfillment. Appropriately, adult educators today extensively investigate the motives and interests of adult students.[152] Their idea of evaluating adult education is to distribute questionnaires to measure student satisfaction with courses. During the 1920s the New School intellectuals tried to steer adult education in a different direction by linking it to the development of a more critical public, an objective that persisted in the 1950s in the work of the Fund for Adult Education. But in retrospect these attempts have been the exceptions rather than the rule. In trying to forge liberal education into a tool of social criticism, Charles Beard and James Harvey Robinson were compelled to dismiss most of the motives that in their day drew adult students back to school. There have been undercurrents of support for liberal education within the adult-education establishment, but most professionals have preferred to define their field's objectives in the all-encompassing terms signified by "lifelong learning" and the "learning society."

Arguably, these terms are empty vessels. Phrases that purport to describe everything usually fail to delineate anything in particular. But such phrases underscore a significant aspect of American adult education and the broader history of self-improvement from which it sprang. By counting an extremely broad range of activities as educational, Americans not only have indicated their broad definition of utility but they also have given evidence of their persistent belief that the very act of studying, the *pursuit* of knowledge under difficulties, is meritorious in itself.

Bridges Across the Water

There are signs of a growing convergence between the American and British movements for adult education. These movements fertilized each other during much of the nineteenth century and then in the mid-1890s began to move in opposite directions. In the early 1900s the contours of adult education in Britain were shaped by two forces alien to the United States: a tradition of restrictive access to higher education, and the allegiance of intellectuals to the working class. American educators preferred to address the public rather than the working class, and they assumed that higher education in the United States was inherently if not always actually democratic.

The early collaboration between the Workers' Educational Association (WEA) and the universities imparted a liberal orientation to adult education in Britain, in sharp contrast to the vocational and public-service activities that permeated educational extension in the United States between 1900 and 1920. But in 1919 the British Ministry of Reconstruction's *Adult Education Report*, which equated adult education with non-vocational study, received a warm welcome from American intellectuals, who despaired at the utilitarianism that had overtaken educational extension in the United States. These intellectuals sought to rescue liberal education from the clutches of Chautauqua, and they greeted the contemporary movement for workers' education as a likely vehicle for addressing the broader public. In reality, workers' education would prove a disappointment, but in the 1930s, forums, adult institutes, and WPA classes offered a mixture of liberal, vocational, and avocational courses to satisfy diverse middle-class interests.

Throughout the late 1940s and 1950s, American educators continued to experiment with ways to popularize nonvocational liberal education. Both the Fund for Adult Education and the Great Books venture owed a great deal to the spirit of the New School intellectuals of the 1920s. Professionals in adult education paid only modest attention to these developments, which appeared to lack popular potential. But in the 1960s the cause of popularizing the humanities received a boost from the establishment in 1965 of the National Endowment on the Arts and the Humanities, which soon split into the National Endowment for the Arts (NEA) and the National Endowment for the Humanities (NEH).

Marking a significant incursion by the federal government into adult education, at its inception the NEH reflected the Kennedy/Johnson and Khrushchev phase of superpower competition in values and images; in essence, Congress began to subsidize the humanities because it wanted to assassinate the Ugly American, the international image of the United States as a boorish and ignorant colossus of wealth. This objective pushed the NEH in its early days to enhance the quality of the humanities by devising programs to train teachers rather than to popularize the humanities. Under congressional prodding to broaden its impact, the NEH began in 1971 to support humanistic programming by affiliated state councils in order to enhance its direct impact on the public. The civil rights and women's movements, as well as the agitation surrounding the Vietnam War, facilitated this approach by seeding college faculties with young men and women eager to make their knowledge relevant to social issues and by encouraging disadvantaged subpopulations to search for viable pasts. With strong ties from its inception to historical commissions (the federal government has supported the National Historical Publications Commission since 1934), the NEH was well positioned to capitalize on the heightened emphasis of scholars and intellectuals in the 1970s and 1980s on multiculturalism and pluralism. By 1979 Joseph Duffey, chairman of the NEH, could report with pride that the endowment would enable residents of a dozen Ozark Mountain communities to view films on their region's traditional cultural forms, and that youngsters in Watts would learn about the cultures that had contributed to contemporary Los Angeles. Multiculturalism has become to the NEH what the humanistic analysis of values was to the FAE.[153]

State councils on the humanities grappled throughout the 1970s and 1980s with determining the appropriate role of colleges and universities in their programs. The residue of late 1960s' and 1970s' social agitation caused some councils to worry whenever the proportion of their aid allotted to university-sponsored programs crept over 25 percent.[154] State councils seem to have been beset by a conflict over whether to adopt a "to the people" approach or a more cautious tactic that would build on existing intellectual and cultural centers such as universities and museums. The latter strategy ran the risk of preaching to the converted, the former of engendering popular misunderstanding and mistrust of the humanities. For example, a photo exhibit on the "Hidden Holyoke" (sponsored by the Massachusetts Foundation for Humanities and Public Policy in the early 1980s) spurred criticism by local Hispanics on the grounds that its portrayal of downtrodden Hispanic workers in the city's industrial past, while appealing to intellectuals as a vivid reminder of America's underside, merely reinforced stereotypes of Hispanics as poor and miserable.[155]

The NEH has been concerned with the same issue that gripped Beard and Robinson in the 1920s and that long has been the focus of adult educators in Britain: how to make the humanities and social sciences relevant to the interests of adults.[156] The entry and reentry of so many older students to colleges and universities in the 1970s and 1980s reinforced the work of the NEH by spurring new programs, such as masters degrees in liberal studies, that also aimed at relating the liberal arts to modern conditions.

While Americans have been returning to some of the types of educational extension that they had abandoned early in the twentieth century, British educators have found it necessary to introduce more flexibility into their approach to adult education. As the British public's level of educational attainment has risen, British adult educators have become more interested in the American model, with its more malleable response to middle-class interests. Even in the 1920s some adult educators in Britain were chafing at the hegemony of the WEA and at the rigid model of the tutorial class. It was obvious in Britain by the 1930s that the WEA no longer spoke for the working class, let alone the public. Starting in the 1920s university extramural departments began to challenge the WEA. Gradually, extramural departments broke the lock of the tutorial and the university honours standard on higher adult education—they varied the length and content of their courses to satisfy middle-class clients who possessed high levels of educational attainment and who evinced little interest in becoming socialist intellectuals.

More recently, adult educators in Britain have had to accommodate the desire of their clients for vocational courses. As late as 1958 a British government inspector warned that management courses for adults were inherently dangerous, "since people would be increasingly drawn into courses from which they might derive material advantage."[157] But the 1944 Education Act had already opened the door to the provision of vocational courses for those beyond the compulsory school age by Local Education Authorities (LEA's, roughly the equivalent of American school boards).[158] In addition, the so-called polytechnics, which were established in the wake of a 1966 White Paper, have offered vocational education to part-time students beyond the compulsory school age.[159] Adult educators in Britain have also moved to meet the desire of students for certificates and degrees, which by tradition were denied to all but resident university students.[160] Significantly, the major British innovation in adult education during the last few decades, the Open University, launched in the late 1960s by the Labour government, has employed a mixture of televised courses and instruction by mail to widen the public's opportunities for both liberal education and university degrees.[161]

Conclusion

World War II had a transforming effect on American higher education. Military personnel who took courses through the USAFI enrolled in colleges and universities after the war under the provisions of the G.I. Bill. The war also stimulated innovations in testing and helped to transform a relatively dim star on the prewar horizon, the junior college, into a major instrument for democratizing higher education.

Little of this had been foreseen before the war, when educators who talked of prolonging the average level of educational attainment spoke of expanding "post-secondary" rather than higher education, a term that underscored their reservations about the potential appeal of existing colleges and universities. In the late 1940s the Zook commission failed to detect any long-term significance in the wave of veterans who entered universities after the war. Well into the 1960s most educators equated democratizing higher education with opening it to ever-widening circles of eighteen-year-olds, and they continued to associate adult education with avocational interests.

In the 1970s several factors conspired to propel adults back into higher education. The women's movement was prominent among these. Increasingly, equal rights came to mean equal access to desirable jobs, for which educational credentials were indispensable. At the same time, colleges and universities, fearful of the implications for their enrollments portended by the declining proportion of eighteen-year-olds in the population, became more receptive to older students, and in this they were eagerly joined by the community colleges, which by 1970 had several decades of experience with part-time students and which long had searched for new pools of students.

These developments placed stress on inherited conceptions of adult education as leisurely, avocational self-improvement. Many of the new students of the 1970s, like those who took advantage of the G.I. Bill in the late 1940s, sought credits and degrees, and after 1970 even some noncredit collegiate courses, notably those relating to CPE, had acquired a mandated quality. Yet while it is plausible to interpret the surge of college reentry as driven by coercive state relicensure requirements and corporate expectations, it seems more reasonable to assume that people usually do what they choose to do. Ultimately, job improvement is a voluntary motive, and returning collegians have found many opportunities in higher education for self-fulfillment as well as economic advancement. Although professional adult educators have been slow to grasp the point, the expansion of higher education and the increasing prominence of colleges and universities as providers of further education have contributed to narrowing the gap, once majestic in its proportions, between job improvement and adult education.

Epilogue

In contrast to histories of education that focus on formal schools and the school-aged population, this work has viewed American education from the perspective of private study and mutual improvement, mechanics' institutes and lyceums, Chautauqua and women's clubs, university extension and evening colleges, correspondence schools and adult institutes, corporate training programs and community-college adult classes. Taken collectively, these means of education have constituted a kind of alternative educational sphere or ladder, but one lacking a convenient name. "Adult education" became an accepted descriptive phrase in the 1920s and 1930s; the early conferences of the American Association for Adult Education included educators with ties to all of the institutions named above that were then in operation, save for correspondence schools, and even the correspondence schools were recognized as a rung, albeit a disreputable one, on the ladder. But after 1960 the term "adult education" had to compete with other names, including "lifelong learning" and "continuing education," and before 1920 none of these terms enjoyed much currency. At the end of the nineteenth century, Herbert Baxter Adams identified university extension as a species of "popular education," for which he found precedents in Chautauqua and in the practices of lyceums and mechanics' institutes. Just after World War I, Charles R. Mann baptized an "American tradition in education," which he equated with the principle that theories were best learned when linked to practice and which he viewed as the basis of "short courses and extension work."[1]

To be sure, Adams and Mann were identifying distinguishable historical impulses and tracing somewhat different lines of development. Adams's "popular education" referred to educational institutions that diffused the rays of enlightenment beyond the circle of formal education, while Mann bemoaned the academicism of engineering colleges and sought to make technical education more practical. Inclined to the view that anything really important in America had to have a British germ, Adams started with early nineteenth-century English radicals, William Cobbett and Francis Place, who favored broader suffrage and education for the common people; moved on to lyceums and popular scientific lectures; skipped the Morrill Act (which funded institutions of formal education and hence did not fit his conception of popular education); and alighted on Chautauqua, public libraries, home study, and the early university extension movement. In contrast, Mann, who wanted to probe "the national intuitions and instincts," began with Franklin, the inventive autodidact whose quest for knowledge blended at every turn with his personal experiences and ambitions; proceeded to Peter Cooper, Cyrus McCormick, and other self-instructed industrialists for whom the "school of experience" was critical; celebrated the Hofwyl experiments for their reliance on teaching through experience, lauded Jonathan Baldwin Turner's view that "a suitable combination of learning and labor would yield mental culture and refinement of taste as well as increased production and practical skill"; and then outlined the gradual subversion of the principle of "learning from experience" in late nineteenth-century engineering colleges.[2]

While distinguishable, these impulses often converged, for, as Mann recognized, the most convenient way to relate formal education to practical experience was to devise institutions for those already at work. Starting from different points on the compass, both Adams and Mann praised Stephen Van Rensselaer's plan in the 1820s to extend scientific knowledge to the whole community, and each viewed natural-history societies, scientific cabinets, associations to improve agriculture and manufacturing, and university extension as threads in a common fabric of education that was related to living and universally accessible. Not surprisingly, advocates of the institutions that Adams admired recognized their kinship with many of the individuals praised by Mann. Franklin and his Junto impressed Chautauqua's John H. Vincent as examples of the successful pursuit of knowledge beyond formal education and under difficulties. Proponents of public libraries, the likeliest base for "university extension" in the eyes of Adams and others at the start of the 1890s, constructed a pantheon that included Nathaniel Bowditch and Elihu Burritt as well as Franklin. The British radicals cherished mechanics' institutes, with their debt to Franklin and resemblances to lyceums, and they certainly would have admired Peter Cooper's famed Union. As a technical institute, Cooper Union targeted the kind of working adults who would enroll in correspondence schools; and as a popular debating forum, it became the locus in the 1920s of the

People's Institute. In turn, the moving spirits behind the People's Institute had ties to the New School for Social Research, and some of them survived to organize the Great Books enterprise in the 1950s.

Allowing for these convergences, a basic difference in tone or mood separated Adams and Mann. Optimistic to the point of complacency, Adams described an irresistible propensity toward the ever-wider diffusion of knowledge. His heroes acted as little more than midwives of what he termed "the nineteenth-century movement toward educational democracy." Writing only two decades later, Mann identified as heroes those who struggled in the face of an academic hailstorm to bring the "national intuitions and instincts" to fruition. Everywhere he saw evidence of a conspiracy of university officials to subvert practical education to academic refinement.

On one level, this difference in mood can be explained by Mann's explicit commitment to practical, vocationally useful education. Whereas Adams depicted the progressive drive toward the diffusion of literature and philosophy, Mann often bemoaned the low regard attached to teaching vocational skills throughout the nineteenth century. Mann approvingly noted the nineteenth-century movement to dignify agriculture and the mechanic arts by teaching them in universities, but he never quite grasped the point that this very emphasis on elevation subordinated trade training to academic goals.

On a deeper level, Mann's rather negative assessment of historical developments reflected the fact that he (and numerous other educators of the early twentieth century) were retargeting the clientele of educational extension in ways that made success more elusive and difficult to define. Whereas Adams and his cohort of nineteenth-century educators primarily addressed those with some predisposition to gentility and intellectual refinement, twentieth-century advocates of educational extension were more likely to aim at those apparently lacking such a predisposition: dirt farmers (cooperative demonstration work), immigrants (Americanization classes), illiterates (WPA programs), and workers eager to acquire new vocational skills (Mann's "short courses and extension work"). Without exception, the institutions that Adams admired—lyceums, Chautauqua, and university extension as practiced in the early 1890s—depended on voluntary learners who sought knowledge in a digestible, popular format. It was plausible for Adams to think of this clientele as democratic, for it included women as well as men, farmers (the Grange and Alliance), and workers (the Knights of Labor), but it was a more intellectually curious clientele than the one Mann targeted. From this perspective, Mann's preference for vocational education can be seen as a device to render education more democratic than anything imagined by Adams by grounding it on occupations, on activities that affected everyone. The same emphasis on democracy led educators of Mann's day gradually to equate culture with activities—customs and behaviors—rather than with ideals.

Of the myriad factors that led educators after the turn of the twentieth century to redefine the clientele of educational extension, one stands out: they became disillusioned with the results of both Chautauqua and the university extension movement of the 1890s, and with this disillusion came a disenchantment with the objective of popular gentrification. From Josiah Holbrook to Herbert Baxter Adams, cultural missionaries had sought to induce their society to value what they valued—not only refined knowledge but refinement. Antebellum literary societies drew up long lists of rules to govern their members' behavior. Public librarians told patrons to wash their hands. Bishop Vincent advised Chautauquans how to eat on trains and how to speak correctly. During the 1890s the experiences of educators with methods of the "Chautauqua-type" had persuaded them that gentrification, while widely appealing, only affected successive generations of the same kind of people, that its clients disproportionately were female and middle class, and that the traditional diffusion of knowledge and culture could not be made a means of social reform.

With support for Arnoldian culture in free-fall, educators framed new goals for extension and devised new strategies. Those sympathetic to John Dewey's call for integrating work and culture became increasingly attuned to popular vocational aspirations, and they borrowed tactics from agricultural education rather than from Chautauqua. Ironically, this new preoccupation with adapting knowledge to the experiences of ordinary citizens encouraged an unprecedented reliance on bureaucracy. Nineteenth-century missionaries of culture had repeatedly demonstrated their knack for managing large organizations. When artisans had failed in the 1830s and 1840s to flock to serious lectures on science, the managers of mechanics' institutes had introduced more diverting lectures on popular science. John H. Vincent devised the Chautauqua Literary and Scientific Circle to teach adults by mail, and public librarians of the Gilded Age employed a variety of new techniques to extend the influence of libraries. But none of this entailed the specialization characteristic of bureaucracy. Individuals like Holbrook, Vincent, and Adams were simultaneously theorists and organizers of popular education and participants in it. In contrast, in the early 1900s universities established separate extension divisions, which quickly fragmented into subdivisions. Now educational theory became the work of specialized professors in departments of philosophy, sociology, or education, while the details of management were left to staff professionals who engaged in neither theory nor teaching.

This move toward bureaucracy arose less because of changes in the scale of extension work than because of shifts in its goals. As long as institutions of popular education like lyceums and Chautauqua aimed at the gentrification and uplift of those with a taste for culture, missionaries for culture had every reason to involve themselves in institutions. What mattered for these individuals was the personal touch. Lectures were important to people like Holbrook, Vincent, and Adams not because they were especially convenient or efficient ways to impart knowledge, but because they required the physical presence of a representative of culture, the speaker. When lectures failed, rituals might substitute. It was a mark of Vincent's genius that he could devise rituals to transform even the mail-order knowledge of the Chautauqua circles into a means of uplift. In contrast, the abandonment of Arnoldian culture meant that the personal touch became relatively unimportant. Rather than reaching out to existing circles of voluntary learners, extension divisions now needed agents to persuade potential students to become actual students, just as the Agricultural Extension Service had to maintain a force of county agents to persuade skeptical farmers of their need for knowledge.

In turn, bureaucracy tended to nurture a preoccupation with institutional self-preservation. Toward the end of the 1880s, the land-grant colleges had glimpsed the possibility that agricultural extension would blunt public and legislative criticism of their failure to enroll students in their campus agricultural courses, and after 1900 state universities discovered that they could curry legislative favor by establishing separate extension divisions. Institutional priorities subsequently drove a great deal of educational extension. Having abandoned Arnoldianism, with its privileging of masterpieces and claims to spiritual elevation, and substituted the servicing of the interests of diverse subpopulations, the institutions of educational extension were left with enrollment figures as the only measure of their success. This was true not only of the university extension divisions of the early 1900s but also of the junior- and community-college officials who later would search at great length for new sources of students, including adults, in order to secure their position in higher education. Since 1970 all sorts of colleges and universities have launched programs for adults in response to the threat of declining enrollments as the baby boom leveled off.

Yet none of these post-1900 changes ever really bumped the popular quest for intellectual refinement off the alternative ladder. The quest for broad intellectual elevation has persisted in twentieth-century adult education, which can draw on diverse and rich traditions. For various reasons historians have not paid much attention to this ladder, which indeed is more than a little crooked. The configurations of this alternative means of acquiring knowledge have been shaped less by the kind of momentous debates about educational objectives that historians like to analyze than by the meandering interests of voluntary students. The steady expansion of formal education has often threatened to topple the ladder by negating one of its main functions: second-chance education. In addition, the institutions and traditions studied in this work have been marked by a seeming marginality; they have attracted learners who have splashed in the streams rather than swum in the river.

Nonetheless, viewing history through the lens of voluntary education affords a valuable perspective on American education and culture. This perspective makes it clear, for example, that schooling as a continuous, uninterrupted preparation for experience—supposedly the "normal" or mainstream route—has characterized only a relatively brief period of American history. With their notion of a graceful pyramid of schools that would encourage practical education in literary institutions, the republican educators of the late eighteenth century favored such schooling, but their ideal was scarcely embodied in their own society or in the antebellum period, when the academies achieved extraordinary popularity by harmonizing their terms with work cycles—by becoming, in effect, institutions of discontinuous education. To a degree, the same was true of antebellum collegians, who not infrequently entered colleges at what seem to us abnormally late ages. Indeed, the ideal of continuous, uninterrupted schooling had relatively little practical impact beyond the elementary grades before the late nineteenth century. Between 1880 and 1930 elite educators devised professional schools that purported to provide a complete preparation for practical activity, but the spread of vocational and professional education from high schools to universities scarcely swept away such alternative institutions as evening colleges and proprietary schools. Rather, the growing prestige of continuous education among elite educators seems to have indirectly spurred the quest for vocational and professional education among adults who could not afford the continuous version and who patronized schools that pretended to do no more than supplement practical experience. In the 1930s the Depression undercut this scaffolding of proprietary and evening schools, and the apparent triumph of democratic higher education after World War II seemed to have negated the need for alternative institutions. Yet the phenomenon of college reentry in recent decades reminds us that in education, as in politics, democracy seems only to whet appetites for more democracy, that each advance in educational opportunity is accompanied by a new wave of learners eager to pursue knowledge under difficulties.

Reference Matter

Notes

Chapter 1

1. James McLachlan, "The Choice of Hercules: American Student Societies in the Early Nineteenth Century," in Lawrence Stone, ed., *The University in Society* (2 vols.; Princeton, N.J., 1974), vol. 2, p. 487; Jerrold E. Siegel, *Rhetoric and Philosophy in Renaissance Humanism: The Union of Eloquence and Wisdom, Petrarch to Valla* (Princeton, N.J., 1968); Wilbur Samuel Howell, *Eighteenth-Century British Logic and Rhetoric* (Princeton, N.J., 1971).

2. Samuel E. Morison, *The Intellectual Life of Colonial New England* (4th ed.; New York, 1970), p. 32.

3. Samuel E. Morison, *The Founding of Harvard College* (Cambridge, Mass., 1935), pp. 8, 27.

4. Samuel Miller, *A Brief Retrospect of the Eighteenth Century* (2 vols.; New York, 1803), vol. 1, chaps. 1, 3, 9, and 10. See also Paoli Rossi, *Francis Bacon: From Magic to Science*, trans. Sacha Rabinovitch (London, 1968), pp. 9–13 and *passim*.

5. Charles Rollin, *The Method of Teaching and Studying the Belles Lettres* (7th ed., 4 vols.; London, 1770), vol. 1, p. 51; vol. 3, pp. 9, 151–53.

6. Morison, *Founding*, p. 51; Joan Simon, *Education and Society in Tudor England* (Cambridge, Eng., 1966), pp. 351–53.

7. Morison, *Founding*, pp. 51–53.

8. Quoted in Simon, *Education and Society*, pp. 351–52.

9. Ibid., pp. 341–42.

10. Moody E. Prior, "Bacon's Man of Science," *Journal of the History of Ideas*, 15 (June 1954), pp. 352–53.

11. Larzer Ziff, "Upon What Pretext?: The Book and Literary History," *Proceedings of the American Antiquarian Society*, 95, pt. 2 (1985), p. 304; David D.

Hall, *Worlds of Wonder, Days of Judgment: Popular Religious Belief in Early New England* (New York, 1989), p. 243. Both Ziff and Hall identify a shift in the early eighteenth century toward Puritan interest in books as embodiments of literary values rather than as mere revelations of the Word. One might add that such an interest was a precondition for the ideal of self-improvement, which emphasized the refinement of faculties rather than the immediate discovery of truth.

12. Cotton Mather, *The Christian Philosopher: A Collection of the Best Discoveries in Nature with Religious Improvements* (orig. ed. 1721; Gainesville, Fla., 1968), p. 2; Morison, *Intellectual Life*, pp. 17–18; John Morgan, *Godly Learning: Puritan Attitudes Towards Reason, Learning, and Education* (Cambridge, Eng., 1986), p. 306.

13. John Maclean, *History of the College of New Jersey, From Its Origin in 1746 to the Commencement of 1814* (2 vols.; Philadelphia, 1877), vol. 2, pp. 8–9, 11.

14. John F. Kasson, *Rudeness and Civility: Manners in Nineteenth-Century Urban America* (New York, 1990), pp. 20–21.

15. Gerald W. Gawalt, *The Promise of Power: The Legal Profession in Massachusetts, 1760–1840* (Westport, Conn., 1979), p. 13; Richard D. Brown, *Knowledge Is Power: The Diffusion of Information in Early America, 1700–1865* (New York, 1989), pp. 96–97. See also "Dr. Ephraim Eliot's Account of the Physicians of Boston," *Proceedings of the Massachusetts Historical Society*, 7 (1863–1864), p. 180.

16. Gawalt, *The Promise of Power*, pp. 18–19.

17. William Tudor, *The Life of James Otis of Massachusetts* (Boston, 1827), pp. 9, 11; Dumas Malone, *Jefferson the Virginian* (New York, 1948), pp. 65–67; Joyce Blackburn, *George Wythe of Williamsburg* (New York, 1975), p. 44. Similarly, the course of reading that Theophilus Parsons assigned to his legal apprentice John Quincy Adams included historical works by Gibbon and Hume as well as texts on the law; see James Willard Hurst, *The Growth of American Law: The Law Makers* (Boston, 1950), p. 266. After Independence, this bond between law and literature tightened, not only in the sense that lawyers cultivated literature but also in that "the broad cultural responsibilities of the professional man and the writer's imperatives [to educate the citizenry in republicanism] could be made to appear the same"; see Robert A. Ferguson, *Law and Letters in American Culture* (Cambridge, Mass., 1984), p. 24.

18. Joseph F. Kett, *The Formation of the American Medical Profession: The Role of Institutions, 1780–1860* (New Haven, Conn., 1968), pp. 9–11.

19. Gilbert Tennent, "The Danger of an Unconverted Ministry," in Douglas Sloan, ed., *The Great Awakening and American Religion: A Documentary History* (New York, 1973), p. 100.

20. George W. Corner, ed., *The Autobiography of Benjamin Rush* (Princeton, N.J., 1968), p. 32.

21. Ibid.

22. Archibald Alexander, *Biographical Sketches of the Founder and Principal Alumni of the Log College* (Philadelphia, 1851), pp. 124–25.

23. Sloan, ed., *Great Awakening*, p. 41; see also Alan Heimert, *Religion and the American Mind from the Great Awakening to the Revolution* (Cambridge, Mass., 1966), pp. 159–66.

24. Alvah Hovey, *A Memoir of the Life of the Rev. Isaac Backus, A.M.* (Boston, 1859), p. 32.

25. Donald M. Scott, *From Office to Profession: The New England Ministry, 1750–1850* (Philadelphia, 1978).

26. Thomas Jefferson to Peter Carr, Aug. 19, 1785, in Julian Boyd, ed., *The Papers of Thomas Jefferson* (23 vols., Princeton, N.J., 1950–1990), vol. 8., p. 408; Rollin, *Teaching and Studying the Belles Lettres*, vol. 1, p. 8.

27. Brown, *Knowledge Is Power*, pp. 93–99.

28. The literature on republicanism is voluminous, but for a brief discussion see J. G. A. Pocock, "Virtue and Commerce in the Eighteenth Century," *Journal of Interdisciplinary History*, 2, (Summer 1972), pp. 119–34.

29. John Adams, "A Dissertation on the Canon and Feudal Law," in *The Works of John Adams* (10 vols.; Boston, 1856), vol. 3, p. 448.

30. Irving Brant, *James Madison: The Virginia Revolutionist* (Indianapolis, Ind., 1941), chap. 6.

31. Frederick Rudolph, *Curriculum: A History of the American Undergraduate Course of Study Since 1636* (San Francisco, 1977), pp. 49–51.

32. Leonard W. Labaree, ed., *The Papers of Benjamin Franklin* (29 vols.; New Haven, Conn., 1959–1992), vol. 3, pp. 397–421; the phrase "youth will come out of this school fitted for learning any Business, Calling or Profession" comes from a sequel to the *Proposals*, which Franklin wrote in 1751 under the title *The Idea of an English School*; see *Papers*, vol. 4, p. 108.

33. Quoted in Rudolph, *Curriculum*, p. 47.

34. Thomas Jefferson to Peter Carr, Sept. 7, 1814, in Andrew A. Lipscomb, ed., *The Writings of Thomas Jefferson* (20 vols.; New York, 1903–4), vol. 19, p. 218.

35. Edward P. Cheyney, *History of the University of Pennsylvania, 1740–1940* (Philadelphia, 1940), p. 31.

36. David C. Humphrey, *From King's College to Columbia, 1746–1800* (New York, 1976), pp. 106–9; Joseph F. Kett, "Education," in Merrill D. Peterson, ed., *Thomas Jefferson: A Reference Biography* (New York, 1986), pp. 245–47.

37. Quoted in McLachlan, "Choice of Hercules" (cited in n. 1), p. 487.

38. On these complements and alternatives to university education see Simon, *Education and Society* (cited in n. 6), pp. 355–56, 347–48, 366–67.

39. Quoted in Morison, *Intellectual Life* (cited in n. 2), p. 61.

40. Robert Middlekauf, *Ancients and Axioms: Secondary Education in Eighteenth-Century New England* (New Haven, Conn., 1963), p. 64.

41. Ibid., chap. 7.

42. Ibid., p. 121.

43. Quoted in ibid., p. 155.

44. Kenneth Cmiel, *Democratic Eloquence: The Fight over Popular Speech in Nineteenth-Century America* (New York, 1990), pp. 24–31; Bruce Kimball, *Orators and Philosophers: A History of the Idea of Liberal Education* (New York, 1986), pp. 111–12.

45. Charles F. Adams, Jr., *Letters of John Adams to His Wife* (2 vols.; Boston, 1891), vol. 2, p. 68.

46. Middlekauf, *Ancients and Axioms*, chap. 9.

47. Ibid., p. 131.

48. Clinton Rossiter, *1787: The Grand Convention* (New York, 1966), pp.

146–47. All but two of the 23 had studied at American colleges; Princeton alone produced nine members of the convention.

49. This figure is merely an estimate. The 1790 census broke the white male population into only two categories: those aged under 16 and those aged 16 and over. The 1800 census employed more categories, including those aged 26 to 44 and 44 and over. To simplify, I calculated the proportion of the white male population in 1800 aged 26 and over (31.5 percent) and applied this percentage to the 1790 population.

50. James McLachlan, *Princetonians, 1748–1768: A Biographical Directory* (Princeton, N.J., 1976), pp. 673–75.

51. Ibid., p. xxii.

52. Ibid., p. 252.

53. Ibid., p. xxi.

54. George W. Pierson, *A Yale Book of Numbers: Historical Studies of the College and University, 1701–1976* (n.p., 1963), pp. 106–16.

55. McLachlan, *Princetonians*, pp. 29–30, 99–100.

56. Ibid., p. xxi. I have calculated the average age at graduation for lawyers and physicians from McLachlan's biographies. Inasmuch as many individuals followed more than one profession, I have sought to identify the primary profession of each.

57. Joseph J. Ellis, *After the Revolution: Profiles in Early American Culture* (New York, 1979), pp. 76–79; Claude M. Newlin, *The Life and Writings of Hugh Henry Brackenridge* (Princeton, N.J., 1932), pp. 1–7.

58. Rudolph, *Curriculum* (cited in n. 31), p. 26.

59. Morison, *Intellectual Life*, p. 146.

60. Paul L. Ford, ed., *The Writings of Thomas Jefferson* (10 vols.; New York, 1892–98), vol. 1, p. 340.

61. Oscar Handlin and Mary F. Handlin, *Commonwealth: The Role of Government in the Massachusetts Economy: Massachusetts, 1774–1861* (New York, 1948), pp. 99–100, 168.

62. Peter D. Hall, *The Organization of American Culture, 1700–1900: Private Institutions, Elites, and the Origin of American Nationality* (New York, 1982), p. 52.

63. William C. Lang, "The Telltale, 1721," *Publications of the Colonial Society of Massachusetts*, 12 (1909), pp. 220–29.

64. McLachlan, "The Choice of Hercules" (cited in n. 1), pp. 449–94; Henry D. Sheldon, *Student Life and Customs* (New York, 1901). Although colleges taught rhetoric as part of their curriculum, they restricted the emphasis on persuasion and, as their commencement exercises indicate, continued to esteem orations in Latin; see George V. Bohman, "The Colonial Period," in William Norwood Brigance, ed., *A History and Criticism of American Public Address* (2 vols.; New York, 1943), vol. 1, pp. 18–19, 44.

65. Rudolph, *Curriculum*, pp. 51–52.

66. Corner, ed., *Autobiography of Benjamin Rush* (cited in n. 20), pp. 42–43.

67. John Locke, "A New Method of a Common Place-Book," in *Works of John Locke in Ten Volumes* (11th ed.; London, 1812), vol. 3, pp. 305–23.

68. William T. Hutchinson and William M. E. Rachal, eds., *The Papers of James Madison* (17 vols.; Chicago, 1962–83), vol. 1, pp. 7–32.

69. Gilbert Chinard, ed., *The Literary Bible of Thomas Jefferson: His Commonplace Book of Philosophers and Poets* (Baltimore, Md., 1928), p. 4.

70. Hutchinson and Rachal, eds., *Papers of James Madison*, vol. 1, p. 6.

71. Isaac Watts, *The Improvement of the Mind; or, a Supplement to the Art of Logic* (London, 1801), p. 18.

72. Hutchinson and Rachal, eds., *Papers of James Madison*, vol. 1, pp. 73, 99.

73. Simeon Baldwin, *Life and Letters of Simeon Baldwin* (New Haven, Conn., 1919), p. 160.

74. Tudor, *James Otis* (cited in n. 17), pp. 9, 11; Malone, *Jefferson* (cited in n. 17), pp. 65–67.

75. "Memoir of Nathaniel Emmons, D.D.," in *The Works of Nathaniel Emmons, D.D.*, (2 vols.; Boston, 1842), vol. 1, p. xx.

76. Mathew L. Davis, ed., *Memoir of Aaron Burr, with Miscellaneous Selections from his Correspondence* (New York, 1971), pp. 45–47.

77. Quoted in Nicholas Hans, *New Trends in Education in the Eighteenth Century* (London, 1951), pp. 166–69.

78. Quoted in ibid., p. 169.

79. Ibid., pp. 166–69.

80. Thomas Bender, *New York Intellect* (New York, 1987), p. 17; see also Carl Bridenbaugh, *Rebels and Gentlemen: Philadelphia in the Age of Franklin* (New York, 1942), pp. 22, 24; Carl Bridenbaugh, "The Press and the Book in Eighteenth-Century Philadelphia," *Pennsylvania Magazine of History and Biography*, 65 (Jan. 1941), pp. 1–30; Neil Harris, *Cultural Excursions: Marketing Appetites and Cultural Tastes in Modern America* (Chicago, 1990), p. 15.

81. Humphrey, *King's College to Columbia* (cited in n. 36), pp. 267–305.

82. John F. Roche, "The Uranian Society: Gentlemen and Scholars in Federal New York," *New York History*, 52 (Apr. 1971), pp. 121–31.

83. Van Wyck Brooks, *The World of Washington Irving* (New York, 1944), pp. 39–41; Eleanor Bryce Scott, "Early Literary Clubs in New York City," *American Literature*, 5 (1933–34), pp. 3–16; Stanley T. Williams, *The Life of Washington Irving* (2 vols.; New York, 1935), vol. 1, p. 16.

84. Kenneth Silverman, *A Cultural History of the American Revolution* (New York, 1987), p. 444; Ellis, *After the Revolution* (cited in n. 57), pp. 3–4.

85. Frank L. Mott, *A History of American Magazines, 1741–1850* (New York, 1930), p. 29; Silverman, *Cultural History*, p. 488.

86. *Memoirs of the Life of Lindley Murray. In a Series of Letters Written by Himself* (York, Eng., 1826), p. 31.

87. Williams, *Washington Irving*, vol. 1, p. 26.

88. David L. Clark, *Charles Brockden Brown: Pioneer Voice of America* (Durham, N.C., 1952), p. 43.

89. Quoted in Paul Allen, *The Late Charles Brockden Brown* (Columbia, S.C., 1956), p. 22.

90. Bender, *New York Intellect*, p. 29.

91. Thomas Jefferson, "Notes on the State of Virginia," in Adrienne Koch and William Peden, eds., *The Life and Selected Writings of Thomas Jefferson* (New York, 1964), p. 214; Benjamin Rush, *An Eulogium, Intended to Perpetuate the Memory of David Rittenhouse, Late President of the American Philosophical Society* (Philadelphia, 1796), pp. 23–24. Jefferson also took an interest in the ac-

complishments of the astronomer and almanacker Benjamin Banneker, but less because Banneker was self-taught (he had taught himself calculus and trigonometry in order to make his astronomical calculations) than because Banneker was an African-American. Banneker's accomplishments challenged Jefferson's ruminations about black mental inferiority, and Quaker abolitionists often cited Banneker to prove that "the powers of the mind are disconnected with the colour of the skin"; see Silvio A. Bedini, *The Life of Benjamin Banneker* (New York, 1972), pp. 157–60; Gary B. Nash, "Benjamin Banneker," in Eric Foner and John A. Garraty, eds., *The Reader's Companion to American History* (Boston, 1991), pp. 82–83.

92. Clark A. Elliott, *Biographical Dictionary of American Science: The Seventeenth Through the Nineteenth Centuries* (Westport, Conn., 1979), p. 4.

93. Walter M. Whitehill, "Early Learned Societies in Boston and Vicinity," in Alexandra Oleson and Sanborn C. Brown, eds., *The Pursuit of Knowledge in the Early American Republic: American Scientific and Learned Societies from Colonial Times to the Civil War* (Baltimore, Md., 1967), p. 157. The same was true of the American Philosophical Society, nearly a fifth of whose members in 1770 were M.D.'s or "Drs."

94. Thomas Hamilton, *Men and Manners in America* (new ed.; Edinburgh, 1843), pp. 195–96.

95. Edward Ford, *David Rittenhouse: Astronomer-Patriot, 1732–1796* (Philadelphia, 1946), pp. 7–50; William Barton, *Memoirs of the Life of David Rittenhouse* (Philadelphia, 1813), p. 150 and *passim*. This William Barton, Rittenhouse's first biographer, was the son of his patron.

96. Donald H. Meyer, *The Democratic Enlightenment* (New York, 1976), pp. 65–68.

97. Carl Van Doren, *Benjamin Franklin* (New York, 1941), pp. 44–45; Roy M. Lokken, "The Social Thought of James Logan," *William and Mary Quarterly*, 27 (Jan. 1970), pp. 68–69.

98. Thomas Jefferson, *Notes on the State of Virginia* (Chapel Hill, N.C., 1955), p. 64.

99. Quoted in Middlekauf, *Ancients and Axioms*, p. 119.

100. Carl Bridenbaugh, *Myths and Realities: Societies of the Colonial South* (Baton Rouge, La., 1952), p. 39.

101. George Tucker, *Life of Jefferson* (2 vols.; Philadelphia, 1837), vol. 1, p. 18.

102. Rhys Isaac, "Books and the Social Authority of Learning: The Case of Mid-Eighteenth Century Virginia," William Joyce et al., eds., *Printing and Society in Early America* (Worcester, Mass., 1983), p. 231; Rhys Isaac, "Dramatizing the Ideology of the Revolution: Popular Mobilization in Virginia, 1774–1776," *William and Mary Quarterly*, 33 (July 1976), p. 362.

103. Joseph F. Kett and Patricia A. McClung, "Book Culture in Post-Revolutionary Virginia," *Proceedings of the American Antiquarian Society*, 94, pt. 1 (Apr. 1984), pp. 97–147.

104. Douglas Adair, ed., "The Autobiography of the Reverend Devereux Jarratt, 1732–1763," *William and Mary Quarterly*, 3d ser., vol. 9 (July 1952), pp. 346–93.

105. Ibid., pp. 361, 360.
107. Ibid., p. 366.
109. Ibid.
111. Ibid., p. 379.
113. Ibid., p. 380.

106. Ibid., p. 363.
108. Ibid., p. 373.
110. Ibid., pp. 374, 377–79.
112. Ibid., p. 370.

114. Cynthia Stiverson and Gregory A. Stiverson, "The Colonial Retail Book Trade: Availability and Affordability of Reading Material in Mid-Eighteenth Century Virginia," in Joyce et al., eds., *Printing and Society*, pp. 152, 169.

115. Kett and McClung, "Book Culture," pp. 106–35.

116. William B. Sprague, *Annals of the American Pulpit* (9 vols.; New York, 1857–69), vol. 7, p. 156; vol. 3, p. 507.

117. William Plumer, Jr., *Life of William Plumer* (Boston, 1857), p. 20. On print culture in colonial New England, see Hall, *Worlds of Wonder* (cited in n. 11), chap. 1; see also James Gilreath, "American Book Distribution," *Proceedings of the American Antiquarian Society*, vol. 95, pt. 2 (1985), pp. 506–37.

118. Plumer, *Life of William Plumer*, p. 20.

119. Hall, *Worlds of Wonder*, pp. 43–61; Victor Neuburg, "Chapbooks in America: Reconstructing the Popular Reading of Early America," in Cathy N. Davidson, ed., *Reading in America: Literature and Social History* (Baltimore, Md., 1989), pp. 81–113.

120. On the relationship between chapbooks and broadsides and the oral culture of the common people, see Roger Chartier, ed., *The Culture of Print: Power and the Uses of Print in Early Modern Europe*, trans. by Lydia G. Cochrane (Princeton, N.J., 1987), pp. 8–9.

121. Franklin D. Praeger, ed., *The Autobiography of John Fitch* (Philadelphia, 1976), p. 25.

122. Ibid., p. 20.

123. Ibid., p. 26.

124. See Benjamin Rush, "Plan for the Establishment of Public Schools," in Frederick Rudolph, ed., *Essays on Education in the Early Republic* (Cambridge, Mass., 1965), p. 8.

125. Quoted in Oscar A. Hansen, *Liberalism and American Education in the Eighteenth Century* (New York, 1926), p. 232.

126. Quoted in ibid., p. 237.

127. Ibid., pp. 131, 183–84.

128. Kett, "Education" (cited in n. 36), pp. 235–39.

129. Jefferson to Peter Carr, Sept. 7, 1814, in Andrew A. Lipscomb, ed., *The Writings of Thomas Jefferson* (20 vols.; New York, 1904), vol. 19, p. 214.

130. Ibid., pp. 218–19.

131. Hansen, *Liberalism*, p. 191.

132. Labaree, ed., *Papers of Benjamin Franklin* (cited in n. 32), vol. 3, pp. 417–18.

133. Noah Webster, "On the Education of Youth in America," in Rudolph, *Essays*, p. 56.

134. Ibid., p. 54.

135. Ibid., p. 56.

136. Ibid., p. 55.

137. Ibid., p. 69; see also Benjamin Rush, "Thoughts upon Female Education," in Rudolph, *Essays*, pp. 27–40; Linda K. Kerber, "Daughters of Columbia: Educating Women for the Republic, 1787–1805," in Stanley Elkins and Eric McKittrick, eds., *The Hofstadter Aegis: A Memorial* (New York, 1974), pp. 45–48.

138. Labaree, ed., *Papers of Benjamin Franklin*, vol. 3, pp. 405–08.

139. Quoted in Linda Kerber, *Federalists in Dissent: Images and Ideology in Jeffersonian America* (Ithaca, N.Y., 1970), p. 114.

140. Benjamin Rush, "Observations upon the Study of the Latin and Greek Languages as a Branch of Liberal Education, with Hints of a Plan of Liberal Instruction," in *Essays, Literary, Moral and Philosophical* (2d ed., Philadelphia, 1806), pp. 43–44. Rush first published this essay anonymously in 1789; it was reprinted in the first edition of his *Essays* in 1798.

141. Benjamin Rush, "Thoughts upon the Mode of Female Education Proper in a Republic," in Rudolph, *Essays*, pp. 19–20.

142. Kerber, *Federalists in Dissent*, pp. 114–34.

143. On the various meanings attached in the eighteenth century to terms like useful and ornamental education, see Eva T. H. Brann, *Paradox of Education in a Republic* (Chicago, 1979), pp. 33–36, 60.

144. "Introduction: Address to the Youth of These States," *Christian's, Scholar's, and Farmer's Magazine*, vol. 1 (Apr.-May 1789), p. 51. I thank James D. Watkinson for calling this reference to my attention.

Chapter 2

1. Joseph Story, "Characteristics of the Age," in William W. Story, ed., *Miscellaneous Writings of Joseph Story* (Boston, 1852), p. 344.

2. Josiah Holbrook, "Associations of Adults for Mutual Improvement," *American Journal of Education*, 1 (Sept. 1826), pp. 594–97; Carl Bode, *The American Lyceum: Town Meeting of the Mind* (Carbondale, Ill., 1968), pp. 11–12; Josiah Holbrook, *The American Lyceum, or Society for the Improvement of Schools and Diffusion of Useful Knowledge* (Boston, 1829).

3. Manuel D. Lopez, "Books and Beds: Libraries in Nineteenth and Twentieth-Century American Hotels," *Journal of Library History*, 9 (July 1974), pp. 196–221; on the penny press, see Michael Schudson, *Discovering the News: A Social History of American Newspapers* (New York, 1978), chap. 1.

4. William J. Gilmore, *Reading Becomes a Necessity of Life: Material and Cultural Life in Rural New England, 1780–1835* (Knoxville, Tenn., 1989), pp. 98, 274–75, 42–50, 348. Richard L. Bushman has linked the nineteenth-century "exaltation of books" with earlier traditions of cultivation; see Bushman, *The Refinement of America: Persons, Houses, Cities* (New York, 1992), p. 283.

5. David D. Hall has traced the transition from "traditional literacy," the reading and re-reading of a few (usually sacred) books in the seventeenth century to a more pragmatic approach to reading that characterized the nineteenth century; see Hall, "The Uses of Literacy in New England, 1600–1850," in William Joyce et al., eds., *Printing and Society in Early America* (Worcester, Mass., 1983), pp. 1–47. On the relationship between lyceum lecturers and their audiences, see Donald

M. Scott, "The Popular Lecture and the Creation of the Public in Mid-Nineteenth-Century America," *Journal of American History*, 66 (Mar. 1980), pp. 806–8.

6. Words like "popular" and "knowledge" are open to misunderstanding and hence a few definitions are in order. By knowledge I mean "polite" or refined knowledge, the kind of knowledge associated with the elite gentry in the eighteenth century. True, others in the eighteenth century besides the gentry could gain access to this knowledge (e.g., Franklin, Rittenhouse, Devereux Jarratt), but only on terms framed by the gentry, such as joining a learned and decidedly genteel society or finding a genteel patron. By "popular" I do not mean "plebeian," but refer instead to the process by which a wide range of social classes in the nineteenth century could gain access to knowledge in neutral settings, for example, by renting rooms or constructing a building for a literary society rather than necessarily meeting in a parlor. Similarly, lyceum lectures were popular in several respects: they attracted diverse audiences, met in places open to the public, and admitted those who paid a fee rather than invitees. In so using words like "popular," "diffusion," and "popularization," I am staying close to the language of contemporaries; for example, the verb "to popularize" was coined at the end of the eighteenth century and applied specifically to knowledge.

7. Donald H. Meyer, *The Democratic Enlightenment* (New York, 1976), p. 71; see also Gordon Wood, "The Democratization of Mind in the American Revolution," in Robert H. Horwitz, ed., *The Moral Foundations of the American Republic* (Charlottesville, Va., 1977), pp. 102–28.

8. Robert Middlekauf, *Ancients and Axioms: Secondary Education in Eighteenth-Century New England* (New Haven, Conn., 1963), pp. 129–35, 151. In 1789 Massachusetts, Connecticut, and New Hampshire relieved their smaller towns of the requirement to maintain Latin grammar schools, a move that contributed to the growth of academies.

9. Ibid., pp. 146–47.

10. Bernard Bailyn, "Education as a Discipline: Some Historical Notes," in John Walton and James C. Keuthe, eds., *The Discipline of Education* (Madison, Wis., 1963), p. 135.

11. Quoted in Middlekauf, *Ancients and Axioms*, p. 150; on educational opportunities for women, see David Tyack and Elisabeth Hansot, *Learning Together: A History of Coeducation in American Public Schools* (New Haven, Conn., 1990), pp. 18–27.

12. "History of Leicester Academy," in Emory Washburn, *Historical Sketches of the Town of Leicester, Massachusetts, During the First Century from Its Settlement* (Boston, 1860), p. 10.

13. Bailyn, "Education as a Discipline," p. 133.

14. Washburn, "History of Leicester Academy," p. 39.

15. Ibid., p. 45.

16. Ibid., p. 31. For an example of an edition of Watts designed for schools, see *The Improvement of the Mind, by Isaac Watts, D.D., with Corrections, Questions, and Supplement by Joseph Emerson* (rev. ed.; Boston, 1858). Although the subject of women's self-education will be taken up more fully later in this chapter, it bears noting here that Emerson was well recognized as a promoter of female ed-

ucation and that he had a major influence on both Mary Lyon and Zilpah Grant. Jane Marcet's *Conversations* went through several American editions; see, for example, J. L. Comstock [Jane Marcet], *Conversations on Chemistry; in which are added The Elements of That Science* (8th American ed. from 6th London ed.; Hartford, 1822). The generation of female educators represented by Lyon, Grant, Emma Willard, and Almira Phelps found Marcet's approach simplistic and patronizing; see a later section in Chapter 2.

17. Jesse Shera, *Foundations of the Public Library: The Origins of the Public Library Movement in New England, 1729–1855* (Chicago, 1949), p. 7.

18. Ibid., pp. 58–59.

19. Ibid., p. 69. Shera identified a total of 1,107 social libraries founded in New England before 1850. Of these, 51 were established before 1781 and another 59 between 1781 and 1790. In contrast, the four decades after 1790 accounted for 788 of the 1,107 libraries (71.1 percent); over 40 percent of the 1,107 were established between 1791 and 1810.

20. For an example of an elite eighteenth-century social library, see David King, *An Historical Sketch of the Redwood Library and Athenaeum in Newport, Rhode Island* (Boston, 1860); see also Harold L. Burstyn, "The Salem Philosophical Library," *Essex Institute Historical Collections*, 96 (July 1960), pp. 169–206. For examples of female shareholders, see George F. Dow, *History of Topsfield, Massachusetts* (Topsfield, 1940), pp. 437–38; Joseph D. Eggleston, ed., "The Minute Book of the Buffalo Circulating Library," *Virginia Magazine of History and Biography*, 49 (Apr. 1941), p. 161; Harry M. Lydenberg, "The Berkshire Republican Library at Stockbridge, Massachusetts, 1794–1818," *Proceedings, American Antiquarian Society*, 50 (1940), pp. 111–62. Of the 82 proprietors of the Andover, Massachusetts, social library in 1823, 11 were women; see *Laws and Regulations of the Social Library, Andover* (Haverhill, Mass., 1823). Library companies sprang up in the unlikeliest places. One was formed in 1806 at Vincennes, Indiana Territory, which at the time had only 700 inhabitants, including French and Indians; see J. Robert Constantine, ed., "The Vincennes Library Company: A Cultural Institution in Pioneer Indiana," *Indiana Magazine of History*, 61 (Dec. 1965), pp. 306–20.

21. Levi W. Leonard and Josiah L. Seward, *The History of Dublin, New Hampshire* (Dublin, N.H., 1920), p. 136; Samuel Sewall, *The History of Woburn, Middlesex County, Mass.* (Boston, 1868), pp. 521–23.

22. Linda K. Kerber, *Women of the Republic: Intellect and Ideology in Revolutionary America* (Chapel Hill, N.C., 1980), pp. 203–8.

23. Cathy N. Davidson has shown numerous connections between the novels of the early republic and other literary genres; see Davidson, *Revolution and the Word: The Rise of the Novel in America* (New York, 1986), p. 79; see also Joan Jacobs Brumberg, *Mission for Life: The Judson Family and American Evangelical Culture* (New York, 1984), chaps. 3–5.

24. Shera, *Foundations of the Public Library*, p. 113; Thaddeus M. Harris, *A Selected Catalogue of Some of the Most Estimated Publications in the English Language, Proper to Form a Social Library* (Boston, 1793).

25. Shera, *Foundations of the Public Library*, pp. 108, 103, table 12. In 1787 the members of the social library at Royalston, Massachusetts, limited divinity

purchases to 30 percent, while allowing purchases of 30 percent for history and biography, 20 percent for arts and sciences, 10 percent for law and medicine, and 10 percent for poetry. Of the social libraries whose contents were analyzed by Shera and that were founded between 1785 and 1818, the proportion of books on theology ranged from a high of 38 percent to a low of 9 percent; the average was 26 percent. (I have calculated these percentages from Shera's data.) For a similar distribution of titles in a social library outside of New England, see Larry E. Sullivan, "The Reading Habits of the Nineteenth-Century Baltimore Bourgeoisie: A Cross-Cultural Analysis," *Journal of Library History*, 16 (Spring 1981), pp. 227–32. Of course there were exceptions in the form of libraries tilted toward polemical literature for or against religious orthodoxy. Nearly half of the titles of the Charitable Library Society of Concord, Massachusetts, fell into the category of religion and moral philosophy; see Robert Gross, "Reconstructing Early American Libraries: Concord, Massachusetts, 1795–1850," *Proceedings of the American Antiquarian Society*, vol. 97, pt. 2 (1987), pp. 331–51. The proprietors of the Buffalo Circulating Library (despite its title, a social rather than circulating library) mainly purchased counter-polemics to deism; see Eggleston, ed., "Minute Book," pp. 163–64. At the other extreme, the holdings of the Berkshire Republican Library, founded in Stockbridge, Massachusetts, in 1794, read like a catalogue of the Age of Reason: Lord Kames, Gibbon, Rousseau, Voltaire; see Lyndenberg, "Berkshire Republican Library," pp. 111–62.

26. Quoted in Shera, *Foundations of the Public Library*, p. 151. Shera surveyed eleven circulating libraries in New England between 1765 and 1816 and found that the proportion of fiction ranged from a low of 12 percent to a high of 45 percent. Six of the eleven libraries contained more than 30 percent fiction, and two more than 40 percent. In contrast, of thirteen social libraries established between 1760 and 1814 which Shera examined, only two contained over 20 percent fiction and none over 30 percent (p. 102, table 12).

27. In some instances each purchase had to be approved by a majority of the shareholders; see James O. Lyford, *History of the Town of Canterbury, New Hampshire, 1727–1912* (2 vols.; Concord, N.H., 1912), vol. 1, p. 207. For examples of social library holdings, see Sarah J. Cutler, "The Coonskin Library," *Ohio State Archaeological and Historical Quarterly*, 26 (1917), pp. 74–75; James R. Jackson, *History of Littleton, New Hampshire* (3 vols.; Cambridge, Mass., 1905), vol. 2, pp. 440–41.

28. A. Growoll, *American Book Clubs: Their Beginnings and History, and a Bibliography of Their Publications* (New York, 1897), pp. vi, 7–8.

29. Frank L. Mott, *A History of American Magazines, 1741–1850* (Cambridge, Mass., 1970), p. 200. On the predominance of localism in publishing before 1820, see William Charvat, *Literary Publishing in America* (Philadelphia, 1959), pp. 25–26. For an example of one such local coterie in Walpole, New Hampshire, see Porter G. Perrin, *The Life and Works of Thomas Green Fessenden*, Univ. of Maine Studies, 2d ser., no. 4 (Orono, 1925), pp. 16–23.

30. Frank L. Mott, *American Journalism: A History, 1690–1960* (3d ed.; New York, 1962), p. 13. Although still subordinate to the dominant eclecticism, specialization was starting to develop. One form that it took was the religious periodical press, which developed especially in the wake of the religious revivals of the

1790s and early 1800s; see Neal Edgar, *A History and Bibliography of American Magazines, 1800–1820* (Metuchen, N.J., 1975), p. 61. Little is known about the readers of the early periodicals, but see David Paul Nord, "A Republican Literature: Magazine Readers and Reading in Late-Eighteenth-Century New York," in Cathy N. Davidson, ed., *Reading in America: Literature and Social History* (Baltimore, Md., 1989), pp. 119–24. Comparing a subscribers' list in the first (1790) volume of the *New-York Magazine; or, Literary Repository* and city directories, Nord found that professionals (especially lawyers) and merchants were overrepresented (about half of the subscribers versus 15 percent of directory listings), but that nearly half of the subscribers were shopkeepers and artisans, who together composed 67 percent of directory listings. While its tone clearly represented aspirations to refinement, the magazine's readership was by no means elite. Neither was it in any respect low; unskilled workers did not subscribe.

31. Benjamin Lewis, "A History and Bibliography of American Magazines," Ph.D. diss., Library Science, Univ. of Michigan, 1955, p. 5.

32. King, *Historical Sketch* (cited in n. 20), pp. iii–v.

33. Charles W. Turner, "The Franklin Society, 1800–1891," *Virginia Magazine of History and Biography*, 66 (Oct. 1958), pp. 432–47.

34. "The Young Men's Society of Detroit," *Collections, Michigan Pioneer and Historical Society*, 12 (1887), p. 370.

35. H. Perry Smith, *History of the City of Buffalo and Erie County* (2 vols.; Syracuse, N.Y., 1884), vol. 2, pp. 531, 533; William G. Rose, *Cleveland: The Making of a City* (Cleveland, Ohio, 1950), pp. 152, 162; Bayrd Still, *Milwaukee: The History of a City* (Madison, Wis., 1948), p. 214; Letha P. McGuire, "A Study of the Public Library Movement in Iowa," *Iowa Journal of History and Politics*, 35 (Jan. 1937), pp. 30–31.

36. Quoted in Sidney L. Jackson, *America's Struggle for Free Schools, 1827–1842* (Washington, D.C., 1941), p. 103.

37. Scott, "Popular Lecture" (cited in n. 5), p. 791.

38. George T. Fleming, *History of Pittsburgh and Environs* (5 vols.; New York, 1922), vol. 5, pp. 593–621.

39. David N. Johnson, *Sketches of Lynn, or the Changes of Fifty Years* (Westport, Conn., 1970 [orig. ed. 1880]), pp. 234–55; for a general survey of societies for young men, see Wallace K. Schoenberg, "The Young Men's Association, 1833–1876: The History of a Socio-Cultural Organization." Ph.D. diss., History, New York Univ., 1962; Luella M. Wright, "The Cedar Falls Parlor Reading Circle," *Iowa Journal of History and Politics*, 34 (Oct. 1936), pp. 39–44; see also Calvin W. Gower, "Lectures, Lyceums, and Libraries in Early Kansas, 1854–1864," *Kansas Historical Quarterly*, 36 (Summer 1970), pp. 174–82; James C. Malin, "The Burlington, Iowa, Apprenticeship of the Kansas Poet Eugene Fitch Ware, 'Irongull'," *Iowa Journal of History and Politics*, 57 (July 1959), p. 200.

40. See the sketches of Murray by C. Conrad Wright and of Adams by Janet Wilson James in Edward T. James, ed., *Notable American Women: A Biographical Directory* (3 vols.; Cambridge, Mass., 1971), vol. 2, pp. 603–5; vol. 1, pp. 9–11. See also *Memoir of Mrs. Hannah Adams, Written By Herself* (Boston, 1832); Benita Eisler, ed., *The Lowell Offering: Writings of New England Mill Women (1840–1845)* (New York, 1977), pp. 31–34; Mary A. Livermore, *The Story of My Life*

(Hartford, Conn., 1897), p. 399; on voluntary associations and "group consciousness" among women, see Nancy F. Cott, *The Bonds of Womanhood: "Women's Sphere" in New England, 1780–1835* (New Haven, Conn., 1977), pp. 199–204; Kerber, *Women of the Republic*, p. 241. There is material on antebellum women's study clubs in Grace P. Courtney, *History, Indiana Federation of Clubs* (Fort Wayne, Ind., 1939), pp. 1–16.

41. Dorothy B. Porter, "The Organized Educational Activities of Negro Literary Societies, 1828–1846," *Journal of Negro Education,* 5 (Oct. 1936), pp. 558–76; Daniel Perlman, "Organizations of the Free Negro in New York City," *Journal of Negro History,* 56 (July 1971), pp. 188–90; Wilson J. Moses, *Alexander Crummell, A Study of Civilization and Discontent* (New York, 1989), p. 9; see also the sketch of Samuel Eli Cornish in Jane H. Pease and William H. Pease, *Bound Them with Chains: A Biographical History of the Antislavery Movement* (Westport, Conn., 1972), pp. 140–61.

42. The comment on Emerson's epigrammatic style comes from a Cincinnati newspaper quoted in David Mead, *Yankee Eloquence in the Middle West: The Ohio Lyceum, 1850–1870* (East Lansing, Mich., 1951), p. 42; the bead-string metaphor was voiced by young Rutherford B. Hayes, who was in the early 1850s a member of the literary club that sponsored Emerson's first midwestern lectures; see Charles R. Williams, ed., *Diary and Letters of Rutherford B. Hayes* (4 vols.; Columbus, Ohio, 1922), vol. 1, p. 30; see also Louise Hastings, "Emerson in Cincinnati," *New England Quarterly,* 11 (Sept. 1938), p. 448. Emerson's popularity as a lecturer resulted at least partly from his ability to distinguish himself from pedantic scholarship while introducing his audience to higher verities; for an illustration see his lecture "Beauty," in *Conduct of Life* (*Complete Works,* 12 vols.; Boston, 1882), vol. 6, p. 281. Although they often had difficulty following his thread, his listeners seem to have appreciated his comprehensive overview of a subject; see Frederick E. Schortemeier, "Indianapolis Newspaper Accounts of Ralph Waldo Emerson," *Indiana Magazine of History,* 49 (Sept. 1953), p. 309. As his reputation grew, many came simply to see him; see Donald F. Tingley, "Ralph Waldo Emerson on the Illinois Lecture Circuit," *Journal of the Illinois State Historical Society,* 64 (Summer 1971), p. 204. See also Mary K. Cayton, "The Making of an American Prophet: Emerson, His Audiences, and the Rise of the Culture Industry in Nineteenth-Century America," *American Historical Review,* 92 (June 1987), pp. 597–620. Distinctions between literary societies in the same town or city were sometimes based on the interests of the members and sometimes on age. As an example of the latter, the "Literary Club," started in a Cincinnati law office in 1859 by twelve "young men" (including Rutherford B. Hayes), attracted those in their twenties, while the city's established literary society drew the middle-aged; see Elsie Ashbury, "The Literary Club," *Cincinnati Historical Society Bulletin,* 32 (Fall 1974), pp. 105–21.

43. Charles H. Foster, ed., *Down East Diary by Benjamin Browne Foster* (Orono, Maine, 1975), pp. 43–45, 165.

44. Philip E. Mackey, ed., *A Gentleman of Much Promise: The Diary of Isaac Mickle, Jr., 1837–1845* (2 vols.; Philadelphia, 1977), vol. 1, pp. 54, 52, xxiii–xxv, 10. Mickle's diary has been discussed by Richard D. Brown, *Knowledge Is Power: The Diffusion of Information in Early America, 1700–1865* (New York, 1989),

pp. 219–27. Mickle's belief that knowledge would not be amiss in any calling resembled the conviction of young Merrill Ober of Monkton, Vermont, who wrote: "I am now [1848] 16 and have not decided what business I will follow through life. But I will probably teach for a spell anyway. I must keep on studying and learn all that I can. A man can not learn too much. If what he learns is of no temporal use, it certainly will be of no mental use." See Wilson O. Clough, "A Journal of Village Life in Vermont in 1848," *New England Quarterly*, 1 (Jan. 1848), p. 35.

45. Mackey, ed., *Gentleman of Much Promise*, vol. 1, p. 54.

46. Ibid., vol. 1, p. 27.   47. Ibid., vol. 1, p. 100.

48. Ibid., vol. 1, p. xv; vol. 2, p. 285.   49. Ibid., vol. 1, p. 95.

50. Timothy Dwight, *Travels in New England and New York* (4 vols.; Cambridge, Mass., 1969), vol. 4, pp. 253–55.

51. For examples of phrenological lecturing see Nelson Sizer, *Forty Years in Phrenology* (New York, 1884), pp. 81–82, 84–86; see also Allan S. Horlick, "Phrenology and the Social Education of Young Men," *History of Education Quarterly*, 11 (Spring 1971), pp. 23–28.

52. Stuart M. Blumin, "The Hypothesis of Middle-Class Formation in Nineteenth-Century America: A Critique and Some Proposals," *American Historical Review*, 90 (Apr. 1985), pp. 313–15.

53. Leonard D. White, *The Jeffersonians: A Study in Administrative History* (New Haven, Conn., 1951), pp. 381, 397.

54. Cadwallader Colden had observed in 1765 that "few men except in the profession of Law have any kind of literature"; quoted in Thomas Bender, *New York Intellect* (New York, 1987), p. 16.

55. Benjamin Lease, *That Wild Fellow: John Neal and the American Literary Revolution* (Chicago, 1972), pp. 15–17, 21; John Neal, *Recollections of a Somewhat Busy Life* (Boston, 1869), p. 49.

56. William T. Coggeshall, *Poets and Poetry of the West: With Bibliographical and Critical Notices* (New York, 1864).

57. Ibid., pp. 90, 119.

58. I have derived this composite picture from Charles H. Bell, *The Bench and Bar of New Hampshire* (Boston, 1894).

59. James H. Matheny, "A Modern Knight-Errant—Edward Dickinson Baker," *Journal of the Illinois Historical Society*, 9 (Apr. 1916), p. 27.

60. Ibid.

61. Frances L. McCurdy, *Stump, Bar, and Pulpit: Speechmaking on the Missouri Frontier* (Columbia, Mo., 1969), pp. 81, 44.

62. Ibid., p. 115. Kenneth Cmiel has identified inflated speech as one of the hallmarks of the "middling poetics" (or decorum) that arose in the nineteenth century. "Politicians, ministers, and newspapermen," he writes, "produced pompous and often meaningless language to impress their audiences with the importance of the occasion and the learnedness of the speaker." Such speech was "middling" in the sense that leaders used it to communicate with the populace rather than merely with gentlemen, and also in its congruence with "code switching"—the concomitant employment of coarse or familiar language to establish the similarity between speaker and audience. See Cmiel, *Democratic Eloquence: The Fight over Popular Speech in Nineteenth-Century America* (New York, 1990), pp. 64–65, 35.

63. Quoted in Jessie McHarry, "John Reynolds," *Journal of the Illinois State Historical Society*, 6 (Apr. 1913), p. 30.

64. Ibid.

65. Ibid., pp. 32, 29.

66. John Reynolds, *My Own Times, Embracing Also the History of My Life* (Belleville, Ill., 1855), p. 133.

67. McHarry, "John Reynolds," p. 32.

68. "Young Men's Society of Detroit" (cited in n. 34), p. 366.

69. Nathan O. Hatch, *The Democratization of American Christianity* (New Haven, Conn., 1989), chap. 2.

70. Peter Cartwright, *Autobiography of Peter Cartwright* (New York, 1956), p. 65; Hatch, *Democratization of American Christianity*, pp. 88–89.

71. Joseph F. Kett, *The Formation of the American Medical Profession: The Role of Institutions, 1780–1860* (New Haven, Conn., 1968), chap. 4.

72. Ibid., pp. 102–3; Elias Smith, *Life, Conversion, Preachings, Travels and Sufferings of Elias Smith* (Portsmouth, N.H., 1816), pp. 46–47.

73. Cartwright, *Autobiography*, p. 64.

74. Ibid., p. 268.

75. John Brooks, *Life and Times of the Rev. John Brooks* (Nashville, Tenn., 1848), p. 104; Hatch, *Democratization of American Christianity*, p. 143.

76. William P. Stackhouse, ed., *Autobiography of Dan Young: A New England Preacher of Olden Time* (New York, 1860), p. 60.

77. Hatch, *Democratization of American Christianity*, pp. 141–46, 204.

78. Quoted in Constance Noyes Robertson, ed., *Oneida Community: An Autobiography, 1851–1876* (Syracuse, N.Y., 1970), pp. 176–77.

79. John E. Todd, ed., *John Todd: The Story of His Life, Told Mainly by Himself* (New York, 1876), p. 65.

80. Paul Stoddard, "The American Lyceum." Ph.D. diss., History, Yale Univ., 1947, p. 55; see also Russel B. Nye, "Marius Robinson, A Forgotten Abolitionist Leader," *Ohio State Archaeological and Historical Quarterly*, 55 (Apr.-June 1946), p. 139.

81. Matthew Hale Smith, *Universalism Examined, Renounced, Exposed* (Boston, 1843), pp. 8–9; John Bangs, *Autobiography of John Bangs* (Boston, 1846), p. 29; Orestes A. Brownson, *The Convert, or Leaves From My Experience* (New York, 1857).

82. David F. Allmendinger, Jr., "New England Students and the Revolution in Higher Education, 1800–1900," *History of Education Quarterly*, 11 (Winter, 1971), p. 382; see also Allmendinger, *Paupers and Scholars: The Transformation of Student Life in Nineteenth-Century New England* (New York, 1975).

83. Colin B. Burke, *American Collegiate Populations: A Test of the Traditional View* (New York, 1982), p. 104. A similar tendency marked midwestern colleges after 1830; see ibid., p. 127.

84. Daniel W. Howe, *The Unitarian Conscience: Harvard Moral Philosophy, 1805–1861* (Cambridge, Mass., 1970), p. 256.

85. Louise L. Stevenson, *Scholarly Means to Evangelical Ends: The New Haven Scholars and the Transformation of Higher Learning in America, 1830–1890* (Baltimore, Md., 1986), p. 2.

86. Emory S. Bucke et al., *The History of American Methodism* (3 vols.; New York, 1964), vol. 1, p. 568.

87. Hatch, *Democratization of American Christianity*, p. 205.

88. David P. Potts, "American Colleges in the Nineteenth Century: From Localism to Denominationalism," *History of Education Quarterly*, 11 (Winter 1971), p. 367.

89. Daniel Drake, *Pioneer Life in Kentucky* (New York, 1948), pp. 161–62.

90. William H. Venable, *Beginnings of Literary Culture in the Ohio Valley: Historical and Biographical Sketches* (New York, 1949), pp. 129–30.

91. Elias P. Fordham, *Personal Narrative of Travels in Virginia, Maryland, Pennsylvania, Ohio, Indiana, Kentucky: And of a Residence in the Illinois Territory, 1817–1818* (Cleveland, Ohio, 1906), p. 27.

92. Quoted in Henry D. Shapiro and Zane L. Miller, eds., *Physician to the West: Selected Writings of Daniel Drake on Science and Society* (Lexington, Ky., 1970), pp. 304, 59.

93. Samuel Gross, *Autobiography of Samuel Gross, M.D., with Sketches of His Contemporaries* (2 vols.; Philadelphia, 1887), vol. 1, pp. 203–4.

94. Ibid., vol. 2, pp. 272–73.

95. Shapiro and Miller, eds., *Physician to the West*, p. 57.

96. Bender, *New York Intellect* (cited in n. 54), pp. 67–68.

97. John C. Greene, "Science, Learning, and Utility: Patterns of Organization in the Early American Republic," in Alexandra Oleson and Sanborn C. Brown, eds., *The Pursuit of Knowledge in the Early American Republic* (Baltimore, Md., 1976), pp. 4, 11. The insecurity of the American scientific community before 1830 and the consequent tendency of learned societies to broaden their appeal by extending their domain is well described in Sally G. Kohlstedt, *The Formation of the American Scientific Community: The American Association for the Advancement of Science, 1848–1860* (Urbana, Ill., 1976), p. 28; see also George Daniels, *American Science in the Age of Jackson* (New York, 1968), p. 34.

98. Patsy A. Gerstner, "The Academy of Natural Sciences of Philadelphia, 1812–1850," in Oleson and Brown, *Pursuit of Knowledge*, p. 174; Kohlstedt, *Formation of the American Scientific Community*, p. 33; Linda Kerber, "Science in the Early Republic: The Society for the Study of Natural Philosophy," *William and Mary Quarterly*, 39 (Apr. 1972), p. 263.

99. Bender, *New York Intellect*, p. 65; John T. Flanagan, "James Hall and the Antiquarian and Historical Society of Illinois," *Journal of the Illinois State Historical Society*, 34 (Dec. 1941), pp. 442–43.

100. Walter M. Whitehill, "Early Learned Societies in Boston and Vicinity," in Oleson and Brown, *Pursuit of Knowledge*, p. 165. Some societies continued to mix natural history and antiquities; see Ralph W. Dexter, "The Essex County Natural History Society, 1833–1848," *Essex Institute Historical Collections*, 133 (Jan. 1977), pp. 38–53; see also George H. Callcott, *History in the United States, 1800–1860: Its Practice and Purpose* (Baltimore, Md., 1970).

101. Quoted in Gerstner, "Academy of Natural Sciences," p. 175.

102. Ibid., p. 79; for more on Maclure, see Chapter 4.

103. Quoted in Ralph S. Bates, *Scientific Societies in the United States* (New York, 1945), p. 36.

104. Ibid., pp. 48–50, 41–47, 53–54. Bates identified 4 local scientific societies in operation in 1805, 7 by 1815, and 23 by 1825.

105. Johnson, *Sketches of Lynn* (cited in n. 39), pp. 235, 237.

106. Quoted in Otto Juettner, *Daniel Drake and His Followers: Historical and Biographical Sketches* (Cincinnati, Ohio, 1909), pp. 175–79.

107. George Daniels, "The Process of Professionalization in American Science: The Emergent Period, 1820–1860," *Isis*, 58 (Summer 1967), pp. 153–54; Kohlstedt, *Formation of the American Scientific Community*, pp. 54–58; see also Wilcomb E. Washburn, "Joseph Henry's Conception of the Purpose of the Smithsonian Institution," in Whitfield Bell, ed., *A Cabinet of Curiosities* (Charlottesville, Va., 1967), pp. 106–66.

108. Douglas Sloan, "Science in New York City, 1867–1907," *Isis*, 71 (Mar. 1980), pp. 35–78; William DePrez Inlow, "The Indiana Geologist and Naturalist," *Indiana Magazine of History*, 56 (Mar. 1960), pp. 1–35; Walter B. Hendrickson, "Nineteenth-Century Natural History Organizations in Illinois," *Journal of the Illinois State Historical Society*, 54 (Aug. 1961), pp. 246–67; Ralph W. Dexter, "History of the Pottsville, (Pa.) Scientific Association, 1854–1862," *Science Education*, 53 (Feb. 1969), pp. 29–32; Dexter, "Essex County Natural History Society," pp. 38–53; Nadine K. Fichter, "The Brookside Society of Natural History," *Indiana Magazine of History*, 42 (Dec. 1946), pp. 305–10.

109. James S. Loring, *The Hundred Boston Orators* (Boston, 1852), pp. 664–66.

110. Edward W. Emerson, ed., *The Early Years of the Saturday Club, 1855–1870* (Boston, 1918), p. 118.

111. Edwin P. Whipple, *Lectures on Subjects Connected with Literature and Life* (Boston, 1853).

112. "Mercantile Miscellanies," *Hunt's Merchants' Magazine*, 6 (Mar. 1842), p. 268.

113. Loring, *Hundred Boston Orators*, p. 667.

114. On the New York Society Library, see Virginia D. Harrington, *The New York Merchants on the Eve of the Revolution* (New York, 1935), pp. 33–36; see also Ronald Story, "Class and Culture in Boston: The Athenaeum, 1807–1860," *American Quarterly*, 27 (May 1975), pp. 182, 196.

115. Allan Nevins, ed., *The Diary of Philip Hone, 1821–1851* (New York, 1936), p. xiv; see also Allan S. Horlick, *Country Boys to Merchant Princes: The Social Control of Young Men in New York* (Lewisburg, Pa., 1975), p. 304.

116. George Putnam, "Lectures on the Moral and Intellectual Culture of American Merchants," *Hunt's Merchants' Magazine*, 8 (Apr. 1843), p. 304.

117. "Mercantile Library Association," *Hunt's Merchants' Magazine*, 1 (July 1839), pp. 77–78.

118. Ibid., p. 76.

119. "Annual Report of the Mercantile Library Association," *Hunt's Merchants' Magazine*, 2 (Feb. 1840), p. 165.

120. "The American Merchant," *Hunt's Merchants' Magazine*, 2 (June 1840), p. 505.

121. "What Constitutes a Merchant," *Hunt's Merchants' Magazine*, 1 (Oct. 1839), pp. 295, 299.

122. On the recruitment of clerks from the country see Joseph Scoville [Walter Barrett, pseud.], *The Old Merchants of New York City* (4 vols.; New York, 1863–66), vol. 2, p. 102. See also F. B. Perkins, "Young Men's Mercantile Libraries," in U.S. Department of the Interior, Bureau of Education, *Public Libraries in the United States of America. Part 1* (Washington, D.C., 1876), p. 381; see also "Nineteenth Annual Report of the Mercantile Library Association," in *Hunt's Merchants' Magazine*, 2 (Feb. 1840), pp. 167–68. On the tendency of young men's associations to draw recent immigrants to the cities, see "An Apology of the Young Men's Society," *Pittsburgh Gazette*, Mar. 5, 1833.

123. New York Mercantile Library Association, *Catalogue of Novels, Tales, Etc., . . . May, 1856* (New York, 1856); see also Richmond [Va.] Mercantile Library Association, *Catalogue of Books, Nov. 15, 1839* (Richmond, 1839).

124. Quoted in Ron Butchart, "Education and Culture in the Trans-Mississippi West: An Interpretation," *Journal of American Culture*, 3 (Summer 1980), p. 353.

125. Donald H. Stewart, *The Opposition Press in the Federalist Period* (Albany, N.Y., 1969), p. 16.

126. Schudson, *Discovering the News*, chap. 1.

127. Quoted in W. J. Rorabaugh, *The Craft Apprentice: From Franklin to the Machine Age in America* (New York, 1986), p. 151.

128. William Dean Howells, *Years of My Youth and Three Essays* (Bloomington, Ind., 1975), p. 15.

129. Kenneth S. Lynn, *William Dean Howells: An American Life* (New York, 1970), p. 21.

130. Ibid., pp. 33–36, 54.

131. John L. Thomas, *The Liberator, William Lloyd Garrison: A Biography* (Boston, 1963), pp. 42–43; Harriet A. Weed, ed., *Autobiography of Thurlow Weed* (Boston, 1884), p. 62.

132. Howells, *Years of My Youth*, pp. 154–55; Lynn, *William Dean Howells*, p. 71–72; Rodney D. Olsen, *Dancing in Chains: The Youth of William Dean Howells* (New York, 1991), pp. 61–63.

133. Rhoda C. Ellison, *Early Alabama Publications: A Study in Literary Interests* (University, Ala., 1947), pp. ix–x, 41, 45, 77–79, 105.

134. Walter M. Merrill, ed., *The Letters of William Lloyd Garrison* (4 vols.; Boston, 1889), vol. 1, pp. 11, 5–6, 16–20.

135. *William Lloyd Garrison, 1805–1879: The Story of His Life, Told by His Children* (4 vols.; Boston, 1889), vol. 1, p. 56.

136. James B. Stewart, *Holy Warriors: The Abolitionists and American Society* (New York, 1876), p. 37.

137. Carl F. Kaestle and Maris A. Vinovskis, *Education and Social Change in Nineteenth-Century Massachusetts* (Cambridge, Eng., 1980), pp. 25–26, 40, 202–6. Massachusetts's widely copied 1789 law, which relieved the smaller towns of the obligation to maintain Latin grammar schools, authorized residents of outlying areas to establish "district schools," in effect, rural primary schools.

138. Paul H. Mattingly, *The Classless Profession: American Schoolmen in the Nineteenth Century* (New York, 1975), pp. 5, 28; "Extract from an Address [by Samuel Ells] Before the College of Teachers," *Common School Advocate*, 2 (Jan. 1838), p. 81.

139. William A. Alcott, *Confessions of a School Master* (Reading, Pa., 1856), p. 25.

140. Richard L. Herrnstadt, ed., *The Letters of A. Bronson Alcott* (Ames, Iowa, 1969), p. 9.

141. Mary Beth Norton, *Liberty's Daughters: The Revolutionary Experience of American Women, 1750–1800* (Boston, 1980), p. 268.

142. Nancy F. Cott, *The Bonds of Womanhood: Woman's Sphere in New England, 1780–1835* (New Haven, Conn., 1977), pp. 112–13.

143. Ibid., pp. 118–20; Norton, *Liberty's Daughters*, pp. 265–66; Kerber, *Women of the Republic*, pp. 24–25, 32. Mercantile Library Association, *Catalogue of Books, Nov. 15, 1839* (Richmond, Va., 1839). Mary Ryan has noted that in Utica in the 1830s, 90 percent of the members of the Young Men's Literary Club were boarders; see Ryan, *Cradle of the Middle Class: The Family in Oneida County, New York, 1790–1865* (Cambridge, Eng., 1981), pp. 128–29.

144. Alma Lutz, *Emma Willard: Pioneer Educator of American Women* (Boston, 1964), chaps. 3–5; Emma Lydia Bolzau, *Almira Hart Lincoln Phelps: Her Life and Work* (Philadelphia, 1936), pp. 24–33.

145. Helen L. Horowitz, *Alma Mater: Design and Experience in the Women's Colleges from Their Nineteenth-Century Beginnings to the 1930s* (Boston, 1984), pp. 10–11.

146. Lutz, *Emma Willard*, pp. 24, 40–41, 54–56; Bolzau, *Almira Hart Lincoln Phelps*, chap. 7. For more on Eaton, see Chapter 4. Eaton also had a pronounced influence on Mary Lyon; see Marion Lansing, ed., *Mary Lyon Through Her Letters* (Boston, 1937), pp. 53–56.

147. Sydney R. Maclean, "Emily Dickinson at Mt. Holyoke," *New England Quarterly*, 7 (Mar. 1934), p. 27.

148. Almira Phelps, *The Fireside Friend, or Female Student* (New York, 1847), pt. 3; Margaret Coxe, *The Young Lady's Companion in a Series of Letters* (Columbus, Ohio, 1839), letter 12; Susan P. Conrad, *Perish the Thought: Intellectual Women in Romantic America* (New York, 1976), pp. 22–23.

149. See Chapter 4.

150. Lydia H. Sigourney, *Letters to Young Ladies* (2d ed., Hartford, Conn., 1835), pp. 32, 35.

151. See, for example, Eliza W. Farrar, *The Young Lady's Friend* (Boston, 1836).

152. See Chapter 5.

Chapter 3

1. Quoted in Frederick Rudolph, ed., *Essays on Education in the Early Republic* (Cambridge, Mass., 1965), p. 22.

2. Rush Welter, *Popular Education and Democratic Thought in America* (New York, 1962), pp. 32–33; Joseph F. Kett, "Education," in Merrill D. Peterson, ed., *Thomas Jefferson: A Reference Biography* (New York, 1986), pp. 241–43.

3. Welter, *Popular Education*, pp. 34–35; Carl F. Kaestle, *The Evolution of an Urban School System: New York City, 1750–1850* (Cambridge, Mass., 1973), pp. 80–88; Lawrence A. Cremin, *American Education: The National Experience,*

1783–1876 (New York, 1980), p. 164. On the workingmen and educational issues, see Sidney L. Jackson, *America's Struggle for Free Schools: Social Tension and Education in New York and New England, 1827–1842* (Washington, D.C., 1941); on the workingmen's parties, see Sean Wilentz, *Chants Democratic: New York City and the Rise of the American Working Class, 1788–1850* (New York, 1984); see also Welter, *Popular Education*, pp. 45–59.

4. Jonathan Messerli, *Horace Mann: A Biography* (New York, 1972), p. 343; David B. Tyack, *The One Best System: A History of American Urban Education* (Cambridge, Mass., 1974), pp. 39–59 ; David B. Tyack, "Onward Christian Soldiers: Religion in the American Public Schools," in Paul Nash, ed., *History and Education* (New York, 1970), pp. 212–55.

5. Messerli, *Horace Mann*, p. 307.

6. Carl F. Kaestle and Maris A. Vinovskis, *Education and Social Change in Nineteenth-Century Massachusetts* (Cambridge, Eng., 1980), pp. 46–71.

7. Ibid., p. 36.

8. Noah Webster, "On the Education of Youth in America," in Rudolph, ed., *Essays on Education*, p. 72. School reformers favored tax-supported public high schools, but they did not envision these as even potentially universal institutions. The workingmen's parties usually opposed tax support for high schools, which would be patronized mainly by the children of the middle class. As late as 1879 the Workingmen's Party in California sought to exclude high schools from the state's public school system, mainly on grounds that public schools should instruct "in the elements only." See David Tyack and Elisabeth Hansot, *Learning Together: A History of Coeducation in American Public Schools* (New Haven, Conn., 1990), p. 119.

9. Messerli, *Horace Mann*, pp. 306–7.

10. Horace Mann addressed some of these in his *Lectures on Education* (Boston, 1855), pp. 276–80, 303–38.

11. Robert Rantoul, Jr., "An Address to the Workingmen of the United States of America," in Luther Hamilton, ed., *Memoirs, Speeches and Writings of Robert Rantoul, Jr.* (Boston, 1854), p. 242. Marvin Meyers has described Rantoul as a progressive Jacksonian who combined moralism (especially on educational issues) with a defense of acquisitiveness. In this respect, his political values resembled those of the predominantly Whig school reformers. See Meyers, *The Jacksonian Persuasion: Politics and Belief* (New York, 1960), pp. 206–33.

12. John Locke, "A Treatise on the Conduct of the Understanding," in Locke, *An Essay Concerning Human Understanding, To Which Are Now Added A Treatise on the Conduct of the Understanding, . . .* (22d ed., 2 vols.; London, 1812), vol. 2, pp. 354–55; Lawrence A. Cremin, *American Education: The Colonial Experience, 1607–1783* (New York, 1970), pp. 394–95.

13. C. C. Felton, "An Address Pronounced on the Anniversary of the Concord Lyceum, November 4, 1829," in Kenneth W. Cameron, ed., *The Massachusetts Lyceum During the American Renaissance* (Hartford, n.d.), p. 43.

14. Carl Bode, *The American Lyceum: Town Meeting of the Mind* (Carbondale, Ill., 1968), chap. 9.

15. William E. Channing, "The Present Age," in *Works of William Ellery Channing, D.D., with an Introduction* (Boston, 1880), p. 159.

16. See Channing, "Self-Culture" (pp. 12–36), and "On the Elevation of the Laboring Classes" (pp. 36–65) in *Works of William Ellery Channing*.

17. Channing, "Present Age," pp. 159, 161.

18. Ibid., p. 171.

19. Richard D. Brown, *Knowledge Is Power: The Diffusion of Information in Early America* (New York, 1989), p. 221.

20. Channing, "On the Elevation of the Laboring Classes," in *Works of William Ellery Channing*, p. 42.

21. John G. Cawelti, *Apostles of the Self-Made Man* (Chicago, 1965), p. 85; "Some Reflections on Self-Education, Considered with Reference to the State of Literature in This Country," *Christian Examiner*, 9 (n.s. 4; Sept. 1830), pp. 296–300; Merle Curti, *The Learned Blacksmith: The Letters and Journals of Elihu Burritt* (New York, 1937), p. 5.

22. Daniel W. Howe, *The Unitarian Conscience: Harvard Moral Philosophy, 1805–1861* (Cambridge, Mass., 1970). Although many Unitarians were led to self-culture by their revulsion from the psychology of revivalism, the ideal had many sources in German and English thought; see Walter H. Bruford, *The German Tradition of Self-Cultivation: 'Bildung' from Humboldt to Thomas Mann* (London, 1975).

23. Orson Fowler, *Memory and Intellectual Improvement Applied to Self-Education and Juvenile Instruction* (New York, 1893), p. 13. See also Fowler, *Self-Culture and Perfection of Character. Including the Management of Youth* (New York, 1893), p. xv.

24. Samuel Bates, *Lectures on Mental and Moral Culture* (New York, 1866).

25. Ibid., pp. 229–63.

26. Ibid., pp. 195–97.

27. Ibid., p. 195.

28. Quoted in Cawelti, *Apostles of the Self-Made Man*, p. 41.

29. James Parton, *The Life of Horace Greeley* (New York, 1855), p. 435.

30. Rantoul, "An Address to the Workingmen of the United States of America," p. 240; William Grier, *The Modern Mechanic: A Scientific Guide and Calculator* (Boston, 1855), p. 9. The latter was originally published in Britain.

31. Quoted in "Edward Everett," *American Journal of Education* (1859), p. 365.

32. "Importance of Education to the Practical Artizan," *Mechanics' Magazine and Register of Inventions and Improvements*, 1 (June 1833), p. 286.

33. Bates, *Lectures*, p. 201.

34. Ibid., pp. 213–18. Bowditch, a distinguished mathematician, translator of scientific works, and writer on navigation, had no formal education beyond his tenth year, but he read widely and in particular made extensive use of the Salem Athenaeum. See Robert E. Berry, *Yankee Stargazer: The Life of Nathaniel Bowditch* (New York, 1941). Watt never attended a university, but he was employed by the College of Glasgow to clean instruments, read books in the college's library, and had access in the college to an atmospheric engine. See H. L. Dickinson, *A Short History of the Steam Engine* (2d ed.; London, 1963), pp. 66–68.

35. Bates, *Lectures on Mental and Moral Culture*, p. 226.

36. Ibid., p. 207; see ibid., p. vii on Bates's audience.

37. Ibid., p. 222.

38. "Craik's English of Shakespeare," *North American Review*, 105 (July 1867), p. 302.

39. George L. Craik, *The Pursuit of Knowledge Under Difficulties* (London, 1865), chap. 9.

40. Quoted in Charles Knight, *Passages of a Working Life During Half a Century* (3 vols.; London, 1864), vol. 2, pp. 133–34.

41. See Craik, *Pursuit of Knowledge*, pp. v–vi, and Knight, *Passages of a Working Life*, pp. 133–35.

42. Knight, *Passages of a Working Life*, pp. 134–35.

43. Ibid.

44. Carl F. Kaestle, "'Between the Scylla of Brutal Ignorance and the Charybdis of a Literary Education': Elite Attitudes Toward Mass Schooling in Early Industrial England and America," in Lawrence Stone, ed., *Schooling and Society: Studies in the History of Education* (Baltimore, Md., 1976), pp. 177–91.

45. Bela B. Edwards, *Biography of Self-Taught Men: With an Introductory Essay* (Boston, 1859).

46. Colin B. Burke, *American Collegiate Populations: A Test of the Traditional View* (New York, 1982), pp. 104, 127.

47. Edwards, *Biography of Self-Taught Men*, pp. 16–17.

48. Ibid., pp. 487–88.

49. Ibid., p. 488.

50. William Charvat, *The Origins of American Critical Thought, 1810–1835* (Philadelphia, 1936), pp. 46–47.

51. Burke, *American Collegiate Populations*, pp. 14, 54.

52. Ibid., pp. 54–55.

53. Quoted in Charles A. Coon, *Education in North Carolina: A Documentary History* (Raleigh, N.C., 1915), p. 733.

54. "The Educational Interest of the United States," *American Journal of Education*, 1 (1855–56), p. 368. Bernard Bailyn, "Education as a Discipline: Some Historical Notes," in John Walton and James C. Keuthe, eds., *The Discipline of Education* (Madison, Wis., 1963), p. 136. The U.S. Census of 1850 reported a roughly similar number of academies and by 1860 nearly 7,000; see U.S. Office of the Census, *Seventh Census*, p. 60, table 42, and *Eighth Census*, vol. 4, p. 506.

55. Bailyn, "Education as a Discipline," p. 136. The compliant North Carolina academy was Fayetteville Academy; see Coon, *Education in North Carolina*, p. 66.

56. Quoted in Coon, *Education in North Carolina*, p. 90.

57. Ibid.   58. Ibid.

59. Quoted in ibid., p. 746.   60. Ibid., pp. 82, 84, 181, 199.

61. Joseph F. Kett, *Rites of Passage: Adolescence in America, 1790–Present* (New York, 1977), pp. 18–20.

62. Rena Vassar, ed., "The Life of Silas Felton, Written by Himself," *Proceedings of the American Antiquarian Society*, vol. 69, pt. 2 (Oct. 1959), pp. 128, 131, 152–53.

63. Frank E. Stevens, "Autobiography of Stephen A. Douglas," *Journal of the Illinois State Historical Society*, 5 (Oct. 1912), p. 329.

64. Alexis de Tocqueville, *Democracy in America*, trans. by Henry Reeve (new

ed., 2 vols.; London, 1862), vol. 2, p. 19; see also Thomas Hamilton, *Men and Manners in America* (new ed.; Edinburgh, 1843), p. 206.

65. Mildred Eversole, ed., "Canton College: An Early Attempt at Higher Education in Illinois," *Journal of the Illinois State Historical Society*, 34 (Sept. 1941), quoted p. 337.

66. Ibid., pp. 339–43.

67. Ibid., pp. 340–41.

68. Burke, *American Collegiate Populations*, p. 301.

69. Frederick Rudolph, *Curriculum: A History of the American Undergraduate Course of Study Since 1636* (San Francisco, 1977), pp. 108–9.

70. Ibid., p. 109; Burke, *American Collegiate Populations*, p. 39.

71. Bates, *Lectures* (cited in n. 24), pp. 230–63.

72. Channing, "Self–Culture," in *Works of William Ellery Channing*, p. 14.

73. Channing, "On the Elevation of the Laboring Classes," in *Works of William Ellery Channing*, p. 37.

74. Bates, *Lectures*, p. 260.

75. Noah Webster, "On the Education of Youth in America" (cited in n. 8), pp. 67, 66.

76. Bates, *Lectures*, pp. 249–50, 252–53, 257–58.

77. "The American Society for the Diffusion of Useful Knowledge," *American Journal of Education*, 15 (1865), pp. 238–45. A contributor to an agricultural journal contended that the American Society for the Diffusion of Useful Knowledge existed mainly to sell books to school libraries at inflated prices; see S.H., "American Society for the Diffusion of Useful Knowledge," *Cultivator*, 5 (Jan. 1839), p. 191.

78. Messerli, *Horace Mann* (cited in n. 4), p. 345; Mann, *Lectures on Education* (cited in n. 10), pp. 269–302.

79. Bates, *Lectures*, p. 258.

80. William Hosmer, *Self-Education: Or The Philosophy of Mental Improvement* (Havana, N.Y., 1847), p. 12.

81. Lester F. Ward, *Applied Sociology: A Treatise on the Conscious Improvement of Society by Society* (Boston, 1906), pp. 246–76. On Ward's education, see Clifford H. Scott, *Lester Frank Ward* (Boston, 1976), pp. 13–19; see also Bernhard J. Stern, ed., *Young Ward's Diary* (New York, 1935). Ward raised the same issue in his *Dynamic Sociology* (2 vols.; New York, 1883), vol. 2, pp. 559–71. Here Ward referred to education by "experience," which he equated with the widely held notion that "contact with the world and observation on its ways are better guides than any form of artificial instruction."

82. Ward was contributing to a debate over nature and nurture within the context of evolutionary thought. The key book in the debate was Francis Galton, *English Men of Science: Their Nature and Nurture* (London, 1874). This debate, including Ward's role in it, is reviewed by Edwin L. Clarke, *American Men of Letters: Their Nature and Nurture* (New York, 1916), chap. 1. Clarke's volume, inspired by his reading of Ward, was representative of scholarly attempts to investigate the issue. Ward also was familiar with the work of Charles Horton Cooley, specifically Cooley's "Genius, Fame, and the Comparison of Races," *Annals of the American Academy of Political and Social Sciences*, 9 (May 1897), pp. 317–58.

83. David Starr Jordan, *Leading American Men of Science* (New York, 1910).

84. John M. Coulter, "Asa Gray," ibid., p. 212; Simon Newcomb, "Joseph Henry," ibid., p. 121.

85. J. McKeen Cattell, "A Statistical Study of American Men of Science, III," *Science*, n.s. 24 (Dec. 7, 1906), pp. 732–42.

86. For a description of Henry's mixture of formal and self-education, see Nathan Reingold, "The New York State Roots of Joseph Henry's National Career," *New York History*, 54 (Apr. 1973), pp. 133–44.

87. Clark A. Elliott, *Biographical Dictionary of American Science: The Seventeenth Through the Nineteenth Centuries* (Westport, Conn., 1979), p. 4.

88. "An Address in Commemoration of William C. Redfield, First President of the Association," *Proceedings of the American Association for the Advancement of Science, Eleventh Meeting, August, 1857* (Cambridge, Mass., 1858), pp. 9–12.

89. Quoted in Nathan Reingold, ed., *The Papers of Joseph Henry* (2 vols.; Washington, D.C., 1972), vol. 1, p. 436.

90. Elliott, *Biographical Dictionary*, p. 82.

91. Ibid., pp. 102–3.

92. Charles S. Osborn and Stellanova Osborn, *Schoolcraft, Longfellow, Hiawatha* (Lancaster, Pa., 1942); Henry Rowe Schoolcraft, *Personal Memoirs of a Residence of Thirty Years with the Indian Tribes on the North American Frontier: With Brief Notices of Passing Events, Facts, and Opinions, A.D. 1812 to A.D. 1842* (Philadelphia, 1851), pp. xxxiv–xxxv.

93. Elliott, *Biographical Dictionary*, p. 4.

94. Ward, *Applied Sociology* (cited in n. 81), p. 246.

Chapter 4

1. For the text of the Morrill Act and later amending acts, see Benjamin F. Andrews, "The Land Grant Act of 1862 and the Land-Grant Colleges," U.S. Department of the Interior, Bureau of Education, *Bulletin, 1918, No. 13* (Washington, D.C., 1928), pp. 7–10.

2. Useful arts societies attracted those who thought that the American Philosophical Society had become too theoretical; see George H. Daniels, *Science and American Society: A Social History* (New York, 1971), p. 154.

3. Quoted in Brooke Hindle, "The Underside of the Learned Society, New York, 1754–1854," in Alexandra Oleson and Sanborn C. Brown, eds., *The Pursuit of Knowledge in the Early American Republic: American Scientific and Learned Societies from Colonial Times to the Civil War* (Baltimore, Md., 1976), p. 89.

4. Ibid., pp. 93–95.

5. Margaret Rossiter, "The Organization of Agricultural Improvement," in Oleson and Brown, eds., *Pursuit of Knowledge*, p. 285.

6. Ibid.

7. Ibid., p. 286.

8. Quoted in John C. Greene, "Science, Learning, and Utility: Patterns of Organization in the Early American Republic," in Oleson and Brown, eds., *Pursuit of Knowledge*, p. 14.

9. Elkanah Watson, *History of the Rise, Progress, and Existing State of the Berkshire Agricultural Society in Massachusetts* (Albany, N.Y., 1819), p. 2.

10. Ibid., p. 44. Richard D. Birdsall, *Berkshire County: A Cultural History* (Westport, Conn., 1978), p. 171.

11. Wayne C. Neely, *The Agricultural Fair* (New York, 1935), pp. 64–65; Hindle, "Underside of a Learned Society," p. 98.

12. Albert L. Demaree, *The American Agricultural Press, 1819–1860* (New York, 1941), pp. 13–19; George F. Lemmer, "Early Agricultural Editors and Their Farm Philosophies," *Agricultural History*, 3 (Oct. 1957), pp. 3–22.

13. Thurlow Weed voiced a widespread nineteenth-century sentiment when he said that no one ever raised a crop with a straight back and that farmers doubted that lawyers, physicians, merchants, and other stalwarts of agricultural improvement societies could tell them anything about farming; see Harriet A. Weed, ed., *Autobiography of Thurlow Weed* (Boston, 1884), pp. 78–79.

14. Ronald E. Shaw, *Erie Water West: A History of the Erie Canal, 1792–1854* (Lexington, Ky., 1966), pp. 23–25.

15. Dorothy Bobbé, *De Witt Clinton* (New York, 1933), p. 65; John A. Krout, "New York's Early Engineers," *New York History*, 26 (July 1945), p. 270.

16. Shaw, *Erie Water West*, p. 233.

17. Ibid., pp. 233–34.

18. Quoted in Ray P. Baker, *A Chapter in American Education: Rensselaer Polytechnic Institute, 1824–1924* (New York, 1924), p. 6.

19. Quoted in Charles A. Bennett, *History of Manual and Industrial Education up to 1870* (Peoria, Ill., 1926), p. 351. See also Daniel H. Calhoun, *The American Civil Engineer: Origins and Conflict* (Cambridge, Mass., 1960), pp. 49–50.

20. Anthony F. C. Wallace, *Rockdale: The Growth of an American Village in the Early Industrial Revolution* (New York, 1978), pp. 114–15, 211–17.

21. Ibid., pp. 187, 201.

22. For a list of "technological" societies in the early republic see Evald Rink, *Technological Americana: A Checklist of Technical Publications Before 1831* (Millwood, N.Y., 1931), pp. 51–56.

23. S.H.C., "Portland Mechanics' Lyceum," *Young Mechanic*, 1 (Sept. 1832), p. 137.

24. Sidney Ditzion, "Mechanics' and Mercantile Libraries," *Library Quarterly*, 10 (Apr. 1940), pp. 197–99.

25. John F. Lewis, *History of the Apprentices' Library of Philadelphia* (Philadelphia, 1924), pp. 23–24.

26. F. B. Perkins, "Young Men's Mercantile Libraries," U.S. Department of the Interior, Bureau of Education, *Public Libraries in the United States of America, Part 1* (Washington, D.C., 1876), p. 385; Lewis, *History of the Apprentices' Library*, p. 21.

27. "List of Societies in Boston, Whose Objects are Entirely or in Part the Improvement of the Mind," *Young Mechanic*, 1 (May 1832), pp. 91–92.

28. Clarence R. Aurner, "Mechanics' Institutes," *Iowa Journal of History and Politics*, 19 (July 1921), pp. 389–413.

29. Timothy Claxton, *Memoir of a Mechanic* (Boston, 1839), pp. 151–52, 90; S.H.C., "Portland Mechanics' Lyceum," pp. 137–38.

30. Stephen Simpson, *The Working Man's Manual* (Philadelphia, 1831), p. 205.

31. Chester W. New, *The Life of Henry Brougham to 1830* (Oxford, Eng., 1961), pp. 332–33; see also Frances Hawes, *Henry Brougham* (New York, 1956), pp. 163–64; Thomas Kelly, *George Birkbeck: Pioneer of Adult Education* (Liverpool, 1957), p. 107.

32. New, *Brougham*, pp. 336–37.

33. Quoted in New, *Brougham*, p. 348; on the possible influence of the New York Mechanic and Scientific Institute on the Glasgow Mechanics' Institute, see Bruce Sinclair, *Philadelphia's Philosopher Mechanics: A History of the Franklin Institute* (Baltimore, Md., 1974), p. 8, note 16.

34. Edward Everett, "The Husbandman, Mechanic, and Manufacturer," *Orations and Speeches on Various Occasions* (4 vols.; Boston, 1856), vol. 3, p. 89; Gulian Verplanck, *A Lecture Introductory to a Course of Lectures Before the Mechanics' Institute of the City of New-York* (New York, 1833), p. 10. Verplanck typified the entrepreneurial wing of the Democratic party; see Edward K. Spann, *Ideals and Politics: New York Intellectuals and Liberal Democracy, 1820–1880* (Albany, N.Y., 1972), pp. 91–92. Similarly, Abraham Lincoln proclaimed in 1859 that "the mechanical branches of Natural Philosophy are ready to help in almost everything; but especially in reference to implements and machinery." See Lincoln's "Address Before the Wisconsin State Agricultural Society, September 30, 1859," in Roy Basler, ed., *The Collected Works of Abraham Lincoln* (9 vols.; New Brunswick, N.J., 1953–55), vol. 3, p. 481.

35. Claxton, *Memoir*, p. 82.

36. Ibid., pp. 88–90.

37. New, *Brougham*, pp. 340–41.

38. Sinclair, *Philadelphia's Philosopher Mechanics*, p. 4.

39. Ibid., pp. 29–30.

40. Monte A. Calvert, *The Mechanical Engineer in America: Professional Cultures in Conflict, 1830–1910* (Baltimore, Md., 1967), p. 7.

41. Ibid., pp. 32–33.

42. "To the Young Mechanic," *Young Mechanic*, 1 (Jan. 1832), p. 1. The *Young Mechanic* was the original title of Light's *Boston Mechanic*.

43. Quoted in Calvert, *Mechanical Engineer*, p. 30.

44. Andrew E. Ford, *History of the Origin of the Town of Clinton, Massachusetts, 1657–1835* (Clinton, Mass., 1896), pp. 192–97.

45. Quoted in ibid., p. 200.   46. Quoted in ibid.

47. Ibid., pp. 200–201.   48. Quoted in ibid., p. 409.

49. Ibid., p. 407 for a list of petitioners and *passim* for biographical information.

50. Ibid., p. 275.

51. Ibid., p. 411.

52. Wallace, *Rockdale* (cited in n. 20), p. 237.

53. "Chemistry," *Mechanic Apprentice*, 1 (Apr. 1846), p. 87.

54. Claxton, *Memoir*, p. 92.

55. Sinclair, *Philadelphia's Philosopher Mechanics*, p. 110.

56. Edward N. Clopper, "The Ohio Mechanics' Institute: Its 125th Anniversary," *Bulletin of the Historical and Philosophical Society of Ohio*, 11 (July 1953), p. 181.

57. Edward Royle, "Mechanics' Institutes and the Working Class, 1840–1860," *The Historical Journal*, 14 (June 1971), p. 305; Mabel Tylecote, *The Mechanics' Institutes of Lancashire and Yorkshire Before 1851* (Manchester, Eng., 1957), p. 130.

58. Quoted in "Edward Everett," *American Journal of Education*, 7 (1859), p. 362.

59. Edward Everett, "The Boyhood and Youth of Franklin," *Orations and Speeches on Various Occasions*, 2, pp. 1–42. See also Edward Everett, "A Lecture on the Working Men's Party," in Leon Stein and Philip Taft, eds., *Religion, Reform, and Revolution: Labor Panaceas in the Nineteenth Century* (New York, 1969), pp. 29, 33; Gulian C. Verplanck, "Of the Pleasures and Advantages of Science," *Mechanics' Magazine and Register of Inventions and Improvements*, 2 (Jan. 1833), p. 4.

60. "To the Reader," *Young Mechanic*, 2 (Jan. 1833), pp. 2–3; see also this column in *Young Mechanic*, 1 (Apr. 1832), pp. 72–74 and (May 1832), p. 61.

61. "Science at Yale College," *Boston Mechanic*, 4 (Aug. 1835), pp. 125–27; "Account of Harvard College," *Boston Mechanic*, 4 (June 1835), pp. 77–84.

62. James M. Porter, "An Address to the Mechanics of Easton, Pennsylvania, Delivered at Their Request, July 4, 1835," *Mechanics' Magazine and Register of Inventions and Improvements*, 6 (Oct. 1835), p. 197.

63. *Young Mechanic*, 1 (Jan. 1832), p. 1.

64. Quoted in Howard B. Rock, *Artisans of the New Republic: The Tradesmen of New York in the Age of Jefferson* (New York, 1979), p. 138. Maxine Berg has observed that the same was true in Britain: working-class traditions of mutual improvement were compatible with the more paternalistic motives of employers in furthering mechanics' institutes. See Berg, *The Machine Question and the Making of Political Economy, 1815–1848* (London, 1980), pp. 148–49.

65. Stephen Simpson, *The Working Man's Manual*, unpaginated advertisement.

66. Seth Luther, *An Address to the Working-Men of New England, on the State of Education, and on the Condition of the Producing Classes in Europe and America* (Boston, 1832), p. 28; see also Edward Pessen, "The Workingmen's Movement of the Jacksonian Era," *Mississippi Valley Historical Review*, 43 (Dec. 1956), pp. 430–41; Louis Hartz, "Seth Luther: The Story of a Working-Class Rebel," *New England Quarterly*, 13 (Sept. 1940), pp. 401–18.

67. James D. Watkinson, "Educating the Million: Institutions, Ideology, and the Working Class, 1787–1920," Ph.D. diss. in progress, History, Univ. of Virginia, chap. 1.

68. Sean Wilentz, *Chants Democratic: New York City and the Rise of the American Working Class, 1788–1850* (New York, 1984), p. 272.

69. Tylecote, *The Mechanics' Institutes of Lancashire and Yorkshire*, pp. 70–73, 184–87, 267–69.

70. Ibid., pp. 184–86.

71. Quoted in Harold Silver, *The Concept of Popular Education: A Study of Ideas and Social Movements in the Early Nineteenth Century* (London, 1977 [orig. ed. 1965]), p. 19.

72. Rush Welter, *Popular Education and Democratic Thought in America*

(New York, 1962), pp. 6–82; see also [Orville Dewey], "Popular Education," *North American Review*, 36 (Jan. 1833), p. 73.

73. Sinclair, *Philadelphia's Philosopher Mechanics*, p. 125.

74. Clopper, "Ohio Mechanics' Institute" (cited in n. 56), p. 186.

75. Ibid.

76. John H. Griscom, *Memoir of John Griscom, LL.D., . . . Compiled from an Autobiography and Other Sources* (New York, 1859), p. 23.

77. Ibid., pp. 49–50.

78. Ethel M. McAllister, *Amos Eaton, Scientist and Educator* (Philadelphia, 1941). Josiah Holbrook also attended Silliman's lectures, but not until over a decade after his graduation from Yale; see "Josiah Holbrook," *American Journal of Education*, 8 (1860), p. 230.

79. Sally G. Kohlstedt, *The Formation of the American Scientific Community: The American Association for the Advancement of Science, 1848–1860* (Urbana, Ill., 1976), p. 17.

80. John C. Burnham, *How Superstition Won and Science Lost: Popularizing Science and Health in the United States* (New Brunswick, N.J., 1987), pp. 4, 32–34, 226.

81. Edward Hitchcock, "The Wonders of Science Compared with the Wonders of Romance," in *Religious Truth, Illustrated from Science in Addresses and Sermons on Special Occasions* (Boston, 1857), pp. 132–91.

82. Ibid., p. 135. The compatibility of popular science and religious motifs is traced in Theodore Dwight Bozeman, *Protestants in an Age of Science: The Baconian Ideal in Antebellum American Religious Thought* (Chapel Hill, N.C., 1977).

83. Margaret W. Rossiter, "Benjamin Silliman and the Lowell Institute: The Popularization of Science in Nineteenth-Century America," *New England Quarterly*, 44 (Dec. 1971), pp. 613–14. Silliman helped to found New Haven's Franklin Institute; see Rollin G. Osterweiss, *Three Centuries of New Haven, 1636–1938* (New Haven, Conn., 1953), p. 231.

84. George P. Fisher, *Life of Benjamin Silliman, M.D., LL.D.* (2 vols; New York, 1866), vol. 2, p. 3.

85. Ibid. One of the goals of the Lowell Institute's managers was to afford more serious and systematic lectures than those of the lyceums; see Edward Weeks, *The Lowells and Their Institute* (Boston, 1966), p. 11.

86. Rossiter, "Benjamin Silliman and the Lowell Institute," p. 619.

87. Rocco Zappone, "The Diffusion of Knowledge in Baltimore, 1820–1900," Ph.D. diss. in progress, History, Univ. of Virginia, chap. 1.

88. Thomas Earle and Charles T. Congdon, eds., *Annals of the General Society of Mechanics and Tradesmen of the City of New York, from 1785 to 1880* (New York, 1882), pp. 93–98, 118–24.

89. "Waterspouts," *Mechanics' Advocate* (Dec. 10, 1846), pp. 10–11.

90. See Chapter 7.

91. Nick Cullather, "Lessons of the 35th Congress: The Morrill Land Grant College Act," *Essays in History*, 31 (Corcoran Department of History, Univ. of Virginia, Charlottesville, 1988), pp. 8–17; see also Leonard P. Curry, *Blueprint for*

Modern America: Nonmilitary Legislation of the First Civil War Congress (Nashville, Tenn., 1968), p. 114.

92. Among the few who did call for such universities was John D. Craig, the founder of the Ohio Mechanics' Institute, who in the 1820s urged each state to establish a public institution to afford young men in the agricultural and mechanical trades an opportunity to learn the principles behind their vocations; see Clopper, "Ohio Mechanics' Institute," p. 180. Several colleges established chairs of agriculture or agricultural chemistry—Columbia as early as 1792—but no one envisioned higher education for farmers and mechanics as a matter of course.

93. "Education Among Mechanics," *Boston Mechanic*, 4 (Mar. 1835), pp. 9–11.

94. Baker, *A Chapter in American Education* (cited in n. 18), pp. 22–23.

95. Ibid., p. 19.

96. Much has been written on producerism as an ideology, but to my mind the most insightful treatment remains that of Marvin Meyers; see Meyers, *The Jacksonian Persuasion: Politics and Belief* (New York, 1960), pp. 21–24. Recently, Christopher Lasch has emphasized the centrality of producerism in nineteenth-century American radicalism; see Lasch, *The True and Only Heaven: Progress and Its Critics* (New York, 1991), pp. 223–24, 209–21.

97. James D. Anderson, *The Education of Blacks in the South, 1860–1935* (Chapel Hill, N.C., 1988), pp. 33–36, 47, 239.

98. Quoted from Fellenberg in Bennett, *History of Manual and Industrial Education* (cited in n. 19), p. 135.

99. "Sketch of the Rise and Progress of the New York Horticultural Society," *New York Farmer*, 1 (Mar. 1828), p. 65.

100. Bennett, *History of Manual and Industrial Education*, p. 349; "Reviews," *United States Literary Gazette*, 2 (Aug. 15, 1825), pp. 361–67.

101. Bennett, *History of Manual and Industrial Education*, pp. 187–88.

102. Ibid., p. 191; "Sketch of Professor Coffin," *Popular Science Monthly*, 3 (Aug. 1873), p. 503.

103. In addition to Weld, Henry B. Stanton, who married Elizabeth Cady, was a student at Oneida, and Lewis Tappan sent his sons there. Oneida Institute was a staging ground for the Lane rebels in Cincinnati; in 1832 Asa A. Stone, a student and preceptor at Oneida before becoming one of the Lane seminarians, wrote to Weld that "every 19th century manual labor student should locate himself at the Lane Seminary." See Gilbert H. Barnes and Dwight Dumond, *Letters of Theodore Dwight Weld, Angelina Grimké Weld, and Sarah Grimké, 1822–1844* (2 vols.; Gloucester, Mass., 1965), vol. 1, p. 84. On the psychology of Weld's generation, see James B. Stewart, *Holy Warriors: The Abolitionists and American Slavery* (New York, 1976), pp. 36–44.

104. Quoted in Arthur E. Bestor, *Education and Reform at New Harmony: Correspondence of William Maclure and Marie Duclos Fretageot, 1822–1833* (Indianapolis, Ind., 1948), p. 293; see also George Lockwood, *The New Harmony Movement* (New York, 1905), p. 261; William P. Sears, *Roots of Vocational Education* (New York, 1931), p. 99.

105. 3 vols., 1828.

106. Ibid., vol. 1, p. 75.

107. Ibid., vol. 1, pp. 56–57.

108. Ibid., vol. 1, pp. 57, 64; see also W. H. G. Armytage, "William Maclure, 1763–1840: A British Interpretation," *Indiana Magazine of History*, 47 (Mar. 1951), pp. 1–20. Maclure once proclaimed that he would not trade "a single fact of the operations of the laws of nature, for all the antiquities that exist." See ibid., p. 18.

109. Quoted in Bestor, *Education and Reform*, p. 301.

110. Armytage, "William Maclure," p. 4.

111. Quoted in Bestor, *Education and Reform*, p. 301.

112. Quoted in ibid., p. 310.

113. Lockwood, *New Harmony Movement*, pp. 241–43.

114. Quoted in Harry J. Carmen, "Jesse Buel, Early Nineteenth-Century Agricultural Reformer," *Agricultural History*, 17 (Jan. 1943), p. 4; see also William P. Ogilvie, *Pioneer Agricultural Journalists* (Chicago, 1927), p. 42.

115. Quoted in Calvert, *The Mechanical Engineer in America*, p. 39. See also "Knowledge—Association," *Mechanics' Advocate*, 1 (Dec. 3, 1846), p. 3; "Mechanic Associations: Maine," *New York State Mechanic*, 1 (Nov. 20, 1841), p. 5.

116. "Political Action," *Mechanics' Advocate*, 1 (Dec. 10, 1846), p. 12. Similar complaints about lawyers and calls for equal education for farmers dotted the agricultural press; see, for example, "Education for Farmers' Sons," *Kennebec Farmer and Journal of Useful Arts* (Feb. 4, 1833), p. 20.

117. Walter P. Rogers, "The People's College Movement in New York State," *New York History*, 26 (Oct. 1945), pp. 419–21.

118. Quoted in Earle D. Ross, *Democracy's College: The Land-Grant Movement in the Formative Stage* (Ames, Iowa, 1942), pp. 25–26.

119. Rogers, "The People's College Movement," pp. 441–42.

120. Margaret W. Rossiter, *The Emergence of Agricultural Science: Justus Liebig and the Americans* (New Haven, Conn., 1975), pp. 49–88.

121. Rossiter, "Organization of Agricultural Improvement" (cited in n. 5), p. 281.

122. Ibid.

123. Lyman Carrier, "The United States Agricultural Society, 1852–1860: Its Relations to the Origins of the United States Department of Agriculture and the Land Grant Colleges," *Agricultural History*, 11 (Oct. 1937), pp. 278–88.

124. Clarence H. Danhof, *Change in Agriculture: The Northern States, 1820–1870* (Cambridge, Mass., 1969), p. 72.

125. Winton U. Solberg, *The University of Illinois, 1867–1894: An Intellectual and Cultural History* (Urbana, Ill., 1968), p. 40.

126. Turner's speech is printed in Edmund J. James, *The Origin of the Land Grant Act of 1862*, Univ. of Illinois Studies, no. 4 (Urbana, Nov. 1910), pp. 66–84.

127. Quoted in ibid., p. 73.

128. Ibid., p. 66.

129. Quoted in Mary Turner Carriel, *The Life of Jonathan Baldwin Turner* (Urbana, Ill., 1961), p. 55; ibid., pp. 52–53.

130. Ibid., p. 45.

131. Quoted in James, *Origin of the Land Grant Act*, p. 78.

132. Ibid., p. 70.

133. Ibid., p. 73. Between the 1860s and the 1890s, a score of states made manual labor compulsory in the land-grant colleges, in part to emphasize that the colleges were for the children of working farmers and in part to head off criticism of silk-hatted and kid-gloved professors of agriculture; see Earle D. Ross, "Manual Labor in the Land-Grant Colleges," *Mississippi Valley Historical Review*, 21 (Mar. 1935), pp. 513–28.

134. In a memorial composed in 1853, in which he called upon Congress to endow industrial universities, Turner spoke of "the more liberal and practical education of our industrial classes and their teachers in their various pursuits." This may have been the source of the Morrill Act's language ("to promote the liberal and practical education of the industrial classes in the several pursuits and professions of life"); see Solberg, *University of Illinois*, pp. 50, 54.

135. James, *Origin of the Land Grant Act*, pp. 71–73, 79.

136. Solberg, *University of Illinois*, pp. 48–53.

137. Earle D. Ross, "The 'Father' of the Land-Grant College Act," *Agricultural History*, 12 (Apr. 1938), pp. 151–86.

138. William B. Parker, *The Life and Public Service of Justin Smith Morrill* (Boston, 1924), p. 273.

139. Quoted in ibid.

140. Ibid., pp. 23–24; Morrill's shifting pronouncements about the purpose of the law that bore his name can be traced in Isaac M. Kandel, *Federal Aid for Vocational Education*, Carnegie Foundation for the Advancement of Teaching, Bulletin no. 10 (New York, 1917), pp. 20, 25, 28.

Chapter 5

1. Edmund J. James, "Introduction," in George F. James, ed., *Handbook of University Extension* (2d ed., Philadelphia, 1893), p. viii.

2. James Russell Lowell, "An Address at the Opening of the Free Public Library in Chelsea, Massachusetts, 22 November, 1885," in Lowell, *Literary, Political Addresses* (10 vols.; Boston, 1895), vol. 6, p. 84. Cf. Emerson: "Consider what you have in the smallest chosen library. A company of the wisest and wittiest men that could be picked out of all civil countries in a thousand years have set in best order the results of their learning and wisdom;" see Emerson, "Books," *Emerson's Complete Works* (12 vols; New York, 1923–26), vol. 7, p. 190.

3. Matthew Arnold, *Culture and Anarchy* (Cambridge, Eng., 1950), p. 70. Arnold in places also referred to the best that has been "thought and said."

4. John Aldington Symonds, "Culture: Its Meaning and Uses," *New Review*, 7 (July 1892), pp. 107–8; Daniel J. Czitrom, *Media and the American Mind: From Morse to McLuhan* (Chapel Hill, N.C., 1982), pp. 30–31; Lionel Trilling, *Matthew Arnold* (New York, 1939), p. 268. On the changing meanings of culture, see Raymond Williams, *Keywords: A Vocabulary of Culture and Society* (rev. ed.; New York, 1983), pp. 87–93.

5. John H. Raleigh, *Matthew Arnold and American Culture* (Berkeley, Calif., 1957), chap. 2. In Arnold's typology, "Philistine" usually connoted a middle-class

Dissenter of narrow outlook. See Patrick J. McCarthy, *Matthew Arnold and the Three Classes* (New York, 1964), pp. 106–7. See also Chisholm H. Leonard, "Arnold in America: A Study of Matthew Arnold's Literary Relations with America and of His Visits to This Country." Ph.D. diss., English, Yale Univ., 1932, pp. 182–86; Henry A. Beers, "Matthew Arnold in America," *Century*, 27 (Nov. 1883), p. 156.

6. Laurence Veysey has shown how professionals and amateurs commingled in late-nineteenth-century literary organizations; see Veysey, "The Plural Organized Worlds of the Humanities," in Alexandra Oleson and John Voss, eds., *The Organization of Knowledge in Modern America, 1860–1920* (Baltimore, Md., 1979), pp. 75–82. Similarly, Kenneth Cmiel observes that in the late 1860s and 1870s genteel literary critics saw university philologists as potential allies in asserting the values associated with culture; see Cmiel, *Democratic Eloquence: The Fight over Popular Speech in Nineteenth-Century America* (New York, 1990), pp. 169–71. Although the potential for conflict—for example, between philologists who valued a scientific approach to language (with its implicit tolerance of linguistic custom) and literary critics for whom polish and refinement were everything—was present from the start, and although the debate within colleges between advocates of research and supporters of culture became rancorous by 1890, the broad field of literary (including historical) organizations outside of universities was not greatly affected by professional/amateur divisions before 1900.

7. F. B. Perkins, "Young Men's Mercantile Libraries," in *Public Libraries in the United States of America, Part 1* (Boston, 1876), p. 380; see Chapter 6.

8. William R. Johnson, *Schooled Lawyers: A Study in the Clash of Professional Cultures* (New York, 1978), p. 52.

9. Richard Hofstadter, *Anti-Intellectualism in American Life*, (New York, 1966 [orig. ed. 1963]), pp. 247–50.

10. Janice Weiss, "Educating for Clerical Work," *Journal of Social History*, 14 (Spring 1981), p. 411.

11. Stephen N. Noland, *Indianapolis Literary Club: Summarized Record, 1877–1934* (Indianapolis, Ind., 1934), p. 104.

12. Kenny J. Williams, *Prairie Voices: A Literary History of Chicago from the Frontier to 1893* (Nashville, Tenn., 1980), pp. 201–3, 151.

13. Ibid., p. 204; Kathleen D. McCarthy, *Noblesse Oblige: Charity and Cultural Philanthropy in Chicago, 1849–1929* (Chicago, 1982), pp. 77–78. Thomas Bender's valuable interpretation of the transformation of cultural institutions in the nineteenth century stresses the causative role of population growth more than I do; see Bender, "The Erosion of Public Culture: Cities, Discourses, and Professional Disciplines," in Thomas L. Haskell, ed., *The Authority of Experts* (Bloomington, Ind., 1984), pp. 84–106.

14. Carl Bode, *The American Lyceum: Town Meeting of the Mind* (Carbondale, Ill., 1968 [orig. ed. 1955]), pp. 251–52.

15. [Josiah G. Holland], "Lecture-Brokers and Lecture-Breakers," *Scribner's Monthly*, 1 (Mar. 1871), p. 650.

16. "Editor's Easy Chair," *Harper's New Monthly Magazine*, 46 (Dec. 1872), p. 137.

17. [Josiah G. Holland], "Triflers on the Platform," *Scribner's Monthly*, 3 (Feb. 1872), p. 489.

18. John R. Godley, *Letters from America* (2 vols.; London, 1844), vol. 2, p. 48.

19. Dionysius Lardner, *Popular Lectures on Science and Art, Delivered in the Principal Cities and Towns of the United States* (2 vols.; New York, 1849), vol. 2, p. 399.

20. Josiah G. Holland, *Every-Day Topics: A Book of Briefs* (New York, 1876), pp. 260–61.

21. James B. Pond, *Eccentricities of Genius: Memories of Famous Men and Women of the Platform and Stage* (London, 1901), pp. 543, 547–54.

22. Eva Draegert, "Cultural History of Indianapolis, Literature, 1875–1890, II," *Indiana Magazine of History*, 52 (Dec. 1956), pp. 358–60; see also Pond, *Eccentricities of Genius*, p. 552. Pond noted that churches and church-related organizations were becoming more receptive to sponsoring lectures, but this by no means meant that lectures were becoming more religious. Rather, as Pond recognized, churches were growing more sympathetic to engaging in ethical but essentially secular activities.

23. Draegert, "Cultural History of Indianapolis," pp. 346–48.

24. E. L. Godkin, "The Chromo-Civilization," in *Reflections and Comments, 1865–1895* (New York, 1895), pp. 199–205.

25. Cmiel, *Democratic Eloquence*, pp. 204, 142. On the self-styled best men, see John L. Tomsich, *A Genteel Endeavor: American Culture and Politics in the Gilded Age* (Stanford, Calif., 1971).

26. "A New Field for Lectures," *Nation*, 29 (Nov. 6, 1879), p. 305; "A Suggestion for Our City Colleges," *Nation*, 29 (Oct. 30, 1879), p. 291.

27. "Suggestion for Our City Colleges," p. 291.

28. F. W. Clarke, "Scientific Dabblers," *Popular Science Monthly*, 1 (Sept. 1872), pp. 595, 600.

29. E. L. Youmans, "Plan and Purpose of Our Enterprise," *Popular Science Monthly*, 1 (May 1872), p. 115. On Youmans's career as a popularizer, see John Fiske, *Edward Livingston Youmans: Interpreter of Science for the People* (New York, 1894), pp. 65, 69, 82, 88, 258–59. See also Charles M. Haar, "E. L. Youmans: A Chapter in the Diffusion of Science in America," *Journal of the History of Ideas*, 9 (Apr. 1948), pp. 193–213.

30. I. L. Kandel, *History of Secondary Education: A Study of the Development of Liberal Education* (New York, 1931), pp. 453–56.

31. Ralph W. Emerson, "Education," in *Works* (cited in n. 2), vol. 10, p. 125.

32. Thomas Woody, *A History of Women's Education* (2 vols.; New York, 1929), vol. 2, pp. 239–45; Helen L. Horowitz, *Alma Mater: Design and Experience in the Women's Colleges from Their Nineteenth-Century Beginnings to the 1930s* (Boston, 1984), pt. 1.

33. Theodora Penny Martin, *The Sound of Our Own Voices: Women's Study Clubs, 1860–1910* (Boston, 1987), p. 175.

34. U.S. Department of the Interior, Bureau of Education, *Report of the Commissioner of Education, 1886–1887* (Washington, D.C., 1888), pp. 642–55.

35. David Tyack and Elizabeth Hansot, *Learning Together: A History of Co-education in American Public Schools* (New Haven, Conn., 1990), chap. 5.

36. John H. Vincent, *The Chautauqua Movement* (Boston, 1886), p. 137; see also "C.L.S.C. Notes and Letters," *Chautauquan*, 1 (Feb. 1881), p. 227. The novelist Zona Gale wrote that "women of the Middle-West university and college towns were ardent in the [women's club] movement, as became those whose look had long been toward the threshold which they never crossed." See Gale, "Katytown in the Eighties," *Harper's*, 157 (Aug. 1928), p. 288.

37. William I. Fletcher, *Public Libraries in America* (Boston, 1895), pp. 11–12.

38. For illustrations of the dependence of women on random reading in private (household) libraries, see Anna B. Warner, *Susan Warner* (New York, 1909), p. 116; Mary E. Dewey, ed., *Life and Letters of Catharine M. Sedgwick* (New York, 1871), pp. 247, 329, 343; Annie Fields, *Life and Letters of Harriet Beecher Stowe* (Boston, 1898), pp. 27, 37. In her short story "Odd Miss Todd," the novelist Rose Terry Cooke described how her protagonist, "Miny" Todd, "found her way to the miscellaneous library that lay heaped on chairs, bureaus, tables, even the floor, everywhere in the old house. . . . There were, no doubt, good materials for a liberal education, in these books, but, taken at haphazard, they were devoured on principles of natural selection." See Rose Terry Cooke, *Huckleberries Gathered from New England Hills* (Cambridge, Mass., 1969 [orig. ed. 1891]), pp. 87–88.

39. Clarence B. Cook, ed., *A Girl's Life Eighty Years Ago: Selections from the Letters of Eliza Southgate Bowne* (New York, 1887), pp. 56–57.

40. Eliza W. Farrar, *The Young Lady's Friend* (Boston, 1836); Margaret Coxe, *The Young Lady's Companion in a Series of Letters* (Columbus, Ohio, 1839).

41. Tyack and Hansot, *Learning Together*, pp. 138–43.

42. Susan P. Conrad, *Perish the Thought: Intellectual Women in Romantic America, 1830–1860* (New York, 1976), pp. 54–55.

43. Ralph W. Emerson et al., *Memoirs of Margaret Fuller Ossoli* (2 vols.; Boston, 1852), vol. 1, p. 53.

44. Farrar, *Young Lady's Friend*, pp. 259–60; Daniel Wise, *The Young Lady's Counsellor* (Boston, 1852), pp. 189–90.

45. Farrar, *Young Lady's Friend*, p. 23.

46. Martin, *Sound of Our Own Voices* (cited in n. 33), p. 7.

47. Charles Capper, "Margaret Fuller as Cultural Reformer: The Conversations in Boston," *American Quarterly*, 39 (Winter 1987), p. 515; Mason Wade, *Margaret Fuller: Whetstone of Genius* (New York, 1940), pp. 76–79. Fuller's Conversations, a method of teaching that she picked up from the Transcendentalist Bronson Alcott, attracted a much more elite audience than did lyceum lecturers, in part because they were expensive to attend. At a time when a subscription to a lyceum series cost $2, a ticket to a series of ten of Fuller's Conversations cost $20.

48. Ednah Dow Cheney, *Reminiscences of Ednah Dow Cheney* (Boston, 1902), p. 20.

49. Ellen M. Henrotin, "The Attitude of Women's Clubs and Associations Toward Social Economics," U.S. Department of Labor, *Bulletin, No. 23, July, 1899* (Washington, D.C., 1899), pp. 501–45.

50. Mrs. John Sherman, "The Women's Clubs of the Middle Western States," *Annals of the American Academy of Political and Social Science*, 28 (July-Dec.

1906), p. 228; Martin, *Sound of Our Own Voices*, pp. 3–4; see also Karen J. Blair, *The Clubwoman as Feminist* (New York, 1980).

51. Jane C. Croly, *The History of the Woman's Club Movement in America* (New York, 1898); Martin, *Sound of Our Own Voices*, p. 53.

52. Julia LeClerc Knox, "The Julia L. Dumont Club of Vevay, Indiana," *Indiana Magazine of History*, 46 (June 1950), p. 167; Gale, "Katytown in the Eighties" (cited in n. 36), p. 288. The survey published by the Department of Labor, which classified two-thirds of the clubs in 1899 as primarily literary rather than social, probably understated the proportion of literary clubs, mainly because it underreported small-town clubs, which were more likely to be literary. An investigation of women's clubs in Wisconsin found that three-fourths were "distinctly literary in character" in 1896; see Mrs. Charles S. Morris, "Women's Club Movement in Wisconsin," typescript, State Historical Society of Wisconsin (Madison, 1896). Historians are only beginning to study the history of black women's clubs, which developed on a parallel track to those for white women. (In 1900 the General Federation of Women's Clubs refused to seat a black delegate from Kansas.) After 1900, black clubwomen devised their own agenda of social issues, including attacks on segregated schools and calls for an anti-lynching law, but in the 1880s and 1890s the black clubs resembled those for whites in their stress on education and culture. In Kansas their state organization called itself the Federation of Women's Arts Clubs; local black clubs exhibited needlework and studied Shakespeare. See Marilyn D. Brady, "Kansas Federation of Colored Women's Clubs, 1900–1930," in Darlene Clark Hine, ed., *Black Women in American History: The Twentieth Century* (4 vols.; Brooklyn, N.Y., 1990), vol. 1, pp. 99–105; see also, in vol. 4, Erlene Stetson, "Black Feminism in Indiana, 1893–1933," pp. 1139–45, and, in vol. 2, Cynthia Neverdon-Morton, "Self-Help programs as Educative Activities of Black Women in the South, 1895–1925," pp. 921–35. An additional perspective is offered by Gerda Lerner, "Early Community Work of Black Club Women," *Journal of Negro History*, 59 (Apr. 1974), pp. 158–67.

53. Paul R. Anderson, "Quincy: An Outpost of Philosophy," *Journal of the Illinois State Historical Society*, 34 (Mar. 1941).

54. Martin, *Sound of Our Own Voices*, p. 21.

55. Caroline H. Stanley, "A Successful Woman's Club," *New England Magazine*, n.s. 2 (Mar.-Aug. 1890), pp. 54–62.

56. Mary L. Ely and Eve Chappell, *Women in Two Worlds* (New York, 1938), pp. 138–39, 135.

57. Martin, *Sound of Our Own Voices*, p. 5.

58. Ibid., pp. 51, 49, 63, and chap. 6.

59. Henry Baldwin, "An Old-Time Sorosis," *Atlantic Monthly*, 74 (Dec. 1894), p. 752.

60. Luella M. Wright, "The Cedar Falls Parlor Reading Circle," *Iowa Journal of History and Politics*, 34 (Oct. 1936), p. 352.

61. Herbert Baxter Adams, "Educational Extension in the United States," U.S. Department of the Interior, Bureau of Education, *Report of the Commissioner, 1899–1900* (2 vols.; Washington, D.C., 1900), vol. 1, p. 313.

62. For a good general history of Chautauqua see Theodore Morrison, *Chautauqua: A Center for Education, Religion, and the Arts in America* (Chicago,

1974); see also Joseph Gould, *The Chautauqua Movement: An Episode in the Continuing American Revolution* (Albany, N.Y., 1961). There is a crisp sketch in Arthur E. Bestor, *Chautauqua Publications: An Historical and Bibliographical Guide* (New York, 1934), pp. 4–10; the "half-pathetic hunger for knowledge" was noted by the novelist Hjalmar H. Boyeson, "The Chautauqua Movement," *Cosmopolitan*, 19 (1895), p. 155. For a regional study, see Harrison J. Thornton, "Chautauqua and the Midwest," *Wisconsin Magazine of History*, 33 (Dec. 1949), pp. 152–63; see also Vincent, *Chautauqua Movement* (cited in n. 36). Although Chautauqua was run mainly by men, Vincent's appeal primarily was to women. Ida Tarbell, who helped to edit the *Chautauquan* before passing on to a career in journalism and muckraking, averred that Vincent appealed principally to women over 30 whose desire for knowledge had been spurred by the women's movement but who lacked the opportunity to attend college. See Ida M. Tarbell, *All in a Day's Work: An Autobiography* (New York, 1939), p. 70.

63. Elwood Hendrick, *Lewis Miller: A Biographical Essay* (New York, 1925); Leon H. Vincent, *John Heyl Vincent: A Biographical Sketch* (New York, 1925). The son of a German immigrant, Miller was a successful manufacturer of agricultural implements, inventor, prominent Methodist layman, and the father-in-law of Thomas A. Edison. Vincent went through a long struggle in his youth over whether a devout Christian could pursue intellectual culture for its own sake. See Rebecca Richmond, *Chautauqua: An American Place* (New York, 1943), p. 43.

64. T. Scott Miyakawa, *Protestants and Pioneers: Individualism and Conformity on the American Frontier* (Chicago, 1964), pp. 109–11; Fernandez C. Holliday, *Indiana Methodism: Being an Account of the Introduction, Progress, and Present Position of Methodism in the State* (Cincinnati, Ohio, 1873), pp. 317–19.

65. Charles W. Ferguson, *Organizing to Beat the Devil: Methodists and the Making of America* (Garden City, N.Y., 1971), pp. 280–82.

66. Quoted in Vincent, *John Heyl Vincent*, p. 260.

67. Ferguson, *Organizing to Beat the Devil*, pp. 306–14; Miyakawa, *Protestants and Pioneers*, p. 106. John H. Vincent explicitly evoked the image of Wesley as a scholarly popularizer "who put secular culture in the hands of the people so they could be broad as well as intense"; see Vincent, *Chautauqua Movement*, p. 89.

68. Vincent, *John Heyl Vincent*, pp. 3–4, 91. Vincent's interest in Palestine reflected a debate that developed among Protestants in the wake of eighteenth-century deprecations by Gibbon and Volney of the Holy Land as a wilderness. Published in 1858, William Maclure Thomson's *The Land and the Book* became a best-seller, and in 1860 it sold more copies in the United States than any other American book save *Uncle Tom's Cabin*; see Herbert Hovenkamp, *Science and Religion in America, 1800–1860* (Philadelphia, 1978), pp. 150–58.

69. Hendrick, *Lewis Miller*, p. 147.

70. Vincent, *Chautauqua Movement*, p. 13; Morrison, *Chautauqua*, p. 43.

71. Vincent, *Chautauqua Movement*, p. 50.

72. Ibid.

73. Ibid., p. 66.

74. Kathleen A. Froome, "The Sacred and Secular Landscape of Chautauqua,

1874–1890," M.A. thesis, Architectural History, Univ. of Virginia, 1988, p. 21. See also Adams, "Educational Extension" (cited in n. 61), p. 987.

75. William W. Sweet, *Methodism in American History* (Nashville, Tenn., 1961), p. 333. On the return to simplicity, see John Higham, "The Reorientation of American Culture in the 1890s," in H. John Weiss, ed., *The Origins of Modern Consciousness* (Detroit, 1965), p. 27; David Shi, *The Simple Life: Plain Living and High Thinking in American Culture* (New York, 1985), pp. 156–60.

76. John H. Vincent, "The Means and Ends of Culture to Be Provided for the American People Beyond the Ordinary Secondary School Period," *Proceedings, National Education Association, 1887* (Salem, Mass., 1888), p. 183. For a similar, contemporary explanation of Henry's success, see James C. Welling, *Notes on the Life and Character of Joseph Henry* (Philadelphia, 1878), p. 208.

77. J. Clinton Ransom, *The Successful Man in His Manifold Relations with Life* (Greensboro, N.C., 1886), p. 368. In his study of adult education in England, J. F. C. Harrison summarizes the leading features of the autodidact tradition: reading whatever books came to hand, almost no idea of progression from the simple to the more complex, and no guidance in the selection of books; see Harrison, *Learning and Living, 1790–1960: A Study in the History of the English Adult Education Movement* (Toronto, 1961), pp. 48–49.

78. Vincent, *Chautauqua Movement*, p. 74.

79. *Society to Encourage Studies at Home: Founded in 1873 by Anna Eliot Ticknor* (Cambridge, Mass., 1897). Anna Ticknor was the daughter of George Ticknor, the historian and Harvard professor.

80. Herbert B. Adams, "Chautauqua: A Social and Educational Study," U.S. Department of the Interior, Bureau of Education, *Report of the Commissioner of Education, 1894–95* (2 vols.; Washington, D.C., 1896), vol. 1, pp. 1001–2. Adams put the number of local Chautauqua circles active in 1894 at "at least 1,000" and estimated that 10,000 new members were enrolling each year.

81. Kate F. Kimball, "Twenty-Five Years of Chautauqua Circle Work," *Chautauquan* 37 (July 1903), p. 387. See also Harrison J. Thornton, "Chautauqua in the Midwest," *Wisconsin Magazine of History*, 33 (Dec. 1949), pp. 152–63. The first few C.L.S.C. classes were composed mainly of evangelical Christians who welcomed books with titles like *Primitive Piety Revived* and *Philosophy of the Plan of Salvation*. But as George Edgar Vincent (John H.'s son) noted, as the circles' membership became more varied, protests arose against theological books. The last book specifically designed to encourage piety appeared on the C.L.S.C. reading list in 1893–94; see George E. Vincent, "The Evolution of the Reading Course," *Chautauquan*, 37 (July 1903), p. 384. As was true of most women's clubs, individual circles usually were small enough to meet in a parlor, but some towns had several circles; see Barry D. Cytron, "The Chautauqua Literary and Scientific Circle in Iowa, 1880–1900," *Palimpsest*, 59 (Nov.-Dec. 1978), p. 171; Cytron notes that seven circles met in Oskaloosa, Iowa, in the 1880s.

82. "Social Life in the C.L.S.C.," *Chautauquan*, 3 (July 1883), p. 603.

83. Bestor, *Chautauqua Publications* (cited in n. 62), p. 12.

84. "C.L.S.C. Round Table," *Chautauquan*, 1 (Jan. 1881), p. 177; *Chautauquan*, 3 (June 1883), p. 525; *Chautauquan*, 10 (Oct. 1889), p. 89.

85. "Local Circles," *Chautauquan*, 3 (June 1883), p. 525.

86. "C.L.S.C. Notes and Letters," *Chautauquan*, 1 (Dec. 1880), p. 118; see also *Chautauqua Literary and Scientific Circle: Membership Book, 1890* (Meadville, Pa., 1890). However vast, no topic was immune to the question and answer approach; for example, Chautauquans in 1890 were asked to name the "general characteristics of French literature." See ibid.

87. Dan Lacy, "Liberty and Knowledge, Then and Now: 1776, 1876, 1976," in Harold Goldstein, ed., *Milestones to the Present: Papers from Library History Seminar V"* (Syracuse, N.Y., 1978), p. 13.

88. George Cary Eggleston, *How to Educate Yourself: With or Without Masters* (New York, 1872).

89. Ibid., p. 2.

90. Ibid., p. 9.

91. Ari Hoogenboom, *Outlawing the Spoils: A History of the Civil Service Reform Movement, 1865–1883* (Urbana, Ill., 1961), p. 89 and *passim*.

92. Ibid., pp. 17, 124, 257–58. For examples of the examinations used in the federal civil service, see John M. Comstock, *The Civil Service in the United States, from the Reports of 1884* (New York, 1885). On home study as a way to prepare for civil service examinations see *Home Culture: A Self-Instructor and Aid to Social Hours at Home* (New York, 1884), p. 12. On women in the civil service, see Cindy S. Aron, *Ladies and Gentlemen of the Civil Service: Middle-Class Workers in Victorian America* (New York, 1987). Aron notes that "in the four decades after the Civil War, thousands of middle-class families called upon their daughters and wives and mothers to assume roles as wage earners" (p. 41).

93. Mary L. Smallwood, *An Historical Study of Grading Systems and Examinations in Early American Universities* (Cambridge, Mass., 1935), p. 9; R. J. Montgomery, *Examinations: An Account of Their Evolution as Administrative Devices in England* (Pittsburgh, 1965), p. 38.

94. I. L. Kandel, *Examinations and Their Substitutes in the United States*, Carnegie Foundation for the Advancement of Teaching, Bulletin no. 28 (New York, 1936), p. 26. Mann argued that written examinations afforded "a sort of Daguerrotype likeness" of the minds of students, "by which schools may be compared with each other or each school may measure its own progress" (p. 99).

95. The Boston school committee in 1845 identified an incontrovertible reason for written examinations: "Committee-men could no longer be found who would find time to examine [orally] over 7,000 children." Quoted in ibid, p. 25.

96. Albert Cook, "Chautauqua: Its Aims and Influence," *Forum*, 19 (1895), p. 697; Frederic P. Noble, "Chautauqua as a New Factor in American Life," *New England Magazine*, 8, n.s. 2 (Mar.-Aug. 1890), p. 95. Kate F. Kimball stated in 1883 that nearly 85 percent of C.L.S.C. members were women and that women predominated over men at the Lake Chautauqua summer assembly by nearly five to one; see Kate F. Kimball, "Graduates of the C.L.S.C.," *Chautauquan*, 3 (Feb. 1883), pp. 298–301.

97. U.S. Department of the Interior, Bureau of Education, *Report of the Commissioner of Education, 1886–1887* (Washington, D.C., 1888), table 23, p. 456.

98. For a state by state review of licensing requirements, see U.S. Department

of the Interior, Bureau of Education, *Circulars of Information, Number 1, 1883* (Washington, D.C., 1883), pp. 1–45.

99. Ibid., pp. 14–18 and *passim.*

100. *Report of the Commissioner, 1886–1887,* pp. 404–6, 408–52.

101. Ibid.

102. Bestor, *Chautauqua Publications* (cited in n. 62), p. 11; Cook, "Chautauqua: Its Aims and Influence," pp. 693–95. High attrition rates did not necessarily result from indifference to self-instruction, for members of some circles subscribed to the *Chautauquan* and then embarked on their own reading courses; see "Local Circles," *Chautauquan,* 3 (Feb. 1883), p. 284, and *Chautauquan,* 3 (Mar. 1883), pp. 347–48.

103. The statement that the C.L.S.C. was ill-suited to laboratory science, while accurate, should not obscure the fact that it did offer courses in descriptive sciences. In addition, Chautauqua textbooks described the different branches of the higher mathematics, so that a student, for example, could learn the difference between the integral and differential calculus. See "Readings on Mathematics," *Chautauquan,* 2 (Apr. 1882), pp. 391–95 and *Chautauquan,* 2 (May 1882), p. 458. The textbook was Charles Merrivale, *A General History of Rome* (London, 1875); see also *Catalogue of the Officers and Students of the University of Virginia, 1885–1886* (Richmond, Va., 1886), p. 26. George E. Vincent, who studied as an undergraduate at Yale, observed Yale students using the same outlines of Greek and Roman history as Chautauquans in order to cram for exams; see Vincent, "Evolution of the Reading Course" (cited in n. 81), p. 383.

104. Carol F. Baird, "Albert Bushnell Hart: The Rise of the Professional Historian," in Robert Church et al., *Social Sciences at Harvard, 1860–1920: From Inculcation to the Open Mind* (Cambridge, Mass., 1965), pp. 134–35, 137, 142.

105. Herbert Baxter Adams to William Rainey Harper, Feb. 10, 1897, Herbert Baxter Adams Papers, Johns Hopkins Univ., Baltimore, Md.

106. George E. Vincent to Herbert Baxter Adams, Nov. 14, 1888, Adams Papers.

107. George E. Vincent to Herbert Baxter Adams, Nov. 14, 1888, Adams Papers; Morrison, *Chautauqua* (cited in n. 62), p. 65; "C.L.S.C. Testimony," *Chautauquan,* 3 (Jan. 1883), p. 233; Vincent, *Chautauqua Movement* (cited in n. 36), p. 65. A textbook issued by the Chautauqua Press in 1886 and accurately if incongruously entitled *The Preparatory Latin Course in English* assured Chautauquans that, while they would not learn Latin and Greek, they would put themselves on a footing to discuss ancient literature with college students; see Gale, "Katytown in the Eighties" (cited in n. 36), p. 294. In 1883 John H. Vincent secured a charter from New York State for "Chautauqua University." He hoped that Chautauqua would become a leader in university extension, a development already under way in England, and that the Chautauqua University would confer degrees on advanced correspondence students. According to Vincent's son, the antagonism of university officials led the elder Vincent to back off. See George Edgar Vincent to Herbert Baxter Adams, May 26, 1891, Adams Papers. Before finally surrendering its power to grant degrees in 1898, Chautauqua University conferred only 21 degrees, of which seventeen were bachelors of divinity; see Bestor, *Chautauqua Pub-*

lications, p. 8. On Hampton Institute teachers, see *Southern Workman and Hampton School Record*, 15 (Dec. 1886), p. 121.

108. Caroline L. Hunt, *The Life of Ellen H. Richards* (Boston, 1912), chaps. 8, 9; Janet Wilson James, "Ellen Henrietta Swallow Richards," in Edward T. James, ed., *Notable American Women: A Biographical Dictionary* (3 vols.; Cambridge, Mass., 1971), vol. 3, pp. 143–46; Margaret W. Rossiter, *Women Scientists in America: Struggles and Strategies to 1940* (Baltimore, Md., 1982), pp. 68–69.

109. W. W. Willoughby, "The History of Summer Schools in the United States," in U.S. Department of the Interior, Bureau of Education, *Report of the Commissioner, 1891–1892* (2 vols.; Washington, D.C., 1892), vol. 2, pp. 899–905; Edwin G. Dexter, *A History of Education in the United States* (New York, 1919), pp. 514–40; Charlotte Haywood, "Cornelia Maria Clapp," in James, ed., *Notable American Women*, vol. 1, pp. 336–38; Rossiter, *Women Scientists in America*, pp. 86–88.

110. Willoughby, "History of Summer Schools," pp. 909–12; Kenneth W. Cameron, *Concord Harvest: Publications of the Concord School of Philosophy and Literature* (Hartford, Conn., 1970).

111. Willoughby, "History of Summer Schools," pp. 915–17.

112. Ibid., pp. 912–14.

113. For more on Davidson, see Chapter 6; on the university summer sessions, see Chapter 8.

114. Willoughby, "History of Summer Schools," pp. 946–50.

115. George E. Vincent, "Summer Schools and University Extension," in Nicholas M. Butler, ed., *Monographs on Education in the United States* (Albany, N.Y., 1904), p. 15; Willoughby, "History of Summer Schools," p. 922.

116. Boyeson, "Chautauqua Movement" (cited in n. 62), p. 151.

117. W. Stuart Towns, "The Florida Chautauqua: A Case Study in American Education," *Southern Speech Communications Journal*, 42 (Spring 1977), pp. 228–48; Benjamin W. Griffith, "Csardas at Salt Springs: Southern Culture in 1888," *Georgia Review*, 26 (Spring 1972), pp. 53–59.

118. Willoughby, "History of Summer Schools," pp. 940–41, 945; Griffith, "Csardas at Salt Springs," p. 57.

119. Quoted in Bestor, *Chautauqua Publications*, pp. 8–9.

120. Quoted in Willoughby, "History of Summer Schools," p. 943. For a survey of courses offered at the independents, see pp. 937–45.

121. Keith Fennimore, *The Heritage of Bay View, 1875–1895* (Grand Rapids, Mich., 1975); Willoughby, "History of Summer Schools," pp. 942, 944, 939. On the number of independents, see Gould, *Chautauqua Movement* (cited in n. 62), p. 10.

122. Willoughby, "History of Summer Schools," p. 941.

123. Towns, "Florida Chautauqua," p. 235; Jean H. Speer, "Cowboy Chautauqua: An Account of Its Origin in Central Texas, 1885–1890," *Southern Speech Communications Journal* 45 (Spring 1980), p. 286.

124. Fennimore, *Heritage of Bay View*, p. 103.

125. Otto W. Snarr, *The Education of Teachers in the Middle States* (Chicago, 1945), pp. 170, 168–69.

126. Frederick J. Logan, *The Growth of Art in American Schools* (New York,

1955), p. 88; Stuart Macdonald, *The History and Philosophy of Art Education* (New York, 1970), pp. 255–57.

127. See Frank Lloyd Wright's recollections of the artistic effect of his kindergarten education in *An Autobiography* (New York, 1977 [orig. ed. 1932]), pp. 34–35.

128. A. D. Mayo, "Southern Women in the Recent Education Movement," in U.S. Department of the Interior, Bureau of Education, *Circulars of Information, No. 1, 1892* (Washington, D.C., 1892), p. 57. Librarianship, which was also undergoing feminization in the late nineteenth century, was another vocation for which a Chautauqua-type preparation was useful. After 1890 examinations for library positions became fairly common in urban areas, and the questions posed on these examinations put a premium on cultural information. For example, to be admitted to the training classes conducted by the Los Angeles Public Library, a candidate had to be able to name three scientists, five painters, and five musical composers, or name the works in which Maggie Tulliver, Shylock, Becky Sharp, Jean Valjean, and Simon Legree appear; see "Library Examinations and Methods of Appointment," *Library Journal*, 26 (June 1901), p. 323.

129. The textbook was L. T. Townshend, *The Art of Speech* (Boston, 1881).

130. J. C. Zachos, *Analytic Elocution* (New York, 1868), pp. ix, xxiv–xxv; J. H. McIlvaine, *Elocution: The Source and Elements of Its Power* (New York, 1872), chap. 2; Barnet Baskerville, *The People's Voice: The Orator in American Society* (Lexington, Ky., 1979), pp. 167–68.

131. Willoughby, "History of Summer Schools," pp. 938, 940; Fennimore, *Heritage of Bay View* (cited in n. 121), pp. 103, 144.

132. See Chapter 8.

133. Charles F. Horner, *Strike the Tents: The Story of the Chautauqua* (Philadelphia, 1954); Gay MacLaren, *Merrily We Roll Along* (Boston, 1938); Lewis Atherton, *Main Street on the Middle Border* (Bloomington, Ind., 1954); Victoria and Robert O. Case, *We Called It Culture* (Freeport, N.Y., 1970); David L. Cohn, *The Good Old Days: A History of American Morals and Manners as Seen Through the Sears Roebuck Catalogs, 1905 to the Present* (New York, 1940).

134. Morrison, *Chautauqua* (cited in n. 62), p. 69; May E. Tomkins, *Ida M. Tarbell* (New York, 1974), pp. 31, 37, 40, 43; see also Cohn, *Good Old Days*, pp. 66, 82, 100.

135. Harold S. Wilson, *McClure's Magazine and the Muckrakers* (Princeton, 1970), p. 66; Tomkins, *Ida M. Tarbell*, pp. 37, 43.

136. Frank L. Mott, "The Magazine Revolution and Popular Ideas in the Nineties," *Proceedings, American Antiquarian Society*, 64 (1954), pp. 195–214; see also George Britt, *Forty Years—Forty Millions: The Career of Frank A. Munsey* (New York, 1935), p. 82. John Brisben Walker competed with the C.L.S.C. not only by launching *Cosmopolitan* as an inexpensive culture magazine but also by starting a correspondence university, which in 1897 enrolled some 20,000 students. See Theodore Peterson, *Magazines in the Twentieth Century* (Urbana, Ill., 1964), p. 14.

137. Herbert Fleming, "The Literary Interests of Chicago, VI and VII," *American Journal of Sociology*, 12 (July 1906), pp. 76–78.

138. Rosalind Rosenberg, *Beyond Separate Spheres: Intellectual Roots of Modern Feminism* (New Haven, Conn., 1982), p. 44.

139. Martin, *The Sound of Our Own Voices* (cited in n. 33), p. 172.

140. Robert S. Lynd and Helen M. Lynd, *Middletown: A Study in Contemporary American Culture* (New York, 1929), p. 291, note 26.

141. Robert L. Utlant, "The Role of the Chautauqua Movement in the Shaping of Progressive Thought at the End of the Nineteenth Century." Ph.D. diss., History, University of Minnesota, 1972.

142. Blair, *Clubwoman as Feminist* (cited in n. 50), pp. 99–101.

143. "The C.L.S.C. Classes," *Chautauquan*, 25 (May 1897), p. 218.

144. "Longfellow's Birthday," *Chautauquan*, 3 (May 1883), p. 459; see also *Chautauquan* 2 (Oct. 1882), p. 44.

145. Wright, "Cedar Falls Parlor Reading Circle" (cited in n. 60), p. 357.

146. Stanley, "Successful Woman's Club" (cited in n. 55), pp. 59–60.

147. Leonard, "Arnold in America" (cited in n. 5), pp. 183–86.

148. Jack Goody, "Against Ritual: Loosely Structured Thoughts on a Loosely Defined Topic," in Sally F. Moore and Barbara G. Meyerhoff, *Secular Ritual* (Amsterdam, 1977), pp. 25–35; see also Moore and Meyerhoff, "Secular Ritual: Forms and Meanings," *Secular Ritual*, pp. 3–24.

149. Herbert Baxter Adams described Chautauqua as a religious revival; perhaps more accurately, Chautauquans accorded culture a kind of religious veneration; see Adams, "Educational Extension" (cited in n. 61), p. 318.

150. Robert Bocock, *Ritual in Industrial Society: A Sociological Analysis of Ritualism in Modern England* (London, 1974), p. 37.

151. Howard M. Jones, *The Age of Energy: Varieties of American Experience, 1865–1915* (New York, 1973), p. 216.

152. Bliss Perry, *A Study of Prose Fiction* (rev. ed.; Cambridge, Mass., 1920), pp. 372–74.

153. Edmund C. Stedman, *Victorian Poets* (New York, 1875).

154. Howard M. Jones, "Introduction," in William C. Brownell, *American Prose Masters* (Cambridge, Mass., 1967), p. x. See also Robert J. Scholnick, *Edmund Clarence Stedman* (Boston, 1977), pp. 38–39.

155. Scholnick, *Stedman*, pp. 41–42.

156. Howard M. Jones, "Arms of the Anglo-Saxons," in Jones, *The Theory of American Literature* (2d ed.; Ithaca, N.Y., 1965), pp. 86–87.

157. Wright, "Cedar Falls Parlor Reading Circle," pp. 357, 343; see also Nathaniel H. Egleston, *Village and Village Life, with Hints for Their Improvement* (New York, 1878), pp. 300–305.

158. H. M. Plunkett, *Josiah Gilbert Holland* (New York, 1894), p. 99; see also Harry H. Peckham, *Josiah Gilbert Holland in Relation to His Times* (Philadelphia, 1940). Like Vincent, Holland counseled his readers on how to behave in public, not just on what to read in private; see Holland, *Every-Day Topics* (cited in n. 20), pp. 260–61, 385–86.

159. William James, "What Makes Life Significant," in John J. McDermott, ed., *The Writings of William James* (New York, 1967), p. 647.

160. Rudyard Kipling, *Abaft the Funnel* (New York, 1909), pp. 164–84; Hamilton W. Mabie, "Concerning Culture," *Outlook*, 48 (Dec. 9, 1893), p. 1073; see

also James L. Ford, "The Fad of Imitation Culture," *Munsey's Magazine*, 24 (Oct. 1900), pp. 153–54.

161. Charles D. Warner, "What Is Your Culture to Me?" *Scribner's Monthly*, 4 (Aug. 1872), pp. 473–78.

Chapter 6

1. I confess to a bias against explanations of cultural change rooted in "social forces" or in such old and recent paradigms as the transition from *Gemeinschaft* to *Gesellschaft*, the rise of the mass society and the concomitant loss of unifying values and personal autonomy, the erosion of "island" communities, or the emergence of "interdependence." As a corollary, I prefer to examine individuals who interpret change to the public on the basis of their experience, "read" public responses (a reading heavily influenced by the cultural heritage of the interpreters), and devise new directions. Thus I assume that social forces (urbanization, industrialization, interdependence) are open to any number of interpretations. The trick is to explain why a particular interpretation and a specific direction seem plausible in one period and not in another, or in one nation and not another.

2. Philip Butcher, *George Washington Cable: The Northampton Years* (New York, 1959), pp. 75–91; Jane Addams, "Successful Efforts to Teach Art to the Masses," *Forum*, 19 (July 1895), pp. 606–17; Herbert B. Adams, "Educational Extension in the United States," U.S. Department of the Interior, Bureau of Education, *Report of the Commissioner of Education, 1899–1900* (2 vols.; Washington, D.C., 1900), vol. 1, p. 342. On Addams's relations with the University of Chicago faculty, see Mary Jo Deegan, *Jane Addams and the Men of the Chicago School, 1892–1918* (New Brunswick, N.J., 1988), p. 107.

3. See her essay "The Subjective Necessity of Social Settlements," in Jane Addams, *Philanthropy and Social Progress* (New York, 1893), pp. 1–26.

4. Jane Addams, *Twenty Years at Hull-House: With Autobiographical Notes* (New York, 1949), p. 430. On the University of Chicago's early extension lecturers, see Harold B. Dunkel and Maureen A. Fay, "Harper's Disappointment: University Extension," *Adult Education*, 29 (Fall 1978), pp. 3–16.

5. Addams, *Twenty Years at Hull-House*, p. 383.

6. Mina Carson, *Settlement Folk: Social Thought and the American Settlement Movement* (Chicago, 1990), pp. 110–19; see Chapter 9.

7. Andrew D. White, *Autobiography of Andrew Dickson White* (2 vols.; New York, 1905), vol. 1, pp. 268–69.

8. Adams, "Educational Extension," pp. 314–15. On Adams's theory of history, see Ray A. Billington, *Frederick Jackson Turner: Historian, Scholar, Teacher* (New York, 1973), pp. 65, 67. On Ely, see Benjamin G. Rader, *The Academic Mind and Reform: The Influence of Richard T. Ely in American Life* (Lexington, Ky., 1966), pp. 64–65.

9. George E. Vincent to Herbert Baxter Adams, Dec. 5, 1888, and May 26, 1891, Adams Papers, Johns Hopkins Univ.

10. W. W. Willoughby, "The History of Summer Schools in the United States," in U.S. Department of the Interior, Bureau of Education, *Report of the Commissioner, 1891–1892* (Washington, D.C., 1892), p. 921.

11. George Woytanowitz, *University Extension: The Early Years in the United States* (n.p., 1974), p. 310. N. A. Jepson, *The Beginnings of English University Adult Education: Policy and Problems: A Critical Study of the Early Cambridge and Oxford University Extension Lecture Movements Between 1873 and 1907, with Special Reference to Yorkshire* (London, 1973), chaps. 2, 3, 12, 19, 21.

12. Herbert B. Adams, "Seminary Libraries and University Extension," *Johns Hopkins University Studies in Historical and Political Science*, ser. 5, no. 11 (Baltimore, Md., 1887), p. 25; see also Adams, "Educational Extension," p. 303.

13. Herbert B. Adams, "University Extension in America," *Forum*, 11 (July 1891), p. 523.

14. Francis N. Thorpe, *William Pepper, M.D., LL.D. (1843–1898)* (Philadelphia, 1904), p. 427. Pepper's interest in university extension coincided with his attempts to attract support for the university's archaeology program. When a group of leading Philadelphians financed an expedition to the Euphrates River, Pepper used his influence to have it named the "expedition of the University of Pennsylvania."

15. Quoted in Woytanowitz, *University Extension*, p. 40.

16. Ibid., pp. 40–41.

17. Ibid., p. 76, pp. 43–45. ASEUT's relations with Chautauqua were far from smooth. George E. Vincent complained that ASEUT was copying Chautauqua without due acknowledgment; see George E. Vincent to Herbert Baxter Adams, Mar. 7, 1891, Adams Papers.

18. President Daniel Coit Gilman's original plan for Hopkins excluded undergraduates, who were more likely than graduate students to be drawn from the local community. Gilman gradually bowed to community pressure to include undergraduates, but throughout the 1880s Hopkins had few undergraduates compared to other universities or to the number of its graduate students; see Hugh Hawkins, *Pioneer: A History of The Johns Hopkins University, 1874–1889* (Ithaca, N.Y., 1960), pp. 22, 238–39, 243.

19. Herbert B. Adams, "Public Educational Work in Baltimore," *Johns Hopkins University Studies in Historical and Political Science*, ser. 17, no. 12 (Baltimore, Md., 1899), pp. 8–36.

20. Adams, "Educational Extension," p. 306.

21. Richard S. Storr, *A History of the University of Chicago: Harper's University. The Beginnings* (Chicago, 1966), pp. 196, 203.

22. Annie M. McLean, "Twenty Years of Sociology by Correspondence," *American Journal of Sociology*, 28 (Jan. 1923), pp. 461–64. Although John H. Vincent included examples of self-improving workers in Chautauqua's promotional literature, these were mainly trophies to display rather than evidence of significant working-class interest in Chautauqua. A study of Pennsylvania's anthracite coal communities disclosed that most members of reading circles were women, usually teachers or the wives of ministers, physicians, and lawyers. In Mohonoy City, not a single person among the 12,000 inhabitants who depended on the mines for a living belonged to any of the city's reading circles; see Peter Roberts, *Anthracite Coal Communities: A Study of the Demography, the Social, Educational and Moral Life of the Anthracite Regions* (New York, 1904), pp. 195–97.

23. Frederick M. Rosenstreter, *The Boundaries of the Campus: A History of*

the University of Wisconsin Extension Division, 1885–1945 (Madison, Wis., 1957), p. 32. Ely's Chautauqua connection is treated in Benjamin G. Rader, "Richard T. Ely: Lay Spokesman for the Social Gospel," *Journal of American History*, 53 (June 1966), pp. 61–74.

24. Billington, *Frederick Jackson Turner*, pp. 97–104.

25. Rosenstreter, *Boundaries of the Campus*, p. 33; see also Edgar B. Wesley, *Owatonna: The Social Development of a Minnesota Community* (Minneapolis, 1938), p. 147.

26. Ely's move to Wisconsin illustrates this point. Long unhappy with his subordination to Adams at Johns Hopkins, he was ready to jump when the University of Wisconsin, prodded by Ely's former student Frederick Jackson Turner, refashioned a chair in Finance and Statistics into a new School of Economics, Political Science, and History. Almost immediately, Ely found that businessmen in Wisconsin were tightfisted when it came to endowing chairs and schools. His extension activities at Wisconsin aimed partly at publicizing his "school" (really a department) as well as at enhancing the university's reputation in the Midwest; see Rader, *Academic Mind and Reform* (cited in n. 8), chap. 5.

27. Edmund J. James, "Introduction," in George F. James, ed., *Handbook of University Extension* (2d rev. ed.; Philadelphia, 1893), p. xix.

28. George E. Vincent, "Summer Schools and University Extension," in Nicholas M. Butler, ed., *Monographs on Education in the United States* (Albany, N.Y., 1904), pp. 858–59; see also Woytanowitz, *University Extension*, pp. 140–41; and Adams, "Educational Extension," pp. 303–311.

29. Adams, "Educational Extension," p. 305.

30. Quoted in Woytanowitz, *University Extension* (cited in n. 11), p. 60.

31. Ibid., p. 82.

32. Ibid., p. 13.

33. Charles McLean Andrews, "Is It Sufficient to Stimulate?" *Book News Monthly*, 9 (May 1891), p. 361.

34. Woytanowitz, *University Extension*, p. 75.

35. Ibid., pp. 58–60.

36. Ibid., p. 60.

37. N. A. Jepson, *The Beginnings of English University Adult Education—Policy and Problems* (London, 1973), p. 127.

38. Woytanowitz, *University Extension*, p. 101.

39. For a bibliography of Adams and his students, see Johns Hopkins University, *Herbert B. Adams; Tributes of Friends, with a Bibliography of the Department of History, Politics and Economics, 1876–1901* (Baltimore, Md., 1902).

40. Edmund K. Alden, "Progressive Methods of Church Work: The Berkeley Temple To-Day," *Christian Union*, 46 (Jan. 9, 1892), 78; "Progressive Methods of Church Work: The Jersey City Tabernacle and People's Palace," *Christian Union* 45 (Nov. 21, 1891), pp. 992–93; "Progressive Methods of Church Work: The Temple, Philadelphia," *Christian Union* 47 (Mar. 18, 1893), p. 508.

41. Herbert B. Adams, "The Church and Popular Education," *Johns Hopkins University Studies in Historical and Political Science*, ser. 18, nos. 8–9 (Baltimore, Md., 1900), pp. 15–83.

42. Ibid., p. 68.

43. Ibid., pp. 21–22.

44. Walter Besant, *All Sorts and Conditions of Men* (New York, 1889 [orig. ed. 1882]), p. 389.

45. Johns Hopkins Univ. Seminary Records, Nov. 13, 1889, manuscript. I am indebted to Dorothy Ross for this reference.

46. Ethel M. Hogg, *Quintin Hogg: A Biography* (London, 1904), pp. 56–57, 81–97, 139–60.

47. Quoted in ibid., p. 89; on Christian Socialism in England, see Edward Norman, *The Victorian Christian Socialists* (Cambridge, Eng., 1987).

48. Raymond Williams, *Culture and Society, 1780–1950* (New York, 1958), pp. 118–19.

49. Adams, "Seminary Libraries and University Extension," p. 468; see also Adams, "University Extension in America," pp. 510–23. In 1891 Adams described university extension as "the Salvation Army of education." See Adams, "'University Extension' and Its Leaders," *American Monthly Review of Reviews*, 3 (July 1891), p. 593.

50. Richard T. Ely, *The Labor Movement in America* (New York, 1886), chap. 5.

51. Ibid., p. 124, note 1, pp. 125–28.

52. Terence V. Powderly, *The Path I Trod*, ed. Henry David and Paul Guthrie (New York, 1940), pp. 198–99; Knights of Labor, *Records of the Proceedings of the Seventh Regular Session of the General Assembly, 1883*, p. 410.

53. Quoted in Gregory S. Kealey and Bryan D. Palmer, *Dreaming of What Might Be: The Knights of Labor in Ontario, 1880–1900* (Cambridge, Eng., 1982), p. 110.

54. Knights of Labor, *Records of the Proceedings of the Sixth Regular Session of the General Assembly, 1882*, p. 293, and *Records of the Proceedings of the Fourth Regular Session of the General Assembly, 1880*, pp. 196, 186.

55. Norman Ware, *The Labor Movement in the United States, 1860–1895: A Study in Democracy* (New York, 1929), pp. 88–89.

56. Kealey and Palmer, *Dreaming of What Might Be*, p. 110.

57. *John Swinton's Paper*, Nov. 1884; Melton McLaurin, *The Knights of Labor in the South* (Westport, Conn., 1978), p. 120.

58. Quoted in Richard T. Ely, *The Labor Movement in America* (rev. ed.; New York, 1886), p. 128; see also Ware, *Labor Movement in the United States*, p. 96.

59. For a trenchant review of the literature on the Knights, see Kealey and Palmer, *Dreaming of What Might Be*, pp. 4–15.

60. Ibid., p. 382; Ware, *Labor Movement in America*, p. 169. McGuire, it needs to be said, was shifting his ground in the 1880s. In 1886 he became one of the founders of the AFL and served as its first secretary; by then his earlier radicalism was cooling.

61. Robert A. Christie, *Empire in Wood: A History of the Carpenter's Union* (Ithaca, N.Y., 1955), pp. 43, 47.

62. George E. McNeill, ed., *The Labor Movement: The Problem of To-Day. Comprising a History of Capital and Labor in its Present Status* (New York, 1888).

63. Ibid., pp. 45–66.

64. On the cooperative principle in the Grange and Farmers' Alliance, see Lawrence Goodwyn, *Democratic Promise: The Populist Movement in America* (New York, 1976), pp. 45–47, 40–43.

65. Oliver H. Kelley, *Origin and Progress of the Order of the Patrons of Husbandry in the United States: A History From 1866 to 1873* (Philadelphia, 1875), p. 22; Roy V. Scott, *The Reluctant Farmer: The Rise of Agricultural Extension to 1914* (Urbana, Ill., 1970), pp. 42, 51–52.

66. Jennie Buell, *The Grange Master and the Grange Lecturer* (New York, 1921), p. 19.

67. C. S. Walker, "The Farmers' Movement," *Annals of the American Academy of Political and Social Science*, 4 (Mar. 1894), pp. 793–94. See also Solon H. Buck, *The Granger Movement* (Cambridge, Mass., 1913), pp. 279, 287, note 4, p. 288; Theodore Reed Mitchell, "Oppositional Education in the Southern Farmers' Alliance: 1890–1910," Ph.D. diss., Education, Stanford Univ., 1983; W. Scott Morgan, *History of the Wheel and Alliance in the Impending Revolution* (New York, 1968 [orig. ed. 1891]), p. 205; for examples of the topics discussed by a local grange, see *History of Bedford, New Hampshire, from 1737* (Concord, N.H., 1903), pp. 561–66.

68. Donald B. Martin, "Woman's Work in the Grange: Mary Ann Mayo of Michigan, 1882–1903," *Agricultural History*, 56 (Apr. 1982), p. 442.

69. Ely, *Labor Movement in America*, p. 129.

70. Jepson, *Beginnings of English University Adult Education* (cited in n. 37), pp. 127, 140.

71. Ely, *Labor Movement in America*, pp. 201, 207.

72. Ibid., p. 200. 73. Ibid.

74. Ibid., p. vii. 75. Ibid., p. 288.

76. Ibid., p. vii. On the fluid relations between socialism and liberalism in the thought of American social scientists in the 1880s, see Dorothy Ross, "Socialism and American Liberalism: Academic Social Thought in the 1880s," *Perspectives in American History*, 11 (1977–78), pp. 5–79.

77. Quoted in Herbert Baxter Adams, "Public Educational Work in Baltimore," *Johns Hopkins Univ. Studies in Historical and Political Science*, ser. 17, no. 12 (Baltimore, Md., 1899), p. 8.

78. Ibid., pp. 8–12.

79. Adams, "Church and Popular Education" (cited in n. 41), p. 68.

80. Adams, "Public Educational Work in Baltimore," p. 12.

81. Quoted in Margaret Hodgen, *Workers' Education in England and the United States* (London, 1925), p. 193. See also William M. Dick, *Labor and Socialism in America: The Gompers Era* (Port Washington, N.Y., 1972), p. 184.

82. Hodgen, *Workers' Education*, pp. 183–84.

83. Goodwyn, *Democratic Promise* (cited in n. 64), pp. 150–53.

84. Oliver E. Wells, "The College Anarchist," *Nation*, 59 (July 12, 1894), p. 27.

85. Ibid. See also Rader, *Academic Mind and Reform* (cited in n. 8), pp. 136–50. The political reaction against Ely is also discussed in Mary Furner, *Advocacy and Objectivity: A Crisis in the Professionalization of American Social Science, 1865–1905* (Lexington, Ky., 1975), pp. 152–53, 157.

86. Furner, *Advocacy and Objectivity*, chap. 8.

87. Edward A. Ross, *Seventy Years of It: An Autobiography* (New York, 1936), p. 65.

88. Ibid., p. 68.

89. Adams, "Church and Popular Education," pp. 68–69.

90. Jepson, *Beginnings of English University Adult Education* (cited in n. 37), pp. 127, 140.

91. A. M. McBriar, *Fabian Socialism and English Politics, 1884–1918* (Cambridge, Eng., 1962), p. 27.

92. George E. Vincent, "Summer Schools and University Extension," in Nicholas M. Butler, ed., *Monographs on Education in the United States* (Albany, N.Y., 1904), pp. 33–34. Vincent cited as one notable exception George H. Palmer, "Doubts About University Extension," *Atlantic Monthly*, 69 (Mar. 1892), pp. 367–74. Palmer identified one of the key differences between Britain and the United States: whereas in Britain there were more trained scholars than university positions, in America the reverse was true. In his view, the abundance of college and university teaching positions in the United States would make it impossible to build a staff of professional extension lecturers. ASEUT's reliance on staff lecturers imported from Britain reinforces Palmer's contention.

93. Louis Levine, *The Women's Garment Workers: A History of the International Ladies' Garment Workers Union* (New York, 1924), pp. 28–29, 31; Morris Hillquit, *Loose Leaves from a Busy Life* (New York, 1934), pp. 1–11, 17, 39; M. E. Ravage, *An American in the Making: The Life Story of an Immigrant* (New York, 1917), p. 147.

94. Abraham Bisno, *Abraham Bisno, Union Pioneer: An Autobiographical Account of Bisno's Early Life and the Beginnings of Unionism in the Women's Garment Industry* (Madison, Wis., 1967), pp. 85–86, 106–7, 115–26; Benjamin Stolberg, *Tailor's Progress: The Story of a Famous Union and the Men Who Made It* (Garden City, N.Y., 1944), p. 284.

95. Thomas Davidson, *The Education of the Wage-Earners* (Boston, 1904), pp. 96–123; for a sketch of Davidson, see William James, *Memories and Studies* (London, 1912), pp. 73–104.

96. Davidson, *The Education of the Wage-Earners*, pp. 101, 102–23. See also "Account of Lectures and Classes Under the Auspices of New York People's Institute," Thomas Davidson Papers, Yale Univ., box 26. Davidson avowed that his lectures aimed to abolish "all class feeling and intellectual hatred"; see p. 25.

97. Leipziger's papers are in the New York Public Library. See especially Henry M. Leipziger, "Address at the 20th Annual Re-Union of the Lecture Corps of the City of New York, April 24, 1909"; "Address by Dr. Henry M. Leipziger on Education of Adults at the Meeting of the American Social Science Association, May 14, 1904"; and "Address of Dr. Henry M. Leipziger on 'School Extension' at the Brooklyn League, May 12, 1903." Leipziger initially envisioned lectures on natural science, but he gradually broadened the program's scope to include such standard Progressive topics as women's wages, the Gary schools, and urban parks. For his original conception, see his manuscript, "Report of the Addresses at the Ninth Annual Reunion and Dinner of the Lecturers, Held at the Hotel Manhattan, . . . May 4, 1899." See also Department of Education, City of New York, *Report of Public Lectures . . . for the Year 1915–1916* (New York, 1916), pp. 10, 94.

98. Lyman Powell, "Ten Years of University Extension," *Atlantic Monthly*, 88 (1901), pp. 396–98.

99. Quoted in William I. Fletcher, *Public Libraries in America* (Boston, 1895), p. 12.

100. David Macleod, *Carnegie Libraries in Wisconsin* (Madison, Wis., 1968), pp. 106–7.

101. Quoted in Sidney Ditzion, *Arsenals of a Democratic Culture: A Social History of the American Public Library Movement in New England and the Middle States from 1850 to 1940* (Chicago, 1947), p. 103.

102. Fletcher, *Public Libraries*, p. 36.

103. Ibid., p. 37.

104. George S. Hillard, comp., *Life, Letters and Journals of George Ticknor* (2 vols.; Boston, 1909), vol. 2, p. 301. Addressing the Massachusetts House of Representatives in 1859, Wendell Phillips voiced a common variation on this theme: public libraries would institutionalize the autodidactic spirit. Citing Nathaniel Bowditch ("You know his family story"), Phillips claimed that libraries would educate "a community of Bowditches." See Phillips, "The Education of the People," in *Speeches, Lectures, and Letters. Second Series* (Boston, 1891), pp. 319–20.

105. David B. Tyack, *George Ticknor and the Boston Brahmins* (Cambridge, Mass., 1967), p. 208.

106. Dee Garrison, *Apostles of Culture: The Public Librarian and American Society, 1876–1920* (New York, 1979), p. 23.

107. Ibid., p. 26.

108. Edward G. Holley, "Scholars, Gentle Ladies, and Entrepreneurs: American Library Leaders, 1876–1976," in Harold Goldstein, ed., *Milestones to the Present: Papers from Library History Seminar V* (Syracuse, N.Y., 1978), p. 85.

109. Paul Finckelman, "Class and Culture in Late Nineteenth Century Chicago: The Founding of the Newberry Library," *American Studies*, 16 (Spring 1975), p. 8.

110. Ibid.

111. Michael Harris, "The Purpose of the American Public Library," *Library Journal*, 98 (Sept. 15, 1973), p. 2511.

112. Quoted in *Life and Journals of George Ticknor*, vol. 2, p. 302.

113. Ibid.

114. Justin Winsor, "Reading in Popular Libraries," U.S. Department of the Interior, Bureau of Education, *Public Libraries in the United States of America. Part 1* (Washington, D.C., 1876), p. 432.

115. Ibid.

116. William F. Poole, "The Organization and Management of Public Libraries," in ibid., p. 479; see also Gwladys Spencer, *The Chicago Public Library: Origins and Backgrounds* (Chicago, 1943), pp. 353–54.

117. Walter M. Whitehill, *Boston Public Library: A Centennial History* (Cambridge, Mass., 1956), p. 431.

118. Winsor, "Reading in Public Libraries," p. 431.

119. Garrison, *Apostles of Culture*, p. 25.

120. William L. Williamson, *William Frederick Poole and the Modern Library*

Movement (New York, 1963), pp. 71, 57; see also Linda A. Eastman, *Portrait of a Librarian: William Howard Brett* (Chicago, 1964), p. 35.

121. Quoted in Michael H. Harris, ed., *The Age of Jewett: Charles Coffin Jewett and American Librarianship, 1841–1868* (Littleton, Colo., 1975), p. 27.

122. Rosemary R. Du Mont, *Reform and Reaction: The Big City Public Library in American Life* (Westport, Conn., 1977), p. 25.

123. Samuel S. Green, *The Public Library Movement in the United States* (Boston, 1913), p. 18.

124. U.S. Department of the Interior, Bureau of Education, *Report of the Commissioner, 1886–1887* (Washington, D.C., 1888), pp. 904–16.

125. Ibid., pp. 941–52, 954–60.

126. Spencer, *Chicago Public Library*, p. 227.

127. Carleton B. Joeckel, *The Government of the American Public Library* (Chicago, 1935), p. 24.

128. Clifton J. Phillips, *Indiana in Transition: The Emergence of an Industrial Commonwealth, 1880–1920* (Indianapolis, Ind., 1968), p. 402; Edgar B. Wesley, *Owatonna: The Social Development of a Minnesota Community* (Minneapolis, 1938), p. 75; "The Peoria Public Library," *Library Journal*, 22 (Mar. 1897), p. 145; Robert W. Lovett, "From Social Library to Public Library: A Century of Library Development in Beverly, Massachusetts," *Essex Institute Historical Collections*, 88 (July 1952), pp. 219–53.

129. D. Hamilton Hurd, comp., *History of Worcester County, Massachusetts* (2 vols.; Boston, 1879), vol. 2, p. 642.

130. Ibid., p. 362.

131. Ibid., p. 156. Library philanthropy affected other regions besides the Northeast; see John C. Colson, "Public Spirit at Work: Philanthropy in Nineteenth-Century Wisconsin," *Wisconsin Magazine of History*, 59 (Spring 1976), p. 198.

132. Sidney A. Bull, *History of the Town of Carlisle, Massachusetts, 1754–1920* (Cambridge, Mass., 1920), p. 110.

133. Albert Annett and Alice E. E. Lehtinen, *History of Jaffrey (Middle Monadnock), New Hampshire* (2 vols.; Jaffrey, N.H., 1937), vol. 1, p. 464.

134. A. F. Bixby and A. Howell, comps., *Historical Sketches of the Ladies' Library Associations of the State of Michigan* (Adrian, Mich., 1876). The ladies' library associations described by Bixby and Howell did not necessarily call themselves women's clubs, but they engaged in some of the same activities, including mutual improvement in culture. See also Anne F. Scott, "Women and Libraries," *Library Journal*, 21 (Spring 1986), pp. 400–405.

135. Phillips, *Indiana in Transition*, p. 403. The multiplicity of arrangements by which libraries were governed defies easy description. As late as 1930 more than one-sixth of all public libraries in cities of 30,000 or more were hybrids, partly supported by municipalities and partly by private societies. See Haynes McMullen, "The Very Slow Decline of the American Social Library," *Library Quarterly*, 55 (Apr. 1985), p. 223.

136. U.S. Department of the Interior, Bureau of Education, *Report of the Commissioner, 1899–1900* (Washington, D.C., 1901), pp. 946–1165.

137. Fletcher, *Public Libraries in America* (cited in n. 99), p. 28.

138. Scott, "Women and Libraries," pp. 400–405. William I. Fletcher observed in 1895 that the "experience of towns and cities has shown that any fee, no matter how small, marks the difference between a meagre constituency for a library and its general use by the public"; see Fletcher, *Public Libraries in America*, p. 11.

139. Colson, "Public Spirit at Work," p. 209.

140. Harry S. Nourse, "The Free Library Movement of Massachusetts," *Library Journal*, 21 (Jan. 1896), pp. 10–13.

141. "Recent Library Legislation," *Library Journal*, 26 (Jan. 1901), p. 337.

142. John C. Larson, "'All This from Books We Could Not Own': The Story of Michigan's Travelling Libraries," *Michigan History*, 61 (Spring 1977), pp. 48, 33–38.

143. Ibid., p. 48.

144. McMullen, "Very Slow Decline," p. 222.

145. Louis R. Wilson, *The Geography of Reading* (Chicago, 1938), p. 72, table 19.

146. See Chapter 11.

147. Macleod, *Carnegie Libraries in Wisconsin* (cited in n. 100), pp. 83, 91–92.

148. A. L. Peck, "What May a Librarian Do to Influence the Reading of the Community?" *Library Journal*, 22 (Feb. 1897), p. 77.

149. John C. Dana, "The Invasion of the Printed Page," *Library Journal*, 26 (Mar. 1901), p. 122. Similarly, Mary W. Plummer declared in 1903 that "the continual increase of libraries in this country and the constant expansion of those already established bid fair to cover the land with a network of these intellectual centers whose influences radiate in every direction"; see Plummer, "The Library of the Future in 'Light and Leading,'" *Library Journal*, 26 (Feb. 1901), p. 63.

150. Arthur Bostwick, "Is Individual Reading Increasing or Decreasing?" *Library Journal*, 27 (Mar. 1902), pp. 124–25.

151. R. R. Bowker, "Libraries and the Century in America: Retrospect and Prospect," *Library Journal*, 26 (Jan. 1901), pp. 5–6.

152. Quoted in Esther J. Carrier, *Fiction in Public Libraries, 1876–1900* (New York, 1965), p. 47.

153. Garrison, *Apostles of Culture* (cited in n. 106), p. 168, note.

154. Frederick B. Perkins, *Best Reading: Hints on the Selection of Books, on the Formation of Libraries, Public and Private, On Courses of Reading, Etc.* (2d ed.; New York, 1877); Evelyn Geller, *Forbidden Books in American Public Libraries, 1876–1939: A Study in Cultural Changes* (Westport, Conn., 1984), chap. 2; Theresa H. West, "Improper Books: Methods Employed to Discover and Exclude Them," *Library Journal*, 20 (Dec. 1895), pp. 32–34; J. N. Larned, "Improper Books," *Library Journal*, 20 (Dec. 1895), p. 35.

155. Dee Garrison, "Immoral Fiction in the Late Victorian Library," *American Quarterly*, 28 (Spring 1976), pp. 70–89; Garrison, *Apostles of Culture*, pp. 74–87; Carrier, *Fiction in Public Libraries*, pp. 267–69.

156. Quoted in Frank Kingdon, *John Cotton Dana: A Life* (Newark, N.J., 1940), pp. 48–49. The attack on fiction was not entirely without effect. It was not uncommon for librarians to exclude works by specific authors or to devise awkwardly paternalistic ploys like allowing patrons to take out two books at a time

provided that one was not a novel; see Carrier, *Fiction in Public Libraries*, p. 269; Garrison, *Apostles of Culture*, p. 91; Geller, *Forbidden Books*, pp. 26–27, 32–35.

157. Quoted in Geller, *Forbidden Books*, p. 43.

158. John Ballinger, "The Public's Aims in Bookbuying," *Library Journal*, 31 (Mar. 1906), p. 122.

159. John C. Dana, "Fiction in Public Libraries," *Library Journal*, 23 (Apr. 1898), p. 155. Whether practiced by editors, publishers, or librarians, book censorship only started to become controversial in the 1910s and did not become intensely so until the 1920s. When the anti-vice crusader Anthony Comstock died in 1915, he was eulogized even by liberal journals like the *New Republic*. See Paul S. Boyer, *Purity in Print: The Vice-Society Movement and Book Censorship in America* (New York, 1968), p. 29.

160. Agnes Hill, "The Public Library and the People," *Library Journal*, 27 (Jan. 1902), pp. 12–13.

161. Lindsay Swift, "Paternalism in Public Libraries," *Library Journal*, 24 (Nov. 1899), pp. 609–18.

162. Quoted in Carl. M. White, *The Origin of the American Library School* (New York, 1961), p. 62.

163. Melvil Dewey, "Advice to Librarians," *Public Libraries*, 2 (1897), p. 267; see also W. Boyd Rayward, "Melvil Dewey and Education for Librarianship," *Journal of Library History*, 3 (Oct. 1968), pp. 297–312.

164. Garrison, *Apostles of Culture*, p. 92.

165. Victor P. Haas, "Looking Homeward: A Memoir of Small-Town Life in Wisconsin," *Wisconsin Magazine of History*, 65 (Spring 1982), p. 189.

166. Melvil Dewey, "Libraries as Related to the Educational Role of the State," in Sarah K. Vann, ed., *Melvil Dewey: His Enduring Presence in Librarianship* (Littleton, Colo., 1978), p. 134.

167. Macleod, *Carnegie Libraries in Wisconsin* (cited in n. 100), p. 82.

168. W. M. Stevenson, "Weeding Out Fiction in the Carnegie Free Library of Allegheny, Pa.," *Library Journal*, 22 (Mar. 1897), pp. 134–35.

169. Bowker, "Libraries and the Century" (cited in n. 151), p. 7.

170. Peck, "What May a Librarian Do?" (cited in n. 148), p. 79.

171. Lindsay Swift, "Proprietary Libraries and Public Libraries," *Library Journal*, 31 (1906), p. 274; see also "Free Libraries and Subscription Libraries: Some Comparisons," *Library Journal*, 26 (Sept. 1901), pp. 687–88.

172. Du Mont, *Reform and Reaction* (cited in n. 122), p. 86.

173. Josephus N. Larned, "The Education of a Reading Public," *Library Journal*, 32 (Apr. 1907), pp. 149–50.

174. Louis R. Wilson, "The Public Library as an Educator," *Library Journal*, 35 (Jan. 1910), p. 9.

175. Quoted in Michael A. Overington, *The Subject Departmentalized Public Library* (London, 1969), p. 22.

176. Sophie Hulsizer, "How To Make a Library Useful in a Small Town," *Library Journal*, 34 (June 1909), pp. 258–59.

177. William S. Learned, *The American Public Library and the Diffusion of Knowledge* (New York, 1924).

178. Katherine F. Gerould, "The Extirpation of Culture," *Atlantic Monthly*,

116 (Oct. 1915), pp. 445–55; "The Decline and Fall of Culture," *North American Review*, 202 (Nov. 1915), pp. 663–64; F. H., "Books and Things," *New Republic* (Oct. 9, 1915), p. 4; "Culture Under Fire," *Nation*, 91 (Sept. 22, 1910), pp. 258–59; "Culture for the Million," *Living Age*, 279 (Dec. 13, 1913), pp. 701–2; William C. Greene, "Culture," *North American Review*, 204 (Oct. 1916), pp. 610–19.

179. Herbert J. Gans, *Popular Culture and High Culture: An Analysis and Evaluation of Taste* (New York, 1974), pp. 81–84, 89; Laurence Veysey, "The Plural Organized Worlds of the Humanities," in Alexandra Oleson and John Voss, eds., *The Organization of Knowledge in Modern America, 1860–1920* (Baltimore, Md., 1979), p. 88.

180. Vida D. Scudder, *Social Ideals in English Letters* (Boston, 1898), pp. 235, 238.

181. Edward B. Tylor, *Primitive Culture: Researches into the Development of Mythology, Philosophy, Religion, Art, and Custom* (2 vols.; New York, 1877), vol. 1, p. 1.

182. On the rise of the anthropological definition of culture see Daniel J. Czitrom, *Media and the American Mind: From Morse to McLuhan* (Chapel Hill, N.C., 1982), p. 31. On John Dewey's efforts to reconcile culture with experience, see Chapter 9. On this score Dewey resembled the literary critic Van Wyck Brooks, who in 1915 complained that America lacked a "genial middle ground" between "transcendent theory" and "catchpenny realities." Unlike the anthropologists, both Dewey and Brooks used "culture" prescriptively even as they assailed residual Arnoldianism (which Brooks preferred to call "Puritanism"). See Van Wyck Brooks, *America's Coming-of-Age* (New York, 1915), p. 7.

183. For a general discussion of the transition from "public" to "society" in Europe, see Jürgen Habermas, *The Structural Transformation of the Public Sphere: An Inquiry into a Category of Bourgeois Society*, trans. Thomas Burger (Cambridge, Mass., 1989).

Chapter 7

1. Jo Ann Boydston, ed., *John Dewey: The Middle Works, 1899–1924* (15 vols.; Carbondale, Ill., 1976–83), vol. 8, p. 314; John Dewey, *Democracy and Education* (New York, 1916), p. 241.

2. Boydston, ed., *Dewey*, vol. 8, p. 315.

3. John Dewey, "Culture and Culture Values," in Paul Monroe, ed., *A Cyclopedia of Education* (5 vols.; New York, 1911–13), vol. 2, p. 239; Robert B. Westbrook, *John Dewey and American Democracy* (Ithaca, N.Y., 1991), pp. 345–46.

4. Boydston, ed., *Dewey*, vol. 8, pp. 315, 314; vol. 6, p. 406.

5. On meager public support for agricultural research in the 1870s and 1880s, see Margaret W. Rossiter, *The Emergence of Agricultural Science: Justus Liebig and the Americans, 1840–1880* (New Haven, Conn., 1975), pp. 170–71.

6. Earle Ross, *Democracy's College: The Land-Grant Movement in the Formative Years* (Ames, Iowa, 1942), p. 87.

7. John K. Bettersworth, *People's College: The Centennial History of Mississippi State* (Jackson, Miss., 1980), pp. 11, 153.

8. Monte A. Calvert, *The Mechanical Engineer in America, 1830–1910: Professional Cultures in Conflict* (Baltimore, Md., 1967), pp. 45–46, 97, 103. Land-grant college graduates were more likely to enter engineering than any other profession; see Mary J. Bowman, "The Land-Grant Colleges and Universities in Human Resource Development," *Journal of Economic History*, 22 (Dec. 1962), p. 531.

9. Alfred D. Chandler, Jr., *The Visible Hand: The Managerial Revolution in American Business* (Cambridge, Mass., 1977), pp. 209–39; Robert R. Locke, *The End of the Practical Man: Higher Education and the Industrialization of Entrepreneurial Performance in Germany, France, and Great Britain—1880–1940* (Greenwich, Conn., 1984), pp. 93–95; Joseph A. Litterer, "Systematic Management: The Search for Order and Integration," *Business History Review*, 35 (Spring 1961), p. 467.

10. Charles R. Mann, *A Study of Engineering Education*, Carnegie Foundation for the Advancement of Teaching, Bulletin no. 11 (New York, 1918), p. 25.

11. Ibid., p. 18.

12. Edmund J. James, "Commercial Education," in Nicholas M. Butler, ed., *Monographs on Education in the United States*, no. 13 (Albany, N.Y., 1904), pp. 38–39, 44–45.

13. Helen L. Horowitz, *Campus Life: Undergraduate Culture from the End of the Eighteenth Century to the Present* (New York, 1989), p. 79; Olivier Zunz, *Making America Corporate: 1870–1920* (Chicago, 1990), pp. 81–87. A study by the National Industrial Conference Board in the early 1920s, which surveyed the graduates of five engineering colleges, found that in the first five years after graduation graduates usually followed one or more of the engineering lines in which they had been trained, but thereafter most moved into different lines. A small fraction switched to engineering lines not studied in college, while most left engineering altogether. Although the survey did not identify subsequent occupations, it noted that mechanical engineers were the least likely to remain in engineering, and it surmised that mechanical engineering's ties to "factory industry" prompted many mechanical engineers to enter management. See National Industrial Conference Board, *Engineering Education and American Industry, Special Report no. 23* (n.p., 1923), pp. 15–16.

14. Quoted from Edmund J. James in Frances Ruml, "The Formative Period of Higher Commercial Education in American Universities," in L. C. Marshall, ed., *The Collegiate School of Business: Its Status at the Close of the First Quarter of the Twentieth Century* (Chicago, 1928), p. 55.

15. Thomas C. Clarke, "The Education of Civil Engineers," *Transactions, American Society of Civil Engineers*, 3 (Nov. 1874), p. 255.

16. Laurence A. Veysey, *The Emergence of the American University* (Chicago, 1965), pp. 70–73; Berenice Fisher, *Industrial Education: American Ideals and Institutions* (Madison, Wis., 1967), pp. 53–55.

17. Arthur O. Jones, "The Continuation School in the United States," U.S. Department of the Interior, Bureau of Education, *Bulletin, 1907, no. 1* (Washington, D.C., 1907), p. 81.

18. Calvin M. Woodward, *The Manual Training School* (Boston, 1887), p. 29.

19. Shan Nelson-Rowe, "Markets, Politics, and Professions," Ph.D. diss., Sociology, State Univ. of New York, Stony Brook, 1988, p. 99.

20. Woodward, *Manual Training School*, p. 267; Morrill's comment is quoted in Isaac M. Kandel, *Federal Aid for Vocational Education*, Carnegie Foundation for the Advancement of Teaching, Bulletin no. 10 (New York, 1917), p. 5.

21. Woodward, *Manual Training School*, p. 267.

22. Woodward's own study of the occupations of the school's graduates disclosed that 153 became bookkeepers; 100, merchants or manufacturers; 75, engineers; 44, salesmen or agents; 41, teachers; and 39, lawyers. See ibid., p. 223. Michael Sedlack's study of the graduates of the Chicago Manual Training School (private communication to author) reveals a similar pattern. Sedlack notes that an institution founded to train machinists and draftsmen was employed by middle-class and upper-working-class families to launch their sons on professional careers.

23. Lewis F. Anderson, *History of Manual and Industrial School Education* (New York, 1926), pp. 186, 85–91; A. Ross Smith, *Development of Manual Training in the United States* (Lancaster, Pa., 1931), pp. 1–47. Jackson Lears has noted that manual training "served as therapeutic socialization for the bourgeoisie." Much like the contemporary Arts and Crafts movement, it promised to provide "affluent children—especially boys—with nourishing roughage amid the sweetmeats served up by polite education." In this respect, manual training addressed late-nineteenth-century fears that middle-class boys had become effeminate, a theme that complemented Woodward's insistence that they or their parents had become too greedy to esteem honest manual work. See Jackson Lears, *No Place of Grace: Antimodernism and the Transformation of American Culture, 1880–1920* (New York, 1981), p. 81.

24. William E. Wickenden, *A Study of Technical Institutes* (Lancaster, Pa., 1931), pp. 1–47; Jones, "Continuation School," p. 96; on trade high schools, see Jones, "Continuation School," pp. 95–96, and U.S. Department of the Interior, Bureau of Education, *Report of the Commissioner of Education, 1887–1888* (Washington, D.C., 1889), pp. 923–24; on the Pratt Institute, see Nelson-Rowe, "Markets, Politics, and Professions," pp. 174–79.

25. Edward C. Mack, *Peter Cooper: Citizen of New York* (New York, 1949), pp. 34–37, 218–73; Rossiter W. Raymond, *Peter Cooper* (Boston, 1901), pp. 72–73.

26. Mack, *Peter Cooper*, pp. 264–67.

27. James D. Watkinson, "Educating the Million: Institutions, Ideology, and the Working Class, 1787–1920," Ph.D. diss. in progress, History, Univ. of Virginia, chap. 3.

28. Mack, *Peter Cooper*, p. 269.

29. Wickenden, *Study of Technical Institutes*, p. 14.

30. Roderick C. Floud, "Technical Education and Economic Performance: Britain, 1850–1914," *Albion*, 14 (Summer 1982), p. 160.

31. "Private Commercial and Business Schools, 1917–1918," U.S. Department of the Interior, Bureau of Education, *Bulletin, 1919, no. 91* (Washington, D.C., 1921), pp. 387–99; see also Janice Weiss, "Education for Clerical Work: the Nine-

teenth-Century Private Commercial School," *Journal of Social History*, 14 (Spring 1981), pp. 407–23.

32. Ibid., p. 397.

33. Frank H. Palmer, "Correspondence Schools," *Education*, 31 (Sept. 1910), pp. 47–52.

34. Stuart Chase, "Job Improvement Inc.," *Fortune*, 7 (June 1933), p. 67.

35. George Creel, "Making Doctors While You Wait," *Harper's Weekly*, 60 (Apr. 3, 1915), pp. 319–21; Norman Gevitz, *The D.O.'s: Osteopathic Medicine in America* (Baltimore, Md., 1982), p. 57.

36. Lee Galloway, "Correspondence School Instruction by Non-Academic Institutions," *Annals of the American Academy of Political and Social Science*, 67 (Sept. 1916), p. 202.

37. *Anniversary Letters, 1897–1907: American School* (n.p., 1937), unpaginated.

38. Quoted in Edwin P. Hoyt, *Horatio's Boys: The Life and Works of Horatio Alger, Jr.* (Radnor, Pa., 1974), p. 91.

39. Correspondence schools started to spread in the 1890s and grew most strikingly between 1900 and 1925. This period was also marked by the high point of state legislation pertaining to the licensing of occupations. Between 1901 and 1925 state legislatures passed 492 such statutes; in contrast, only 24 such statutes were enacted before 1871, and of the 171 enactments between 1871 and 1900, 84 occurred from 1891 to 1900. After 1925 the rate of enactment slumped; only 274 statutes were enacted between 1926 and 1950. The occupations that drew extensive licensing legislation between 1900 and 1925 included nursing (47 laws), accountancy (44), chiropractic (33), osteopathy (29), veterinary medicine (27), embalming (26), and real-estate brokerage (20). See Council of State Governments, *Occupational Licensing in the United States* (Chicago, 1952), p. 23.

40. *Anniversary Letters, 1897–1937: American School*.

41. Ibid.

42. Thomas Foster, "The International Correspondence Schools: Something of Their Origin and the Methods of Their Management," *American Machinist*, 29 (Nov. 1, 1916), p. 583.

43. Ibid., p. 584; see also J. J. Clark, "The Correspondence School—Its Relation to Technical Education," *Science*, n.s. 24 (Sept. 14, 1906), p. 328. For typical ICS advertisements, see *Saturday Evening Post*, May 5, 1906, p. 29; Feb. 23, 1907, p. 31; and Mar. 23, 1907, p. 33.

44. Foster, "International Correspondence Schools," p. 584.

45. Ibid., p. 585.

46. Ibid., p. 586.

47. Chase, "Job Improvement Inc." (cited in n. 34), p. 67.

48. Foster, "International Correspondence Schools," p. 584.

49. Allan Nevins, *Ford: The Times, the Man, the Company* (New York, 1954), pp. 269–70.

50. *Report of the Commissioner of Education, 1887–1888* (cited in n. 24), p. 926.

51. Watkinson, "Educating the Million" (cited in n. 27), chap. 4.

52. *The I.C.S. System of Instruction by Mail* (Scranton, Pa., 1905).

53. It is possible that persistent students possessed significantly different characteristics than the total body of ICS enrollees, but an executive of the company did not think so. The company's practice of shipping all the textbooks of a course to each student upon enrollment virtually invited students to sign up and then not complete the course. The executive believed that those who failed to complete the course continued to study on their own.

54. Watkinson, "Educating the Million," chap. 4.

55. Burton Bledstein has noted that "success [in the late-nineteenth-century] middle class increasingly depended upon providing a service based on a skill"; see Bledstein, *The Culture of Professionalism: The Middle Class and the Development of Higher Education in America* (New York, 1977), p. 34.

56. J. Shirley Eaton, "Education for Efficiency in the Railroad Service," U.S. Department of the Interior, Bureau of Education, *Bulletin, 1919, no. 10* (Washington, D,C., 1909), p. 22.

57. Ibid., p. 89.

58. Quoted in ibid., p. 96.

59. Isaac F. Marcosson, *Wherever Men Trade: The Romance of the Cash Register* (New York, 1948), pp. 30–39, chap. 5; F. C. Henderschott, "Corporation Schools," *Independent*, 84 (Mar. 6, 1913), pp. 519–23.

60. Donald Wilhelm, "The 'Big Business Man' as a Social Worker: A Series of Portraits—Dr. Steinmetz of the General Electric Company," *Outlook*, 108 (Sept.-Oct. 1914), pp. 499, 500. Improved labor relations rather than job training motivated some corporate educational endeavors. An authority on corporation schools noted in 1923 that "many companies conduct classes in dancing, swimming, economics, millinery, home gardening, domestic science, automobile repairing and many other irrelevant subjects, solely for the interest and goodwill which they will engender." See Henry C. Link, *Education and Industry* (New York, 1923), p. 15.

61. Shan Nelson-Rowe, "Corporation Schooling and the Labor Market at General Electric," *History of Education Quarterly*, 31 (Spring 1991), pp. 32–33.

62. Quoted in Wickenden, *Study of Technical Institutes* (cited in n. 24), p. 96.

63. Nelson-Rowe, "Corporation Schooling," p. 31.

64. Eaton, "Education for Efficiency," p. 20.

65. Ibid., p. 21.

66. For the YMCA's initial indifference to evening classes, see International Committee of the YMCA, *The Jubilee of Work for Young Men in North America* (New York, 1891), p. 391. The rise of evening class instruction coincided with the decline of literary societies in local associations. In 1860 there was one literary society for every two local associations; by 1900 the ratio had dropped to one in four (p. 390). The rise of YMCA educational work is described in C. Howard Hopkins, *History of the Y.M.C.A. in North America* (New York, 1951), pp. 196–97. See also William F. Hirsch, "Educational Work of the Young Men's Christian Association," U.S. Department of the Interior, Bureau of Education, *Bulletin, 1924, no. 13* (2 vols.; Washington, D.C., 1924), vol. 1, pp. 706–7. The average age of YMCA students in 1922 was 25; in that year nearly half of all students were enrolled in commercial courses, 17 percent in industrial courses, 14.1 percent in academic subjects, and 6.7 percent in "professional subjects." Gradually, degree-granting colleges grew out of some of these evening schools (p. 695). See also Wil-

liam Orr, "Educational Work of the Young Men's Christian Associations," in U.S. Department of the Interior, Bureau of Education, *Bulletin, 1919, no. 53* (Washington, D.C., 1919), p. 3.

67. Daniel T. Rodgers, *The Work Ethic in Industrial America, 1850–1920* (Chicago, 1978), p. 66.

68. Committee on the Reorganization of Secondary Education, "Cardinal Principles of Secondary Education," U.S. Department of the Interior, Bureau of Education, *Bulletin, 1918, no. 35* (Washington D.C., 1918), p. 31.

69. Forest Ensign, *Compulsory School Attendance and Child Labor Laws* (Ames, Iowa, 1921), p. 61.

70. A. Caswell Ellis, "The Money Value of Education," U.S. Department of the Interior, Bureau of Education, *Bulletin, 1917, no. 22* (Washington, D.C., 1917), pp. 3–52. For recent studies of the value of school persistence in the late nineteenth and early twentieth centuries, see Joel Perlmann, *Ethnic Differences: Schooling and Social Structure Among the Irish, Italians, Jews, and Blacks in an American City, 1880–1935* (Cambridge, Eng., 1988), pp. 38–40; Reed Ueda, *Avenues to Adulthood: The Origins of the High School and Social Mobility in an American Suburb* (Cambridge, Eng., 1987).

71. Harvey Kantor, "Vocationalism in American Education: The Economic and Political Context," in Harvey Kantor and David B. Tyack, *Work, Youth, and Schooling: Historical Perspectives on Vocationalism in American Education* (Stanford, Calif., 1982), p. 43.

72. See the exchange between John Dewey and David Snedden in *New Republic*, 2 (May 8, 1915), pp. 40–42; see also Julius T. House, "Two Kinds of Vocational Education," *American Journal of Sociology*, 27 (Sept. 1929), pp. 222–25; Arthur G. Wirth, *Education in the Technological Society: The Vocational-Liberal Studies Controversy in the Early Twentieth Century* (Scranton, Pa., 1972).

73. Quoted in Paul Douglas, *American Apprenticeship and Industrial Education* (New York, 1921), p. 106.

74. Edward Everett Hale, "Half-Time in Schools," *North American Review*, 139 (Nov. 1884), p. 449.

75. Jones, "Continuation School" (cited in n. 17), pp. 82–127.

76. Douglas, *American Apprenticeship and Industrial Education*, pp. 252–68.

77. On the NSPIE, see Fisher, *Industrial Education* (cited in n. 16), pp. 114–37; on Taylorism see Frederick W. Taylor, *The Principles of Scientific Management* (New York, 1911); Donald Nelson, *Frederick W. Taylor and the Rise of Scientific Management* (Madison, Wis., 1980); Samuel Haber, *Efficiency and Uplift: Scientific Management in the Progressive Era, 1890–1920* (Chicago, 1973).

78. Charles A. Prosser and Charles R. Allen, *Vocational Education in a Democracy* (New York, 1925), pp. 72–73.

79. Ibid., pp. 231–32. Paul Douglas averred in 1921 that "many believe that such changing from job to job is good for a child, and that by trying various trades he acquires experience; that by learning what he cannot do, he finds what he can do, and that the hard school of experience teaches him resourcefulness." See Douglas, *American Apprenticeship and Industrial Education*, p. 106.

80. Prosser and Allen, *Vocational Education*, p. 53.

81. Douglas, *American Apprenticeship and Vocational Education*, pp. 257–

59; Arthur B. Mays, *Principles and Practices of Vocational Education* (New York, 1948), p. 56. Snedden made the case against public continuation schools in his one published foray into prophecy, *American High Schools and Vocational Schools in 1960* (New York, 1931), p. 108. Here he insisted that by 1935 the nation would be ready to abandon this type of school because their students "were nearly all working in juvenile vocations which they must presently leave." The future, he was sure, lay with vocational schools for adults; by 1960 there would be 6,500 of these, he averred, one for each clearly defined occupation (p. 115).

82. Charles R. Allen, *The Instructor, the Man, and the Job: A Handbook for Instructors of Industrial and Vocational Schools* (Philadelphia, 1919), pp. 11–12, 39–42. Prosser had argued in a similar vein in 1915, when he contended that workers could only be taught from the standpoint of "direct and immediate values." The alternative, which he called the standpoint of "deferred value," meant "preparation for future needs and deals with abstractions and repetitions rather than practical application." Prosser concluded that the average worker was unfit to learn by the principle of deferred value. See W. A. O'Leary and Charles A. Prosser, "Short-Unit Courses for Wage-Earners and a Factory School Experiment," U.S. Department of Labor, Bureau of Labor Statistics, *Bulletin no. 159, April 1915* (Washington, D.C., 1915), p. 17.

83. David Snedden, *Vocational Education* (New York, 1920), pp. 21–22, and Snedden, *American High Schools*, pp. 108–14.

84. My conclusion about the effectiveness of wartime job training is based on the voluminous publications of the U.S. Training Service. See, for example, U.S. Department of Labor, United States Training Service, *A Successful Apprentice Toolmakers' School* (Washington, D.C., 1919), and *The Foreman* (Washington, D.C., 1919). Many of the same techniques were used to train defense workers in World War II; see Chapter 12.

85. By the late 1920s only a little over 300,000 students were enrolled in public continuation schools. For data see U.S. Department of the Interior, Bureau of Education, *Biennial Survey of Education, 1928–30* (2 vols.; Washington, D.C., 1932), vol. 2, p. 108.

86. Quoted in Percy E. Davidson and H. Dewey Anderson, *Occupational Mobility in an American Community* (Palo Alto, Calif., 1937), p. 64.

87. Paul H. Douglas, "What Is Happening to the White-Collar Job Market?" *System: The Magazine of Business*, 50 (Dec. 1926), pp. 720–21.

88. Ibid., p. 720; see also Margery W. Davies, *Woman's Place is at the Typewriter: Office Work and Office Workers, 1870–1930* (Philadelphia, 1982), pp. 98–101.

89. Douglas, "What Is Happening?" p. 721; see also Ernest L. Talbert, "Opportunities in School and Industry for Children of the Stockyard," in Meyer Bloomfield, ed., *Readings in Vocational Guidance* (Cambridge, Mass., 1924), pp. 433, 437–39. In her recent study of clerical work in Pittsburgh, Ileen A. DeVault stresses that skilled mechanics perceived clerical work as suitable for their daughters on several grounds: it was relatively clean, required education, and occurred in prestigious corporate headquarters; see DeVault, *Sons and Daughters of Labor: Class and Clerical Work in Turn-of-the-Century Pittsburgh* (Ithaca, N.Y., 1990), pp. 102–3 (see also pp. 9–23 for more on the rise of clerical work).

90. J. O. Malott, "Commercial Education," U.S. Department of the Interior, Bureau of Education, *Bulletin, 1928, no. 25* (Washington, D.C., 1928), pp. 252–53; A. L. Prickett, "Development of High School Commercial Curriculum and University Courses," *Accounting Review*, 3 (Mar. 1928), p. 55; U.S. Department of the Interior, Bureau of Education, *Biennial Survey of Education, 1916–1918* (4 vols.; Washington, D.C., 1919), vol. 4, pp. 389, 416–28; David Tyack and Elisabeth Hansot, *Learning Together: A History of Coeducation in American Public Schools* (New Haven, Conn., 1990), pp. 211–15. Tyack and Hansot note that employers were less willing to give girls than boys on-the-job training on grounds that young women would leave employment and thus make it impossible for employers to recoup their investment in training, and they suggest that this contributed to the tendency of girls to seek vocational, specifically commercial, education in school. See also Susan B. Carter and Mark Prus, "The Labor Market and the American High School Girl, 1890–1928," *Journal of Economic History*, 42 (1982), pp. 163–71. On the compatibility of both the commercial and general curricula of high schools with office work, see Walter Licht, *Getting Work: Philadelphia, 1840–1950* (Cambridge, Mass., 1992), pp. 71–72, 94–96.

91. John S. Noffsinger, *Correspondence Schools, Lyceums, Chautauquas* (New York, 1926), pp. 15–16.

92. Ibid., p. 18.

93. Clark, "Correspondence School" (cited in n. 43), pp. 330–31.

94. Noffsinger, *Correspondence Schools*, p. 54.

95. Chase, "Job Improvement Inc." (cited in n. 34), p. 68. See also Richard B. Kennan, *The Private Correspondence School Enrollee*, Teachers College, Columbia Univ., Contributions to Education, no. 796 (New York, 1940), pp. 25, 29, 55.

96. See Chapter 10.

97. See Chapter 8.

98. *Fourteenth Annual Report of the Federal Board for Vocational Education, 1930* (Washington, D.C., 1930), pp. 11–12, 14.

99. L. R. Alderman, "Public Education of Adults," U.S. Department of the Interior, Bureau of Education, *Bulletin, 1928, no. 25*, printed in *Biennial Survey of Education, 1924–1926* (Washington, D.C., 1928), pp. 294–96; L. R. Alderman, "Public Evening Schools for Adults," U.S. Department of the Interior, Bureau of Education, *Bulletin, 1927, no. 21* (Washington, D.C., 1927), pp. 1–22; C. S. Marsh, *Adult Education in a Community: A Survey of the Facilities Existing in the City of Buffalo, New York* (New York, 1926), pp. 55–57.

100. Galloway, "Correspondence School Instruction" (cited in n. 36), pp. 205–6. The Alexander Hamilton Institute sold textbooks on a wide variety of business subjects, but did not actually offer instruction through the mails.

101. Chase, "Job Improvement Inc.," p. 69.

102. Maris Proffitt, "Private Proprietary and Endowed Schools Giving Trade and Industrial Courses," U.S. Department of the Interior, Office of Education, *Bulletin, 1935, no. 8* (Washington, D.C., 1935), pp. 83–87.

103. Ibid., pp. 1–82.

104. Ibid.

105. Noffsinger, *Correspondence Schools*, pp. 57–58.

Chapter 8

1. William S. Learned et al., *The Professional Preparation of Teachers for American Public Schools: A Study Based upon an Examination of Tax-Supported Normal Schools in the State of Missouri*, Carnegie Foundation for the Advancement of Teaching, Bulletin no. 14 (New York, 1920), p. 123.

2. Francis A. Walker, *The Wages Question: A Treatise on Wages and the Wages Class* (New York, 1968 [orig. ed. 1876]), p. 195; see also David A. Wells, *Recent Economic Change* (New York, 1889), p. 61.

3. Quoted in Edward A. Krug, *The Shaping of the American High School* (New York, 1964), p. 124.

4. On the rise of regional accrediting associations and the establishment of the College Entrance Examination Board, see ibid., chap. 7; for an exposition of the history of Carnegie units, see Ellsworth Tompkins and Walter H. Gaumnitz, "The Carnegie Unit: Its Origin, Status, and Trends," in U.S. Department of Health, Education, and Welfare, *Bulletin, 1954, no. 7* (Washington, D.C., 1954), p. 4; on the notion of credits as a by-product of the elective system, see Dietrich Gerhard, "The Emergence of the Credit System in American Education Considered as a Problem of Social and Intellectual History," *American Association of University Professors, Bulletin*, 41 (Winter 1955), pp. 647–68.

5. Alfred Z. Reed, *Present-Day Law Schools in the United States and Canada*, Carnegie Foundation for the Advancement of Teaching, Bulletin no. 21 (New York, 1928), pp. 120–21. Law schools were not exclusively part-time or full-time, for many "mixed" schools offered both types of instruction. Three mixed schools failed to provide Reed with data on their students, an omission that almost certainly forced him to understate the number of part-time law students in 1926, for Reed averred that "undoubtedly" the great majority of students in the mixed schools enrolled only in the evening. See Reed, *Present-Day Law Schools*, p. 121, note 3. Reed's other study of the legal profession was *Training for the Public Profession of the Law*, Carnegie Foundation for the Advancement of Teaching, Bulletin no. 15 (New York, 1921). Reed displayed a strong bias against part-time law schools, but he did not oppose their existence. Rather, he assumed that the less affluent bar candidates, who could not afford full-time schooling, would use the part-time schools to enter the lower rungs of the profession. See Albert Kales's review of *Training for the Law* in "Book Reviews," *Harvard Law Review*, 35 (Nov. 1921), p. 97.

6. Quoted in Robert Stevens, *Law School: Legal Education in America from the 1850s to the 1980s* (Chapel Hill, N.C., 1983), p. 85, note 15.

7. Ibid., p. 85, note 16.   8. Reed, *Training for the Law*, p. 121.

9. Stevens, *Law School*, p. 83.   10. Quoted in ibid., p. 107, note 40.

11. Quoted in ibid., p. 109, note 67.

12. Reed, *Present-Day Law Schools*, pp. 98–99, note 2.

13. William R. Johnson, *Schooled Lawyers: A Study in the Clash of Professional Cultures* (New York, 1978), pp. 40–41.

14. Reed, *Present-Day Law Schools*, p. 45.

15. Quoted in ibid., p. 122.

16. Of the thirty-five law schools represented at the organizational meeting of the AALS in 1901, 24 were exclusively full-time schools in the sense that they of-

fered instruction throughout the day and no instruction at night. In contrast, by 1927–28, when part-time schools accounted for one-third of all law schools in the United States, 90 percent of the AALS's members were exclusively full-time schools; see ibid., p. 119, note 2.

17. Quoted in Stevens, *Law School*, p. 109, note 67.

18. Quoted in Jerold S. Auerbach, *Unequal Justice: Lawyers and Social Change in Modern America* (New York, 1976), p. 114.

19. Quoted in Joseph S. Tinnelly, *Part-Time Legal Education: A Study of the Problems of Evening Law Schools* (Brooklyn, N.Y., 1957), p. 8.

20. Quoted in ibid., p. 7.

21. Johnson, *Schooled Lawyers*, pp. 126–27. Wisconsin made an exception for "special" students, those aged 23 or over, but if these students chose to take the LL.B., they would then have to pass the university's entrance examination for freshmen. Not surprisingly, few special students were awarded the LL.B.

22. Stevens, *Law School*, pp. 77–78.

23. Gleason Archer, *The Educational Octopus: A Fearless Portrayal of Men and Events in the Old Bay State, 1906–1915* (Boston, 1915), pp. 20, 13.

24. Ibid., p. 123.
25. Ibid., p. 135.
26. Ibid., p. 158.
27. Ibid., pp. 226–28.
28. Ibid., p. 277.
29. Ibid., p. 194.
30. Ibid., p. 267.
31. Stevens, *Law School*, p. 174.

32. Some AALS dissidents contended that if the AALS really wanted to elevate the profession, it should concentrate on raising legal requirements for entry into practice and leave the part-time schools alone. See I. Maurice Wormser, "The Problem of Evening Law Schools," *American Law School Review*, 4, no. 10 (1927), p. 547.

33. Reed, *Present-Day Law Schools*, pp. 125–26.

34. Stevens, *Law School*, pp. 177–78.

35. Ibid., p. 177; p. 184, note 54; and pp. 186–87, note 53.

36. Tinnelly, *Part-Time Legal Education*, pp. 24–25. In 1956–57 these 38 law schools served only 4,487 students, roughly a tenth of the number of law students in the nation.

37. Drew VandeCreek, "Power and Order: The Ideology of Professional Business Training at Wharton and Harvard, 1881–1933." M.A. thesis, History, Univ. of Virginia, 1990, pp. 26–28.

38. Lowell described business as "the oldest of the arts and the newest of the professions" in an address at Harvard's 1926 commencement; quoted in J. Hugh Jackson, "Present Tendencies in Commercial Education," *Accounting Review*, 1 (June 1926), p. 1.

39. Edmund J. James, "Commercial Education," in Nicholas M. Butler, ed., *Monographs on Education in the United States, no. 13* (Albany, N.Y., 1904), p. 40; Frances Ruml, "The Formative Period of Higher Commercial Education in American Universities," in L. C. Marshall, ed., *The Collegiate School of Business: Its Status at the Close of the First Quarter of the Twentieth Century* (Chicago, 1928), p. 57.

40. Michael Sedlack and Harold F. Williamson, *The Evolution of Management Education: A History of the Northwestern University J. L. Kellogg Graduate*

School of Management, 1908–1933 (Urbana, Ill., 1983), p. 22; U.S. Department of the Interior, Bureau of Education, *Biennial Survey of Education, 1916–1918* (4 vols.; Washington, D.C., 1921), vol. 3, p. 808; James H. S. Brossard and J. Frederic Dewhurst, *University Education for Business: A Study of Existing Needs and Practices* (Philadelphia, 1931), p. 258. Brossard and Dewhurst noted that evening commercial instruction was chiefly confined to eight urban universities: New York University, Northwestern, Boston University, Temple, Duquesne, and the universities of Pittsburgh, Cincinnati, and Pennsylvania. Only at the University of Pennsylvania did day enrollments exceed evening enrollments. By the late 1920s, day business enrollments had greatly increased from their level in 1918, but evening enrollments nationally still amounted to nearly 70 percent of day enrollments in business courses.

41. Quoted in Sedlack and Williamson, *Evolution of Management Education,* p. 15.

42. Ibid., p. 28.

43. A. C. Littleton, *Accounting Evolution to 1900* (New York, 1966), chap. 21; Sidney Pollard, *The Genesis of Modern Management: A Study of the Industrial Revolution in Great Britain* (Baltimore, Md., 1965), chap. 6; Jeremiah Lockwood, "Early University Education in Accountancy," *Accounting Review,* 13 (June 1938), p. 135.

44. Charles W. Haskins, *Business Education in Accountancy* (New York, 1904), pp. 59–60; on the close connection between the passage of laws regulating accountancy and the rise of education for accountancy, see C. E. Allen, "The Growth of Accounting Instruction Since 1900," *Accounting Review,* 2 (June 1927), pp. 155–59.

45. Sedlack and Williamson, *Evolution of Management Education,* p. 32.

46. For a discussion of how the development of standardized and commodified knowledge has shaped modern professions, see Magali Sarfatti Larson, *The Rise of Professionalism: A Sociological Analysis* (Berkeley, Calif., 1977), pp. 40–47. The process by which universities absorbed traditionally extramural activities is well illustrated by the evolution of the University of Cincinnati under President Charles W. Dabney (1904–20). Under Dabney, the university acquired an independent business school in 1912, the Cincinnati College of Finance, Commerce, and Accounts, which itself had been established in 1906 as an outgrowth of evening classes for bank clerks. During the same period, the university, under Dean Herman Schneider of the College of Engineering, began its widely influential cooperative system of technological education (students alternated between factory and classroom), welded two independent medical schools into its own medical department, started a teachers' college, and dedicated its graduate school of arts and sciences. Research, represented by the graduate school, and outreach to new student constituencies, represented by the colleges of commerce and teaching, did not conflict in Dabney's mind. See Reginald C. McGrane, *The University of Cincinnati: A Success Story in Higher Education* (New York, 1963), chap. 14.

47. Quoted in J. R. Wildman, "Early Instruction in Accountancy," *Accounting Review,* 1 (Mar. 1926), p. 106.

48. Haskins, *Business Education in Accountancy,* pp. 59–60.

49. Sedlack and Williamson, *Evolution of Management Education,* p. 21. New

York University's business school resorted to awarding academic credit for work experience in order to encourage evening students to obtain degrees, but the practice proved controversial within the university and was dropped in 1926. See Theodore R. Jones, ed., *New York University, 1832–1932* (New York, 1933), p. 369.

50. Brossard and Dewhurst, *University Education for Business*, pp. 258–59.

51. Tyrus Hillway, *The American Two-Year College* (New York, 1970), pp. 50–51; J. O. Malott, "Commercial Education," in U.S. Department of the Interior, Office of Education, *Bulletin, 1930, no. 16* (Washington, D.C., 1930), p. 250.

52. Sedlack and Williamson, *Evolution of Management Education*, p. 47.

53. Jones, ed., *New York University*, p. 369.

54. Marshall, "The American Collegiate School of Business," in Marshall, ed., *Collegiate School of Business* (cited in n. 39), p. 27.

55. Brossard and Dewhurst, *University Education for Business*, p. 283.

56. Quoted in Sedlack and Williamson, *Evolution of Management Education*, p. 47.

57. Roy V. Scott, *The Reluctant Farmer: The Rise of Agricultural Extension to 1914* (Urbana, Ill., 1970), pp. 52–54; Vernon Carstensen, "The Origin and Early Development of the Wisconsin Idea," *Wisconsin Magazine of History*, 39 (Spring 1956), p. 183; Liberty H. Bailey, "Farmers' Institutes: History and Status in the United States and Canada," U.S. Department of Agriculture, Office of Experiment Stations, *Bulletin, no. 79* (Washington, D.C., 1900); E. L. Luther, "Farmers' Institutes in Wisconsin, 1885–1933," *Wisconsin Magazine of History*, 30 (Sept. 1946), pp. 59–68; Roy V. Scott, "Farmers' Institutes in Louisiana, 1897–1906," *Journal of Southern History*, 25 (Feb. 1959), pp. 73–90; Roy V. Scott, "Pioneering in Agricultural Education: Oren C. Gregg and Farmers' Institutes," *Minnesota History*, 37 (Mar. 1960), pp. 19–29.

58. James Gray, *The University of Minnesota, 1851–1951* (Minneapolis, 1951), p. 228.

59. Quoted in Carstensen, "Wisconsin Idea," p. 184.

60. Quoted in Edward A. Fitzpatrick, *McCarthy of Wisconsin* (New York, 1944), p. 287.

61. Charles McCarthy, *The Wisconsin Idea* (New York, 1912), p. 16.

62. Ibid., p. x.

63. E. Wenger to William H. Lighty, Feb. 9, 1897, Lighty Papers, Wisconsin Historical Society.

64. Lighty to A. H. Wiseman, Oct. 18, 1899, Lighty Papers.

65. On Reber, see Michael Bezilla, *Engineering Education at Penn State: A Century in the Land-Grant Tradition* (University Park, Pa., 1981), pp. 53–54.

66. Frederick M. Rosenstreter, *The Boundaries of the Campus: A History of the University of Wisconsin Extension Division* (Madison, Wis., 1957), p. 5.

67. Lighty to Charles A. Tuck, July 21, 1903, Lighty Papers.

68. Rosenstreter, *Boundaries of the Campus*, p. 50; McCarthy, *Wisconsin Idea*, p. 133.

69. McCarthy, *Wisconsin Idea*, pp. 143–52.

70. A. R. Mackinnon to Leonard Blackmer, May 6, 1914, Lighty Papers.

71. Edward M. Hyans to Lighty, July 22, 1908; and Walton James to Lighty, Dec. 4, 1908, Lighty Papers.

72. Rosenstreter, *Boundaries of the Campus*, p. 91. A different pattern emerged at Penn State, where the university subordinated correspondence courses in engineering to off-campus classroom instruction in order to avoid antagonizing ICS. See James A. Moyer, "The Extension Class," *Proceedings, First National University Extension Association, 1915* (n.p., n.d.), p. 117.

73. B. G. Elliott, "The History and Development of Engineering Extension," *Proceedings of the National University Extension Association, 1922* (Boston, 1923), pp. 80–81.

74. Rosenstreter, *Boundaries of the Campus*, pp. 53–54.

75. Vernon A. Stadtman, ed. and comp., *The Centennial Record of the University of California* (Berkeley, Calif., 1967), p. 227. Penn State, one of the leaders in engineering extension, also discovered that much of the demand for extension was for courses of sub-university grade. In 1909 the university's engineering department established an evening course in mechanical drawing at the request of the Williamsport school board, but soon handed the experiment over to the state's Department of Public Instruction on grounds that "the level of instruction was not really at the college level." See Bezilla, *Engineering Extension at Penn State*, p. 67. After World War I, Penn State did develop a correspondence program intended for machinists, pattern makers, power-plant employees, foundrymen, and those in similar lines (p. 92).

76. Levering Tyson, "Columbia's Ten Year Experience in Home Study," *Proceedings of the National University Extension Association, 1930* (Bloomington, Ind., 1930), p. 4; Ella Woodyard, *Culture at a Price: A Study of the Private Correspondence School Offerings* (New York, 1940).

77. Michael Bezilla, *Penn State: An Illustrated History* (University Park, Pa., 1985), pp. 85–90.

78. Quoted in Charles R. Mann, "The American Spirit in Education," U.S. Department of the Interior, Bureau of Education, *Bulletin, 1919, no. 3* (Washington, D.C., 1919), p. 44.

79. Ibid., p. 40.

80. Ibid., pp. 53–54.

81. One explanation for this is that university engineering departments rarely offered extension courses; rather, these were conducted by university extension divisions, which lacked any special commitment to technical education as such and which tended to engage in whatever activities their directors believed would raise the universities' public profile. See W. S. Bittner, "The University Extension Movement," U.S. Department of the Interior, Bureau of Education, *Bulletin, 1919, no. 84* (Washington, D.C., 1919), pp. 56–59, 24–37.

82. Quoted in ibid., p. 39.

83. Ibid., pp. 12, 51.

84. Lighty to Charles H. Tuck, Sept. 17, 1908, Lighty Papers.

85. Alfred Hall-Quest, *The University Afield* (New York, 1926), p. 102.

86. Ibid.

87. Raymond Walters, "On the Summer School Campus," *Scribner's Magazine*, 80 (July 1926), p. 60.

88. U.S. Department of the Interior, Office of Education, "National Survey of the Education of Teachers," *Bulletin, 1933, no. 10* (6 vols.; Washington, D.C., 1935), vol. 3, p. 403.

89. Rosalind Rosenberg, *Beyond Separate Spheres: Intellectual Roots of Modern Feminism* (New Haven, Conn., 1982), pp. 115–16.

90. Ibid., p. 404.

91. John A. Burrell, *A History of Adult Education at Columbia University's Extension and the School of General Studies* (New York, 1964), p. 7.

92. Jessie M. Pangburn, *The Evolution of the American Teachers College* (New York, 1932), p. 14.

93. Katherine M. Cook, "State Laws and Regulations Governing Teachers' Certificates," U.S. Department of the Interior, Office of Education, *Bulletin, 1921, no. 22* (Washington, D.C., 1921), pp. 7–10.

94. Ibid., pp. 32–198.

95. "Sympathy and the Certification of Teachers," *School and Society,* 19 (June 28, 1924), p. 761.

96. Cook, "State Laws and Regulations," p. 199.

97. Ibid., p. 26.

98. "National Survey of the Education of Teachers," vol. 6, p. 3.

99. Ibid., vol. 1, p. 1.

100. Charles McKenny, "Extension Work in Teachers Colleges," *Proceedings, National Education Association,* 64 (1926), p. 295.

101. Lorine Pruette, "Summer Schools," *Nation,* 127 (July 25, 1928), p. 87.

102. E.R.B., "Summer School," *New Republic,* 55 (July 11, 1928), p. 196.

103. Hall-Quest, *University Afield* (cited in n. 85), p. 103.

104. "National Survey of the Education of Teachers," vol. 3, p. 407.

105. Ralph L. Henry, "Summer Schools: An Adverse View," *School and Society,* 26 (Dec. 10, 1927), p. 733.

106. Ibid.

107. "Extending the University," *New Republic,* 9 (Jan. 6, 1917), p. 259.

108. William T. Foster, "The State-Wide Campus," *School and Society,* 1 (Jan. 2, 1915), pp. 14–16.

109. "Dangers in University Extension," *Nation,* 100 (March 18, 1915), p. 297; Frank McVey, "Has University Extension Justified Itself?" *School and Society,* 5 (Feb. 24, 1917), p. 214.

110. James Egbert, "Class Instruction and Extension Teaching," *Educational Review,* 50 (June 1915), pp. 44, 47.

111. Louis Reber, "University Extension in the United States," U.S. Department of the Interior, Bureau of Education, *Bulletin, 1914, no. 19* (Washington, D.C., 1914), pp. 6–26; Frederick F. Stephens, *The History of the University of Missouri* (Columbia, Mo., 1962), p. 415.

112. Arthur Klein, "Class Extension Work in the Universities and Colleges of the United States," U.S. Department of the Interior, Bureau of Education, *Bulletin, 1919, no. 62* (Washington, D.C., 1920), p. 16. For a similar assessment, see L. L. Bernard, "Education by Correspondence," *School and Society,* 12 (July 10, 1920), p. 34.

113. See the memos of one such staffer, Arthur T. Nelson, dated May 28, 29, and 31, 1919, Lighty Papers.

114. A. L. P. Dennis to Lighty, July 3, 1907, Lighty Papers.

115. Gray, *University of Minnesota* (cited in n. 58), pp. 209–17.

116. Burrell, *Adult Education at Columbia* (cited in n. 91), pp. 28–29.

117. Mary B. Orvis, "Extension Publicity," *Proceedings, National University Extension Association, 1921, 1922* (Boston, 1922), pp. 96–97.

Chapter 9

1. Sol Cohen, *Progressives and Urban School Reform: The Public Education Association of New York City, 1895–1954* (New York, 1964); David B. Tyack, *The One Best System: A History of American Urban Education* (Cambridge, Mass., 1974), pp. 193–98. The term "progressive education" did not come into fashion until after 1920, and then with the principal connotation of child-centered schools (which Dewey criticized). I have preferred the more cumbersome "educators of the Progressive era" (and several equally cumbersome variations) to convey my view that reformist educators between 1900 and 1920 had a much broader agenda for education than child-centeredness.

2. Jo Ann Boydston, ed., *John Dewey: The Middle Works, 1899–1924* (15 vols.; Carbondale, Ill., 1976–83), vol. 6, p. 405.

3. Self-professed reformers of the early 1900s so often clashed with each other—advocates of social engineering versus neo-Jeffersonians, Rooseveltians versus Bryanites, corporate liberals versus settlement workers, and so on—that some historians have advised dropping phrases like the "Progressive movement" from the historian's lexicon. For an informed and lively riposte to these urgings, see Daniel T. Rodgers, "In Search of Progressivism," *Reviews in American History*, 10 (Dec. 1982), pp. 113–32. Like Rodgers (but for somewhat different reasons), I am comfortable with terms like "Progressivism" and the "Progressive movement." As I see it, even zealous proponents of social engineering and rule by experts sought to, and in fact had to, enlist public sympathy on their behalf, and this imperative directed them toward campaigns for educating the public that were identical with those launched by those who preferred a more decentralized and community-based approach to reform. For a different approach that stresses the role of education in Progressive-era political reform, see Michael E. McGerr, *The Decline of Popular Politics: The American North, 1865–1928* (New York, 1986), pp. 69–106, 138–83.

4. Lester F. Ward, *The Psychic Factors in Civilization* (Boston, 1907 [orig. ed. 1893]).

5. William Fine, *Progressive Evolutionism and American Sociology, 1890–1920* (Ann Arbor, Mich., 1979), p. 309; Dorothy Ross, *The Origins of American Social Science* (New York, 1991), pp. 88–94.

6. George E. Vincent, *The Social Mind and Evolution* (New York, 1897), p. vi.

7. Ward, *Psychic Factors*, p. 324.

8. Ibid., p. 316.

9. Lester F. Ward, *Applied Sociology: A Treatise on the Conscious Improvement of Society by Society* (Boston, 1906), p. 276.

10. Roscoe C. Hinkle, Jr. and Gisela J. Hinkle, *The Development of Modern Sociology* (New York, 1954), pp. 3, 12.

11. Elmer Barnes, "The Place of Albion Woodbury Small in Modern Sociol-

ogy," *American Journal of Sociology*, 32 (July 1926), p. 19; Charles A. Ellwood, *An Introduction to Social Psychology* (New York, 1917), p. 309.

12. Willard Fisher, " 'Coin' and his Critics," *Quarterly Journal of Economics*, 10 (Jan. 1896), p. 201; see also Alfred Bournemann, *J. Lawrence Laughlin: Chapters in the Career of an Economist* (Washington, D.C., 1940), pp. 41ff.

13. Edward A. Ross, *Social Control: A Survey of the Foundations of Order* (New York, 1901).

14. Ibid., p. 441.

15. Fred H. Mathews, *Quest for an American Sociology: Robert E. Park and the Chicago School* (Montreal, 1977), p. 183.

16. Quoted in Thomas L. Haskell, *The Emergence of Professional Social Science: The American Social Science Association and the Nineteenth-Century Crisis of Authority* (Urbana, Ill., 1977), p. 253 and note 31, p. 253. Haskell effectively contrasts the generation of university sociologists represented by Small with the earlier generation of lay social scientists, typified by Franklin Sanborn, who emphasized individual autonomy and voluntarism rather than "interdependence"; see Haskell, *Emergence of Professional Social Science*, pp. 206–7.

17. Clifford H. Scott, *Lester Frank Ward* (Boston, 1976), p. 63; Alfred S. Clayton, *Emergent Mind and Education* (New York, 1943), p. 165; Mary Jo Deegan, *Jane Addams and the Men of the Chicago School, 1892–1918* (New Brunswick, N.J., 1988), p. 107.

18. Herbert Croly, *The Promise of American Life* (New York, 1909), p. 407. In a similar vein the sociologist Charles A. Ellwood wrote: "education exists to adapt individuals to their social life. It is for the purpose of fitting the individual to take his place in the social group." See Ellwood, *Sociology and Modern Social Problems* (New York, 1913), p. 359.

19. Jane Addams, *Twenty Years at Hull-House, with Autobiographical Notes* (New York, 1949), p. 375.

20. Ibid., pp. 393, 389. See also Jane Addams, *The Spirit of Youth and the City's Streets* (New York, 1909), chap. 4.

21. Mina Carson, *Settlement Folk: Social Thought and the American Settlement Movement* (Chicago, 1990), pp. 110–19. Addams certainly was not indifferent to assimilating immigrants, but she attached more importance to acculturating their children, and she could not find any value in Arnoldian culture (in any form) for the latter.

22. Addams, *Twenty Years at Hull-House*, p. 389.

23. Quoted in Scott, *Lester Frank Ward*, p. 30.

24. Simon Newcomb, "Exact Science in America," *North American Review*, 119 (Oct. 1874), pp. 307, 300–301.

25. C. R. Orcutt, "Popularizing Science," *Science*, n.s. 35 (May 17, 1912), p. 776; for similar developments in social science, see Thomas R. Haskell, *The Emergence of Professional Social Science: The American Social Science Association and the Nineteenth-Century Crisis of Authority* (Urbana, Ill., 1977), chap. 9. After 1915 the *Popular Science Monthly* was transformed into a magazine of popular mechanics; see "The Scientific Monthly and the Popular Science Monthly," *Popular Science Monthly*, 86 (Sept. 1915), pp. 307–9.

26. Quoted in Charles McCarthy, *The Wisconsin Idea* (New York, 1912), p. 24.

27. Charles Van Hise, "The University Extension Function of the Modern University," *Proceedings of the First Annual National University Extension Association Conference, 1915* (Madison, Wis., 1915), p. 8.

28. The "aristocratic influence" phrase was McCarthy's; see his *Wisconsin Idea*, p. 8.

29. Edward L. Thorndike, "Education: A Sociologist's Theory," *Bookman*, 23 (Nov. 1906), p. 293.

30. Quoted in Philip P. Jacobs, "The Year's Trend in the Prevention of Tuberculosis," *Survey*, 28 (June 15, 1912), p. 443.

31. R. G. Moulton, "The Humanities in University Extension," *Proceedings, First NUEA Conference*, pp. 255–60.

32. Alfred C. True, "Popular Education for the Farmer," *Yearbook of the United States Department of Agriculture, 1897* (Washington, D.C., 1898), p. 280; Mildred Thorne, " 'Book Farming' in Iowa, 1840–1870," *Iowa Journal of History*, 49 (Apr. 1951), p. 123.

33. On rural mail delivery, see Wayne E. Fuller, *RFD: The Changing Face of Rural America* (Bloomington, Ind., 1964), pp. 13, 291–93, 299–300.

34. Joseph C. Bailey, *Seaman A. Knapp: Schoolmaster of American Agriculture* (New York, 1945); Rodney Cline, *The Life and Work of Seaman A. Knapp* (Nashville, Tenn., 1936), pp. 206–313; Roy V. Scott, *The Reluctant Farmer: The Rise of Agricultural Extension to 1914* (Urbana, Ill., 1970), pp. 76–92; on Knapp's influence see "Transforming One-Mule Farmers," *World To-Day*, 16 (Apr. 1907), p. 437; "Help for Men to Become Independent Farmers," *World's Work*, 20 (May 1910), pp. 12888–89; O. B. Martin, *The Demonstration Work: Dr. Seaman A. Knapp's Contribution to Civilization* (Boston, 1926), p. 3. In a reference to Knapp's term as a superintendent of a school for the blind, Martin wrote: "He must have thought a great deal about how to teach those who cannot see." Less dramatically but probably more decisively, Knapp was influenced by his experience as a farmer in Iowa, where he tried to induce farmers to raise livestock to offset falling grain prices, and as a professor of agriculture at Iowa State, where he sought to break down the barriers between professors of agriculture and working farmers; see Bailey, *Knapp*, pp. 44–108.

35. Bailey, *Knapp*, pp. 149–60.

36. Robert C. Morris, *Reading, 'Riting, and Reconstruction: The Education of Freedmen in the South, 1861–1870* (Chicago, 1981), pp. 157–58; Jacqueline Jones, *Soldiers of Light and Love: Northern Teachers and Georgia Blacks, 1865–1873* (Chapel Hill, N.C., 1980), p. 119; Joe M. Richardson, "Christian Abolitionism: The American Missionary Association and the Florida Negro," *Journal of Negro History*, 30 (Winter 1971), p. 37. Extensive educational programs for adult freedmen began in the Union army even before the end of the war; see John W. Blassingame, "The Union Army as an Educational Institution for Negroes, 1862–1865," *Journal of Negro History*, 34 (Spring 1965), pp. 152–59.

37. Thomas M. Campbell, *The Moveable School Goes to the Negro Farmer* (New York, 1969 [orig. ed. 1936]), pp. 92–132.

38. Harrison Hale, *University of Arkansas, 1871–1948* (Fayetteville, Ark., 1948), p. 7.

39. Jane S. McKimmon, "Home Demonstration Work—Its Beginnings," in R. K. Bliss, ed., *The Spirit and Philosophy of Extension Work* (Washington, D.C., 1952), pp. 67–68; Bailey, *Knapp*, pp. 235–36.

40. While focusing mainly on agricultural topics, the correspondence courses drew on Chautauqua for inspiration and methodology. For example, in 1892 Penn State established its "Chautauqua Course of Home Reading in Agriculture." For information on this and similar courses, see U.S. Department of Agriculture, "Farmers' Reading Courses," *Farmers' Bulletin no. 109* (Washington, D.C., 1900), pp. 7–13.

41. Scott, *Reluctant Farmer*, chap. 10.

42. R. K. Bliss, "Perry Holden. A Great Teacher," in Bliss, ed., *Spirit and Philosophy of Extension Work*, pp. 45–49. See also Virginia E. and Robert W. McCormick, "Agricultural Trains: An Innovative Educational Partnership Between Universities and Railroads," *Ohio History*, 94 (Winter-Spring 1985), pp. 34–45.

43. When the Cornell University faculty voted in 1911 to establish a department of home economics, it affirmed its general opposition to the appointment of women to professorships, but voiced "no objection to their appointment to the Department of Home Economics in the College of Agriculture." Quoted in Ruby G. Smith, *The People's College: A History of the New York State Extension Service in Cornell University and the State, 1876–1948* (Ithaca, N.Y., 1949), p. 84.

44. Bailey, *Knapp*, pp. 245–80. Smith-Lever's prohibition of appropriations for demonstration trains did little to check their spread, especially during World War I.

45. Everett W. Smith, "Raising a Crop of Men," *Outlook*, 89 (July 18, 1908), p. 603.

46. Seaman A. Knapp, "An Agricultural Revolution," *World's Work*, 1 (1906), p. 7737.

47. U.S. Department of Agriculture, Extension Service, *Report of Extension Work in Agriculture and Home Economics, 1931* (Washington, D.C., 1932), p. 20.

48. Charles J. Galpin, "Rural Progress, 1917–1929," *Rural America*, 5 (Oct. 1927), p. 11.

49. Rosalind Rosenberg, *Beyond Separate Spheres: Intellectual Roots of Modern Feminism* (New Haven, Conn., 1982), pp. 111–12, 240–41.

50. Mary S. Routzahn, *Traveling Publicity Campaigns: Educational Tours of Railroad Trains and Motor Vehicles* (New York, 1920), pp. 20–21; see also Mary S. and Evart G. Routzahn, *Publicity for Social Work* (New York, 1928).

51. Taped interview with Flora Rose, Cornell Univ. Archives, undated but circa 1933. Richard K. Means, *A History of Health Education in the United States* (Philadelphia, 1962), p. 86; see also Lloyd D. Taylor, *The Medical Profession and Social Reform* (New York, 1974), pp. 18–43; Frank E. Hill, *Educating for Health: A Study of Programs for Adults* (New York, 1939), pp. 65–66; Eleanor J. MacDonald, *A History of the Massachusetts Department of Public Health* (Boston, 1936), pp. 20–28.

52. Charles Singer and E. Ashworth Underwood, *A Short History of Medicine* (2d ed.; Oxford, Eng., 1962), pp. 473–74.

53. Quoted in Paul Starr, *The Social Transformation of American Medicine: The Rise of a Sovereign Profession and the Making of a Vast Industry* (New York, 1982), p. 190.

54. Nancy Tomes, "The Private Side of Public Health: Sanitary Science, Domestic Hygiene, and the Germ Theory, 1870–1900," *Bulletin of the History of Medicine*, 64 (Winter 1990), pp. 528–29.

55. Singer and Underwood, *Short History of Medicine*, p. 479.

56. Walter H. Page, "The Hookworm and Civilization," *World's Work*, 24 (Sept. 1912), p. 506.

57. "War on the Hookworm—the Rockefeller Sanitary Commission," *Review of Reviews*, 43 (May 1911), pp. 606–7.

58. William H. Glasson, "Report of the Rockefeller Sanitary Commission," *South Atlantic Quarterly*, 10 (Apr. 1911), p. 181.

59. Page, "Hookworm and Civilization," p. 509.

60. Richard H. Shryock, *National Tuberculosis Association, 1904–1954* (New York, 1957), p. 64.

61. Ibid., pp. 66–67.

62. Ibid., pp. 53, 21–22; Taylor, *Medical Profession and Social Reform*, pp. 18–43. During the early 1900s, high-school textbooks on biology and general science increasingly addressed human health issues; see John C. Burnham, *How Superstition Won and Science Lost: Popularizing Science and Health in the United States* (New Brunswick, N.J., 1988), p. 59.

63. Quoted in Sheila Rothman, *Woman's Proper Place: A History of Changing Ideals and Practices, 1870 to the Present* (New York, 1978), p. 124.

64. Ibid., pp. 124–25.

65. Edward T. Devine, *Misery and Its Causes* (New York, 1909), chaps. 2, 3; Shryock, *National Tuberculosis Association*, p. 76; Roy Lubove, *The Progressives and the Slums: Tenement House Reform in New York City, 1890–1917* (Pittsburgh, 1962), pp. 203–5.

66. Ibid., p. 101.

67. Ibid., p. 101; Wilfred B. Shaw, ed., *The University of Michigan: An Encyclopedic Survey* (4 vols.; Ann Arbor, Mich., 1942), vol. 1, p. 343.

68. J. C. Kesler, "Health—the New Attitude, the New Knowledge, the New Responsibility," in James McCulloch, ed., *The New Chivalry—Health: Southern Sociological Conference, Houston, Texas, May 8–11, 1915* (Nashville, Tenn., 1915), p. 454. A public-health officer insisted in 1915 that the typhoid vaccine "should not appeal to us as a general measure," for the key to prevention lay in "education of the people . . . through literature, lectures, and especially demonstrations"; see R. H. von Ezdorf, "Prevention of Typhoid Fever," in McCulloch, ed., *New Chivalry*, pp. 69, 68.

69. Orville G. Brim, *Education for Child Rearing* (New York, 1959), p. 96, pp. 326–29; see also John E. Anderson, "Child Development: An Historical Perspective," *Child Development*, 27 (June 1956), pp. 181–96.

70. Florence B. Sherborn and Elizabeth Moore, "Maternity and Infant Care in Two Rural Counties in Wisconsin," U.S. Department of Labor, Children's Bureau, *Publications, no. 46* (Washington, D.C., 1919).

71. J. Stanley Lemons, *The Woman Citizen: Social Feminism in the 1920s* (Urbana, Ill., 1973), pp. 153–59.

72. Annie S. Veech, "For Blue Grass and Hill Babies," *Survey*, 52 (Sept. 15, 1924), pp. 625–26.

73. On the Progressives' scientific approach to intemperance see James H. Timberlake, *Prohibition and the Progressive Movement, 1900–1920* (New York, 1920), pp. 39–66; on their approach to the brothel and the saloon, see Paul Boyer, *Urban Masses and Moral Order in America, 1820–1920* (Cambridge, Mass., 1978), pp. 191–204. Although strongly committed to an investigative, fact-based approach to social problems, many Progressives incongruously suffused their data with moral outrage (pp. 205–19).

74. Page, "Hookworm and Civilization," p. 510.

75. J. F. Steiner, "An Appraisal of the Community Movement," *Publications of the American Sociological Society*, 23 (1928), p. 21.

76. Read Bain and Joseph Cohen, "Trends in Applied Sociology," in George A. Lundberg, Read Bain, and Nels Anderson, eds., *Trends in American Sociology* (New York, 1929), p. 362.

77. Joseph Kinmont Hart, *Community Organization* (New York, 1921). For similar ideas see Edward J. Ward, *The Social Center* (New York, 1917).

78. Thomas Bender, *Community and Social Change in America* (New Brunswick, N.J., 1978), pp. 17–19.

79. Hart, *Community Organization*, p. 4.

80. Ibid., p. 62. 81. Ibid., p. 114.

82. Ibid., p. 149. 83. Ibid., p. 161.

84. Ibid., p. 172.

85. William L. Bowers, *The Country Life Movement in America, 1900–1920* (Port Washington, N.Y., 1974), p. 13.

86. Ibid., pp. 22–24.

87. Ibid., p. 31.

88. Charles J. Galpin, *The Social Anatomy of an Agricultural Community* (New York, 1911).

89. C. R. Hoffer, "The Development of Rural Sociology," *American Journal of Sociology*, 32 (July 1926), p. 103.

90. Charles J. Galpin, *My Drift into Rural Sociology: Memoirs of Charles J. Galpin* (Baton Rouge, La., 1938), p. 31.

91. George H. M. Lawrence, "Liberty Hyde Bailey, 1858–1955," *Bailey A*, 3 (Mar. 1955), p. 28.

92. Ibid., pp. 31–32.

93. Seaman A. Knapp, "Address at the Ninth Conference on Education in the South, at Lexington, Kentucky, May 4, 1906," in Martin, *Demonstration Work* (cited in n. 34), p. 248.

94. Kenyon Butterfield, *Chapters in Rural Progress* (Chicago, 1916); Liberty H. Bailey, *The Country Life Movement in the United States* (New York, 1920).

95. Liberty H. Bailey to Theodore Roosevelt, Jan. 23, 1909, Bailey Papers, Cornell Univ. Downplaying the importance of political lobbies and legislative measures, the final report of the Country Life Commission assumed that, for the most part, "matters of economics or morality were not the province of legislation.

In the large, the solutions were to be found in education." See Andrew D. Rodgers, III, *Liberty Hyde Bailey: A Story of American Plant Sciences* (Princeton, N.J., 1949), p. 366.

96. On the intentions of the framers of the Smith-Lever Act, see Edmund deS. Brunner and E. Hsin Pao Yang, *Rural America and the Extension Service: A History and Critique of the Cooperative Agricultural and Home Economics Extension Service* (New York, 1949), p. 15. The authors note that debates leading up to the passage of the act defined rural popular education more broadly than did the act itself. Once in operation, the Extension Service emphasized efficient production more than community building, an outlook undoubtedly influenced by the outbreak of World War I. This preoccupation with production grieved Brunner, a leading rural sociologist. Much like Galpin, Brunner had entered the field from the direction of the rural ministry and the social gospel. William Bowers observes that farmers themselves did not accept the social-gospel diagnosis of their problem as a lack of community; see Bowers, *Country Life Movement* (cited in n. 85), pp. 102–27.

97. Bradford Knapp and Mary E. Creswell, "The Effect of Home Demonstration Work on the Community and the County in the South," in U.S. Department of Agriculture, *Yearbook, 1915* (Washington, D.C., 1917), pp. 261–63; see also Joseph F. Kett, "Women and the Progressive Impulse in Southern Education," in Walter Fraser, Jr., R. Franklin Saunders, Jr., and Jon L. Wakelyn, eds., *The Web of Southern Social Relations: Women, Family, and Education* (Athens, Ga., 1985), pp. 166–80.

98. Warren Foster, "A Working Program for Rural Recreation," in McCulloch, ed., *New Chivalry* (cited in n. 68), p. 325.

99. J. S. Peters and W. F. Stinespring, "An Economic and Social Survey of Rockingham County," *University of Virginia Record: Extension Series*, 9 (Sept. 1924), pp. 127–28; Grace E. Frysinger, "Needed Changes in Home Demonstration Work," *Rural America*, 6 (Jan. 1928), p. 7.

100. Ross, *Social Control* (cited in n. 13), p. 440.

101. John C. Campbell, *The Southern Highlander and His Homeland* (New York, 1921), p. 91.

102. Foster, "Rural Recreation," p. 325.

103. Edgar G. Murphy, "The Southern Education Board," *Proceedings of the Tenth Conference for Education in the South, Pinehurst, North Carolina, April 9, 1907* (Richmond, Va., 1907), p. 40.

104. J. D. Eggleston, Jr., "Consolidation and Transportation in Virginia," *Alumni Bulletin, University of Virginia*, 3d ser., 3 (July 1910), pp. 254–56; Charles J. Galpin, *Rural Life* (New York, 1918), p. 166; Mary Mims, with Georgia W. Moritz, *The Awakening Community* (New York, 1932), p. 119.

105. Llewellan MacGarr, *The Rural Community* (New York, 1922), pp. 230–31; Bowers, *Country Life Movement* (cited in n. 85), p. 114.

106. Edward K. Graham, *Education, Citizenship, and Other Papers* (New York, 1919), p. 25.

107. Michael E. Sadler, "Education of Adults in America," in Paul Monroe, ed., *A Cyclopedia of Education* (5 vols.; New York, 1911–13), vol. 1, p. 48.

108. On the freedmen's varied motives for learning, see Richardson, "Christian

Abolitionism," pp. 35–44; James D. Anderson, "Ex-Slaves and the Rise of Universal Education in the New South, 1860–1880," in Ronald K. Goodenow and Arthur O. White, eds., *Education and the Rise of the New South* (Boston, 1981), p. 11, and John B. Meyers, "The Education of Alabama Freedmen During Presidential Reconstruction," *Journal of Negro Education*, 40 (Spring 1971), pp. 163–71.

109. Cora Wilson Stewart, *Moonlight Schools for the Emancipation of Adult Illiterates* (New York, 1922), pp. 124–44.

110. Ibid., pp. 45–46.

111. Kenneth Macgowan, *Footlights Across America: Towards a National Theater* (New York, 1929), pp. 108–9.

112. Ibid., p. 163.

113. Percy MacKaye, *Community Drama: Its Motive and Method of Neighborliness: An Interpretation* (Boston, 1917), p. viii.

114. See MacKaye's "Prefatory Letter" in Louise Burleigh, *The Community Theatre in Theory and Practice* (Boston, 1917), p. xvi; David Glassberg, "History and the Public: Legacies of the Progressive Era," *Journal of American History*, 73 (Mar. 1987), p. 964.

115. Quoted in Glassberg, "History and the Public," p. 966.

116. MacKaye, "Prefatory Letter," p. xxvii.

117. Burleigh, *Community Theatre*, p. 5.

118. Ibid., pp. 163–64.

119. Macgowan, *Footlights Across America*, pp. 24–30, 54.

120. Ibid., p. 156.

121. Mary P. Beegle and John R. Crawford, *Community Drama and Pageantry* (New Haven, Conn., 1916), pp. 20–21, 26–27.

122. Ibid., pp. 20–21.

123. Glassberg, "History and the Public," p. 966; see also Glassberg, *American Historical Pageantry: The Uses of Tradition in the Early Twentieth Century* (Chapel Hill, N.C., 1990), pp. 159–99.

124. Glassberg, "History and the Public," p. 970.

125. Ibid.; see also Glassberg, *American Historical Pageantry*, pp. 143–45.

126. Burleigh, *Community Theatre*, p. 38.

127. Ibid., p. 50; see also Beegle and Crawford, *Community Drama and Pageantry*, p. 7.

128. Walton S. Bittner, "The University Extension Movement," in U.S. Department of the Interior, Bureau of Education, *Bulletin, 1919, no. 84* (Washington, D.C., 1919), p. 25.

129. Routzahn, *Traveling Publicity Campaigns* (cited in n. 50), p. 22; Bittner, "University Extension Movement," p. 27.

130. Bittner, "University Extension Movement," pp. 27–28.

131. Thomas H. Shelby, "General University Extension," U.S. Department of the Interior, Bureau of Education, *Bulletin, 1926, no. 19* (Washington, D.C., 1926), p. 266.

132. In a critique of university extension written in the 1930s, the philosopher Scott Buchanan crisply drew this distinction; see Scott Buchanan, "Methods and Techniques of Adult Education," *University of Virginia Record, Extension Series*, 20 (Oct. 1935), p. 31.

133. John Dewey, *Experience and Education* (New York, 1938), chap. 2.

134. Robert M. Crunden, *Ministers of Reform: The Progressives' Achievement in American Civilization, 1889–1920* (Urbana, Ill., 1984), pp. 195–96. For a keen discussion of the retarded development of the administrative state in the United States, see Brian Balogh, "Reorganizing the Organizational Synthesis: Federal-Professional Relations in Modern America," *Studies in American Political Development*, 5 (Spring 1991), pp. 119–72.

135. John W. Herring, *Social Planning and Adult Education* (New York, 1933), p. 102. For similar experiments, see Jean C. and Jess Ogden, *These Things We Tried: A Five Year Experiment in Community Development, Initiated and Carried Out by the Extension Division of the University of Virginia* (Charlottesville, Va., 1947); Richard W. Poston, *Small-Town Renaissance: A Story of the Montana Study* (New York, 1950). Comparing British and American adult education, Lyman Bryson observed in 1938 that the Americans applied the term "education" to most kinds of voluntary social betterment; see Bryson, "Adult Education," in W. E. Williams, ed., *Adult Education in Great Britain and the United States of America* (London, 1938), p. 83.

136. See Chapter 12.

137. I recognize that by World War I adult education in Britain consisted of more than the WEA and the tutorial classes. The influential report on adult education issued in 1919 by the Ministry of Reconstruction acknowledged the role of other bodies and called for the introduction of drama and craft courses to moderate the literary emphasis of university adult education. Still, the tenor of the report underscores the differences between developments in Britain and contemporaneous developments in the United States. See Great Britain, Ministry of Reconstruction, *A Design for Democracy: An Abridgement of the Report of the Adult Education Committee of the British Ministry of Reconstruction* (New York, 1956), pp. 148–202, 78–90.

138. John A. Blyth, *English University Adult Education, 1908–1958: The Unique Tradition* (Manchester, Eng., 1983), pp. 7–9, 54–55, 107, 112–13, 128, 200; see also Allen Parker and S. G. Raygould, *University Studies for Adults* (London, 1972).

Chapter 10

1. Jesse L. Bennett, *On "Culture" and "A Liberal Education," with Lists of Books Which Can Aid in Acquiring Them* (Baltimore, Md., 1924); see also Joan Shelley Rubin, "Self, Culture, and Self-Culture in Modern America: The Early History of the Book-of-the-Month Club," *Journal of American History*, 71 (Mar. 1985), pp. 787–88; Rubin, *The Making of Middlebrow Culture* (Chapel Hill, N.C., 1992), chap. 3; and Edwin E. Slosson, *Keeping Up with Science: Notes on Recent Progress in the Various Sciences for Unscientific Readers* (New York, 1931).

2. Dedicated to maintaining literary standards that promised to advance society as a whole, the so-called New Humanist critics—Irving Babbitt, Paul Elmer More, and (for a period) Stuart Pratt Sherman—often invoked Matthew Arnold, but they did so in ways that underscored their distance from Gilded Age custodi-

ans of culture. Whereas the latter rarely had argued their case, the New Humanists were forced to engage in polemics against naturalism and modernism at every turn. In addition, although the Gilded Age custodians had energetically promoted popular institutions like libraries and Chautauqua, the New Humanists showed little interest in reproducing their authority outside of the academy. On the New Humanists, see J. David Hoeveler, *The New Humanists: A Critique of Modern America, 1900–1940* (Charlottesville, Va., 1977); see also Rubin, *Making of Middlebrow Culture*, pp. 52–53.

3. Laurence R. Veysey, *The Emergence of the American University* (Chicago, 1965), pp. 252–59; Charles F. Thwing, "The College as a Preparation for Practical Affairs," in William H. Crawford, *The American College* (New York, 1915), pp. 95–107; see also Thwing, *The American College in American Life* (New York, 1897); Bruce Kimball, *Orators and Philosophers: A History of the Idea of Liberal Education* (New York, 1986), pp. 176–77; Warren Susman, "'Personality' and the Making of Twentieth-Century Culture," in John Higham and Paul K. Conkin, eds., *New Directions in American Intellectual History* (Baltimore, Md., 1979), pp. 217–20.

4. Robert S. and Helen M. Lynd, *Middletown: A Study in American Culture* (New York, 1929), p. 299, pp. 287–98.

5. Bruce Barton, "You Can't Fool Your Other Self," *American Magazine*, 92 (Sept. 1921), p. 129.

6. The idea that popularization degraded American education was emphatically voiced by Abraham Flexner, who pilloried Columbia University's Home-Study Department for advertising courses of "university grade" on direct-mail selling; see Flexner, *Universities: American, English, German* (New York, 1930), pp. 133, 135–42.

7. Public schools, which had drawn immigrants to evening English classes before the war, responded to the slackening of immigration after 1914 and to the Immigration Restriction Act of 1924 by expanding their facilities for vocational instruction. See C. S. Marsh, *Adult Education in a Community: A Survey of the Facilities Existing in the City of Buffalo, New York* (New York, 1926), pp. 55–57.

8. Morse A. Cartwright, *Ten Years of Adult Education: A Report of a Decade of Progress in the American Movement* (New York, 1935), chap. 9.

9. Amy D. Rose, "Towards the Organization of Knowledge: Professional Adult Education in the 1920s." Ed.D. diss., Teachers College, Columbia Univ., 1979, pp. 107–9.

10. Abraham Flexner, *Henry S. Pritchett: A Biography* (New York, 1943), pp. 74–76, 108–9; see also Ellen Condliffe Lagemann, *Private Power for the Public Good: A History of the Carnegie Foundation for the Advancement of Teaching* (Middletown, Conn., 1983).

11. Flexner, *Pritchett*, p. 152.

12. William S. Learned, *The American Public Library and the Diffusion of Knowledge* (New York, 1924).

13. Frederick P. Keppel, *Education for Adults and Other Essays* (New York, 1927), pp. 12–14.

14. Carnegie Corporation of New York, *Digest of Proceedings of National Conference on Adult Education, Cleveland, Ohio, Oct. 16–17, 1925* (New York,

1925), pp. 7–8; *Digest of Proceedings of Regional Conference on Adult Education, New York, N.Y., Held on December 15, 1925* (New York, 1925), pp. 7–10; and *Digest of National Conference on Adult Education and First Meeting of American Association for Adult Education, Chicago, Ill.* (New York, 1926), pp. 5–14.

15. Keppel, *Education for Adults*, p. 22. This aversion to equating adult with vocational education, widespread among liberal intellectuals after World War I, drew inspiration from an influential report on adult education in Britain issued in 1919 by the Ministry of Reconstruction. Original copies of this report, which envisioned adult education as a major reform movement, are rare, but it is accessible in an abridgment; see Great Britain, Ministry of Reconstruction, *A Design for Democracy: An Abridgement of the Report of the Adult Education Committee of the British Ministry of Reconstruction* (New York, 1956); for a contemporary American response to the report, see "Adult Education," *New Republic*, 19 (Mar. 29, 1919), p. 282.

16. Keppel, *Education for Adults*, pp. 16–17.

17. Paul M. Rutkoff and William B. Scott, *New School: A History of the New School for Social Research* (New York, 1986), p. 10.

18. Morton G. White, *Social Thought in America: The Revolt Against Formalism* (New York, 1949).

19. James H. Robinson, *The New History: Essays Illustrating the Modern Historical Outlook* (New York, 1912), pp. 5, 65, 99.

20. James H. Robinson, *The Mind in the Making: The Relation of Intelligence to Social Reform* (New York, 1921), p. 13.

21. Ibid., p. 93.

22. James H. Robinson, *The Humanizing of Knowledge* (New York, 1923), p. 74. Italics in original.

23. Ibid., pp. 88–89.

24. Horace Kallen, *Education, the Machine and the Worker: An Essay in the Psychology of Education in Industrial Society* (New York, 1925), pp. 13–15.

25. Robinson, *Humanizing of Knowledge*, p. 23.

26. Charles A. Beard, "The Electric Fire of Thought," *Journal of Adult Education*, 2 (Jan. 1930), pp. 5–7.

27. Rutkoff and Scott, *New School*, p. 23.

28. Walter Lippmann, *Drift and Mastery* (New York, 1914), pp. 165, 169.

29. Rutkoff and Scott, *New School*, p. 29.

30. Alvin Johnson, *Pioneer's Progress: An Autobiography* (New York, 1952), p. 274.

31. Ibid.

32. Ibid., p. 81.

33. Nathaniel Peffer, *New Schools for Older Students* (New York, 1926), p. 48.

34. See, e.g., *New School Bulletin*, 17 (Mar. 24–28, [1930]).

35. Mortimer J. Adler, *Dialectic* (New York, 1927), p. 108.

36. Mortimer J. Adler, *Philosopher at Large; An Intellectual Biography* (New York, 1917), p. 115; Harris Wofford, Jr., *Embers of the World: Conversations with Scott Buchanan* (Santa Barbara, Calif., n.d.), pp. 41–42. There were significant differences between Robinson's conception of humanizing knowledge and

Adler's later Great Books project, most notably the fact that the latter targeted academic positivism rather than popular bigotry. But there were several connecting links. For example, a number of staffers of the People's Institute were also members of Columbia University's general honors faculty, which since 1919 had been engaged in conducting a two-year course on classics of the western tradition; see Philip N. Youtz, "Experimental Classes in Adult Education," *School and Society*, 28 (July 28, 1928), p. 93.

37. Gisela Konopka, *Eduard C. Lindeman and Social Work Philosophy* (Minneapolis, Minn., 1958), p. 27.

38. Eduard C. Lindeman, *The Community* (New York, 1921).

39. Konopka, *Eduard C. Lindeman*, pp. 32–40.

40. Eduard C. Lindeman, "Rural Community," *Survey*, 52 (May 15, 1924), p. 240.

41. Eduard C. Lindeman, "The Future of Agriculture and Rural Life," *Rural America*, 5 (Oct. 1927), pp. 22, 24.

42. Ibid., p. 24.

43. E. L. Bernays, *Public Relations* (Norman, Okla., 1952), p. 66; Bernays, *Biography of an Idea: Memoirs of a Public Relations Counsel* (New York, 1965), p. 59.

44. Walter Lippmann, *Public Opinion* (New York, 1922), pp. 79–80.

45. E. L. Bernays, *Crystallizing Public Opinion* (New York, 1923).

46. Lippmann, *Public Opinion*, p. 31.

47. Ibid., p. 378.

48. Ibid., p. 377.

49. Lindeman, "Future of Agriculture and Rural Life," p. 23.

50. Edward D. Martin, *The Meaning of Liberal Education* (New York, 1926), pp. viii, 313, 349; Eduard C. Lindeman, *The Meaning of Adult Education* (New York, 1926), p. 37; see also Lindeman, "After Lyceums and Chautauqua, What?" *Bookman*, 65 (May 1927), pp. 246–50.

51. James S. Smith, "The Day of the Popularizers: The 1920s," *South Atlantic Quarterly*, 62 (Spring 1963), p. 297.

52. Hugh Hawkins, *Between Harvard and America: The Educational Leadership of Charles William Eliot* (New York, 1972), pp. 291–96; Henry James, *Charles W. Eliot: President of Harvard University, 1869–1909* (2 vols.; New York, 1930), vol. 2, pp. 193–201.

53. William S. Gray and Ruth Munroe, *The Reading Interests of Adults* (New York, 1929), p. 147.

54. Ibid., p. 161.

55. Paul De Kruif, *Microbe Hunters* (New York, 1926), p. 207; I. F. Clarke, *The Pattern of Expectations, 1644–2001* (New York, 1979), pp. 243–44; Nancy Knight, " 'The New Light': X Rays and Medical Futurism," in Joseph J. Corn, ed., *Imagining Tomorrow: History, Technology, and the American Future* (Cambridge, Mass., 1986), pp. 11–13.

56. H. G. Wells, *The New and Revised Outline of History* (Garden City, N.Y., 1931), p. 2.

57. Will Durant, *Philosophy and the Social Problem* (New York, 1927), pp. 234–40.

58. Ibid., p. xi.

59. Will and Ariel Durant, *A Dual Autobiography* (New York, 1977), pp. 58–59.

60. Abraham Bisno, *Abraham Bisno, Union Pioneer: An Autobiographical Account of Bisno's Early Life and the Beginnings of Unionism in the Women's Garment Industry* (Madison, Wis., 1967), p. 120.

61. Durant and Durant, *Dual Autobiography*, p. 92.

62. Emanuel Haldeman-Julius, *The First Hundred Million* (New York, 1928). See also Dale Herder, "Haldeman-Julius," *Journal of Popular Culture*, 4 (Spring 1971), pp. 881–91.

63. This is Durant's version of their original encounter, but Rubin suggests that Durant may have pushed himself to Haldeman-Julius's attention; see Rubin, *Making of Middlebrow Culture* (cited in n. 1), pp. 232–33.

64. Will Durant, *The Story of Philosophy: The Lives and Opinions of the Greater Philosophers* (New York, 1926), p. 186.

65. Ibid., p. xiii.

66. Ibid., p. 205.

67. Clement C. J. Webb, *A History of Philosophy* (New York, 1915).

68. Durant, *Story of Philosophy*, p. 2.

69. Ibid., p. xiii; Rubin, *Making of Middlebrow Culture*, pp. 237–40.

70. Durant and Durant, *Dual Autobiography*, pp. 113–14.

71. Will Durant, *Transition: A Sentimental Story of One Mind and One Era* (New York, 1927), pp. 322–42.

72. Durant and Durant, *Dual Autobiography*, p. 119.

73. Lindeman, *Meaning of Adult Education*, pp. 7, 52, 59.

74. Rutkoff and Scott, *New School* (cited in n. 17), p. 37.

75. Sinclair Lewis, *Main Street* (New York, 1921 [orig. ed. 1920]), pp. 144, 126–27; Harvey N. Davis, "Leisure to Think," *Journal of Adult Education*, 6 (Jan. 1934), p. 5.

76. Robert M. Lovett, "Education," in Harold E. Stearns, ed., *Civilization in the United States: An Inquiry of Thirty Americans* (New York, 1922), p. 83; see also Carl D. Thompson, "Is the Chautauqua a Free Platform?" *New Republic*, 41 (Dec. 17, 1924), pp. 86–88; Mary Austin, "The Town That Doesn't Want a Chautauqua," *New Republic*, 47 (July 7, 1926), pp. 195–97; Bruce Bliven, "Mother, Home and Heaven," *New Republic*, 37 (Jan. 9, 1924), pp. 172–75.

77. Robert Molloy, "The Problem of the Amateur," *Journal of Adult Education*, 2 (Oct. 1930), p. 424.

78. In *Middletown* the Lynds noted that even as the city's middle-class women approached club life with "instrumental" goals, their club meetings continued to be permeated by the language of moral idealism. Thus a paper on the problems of the church in Middletown sounded like an address by Chautauqua's John H. Vincent: "No man with a soul in him can look at the stars and not see God." See Lynd and Lynd, *Middletown*, p. 292.

79. Lindeman, *Meaning of Adult Education*, p. 39.

80. Harlan B. Phillips, "Charles Beard, Walter Vrooman, and the Founding of Ruskin Hall," *South Atlantic Quarterly*, 50 (1951), pp. 186–91; Richard Hofstadter, *The Progressive Historians: Turner, Beard, Parrington* (New York, 1968), pp. 176–79.

81. Ibid., pp. 172, 174–75.

82. On this school, see Robin Miller Jacoby, "The Women's Trade Union League Training School for Women Organizers, 1914–1926," in Joyce L. Kornbluh and Mary Frederickson, eds., *Sisterhood and Solidarity: Workers' Education for Women, 1914–1984* (Philadelphia, 1984), pp. 5–35.

83. Quoted in James Weinstein, *The Decline of Socialism in America* (New York, 1967), p. 11.

84. Louis Levine, *The Women's Garment Workers: A History of the International Ladies' Garment Workers Union* (New York, 1924), p. 284.

85. Benjamin Stolberg, *Tailor's Progress: The Story of a Famous Union and the Men Who Made It* (Garden City, N.Y., 1944), p. 284.

86. Levine, *Women's Garment Workers*, p. 483.

87. Ibid., pp. 235, 485.

88. Quoted in ibid., p. 486.

89. Ibid., pp. 489–92; see also Susan Stone Wong, "From Soul to Strawberries: The International Ladies' Garment Workers' Union and Workers' Education, 1914–1950," in Kornbluh and Frederickson, eds., *Sisterhood and Solidarity*, pp. 42–44.

90. Quoted in Stolberg, *Tailor's Progress*, p. 288.

91. Hilda W. Smith, *Women Workers in the Bryn Mawr Summer School* (New York, 1929); Florence H. Schneider, *Patterns of Workers' Education: The Story of the Bryn Mawr Summer School* (Washington, D.C., 1941); Ernest E. Schwarztrauber, *Workers' Education: A Wisconsin Experiment* (Madison, Wis., 1942); Caroline F. Ware, *Labor Education in Universities: A Study of University Programs* (New York, 1946); Margaret Hodgen, *Workers' Education in England and the United States* (London, 1925), chap. 11; Robert Shafer, "Working People's Education," *North American Review*, 214 (Dec. 1921), p. 788; Anne Withington, "Boston's Central Labor Body's Successful Trade Union College," *Life and Labor*, 9 (Sept. 1919), p. 239.

92. Quoted in Smith, *Women Workers in the Bryn Mawr Summer School*, p. 4. Prejudiced against Jews, immigrants, and blacks and scarcely an egalitarian in either politics or education, Thomas nevertheless approached women's rights with strains of radicalism and militant separatism. When she spoke of women denied access to intellect and spirit, she reflected her own experiences, including the fact that she had been denied entrance to classes at all-male Johns Hopkins University in the late 1870s, even though her father was a trustee of the university. See the sketch of Thomas by Laurence R. Veysey in Edward James, ed., *Notable American Women* (3 vols.; Cambridge, Mass., 1971), vol. 3, pp. 446–50. In addition, Thomas, whose interest in social issues had grown stronger in the 1910s, was familiar with the WEA through contacts with her cousin Alys, the wife of Bertrand Russell, and from her own observations during a 1919–20 world tour; see Rita Heller, "Blue Collars and Bluestockings: The Bryn Mawr Summer School for Women Workers, 1921–1938," in Kornbluh and Frederickson, eds., *Sisterhood and Solidarity*, pp. 111–13.

93. Kallen, *Education, the Machine and the Worker* (cited in n. 24), p. ix.

94. Ware, *Labor Education in Universities*, p. 27.

95. The Industrial Department of the YWCA provided an important link between trade unions and the movement for summer schools for working women;

over half of the 82 students at the first session of the Bryn Mawr school were recruited through it. See Mary Frederickson, "Citizens for Democracy: The Industrial Programs of the YWCA," in Kornbluh and Frederickson, eds., *Sisterhood and Solidarity*, p. 91.

96. For events leading up to this split, see Heller, "Blue Collars and Bluestockings," p. 122. The Bryn Mawr school had a strong impact on labor women, some of whom became active in the industrial unionism movement in the 1930s; see ibid., pp. 123–25 and Susan Ware, *Holding Their Own: American Women in the 1930s* (Boston, 1982), p. 43; see also Rose Schneiderman with Lucy Goldthwaite, *All for One* (New York, 1967), pp. 140–45.

97. Schwarztrauber, *Workers' Education*, pp. 38, 28–30.

98. James H. Maurer, "Labor's Demand for Its Own Schools," *Nation* (Sept. 20, 1922), p. 277.

99. Upton Sinclair, *The Goslings* (New York, 1924), p. 26.

100. Philip Taft, *The A.F. of L. in the Time of Gompers* (New York, 1957), pp. 362–67. Gompers also faced growing opposition within the AFL on the issue of political action. Continued support by AFL socialists for candidates of the Socialist Party of America and the increasing militancy of the railroad unions put pressure on Gompers's opposition to labor support for independent or third-party candidates. In 1922 the railroad unions took the lead in organizing the Conference for Progressive Political Action, which in 1924 supported the presidential candidacy of Wisconsin's Robert M. LaFollette. Never far in the background was the Russian Revolution, which sparked the secession of left-wingers from the Socialist party in 1919 and led to the formation of the Communist party in 1921. By 1922 the AFL faced the possibility of communist infiltration.

101. Hodgen, *Workers' Education*, p. 245.

102. American Federation of Labor, *Workers' Education in the United States: Report of Proceedings, First National Conference on Workers' Education, 1921* (New York, 1921), pp. 7–8.

103. Quoted from Adolph Germer (national secretary of the Socialist party) in Weinstein, *Decline of Socialism in America* (cited in n. 83), p. 215.

104. Ibid., p. 331.

105. J. B. Salutsky, "Class Consciousness as a Factor in Labor Education" (p. 66), and John Brophy, "Miners' Problems in Workers' Education" (p. 124), in American Federation of Labor, *Proceedings, First National Conference on Workers' Education*; "Norman Thomas on Workers' Education," *New Republic*, 34 (May 9, 1923), p. 287; Schwarztrauber, *Workers' Education*, p. 43. Brophy, an ardent reader in his youth, was strongly committed to workers' education, but he observed that most old-line labor leaders saw it as a frill; see John O. P. Hall, ed., *A Miner's Life: John Brophy* (Madison, Wis., 1964), pp. 211, 30–31, 81.

106. Paul Blanshard, "The Rochester Labor College," in American Federation of Labor, *Proceedings, First National Conference on Workers' Education*, pp. 17–18.

107. On the changing profile of students, see Heller, "Blue Collars and Bluestockings," pp. 116–17.

108. Smith, *Women Workers at the Bryn Mawr Summer School*, p. 132, 71–78.

109. Quoted in ibid., p. 95. For a more detailed account of the curriculum of

the Bryn Mawr school see Heller, "Blue Collars and Bluestockings" (cited in n. 92), pp. 118–19.

110. E. E. Cummins, *The Labor Problem in the United States* (New York, 1932), p. 396. Neighborhood adult centers in Jewish working-class areas had similar curricula; see Gustav F. Beck, "Labor Temple Students," in Mary L. Ely, ed., *Adult Education in Action* (New York, 1936), p. 346.

111. Jo Ann Ooiman Robinson, *Abraham Went Out: A Biography of A. J. Muste* (Philadelphia, 1981), chap. 1.

112. Ibid., p. 37.

113. Cummins, *Labor Problem*, pp. 400–401.

114. Robinson, *Abraham Went Out*, pp. 38–39.

115. Schneider, *Patterns of Workers' Education* (cited in n. 91), p. 32; see also Joseph Mize, *Labor Education: A Study Report on Needs, Programs and Approaches* (n.p., 1946), pp. 133–34. There were some exceptions, but they tended to prove the rule. The United Automobile Workers, for example, would occasionally sponsor photo exhibits and arts and crafts classes.

116. Quoted in Schneider, *Patterns of Workers' Education*, p. 32.

117. Ibid., p. 86.

118. Ibid., pp. 87–88.

119. Johnson, *Pioneer's Progress* (cited in n. 30), pp. 272–73; see also "The Object of Workers' Education," *New Republic*, 34 (Apr. 25, 1923), pp. 229–30.

120. Joseph K. Hart, *Light from the North. The Danish Folk High Schools: Their Meaning for America* (New York, 1927).

121. Frederick C. Howe, *Denmark: A Cooperative Commonwealth* (New York, 1921), pp. 1, 65; chap. 4.

122. Ibid., pp. 84–85, 91–97; see also Johannes Knudsen, *Selected Writings of N. F. S. Grundtvig* (Philadelphia, 1976), pp. 148–55.

123. On Danish-American folk schools, see Marion T. Marzolf, *The Danish-Language Press in America* (New York, 1979), pp. 108–11. Ultimately, pressures for assimilation overwhelmed the Danish-American folk schools, which also encountered opposition from Danish pietists, who cared little for the schools' stress on folk singing and folk dancing.

124. Edmund deS. Brunner and E. Hsin Pao Yang, *Rural America and the Extension Service: A History and Critique of the Cooperative Agricultural and Home Economics Extension Service* (New York, 1949), p. 15. In 1919 a mixture of clergymen, educators, rural sociologists, and government officials organized the National Country Life Association. Headed by Kenyon Butterfield, it promoted rural social welfare, recreation, and community organization, all in contrast to the American Farm Bureau Federation, formed in 1920, which united those groups concerned with the farmer's economic problems. See William L. Bowers, *The Country Life Movement in America, 1900–1920* (Port Washington, N.Y., 1920), pp. 91, 95. As noted earlier, World War I boosted the emphasis on production, which persisted into the 1920s. Indirectly, the Smith-Hughes Act promoted the same stress on production, for it sprinkled rural areas with teachers of agriculture who equated adult with vocational education. See Edmund deS. Brunner and Irving Lorge, *Rural Trends in Depression Years: A Survey of Village-Centered Agricultural Communities, 1930–1936* (New York, 1937), p. 223. Brunner and Lorge

observed that "teachers in other branches [than agriculture] have neither the tradition nor the pressure that sends them into adult education; nor do their professional duties bring them as constantly into touch with adults as is the case with teachers of agriculture, whose supervision of their students' farm plots takes them constantly to the students' homes" (p. 224).

125. Quoted in "New People's College," *Rural America*, 6 (May 1928), p. 12.

126. Peffer, *New Schools for Older Students* (cited in n. 33), p. 99.

127. Ibid., p. 101.

128. Ibid., pp. 101–2.

129. Ibid., p. 105.

130. Aimee I. Horton, *The Highlander Folk School: A History of its Major Programs, 1932–1961* (Brooklyn, 1989), pp. 11–27; and Highlander Research and Education Center Papers, Wisconsin Historical Society, box 1, folder 1.

131. Aimee I. Horton, "An Analysis of Selected Programs for the Training of Civil Rights and Community Leaders in the South," Highlander Research and Education Center Papers, box 82, folder 8: Horton, *Highlander Folk School*, pp. 79–163.

132. "Background," Highlander Research and Education Center Papers, box 1, folder 1.

133. Ibid.

134. T. R. Adam, *The Workers' Road to Learning* (New York, 1940), p. 41.

135. Hilda W. Smith, "Workers' Education as Determining Social Control," *Annals, American Academy of Political and Social Science*, 182 (Nov. 1935), p. 87. Smith also assumed charge of the so-called she-she-she camps for unemployed women, which were administered successively through the FERA, WPA, and National Youth Administration; on these see Joyce L. Kornbluh, "The She-She-She Camps: An Experiment in Learning and Living, 1934–1937," in Kornbluh and Frederickson, eds., *Sisterhood and Solidarity*, pp. 255–83.

136. Doak F. Campbell, Frederick H. Bair, and Oswald L. Harvey, *Educational Activities of the Works Progress Administration*, prepared for the Advisory Committee on Education, Staff Study no. 14 (Washington, D.C., 1939), p. 94.

137. Adam, *The Workers' Road to Learning*, pp. 69–71.

138. Beard, "Electric Fire of Thought," p. 5.

139. Rutkoff and Scott, *New School* (cited in n. 17), p. 39; Johnson, *Pioneer's Progress* (cited in n. 30), p. 274.

140. A. J. Muste, "What Is Adult Education?" *Survey*, 55 (Feb. 15, 1926), p. 544.

Chapter 11

1. Robert S. and Helen M. Lynd, *Middletown in Transition: A Study in Cultural Conflict* (New York, 1937), p. 252; see also National Recreation Association, *The Leisure Hours of 5,000 People: A Report of a Study of Leisure Time Activities and Desires* (New York, 1934), p. 20.

2. John W. Studebaker, *The American Way: Democracy at Work in the Des Moines Forums* (New York, 1935), pp. 44, 59.

3. American Association for Adult Education, *Handbook of Adult Education*

in the United States (New York, 1934), pp. 64–69; R. E. Dooley, "A Village Forum," *Journal of Adult Education*, 7 (Apr. 1935), pp. 147–49; see also John W. Studebaker, *Plain Talk* (Washington, D.C., 1936); Lucy W. Adams, "A Mirror of Minds," *Journal of Adult Education*, 7 (Jan. 1935), p. 24. With the assistance of the Works Progress Administration, which put the unemployed to work as staffers on forum projects, the movement for public forums sustained itself throughout the 1930s. See John W. Studebaker and C. S. Williams, "Public Affairs Forums," U.S. Department of the Interior, Office of Education, *Bulletin, 1935, no. 17* (Washington, D.C., 1936). One source of information about local forums can be found in the scrapbook of newspaper clippings kept by Paul Sheats, who served as director of forums in Chattanooga-Hamilton county; see Papers of Paul Sheats, Syracuse Univ. Library, box 3.

4. George E. Vincent, "The Few and the Many," in Mary Ely, ed., *Adult Education in Action* (New York, 1936), p. 326.

5. Lyman Bryson, "What Education Have the Many?" in Ely, ed., *Adult Education in Action*, p. 237.

6. Carl C. Brigham, *A Study of American Intelligence* (Princeton, N.J., 1923), p. 63. On the postwar analysis of the mental tests see Raymond E. Fancher, *The Intelligence Men: Makers of the IQ Controversy* (New York, 1985), pp. 127–30.

7. President's Research Committee on Social Trends, *Recent Social Trends* (2 vols.; New York, 1933), vol. 1, p. 328.

8. Bryson, "What Education Have the Many?" p. 328.

9. William S. Gray and Ruth Munroe, *The Reading Interests and Habits of Adults: A Preliminary Report* (New York, 1930 [orig. ed. 1929]), pp. 48, 17, 59, 98. The Gray-Munroe study and similar investigations in the 1930s arose from the intersection of two forces: studies by librarians of their patrons and the broader influence of the adult-education movement. For background see Stephen Karetzky, *Reading Research and Librarianship: A History and Analysis* (Westport, Conn., 1982). For long-term trends in reading see the essay by Stedman, Tinsley, and Kaestle, "Literacy as a Consumer Activity," in Carl F. Kaestle, Helen Damon-Moore, Lawrence C. Stedman, Katherine Tinsley, and William Vance Trollinger, Jr., *Literacy in the United States: Readers and Reading Since 1880* (New Haven, Conn., 1991), pp. 149–79; see also in the same volume Damon-Moore and Kaestle, "Surveying American Readers" (pp. 180–203).

10. Louis R. Wilson, *The Geography of Reading: A Study of the Distribution and Status of Libraries in the United States* (Chicago, 1938), p. 193.

11. Ibid., pp. 189–90.

12. Ibid., p. 434.

13. W. Lloyd Warner and Paul S. Lunt, *The Social Life of a Modern Community* (New Haven, Conn., 1941), chap. 19. Warner and Lunt concluded: "The reading habits of the people [of "Yankee City"—Newburyport] were highly influenced by class values; they read certain books, magazines, and newspapers in varying percentages according to their place in the class hierarchy" (p. 379). Studies of the use of libraries ultimately reached a similar conclusion; see Bernard Berelson, *The Library's Public* (New York, 1949), pp. 30, 37, *passim*. Some of these conclusions were foreshadowed by Douglas Waples and Ralph W. Tyler, *What*

People Want to Read: A Study of Group Interests and a Survey of Problems in Adult Reading (Chicago, 1931), p. 35 and *passim*.

14. Percy W. Bidwell, "How To Write a Readable Book," in Ely, ed., *Adult Education in Action*, p. 247.

15. William S. Gray and Bernice Leary, *What Makes a Book Readable, with Special Reference to Adults of Limited Reading Ability: An Initial Study* (Chicago, 1935).

16. Ibid., p. 92.

17. Ibid., p. 97.

18. Ibid., p. 98.

19. Ibid., pp. 339–50, 203, 121.

20. Lyman Bryson, "Readable Books for the People," *Publishers' Weekly* (Feb. 18, 1939), pp. 778–79; see also the sketch of Bryson in John F. Ohles, ed., *Biographical Dictionary of American Educators* (3 vols.; Westport, Conn., 1978), vol. 1, pp. 200–201.

21. Joan Shelley Rubin, *The Making of Middlebrow Culture* (Chapel Hill, N.C., 1992), pp. 299–314.

22. Vincent, "The Few and the Many" (cited in n. 4), p. 326; see also Nathaniel Peffer, "A Recantation," *Journal of Adult Education*, 7 (Apr. 1935), pp. 15–29. Peffer wrote that "adult education is limited by the foundation that is laid for it in earlier education and it can go no higher than that education will support. You can not begin educating people at the age of twenty-one" (pp. 125–26). This observation led Peffer to question "the messianic connotations of the enthusiasm the 'forum movement' has generated": "I do not think it is true that you have only to bring people together once or twice a week to hear speeches from two points of view; and lo, there shall be light" (pp. 126–27). See also Seymour Barnard, "May We Be Exclusive," *Journal of Adult Education* 8 (Jan. 1936), pp. 32–35.

23. George A. Lundberg, Mirra Komarovsky, and Mary Alice McInerny, *Leisure: A Suburban Study* (New York, 1934), pp. 341–42.

24. Benjamin Kline Hunnicutt, *Work Without End: Abandoning Shorter Hours for the Right to Work* (Philadelphia, 1988), p. 11.

25. Ibid., chap. 2.

26. Ibid., chap. 4. See, for example, Weaver Pangburn, "The Worker's Leisure and His Individuality," *American Journal of Sociology*, 27 (Jan. 1922), pp. 433–41.

27. President's Research Committee on Social Trends, *Recent Social Trends*, vol. 2, p. 912; Jesse F. Steiner, *Research Memorandum on Recreation in the Depression. Social Science Research Council, Bulletin no. 32, 1937* (New York, 1937), p. 29. The average number of hours worked per week by private nonagricultural wage and salary workers declined from 58.5 in 1900 to 50.6 in 1920, 47.1 in 1930, and 41.7 in 1935; see John D. Owen, *The Price of Leisure: An Economic Analysis of the Demand for Leisure Time* (Rotterdam, N.Y., 1969), p. 67.

28. The debate over shorter hours and leisure was most vocal in the early 1930s. Hunnicutt has shown that by the late 1930s intellectuals and reformers were retreating from the notion of a more leisurely future, and this retreat was evidenced in the drastic decline in the number of listings under "leisure" in the *Education Index*; see Hunnicutt, *Work Without End*, pp. 251–65, 381–82. On the other hand, by the late 1930s the Works Progress Administration and sundry pri-

vate institutions had established a vast network of classes and clubs for adults eager to fill their leisure time more creatively.

29. Stuart Chase, *The Economy of Abundance* (New York, 1934), p. 11.

30. Stuart Chase, *Men and Machines* (New York, 1929), chaps. 10, 11.

31. Chase, *Economy of Abundance*, chap. 9.

32. Ibid., p. 149.

33. Ibid., p. 148.

34. Ibid., p. 24. As new forms of recreation came to the fore, the percentage of their budgets that Americans spent on reading declined between 1900 and 1930; see Owen, *Price of Leisure*, p. 91; for long-term trends in expenditures on reading see Stedman, Tinsley, and Kaestle, "Literacy as a Consumer Activity" (cited in n. 9), p. 156.

35. Stuart Chase, *The Nemesis of American Business and Other Essays* (New York, 1931), p. 134. On rising concern about middle age, see Howard P. Chudacoff, *How Old Are You? Age Consciousness in American Culture* (Princeton, N.J., 1989), pp. 108–9.

36. William Graebner, *The Meaning of Retirement: The History and Function of an American Institution, 1885–1978* (New Haven, Conn., 1980), pp. 24, 30–31.

37. William James, *The Principles of Psychology* (2 vols.; New York, 1893), vol. 2, p. 402.

38. Quoted in Graebner, *Meaning of Retirement*, p. 4.

39. H. L. Hollingworth, *Mental Growth and Decline* (New York, 1927). Hollingworth conceded that "very few experimental data or measures are available on the mental changes after the period of early maturity" (p. 310).

40. E. L. Thorndike, Elsie O. Bregman, J. Warren Tilton, and Ella Woodyard, *Adult Learning* (New York, 1928), p. 177.

41. Ibid., p. 123.

42. Ibid., p. 126, note 1.

43. Waples and Tyler, *What People Want to Read* (cited in n. 13), p. xviii.

44. James T. Adams, *Frontiers of American Culture: A Study of Adult Education in a Democracy* (New York, 1944), p. 140.

45. Walter B. Pitkin, *Life Begins at Forty* (New York, 1932), pp. 82, 102, 106, 158.

46. Kenneth Macgowan, *Footlights Across America: Towards a National Theater* (New York, 1929), pp. 311–25.

47. Frederick P. Keppel and Robert L. Duffus, *The Arts in American Life* (New York, 1933), pp. 35–36, 42.

48. Ibid., pp. 63–68.

49. Macgowan, *Footlights Across America*, pp. 10–11; Robert L. Duffus, *The American Renaissance* (New York, 1928), pp. 93–161.

50. Quoted in Keppel and Duffus, *Arts in American Life*, p. 69.

51. Robert S. and Helen M. Lynd, *Middletown: A Study in Contemporary American Culture* (New York, 1929), p. 301.

52. Ibid., p. 291, note 6, and p. 296.

53. Ibid., p. 250.   54. Ibid., pp. 248–49.

55. Ibid., p. 244.   56. Ibid.

57. Macgowan, *Footlights Across America*, p. 3.

58. Jane De Hart Mathews, *The Federal Theatre, 1935–1939: Plays, Relief, and Politics* (New York, 1980), p. 24.

59. Ibid., p. 23.

60. Frederick H. Koch, "Folk Playmaking," in Samuel Selden and Mary Tom Sphangos, *Frederick Henry Koch, Pioneer Playmaker: A Brief Biography* (Chapel Hill, N.C., 1945), p. 25. See also Samuel Selden, *Frederick Henry Koch: Pioneer Playmaker*, Univ. of North Carolina, Chapel Hill, Extension Publications, 19, no. 4 (July 1954).

61. Quoted in Selden and Sphangos, *Frederick Henry Koch*, p. 61.

62. Marjorie Patten, *The Arts Workshop in Rural America: A Study of the Rural Arts Program of the Agricultural Extension Service* (New York, 1937), p. 3.

63. Ibid., p. 74.

64. Several black colleges in the 1930s and early 1940s organized little theaters that extended beyond their campuses; among the most notable were the Bucket Theatre at Tuskegee Institute, the Log-Cabin Theatre at Wiley College, and programs at Atlanta and Dillard universities. In addition, companies devoted to presenting plays about black life were organized in Chicago, New York, Minneapolis, Cleveland, Washington, and Pittsburgh. Although these companies employed some of the same folk themes as white theaters, they also sought to use the little theater to break down stereotypes of blacks in the theater. See Anne M. Cooke, "The Little Theatre Movement as an Adult Education Project Among Negroes," *Journal of Negro Education*, 14 (Summer 1945), pp. 418–24.

65. Jean Carter and Jesse Ogden, *Everyman's Drama* (New York, 1938), p. 112.

66. Macgowan, *Footlights Across America*, pp. 97–98.

67. Ibid., p. 74.

68. Clarence A. Perry, *The Work of the Little Theaters* (New York, 1933), p. 17.

69. Jane De Hart Mathews, *Federal Theatre*, p. 59. With the support of Frederick P. Keppel of the AAAE, Flanagan had been awarded a Guggenheim fellowship in 1926 to study workers' and peasants' drama in the Soviet Union.

70. Ibid., pp. 38, 198–235.   71. Ibid., pp. 59–60.

72. Ibid., p. 60.   73. Patten, *Arts Workshop*, p. 50.

74. Ruby G. Smith, *The People's Colleges: A History of the New York State Extension Service in Cornell University and the State of New York, 1876–1948* (Ithaca, N.Y., 1949), p. 322, note 1; see also Chapter 10, note 121, and Benson Y. Landis and John D. Willard, *Rural Adult Education* (New York, 1933), pp. 138–39. The Depression intensified the hostility of some farm organizations to the Agricultural Extension Service and its county agents, who were assailed as mere tools of the American Farm Bureau Federation; for example, the Farmers' Educational and Co-operative Union sought to prevent county appropriations for extension work in Iowa during the mid-1930s. See Gladys Baker, *The County Agent* (Chicago, 1939), pp. 14–15.

75. Ibid., p. 323.

76. Patten, *Arts Workshop*, pp. 52–54.

77. Carter and Ogden, *Everyman's Drama* (cited in n. 65), p. 112.
78. William Corbin, "Everybody Wants To Be an Actor," *American Magazine*, 118 (Nov. 1934), p. 119.
79. Ibid., pp. 51, 119–23.
80. Carter and Ogden, *Everyman's Drama*, pp. 10–11.
81. Martin H. Neumeyer and Esther S. Neumeyer, *Leisure and Recreation: A Study of Leisure and Recreation in Their Sociological Aspects* (New York, 1926), pp. 101–2.
82. Ibid. In a book widely cited by American adult educators the British philosopher L. P. Jacks wrote in 1931: "The pleasures which result from external excitement are far inferior to those which result from creative skill." See L. P. Jacks, *The Education of the Whole Man: A Plea for a New Spirit in Education* (London, 1931), p. 120.
83. Marjorie B. Greenbie, *The Arts of Leisure* (New York, 1935), pp. 7, 17.
84. Thomas H. Nelson, *Ventures in Informal Adult Education* (New York, 1933), p. 8.
85. Seymour Barnard, "Informal but Important," *Journal of Adult Education*, 5 (Oct. 1933), p. 443.
86. Nelson, *Ventures in Informal Adult Education*, p. 4.
87. Warren Susman, *Culture as History: The Transformation of American Society in the Twentieth Century* (New York, 1984), p. 165.
88. For biographical details see the sketch by Donald Meyer in *Dictionary of American Biography*, supp. 5, p. 102. In the course of Carnegie's life, *How to Win Friends and Influence People* sold 5,000,000 copies.
89. Henry C. Link, *The Return to Religion* (New York, 1936), p. 86.
90. Ibid., p. 74; see also Susman, *Culture as History*, p. 165.
91. Link, *Return to Religion*, p. 78.
92. Dorothy Rowden, ed., *Handbook of Adult Education in the United States, 1936* (New York, 1936), pp. 234–44.
93. Watson Dickerman, *Outposts of the Public Schools* (New York, 1938), p. 45; S. Alexander Shear, "Highschool Pioneering in Adult Education," *Journal of the National Education Association*, 24 (Jan. 1931), pp. 49–50; Harvey M. Genskow, "Shorewood—A School-Centered Community," *Journal of Adult Education*, 7 (Apr. 1935), p. 174. Dickerman observed that students in adult schools were twice as likely to be females as males.
94. Harlan P. Douglass, *The Suburban Trend* (New York, 1925), pp. 220–21.
95. Edward Yeomans, "The Suburban Deluxe," *Atlantic Monthly*, 125 (Jan. 1920), p. 107; Lewis Mumford, "The Wilderness of Suburbia," *New Republic*, 28 (Sept. 1921), pp. 44–45; and Joseph L. Arnold, *The New Deal in the Suburbs: A History of the Greenbelt Town Program, 1935–1954* (Columbus, Ohio, 1971), p. 12. See also Kenneth T. Jackson, *Crabgrass Frontier: The Suburbanization of the United States* (New York, 1985), pp. 172–89.
96. Douglass, *Suburban Trend*, p. 327.
97. Arnold, *New Deal in the Suburbs*, pp. 14–15.
98. Robert B. Hudson, *Radburn: A Plan of Living. A Study Made for the American Association for Adult Education* (New York, 1934), p. 7.
99. Hudson, *Radburn*, chap. 3.

100. Ibid., p. 12.

101. Douglass, *Suburban Trend*, p. 302.

102. J. Keith Torbert, *The Establishment of an Adult School* (New York, 1936), p. 44.

103. Ibid., p. 103. In descending order of student registrations, the courses ranked as follows: Economic Forum, 298; American Literature, 243; Interior Decorating, 103; Gymnasium, 75; Character Education, 65; History, 58; Best Recipes, 54; Public Speaking, 52; Youth Forum, 50; Appreciation of Music, 49; Writing, 46; Typing, 44; Astronomy, 37; French, 36; Shop, 36; Photography, 36; Theater, 36; Drawing, 35; Sketching, 35; Pottery, 27; Chemistry, 26; Orchestra, 26; Class Piano, 25; and Woodcarving, 23.

104. Philip C. Nash, "The Combination of Community Adult Education with the FERA Emergency Relief School Program," *School and Society*, 41 (June 8, 1935), p. 774; Art Armstrong, "Adult Education in St. Paul," *School and Society*, 43 (May 16, 1935), p. 677; Dickerman, *Outposts of the Public Schools*, p. 49; Genskow, "Shorewood," p. 174.

105. Torbert, *Establishment of an Adult School*, p. 77.

106. Lynd and Lynd, *Middletown in Transition* (cited in n. 1), p. 270.

107. Jean Carter, *Parents in Perplexity* (New York, 1938), p. 10.

108. Ibid. See also Armstrong, "Adult Education in St. Paul," pp. 676–78.

109. Arnold, *New Deal in the Suburbs*, p. 167.

110. Charles F. Searle, *Minister of Relief: Harry Hopkins and the Depression* (Syracuse, N.Y., 1963), p. 73.

111. Doak F. Campbell, Frederick H. Bair, and Oswald L. Harvey, *Educational Activities of the Works Progress Administration*, prepared for the Advisory Committee on Education, Staff Study no. 14 (Washington, D.C., 1939), p. 8.

112. Maris Proffitt, "Adult Education," in U.S. Department of the Interior, Office of Education, *Biennial Survey of Education, 1934–1936* (Washington, D.C., 1940), p. 23. On the decline of vocational education enrollments in the Depression, see Morse A. Cartwright, *Ten Years of Adult Education* (New York, 1934), p. 193; see also Lucy W. Adams, "A Mirror of Minds," *Journal of Adult Education*, 2 (Jan. 1935), p. 21. Although they did not spur much interest among leaders of the adult-education movement at the time, the WPA's literacy classes were important forerunners of the more systematic literacy programs of recent decades; see Edmund deS. Brunner and Irving Lorge, *Rural Trends in Depression Years: A Survey of Village-Centered Agricultural Communities, 1930–1936* (New York, 1937), p. 234. One investigator claimed in 1941 that WPA classes had taught 500,000 blacks to read and write and reduced illiteracy among blacks by one-sixth between 1930 and 1940; see Samuel A. Madden, "Adult Education and the American Negro," *Adult Education Bulletin*, 5 (June 1941), p. 138. For subsequent developments in what is now called "adult basic education," see Maurice C. Taylor, "Adult Basic Education," in Sharan B. Merriam and Phyllis M. Cunningham, eds., *Handbook of Adult and Continuing Education* (San Francisco, 1989), pp. 465–89.

113. Andrew Hendrickson, *Trends in Public School Adult Education in Cities of the United States, 1929–1939* (New York, 1943), pp. 59–63.

114. S. L. Pressy, "Outstanding Problems of Emergency Junior College Students," *School and Society*, 43 (May 30, 1936), pp. 743–47.

115. Nash, "Community Adult Education with the FERA Emergency Relief School Program," p. 774.

116. Hendrickson, *Trends in Public School Adult Education*, pp. 30, 74; Barbara Blumberg, *The New Deal and the Unemployed: The View from New York City* (Lewisburg, Pa., 1979), pp. 170, 180.

117. Irene Freuder, "Adult Education," *Nation*, 140 (Apr. 7, 1935), p. 389; see also Emily M. Danton, "The Federal Emergency Adult Education Program," in Rowden, ed., *Handbook of Adult Education in the United States, 1936*, p. 32; Campbell, Bair, and Harvey, *Educational Activities of the Works Progress Administration*, p. 85; on the relations between the WPA and state educational agencies, see Arthur W. MacMahon, John D. Millett, and Gladys Ogden, *The Administration of Federal Work Relief* (Chicago, 1941), pp. 249–51.

118. Campbell, Bair, and Harvey, *Educational Activities of the Works Progress Administration*, pp. 55–56.

119. Ibid., pp. 56–57.

120. Ibid., p. 82.

121. Alexander Meiklejohn, "Adult Education: A Fresh Start," *Nation*, 80 (Aug. 15, 1934), p. 15.

122. Armstrong, "Adult Education in St. Paul" (cited in n. 104), p. 678.

123. David E. Shi, *The Simple Life: Plain Living and High Thinking in American Culture* (New York, 1985), pp. 241–42, 236.

124. Glenn Frank, "Is Adult Education Overspecializing?" in Ely, ed., *Adult Education in Action* (cited in n. 4), p. 44; for various statements of the emerging philosophy of adult education, see Proffitt, "Adult Education" (cited in n. 112), pp. 6–19.

125. Proffitt, "Adult Education," pp. 6–19.

126. Beulah Amidon, "A Middle-Class Movement?" *Journal of Adult Education*, 10 (Apr. 1938), pp. 163–67.

127. For a critique of adult education along these lines, see Ruth Kotinsky, *Adult Education and the Social Scene* (New York, 1933). This type of criticism has not abated. Christopher Lasch wrote in 1976: "Having no hope of improving their lives in any of the ways that matter, people have convinced themselves that what matters is psychic self-improvement: getting in touch with their feelings, eating health foods, taking lessons in ballet or belly dancing, immersing themselves in the wisdom of the East, jogging, learning how to 'relate,' overcoming the fear of pleasure"; see Christopher Lasch, "The Narcissistic Society," *New York Review of Books*, Sept. 30, 1976, p. 5.

128. See Chapter 12.

129. Charles A. and Mary R. Beard, *The Rise of American Civilization* (New York, 1945 [orig. ed. 1930]), p. vii.

130. "Announcement," *Journal of Adult Education*, 13 (June 1941), p. 309.

131. Malcolm S. Knowles, *A History of the Adult Education Movement in the United States* (Huntington, N.Y., 1977), p. 204.

132. Campbell, Bair, and Harvey, *Educational Activities of the Works Progress Administration*, pp. 133–37. Malcolm Knowles and Paul Sheats were among

those later prominent in professional adult education who got their start in classes (Knowles) or forums (Sheats) supported by the WPA. On Sheats, see above, note 3.

133. Hendrickson, *Trends in Public School Adult Education* (cited in n. 113), p. 56.

Chapter 12

1. *The Autobiography of Malcolm X* (with the assistance of Alex Haley, New York, 1965), pp. 153–54, 157–58, 171–85.
2. K. Patricia Cross, "Adult Learners: Characteristics, Needs, and Interests," in Richard E. Peterson and Associates, *Lifelong Learning in America* (San Francisco, 1979), pp. 78–80; John W. C. Johnstone and Ramon Rivera, *Volunteers for Learning: A Study of the Educational Pursuits of American Adults* (Chicago, 1965), pp. 1–2; Jack London, Robert Wenkert, and Warren O. Hagstrom, *Adult Education and Social Class*, Comparative Research Project no. 1017, Survey Research Center, Univ. of California, (Berkeley, Calif., 1963), pp. 4–5.
3. Cross, "Adult Learners," pp. 79–80.
4. The number of students enrolled in proprietary schools rose from 800,000 in 1949 to 1,400,000 in 1971, a modest proportionate increase in view of the geometric leaps that marked enrollments in colleges during the same period; see Richard B. Freeman, "Occupational Training in Proprietary Schools and Technical Institutes," *Review of Economics and Statistics*, 56 (Aug. 1974), p. 310. On the growth of proprietary schools in the 1970s and 1980s, see Don F. Seaman and Patricia McDivitt, "Proprietary Schools," in Sharan B. Merriam and Phyllis M. Cunningham, *Handbook of Adult and Continuing Education* (San Francisco, 1989), p. 411.
5. For a review of changing attitudes among social scientists on this issue, see Eli Ginzberg, *The Manpower Connection: Education and Work* (Cambridge, Mass., 1975), p. 39.
6. For a concise review of these and related factors, see Dale L. Hiestand, *Changing Careers After Thirty-Five: New Horizons Through Professional and Graduate Study* (New York, 1971), pp. 5–7, chap. 14.
7. Christopher Jencks et al., *Who Gets Ahead: The Determinants of Economic Success in America* (New York, 1979), chap. 5.
8. U.S. Department of Education, National Center for Education Statistics, *Digest of Education Statistics, 1988* (Washington, D.C., 1988), p. 15.
9. Johnstone and Rivera, *Volunteers for Learning*, p. 95. Other investigators reached the same conclusion; see London, Wenkert, and Hagstrom, *Adult Education and Social Class*, pp. 46–47.
10. *Digest of Education Statistics, 1988*, p. 98.
11. David O. Levine, *The American College and the Culture of Aspiration, 1915–1940* (Ithaca, N.Y., 1986), p. 202.
12. Lyman Bryson, *Adult Education* (New York, 1936), p. 196.
13. Marcia Edwards, "The Relation of College Enrollment to Economic Depression," *American Association of Collegiate Registrars, Bulletin*, n.s. 7 (1931–32), pp. 197–218; see also Edwards, "College Enrollment During Times

of Economic Depression," *Journal of Higher Education*, 3 (1932), pp. 11–16; American Association of University Professors, *Depression, Recovery and Higher Education* (New York, 1937), pp. 238, 262.

14. Levine, *American College and the Culture of Aspiration*, p. 191.

15. American Association of University Professors, *Depression, Recovery and Higher Education*, pp. 238, 258.

16. Robert M. Hutchins, "The Threat to American Education," *Colliers*, Dec. 30, 1944, pp. 20–21.

17. Levine, *American College and the Culture of Aspiration*, p. 174.

18. F. W. McDowell, "The Junior College," in U.S. Department of the Interior, Bureau of Education, *Bulletin, 1919, no. 35* (Washington, D.C., 1919), p. 13.

19. Levine, *American College and the Culture of Aspiration*, p. 175.

20. American Association of University Professors, *Depression, Recovery and Higher Education*, p. 262.

21. William S. Learned, *The Quality of the Educational Process in the United States and Europe*, Carnegie Foundation for the Advancement of Teaching, Bulletin no. 20 (New York, 1927), p. 36 and *passim*; Ellen Condliffe Lagemann, *Private Power for the Public Good: A History of the Carnegie Foundation for the Advancement of Teaching* (Middletown, Conn., 1983), pp. 102–3.

22. Carnegie Foundation for the Advancement of Teaching, *State Higher Education in California* (Sacramento, Calif., 1932). For a trenchant discussion of this document, see Steven Brint and Jerome Karabel, *The Diverted Dream: Community Colleges and the Promise of Educational Opportunity in America, 1900–1985* (New York, 1989), pp. 47–52.

23. Quoted in John M. Proctor, ed., *The Junior College: Its Organization and Administration* (Stanford, Calif., 1927), p. 22; see also Walter C. Eells, *The Present Status of Junior College Terminal Education* (Washington, D.C., 1941), p. 18.

24. Eells, *Present Status of Junior College Terminal Education*, pp. 14–19.

25. Commission on the Reorganization of Secondary Education, "Cardinal Principles of Secondary Education," in U.S. Department of the Interior, Bureau of Education, *Bulletin, 1918, no. 35* (Washington, D.C., 1918), pp. 9–11; Edward A. Krug, *The Shaping of the American High School: Volume I* (New York, 1964), pp. 39–65, 388–89.

26. Krug, *Shaping of the American High School*, pp. 378–79.

27. Quoted in ibid., p. 281; see also ibid., pp. 214–15.

28. Brint and Karabel, *Diverted Dream*, pp. 34–35.

29. Quoted in ibid., p. 49.

30. Kramer Rohfleisch, "A Danger in the Terminal Program," *Junior College Journal*, 12 (Nov. 1941), p. 157.

31. For a summary of these surveys, see Coleman Griffith, with the assistance of Hortense Blackstone, *The Junior College in Illinois* (Urbana, Ill., 1945), p. 163. Although these surveys had a considerable impact on contemporaries, both their methodology and assumptions seem flawed. For example, an oft-cited investigation of Mississippi junior-college students concluded that barely one-third went on to four-year colleges; in retrospect, it seems remarkable that in Depression-era Mississippi as many as a third of all junior-college students actually enrolled in four-year colleges.

32. Coleman Griffith, the provost of the University of Illinois, stated in 1941 that the nation was already oversupplied with institutions "offering a classic, traditional education," that "too many youth of the middle and lower orders of inability have attempted to perform tasks devised for abler youth," and that "large numbers of youth do not have an appropriate education at all." See ibid.

33. Rohfleisch, "Danger in the Terminal Program," p. 157.

34. Walter C. Eells, *Why Junior College Terminal Education?* (Washington, D.C., 1941), p. 11.

35. Ibid., pp. 12–13; see also Eells, *Present Status of Junior College Terminal Education*, pp. 211–43.

36. Benjamin Kline Hunnicutt, *Work Without End: Abandoning Shorter Hours for the Right to Work* (Philadelphia, 1988), pp. 254, 257–60, 265.

37. Frank W. Taussig, *Principles of Economics* (4th ed., 2 vols.; New York, 1939), vol. 1, p. 91; Richard T. Ely and G. R. Wicker, *Elementary Principles of Economics* (New York, 1930), pp. 383–84. Significantly, in the third edition of his *Principles of Economics* (2 vols.; New York, 1921), Taussig confined himself to the assertion that education would increase wages rather than narrow wage differences. In this edition he assumed that the children of laborers would acquire no education beyond the age of fourteen, and hence "differences in reward, and the social classes which rest mainly on them, tend to perpetuate themselves." See his *Principles of Economics*, vol. 2, p. 136.

38. Howard M. Bell, *Youth Tell Their Story: A Study of the Conditions and Attitudes of Young People in Maryland Between the Ages of 16 and 24* (Washington, D.C., 1938), pp. 80, 76–79; see also Bell, *Matching Youth and Jobs: A Study of Occupational Adjustment* (Washington D.C., 1940), pp. 99–100, 240–42.

39. Palmer O. Johnson and Oswald Harvey, *The National Youth Administration* (Washington, D.C., 1938), p. 7.

40. National Education Association, Educational Policies Commission, *Education and Economic Well-Being in American Democracy* (Washington, D.C., 1940), pp. 105–32.

41. On curriculum content see Eells, *Present Status of Junior College Terminal Education*, p. 75; also Beulah Nunamaker, "Business Education in Junior Colleges," *Junior College Journal*, 12 (Oct. 1940), p. 92. Eells discussed the conditions under which junior colleges could qualify for federal assistance under the Smith-Hughes and George-Deen acts in his *Present Status of Junior College Terminal Education*, pp. 29–30; see also James M. Greig, "Evening Junior Colleges for Adults," *Junior College Journal*, 12 (Nov. 1941), p. 155.

42. Quoted in Eells, *Why Junior College Terminal Education?*, p. 166.

43. Jesse P. Bogue, *The Community College* (New York, 1950), p. 35.

44. J. E. Carpenter, "Adult Education in Sacramento," *Junior College Journal*, 14 (Jan. 1944), pp. 217–37.

45. Walter C. Eells, "The Junior College Directory, 1944," *Junior College Journal*, 14 (Jan. 1944), pp. 217–37.

46. Lacking competent instructors for skills in demand, junior colleges trained air-raid wardens as well as stock clerks, typists, and stenographers on military bases. See Carpenter, "Adult Education in Sacramento," p. 15; Nora P. Coy, "Adult Students in San Bernardino," *Junior College Journal*, 14 (Feb. 1944), p.

263; Wesley M. Pugh, "One-Third of Modesto's Adults Go To College," *Junior College Journal*, 14 (Jan. 1944), p. 198.

47. George Q. Flynn, *The Mess in Washington: Manpower Mobilization in World War II* (Westport, Conn., 1979), pp. 6–7, 57–59. TWI originated in 1940 under the Labor Policy Advisory Committee, chaired by Sidney Hillman. In 1942 it was absorbed by the War Mobilization Commission, headed by Paul V. McNutt. One of TWI's directors, Channing R. Dooley of Socony-Vacuum, had served during World War I on the U.S. Training Service, which foreshadowed TWI. Both the U.S. Training Service and TWI drew on the ideas of the efficiency educators of the Progressive era, especially Charles R. Allen. Factory managers subdivided job tasks, while master mechanics trained workers, often drawn from the ranks of the unskilled and unemployed, in "single-skill competence." Workers who mastered one skill were quickly upgraded to the next. Interestingly, the federal government, which had subsidized vocational education through the Smith-Hughes Act, largely ignored its handiwork during the war, for vocational graduates were put through the same training program as everyone else. See War Manpower Commission, *The Training Within Industry Report, 1940–1945* (Washington, D.C., 1945), pp. 31, 36, and *Training Workers for Toolroom and Machine Repair* (Washington, D.C., n.d.), pp. 32–33.

48. James B. Young and James M. Ewing, *The Mississippi Public Junior College Story: The First Fifty Years, 1922–1972* (Jackson, Miss., 1972), p. 23.

49. Burton Clark, *Adult Education in Transition: A Study of Institutional Insecurity* (Berkeley, Calif., 1956), pp. 130–41.

50. Bogue, *Community College*, p. 31.

51. John A. Sexson and John W. Harbeson, *The New American College* (New York, 1946), pp. 123–24. I will use the terms "community college" and "junior college" interchangeably throughout the remainder of this chapter, but the reader should keep in mind that the postwar transformation of junior colleges into community colleges was gradual and uneven. In general, junior colleges in sparsely populated areas were much slower than their urban counterparts to change into community colleges.

52. Keith Olson, *The G.I. Bill, the Veterans, and the Colleges* (Lexington, Ky., 1974), pp. 17, 37.

53. Ibid., pp. 21–22, 30–31, 35; see also David R. Ross, *Politics and Veterans During World War II* (New York, 1969), pp. 49–63; William E. Hayes, "The Post-War Liberal Arts College and the G.I. Bill: An Analysis," *Education*, 66 (Sept. 1945), p. 48.

54. Olson, *G.I. Bill, Veterans, and Colleges*, p. 44.

55. Ibid., pp. 51–54.

56. Raymond Walters, "Facts and Figures of Colleges at War," *Annals of the American Academy of Political and Social Science*, 231 (Jan. 1944), p. 8. Walters estimated that by 1943, 288,000 enlistees were taking specialized military courses on some 420 campuses. This was probably the first exposure of most of them to a campus.

57. Cyril O. Houle, Elbert W. Burr, Thomas H. Hamilton, and John R. Yale, *The Armed Forces and Adult Education* (Washington, D.C., 1947), pp. 13–45, 82–89, 39, 105

58. Ibid., pp. 88–101, p. 106.

59. Jackson Toby and David J. Armor, "Carrots or Sticks for High School Dropouts?" *Public Interest*, no. 106 (Winter 1992), pp. 87–89; see also the description of the GED tests' objectives in Lee C. Deighton, ed., *The Encyclopedia of Education* (10 vols.; New York, 1971), vol. 4, p. 111. During the war colleges were reluctant to award credit for military experience, hence the need for new tests of academic proficiency; see Ralph W. Tyler, "Social Credit for Military Experience," *Annals of the American Academy of Political and Social Science*, 231 (Jan. 1944), pp. 58–64.

60. William S. Learned and Ben D. Wood, *The Student and His Knowledge*, Carnegie Foundation for the Advancement of Teaching, Bulletin no. 20 (New York, 1938); Lagemann, *Private Power for the Public Good*, pp. 113–14.

61. Walter V. Bingham, "Inequality in Adult Capacity—From Military Data," *Science*, 16 (Aug. 1946), pp. 148–52.

62. Michael Ackerman, "Standardized Tests and the Democratic Ideal, 1945–1963," seminar paper, History, Univ. of Virginia, 1990, pp. 29–31.

63. President's Commission on Higher Education, *Higher Education for American Democracy* (6 vols.; New York, 1948), vol. 1, p. 32. On the composition of the Zook commission, see Janet Kerr-Tener, "From Truman to Johnson: Ad Hoc Policy Formation in Higher Education," Ph.D. diss., Education, Univ. of Virginia, 1985, pp. 59–62.

64. *Higher Education for American Democracy*, vol. 1, p. 37.

65. Ibid., vol. 1, p. 44.

66. Ibid., vol. 1, p. 39.

67. Olson, *G.I. Bill, Veterans, and Colleges* (cited in n. 52), pp. 44–45.

68. This recommendation provoked a formal dissent from two Catholic members of the commission; see *Higher Education for American Democracy*, vol. 5, pp. 65–68.

69. Ibid., vol. 1, pp. 69, 97.

70. See Chapter 8, note 46 for the work of Charles Dabney at the Univ. of Cincinnati.

71. Brint and Karabel, *Diverted Dream* (cited in n. 22), pp. 32–33.

72. Ervin L. Harlecher, *The Community Dimension of the Community Colleges* (Englewood Cliffs, N.J., 1969), pp. 11–14.

73. James Sloan Allen, *The Romance of Commerce and Culture: Capitalism, Modernism, and the Chicago-Aspen Crusade for Cultural Reform* (Chicago, 1983), chaps. 2, 6, 7.

74. Ibid., chap. 3; Joan Shelley Rubin, *The Making of Middlebrow Culture* (Chapel Hill, N.C., 1992), chap. 4.

75. On the tendency of Great Books discussion groups to attract college-educated and predominantly female participants, see James A. Davis, *Great Books and Small Groups* (Glencoe, Ill., 1960), pp. 31–51.

76. I have constructed this profile from the Fund for Adult Education Papers, Syracuse Univ. Library, esp. boxes 9 and 14, which contain voluminous correspondence between fund representatives and officials in the test cities.

77. Elwood Street to John Osman, Aug. 15, 1955; Osman to Street, Sept. 14, 1955; Street to Osman, Sept. 15, 1955, Fund for Adult Education Papers, box 9. See also the typescript History of the [Kansas City] Project in box 14.

78. Allen, *Romance of Commerce and Culture*, pp. 290–91.

79. Similarly, when the FAE withdrew support from the Kansas City project in 1955, the University of Kansas City absorbed the program; see History of the [Kansas City] Project, Fund for Adult Education Papers, box 14.

80. Jesse P. Bogue, *American Junior Colleges* (4th ed.; Washington, D.C., 1956), p. 40.

81. Leland L. Medsker, *The Junior College: Progress and Prospect* (New York, 1960), p. 43.

82. Ibid., pp. 44–45.

83. W. Max Wise, *They Come for the Best of Reasons* (Washington, D.C., 1958), pp. 7–8.

84. Bogue, *American Junior Colleges*, p. 14.

85. Ibid., p. 5.

86. John W. Thornton, *The Community Junior College* (2nd. ed., New York, 1966), p. 66; see also Ralph R. Fields, *The Community College Movement* (New York, 1962), p. 79. Junior college officials, who were in a position to know, routinely commented on the large number of older students, but none of the categories mentioned in the text—"adult," "special," or "part-time"—necessarily excluded teenagers. "Special student" referred to anyone who took courses without intending to graduate. To confuse matters, regardless of their age, students who took evening courses toward the Associate in Arts degree (A.A.) were classified as "regular" rather than as "special" or "special and adult." See Homer Kempfer, "Adult Education in a Community College," *Junior College Journal*, 21 (Sept. 1950), p. 18.

87. Arthur M. Cohen and Florence B. Brawer, *The American Community College* (2d ed., San Francisco, 1989), pp. 200–207; Leland Medsker and Dale Tillery, *Breaking the Access Barriers: A Profile of Two-year Colleges* (New York, 1971), p. 62.

88. Medsker and Tillery, *Breaking the Access Barriers*, p. 62. For a review of how federal training programs have affected community colleges see Terry W. Hartle and Mark A. Kutner, "Federal Policies: Programs, Legislation, and Prospects," in Richard E. Peterson and Associates, *Lifelong Learning in America* (San Francisco, 1979), chap. 5; see also Dennis L. Nystrom and G. Keith Bayne, *Occupational and Career Education Legislation* (2d ed.; Indianapolis, Ind., 1979).

89. Richard E. Peterson wrote in 1979 that "the field of adult education has evolved a vocabulary unparalleled in its confusion"; see Richard E. Peterson, "Introduction," in Peterson and Associates, *Lifelong Learning in America*, p. 13.

90. Medsker and Tillery, *Breaking the Access Barriers*, pp. 16, 27.

91. Brint and Karabel, *Diverted Dream* (cited in n. 22), p. 84.

92. Ibid.; Medsker and Tillery, *Breaking the Access Barriers*, pp. 18–20.

93. Medsker and Tillery acknowledged in 1971 that "a paucity of information exists about these older students [in community colleges], particularly the ones attending part-time"; see *Breaking the Access Barriers*, p. 49.

94. Elizabeth L. Cless, "The Birth of an Idea: An Account of the Genesis of Women's Continuing Education," in Helen S. Astin, ed., *Some Action of Her Own: The Adult Woman and Higher Education* (Lexington, Mass., 1976), pp. 3–22. Demographic characteristics of the women who participated in CEW centers are well described in Helen S. Astin, "A Profile of the Women in Continuing Education," in Astin, ed., *Some Action of Her Own*, pp. 57–88; see also Jean W. Camp-

bell, "Women Drop Back In: Educational Innovation in the Sixties," in Alice S. Rossi and Ann Calderwood, eds., *Academic Women on the Move* (New York, 1973), pp. 93–124. Campbell records that in 1971, 376 programs aimed at "reentry" women existed in colleges and universities (p. 109). In the mid-1970s, Helen S. Astin found that women who were participating in CEW programs and those who had graduated from them had a higher level of educational attainment than did the general population of college alumnae; see Astin, "A Profile of the Women in Continuing Education," pp. 61–62.

95. Cless, "Birth of an Idea," pp. 16–17.

96. College enrollments (undergraduate and graduate combined) rose from 7,400,000 in 1970 to 13,100,000 in 1988. Much of this growth took place between 1970 and 1979; in the latter year enrollment stood at 11,300,000. Composing 18.2 percent of all students aged 14 to 34 in 1970, those aged 25 to 34 made up 27.3 percent of all students aged 14 to 34 in 1981. In addition, students aged 35 or over flocked into colleges, so much so that government statistics began to record them separately. Unless otherwise indicated, the enrollment statistics above and throughout this section are derived from U.S. Department of Commerce, Bureau of the Census, "Social and Economic Characteristics of Students," *Current Population Reports: Population Characteristics*: ser. P–20, no. 360 (Oct. 1979); no. 400 (Oct. 1981 and 1980); no. 408 (Oct. 1982); no. 413 (Oct. 1983); no. 426 (Oct. 1985 and 1984); no. 429 (Oct. 1986); and no. 443 (Oct. 1988 and 1987). One especially useful source is Table A–4 in the last mentioned volume, which records the age distribution of college students, 1948–88.

97. Medsker and Tillery, *Breaking the Access Barriers*, pp. 20–21. The actual ratio of males probably was higher than 2:1. The 2:1 figure applies only to junior-college students enrolled in degree-credit college-transfer curricula and hence excludes most students in vocational curricula. In the 1960s the latter usually were males.

98. K. Patricia Cross, *Adults as Learners* (San Francisco, 1981), p. 68.

99. Ibid., pp. 68–69.

100. Community colleges' receptivity to part-time students reflects their near obsession with maximizing enrollments to obtain increased state funding; two scholars have described this push for enrollments as "the dominant administrative objective" in community colleges. See David W. Breneman and Susan C. Nelson, *Financing Community Colleges: An Economic Perspective* (Washington, D.C., 1981), p. 217.

101. Arthur M. Cohen and Florence B. Brawer, *American Community Colleges*, (1st ed.; San Francisco, 1982), p. 33; National University Continuing Education Association, *Lifelong Learning Trends: A Profile of Continuing Higher Education* (2d ed.; Washington, D.C., 1992), p. 3.

102. David B. House, *Continuing Liberal Education* (New York, 1991), p. 27.

103. In 1979 the CPS did control for the ages of one specific subpopulation of students: those of Hispanic origin. Over 70 percent of Hispanic students in two-year colleges who were aged 25 to 34, and over 60 percent of those aged 35 and over, stated the intention to secure degrees; see also Carol K. Tittle and Elenor R. Denke, *Returning Women Students in Higher Education: Defining Policy Issues* (New York, 1980), pp. 32–33.

104. Paul P. Van Riper, *History of the United States Civil Service* (Evanston, Ill.,

1958), p. 138; Frederick C. Mosher, *Democracy and the Public Service* (New York, 1968), p. 66; George A. Graham, "Personnel Procedures in Business and Governmental Organizations," in Carl J. Friedrich et al., *Problems of the American Public Service* (New York, 1935), pp. 345–47, 386–87; William H. Whyte, Jr., *The Organization Man* (New York, 1956), pp. 109–28, 171–201. In his seminal analysis of bureaucracy, Max Weber equated examinations and diplomas as tickets of admission. Of course Weber was not primarily addressing the American context, where the two methods of selection conflicted, but his visit to the United States in 1904 had afforded him a quick study in the American suspicion of educational privilege. In the early days of civil-service reform, Weber related, Americans affirmed: "We prefer having people in office whom we can spit upon, rather than a caste of officials who spit upon us, as is the case with you." See H. H. Gerth and C. Wright Mills, trans. and eds., *From Max Weber: Essays in Sociology* (New York, 1958), pp. 110, 240–41.

105. Van Riper, *History of the United States Civil Service*, pp. 140, 216; Mosher, *Democracy and the Public Service*, pp. 81, 96–97, 126–27; Whyte, *Organization Man*, pp. 101–9.

106. Dwight Waldo, *The Administrative State* (New York, 1948), p. 94. In *Organization Man*, William H. Whyte, Jr., observed that business corporations primarily recruited college graduates with specialized majors in branches of business or engineering but then, so far from utilizing their specialties, placed the best into programs to train general managers (pp. 101–9).

107. Magali Sarfatti Larson, *The Rise of Professionalism: A Sociological Analysis* (Berkeley, Calif., 1977), pp. 199–207. On a parallel track, William H. Whyte, Jr., noted that advertising associations and newspaper guilds in the 1950s urged colleges to establish degree programs in advertising; see Whyte, *Organization Man*, pp. 86–87.

108. Harold L. Wilensky, "Work, Careers, and Social Integration," *International Social Science Journal*, 12 (1960), p. 554.

109. Whyte, *Organization Man*, pp. 63–78.

110. For a good discussion of how large corporations use educational attainment as a basis for selecting and promoting employees, see V. Lane Rawlins and Lloyd Ulman, "The Utilization of College-Trained Manpower in the United States," in Margaret S. Gordon, ed., *Higher Education and the Labor Market* (New York, 1974), pp. 216–17. Rawlins and Ulman note that departmental managers rarely consider the overall cost-effectiveness for their firms of the policy of privileging possessors of academic degrees, an observation that is relevant to the debate over whether mounting requirements of educational attainment spring from changes in the economy, such as technological advances that require new skills, or from the unexamined assumption that more highly educated workers will be more energetic and disciplined.

111. Quoted in Wendy Schuman, "Learn: How Education Helps You Get Ahead," *Working Woman*, 3 (Aug. 1978), p. 84.

112. Rates of labor-force participation by women rose between 1950 and 1976 in all age groups from 16 to 64 and most strikingly for women aged 25 to 34 (67.9 percent), 55 to 64 (52.2 percent), and 35 to 44 (47.8 percent). Inasmuch as the trend was long-term, in itself rising labor-force participation by women does not

explain the surge of college reentry. For data on labor-force participation by women since 1950, see Mary Dublin Keyserling, "Women's Stake in Full Employment: Their Disadvantaged Role in the Labor Force," in Ann Foote Cahn, ed., *Women in the U.S. Labor Force* (New York, 1979), p. 26. Between 1947, when statistics began to be collected on a regular basis, and 1978, labor-force participation by women increased in all but four years, but never by more than 1.5 percentage points in any one year; see Ralph E. Smith, "The Movement of Women into the Labor Force," in Ralph E. Smith, ed., *The Subtle Revolution: Women at Work* (Washington, D.C., 1979), p. 2.

113. K. Patricia Cross, *Beyond the Open Door* (San Francisco, 1971), pp. 133–34.

114. Stephen D. McLaughlin, Barbara D. Melber, et al., *The Changing Lives of American Women* (Chapel Hill, N.C., 1988), pp. 32–34.

115. Ibid., pp. 45–47.

116. Quoted in Daniel Yankelovich, *New Rules: Searching for Self-Fulfillment in a World Turned Upside Down* (New York, 1981), p. 30.

117. Diane E. Clayton and Margaret M. Smith, "Motivational Typology of Reentry Women," *Adult Education Quarterly*, 37 (Winter 1987), pp. 90–104; Linda H. Lewis, "Ingredients of Successful Programming," in Linda H. Lewis, ed., *Addressing the Needs of Returning Women* (San Francisco, 1988), pp. 94–114.

118. Peter Clecak, *America's Quest for the Ideal Self: Dissent and Fulfillment in the 60s and 70s* (New York, 1983), pp. 10, 6–8. Clecak emphasizes the positive and evolutionary features of the quest for fulfillment in the postwar era, and he scores Christopher Lasch and other critics for their preoccupation with the pathological ("narcissistic") manifestations of fulfillment in the 1970s (pp. 247–58).

119. Leland Medsker et al., *Extending Opportunities for a College Degree: Practice, Problems, and Potentials* (Berkeley, Calif., 1975), pp. 13, 57–110; see also David Riesman, *On Higher Education: The Academic Enterprise in an Era of Rising Student Consumerism* (San Francisco, 1980), pp. 113–17.

120. National University Continuing Education Association, *Lifelong Learning Trends*, p. 53; House, *Continuing Liberal Education* (cited in n. 102), pp. 90–115.

121. Debbie Goldberg, "Hitting the Books Late," *Washington Post, Educational Review*, Nov. 18, 1990, p. 12.

122. Arthur M. Cohen and John C. Lombardi, "Can the Community College Survive Success?" *Change*, 11 (Nov.-Dec. 1979), p. 25.

123. Cohen and Brawer, *American Community Colleges*, 2d ed. (cited in n. 87), p. 58.

124. Brint and Karabel, *Diverted Dream* (cited in n. 22), pp. 116–24. The revisionist onslaught against community colleges has been developing since the 1970s; see L. Steven Zwerling, *Second Best: The Crisis of the Community College* (New York, 1976) and Zwerling, ed., *The Community College and Its Critics* (San Francisco, 1986).

125. Ivar Berg, *Education and Jobs: The Great Training Robbery* (New York, 1979), pp. xii–xiii, 85–104; Douglas Adkins, "The American Educated Labor Force," in Gordon, ed., *Higher Education and the Labor Market* (cited in n. 110), pp. 112–43; Rawlins and Ulman, "Utilization of College-Trained Manpower"

(cited in n. 110), pp. 198–208, 221–27; Lester C. Thurow, "Measuring the Economic Benefits of Education," in Gordon, ed., *Higher Education and the Labor Market*, pp. 373–418; Thurow, "Education and Economic Equality," *Public Interest*, no. 28 (Summer 1972), pp. 66–81. Neoclassical economists have criticized this stress on the credentialing role of education, but they have done so mainly on theoretical rather than on empirical grounds. Without actually disputing the economic role played by credentials, they have insisted that employers will not persist in hiring expensive credentialed workers in the absence of evidence that such workers are more productive than those with lower educational attainment. See Glen G. Cain, "The Challenge of Segmented Labor Market Theories to Orthodox Theories: A Survey," *Journal of Economic Literature*, 14 (Dec. 1976), p. 1245.

126. Beverly T. Watkins, "Community Colleges and Industry Ally To Provide 'Customized' Job Training," *Chronicle of Higher Education* (Oct. 27, 1982), p. 4.

127. Fred L. Pincus, "Vocational Education: More False Promises," in Zwerling, ed., *Community College and Its Critics*, p. 49; see also Pincus, "The False Promises of Community Colleges: Class Conflict and Vocational Education," *Harvard Educational Review*, 50 (Aug. 1980), pp. 332–59.

128. Gene I. Maeroff, "Community Colleges Defy Recession," *New York Times*, Aug. 22, 1981, sec. 12, p. 31.

129. Nell Eurich, *Corporate Classrooms: The Learning Business* (Princeton, N.J., 1985), pp. 71–73.

130. Ibid., p. 17.

131. Milton A. Stern, "The Universities," in Grover J. Andrews et al., *Power and Conflict in Continuing Education* (Belmont, Calif., 1980), p. 18. The continuing-education establishment has been reluctant to tackle noncollegiate providers directly, in part because collegiate providers are in no position to throw stones—in 1965 the College Entrance Examination Board established the College-Level Examination Program to administer examinations through which students can secure credit without necessarily attending any classes. Rather than directly attacking noncollegiate providers, leaders in continuing education have insisted on their accreditation. In the 1970s the American Council on Education established its Office of Educational Credit to evaluate programs undertaken by noncollegiate providers.

132. Eurich, *Corporate Classrooms*, p. 6; see also Breneman and Nelson, *Financing Community Colleges* (cited in n. 100), p. 13. Breneman and Nelson put revenues of all institutions of higher education at $52 billion in 1981, up from $47 billion in 1978, $21.6 billion in 1970, and $2.5 billion in 1952.

133. Eurich, *Corporate Classrooms*, pp. 40–41; Ernest R. Hilgard, *Psychology in America: An Historical Survey* (San Diego, 1987), pp. 716–17.

134. Eurich, *Corporate Classrooms*, pp. 41, 43–44.

135. Arthur P. Carnevale, Leila J. Gainer, and Janice Villet, *Training in America: The Organization and Strategic Role of Training* (San Francisco, 1990), pp. 30–31.

136. Ray Marshall and Marc Tucker, *Thinking for a Living: Work, Skills, and the Future of the American Economy* (New York, 1992).

137. Nell P. Eurich, *The Learning Industry: Education for Adult Workers* (Princeton, N.J., 1990), p. 244.

138. See above, pp. 435–40.

139. National Center for Education Statistics, U.S. Department of Education, Office of Education Improvement and Research, *Dropout Rates in the United States, 1991* (Washington, D.C., 1992), pp. 7–8, 21.

140. Ibid., p. 245.

141. One figure with a significant impact on adult-education professionals has been Ralph W. Tyler, who chaired the University of Chicago's department of education in the 1940s and who in the 1930s had served as director of evaluation for the Progressive Education Association's Eight-Year Study. In 1949 Tyler defined education as a "process of changing the behavior patterns of people." See Ralph W. Tyler, *Principles of Curriculum and Instruction* (Chicago, 1949), pp. 5–6; on Tyler's pervasive influence on the field, see Cyril O. Houle, *The Design of Education* (San Francisco, 1972), pp. 256–57. It should be recalled that Tyler was the coauthor of one of the early 1930s studies that pointed to the fragmentation of reading interests along class and occupational lines; see Douglas Waples and Ralph W. Tyler, *What People Want to Read: A Study of Group Interests and a Survey of Problems in Adult Reading* (Chicago, 1931); see also Chapter 11. One plausible conclusion that could be drawn from this and similar studies was that literary classics had very little potential as a basis of mass adult education.

142. Eduard C. Lindeman, *The Meaning of Adult Education* (New York, 1926), p. 8. Lindeman's place in the pantheon of adult education appears increasingly secure; see Stephen Brookfield, "Eduard C. Lindeman," in Peter Jarvis, ed., *Twentieth-Century Thinkers in Adult Education* (London, 1987), pp. 120–29. Malcolm Knowles, long a leading figure in adult education, has predicted that "the curriculum and methodology of adult education will become increasingly differentiated from those designed for children and youth. Adult learning experiences will more and more be organized around the problems and processes of real life rather than according to academic subjects." See Knowles, *A History of the Adult Education Movement in the United States* (rev. ed.; Huntington, N.Y., 1977), pp. 270–71.

143. For a critique of adult education's "orthodoxy" by a dissenter within the field, see Stephen Brookfield, "A Critical Definition of Adult Education," *Adult Education Quarterly*, 36 (Feb. 1985), pp. 44–49.

144. For example, see Robert D. Boyd, Jerold W. Epps, and Associates, *Redefining the Discipline of Adult Education* (San Francisco, 1980), p. 5. On Kurt Lewin, see Alfred J. Marrow, *The Practical Theorist: The Life and Work of Kurt Lewin* (New York, 1969).

145. The process of professionalization has contributed to this attitude. Those who hold doctorates in adult education usually have made their way into administration rather than instruction; see William S. Griffiths, "Personnel Preparation," in Grover J. Andrews et al., *Power and Conflict in Continuing Education* (Belmont, Calif., 1980), pp. 209, 201–6. In general, those who see their profession as the articulation of values and directions for adult education are based in institutions that do little direct teaching of adults: university departments of adult education, divisions of continuing education, community-college administration, the testing services, and the foundations. The foundations long have seeded adult-education experiments, in part because they have not seen their task as supporting

established university programs. In addition to the Carnegie and Ford foundations' support, the W. K. Kellogg Foundation has aided the establishment of residential adult-education centers at several universities. On these see Harold J. Alford, *Continuing Education in Action: Residential Centers for Lifelong Learning* (New York, 1968).

146. House, *Continuing Liberal Education* (cited in n. 102), p. 27.

147. "Adult Education Students," *Chronicle of Higher Education* (Nov. 4, 1981), p. 12.

148. Craig L. Scanlon, "Practicing with a Purpose," in Ronald M. Cervero and Craig L. Scanlon, eds., *Problems and Prospects in Continuing Professional Education* (San Francisco, 1985), p. 11; Beverly T. Watkins, "Continuing Education for Professionals," *Chronicle of Higher Education* (Sept. 4, 1979), p. 9.

149. On the growth of CPE, see Eurich, *Learning Industry* (cited in n. 137), p. 188. Highly profitable and conducted by a great variety of providers, CPE has given rise to frequent battles for its control. These have occurred not only among corporations, professional associations, and universities but at times between professional schools and divisions of continuing education within universities. In addition, the notion of mandating continuing education, which developed partly in response to periodic scandals in the administration of nursing homes and daycare centers, remains controversial. But generalizations are risky, for the different providers have often cooperated, and mandated CPE has been sustained not only by state legislatures but in many instances by professional associations. Elements within the National University Continuing Education Association have opposed mandated CPE; see Philip M. Nowlen, *A New Approach to Continuing Education for Business and the Professions* (New York, 1988), pp. 229–32. For a recent review of the issues generated by CPE in several different professions, see Eurich, *Learning Industry*, pp. 185–219. See also D. C. Williams, "The Spectre of Permanent Schooling," *Teachers College Record*, 76 (Sept. 1974), pp. 49–62; D. Lisman and Jo Ohliger, "Must We All Go Back to School?" *Progressive*, 42 (Oct. 1978), pp. 35–37; Milton A. Stern, "The Universities," in Andrews et al., *Power and Conflict in Continuing Education* (cited in n. 131), pp. 2–35.

150. Knowles, *A History of the Adult Education Movement* (cited in n. 142), p. 280.

151. See Chapter 3.

152. Edgar J. Boone, Ronald W. Shearon, Estelle E. White, et al., *Serving Personal and Community Needs Through Adult Education* (San Francisco, 1980), pp. 12–16; Carol B. Aslanian and Henry M. Brickell, *Americans in Transition: Life Changes as Reasons for Adult Education* (New York, 1980).

153. National Endowment for the Humanities, *First Annual Report, Fiscal Year 1966* (Washington, D.C., 1966), pp. 3–5, 19–20; National Endowment for the Humanities, *Fourteenth Annual Report, 1979* (Washington, D.C., 1979), p. ix. See also "Establishing a National Foundation on the Arts and the Humanities," *89th Cong., 1st sess., House Report, no. 618, Senate Report, no. 300.* For comments on the significance of changing college faculties for NEH programming, see "A Proposal to the National Endowment for the Humanities by the Vermont Council on the Humanities and Public Issues," National Endowment for the Humanities (Washington, D.C., June 26, 1975), p. 21.

154. James Veninga, "The Humanities and Public Life: Thoughts on the Work

of the State Humanities Councils," *The Michigan Connection* (special ed.; 1983–84), p. 5.

155. "A Proposal to the National Endowment for the Humanities for the Massachusetts Foundation for Humanities and Public Policy, 1984–1986," vol. 1, app. G, National Endowment for the Humanities (Washington, D.C., n.d.), p. 8.

156. See, for example, Richard Hoggart, *The Uses of Literacy: Changing Patterns in English Mass Culture* (Fair Lawn, N.J., 1957), pp. 260–64.

157. Quoted in John A. Blyth, *English University Adult Education, 1908–1958* (Manchester, Eng., 1983), pp. 310–11.

158. On the role of the LEAs in popular adult education in Britain, see W. A. Devereux, *Adult Education in Inner London, 1870–1970* (London, 1982).

159. Britain has long contained sundry regional and local colleges (some of which developed from nineteenth-century mechanics' institutes) devoted to specialized subjects such as education, food science, music, and art. At their inception the polytechnics were to take over the advanced courses offered by these colleges in order to meet the growing demand for advanced education among adults, and it was assumed that the polytechnics would attact a high proportion of part-time students to what the British prefer to call "further" education. These expectations have not always been met. The proportion of part-time students in polytechnics declined between the 1960s and 1980s, while the polytechnics moved away from their original designation as teaching institutions with a focus on applied knowledge and toward more emphasis on comprehensive higher education and faculty research. The British government now plans to upgrade the polytechnics into universities. One sign of the continuing difference between the educational cultures of the two nations is that the American community colleges, whose rationale bears some resemblance to the original conception of the polytechnics, have not shown much inclination to follow the academic path of the polytechnics or to turn themselves into four-year colleges. On the polytechnics see Leonard M. Cantor and I.F. Roberts, *Further Education Today: A Critical Review* (3d ed.; London, 1986), pp. 116–23.

160. Blyth, *English University Adult Education*, pp. 200–204. The issue of credit for extramural work remains an agitated one in Britain. Professor Walter James of the Open University has remarked that "most universities have only just woken up to the fact that mature students want certificates and diplomas"; quoted in Caroline Ellwood, *Adult Learning Today: A New Role for the Universities* (London, 1976), p. 76.

161. On the Open University, see Jeremy Tunstall, ed., *The Open University Opens* (London, 1974).

Epilogue

1. Herbert B. Adams, "Educational Extension in the United States," U.S. Department of the Interior, Bureau of Education, *Report of the Commissioner of Education, 1899–1900* (2 vols.; Washington, D.C., 1900), vol. 1, pp. 275ff.; Charles R. Mann, "The American Spirit in Education," U.S. Department of the Interior, Bureau of Education, *Bulletin, 1919, no. 30* (Washington, D.C., 1919), pp. 7–63.

2. Mann, "American Spirit in Education," pp. 14, 49.

Index

In this index an "f" after a number indicates a separate reference on the following page, and an "ff" indicates separate references on the two pages following. A continuous discussion over two or more pages is indicated by a span of page numbers, e.g., "pp. 57–59." *Passim* is used for a cluster of references in close but not consecutive sequence.

Library of Congress Cataloging-in-Publication Data

Kett, Joseph F.
The pursuit of knowledge under difficulties: from self-
improvement to adult education in America, 1970-1990 /
Joseph F. Kett.
p. cm.
Includes bibliographical references and index.
ISBN 0-8047-2297-8 (cl.) : ISBN 0-8047-2680-9 (pbk.)
1. Adult education—United States—History.
2. Continuing education—United States—History.
3. Self-culture—History. I. Title.
LC5251.K48 1994 374'.973—dc20
93-41885 CIP

This book is printed on acid-free paper.